The democratic peace and territorial conflict in the twentieth century

This book re-evaluates the foundations of the democratic peace literature and presents three distinct theoretical models of how domestic institutions can influence the foreign policy choices of state leaders – Political Accountability, Political Norms, and Political Affinity. Huth and Allee test their hypotheses against a new and original global data set of 348 territorial disputes from 1919 to 1995. Each territorial dispute is divided into three separate but related stages for empirical analysis: Challenge the Status Quo Stage, Negotiation Stage, and Military Escalation Stage. The authors employ advanced statistical tests to compare the explanatory power of the three theoretical models across each stage of a territorial dispute. Their results provide strong support for the importance of democratic accountability and norms in shaping the diplomatic and military policies of incumbent leaders, and add new insights into understanding when and why democratic leaders engage in highly cooperative or confrontational foreign policies.

PAUL K. HUTH is Professor at the Department of Political Science and Senior Research Scientist at the Center for Political Studies, Institute for Social Research, University of Michigan. Previous publications include *Extended Deterrence and the Prevention of War* (1988) and *Standing Your Ground* (1996).

TODD L. ALLEE is a Ph.D. Candidate at the Department of Political Science of the University of Michigan. His research focuses on the dynamics of international cooperation and conflict, international trade institutions, comparative trade policy, and research methods in world politics.

D0123985

The Democratic Peace and Territorial Conflict in the Twentieth Century

Cambridge Studies in International Relations is a joint initiative of Cambridge University Press and the British International Studies Association (BISA). The series will include a wide range of material, from undergraduate textbooks and surveys to research-based monographs and collaborative volumes. The aim of the series is to publish the best new scholarship in International Studies from Europe, North America and the rest of the world.

CAMBRIDGE STUDIES IN INTERNATIONAL RELATIONS

The democratic peace and territorial conflict in the twentieth century

Paul K. Huth and Todd L. Allee

University of Michigan, Ann Arbor

CAMBRIDGE
UNIVERSITY PRESS

PUBLISHED BY THE PRESS SYNDICATE OF THE UNIVERSITY OF CAMBRIDGE
The Pitt Building, Trumpington Street, Cambridge, CB2 1RP, United Kingdom

CAMBRIDGE UNIVERSITY PRESS
The Edinburgh Building, Cambridge, CB2 2RU, UK
40 West 20th Street, New York, NY 10011-4211, USA
477 Williamstown Road, Port Melbourne, VIC 3207, Australia
Ruiz de Alarcón 13, 28014 Madrid, Spain
Dock House, The Waterfront, Cape Town 8001, South Africa

http://www.cambridge.org

First published 2002

Printed in the United Kingdom at the University Press, Cambridge

Typeface Plantin 10/12 pt   *System* LATEX 2$_\varepsilon$ [TB]

A catalog record for this book is available from the British Library

ISBN 0 521 80115 X hardback
ISBN 0 521 80508 2 paperback

To Eleni, for her constant support and patience
P.H.

To Kris, for her encouragement and support
throughout the duration of this project
T.A.

Contents

Figures

Tables

Acknowledgments

We would like to thank the National Science Foundation and the United States Institute of Peace for their generous financial support of this project. At the University of Michigan we would like to thank the Undergraduate Research Opportunity Program for providing a talented pool of research assistants who helped to collect data on territorial disputes. The research support of many graduate students in the Political Science Department is also deeply appreciated with special thanks to Natsuko Hayashi. Finally, we would like to thank Bruce Russett, Curt Signorino, Jim Morrow, Chris Achen, Rob Franzese, Nick Winter, Doug Lemke, Bill Reed, Kevin Clarke, and Ben Valentino for their comments and willingness to endure many questions about various aspects of the project.

1   Another study of democracy and international conflict?

Introduction

Over the past decade numerous books and countless articles have been published on the theoretical and empirical relationship between democracy and international conflict.[1] The central theoretical claim advanced by scholars is that decisions by state leaders to rely upon either peaceful diplomacy or military force as the means to resolve international disputes are influenced by the political institutions and norms of political competition and conflict resolution within states. As a result, analysts have argued that patterns of international conflict behavior should vary between democratic and non-democratic countries because of differences in the degree of state leaders' political accountability, or the strength of non-violent norms of resolving political conflict among political elites (e.g. Bueno de Mesquita and Lalman 1992; Bueno de Mesquita, Morrow, Siverson, and Smith 1999; Dixon 1993, 1994, 1998; Doyle 1986; Kahl 1998/99; Maoz and Russett 1992, 1993; Owen 1994, 1997; Raymond 1994; Rummel 1983, 1985; Russett 1993; Schweller 1992; Weart 1998).

In empirical research scholars have examined patterns of military conflict between democracies and non-democracies, as well as among the two types of states. Two different conclusions have emerged from empirical findings. The first, more widely accepted, claim is that while democratic states rarely if ever go to war against each other, they do adopt more confrontational diplomatic and military policies towards non-democratic states. Thus, patterns of military conflict between democracies and non-democracies are not very different from patterns of military conflict among non-democracies. Both are characterized by much higher rates of militarized disputes and war than are found between pairs of democratic states (e.g. Chan 1984; Dixon 1993, 1994; Owen 1994, 1997; Maoz 1997; Maoz and Abdolali 1989; Maoz and Russett 1992, 1993; Oneal and Ray 1997; Small and Singer 1976; Weart 1998; Weede 1984,

---

[1] Reviews of much of the literature can be found in Ray 1995: ch. 1, 1998; Maoz 1997, 1998; Chan 1997; and Rousseau, Gelpi, Reiter, and Huth 1996.

1992). The second claim, which is more controversial, is that democracies are less likely to resort to the aggressive threat or use of military force against all other states (e.g. Benoit 1996; Bremer 1992; Hart and Reed 1999; Hermann and Kegley 1995; Hewitt and Wilkenfeld 1996; Huth 1996; Leeds and Davis 1999; Morgan and Schwebach 1992; Oneal and Russett 1997a, 1997b, 1999a, 1999b; Rousseau 1996; Rummel 1995a, 1997; Russett and Oneal 2001; Schultz 2001b). As a result, not only are two democratic states very unlikely to become engulfed in military conflicts with each other, but democratic states are also less likely to initiate crises and wars against non-democratic states. Thus, while it may be true that mixed dyads of democratic and non-democratic states have relatively high rates of military conflict, the reason is because the non-democratic states in the dyads are generally escalating disputes to the point of military confrontations, compelling democratic states to resist and defend themselves with counter-threats and the use of force.

We refer to the body of theoretical and empirical work on domestic political institutions and international conflict as the democratic peace literature. The democratic peace literature, broadly understood, advances claims about the international conflict behavior of *both democratic and non-democratic states*, and seeks to test such claims against the historical record of military conflict in the international system involving either type of state. We want to emphasize that when we refer to the democratic peace literature we are not restricting our attention to the specific question of whether democratic states have engaged in military conflict with other democratic states. Instead, we view the debate about the absence of war among democratic states as one piece of a larger research program on the relationship between domestic political systems and international conflict behavior.

We have already alluded to the two main schools of thought within the democratic peace literature. We refer to the first school as the dyadic version of the democratic peace, since some scholars argue that the incidence of militarized disputes and war is greatly reduced only in relations among democratic states. On the other hand, these same scholars maintain that disputes between pairs of non-democratic states or mixed dyads are much more conflictual and include a pattern of aggressive behavior by democratic states towards non-democratic states. Meanwhile, the second school is termed the monadic version of the democratic peace, since other scholars argue that democratic states are less aggressive than non-democratic countries regardless of whether an international opponent is democratic or not. In this book we critically evaluate the theoretical and empirical foundations of both the dyadic and monadic versions of the democratic peace.

Debates over the democratic peace have been extensive. One area of contention lies with empirical research and findings. Scholars raise questions about the empirical strength and robustness of the finding that democratic states are less likely to rely on military force as an instrument of foreign policy. In particular, analysts frequently debate the strengths and weaknesses of various research designs, the methods used to test hypotheses, the measurement of variables, and whether alternative explanations can account for the democratic peace (e.g. Benoit 1996; Bremer 1992, 1993; Cohen 1995; Crescenzi and Enterline 1999; Dixon 1993, 1994; Elman 1997; Enterline 1996; Farber and Gowa 1995, 1997a, 1997b; Gates, Knutsen, and Moses 1996; Gartzke 1998, 2000; Gleditsch and Hegre 1997; Gowa 1999; Henderson 1998, 1999, 2002; Kegley and Hermann 1995, 1997; Layne 1994, 1995; Mansfield and Snyder 1995; Maoz and Russett 1992, 1993; Mitchell, Gates, and Hegre 1999; Mintz and Geva 1993; Mousseau 2000; Mousseau and Shi 1999; Oneal, Oneal, Maoz, and Russett 1996; Oneal and Ray 1997; Oneal and Russett 1997a, 1997b, 1999a, 1999b, 1999c; Rousseau, Gelpi, Reiter, and Huth 1996; Russett 1993, 1995; Senese 1997b, 1999; Snyder 2000; Spiro 1994, 1995; Thompson and Tucker 1997; Turns 2001; Van Belle 1997; Weede 1992). A second source of controversy focuses more directly on theory, as critics question whether a compelling theoretical argument has been developed to explain how domestic political institutions and norms of political competition influence the foreign policy choices of political leaders. This debate is also often linked to a broader discussion about the relative theoretical power of domestic and international conditions in accounting for international conflict behavior (Bueno de Mesquita and Lalman 1992; Bueno de Mesquita, Morrow, Siverson, and Smith 1999; Cederman 2001; Cohen 1994; Doyle 1986; Farber and Gowa 1995, 1997a, 1997b; Forsythe 1992; Gowa 1999; Henderson 1999; Hermann and Kegley 1995; James and Mitchell 1995; Lemke and Reed 1996; Kacowicz 1995; Kahl 1998/99; Mearsheimer 1990; Morgan and Campbell 1991; Morgan and Schwebach 1992; Oren 1995; Owen 1994, 1997; Rousseau 1996; Rummel 1983, 1985; Russett and Ray 1995; Schultz 2001b; Schweller 1992; Thompson 1996; Weart 1998).

Given that both critics and supporters of the democratic peace have had considerable opportunity to make their case, it is reasonable to ask: Do we really need another study on the relationship between domestic political systems and international military conflict? A skeptic might protest that both sides in the debate have posed the fundamental theoretical questions and presented their best counter-arguments in response to the strongest critiques put forth by the scholarly opposition (e.g. Cohen 1994 vs. Russett and Ray 1995; Farber and Gowa 1997b, Gowa 1999 vs.

Russett and Oneal 2001, Thompson and Tucker 1997; Mansfield and Snyder 1995 vs. Enterline 1996, 1998, Thompson and Tucker 1997, Maoz 1997, 1998, and Oneal and Russett 1999c; Oneal and Russett 1999a, Russett and Oneal 2001 vs. Gartzke 1998, 2000; Spiro 1995, Layne 1994, 1995, Oren 1995 vs. Russett 1995 and Maoz 1997, 1998; Turns 2001 vs. Hermann and Kegley 2001; Weede 1984, 1992 vs. Benoit 1996). Furthermore, this skeptic might insist that by now enough different empirical studies and findings have been produced, dissected, and re-analyzed such that another empirical study is not going to break much new ground. The exasperated skeptic might also say that the debate over the past decade has produced an extensive body of scholarship from which critical observers can draw well-founded conclusions as to the theoretical and empirical veracity of claims about the relationship between regime type and international conflict. As a result, the impact of new work on the subject of the democratic peace may have reached the point of a rather sharply declining marginal rate of return. In short, the skeptic cries out: Please no more!

Alas, while we sympathize with such skeptics, we would in fact argue that there is much more important work to be done on the subject of domestic political institutions and international conflict. Although it is true that a rich literature has developed, several basic questions and puzzles remain to be answered about the existence of and explanation for a democratic peace. Put differently, both the critics (e.g. Cohen 1994; Farber and Gowa 1995, 1997a; Forsythe 1992; Gartzke 1998, 2000; Gates, Knutsen, and Moses 1996; Gowa 1999; Henderson 2002; James and Mitchell 1995; Layne 1994; Mearsheimer 1990; Spiro 1994, 1995; Thompson 1996) and the supporters (Dixon 1993, 1994, 1998; Doyle 1986; Maoz 1997, 1998; Maoz and Russett 1992, 1993; Oneal and Ray 1997; Oneal and Russett 1997a, 1997b, 1999a, 1999b, 1999c; Owen 1994, 1997; Ray 1995, 1998; Raymond 1994; Rummel 1983, 1985; Russett 1993; Russett and Oneal 2001; Russett and Ray 1995; Schweller 1992) of the democratic peace claim that theory and evidence strongly support their position, but neither side's claim is fully persuasive. Nevertheless, while we are not convinced by either side in the democratic peace debate, scholarship over the past decade has clearly advanced our knowledge on the subject and raised new questions. As a result, in this book we address a number of important puzzles and debates and in so doing we draw upon the contributions of both critics and supporters of the democratic peace. In our judgement, more persuasive claims about the democratic peace require both a critical re-examination and development of basic theory as well as the development of new types of statistical tests whose research design and data differ from those commonly employed.

Let's consider a few examples of the general types of arguments advanced by critics and supporters of the democratic peace. Supporters have argued that extensive quantitative tests have confirmed the robustness of the democratic peace finding and that the causal logic which explains dyadic or monadic patterns of behavior has been clearly presented. Thus, while further refinement is possible and even desirable, the basic thrust of the theoretical and empirical analysis has been well established. As a result, useful but marginal returns can be expected from further empirical and theoretical work. Critics, however, have challenged these claims. Case study researchers object that quantitative studies have been long on testing the robustness of statistical results by including various control variables in equations, but short on directly testing the causal process that might link domestic institutions and norms to actual foreign policy choices by state leaders. These scholars argue that empirical research requires more process-tracing of state behavior in specific international disputes in order to assess causal claims about the democratic peace.

A different critique has been offered by scholars who are not empirically oriented, but are more concerned with the logical rigor supporting hypotheses about the democratic peace. Such theorists claim that theory-building efforts have been too inductive and driven by attempts to develop explanations for already-known empirical findings. Instead, they propose a more deductive approach in which analysts try to develop basic theory about the domestic politics of foreign policy choices and then determine if democratic institutions and norms logically result in particular types of dyadic or monadic hypotheses about the democratic peace.

We share the concern of critics that theory-building efforts may have been overly shaped by known empirical results. We also agree that more attention to deductive logic would be desirable and that we should try to ground democratic peace hypotheses in general models that link domestic politics to foreign policy choices. Nevertheless, we think supporters are right that hypotheses about norms of political bargaining or the accountability of leaders to political opposition represent plausible and fruitful theoretical approaches to explaining how domestic political institutions influence the foreign policy choices of state leaders. However, we believe that for both the norms-based and accountability-based approaches, the logical hypotheses to be tested are not adequately established in the existing literature. Through critical re-examination of the theoretical foundations of each approach, we can develop new hypotheses that refine and extend existing arguments.

On the empirical side, we find value in the work of both critics and supporters. For example, case study critics are right in several respects, but we still believe a great deal can be gained from further quantitative tests. We agree that empirical tests should attempt to examine more directly the causal pathways linking domestic institutions to decisions regarding military threats and the use of force. We would also disagree with supporters who might claim that the consistency of results in quantitative tests suggests that only marginal gains in knowledge can be achieved through further statistical tests. We would argue that the research design of many quantitative tests significantly limits the range and type of hypotheses that can be tested. As a result, while useful findings have been and will continue to come from such studies, we believe that alternative statistical tests based on different research designs and new data sets are essential. Thus, while we share the desire of case study researchers for more direct empirical tests, we prefer to rely on statistical tests. Our solution is to create a large data set, which is in some ways composed of many case studies. With such a data set we can test for more specific patterns of diplomatic and military behavior, and at the same time have greater confidence that the findings are generalizable and systematic.

In sum, if we re-examine and extend the basic theory of the democratic peace and then couple it with new data sets and alternative research designs for statistical tests, our results can make important and lasting contributions to an already extensive democratic peace literature. Our objective in this book, then, is to identify central puzzles and questions which persist in the democratic peace literature and to answer them with new theoretical and empirical analyses.

Theoretical debates and empirical puzzles

What are the central theoretical questions and empirical puzzles that need to be addressed by scholars studying the democratic peace? We find five areas in which further work is essential.

The debate over norms vs. institutional accountability

One theoretical debate among scholars seeking to explain the democratic peace has focused on the relative explanatory power of domestic norms of political conflict resolution and the political accountability of democratic institutions. Some scholars hold that democratic norms and institutions produce similar causal effects in international disputes. For example, in the dyadic version of the democratic peace, both democratic norms and democratic institutions encourage negotiated settlements and the avoidance of military conflict between democratic states, and both promote more confrontational policies towards non-democratic states. From this point of view, norms and institutions are complementary causes of the democratic peace and it is very difficult to disentangle their individual causal effects in empirical tests (e.g. Maoz and Russett 1993; Owen 1994, 1997; Ray 1995; Russett 1993). Other scholars, however, insist that while democratic norms and institutions may have similar causal effects, one explanation is in fact more compelling than the other. (Bueno de Mesquita and Lalman 1992; Bueno de Mesquita, Morrow, Siverson, and Smith 1999, and Reiter and Stam 1999a, 2002 favor institutionalist arguments while Dixon 1993, 1994 and Doyle 1986 give greater emphasis to democratic and liberal norms.)

We argue in this book that addressing two broad theoretical problems can advance the debate over the causal effects of norms and institutions. First, we need to develop the basic logic of the norms-based arguments more fully. Norms-based approaches need to ground theoretical arguments more directly in intra-elite patterns of political competition. Then they should develop more carefully the logic of how elite norms of resolving domestic political conflict might influence conflict resolution behavior in international disputes. There is a tendency among scholars, whether critics or supporters of norms-based theories, to argue that democratic norms imply a fairly "dovish" or accommodative approach to conflict resolution in international disputes. This leads both sides in the debate to overstate the strategic weaknesses of democratic states in situations of crisis bargaining with non-democratic adversaries. Our argument, as advanced in Chapter 5, is that a norms-based approach should predict a consistent pattern of "firm-but-flexible" or "tit-for-tat" diplomatic and military policies (Huth 1988) for democratic states in international disputes. Nonviolent norms should socialize leaders to adopt policies of reciprocity in diplomacy and military actions and to reject more extreme policies of unilateral concessions or military aggressiveness.

Second, we re-examine the general consensus in the literature that norms and institutions produce convergent effects. There has not been an adequate dialogue between supporters of the norms-based approach and those scholars who focus on the political accountability created by institutions. As a result, supporters of the norms-based approach have not addressed some recent arguments, which suggest that norms and institutions may in fact exert divergent influences on leaders' actions in international disputes. For example, the norms literature argues that democratic leaders should be more likely to seek negotiated settlements in disputes (e.g. Dixon 1993, 1994; Maoz and Russett 1993; Raymond 1994; Russett 1993).[2] Empirically, however, Huth's (1996) previous research on the settlement of territorial disputes suggests more complex patterns of

---

[2] In the dyadic version of the democratic peace this applies to disputes between democratic states, while in the monadic version it applies more generally to all target states in disputes.

behavior. One of his central findings is that state leaders rarely make territorial concessions for fear of the domestic political consequences of such a policy. Thus, while Huth finds that democratic states are more likely to seek peaceful settlements by offering concessions, it is nevertheless true that in a majority of dispute observations democratic leaders, too, failed to pursue diplomatic initiatives designed to break a stalemate in negotiations (Huth 1996: ch. 6). This suggests powerful domestic political constraints on democratic leaders, which may compete with norms of negotiated conflict resolution. A case in point would be the unwillingness of Indian Prime Minister Nehru either to propose or respond positively to Chinese offers of partial territorial concessions in several rounds of talks from the late 1950s to early 1960s for fear that supporters within his own Congress Party, as well as the leadership of opposition parties, would oppose such policies (Huth 1996: 176). Another example would be the unwillingness of Prime Minister Bhutto in 1972 to sign a treaty in which Pakistan would formally recognize the line of control in disputed Kashmir as the *de jure* international border. Bhutto feared that such a territorial concession would provoke strong domestic opposition from elites in political parties, the military leadership, and the public at large, with the result that the new democratic regime would be toppled (Ganguly 1997: 62–3).

Recent institutionalist arguments may help to explain these empirical puzzles. In models of costly signaling and domestic audience costs, for example, analysts argue that during crises democratic leaders might be particularly worried about compromise for fear of being charged with a diplomatic retreat by political opponents (e.g. Fearon 1994b, 1997; also see Schultz 1998, 1999, 2001a, 2001b). Furthermore, elite and public opinion may strongly support the use of force and oppose compromise as a general policy, in which case democratic leaders would have further reasons to pull back from compromise. Prime Minister Nehru, in fact, was concerned about the domestic political fallout of a territorial exchange with China, while confident that opposition parties would support a firm "forward policy" of military probes in disputed territories (Huth 1996: 176). The broader point derived from these institutionalist models is that democratic accountability may limit the diplomatic flexibility required of state leaders to pursue the peaceful settlement of international disputes. In this book we argue that democratic norms and institutions do not consistently predict the same type of conflict escalation or conflict resolution behavior and that differences in expected behavior should be subjected to empirical tests. In the theory-development chapters later in the book we argue that while democratic norms are expected to produce a consistently moderating effect on diplomatic and military policies, political accountability can push a decision-maker towards either conflictual or cooperative foreign policy behavior. This is because under different conditions of institutional accountability, democratic leaders will weigh the relative advantages of negotiated compromise, military conflict, and continuing diplomatic stalemate quite differently.

Since norms-based and political accountability-based models do not necessarily produce similar hypotheses, one important avenue for theory development is to identify when norms and institutions generate similar incentives for leaders and, conversely, to explain what behavior is to be expected when they collide. The logic of accountability-based arguments suggests that when norms-based incentives to pursue more cooperative policies conflict with institutional incentives to act more aggressively, the latter would have a stronger impact, since they are more directly linked to the political costs and risks of foreign policy decisions. For example, violations of normative principles of nonviolence and compromise in foreign policy may not be so politically costly for leaders when more hostile and conflictual policies either prove successful, or are directed at long-standing international adversaries. In short, democratic norms of conflict resolution may suffer when weighed against the powerful forces of nationalism and expected military success. In such situations, democratic leaders can expect political support for tougher diplomatic and military policies.

On the whole, the debate over democratic norms and institutions as causes of the democratic peace should focus more on the conditions under which differences in foreign policy behavior are predicted by each approach. New empirical tests can then be devised to assess the explanatory power of each theoretical model more directly. The results of empirical tests in Chapters 8 and 9 provide clear evidence that when these two models predict divergent behavior, the hypotheses of the Political Accountability Model are generally supported by the empirical evidence.

The puzzle of intra-regime variation in conflict behavior

One of the central theoretical puzzles of the democratic peace stems from recent empirical findings, which highlight substantial variation in the conflict behavior of both democratic and non-democratic states. That is, some studies provide evidence that military conflict can be quite rare among both democratic and non-democratic states, while other studies report that at other times both democratic and non-democratic states will pursue aggressive policies of military threats and the use of force (e.g. Benoit 1996; Gowa 1999: ch. 6; Hurrell 1998; Huth 1996: ch. 5; Holsti 1996: ch. 8; Kocowicz 1998, 1999; Leeds 1999; Maoz and

Abdolali 1989; Mousseau 1998; Oneal and Russett 1997a, 1997b; Rousseau 1996; Weart 1998). The theoretical challenge is to explain this variation within both types of regimes using a common theoretical framework.

Neither the dyadic nor the monadic version of the democratic peace adequately addresses variation in conflict behavior among non-democratic states. Instead, both approaches focus on explaining patterns of conflict behavior for democratic states, while arguing that non-democratic states should follow a pattern of fewer peaceful settlements of international disputes and more frequent military conflict due to the absence of democratic institutions and norms of conflict resolution (e.g. Dixon 1993, 1994; Doyle 1986; Maoz and Russett 1993; Morgan and Schwebach 1992; Raymond 1994; Russett 1993). The variation in conflict behavior within the category of non-democratic states is a particularly interesting theoretical issue, however. While some studies present empirical findings that suggest both peaceful and conflictual relations among non-democratic states (e.g. Peceny, Beer, and Sanchez-Terry 2002), scholars have not directed sustained theoretical attention to explaining this pattern of behavior and its implications for theories of the democratic peace.

Once again, some empirical findings from the study of territorial disputes are illustrative. In an earlier analysis of military escalation and the peaceful resolution of territorial disputes, Huth found that although democratic states were generally less likely to initiate military threats or use force, some non-democratic states were unlikely to engage in military escalation (Huth 1996: ch. 5). Similarly, while we have already noted that some democratic leaders, such as India's Nehru or Pakistan's Bhutto, may feel constrained by domestic opposition to avoid concessions, the same is often true for many non-democratic leaders, who believe that concessions are a risky policy domestically.

The challenge, then, is to develop theoretical models that can explain how domestic conditions in both democratic and non-democratic regimes affect foreign policy choices. In the theoretical section of this book we develop three different domestic-based models, each of which provides an explanation for differences in conflict behavior among both democratic and non-democratic states. For example, in the Political Affinity Model presented in Chapter 6, cross-national differences or similarities in political institutions and ideologies provide a general theoretical framework for explaining various patterns of foreign policy behavior. The hypotheses derived from this model potentially can help to explain a number of patterns: conflict and cooperation among non-democratic states, generally high levels of military conflict between democratic and non-democratic states, and low levels of military conflict between democratic states. The logical foundations of this model, however, are quite different to those of the more common norms-based or accountability-based models.

The empirical findings from Huth's previous research (1996) suggest that our existing theoretical analysis of political constraints in non-democratic states is underdeveloped in the political accountability literature. When are non-democratic leaders constrained by domestic opposition? How can we develop a theory about variation among non-democratic leaders in terms of the political constraints they face? The same types of questions can also be asked about democratic leaders (see Auerswald 1999, 2000; Elman 2000). How typical is the situation in which Prime Ministers Nehru and Bhutto found themselves – constrained, as democratic leaders, from making concessions while enjoying support for more confrontational foreign policies? More broadly, how can we account for opposing patterns of democratic peace and aggression? If we do account for them, what are the implications for prevailing dyadic and monadic versions of the democratic peace?

In this book we will argue that a worthwhile subject of theoretical work, neglected in the democratic peace literature, is the extent to which political constraints and accountability vary in important ways for the leaders of both democratic and non-democratic governments. The existing democratic peace literature on institutional constraints has focused on broad comparisons between regime types. Another avenue for theoretical elaboration, as we argue in this book, is to focus on the contrasts within each broad category of regime type. While we do not fundamentally disagree with the generalization that political constraints on average are higher in democratic regimes, we do believe that existing arguments about institutional constraints can and should be extended to include a more systematic analysis of differences within a regime type. Thus, just as the basic logic of the norms-based approach can be fruitfully extended, we argue that institutional approaches can be extended by sharpening the focus on the manner in which different domestic conditions produce variation in the degree of political accountability facing democratic and non-democratic leaders. Current scholarship does not exclude the possibility of important differences within each regime type, but has not pursued that path of analysis.[3] Such a path provides an opportunity to

---

[3] Morgan and Campbell (1992) suggest that decisional constraints should be considered carefully in all types of political systems. Rousseau (1996) also pays close attention to variation in constraints among both democratic and non-democratic regimes, as do researchers studying the democratic peace in the context of specific case studies (Elman 1997, 2000 and Auerswald 1999, 2000). In general, however, the tendency has been for scholars working in the democratic peace literature to focus on broad comparisons across regime types.

extend the basic logic of institutional approaches to the democratic peace and to conduct new empirical tests.

Chapter 4 explains variation in political constraints within regime types by focusing on those factors that might be expected to affect a leader's beliefs about the effective threat and power of domestic political opposition. Our comparative analysis of democratic systems centers on the timing of elections and the strength of opposition parties in legislatures and cabinets. Meanwhile, the comparative analysis of non-democratic regimes focuses on variation in the threat of coups during periods of political instability and violent political conflict, or during periods of political change and liberalization. The implication is that the political vulnerability of non-democratic leaders is potentially quite varied despite the prevailing absence of competitive elections, well-organized opposition parties, and politically independent legislatures. In fact, the results of empirical tests in the final section of this book provide considerable support for many of these hypotheses derived from the Accountability Model, as well as several hypotheses from the Norms Model. For example, we find that differences in the diplomatic and military behavior of democratic and non-democratic states are due to variables such as the timing of elections, the strength of opposition parties in legislatures, recent coups, or how recently democratic institutions had been established in a country.

The debate over audience costs and democratic institutions

Two opposing lines of argument have emerged from the theoretical literature which focuses on the impact of democratic institutions. The first and original line of analysis posits that the greater political accountability of democratic systems, stemming from such institutional features as regular competitive elections and independent legislatures, makes political leaders more cautious about the use of military force in international disputes (e.g. Bueno de Mesquita and Lalman 1992: ch. 5; Maoz and Russett 1993; Morgan and Campbell 1992; Russett 1993; Russett and Oneal 2001). The political risk for democratic leaders is that political opposition will arise and challenge incumbent leaders whenever force is used, particularly if the use of force results in high casualties and/or a military defeat. The theoretical analysis here centers on the potential political costs of *using* force. Scholars argue that democratic leaders should be more sensitive to those costs because democratic systems offer greater opportunity for political opposition to contest government policies and, through elections, to remove leaders for pursuing failed policies (see Bueno de Mesquita and Siverson 1995; Bueno de Mesquita,

Siverson, and Woller 1992). Thus, the higher expected domestic audience costs associated with conflictual policies should induce democratic leaders to be more risk-averse to the use of military force and more receptive to negotiated settlements of international disputes.

A more recent literature, however, has shifted the focus of analysis on democratic institutions by considering the political costs democratic leaders incur by *retreating* in a crisis or international dispute (Eyerman and Hart 1996; Fearon 1994b, 1997; Gelpi and Griesdorf 2001; Partell 1997; Partell and Palmer 1999; Schultz 1998, 1999, 2001a, 2001b). The general argument advanced is that threats of military force by democratic leaders are actually more credible because such leaders know that a failure to follow through on such threats will be used by political opponents to charge the political leadership with irresolution and a diplomatic defeat. In contrast, non-democratic leaders can issue strong threats and then decide to back down. For them, the political risks of retreating or bluffing are less threatening because domestic political opposition is in a much weaker position. High domestic audience costs for accommodative policies, then, can provide incentives for democratic leaders to prefer conflictual policies over more accommodating ones.

These two literatures highlight rather different constraints under which democratic leaders operate in international disputes. While scholars on both sides of the debate have developed formal arguments (e.g. Fearon 1994b; Schultz 1998; Smith 1998), there have been few empirical tests of these arguments (see Eyerman and Hart 1996; Gelpi and Griesdorf 2001; Partell 1997; Partell and Palmer 1999; Schultz 1999), and the interpretation of existing results is difficult due to potential problems of selection bias (Schultz 2001a). In Chapter 4 we develop the logic behind both types of audience costs and derive a number of hypotheses. With the new research design we employ for empirical testing, we better address problems of selection bias and find support for the influence of both types of audience costs. These supportive findings are expected, since we develop arguments about audience costs and political institutions in which leaders pay attention to both the expected political costs of using military force and the costs of making concessions. We maintain that it makes logical sense for leaders to attend to both types of costs when choosing among diplomatic and military options.

The debate over the strategic behavior of democratic states
in disputes with non-democratic states

Dyadic and monadic versions of the democratic peace are typically based on quite different arguments about how democratic states perceive their bargaining position in disputes with non-democratic opponents (see Rousseau, Gelpi, Reiter, and Huth 1996). The theoretical debate between advocates of the dyadic vs. monadic democratic peace centers on the question of whether democratic leaders should be expected logically to adopt more intransigent and aggressive policies towards non-democracies. As noted, proponents of the dyadic approach argue that democratic leaders will consistently prefer negotiations to the use of force only in disputes with other democracies, whereas they may be intransigent and aggressive in their policies towards non-democracies. The reason, as argued by some scholars, is that institutional constraints and/or norms of nonviolent conflict resolution place democratic states in a relatively weak position to protect their security interests. For example, high audience costs of using force restrain democratic leaders from adopting timely and credible deterrent policies, while their democratic norms favoring compromise encourage military threats and intransigent negotiating tactics by non-democratic opponents. Recognizing their disadvantaged bargaining position, democratic leaders will reciprocate the more aggressive policies of their opponents, resulting in preemptive military attacks or the breakdown of negotiations as a result of mutual intransigence (e.g. Bueno de Mesquita and Lalman 1992: ch. 5; Maoz and Russett 1993; Morgan and Schwebach 1992; Russett 1993).

The available empirical evidence, however, does not provide strong support for these predictions. For example, in the last two centuries, wars have very rarely been started by preemptive attacks (Reiter 1995; also see Schweller 1992), and decisions by democratic leaders to escalate crises have not been driven by such incentives very often (Rousseau 1996; Rousseau, Gelpi, Reiter, and Huth 1996). Furthermore, we know of no systematic body of evidence indicating that democratic states consistently adopt inflexible bargaining positions in negotiations with non-democratic states. Several studies of US–Soviet arms control negotiations, in fact, suggest a general pattern of reciprocity in concession-making (Druckman and Harris 1990; Jensen 1988a, 1988b; Stoll and McAndrew 1986). Another study of crisis bargaining strategies suggests that democratic states often adopt mixed strategies, combining threats with offers of negotiation as part of carrot-and-stick policies (Leng 1993). At the same time, empirical studies have established that democracies sometimes do adopt more aggressive policies against non-democratic states (e.g. Rousseau 1996; Rousseau, Gelpi, Reiter, and Huth 1996). There are enough cases of democracies initiating and escalating military threats that even if there does exist a very general pattern consistent with a monadic hypothesis, it is important to explain when democratic states are most likely to shift towards more conflictual policies.

Arguing against certain claims of dyadic democratic peace advocates, we question the logic of expecting democratic leaders to believe that they are at a diplomatic and military disadvantage in disputes with non-democratic states. If, as argued in Chapter 5, democratic norms encourage policies of reciprocity in international bargaining, then democratic leaders are actually in a favorable position to protect their country's security interests, since a number of studies suggest that diplomatic and military policies of reciprocity in crises are effective at deterring opponents (e.g. Huth 1988; Gelpi 1997; Leng 1993; also see Eyerman and Hart 1996; Friedberg 2000; Partell 1997; Partell and Palmer 1999). Furthermore, if the institutional constraints faced by democracies can vary to a substantial degree, then we might expect that under certain conditions democratic leaders would not face high audience costs for initiating or reciprocating the use of force. Indeed, it is possible that in some international disputes, domestic pressures push democratic leaders away from compromise and towards military confrontation (Owen 1994, 1997; Rousseau 1996). Nevertheless, we do not expect democratic leaders to simply suspend democratic norms of conflict resolution or to systematically adopt preemptive policies as a way of dealing with vulnerability, as is suggested by some scholars. Indeed, hypotheses from our Accountability and Norms Model predict that in disputes between democratic and non-democratic states the initiation and escalation of military conflicts is generally driven by the more aggressive policies of non-democratic states. The empirical results presented in Chapter 7 are strongly supportive of this claim regarding the initiation of military conflicts. The findings regarding escalation are not as strong, but there is little evidence that democracies aggressively escalate to high levels against non-democracies.

Our argument has important implications for the monadic democratic peace argument, since we specify more clearly the logical conditions under which it is most likely to hold true. For example, in Chapter 4 we argue that the monadic claim is most persuasive when democratic leaders are involved in territorial disputes with states that are not their long-term adversaries and issues of political self-determination for ethnic co-nationals are not at stake. Conversely, democratic aggressiveness, when it does occur, is likely to reflect one of two situations. The first situation is when the military risks of using force are low to moderate, and therefore the threat of domestic opposition to the use of force is not a strong deterrent for democratic leaders. The other scenario under which democratic leaders might turn to force is when the political costs of accommodative policies are high, in which case leaders are unlikely to offer controversial territorial concessions as part of a diplomatic compromise and are more willing to accept the risks of a military conflict.

*The debate over international-level vs. domestic-level explanations
of foreign policy behavior*

The field of international conflict studies has undergone a major re-orientation over the past decade. Scholars have argued forcefully, and with considerable success in our view, that domestic political conditions play a central role in explaining patterns of diplomatic and military conflict among states. Some scholars using a realist theoretical framework have challenged the claim that domestic-level variables provide systematic and powerful findings (e.g. Gowa 1999; Mearsheimer 1990), while other scholars have grappled with the theoretical implications of integrating domestic- and international-level variables in a common theoretical framework (e.g. Bates 1997; Bueno de Mesquita and Lalman 1992; Downs and Rocke 1995; Fearon 1994b, 1998; Gruber 2000; Huth 1996; Kahler 1997; Lamborn 1991, 1997; Martin 2000; Milner 1997; Moravcsik 1997; Morrow 1995; Nincic 1994; Powell 1993; Putnam 1988; Rosenau 1990, 1997; Siverson 1998; Smith 1998; Walt 1996; Wendt 1999). The democratic peace literature has been an integral part of this theoretical debate. Indeed, a persistent line of critique directed at claims of a democratic peace are based on realist-type arguments, which maintain that military power and common national security interests between states can explain the absence of military conflict between states in general, and pairs of democratic states in particular (Elman 1997; Farber and Gowa 1995, 1997a; Gowa 1999; Layne 1994, 1995; Maoz 1998; Mearsheimer 1990). Based on these arguments, then, the absence of war between democracies during the post-World War II period can be explained by the common alliance among most democracies in opposition to the Soviet threat.

The premise of our theoretical analysis in this book is that realist critics have failed to make a compelling logical case that domestic-level variables should not be expected to shape the foreign policy choices of state leaders. Thus, the essential starting point for theory building among advocates of the democratic peace – namely that domestic political institutions and norms of behavior can influence state policy in international disputes – strikes us as logically plausible and worthy of rigorous analysis. At the same time, we think that the diplomatic and military policies of states are quite responsive to the international political and military environment within which states must operate (Huth 1988, 1996, 1998). Therefore, both domestic- and international-level variables logically should be expected to affect state policy in international disputes. Theoretically, the task is to consider foreign policy choices as potentially reflecting the interplay between the two sets of conditions.

Our general theoretical framework might be termed a modified realist approach (Huth 1996, 1998) in which state leaders seek to protect and promote national security interests abroad while also seeking to ensure their tenure and position of political power at home. Theoretical integration is attempted in several ways. For example, success or failure in foreign policy can have important implications for the domestic political tenure of leaders. It is therefore argued that leaders have incentives, even as domestic office holders, to assess the international strategic environment carefully before pursuing diplomatic or military initiatives. Thus, in Chapter 5 our model of domestic political survival requires leaders to think like realists about the prospects for successful foreign policy actions.

We also link the domestic and international levels by arguing that domestic political opponents are likely to condition their challenges of government policy based on an assessment of their government's strategic options and foreign policy outcomes. For example, a military success for an incumbent government will undercut an opposition challenge, while a diplomatic retreat for a militarily powerful government will provoke greater dissent and opposition than a retreat under conditions of military weakness. Furthermore, nationalism can be an important constraint that limits domestic opposition. For example, we argue in Chapter 4 that conflict with an enduring international rival is less likely to provoke dissent from opposition groups, permitting governments greater leeway to threaten force and maintain unyielding diplomatic positions (also see Braumoeller 1997). Finally, we argue that foreign policy choices are most likely to be affected by the domestic political concerns of leaders when they are most insecure about their hold on office and thus have a very short-term time horizon.

Empirically, tests of domestic-level hypotheses still need to account for the potential influence of various international conditions. With such tests, it is possible to assess the joint effects of domestic and international conditions as well as their individual influences on foreign policy behavior. The debate then shifts to questions of: (a) the relative substantive impact of domestic and international variables, (b) the conditions under which domestic political variables matter more or less, and (c) how we can best capture the interactive effects of variables from the two levels of analysis. In sum, while we are not convinced that realist variables are the dominant set of powerful explanatory variables, we certainly do think they are important. Therefore, the focus of our theoretical and empirical research on the democratic peace is to integrate and draw upon both levels of analysis. Empirically, we present very strong and consistent evidence across Chapters 7 to 9 that both international and domestic-level variables are important in explaining state behavior across the different stages of territorial disputes. More specifically, we find that international political-military conditions are central to understanding the initiation and escalation of military confrontations, but offer few insights regarding the initiation or outcome of negotiations. Conversely, while domestic political variables do provide a number of additional insights into the causes of military conflict, they are essential to understanding when and why state leaders seek negotiations and offer concessions over disputed territory. In sum, the threat of war is linked closely to the strategic context of international political-military conditions, while peace and the settlement of international disputes depends crucially on domestic political conditions.

Policy implications of research on the democratic peace

While our primary objective in this book is to advance basic research and scholarship on the democratic peace, we do believe that our research will have policy implications in a number of areas. At present, we will simply outline some of the potential policy issues raised by our research. In the concluding chapter we will return to these policy questions and consider how the results of our research can be of value to policy-makers and analysts.

What are the challenges for democratic leaders when managing disputes with authoritarian regimes?

The debates among scholars regarding the possible ways in which democratic institutions and norms may constrain or shape the policy choices of democratic leaders can clearly be linked to long-standing questions about whether democracy is an asset or liability in the formation and conduct of foreign policy. We believe that our research can clarify and provide new and more compelling evidence on the question of whether non-democratic states generally believe that democratic leaders are more risk averse to military conflict and more inclined to compromise in protracted disputes and negotiations. If critics of democracy are correct, democratic leaders may find it difficult to credibly signal their resolve in military confrontations, or to induce concessions from authoritarian leaders in negotiations. One policy implication that follows from such expectations is that democratic leaders should have limited confidence in their ability to bargain effectively with authoritarian states in crises or during peacetime negotiations. As a result, the escalation of military conflicts should be difficult to avoid, while negotiations will be protracted and rarely produce satisfactory agreements. In our theoretical and empirical analyses in this book we will address important questions about the behavior of non-democratic states that are of central importance to democratic policy-makers. Are democratic states frequently targeted by non-democracies with military threats and probes? Can democratic leaders credibly send deterrent signals in military crises to authoritarian adversaries? Furthermore, our research will examine whether democratic negotiators can signal their intention to stand firm in negotiations and induce concessions from their adversary, or whether democratic leaders often compromise in the face of stalemated negotiations.

Managing the politics of international dispute settlement

We also believe that our research can offer advice to policy-makers on questions of how to promote the resolution of international disputes. For example, our research on electoral cycles and the role played by opposition parties in democratic legislatures can help to identify those domestic situations that are most promising for democratic leaders to pursue negotiations and to offer concessions. That is, when can leaders expect to secure ratification of border agreements at home and, similarly, when are negotiating adversaries most inclined to offer concessions and when will their leaders be capable of securing ratification? The results of our research should therefore be useful for understanding when initiatives to hold talks and pursue negotiations are likely to be successful and conversely when stalemate can be expected. These questions of timing, then, are potentially useful to state leaders who are trying to identify opportune times to push for talks and pressure their adversary to put concessions on the table.

Another way in which our research is policy-relevant concerns the negotiating strategies that democratic states might adopt. For example, the results of our research will address the interesting question of whether democratic leaders who claim that their "hands are tied" by strong domestic opposition can actually induce their negotiating partner to offer more favorable terms for an agreement. In academic scholarship there is a debate about whether such a policy should be an effective bargaining tactic. In our research we will be able to pinpoint whether democratic leaders who are faced with strong opposition parties in their legislature are more likely to secure territorial concessions from other states at the negotiating table.

The interests of third parties in questions of war and peace over disputed territory

Finally, we believe that the results of our research can be of value to third parties, such as Great Powers or the leaders of regional states, who are concerned about the outcomes of territorial disputes. For example, allies of states involved in territorial disputes are likely to be concerned about the outbreak of military confrontations and their possible escalation to war. Our empirical findings will help to identify those domestic and international conditions under which challenger states will threaten force and risk war. Based on these types of results, policy analysts in third party states can develop better forecasts of military conflict and assess what policies might act as powerful deterrents to such conflict. Also, as noted above, if our research can identify those domestic conditions under which democratic leaders are inclined to favor talks and to offer concessions, then diplomatic pressure and efforts at mediation are more likely to succeed. Third parties and mediators need to decide when to invest resources, time, and political capital in pursuit of dispute settlement. We believe that our findings should be quite helpful for understanding the key obstacles to successful negotiations, as well as conditions conducive to achieving progress in negotiations. Put differently, we hope to ascertain when disputes are "ripe" for negotiations that will produce concessions from both parties over issues that have been contested for some time.

A framework for theoretical and empirical analysis

The theoretical and empirical analyses presented in this book are premised on the belief that hypotheses about the democratic peace should be related more directly to the unfolding of international disputes into different stages and pathways. The starting point for justifying this approach is a critique of a common research design used for statistical tests of the democratic peace.

Dyadic studies

A number of statistical studies of the democratic peace have analyzed data sets consisting of pairs of states in which the occurrence of a war or militarized dispute short of war is coded on an annual basis over some specified time period. In some tests the population of dyads consists of all possible pairings of states, while other scholars rely on a smaller set of "politically relevant" dyads (e.g. Bremer 1992, 1993; Gowa 1999; Maoz 1997, 1998; Maoz and Russett 1992, 1993; Oneal and Ray 1997; Oneal and Russett 1997a, 1997b, 1999a, 1999b, 1999c; Ray 1995: ch. 1; Russett and Oneal 2001). These "dyad-year" studies have produced many useful and important findings, but such designs for empirical tests of the democratic peace feature three limitations.

First, these studies simply code whether conflict did or did not occur between two pairs of states in a given year. However, even though two states might be embroiled in a bilateral dispute, each state makes its own decision regarding how to behave in the dispute, even if the states' decisions are interdependent. In most of these dyadic studies the dependent variable is conflict involvement for the countries in the dyad, but patterns of military initiation and response or conflict resolution are not identified. In other words, there is no way to tell which of the two states actually initiated the use of force, or which state raised the ante by escalating its level of force first. This is an important drawback, since hypotheses about democratic institutions and norms of conflict resolution logically predict which state in a dyad should be most likely to initiate militarized disputes, escalate disputes to the brink of war, or seek diplomatic settlements of disputes.

Data on initiation and escalation are particularly important for testing the monadic version of the democratic peace because the occurrence of war, crises, or militarized disputes in a mixed dyad of democratic and non-democratic states does not distinguish between two quite different situations. In the first case, the non-democratic state initiates the large-scale use of force after rejecting compromise proposals, and the democratic state responds by defending itself against the attack. In the second case, the democratic state initiates the large-scale use of force after rejecting compromise proposals and the non-democratic state defends itself. These two cases represent very different pathways to war and therefore suggest different conclusions about the monadic approach to the democratic peace. The second pathway is at variance with a monadic hypothesis, whereas the first pathway is not. Yet statistical tests that use dyads as the unit of analysis cannot distinguish between these two pathways.

The same general point is applicable regarding different pathways to conflict resolution. In one case the dispute is settled by a non-democratic state initiating concessions or withdrawing claims, while in a second case a democratic state takes the initiative to propose concessions that are then accepted by a non-democratic adversary. The first case runs counter to prevailing monadic arguments about democratic norms while the second seems consistent with them. The findings of existing quantitative studies that use dyads, however, do not provide a solid foundation upon which to build conclusions about the monadic version of the democratic peace (Rousseau, Gelpi, Reiter, and Huth 1996). It seems very desirable to disaggregate conflict behavior within a dyad into a more sequential analysis of the decisions made by each state over the course of a dispute.

Furthermore, the use of dyads leads to additional problems when attempting to test hypotheses about the impact of domestic political factors on patterns of conflict initiation, escalation, and resolution. Using dyads, variables that are particular to each state, such as the level of democracy, the timing of elections, or the relative strength of the leader's position, must be combined somewhat unnaturally into some type of joint or composite measure.[4] For instance, the dyadic indicators for such variables generally measure the lowest of the two states' democracy scores, or indicate that a coup has recently taken place in at least one of the two states. As a result, it is often difficult to ascertain causal inference using dyads; there is no clear sense of the "direction" of any estimated relationship. For example, assume one wants to know whether minority governments behave differently than majority governments during negotiations over territory. Using dyads, the researcher would assign a value of "1" to dyads in which one state has a minority government. Perhaps the parameter estimates indicate that minority government is associated with situations of deadlock in talks. One still does not know if minority governments are less likely to make concessions due to their position of domestic weakness, or whether majority governments are the ones who resist making concessions to minority governments, who they perceive as unwilling or unable to offer reciprocal concessions.

In sum, the prevailing focus on dyads makes it difficult to test directly how domestic norms and institutions shape the military and diplomatic behavior of states. Scholars code for the presence or absence of some level of military conflict, but the diplomatic and military interactions and processes that produced the presence or absence of conflict are not analyzed, even though these intermediate causal pathways are very useful for testing and evaluating hypotheses about the democratic peace. The dyad-based data set of conflict outcomes, as commonly used, requires the researcher to make inferences about the causal processes that might have produced patterns of observed dyadic conflict outcomes (also see Bennett and Stam 2000; Dixon 1998).

A second, related limitation of these dyadic studies is that they fail to account for the various stages in an international dispute, most notably the emergence of a dispute between two states. In other words, these studies test hypotheses about international conflict without grounding the empirical analysis in the development and progression of international disputes between states and without carefully considering issues of case selection. In principle one might identify several stages or phases in an international dispute:

---

[4] As Bennett and Stam point out, in dyadic analyses the researcher "must then transform these individual variables to eliminate identity and directionality to create a variable that is usable in nondirected analysis" (Bennett and Stam, 2000: 656).

1. The transition from the status quo to a dispute over some issue.
2. Attempts at negotiation and talks to settle the dispute.
3. The escalation of diplomatic conflict to the point where military force is threatened.
4. The further escalation of these militarized conflicts or crises to war.

Our contention is that any research design devised to test hypotheses about international conflict and cooperation should consider each of these possible stages.

One concern we have about the use of dyads is that when states become involved in a militarized dispute or war, the causal pathway necessarily includes a first stage of a dispute emerging, but we do not think that democratic peace arguments explain why disputes arise – only how they will be managed.[5] As a result, dyads that do not get into disputes for reasons unrelated to democratic institutions or norms may appear as cases in support of the democratic peace. The problem with the typical dyad-year-based data set is that the observed behavior of no militarized dispute or war for certain dyad years could be explained by either of two general processes, one of which is distinct from arguments in the democratic peace literature. Military conflict may be absent because states were able to prevent a dispute from escalating, a situation the democratic peace literature addresses. On the other hand, military conflict may be absent because states were not involved in a dispute in the first place and thus there was no reason for leaders to consider using force (also see Gartzke 1998, 2000). In this second pathway democratic peace explanations are not relevant.

The use of politically relevant dyads helps to reduce this problem of irrelevant no-conflict observations on the dependent variable, but many relevant dyads are not parties to an international dispute that has the potential to escalate to military conflict. In the typical data set that contains both types of zero observations on the dependent variable, estimates for the democratic peace variables are biased unless the statistical test very effectively controls for the conditions that produce disputes in the first place. For example, the negative coefficient on a democratic dyad variable could reflect not only the fact that some democratic leaders managed disputes in a nonviolent way, but also the fact that some democratic dyads were not involved in any disputes for many of the dyad-year observations in the data set. Without question, several of the common control variables included in these tests do help to explain the absence of disputes

<hr/>

[5] One study does argue that democratic states are less likely to initiate certain types of disputes, but not that democratic states are less likely to initiate disputes in general (see Siverson and Bueno de Mesquita 1996).

between states, but we are not confident that the selection process for disputes emerging has been specified so well that the remaining bias is negligible.

In Huth's research on the origins of territorial disputes (1996: ch. 4) he found that common control variables in democratic peace tests, such as alliance ties, did reduce the chances of disputes emerging. But their substantive effect was not that strong, and the measure of the military balance actually had no systematic impact upon the emergence of a dispute. The typical model specification for democratic peace tests does capture to some degree the selection process of moving from the status quo to a dispute, yet there is certainly some slippage at this stage. The inability to fully account for selection processes weakens the conclusions we can draw about what we really want to know, namely how domestic institutions and norms influence the resolution and escalation of international disputes.

The third and final limitation of dyad-year studies is that the use of annual observations not only obscures the fact that there are several stages to an international dispute, but also presents a number of operational problems. For one, there is little reason to think most substantive decisions in international politics are taken on a consistent, annual, or twelve-month basis. While some real-world processes might be regularized, perhaps even on an annual basis, the interactions of governments over disputed issues are not one of these processes. Military interventions, diplomatic initiatives, threats of retaliation, and cease-fires can happen frequently, so it is problematic to measure them only once a year.[6]

In operational terms, the dyad-year framework forces a single observation to summarize the behavior of a pair of states over an entire year, even if patterns of activity do not correspond to that annual framework. In fact, in our territorial dispute data set there are 211 instances in which multiple, unique foreign policy initiatives are taken by a single state in the same year. For example, two states might hold talks twice in one year, perhaps with very different results each time. Or a pair of states might engage in negotiations in March, only to see one state attack the other in October. Furthermore, a strict annual coding scheme also has a

---

[6] Since researchers always aggregate foreign policy activity over some unit of time, they will always be dealing with grouped data. This is a fact of life for empirical researchers (Freeman 1989). When analyzing international interactions, it is very difficult to measure the behavior of a number of cross-sections (whether states or dyads) for short intervals of time, such as minutes, hours, days, or even weeks. Thus our parameter estimates will always entail some degree of inefficiency. Yet higher levels of aggregation eliminate much of the interesting variation in the data compared to lower levels of aggregation. Our contention is that annual observations eliminate too much variation in both the independent and dependent variables.

difficult time accommodating events that linger for a long period of time. Many important events in international relations, such as lengthy rounds of negotiations or protracted military conflicts, span the course of two or more calendar years.[7] The resulting question, then, is how to code the subsequent years in which talks or military conflict is ongoing?[8] One of the goals of our research design is to capture, and measure more accurately, all instances in which negotiations are held or a military encounter takes place.

It may also be problematic to measure many independent variables of interest solely on an annual basis. Many interesting domestic political phenomena entail significant shifts at precise points in time or take the form of discrete events. For example, an annual measure of the degree to which a country is democratic would contain considerable measurement error if there is a significant regime change during the middle of a year. We often dismiss or ignore such concerns, and wonder if any observations in the data really suffer from this feature. We are able to shed light on this question, however, because in compiling our data on territorial disputes we identified the months in which important domestic political events or changes occurred.[9] In fact, more than 10 percent of the countries in our data set experience a change in their *POLITY* net-democracy score during a given year.[10] In a more substantive sense, further examination of our data shows that nearly 6 percent of these same countries experience a full-scale regime change at some point during a given year.[11] The dyad-year framework, then, struggles to capture any middle-of-the-year domestic political changes, such as when a coalition partner drops out of a governing coalition in May, or an opposition party wins an election and assumes power in July.

In addition, many of the variables we think have an important impact on international politics, such an elections or internal coups, are discrete

---

[7] Once again, in the territorial dispute data set there are more than 300 instances in which either a round of negotiations or a military conflict spreads across multiple years.

[8] See Bennett and Stam (2000) for a lengthy discussion of this particular issue.

[9] We first identify the situations in which a country's net-democracy score changes from one year to the next, and then pinpoint the exact month in which the change took place. This allows us to identify the years in which a net-democracy score changes during the course of a calendar year.

[10] For our purposes, the *POLITY* net-democracy score is equal to the democracy score (scaled from -0 to 10) minus the autocracy score (scaled from 0 to -10). In terms of raw numbers, 497 out of 4,792 country-years experience an intra-year change in their net-democracy score.

[11] By "regime change" we mean that a country shifts from one of the following systems of government to another: liberal democracy, hereditary non-democratic monarchy, single-party-dominant communist, single-party-dominant fascist, collective military junta, or a miscellaneous non-democratic regime. See the coding rules employed in Chapter 6 for more details.

events. These events happen at identifiable moments in time, but an annual measure can only indicate that such an event did or did not occur at some point during the course of a year. From a measurement standpoint, however, the timing of these events is of considerable importance. To be able to think in terms of causality, we need to be certain that hypothesized independent variables occur or exist prior to the outcome we measure. For example, we might collect information on the existence of military coups and the initiation of violence abroad if we want to understand whether domestic violence leads to militaristic foreign policy behavior. However, an annual observation would simply indicate that a coup and a military skirmish with a neighboring country both occurred in the same calendar year. In order to draw any type of causal inference we would want to ensure that the domestic coup took place *before* the militarized dispute. But consider the case in which a country launches an unsuccessful series of border attacks in February, and then experiences a successful coup in September. The results based on annual data might indicate that coups do indeed lead to aggressive foreign policy behavior. However, in this case the unsuccessful military action might have contributed to the military coup against the incumbent leadership. The supposed causal relationship would actually be reversed!

In sum, the dyad-year as the unit of analysis aggregates the behavior of both states in multiple stages of an international dispute into a single observation, which makes it difficult for empirical tests to assess the causal processes operating at different stages in the escalation or resolution of disputes. These limitations of previous data sets and statistical tests lead us to believe that new directions for quantitative empirical testing could make very useful contributions to the democratic peace literature.

An alternative research design

Our alternative approach for theoretical and empirical analysis of the democratic peace includes the following:
1. A focus on the behavior of individual states involved in international disputes.
2. An attempt to explain how disputes evolve over time through different stages of diplomatic and military conflict.
3. An analysis of the diplomatic and military actions of challenger and target states at each stage of a dispute, including patterns of initiation and response that takes into account the strategic nature of policy choices adopted by state leaders.

Our theoretical and empirical analyses of the democratic peace are built around the behavior of states involved in specific international disputes. In

Table 1.1 *Territorial disputes between states, 1919–1995*

Region	Number of disputes	Pre-1945	Post-1945	Across both periods
Europe	95	60	27	8
Middle & Near East	89	36	32	21
Africa	48	17	26	5
Asia	65	14	42	9
Americas	51	30	6	15
Total	348	157	133	58

particular, we focus on disputes over opposing claims to national territory, and we examine the diplomatic and military behavior of states seeking to change the status quo and those preferring to preserve it (see Table 1.1 and Figure 1.1).[12] We have assembled a data set of 348 territorial disputes from 1919–95 that includes disputes from all regions of the globe. We have attempted to identify the population of such disputes, along with information about the diplomatic and military history of the dispute throughout its duration. Given our interest in testing arguments about the democratic peace, the existence of a territorial disagreement is a logical place to begin the analysis, since arguments about democratic norms and institutions focus on how state leaders can manage conflicts of interest and not why conflicts of interest emerge to begin with.

Our data set provides a useful way to directly test hypotheses about the relationship between domestic political factors and conflict behavior. First of all, by examining cases of territorial disagreement we control for much of the unexplained and unimportant variance across cases and ensure that the states in our data set have at least the possibility for interaction. As we discuss in Chapter 2, states with territorial claims consistently possess three options: accept the status quo and do nothing, call for negotiations over the disputed territory, or threaten force in an attempt to acquire territory. Since all states with territorial claims in principle face these same options at all times, we can isolate hypothesized factors of interest and see how variation in these factors affects patterns of territorial challenges. A time-series cross-sectional design also works nicely in this situation. We can focus on both cross-sectional variation in state behavior under similar strategic scenarios, as well as temporal variation in state behavior to see how changes in international and domestic factors affect a state's pursuit of a territorial claim over time.

---

[12] See Appendix A for a discussion of the coding rules for identifying cases of territorial disputes and Appendices B–F for a more detailed listing and summary description of the individual disputes by region.

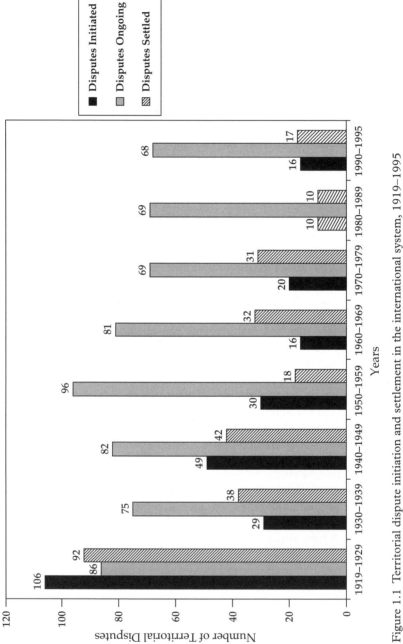

Figure 1.1 Territorial dispute initiation and settlement in the international system, 1919–1995

Table 1.2 *Negotiations over disputed territory, 1919–1995*

Region	Territorial disputes	Number of rounds of talks	Number of rounds with concessions by challenger states
Europe	95	268	113
Middle & Near East	89	423	162
Africa	48	172	60
Asia	65	362	114
Americas	51	303	119
Total	348	1528	568

Note: The totals listed for concessions include cases in which the challenger made either limited or major concessions over disputed territory.

Our research design also addresses many of the concerns with measurement and the selection of units of observation discussed in the previous section. For one, independent variables that change during the course of a year are measured monthly instead of yearly. Similarly, the dates of any actions are recorded in a month-specific manner in order to more accurately capture the timing of foreign policy decisions. Instead of coding one outcome per year and fitting the timing of talks and militarized disputes into an annual period, the actual rounds of talks and militarized disputes themselves serve as the units of observation.[13] In other words, each "episode" of interaction during a stage of a territorial dispute (see Chapter 2) constitutes a unit of observation. Not only are variables measured more precisely, the sequencing of events is also captured properly since events are attributed to the actual month in which they occurred.

The precise nature of our data on negotiations and military conflicts over disputed territory gives us the leverage to test for patterns of dispute settlement and deadlock in talks as well as patterns of initiation, escalation, and response in militarized disputes (see Tables 1.2 and 1.3). Thus, while we retain a statistical approach to testing a large data set, this particular data set, with its greater attention to micro-level information on diplomatic and military behavior, enables more direct tests of the controversial theoretical issues of the democratic peace in Chapters 7 through 9.

The final advantage of this alternative research design is that we can capture more directly the strategic behavior of foreign policy leaders and thus assess more carefully the substantive effects of variables at different stages in the evolution of disputes. For example, recent studies

[13] The idea of a "decision to do nothing" is a bit more complicated. One must conceptualize the idea that a state has decided to do nothing and must consider how to determine and code the times at which it decided to do.

Table 1.3 *Military confrontations over disputed territory,*
1919–1995

Region	Territorial disputes	Number of Militarized disputes	Number of wars
Europe	95	56	9
Middle & Near East	89	130	15
Africa	48	27	3
Asia	65	109	12
Americas	51	52	1
Total	348	374	40

Note: The totals listed for militarized disputes include only those initiated by challenger states while the totals for wars include all military confrontations in which both challenger and target states resorted to the large-scale use of force.

(e.g. Achen 1986; Bueno de Mesquita, Morrow, and Zorick 1997; Downs, Rocke, and Barsoom 1996; Fearon 1994a; Hart and Reed 1999; Reed 2000; Reed and Clark 2000; Rousseau, Gelpi, Reiter, and Huth 1996; Schultz 2001; Signorino 1999; Smith 1995, 1999) suggest that strategic behavior can produce selection effects which threaten the accuracy of our conclusions from empirical tests. These studies caution us to be more careful and precise about theoretical generalization. If the general logic of strategic behavior is applied to the democratic peace, it raises the possibility that the results of statistical tests may be inaccurate and that the causal effects of democratic institutions and norms may vary across different stages of a dispute. For example, some empirical studies suggest that democratic institutions and norms are much stronger in explaining whether democratic leaders initiate crises as opposed to whether they escalate these crises (Reed 2000; Rousseau 1996; Rousseau, Gelpi, Reiter, and Huth 1996). Thus, the effects of democracy may be relatively strong in channeling disputes down a path of negotiations and away from crises, yet once in crises, democratic leaders may find it more difficult to make concessions and may become more willing to use force. The general finding of few if any wars between democracies may be due primarily to the ability of democratic states to defuse and settle disputes before they escalate to the point of crisis, not because of their ability to manage crises more peacefully.

Territorial disputes and testing the democratic peace

We will test hypotheses about the democratic peace on our data set of 348 territorial disputes between states from 1919 through 1995 (see Table 1.1

and Appendices A–F). The diplomatic and military behavior of states in territorial disputes provides a particularly demanding and critical test of the democratic peace. This is because territorial disputes are a central issue over which militarized disputes, crises, and wars have erupted. For example, scholars using a variety of different types of data sets have produced consistent and convergent findings that the presence of a territorial dispute is correlated with the initiation and escalation of militarized disputes and international crises, as well as the emergence of enduring interstate rivalries and their repeated escalation to military conflicts and war (Brecher 1993: 72; Brecher and Wilkenfeld 1997: 821; Hensel 1996a, 1996b; Holsti 1991; Kocs 1995; Leng 1993; Luard 1986; Rousseau, Gelpi, Reiter, and Huth 1996; Senese 1996, 1997a; Vasquez 1993, 1995, 1996; Vasquez and Henehan 2001).

It seems clear, then, that issues of territorial sovereignty have been and remain a central concern of state leaders. Currently, more than sixty territorial disputes persist, and many regional conflicts remain linked to unresolved territorial claims. Furthermore, more recent trends of increased civil war (Byman and Van Evera 1998; Holsti 1996) threaten the dissolution of states due to ethnic conflicts and struggles for political self-determination. The break-up of states, however, is likely to produce a number of new territorial disputes, as leaders from the new and old states struggle to define where the new international border is to be located (e.g. Estonia and Latvia vs. Russia, Eritrea vs. Ethiopia, Croatia vs. Yugoslavia).

Why is it that territorial disputes significantly increase the risks of armed conflict and war? We argue for three factors that, taken together, help explain this connection:[14]

1. State leaders place a high utility on controlling disputed territory.
2. Foreign policy leaders can mobilize domestic support for territorial claims.
3. Military force is an effective instrument for achieving territorial goals.

The combined effect of these three factors is that generally, for challenger states, expected utilities for disputing territorial claims and escalating territorial disputes are higher than expected utilities for making concessions or accepting the status quo.

If territorial disputes are more likely than others to escalate to the level of military confrontations, then the study of such disputes provides a demanding test for the impact of democratic norms and institutional accountability on the conflict behavior of foreign policy leaders. If democratic political institutions and norms have the capacity to discourage military conflict and promote peaceful resolution of disputes, then territorial

---

[14] For a more detailed discussion of theoretical explanations for the strong empirical correlation between territorial disputes and international conflict see Huth (2000).

disputes – in which nationalism, high stakes, and the utility of military force all encourage leaders to choose military conflict – will push that capacity to its limits. Analyzing the effects of domestic political factors on democratic leaders involved in territorial disputes is an appropriate, though difficult, test of the democratic peace literature. If the theoretical arguments within the democratic peace literature are insightful and generalizable, then they should help to explain in a systematic way patterns of state behavior with respect to territorial disputes. Stated more generally, much recent scholarship has argued that it is essential to consider domestic factors, broadly conceived, when developing theoretical models of international conflict behavior. The careful empirical analysis of territorial disputes provides a set of potentially critical results for evaluating the utility of models which assign a prominent explanatory role to domestic-level variables.

The application of the democratic peace literature to the study of territorial conflict is an important step, then, in the democratic peace research program. If democratic peace theories cannot explain patterns of conflict over disputed territory, then there are serious reasons to question their logic and power. Conversely, if the empirical findings are clearly supportive, then our confidence in the theoretical arguments about the democratic peace should be greatly enhanced.

Conclusion

The premise of this book is that while scholars have made important contributions to our understanding of international conflict by analyzing how democratic institutions and norms affect foreign policy behavior, three problems nevertheless can be identified:

1. A number of theoretical arguments in the democratic peace literature need to be extended and revised through a re-examination of basic logic and the integration of existing arguments.
2. Quantitative empirical tests of the democratic peace have been somewhat restrictive, focusing on dyad-years as the unit of analysis. As a result, important theoretical questions have been difficult to address. Thus, while the empirical results of many such studies support the democratic peace, they are not as persuasive as they could be.
3. Recent findings on territorial disputes suggest that disputed territorial claims are one of the most contentious issues that state leaders can disagree over. The study of territorial disputes should provide an excellent opportunity to test the theoretical power of democratic peace arguments. Existing studies, however, have not tested democratic peace hypotheses against the historical record of state behavior in territorial disputes.

The research agenda, then, is twofold. First, we hope to develop the deductive logic of different models of the democratic peace more fully, seeking to explain the broad spectrum of diplomatic and military policies that state leaders may adopt in international disputes. Second, we venture to devise new and compelling statistical tests of theoretical models of the democratic peace. The remainder of this book is structured as follows. Chapters 2 through 6 present a series of theoretical models to explain the diplomatic and military decisions of state leaders involved in territorial disputes. The theory-building efforts begin with an analysis of international conditions in Chapter 3, but the key chapters are 4, 5, and 6, which develop three different domestic-based models of the democratic peace. Chapters 7, 8, and 9 present the results of a series of empirical tests of the democratic peace. In Chapter 10, we conclude with a summary analysis of the empirical findings and discuss their implications for democratic peace theories and the study of international conflict.

2 Pathways to conflict escalation and resolution in international disputes

Alternative paths to conflict and cooperation

The leaders of both democratic and authoritarian states engage in varied patterns of diplomatic and military behavior. In some international disputes we find examples of the aggressive use of military force and intransigent bargaining strategies, while in other disputes military inaction and accommodative diplomacy are equally evident. When and why do democratic and authoritarian leaders at times pursue conflictual policies? Conversely, why do they at other times seek the resolution of international disputes through compromise and concessions? Do differences in the domestic political institutions of states influence the foreign policy choices of political leaders in a consistent and systematic fashion, such that domestic politics models can explain patterns of international conflict escalation and resolution? These are the critical questions that motivate our efforts at theory building in this book.

The starting point for developing theory is to think broadly about the causal pathways that are associated with (a) the presence or absence of military conflict between states, and (b) the continued stalemate or settlement of international disputes. Figure 2.1 presents four different stages that are associated with the development of international disputes over time, along with some of the principal pathways leading to different diplomatic and military outcomes. The Dispute Initiation Stage centers on the emergence of a dispute or disagreement between countries in which a challenger state seeks to alter the prevailing status quo over some issue(s). If a target state rejects the challenger's claims, then a dispute exists. For example, after the 11 September 2001 terrorist attack on the World Trade Center and Pentagon, the United States demanded that the Taliban regime in Afghanistan cooperate with the United States in locating and arresting Osama Bin Laden and the leadership of the Al-Qaeda terrorist network within its national borders. The leadership of the Taliban government refused to cooperate and thus a new dispute had emerged between the two governments over anti-terrorism policy. Next, in the

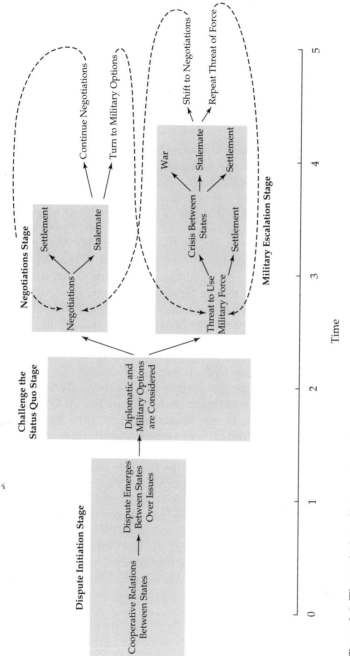

Figure 2.1 The evolution of international disputes

Challenge the Status Quo Stage, the challenger state assesses its policy options and decides when to press its claims in a dispute and by what means of diplomatic or military pressure. Thus, the Bush Administration had to decide how to respond to the initial refusal of the Taliban leadership to comply with its demands. For example, should various diplomatic options be pursued in which negotiations would be entered into with the Taliban regime, or should the United States prepare to undertake military actions in Afghanistan against the Taliban regime and Al-Qaeda network?

In the Negotiations Stage, the challenger and target have entered into talks and both states must decide whether to offer any concessions over the disputed issues. If a settlement is reached in the negotiations, the dispute ends; otherwise, the dispute persists and the challenger considers its policy options in another iteration of the Challenge the Status Quo Stage. The Bush Administration rejected the option of negotiations over the possible terms of arresting Osama Bin Laden and the Al-Qaeda leadership and instead demanded swift compliance with United States calls for a forceful crackdown on the Al-Qaeda network. Thus the United States never even entered into the Negotiations Stage.

On the other hand, if a challenger state initiates a military threat in an attempt to alter the status quo, then a Military Escalation Stage ensues. When the threatened target state responds with a counter-threat, a crisis emerges in which the leaders of both states must decide whether to resort to the large-scale use of force. In fact, the United States warned the Taliban regime that if it did not comply with its demands, then United States military forces would attack both Taliban and Al-Qaeda forces within Afghanistan. The Taliban leadership responded with counter-threats and warned the United States that it would become involved in another long and costly civil war if it intervened in Afghanistan. At this point, the two states had moved into the Military Escalation Stage.

The outcome of the international crisis determines whether the dispute continues and what foreign policy choices need to be reconsidered. For example, if war breaks out, a decisive victory by one side is likely to end the dispute whereas a stalemate on the battlefield will lead to the persistence of the dispute in the post-war period. Conversely, the avoidance of war may mean ending the dispute through a negotiated agreement, while a standoff in the crisis will result in the continuation of the dispute. In either case where the dispute persists, state leaders find themselves reconsidering their diplomatic and military options in another iteration of the Challenge the Status Quo Stage. In the current example, the United States resorted to the large-scale use of military force in early October, and by the end of December the Taliban regime had been removed from power and its armed forces (as well as those of the Al-Qaeda

Table 2.1 *Military confrontations initiated by challengers in territorial disputes, 1919–1995*

Total number of disputes	Number of disputes that involved various numbers of military conflicts					
		Number of military conflicts				
348		0	1	2–5	6–9	>10
	Total	196	75	64	8	5
		(56%)	(22%)	(18%)	(2%)	(1%)

Note: The percentages are calculated by dividing the totals for each category of military conflict by the total number of territorial disputes. The percentages may not add up to 100% due to rounding.

network) were defeated. As a result, a dispute between the United States and Afghan governments no longer existed, since the new interim regime pledged its full support for the policy of eliminating what remained of the Al-Qaeda network within Afghanistan.

Over the duration of a dispute, decision-makers must make repeated choices regarding the pursuit of negotiations and dispute settlement, the use of coercive pressure by means of military force, or the maintenance of the status quo and the avoidance of conflict. This sequence of choices over time produces various diplomatic and military outcomes characterized by quite different pathways. For example, continued stalemate may reflect a history of infrequent attempts at negotiation and no military conflict, whereas dispute resolution could reflect a short but violent history of armed conflict in which the victor imposed a settlement on the defeated party (United States policy in Afghanistan after the defeat and removal of the Taliban regime). Furthermore, even the same outcome could have been preceded by very different patterns of diplomatic and military interaction. Consider the outcome of a negotiated settlement reached through mutual concessions. In one dispute this could come about by peaceful talks and mutual compromise in a short period of time, whereas in another dispute a mutually agreeable settlement may only come about after repeated military conflicts and then difficult and protracted negotiations.

These various patterns of diplomatic and military behavior are evident in our data set of 348 territorial disputes from 1919 through 1995, which provides the empirical foundation for the statistical tests in Chapters 7 through 9.[1] Table 2.1 shows that in 56 percent of the disputes

---

[1] The concept of a territorial dispute and the coding issues that have arisen while constructing a territorial dispute data set are discussed in Appendix A. In Appendices B–F case summaries of territorial disputes by region are presented.

Table 2.2 *Rounds of negotiations in territorial disputes, 1919–1995*

Total number of disputes		Number of disputes that involved various numbers of negotiation rounds				
		Number of rounds				
348		0	1	2–5	6–9	>10
	Total	44	75	140	46	43
		(13%)	(22%)	(40%)	(13%)	(12%)

Note: The percentages are calculated by dividing the totals for each category of rounds by the total number of territorial disputes.

(196/348) challenger states did not even once resort to the threat or use of military force in their attempts to change the status quo, while in 21 percent of the disputes (77/348) challengers turned to coercive military pressure multiple times (two or more military conflicts). For example, in the long-standing dispute over Northern Ireland, Ireland has not initiated any military confrontations against the British in an attempt to coerce a change in policy. In contrast, in the dispute over Kashmir, Pakistan initiated fourteen military confrontations during the period 1947–95, with two confrontations escalating to war. If we shift from comparisons regarding the frequency of military conflict to reliance on negotiations, we also see considerable variance across disputes. In Table 2.2 we find that in over 22 percent of the disputes (75/348) there was only one round of talks, while in just over one-quarter of the disputes (89/348) challengers held six or more rounds of talks with their adversaries. Once again, Ireland has pursued twenty-seven rounds of negotiations with the British over Northern Ireland, while China only held four rounds of talks with Japan over the disputed Senkaku Islands during the period 1951–95.

The data set also provides evidence of different pathways to armed conflict. For example, Table 2.3 shows that in most disputes the decision by challenger states to shift from diplomacy to coercive military pressure was made within five years of the beginning of the dispute (94/152 or 62 percent), but in about 14 percent of the cases (21/152) a dispute persisted for over twenty years before such a decision was reached. For example, Arab territorial claims to Israel immediately escalated to a war in 1948, while Argentina's dispute with Chile over their land border and the Beagle Channel remained free of any military conflicts for many decades until limited military confrontations in the 1950s and a period of frequent crises in the 1970s. Another way to look at the pathway to armed conflict is to consider the frequency of talks and negotiations prior to military conflicts. In Table 2.4 the data reveal that in over 40 percent of the territorial

Table 2.3 *Timing of military threats to the status quo by challengers in territorial disputes, 1919–1995*

Total number of disputes	Number of disputes of various duration prior to first military confrontation				
	Number of dispute years				
152	1–5	6–10	11–20	21–30	>30
Total	94	16	21	8	13
	(62%)	(11%)	(14%)	(5%)	(9%)

Note: The percentages are calculated by dividing the totals for each category of dispute years by the total number of territorial disputes. The percentages may not add up to 100% due to rounding. Given our focus on the period 1919–1995 dispute years are counted from 1919 onward, although a small number of disputes had begun prior to 1919.

Table 2.4 *Shift from negotiations to military threats by challengers in territorial disputes, 1919–1995*

Total number of disputes	Number of disputes involving various numbers of negotiation rounds before first military confrontation				
	Number of rounds				
152	0	1–5	6–10	11–20	21–30
Total	61	51	21	15	4
	(40%)	(34%)	(14%)	(10%)	(3%)

Note: The percentages are calculated by dividing the totals for each category of rounds by the total number of territorial disputes. The percentages may not add up to 100% due to rounding. Given our focus on the period 1919–1995 we do not include in this table any rounds of talks that occur in some pre-existing disputes prior to 1919.

disputes involving a military conflict (61/152), challengers turned to military force despite no previous rounds of negotiations. However, nearly 13 percent of the disputes (19/152) involved more than ten rounds of talks before the challenger initiated a military confrontation. For example, Soviet territorial demands on its Baltic neighbors in 1939 quickly escalated to military threats and occupation. In contrast, Argentina held multiple rounds of talks with Chile from the 1920s to early 1950s before the first military confrontation.

Alternative pathways to compromise and dispute resolution are clearly present in the data set as well. One indicator of this is the duration of disputes before the challenger state offers or makes concessions in talks. In Table 2.5 we see that over 23 percent of the cases (23/103) in which

Table 2.5 *Duration of territorial disputes and major concessions by challengers in negotiations, 1919–1995*

Total number of disputes		Number of disputes of various durations before first offer of major concessions				
		Number of dispute years				
103		1–5	6–10	11–20	21–40	>40
	Total	34	23	23	15	8
		(33%)	(22%)	(22%)	(15%)	(8%)

Note: The percentages are calculated by dividing the totals for each category of dispute years by the total number of territorial disputes. Due to our focus on the period 1919–1995 dispute years are counted from 1919 onward, although a small number of disputes had begun prior to 1919.

Table 2.6 *Timing of major concessions by challengers in negotiations over disputed territory, 1919–1995*

Total number of disputes		Number of disputes involving various numbers of negotiation rounds before first offer of major concessions			
		Number of rounds			
103		0	1–5	6–10	11–20
	Total	23	61	11	8
		(22%)	(59%)	(11%)	(8%)

Note: The percentages are calculated by dividing the totals for each category of rounds by the total number of territorial disputes. Given our focus on the period 1919–1995 we do not include in this table any rounds of talks that occur in some pre-existing disputes prior to 1919.

concessions were offered by challengers occurred more than twenty years after the dispute had begun, while in 33 percent of the cases (34/103) challenger states made such concessions within the first five years of the dispute. In the Persian Gulf, the emergence in the 1930s of disputes between Saudi Arabia and the British over what would become the borders of the United Arab Emirates and South Yemen were characterized by British concessions on several occasions during multiple rounds of talks in the mid-to-late 1930s. In contrast, Syria has remained steadfast in its claims to regain the Golan Heights after 1967 and has only offered limited non-territorial concessions in talks held in the 1990s. Another useful measure is the number of rounds of talks that preceded decisions by challengers to make concessions. We see in Table 2.6 that 22 percent of the

Table 2.7 *Military conflict and major concessions by challengers in negotiations over disputed territory, 1919–1995*

Total number of disputes	Number of disputes in which military conflict did/did not precede first offer of major concessions	
103	History of military conflict	Absence of military conflict
Total	33	70
	(32%)	(68%)

Note: The percentages are calculated by dividing the totals for each category of military conflict by the total number of territorial disputes. The presence or absence of military conflict is based on the period from 1919 onward, although a small number of disputes had begun prior to 1919.

challengers (23/103) were willing to concede without first testing the resolve of the target in previous rounds of talks, but in about 19 percent of the cases (19/103) many rounds of talks (six or more) were required before challengers would concede. For example, Britain and France were able to reach an agreement based on mutual concessions quickly between 1919 and 1920 to settle disputes over the borders of British and French-controlled Syria, Jordan, and Palestine. In contrast, in the 1990s Syria finally offered limited concessions to Israel regarding the Golan Heights after many earlier rounds of talks had ended in stalemate.

Another interesting aspect of the pathway to dispute resolution is the history of prior armed conflict in these territorial disputes. Table 2.7 presents data on whether militarized conflicts preceded the decisions of challengers to make concessions in negotiations. The challengers' path to seeking a settlement was nonviolent in about 68 percent of the cases (70/103), while in the remaining 32 percent of cases concessions were preceded by one or more military confrontations. For example, major Iraqi concessions over the Shatt-al-Arab during 1974–5 were preceded by a series of military confrontations, while China and Pakistan settled their border through negotiations from 1960–3 without any prior military confrontations.

Overall, the theoretical models developed in Chapters 3 through 6 seek to explain the varied patterns of behavior summarized in the tables above: (a) the repeated choices of state leaders regarding diplomacy and military force, and therefore (b) which pathways to war, dispute settlement, and stalemate are selected by foreign policy decision-makers.

Figure 2.1 and the patterns presented in Tables 2.1 through 2.7 have five important implications for our theory building efforts:

1. Conflict escalation to the level of international crises and the outbreak of war almost always take place within the context of an existing international dispute over some set of contested issues. As a result, international disputes rarely escalate to military confrontations without a history of prior diplomacy and negotiations. Furthermore, most international disputes do not evolve into military confrontations. This prior stage of diplomacy and the transition from nonviolent to violent conflict is a critical feature in the evolution of international disputes over time.

2. A similar point can be made about the pathway to the settlement of international disputes. That is, state leaders often engage in several, if not many, efforts at negotiations before deciding to make major concessions. In fact, they may even turn to coercive force before making significant concessions. As a result, disputes are rarely settled without the parties involved seeking to shift the burden of concession-making on to their adversary. Therefore, theoretical models of the democratic peace (and empirical tests of such models) should account for these different pathways to outcomes such as international crises, wars, or dispute settlement through negotiations. Powerful theoretical models should be able to help us understand these earlier stages in the development of international disputes as well as the dynamics of state leaders' decisions to shift from diplomacy to military force, or to quit holding out for concessions and instead to offer substantial concessions themselves.

3. Since international disputes unfold over time and repeated choices are made by state leaders, theoretical models will need to consider: (a) how the past history of a dispute influences the current diplomatic and military policies of state leaders, and (b) how the larger strategic context of a state's foreign policy affects how policy-makers must manage their country's concurrent involvement in multiple international disputes. As a result, the theoretical models presented in Chapters 3 through 6 will need to account for periods of continuity as well as change in the diplomatic and military behavior of states. If international disputes persist over time, however, political institutions within states may change and the foreign policy choices should then vary as a result of those domestic institutional changes.

4. The decisions reached at various stages of a dispute reflect the influence of (a) prior conditions that help explain why a certain pathway has been selected by decision-makers, but also (b) the more current short-term actions and changes in prevailing conditions that can lead decision-makers to update their beliefs and to change their initial assessment of policy options. The theoretical analysis of state behavior

Table 2.8 *Military escalation by challengers in territorial disputes, 1919–1995*

Number of military confrontations	Number of military confrontations that escalated to war or brink of war
374	89 (24%)

at different stages should incorporate new information and conditions that have arisen since the initial choice of state leaders shifted the dispute into a new stage.

For example, a decision by a challenger state to issue a threat of force does not necessarily reflect a firm decision to escalate to the large-scale use of force. The territorial dispute data set contains 374 cases of military confrontations initiated by challengers, but in only about 89 of these confrontations (24 percent) does the challenger either resort to the large-scale use of force or seem resolved to do so (see Table 2.8). As a result, a theoretical distinction between the initiation and escalation of militarized conflicts should be drawn. Challengers may initiate a militarized dispute without knowing whether they would escalate further. A threat of force may be designed to probe the intentions and resolve of a target state, to induce the target to resume talks by signaling the dangers of a continued stalemate, or to pressure the target into making concessions in an upcoming round of talks. Furthermore, militarized disputes and crises can unfold over months, and during that time domestic political conditions can change, other international disputes can arise, third parties can intervene, and the target state's own behavior can signal new information about its resolve and military strength. Certainly, the challenger had beliefs about possible escalation outcomes when it made its initial threat, but its beliefs and even goals may change in response to the short-term actions of the target and third parties, as well as to changes in domestic and international conditions that occurred after the militarized dispute was initiated.

5. The three models of domestic political institutions presented in Chapters 4 through 6 are applicable to explaining each of the stages in Figure 2.1 except for the very first stage, which examines the emergence of a dispute between countries. If a theoretical model were to explain that preliminary stage, it would focus on answering two questions: (a) what issues are likely to arise that might be disputed and why do such issues emerge among certain states? and (b) if contentious

issues potentially exist between states, why is it that only some of those latent disputes become explicit and direct conflicts? Why are some states deterred from even raising the issue of a disagreement to begin with? In our judgement, the domestic-level models presented in Chapters 4 through 6 are not well suited to answer these questions. Instead, each of the models is better situated to explain how conflictual or cooperative state leaders will be in their attempts to pursue their claims in a dispute. As a result, we do not attempt to analyze theoretically why countries initially become embroiled in conflicts over disputed territory.[2]

Analyzing territorial disputes

The models that we develop in Chapters 3 through 6 attempt to explain a series of basic foreign policy choices confronted by state leaders who are involved in a territorial dispute. These critical choices are represented in simplified form in Figures 2.2 to 2.4. In the Challenge the Status Quo Stage, the theoretical focus is directed at the decision of the challenger state – whether it will seek a change in the status quo and, if so, by what mix of diplomacy and/or military force. The next stage depends upon what choice was initially selected by the challenger. If the challenger pursues neither diplomatic nor military initiatives, the status quo persists. If the challenger decides to rely on negotiations, then the next stage to be analyzed is what we term the Negotiations Stage. In this stage of the dispute each of the theoretical models seeks to explain the choices of both challenger and target to offer or withhold concessions. However, if the challenger contests the status quo through the movement or use of their country's regular armed forces in disputed territory against the target state, then the analysis shifts to the Military Escalation Stage. Both parties now must decide whether to risk war in pursuit of their territorial claims. The outcomes of the Negotiations and Military Escalation Stages determine whether the dispute persists or comes to an end. If the dispute

[2] In previous work Huth (1996: ch. 4) has analyzed when states do become involved in territorial disputes and we have incorporated into our theoretical and empirical analyses in this book several of the variables that were found to help explain the emergence of territorial disputes. As a result, while we do not model the initial stage of territorial dispute initiation, we do try to control for factors that help to account for this first stage of the selection process. While scholars studying the causes of war have become increasingly aware of selection bias issues in studying the escalation of international crises and militarized disputes (e.g. Bueno de Mesquita, Morrow, and Zorick 1997; Fearon 1994a, b; Hart and Reed 1999; Morrow 1989; Reed 2000; Schultz 2001a; Smith 1996), less attention has been directed to developing and testing models which seek to explain why disputes might initially arise between states. A promising effort in this direction is the recent work of Bueno de Mesquita, Morrow, Siverson, and Smith (1999).

Table 2.9 *Challenges to the status quo in territorial disputes, 1919–1995*

Number of dispute observations involving various diplomatic and military policies adopted by challenger states			
Total number of observations	Maintain status quo	Seek negotiations	Threaten force
6542	4370	1782	390
	(67%)	(27%)	(6%)

Note: The percentages are calculated by dividing the totals for each category of policies by the total number of dispute observations.

persists, then the next iteration of the dispute is analyzed, beginning once again with the challenger's choice regarding the status quo. In this new iteration of the dispute, domestic and international conditions may now have changed, and previous diplomatic and military outcomes in the dispute might influence the current choices of both challenger and target. We now turn to each of these three stages in more detail.

The decision to challenge the status quo

At this stage (see Figure 2.2) the challenger state has to decide whether to try to alter the territorial status quo through a foreign policy initiative. If so, should the initiative be only diplomatic in nature, should it be largely coercive based on the use of military force, or should it consist of diplomacy backed by the coercive threat of force? The challenger's policy options can be grouped in three categories, ranging from a non-coercive diplomatic initiative to a very coercive policy of seeking to compel a change in the status quo by a military victory:

1. Category one: No attempt to change the status quo by direct negotiations or military actions
2. Category two: An attempt to alter the status quo by only diplomacy and negotiations
3. Category three: A direct threat or use of military force

For the territorial dispute data set, Table 2.9 summarizes the distribution of values across these three categories of policy options. To help illustrate the options available to state leaders in the Status Quo Stage, consider as an example the options available to the Pakistani political and military leadership at the time the dispute with India over Kashmir emerged in the summer of 1947. Pakistan sought to incorporate Kashmir as part of Pakistan, while India preferred that Kashmir join the Indian union. At the time of independence for both India and Pakistan, the maharaja of Kashmir had refused to accede to either country. In October, however,

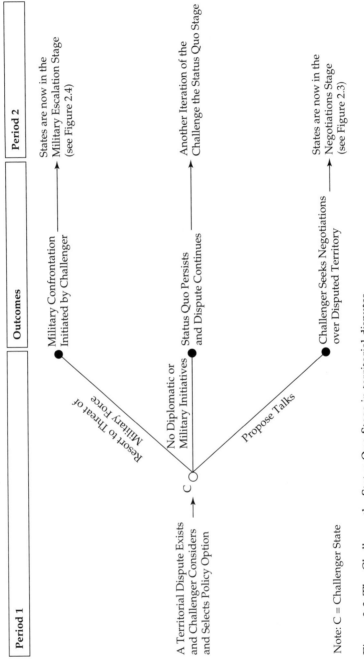

Period 1

Outcomes

Period 2

A Territorial Dispute Exists
and Challenger Considers
and Selects Policy Option

Resort to Threat of
Military Force

Military Confrontation
Initiated by Challenger

States are now in the
Military Escalation Stage
(see Figure 2.4)

No Diplomatic or
Military Initiatives

Status Quo Persists
and Dispute Continues

Another Iteration of the
Challenge the Status Quo Stage

Propose Talks

Challenger Seeks Negotiations
over Disputed Territory

States are now in the
Negotiations Stage
(see Figure 2.3)

Note: C = Challenger State

Figure 2.2 The Challenge the Status Quo Stage in territorial disputes

the maharaja acceded to India and large numbers of Indian armed forces moved into Kashmir to oppose Azad Kashmir rebel forces backed by Pakistan. At this time, Pakistan had a variety of options to consider ranging from: accepting the accession of Kashmir to India, relying on diplomacy and negotiations to persuade the maharaja and India to change their policies, or contesting the accession of Kashmir to India by direct military means and therefore possibly risking war with India (for a summary see Brecher and Wilkenfeld 1997: 166–7).

The theoretical focus in the Status Quo Stage is on explaining active bilateral efforts by the challenger state to change the status quo. The premise is that to change the status quo the challenger needs to engage the target state directly by some combination of diplomacy and/or military force. In the absence of such policy initiatives, the target is very unlikely to change its policies and concede territory.

We can think of category one as the status quo policy. The important question is whether the challenger will initiate more direct diplomatic or military actions in the future in an attempt to change the status quo. This status quo category does not necessarily imply that the challenger is passive, since it could include the following actions by the challenger: (a) rhetoric and statements which are hostile and critical of the target, (b) reiteration of its claims and the legitimacy of its position in the dispute and/or statements that if a deadlock is to be broken, the target needs to change its policies, (c) continuing conflictual bilateral relations characterized by economic sanctions and severed diplomatic ties, and/or (d) attempts to gather support from third parties for its territorial claims. In sum, maintaining the status quo can imply a hostile relationship between the challenger and target in which the challenger remains firmly committed to the policy of overturning the status quo. It could also include a situation in which the challenger maintains a normal state of bilateral relations and simply does not make any effort to press its territorial claim. The one common and theoretically critical defining feature, however, is that in either of these two cases the challenger essentially refrains from direct engagement with the target over the disputed territorial issue.

Category two represents a decision by the challenger to forgo the military option and instead rely on negotiations. Reliance on diplomacy and talks seemingly could be viewed as a less coercive policy approach for the challenger. In particular, the decision to pursue negotiations could reflect an interest in dispute settlement through concessions. The decision to seek negotiations, however, could also be motivated by other incentives, such as (a) the desire to respond to international or domestic political pressures and to counter charges of being truculent and unwilling to negotiate, or (b) the desire to test the resolve of the target and to determine if territorial concessions can be gained without incurring the risks of military action. Given these varied motivations for pursuing talks, we are hesitant to draw any strong inferences that proposing negotiations represents a cooperative approach to territorial dispute settlement.

Category three clearly represents a coercive approach to changing the status quo. This category does not imply that diplomacy and talks have been rejected by the challenger. Indeed, diplomacy backed by the active threat of force is an enduring feature of statecraft. The critical theoretical distinction associated with this third category is that the challenger initiates military actions that risk a direct and larger military confrontation with the target. That is, the political leadership of the challenger threatens or, in fact, engages its armed forces in an attack against the military forces of the target.

As noted above, the threat or initiation of force by the challenger at this stage does not necessarily mean that the challenger has decided to resort to the large-scale use of force. That is, given that the challenger has initiated a threat, we should not assume that the challenger will escalate to the large-scale use of force. The initiation of the threat of force could represent any of the following:

1. A probe to test the resolve of the target and possibly third parties. In this case the decisions of the challenger to initiate and escalate are sequential and separate choices.

2. A policy to put pressure on the target (or third parties) to resume talks or to soften its position in ongoing or future talks. The challenger's estimates of the risks and payoffs from escalation may not be central to the decision to initiate a threat, since the purpose of the limited threat is to bolster its bargaining position in subsequent talks.

3. A policy to divert the attention of domestic political actors away from internal problems towards an international adversary. In this scenario it is difficult to generalize about whether the challenger's decision to initiate is tightly linked to calculations of expected escalation outcomes. On the one hand, the challenger may only be seeking a low-level confrontation to generate domestic rally effects, in which case estimates of military escalation would not figure centrally in the initial decision. On the other hand, if the challenger is not confident about its ability to limit escalation, then it would not want to initiate a threat unless it thought that its chances in a large-scale military conflict were favorable, since a military setback would only worsen the domestic political problems of the leadership. In this latter case, it seems reasonable to draw a more direct connection between initiation and escalation choices.

4. The first stage in a plan to use large-scale force to take control of disputed territory. This is a case in which the decisions to initiate and escalate are essentially one and the same.

If we return to our example of Pakistani policy options in the October of 1947 over Kashmir, we see that Pakistani leaders refused to accept the new status quo established by Kashmir's accession to India. Pakistan then had to consider the diplomatic and military options available to contest the new status quo. Pakistan rejected reliance on diplomacy and negotiations and therefore began preparations for direct military intervention. By March of 1948 Pakistani armed forces launched their first attack against Indian armed forces. The goal of the military intervention was to prevent a decisive victory by the Indian army and to compel India to resume negotiations over the status of Kashmir (Brecher and Wilkenfeld 1997: 166–7).

The decision to concede in negotiations

Suppose the challenger initiates negotiations with the target and does not threaten or use force to support its bargaining position. For the challenger and target the critical question now becomes: What concessions, if any, should be offered to resolve the dispute at this time?

The theoretical analysis in this negotiating stage (see Figure 2.3) centers on the extent of concessions by challenger and target in a given round of talks: (a) no concessions, (b) limited concessions, or (c) major concessions.

The outcome of no concessions represents a very firm and unyielding bargaining position in which state leaders refuse to make any changes in policy. In some cases this type of policy may reflect an equally intransigent negotiating position by the other party, yet in other cases the refusal to make any concessions may have been maintained despite concessions by the other side. Limited concessions implies that the challenger or target either proposed or actually made concessions regarding (a) non-territorial issues that are part of the talks, or (b) a small amount of the disputed territory. Once again, these limited concessions may or may not have been reciprocated by the other party. Finally, the outcome of major concessions by one party implies that it acceded to many if not all of the territorial demands of the other party. In some cases it is possible that both sides make major concessions over different sections of disputed territory (see Table 2.10 for the distribution of outcomes in the Negotiations Stage).

The territorial dispute is very likely to end if one or both parties make major concessions. Limited concessions by the target, however, are unlikely to settle the dispute. In this case the challenger returns to the Status Quo Stage and has to decide whether to pursue further negotiations, turn to military force, or accept the revised status quo for the time being. Similar decisions have to be made by the challenger in the event that the negotiations end in deadlock with neither side making concessions.

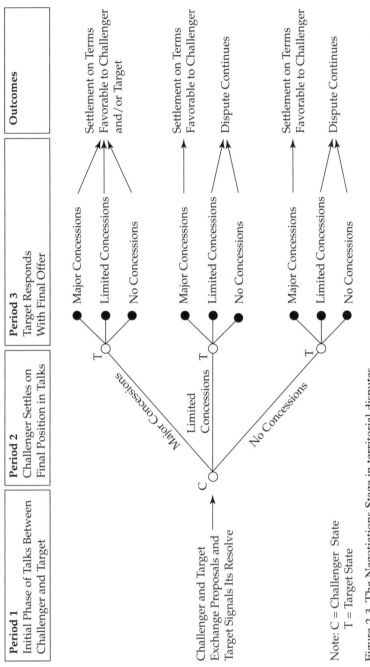

| Period 1 | Period 2 | Period 3 | Outcomes |
| Initial Phase of Talks Between Challenger and Target | Challenger Settles on Final Position in Talks | Target Responds With Final Offer | |

Major Concessions

Limited Concessions

No Concessions

Settlement on Terms Favorable to Challenger and/or Target

Major Concessions

Limited Concessions

No Concessions

Settlement on Terms Favorable to Challenger

Dispute Continues

Major Concessions

Limited Concessions

No Concessions

Settlement on Terms Favorable to Challenger

Dispute Continues

T

T

T

Major Concessions

Limited Concessions

No Concessions

C

Challenger and Target Exchange Proposals and Target Signals Its Resolve

Note: C = Challenger State
T = Target State

Figure 2.3 The Negotiations Stage in territorial disputes

Table 2.10 *Concessions by states in negotiations over disputed territory, 1919–1995*

| Total number of rounds of talks | I. Challenger Outcomes of talks | |
	No concessions	Limited or major concessions
1528	960 (63%)	568 (37%)

| Total number of rounds of talks | II. Target Outcomes of talks | |
	No concessions	Limited or major concessions
1528	983 (64%)	545 (36%)

Note: The percentages are calculated by dividing the totals for each negotiation outcome category by the total number of rounds of talks.

Once again we can use the Kashmir dispute to illustrate this description of the Negotiations Stage. Pakistani diplomatic initiatives and efforts between October 1947 and March 1948 failed to bring about any changes in Kashmir, as both sides refused to concede on the central issues. India insisted that the maharaja's decision to accede to the Indian union followed accepted procedures and was therefore legal and legitimate. Pakistan, however, contested the legitimacy of the accession proclamation and insisted that the rights of self-determination for the Kashmiri population had been thwarted. From the Pakistani perspective diplomacy and attempts at negotiations had ended in failure and therefore the military option was then chosen.

The decision to escalate and risk war

The challenger and target are now in a military confrontation over disputed territory (see Figure 2.4). The theoretical analysis at this stage focuses on explaining the decisions of leaders in each state to escalate a military confrontation that was initiated by the challenger. The question for both parties is twofold: Should territorial claims be maintained at the risk of war, and what level of military force should be employed in support of such claims? For the challenger the question can be posed as follows: Having initiated a militarized dispute, is further military escalation required to achieve a favorable change in the status quo? We want to

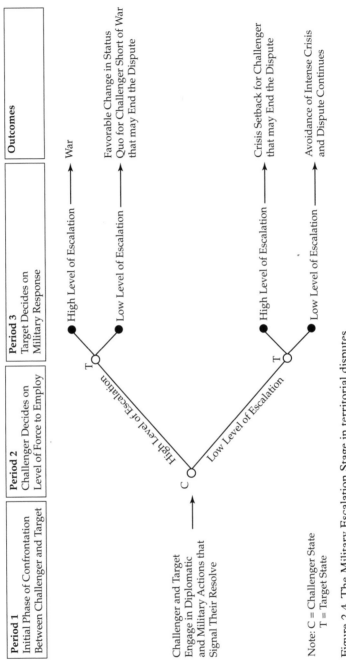

Period 1 Initial Phase of Confrontation Between Challenger and Target	Period 2 Challenger Decides on Level of Force to Employ	Period 3 Target Decides on Military Response	Outcomes

High Level of Escalation ⟶ War

Low Level of Escalation ⟶ Favorable Change in Status Quo for Challenger Short of War that may End the Dispute

High Level of Escalation ⟶ Crisis Setback for Challenger that may End the Dispute

Low Level of Escalation ⟶ Avoidance of Intense Crisis and Dispute Continues

T

High Level of Escalation

Low Level of Escalation

T

C

Challenger and Target
Engage in Diplomatic
and Military Actions that
Signal Their Resolve

Note: C = Challenger State
        T = Target State

Figure 2.4 The Military Escalation Stage in territorial disputes

reiterate that the challenger's choice at this stage depends not only upon the conditions and incentives that motivated the initial threat but also upon new conditions and updated beliefs that may have emerged over time as a result of the diplomatic and military interactions between the challenger and target since the threat was first issued.

The challenger's choices can be portrayed as falling into one of two policy categories: (a) no further escalation or only limited escalation, or (b) a high level of escalation. A policy of no further escalation indicates that the challenger engages in little if any further military build-up or preparations beyond the level of the initial threat, even if the target escalates to higher levels of military preparedness and refuses to make any substantial concessions. In addition, the challenger may even offer territorial concessions as part of a policy to further reduce the risk of war. Limited escalation implies that the challenger increases the size and readiness of military forces beyond the initial level of threat but does not resort to the large-scale use of force, despite the target's refusal to offer concessions. In this scenario, the challenger seems willing to increase the military pressure on the target, but is not prepared to cross the critical threshold of risking war by initiating the large-scale use of force. Escalation to high levels occurs when the challenger refuses to offer any territorial concessions and resorts to the large-scale use of force when the target stands firm and refuses concessions. The challenger clearly risks war by initiating an attack against a target that seems resolved to defend its disputed territory. If the challenger escalates to the large-scale threat of force and refuses to offer concessions but does not resort to an attack because the target retreats and agrees to major concessions, we would nevertheless place the challenger in the high escalation category. In this latter type of crisis, we do not know if the challenger would have attacked, but its behavior was fully consistent with the actions of a state that is prepared to do so.

For the target the question can be posed as: Faced with a challenger threatening a military conflict, should we stand firm and use whatever force is necessary, or should we try to avoid further military escalation even at the price of concessions? The target's resolve to stand firm at the risk of war can be categorized in terms very similar to those used above for the challenger: (a) low or limited escalation, or (b) tit-for-tat to high escalation. With a policy of low or limited escalation the target does not reciprocate the escalation of the challenger and may even propose unilateral concessions. Tit-for-tat and high escalation, on the other hand, implies that the target offers no concessions on territorial issues and matches, if not exceeds, the level of military escalation reached by the challenger. This is the behavior pattern of targets who not only seem

Table 2.11 *Escalation by states in military confrontations over disputed territory, 1919–1995*

	I. Challenger level of escalation	
Total number of military conflicts	Low or limited escalation	High escalation
374	285	89
	(76%)	(24%)
	II. Target level of escalation	
Total number of military conflicts	Low or limited escalation	High escalation
374	307	67
	(82%)	(18%)

Note: The percentages are calculated by dividing the totals for each category of escalation by the total number of military conflicts.

willing to push a crisis to the brink of war, but are also willing to go to war to protect their territorial interests if attacked or severely threatened. Table 2.11 reports the distribution of outcomes in the Military Escalation Stage.

There are several possible outcomes to the Military Escalation Stage. For example, the challenger or target could back down and offer territorial concessions, thereby diffusing the crisis. Or the crisis could end in a stalemate with no armed conflict and no change in the status quo. In the latter case, the challenger returns to the Status Quo Stage for another iteration of the dispute. If the crisis does escalate, it is possible that the challenger could take control of the disputed territory without armed resistance. The target would then have to decide whether to accept the loss of territory, or maintain its claims and assume the role of a challenger to the new territorial status quo that has been established. Finally, if the target resists an attack the ensuing war could result in a victory by one side, which might bring an end to the dispute. A war ending in stalemate, however, would place the challenger once again in the Status Quo Stage in the aftermath of the war.

If we apply this general discussion of the Military Escalation Stage to the Kashmir case, we see that in March of 1948 the Pakistani leadership had decided to turn to the direct use of military force against India. In the ensuing military conflict both sides committed large numbers of military forces and, as a result, the dispute over Kashmir escalated to a war between the two countries with fighting continuing until late 1948. When a cease-fire agreement went into effect in January 1949, India had achieved a clear but not complete military victory. Roughly two-thirds of Kashmir was under Indian occupation, with Pakistan controlling the remaining one-third. Even though Pakistan failed to dislodge Indian forces from much of Kashmir, its leadership refused to accept the unfavorable status quo and maintained that if given the free and fair opportunity to exercise its right of self-determination, the majority of the Kashmiri (Muslim) population would vote for union with Pakistan. Thus, by January 1949 the initial phase of the Kashmir dispute had been played out with India establishing a new line of control in Kashmir that was quite favorable to its interests, while Pakistan refused to reconcile itself to the loss of much of Kashmir (Brecher and Wilkenfeld 1997: 166–7).

Conclusion

We began this chapter by arguing that the theoretical analysis of international disputes should be disaggregated into a series of stages in which state leaders make repeated choices about the use of diplomacy and military force. Over time the sequence and pattern of such choices can produce very different pathways to escalation and war as well as to dispute settlement. We then applied these general points to the study of territorial disputes and presented in more detail the different stages through which such disputes can progress. We summarized the principal foreign policy choices that need to be explained by theoretical models. In the next four chapters we present a series of models that portray foreign policy choices over disputed territory as a function of domestic and international political calculations. As already noted, the choices of challenger and target states regarding the use of diplomacy and military force are repeated many times over the duration of a dispute. The past history of diplomatic and military outcomes potentially influences current choices, and states can alter policies over time as domestic and/or international conditions change. The focus of the theoretical analysis is directed at the domestic level in Chapters 4 through 6. These chapters contain three different models of how domestic political institutions shape foreign policy choices. However, before turning to these different domestic models, in Chapter 3 we offer a simple model of international politics that provides a starting point for theoretical analysis, which is then supplemented with the domestic models in subsequent chapters.

3 The international strategic context

In the previous chapter we summarized the stages associated with the evolution of territorial disputes and the corresponding set of policy options from which state leaders can choose. In this and the next three chapters we present a series of models that attempt to explain which diplomatic and military policies will be adopted by political leaders in territorial disputes. The thrust of the theoretical analysis is directed at the domestic level, particularly in Chapters 4 through 6. In this chapter, however, we develop a model of international politics as a starting point for theoretical analysis. For each model presented in this and subsequent chapters, the underlying theoretical foundations are first described and then a number of hypotheses are proposed and discussed. Each chapter concludes with a discussion of how the hypotheses will be operationalized for empirical testing.

A model of international politics

In this model the explanation of the foreign policy choices of state leaders centers on calculations about international political and military conditions. We begin with a model of international politics because each of the domestic-based models in Chapters 4 through 6 must be placed in a broader international strategic context. Before turning to each of these domestic models, it is necessary to identify the general incentives and constraints on decision-makers that are associated with pursuing foreign policy goals in an anarchic international system.

We want to reiterate that we do not consider the International Politics Model presented in this chapter to be logically incompatible with the domestic models that focus on political institutions in Chapters 4 through 6. As Huth has argued elsewhere (1996, 1998), compelling theoretical accounts of foreign policy behavior require that analysts consider how both domestic and international conditions influence the decisions of policymakers. While we argue in this chapter that international political-military conditions systematically shape policy choices in territorial disputes, we expect that domestic-level variables will also produce strong causal effects. Put differently, the International Politics Model (with its realist underpinnings) establishes a theoretical starting point for the analysis of territorial disputes that is then strengthened in subsequent chapters by considering how the domestic political context shapes foreign policy choices.

Premises and hypotheses

A general note is required about the presentation of the hypotheses for the international and domestic politics models. In an effort to avoid repetition, when discussing predicted state behavior during rounds of talks or military confrontations we will state the hypotheses in terms as general as possible. As a result, designations of challenger and target status are avoided in most cases since the logic of the hypotheses holds equally well for either party. When stating each hypothesis formally we typically begin with propositions regarding challenges to the status quo, followed by those regarding concessions in negotiations and then those concerning the escalation of military confrontations.

Premise 1: International anarchy and the pursuit of foreign policy goals

State leaders are charged with the responsibility of pursuing territorial claims in the political context of international anarchy.

Given that there is no generally recognized international actor with the authority and power to enforce the settlement of international disputes, state leaders must ultimately rely on their own domestic and foreign policies to ensure their country's national security goals. We make no general premise, however, regarding the intentions of state leaders. Political leaders can have varied foreign policy goals ranging from the defensive protection of the status quo to aggressive designs to challenge it (e.g. Glaser 1994/95, 1997; Kugler and Lemke 1996; Schweller 1998; Zakaria 1997). If we refer back to Figures 2.2 through 2.4 in Chapter 2, states which are termed challengers are dissatisfied with the territorial status quo, while states deemed as targets are satisfied with existing boundaries or effective control over bordering regions or islands. In the absence of any challenger initiatives, the status quo will prevail since targets are very unlikely to concede territory unless challengers apply diplomatic and/or military pressure. As a result, questions of military conflict, war, and the negotiated settlement of territorial disputes revolve around initiatives pursued by challenger states.

One implication of this first premise is that ensuring military security is a central policy goal of state leaders and therefore they should assess the value of disputed territory in terms of whether control over territory will have important consequences for their country's military security. As a result, disputed territory with military or strategic value should be highly desired by state leaders. A second implication is that state leaders generally prefer to rely upon their own country's economic, military, and human resources to counter threats and to achieve foreign policy goals. There are two principal reasons for this preference. First, allies may not be fully reliable in times of international crisis and conflict.[1] Second, external support from allies is typically based on some type of political exchange wherein the recipient of support is expected in turn to support certain foreign policy goals of its ally. As a result, dependence on allies can create problems of entrapment in which dependent states become engulfed in their allies' conflicts, which may be peripheral to their own security needs (e.g. Cha 2000; Lake 1999; Snyder 1984, 1997; Stein 1990: ch. 6). Furthermore, problems of moral hazard may arise as states pursue more intransigent policies in their disputes with other states because they are more confident of support from their allies if the dispute escalates to the threat or use of force (e.g. Smith 1995, 1996).

Despite these risks, foreign policy leaders at times do conclude that they cannot achieve foreign policy goals without the assistance and cooperation of other states (Christensen and Snyder 1990; Lake 1999; Morrow 1991, 1993, 1994a; Powell 1999; Reiter 1996; Smith 1995; Sorokin 1994; Walt 1987). As a result, various forms of security cooperation between states, ranging from formal alliance ties to close alignment, are signals that states value the ally's support so highly that they are willing to accept or risk some loss of autonomy over their own foreign policies.

Premise 2: The value of relative military strength
The threat or use of military force is a critical source of bargaining leverage for state leaders, especially for those engaged in territorial disputes.

We believe that the threat or use of military force is not equally effective in support of foreign policy goals across a wide range of issue areas (e.g.

---

[1] While some scholars argue that military allies are quite unreliable (e.g. Sabrosky 1980), Huth in his empirical research (Huth 1998; Huth and Russett 1984, 1988) has found consistent evidence that states honor alliance commitments in crises or when deterrence fails (also see Leeds, Long, and Mitchell 2000). Nevertheless, even though we believe that alliance ties are important signals of commitment, they do not ensure support and intervention. Also see Bennett, Lepgold, and Unger (1994); Christensen and Snyder (1990); Fearon (1997); Gelpi (1999); Krebs (1999); and Smith (1996) for useful discussions of the alliance reliability literature and analyses of intra-alliance relations.

Baldwin 1979, 1985; Keohane and Nye 1977; Lamborn 1997). Instead, we argue that military force is particularly effective in support of territorial goals. The goal of translating a military victory on the battlefield into clear diplomatic and political concessions by an adversary can be quite difficult to attain, but the ability to establish physical control of disputed territory is a consistent consequence of defeating the armed forces of another country. As a result, state leaders in territorial disputes should view relative military strength as a critical factor determining their ability to achieve territorial goals.

An implication of this second premise is that state leaders should be selective in threatening or using force in foreign policy so as to avoid overextending their country's military capabilities. The reason is that overextension would risk undermining their ability to threaten force credibly in support of diplomacy in international disputes. Two intuitive propositions follow. First, state leaders should be less willing to threaten or use force when the issues at stake in an international dispute do not involve important policy objectives. Second, state leaders should generally be wary of placing themselves in the strategically difficult position of taking on simultaneous military commitments in multiple disputes.

Premise 3: Uncertainty in estimating the military strength and resolve of adversaries

State leaders have beliefs about the balance of military power and the resolve of adversaries to use force, but they may lack confidence that their beliefs are fully accurate. As a result, leaders will have greater confidence in their ability to predict the outcomes of military confrontations when their uncertainty about their adversaries' power and resolve is relatively low.

There are several reasons why state leaders may not possess complete and accurate information about the military capabilities of other states or the resolve of their leaders:

1. States often try to conceal information about the size, quality, and readiness of their military forces (e.g. Fearon 1995).
2. Even if information is available, qualitative dimensions of military power can be particularly difficult to assess but can have important effects on military performance (Bennett and Stam 1996, 1998; Bueno de Mesquita, Morrow, and Zorick 1997; Millett and Murray 1987–8; Reiter and Stam 1998 a, b, 2002; Rosen 1996; Stam 1996).
3. The resolve of state leaders can be difficult to judge. For one, leaders have incentives to bluff and act tough in order to get other states to retreat (Fearon 1994b; Jervis 1970; Nalebuff 1991; Schelling 1966). Furthermore, misunderstandings can arise about what issues are at

stake in a dispute, or how salient those issues are to an opponent, particularly to states that might intervene. As a result, unexpected third-party military interventions may overturn estimates of the local military balance and radically change military outcomes (Gartner and Siverson 1996; Wang and Ray 1994).

One implication of this third premise is that the threat and use of military force is a foreign policy option for state leaders that typically entails some degree of policy risk. The extent of risk will vary across situations, however. As a result, the uncertainties of predicting crisis and military outcomes will be limited in some cases and high in others. A second implication is that state leaders have an incentive to try and reduce their uncertainty in order to better gauge the likely risks of a military confrontation. Therefore, leaders may revise their beliefs when their adversaries' actions provide new information about their military power and resolve (e.g. Wagner 2000).

Hypotheses

We now propose a series of intuitive hypotheses that draw upon one or more of these three premises.

IP1: When common security ties and interests exist between states, political leaders are:

a. less likely to threaten force in an attempt to change the territorial status quo,
b. more likely to make concessions in negotiations over disputed territory, and
c. less likely to resort to higher levels of escalation in military confrontations over disputed territory.

While some states are able to rely largely on their own diplomatic and military means to achieve foreign policy goals, others may find it necessary to develop cooperative security ties with other countries in order to gain diplomatic and/or military support. However, as noted in the discussion of Premise 1, the support of other countries usually comes at some cost to freedom of action in foreign policy, since recipient countries are expected to coordinate diplomatic and even military policies with their allies. Nevertheless, allies on security issues can enhance a country's own military strength by making positive commitments of direct military and/or diplomatic support, making negative assurances to not oppose that country in the event of war, or providing arms or finances to support weapons purchases.[2] Given these security benefits we should expect that in disputes between states that share cooperative security ties and interests,

---

[2] Scholars also argue that economic cooperation with allies can have positive security consequences by increasing the economic and financial resource base of allies, which can then be translated into military power (e.g. Gowa 1994; Gowa and Mansfield 1993).

both parties would seek to avoid military conflicts and the escalation of such conflicts, as well as be more inclined to make concessions in pursuit of a territorial settlement. Diplomatic and military conflict over disputed territory, in contrast, would put at risk the cooperation of one's ally in countering security threats. Therefore, more accommodative policies would be expected in an attempt to secure the continued benefits of security cooperation with the ally.

The next hypothesis draws upon Premises 2 and 3.

IP2: As a country's relative military strength increases state leaders are:

a. more likely to threaten force or seek negotiations rather than to accept the status quo, and are especially likely to threaten the use of force in an attempt to change the status quo,

b. less likely to make concessions in subsequent negotiations over disputed territory, and

c. more likely to resort to higher levels of escalation in military confrontations over disputed territory.

The willingness of state leaders to risk a military confrontation depends in part on the attractiveness of any alternative negotiated settlement in the absence of a military confrontation. The logic of **IP2** begins with the argument that most state leaders would prefer to resolve a territorial dispute short of a military confrontation by gaining unilateral concessions from the other party. A military advantage should increase the confidence of leaders to pursue negotiations based on the expectation that their country's military strength will provide leverage in talks and increase the chances that their adversary will offer territorial concessions. Thus, even though leaders from militarily strong states should initially seek negotiations, they should nevertheless be less willing to make concessions during the course of negotiations. The reason is that the willingness of policy-makers to make concessions should be influenced by expectations about their ability to secure territorial gains through the alternative policy of threatening or using military force. As a result, state leaders who are relatively confident that their country possesses a military advantage should have stronger beliefs that military coercion can be utilized successfully with less risk and therefore should be less willing to make concessions. Instead, they should adopt more intransigent positions in negotiations with the expectation that their weaker adversary will be more likely to back down when the leaders of more powerful states signal their resolve to stand firm in negotiations.

However, if the adversary fails to make concessions we expect the stronger party to be more inclined to initiate a militarized dispute. In such a case the stronger side anticipates either that the opponent will make concessions under the threat of war, or, if the target refuses to back down diplomatically, that victory will follow in an armed conflict.[3] In sum, military strength then should induce political leaders to hold out for more favorable terms in any negotiated settlement and to be more willing to supplement diplomacy with coercive force to secure territorial goals.

The next hypothesis builds upon Premises 1 and 2.

IP3: When state leaders claim territory of strategic value, they are:

a. more likely to threaten force or seek negotiations rather than to accept the status quo, and especially likely to threaten the use of force in an attempt to change the status quo,
b. less likely to make concessions in negotiations over disputed territory, and
c. more likely to resort to higher levels of escalation in military confrontations over disputed territory.

The logic is that securing strategically valuable territory should be a highly salient goal for policy-makers in a territorial dispute. Given the high value of securing such territory, political leaders should be more motivated to challenge the status quo by diplomatic pressure. Furthermore, the value of strategic territory should induce leaders to apply even further pressure and to resort more frequently to the riskier option of military threats. Once diplomatic and military initiatives have been pursued, these leaders should be less willing to offer substantial concessions in negotiations since territorial concessions would entail losing control over highly valued territory. Similarly, political leaders should be more resolved to escalate military confrontations in an attempt to compel the adversary to concede control over strategic territory. Thus, these types of challengers will be more difficult to deter in military conflicts since high levels of expected gains will help to offset the higher expected military costs associated with the large-scale use of force.

The final set of hypotheses build upon Premises 2 and 3 and are as follows.

IP4i: When a state engaged in a territorial dispute is also currently involved in militarized conflicts with other countries, its policies in the territorial dispute will shift towards inaction and risk avoidance. As a result, state leaders are:

a. less likely to attempt to change the territorial status quo, whether by threatening force or seeking negotiations,
b. more likely to make concessions in negotiations over disputed territory, and

---

[3] This hypothesis does not preclude militarily weak states from becoming more aggressive in the aftermath of failed negotiations since the general logic holds that for these leaders the likely terms associated with a peacefully negotiated settlement should look unattractive (e.g. Wagner 2000). Nevertheless, our claim is that militarily strong states should be even more aggressive.

c. less likely to resort to higher levels of escalation in military confrontations over disputed territory.

A similar logic applies to the behavior of states whose territorial dispute adversary is simultaneously involved in other military conflicts. In this case a state is more likely to make demands upon its distracted adversary.

IP4ii: A state whose territorial dispute adversary is involved in one or more militarized conflicts with other countries is:

a. more likely to threaten force or seek negotiations rather than to accept the status quo, and is especially likely to threaten the use of force in an attempt to change the status quo,
b. less likely to make concessions in negotiations over disputed territory, and
c. more likely to resort to higher levels of escalation in military confrontations over disputed territory.

When a given dispute has escalated to the point of military threats and armed conflicts, the leaders of the states involved are likely to focus diplomatic and military efforts at managing the threatening situation in that particular dispute. Therefore, states should not be expected to initiate new rounds of talks or risk new military confrontations in additional territorial disputes when they are already involved in military conflicts elsewhere. If they do enter into negotiations in another dispute they are likely to be more accommodative so that their territorial adversary does not consider resorting to force as a result of stalemated talks. Furthermore, state leaders should be wary of risking a military confrontation over disputed territory if they are already engaged in a military dispute. Leaders risk spreading their forces too thin and undermining their ability to credibly deter or compel their adversaries if they permit their country's armed forces to be committed to multiple military conflicts at the same time. Thus, for a given territorial dispute, challengers should avoid initiating and escalating military action against the target if they are already involved in military confrontations with other states.

In **IP4ii** the analysis shifts to the behavior of adversaries who observe that their territorial dispute opponent is involved in military conflict with other states. The strategic course of action for adversaries is to apply more diplomatic and military pressure at this time to see if their opponent will offer concessions in order to avoid another crisis or military conflict.

Measurement of variables for empirical tests

The hypotheses to be tested from the International Politics Model are listed in Table 3.1. In the following section we describe the operational measures that are used to test each of these hypotheses. To test the

Table 3.1 *Summary of hypotheses to be tested from the International Politics Model*

Hypotheses regarding	Predicted relationships in equation to be tested			
	Status quo stage		Negotiations stage	Escalation stage
	Force	Talks		
Common security ties (**IP1**)	−	−	+	−
Military balance (**IP2**)	+	+	−	+
Strategic value of territory (**IP3**)	+	+	−	+
Involvement of state in another dispute (**IP4i**)	−	−	+	−
Adversary's involvement in another dispute (**IP4ii**)	+	+	−	+

Note: A positive sign (+) indicates that in the statistical tests the estimated coefficient should have a value greater than zero; a negative sign (−) indicates that in the statistical tests the estimated coefficient should have a value less than zero.

hypotheses in this and the following three chapters, we often create multiple operational indicators to measure a given theoretical concept. However, only one operational measure for each concept is included in any empirical model. We simply substitute one measure for another to check the robustness of our results.

We draw upon several indicators and conduct these robustness checks for a number of reasons. Since the quality of available data often varies and measurement error could be a problem, we insert multiple measures to mitigate these broad concerns. Furthermore, there are often multiple valid measures for a general concept, and therefore it seems unwise to ignore or eliminate any such measures *ex ante*. Finally, at times our theory is not precise enough to dictate one single, precise measure. For example, we often do not know whether a one-, two-, or five-year lag best captures the idea of a "recent" stalemate or a "recent" militarized dispute. In such scenarios we employ multiple lags or multiple plausible measures in order to gain greater confidence in any results we might find.

Military balance

To test **IP2** in each of the three stages summarized in Table 3.1, we construct a short-term military balance variable that measures the military capabilities of each state relative to its territorial dispute adversary. We take the average of three different ratios of military capabilities to come up with an overall measure of the short-term military balance. Our final measure is thus an average of the two states': (a) relative military personnel, (b) relative military expenditures, and (c) relative expenditures per soldier.[4] In calculating each of these three individual ratios, we adjusted the capabilities of each state for distance if the territorial dispute was located overseas from the state's homeland territory (see Bueno de Mesquita 1981: 105). We also included the military capabilities of a target's ally as part of the capabilities of the target if the ally's military forces were stationed on the target's territory and the ally had a defense pact with the target.[5] In operational terms, each of the three component ratios, as well as the final average ratio, is translated to a continuous scale that ranges from 0 to 1. Logically, the ratios for the challenger and target sum to 1. Values near 0.5 indicate that a state is near military parity with its adversary, while values above 0.5 indicate a state has a military balance advantage and values below 0.5 indicate the state is at a military disadvantage.

The primary source for data on these three indicators is the Correlates of War (COW) data set on national capabilities, which contains annual data for countries through 1992. For the years 1993–5 and for missing data prior to 1993, information on military capabilities was collected from several additional sources (i.e. Banks Cross-Polity Data Set, *The Military Balance, SIPRI Yearbook, World Military Expenditures and Arms Transfers*).[6]

To test **IP2** in the Military Escalation Stage we utilize an additional measure of the military balance. This second measure attempts to tap the local or more immediately available military forces that each side has positioned for a possible military conflict (Huth 1988). These are the forces that each side has mobilized or built up during a militarized dispute and they are the forces that can be committed at the outset or very early stages of an armed conflict. Due to the varying quality and availability of data on local forces, a precise ratio of challenger to target forces cannot be determined with confidence. Instead, the local balance is simply coded as a dummy variable.

---

[4] In rare cases where data on one or more of these indicators could not be calculated, the remaining available ratio(s) were used.

[5] In the Middle East, British military capabilities were added to those of Iraq in 1932–47, Kuwait in 1961–7, Jordan in 1946–56, and Egypt in 1922–5. In Asia, the Soviet Union's military capabilities were added to those of Outer Mongolia in 1936–40 and 1946–62, British capabilities were added to those of Malaysia in 1962–70, and US capabilities were added to those of South Korea in 1953–95. In the Americas, British capabilities were added to those of Belize in 1981–93. Finally, in Europe, British, French, and West German military capabilities were added to those of the US (the dispute over West Berlin) in 1955–71 and the Soviet Union's military capabilities were added to those of Czechoslovakia in 1955–73, East Germany in 1955–72, and Poland in 1955–70.

[6] In some cases missing data for selected years were filled in by extrapolating from data that were available for years prior to and after the missing data.

There are two situations in which the challenger or target is coded as possessing such an advantage. The first situation is when a state holds at least a two-to-one advantage in the estimated ratio of local ground forces and also possesses any advantage in the ratio of expenditures per soldier (as described above). The second scenario for a local advantage is when the state does not enjoy a clear numerical advantage in the local balance of ground forces (i.e. relative parity exists), but does possess a very strong advantage in the ratio of expenditures per soldier (the ratio was greater than two-to-one). In this second case the challenger's (target's) superior quality of forces coupled with quantitative parity is treated as constituting a strong overall advantage in the local balance of forces. Data on the local balance of forces were collected from a wide range of historical and secondary sources for each dispute and from Huth's data set on extended-immediate deterrence (see the bibliography of case sources in Appendix A and Huth 1988). If third parties threatened or intervened with military force in support of either challenger or target during a militarized dispute, the capabilities of the third party are included in the measure of the local balance of forces.

Other military dispute involvement for challenger and target

To test **IP4i** and **IP4ii** we collect data on the beginning and end month and year of any war or militarized dispute in which either the challenger or the target was involved, other than the territorial dispute between them. We then construct two dummy variables – one for the challenger and one for the target – with a value of one indicating that the state is simultaneously involved in a military campaign elsewhere. The primary data sources are the COW data set on militarized inter-state disputes during the period 1816–1992, as well as our data set of military confrontations over disputed territory. Additional coding sources, consulted to cover the years 1993–5 as well as prior years, include Bercovitch and Jackson (1997), Brecher and Wilkenfeld (1997), Tillema (1991), and Wallensteen and Sollenberg (1996).

Common security ties

To test **IP1** we construct three alternative measures for common security ties. We first consider whether the challenger and target share alliance ties. We record a value of one for our military alliance indicator if the challenger and target currently have a defense pact or entente military alliance, and record a value of zero if they simply have a non-aggression pact or do not share a military alliance. The updated COW data set on inter-state alliances are used to code this variable. The second measure is whether the challenger and target currently face a common territorial dispute opponent. A value of one is recorded if both are embroiled in separate territorial disputes with a common adversary during a given time period. The data for coding this variable are taken from Appendix A. The final indicator considers whether the challenger and target have shared a common adversary in a militarized dispute or war within the past two years.[7] The data on wars and militarized disputes are taken from the COW data sets and our territorial disputes data set, as well as from Bercovitch and Jackson (1997), Brecher and Wilkenfeld (1997), Tillema (1991), and Wallensteen and Sollenberg (1996).

Strategic value of disputed territory
To test **IP3** we construct a dummy variable to measure the strategic value of a territory.[8] This dummy variable is equal to one if the territory is strategically located or if it contained (or was believed to contain) natural resources that were used by the state in the production of military weapon systems. The definition and sources relied upon to code for strategic location of territory as well as strategic natural resources are taken from Huth (1996: 256 and 1988: 65).

Conclusion

In this chapter we presented a series of hypotheses based on a set of premises about the international political-military environment within which state leaders make choices about diplomacy and military force in territorial disputes. These hypotheses make no direct mention of domestic political institutions within states, nor consider how differences in such institutions might influence foreign policy choices. In each of the next three chapters we shift the theoretical analysis to the domestic level, and by doing so, we develop a richer set of theoretical propositions. We begin in the next chapter with what we term the Political Accountability Model, and then turn to the Political Norms and Political Affinity Models in Chapters 5 and 6.

---

[7] To check the robustness of results a second dummy variable was constructed in which a common adversary was coded on the basis of a five-year period.

[8] To check for robustness we also created a variable to indicate whether the territory is of economic value to the disputing states.

4 Domestic institutions and the Political Accountability Model

As we argued in the previous chapter, the foreign policy choices of state leaders reflect calculations about the constraints and opportunities for pursuing territorial claims in the strategic setting of international politics. This chapter, as well as the two following chapters, constitute the central theoretical chapters of the book, in which domestic political institutions are given center-stage in three models that seek to explain what types of diplomatic and military policies will be adopted by political leaders in territorial disputes. These three models can be viewed as related, but nevertheless distinct, theoretical approaches for analyzing the democratic peace. Their common foundation is that each considers how domestic political institutions shape foreign policy choices. Each model, however, focuses on a different causal mechanism that links domestic institutions to the choices made by political leaders:

1. Institutions are a source of political accountability for leaders' decisions on matters of foreign policy (Political Accountability Model).
2. Institutions are a source of norms for bargaining and conflict resolution in international disputes (Political Norms Model).
3. The similarity of institutions between states is a source of international threat perception and political alignment for state leaders (Political Affinity Model).

The Political Accountability Model centers on the ability of political opposition to punish and reward political leaders for the success or failure of the diplomatic and military policies they pursue. The Political Norms Model views domestic institutions as influencing the principles by which political elites bargain and resolve political conflict. These domestic-based principles, then, also influence how leaders bargain internationally. Finally, the Political Affinity Model argues that the similarity of institutions in different states can be an important foundation for shared political interests between political leaders, which in turn enables leaders to differentiate between potential allies and potential security threats.

This chapter is devoted to presenting the theoretical foundations and then hypotheses of the Political Accountability Model.

Differences Between States in Accountability of Executive to Domestic Political Opposition	Differences in Domestic Political Risks/ Rewards of Varying Foreign Policy Outcomes for Executive	Differences in Political Accountability Lead to Different Choices by Foreign Policy-makers Regarding Negotiations and Military Force in Territorial Disputes

Figure 4.1 Summary of logic in Political Accountability Model

Political Accountability Model

Figure 4.1 summarizes the logical foundations of the Political Account-ability Model. One of the defining features of political systems is the extent to which political opposition can hold leaders accountable for the policies and decisions they adopt. Political institutions are one key factor which determine levels of accountability, since they can restrict or expand the means and opportunities available to opposition groups for challeng-ing and contesting governmental policies. Leaders who are accountable for their policies risk the loss of political authority and influence, if not removal from office, for policy setbacks or for pressing ahead with un-popular programs. In political systems where accountability is relatively high, the domestic political consequences of pursuing failed or contro-versial foreign policy actions can be substantial. As a result, foreign policy leaders who are more accountable to political opposition should be more attentive to potential setbacks in foreign policy and risk-averse to initi-ating diplomatic and military policies that are likely to be controversial. Conversely, foreign policy successes are likely to disarm political opposi-tion and bolster the political authority and power of incumbents. Thus, in political systems where accountability is relatively high, leaders should also have stronger incentives to seek the political payoffs of successful diplomatic and military initiatives in foreign policy.

Premises of the model

The causal links summarized in Figure 4.1 are based on a number of theoretical premises.

Premise 1: The primacy of retaining office for incumbent leaders

A critical goal of incumbent leaders is to maintain their position of politi-cal leadership and to protect their hold on office from political opposition.

The importance of staying in power can reflect a variety of motivations: a personal drive for political power and leadership status, the attempt to secure financial and material gains, or the desire to achieve certain public policy goals by means of legislation and governmental programs. In sum, the maintenance of political office can advance personal as well as broader public policy goals for leaders. One implication is that political leaders should be strategic in their pursuit of both domestic and foreign policies and try to anticipate the domestic political responses to various policies that they might adopt. Leaders should not be expected generally to choose policies that are likely to produce high political risks and significant costs; they should instead prefer policies that will improve their political standing.

Premise 2: The strategic behavior of political opposition

In all political systems there are political elites who seek to remove the current leadership from office and to assume positions of political power themselves. Opposition elites, however, are strategic in deciding when to challenge incumbents and seek their removal.

Elites who aspire to positions of national leadership recognize that an incumbent's political vulnerability varies over time. They are more likely to challenge leaders at a time when they are confident of political support from other groups and when the incumbent's supporting coalition is divided (e.g. Auvinen 1997; DeNardo 1985; Dudley and Miller 1998; Hardin 1995; Huber 1996; Laver and Schofield 1998; Lichbach 1995; Lupia and Strom 1995; Tarrow 1994; Zimmermann 1983). Unsuccessful political challenges against an incumbent can be costly for leaders of the opposition. At a minimum, they risk the loss of political standing among potential allies. There is also the potential for a political counter-attack by the incumbent. In authoritarian systems the counter-attack may result in opposition elites becoming the target of political violence and repression. The first implication of Premise 2 is that counter-elites and political opposition will be more active in challenging incumbents when the latter's policy initiatives have failed or proven controversial. The policy performance of a given regime on domestic and foreign policy issues plays an important role, therefore, in determining when incumbent leaders face strong political opposition (see e.g. Aldrich, Sullivan, and Borgida 1989; Bueno de Mesquita and Siverson 1995; Bueno de Mesquita, Morrow, Siverson, and Smith 1999; Bueno de Mesquita, Siverson, and Woller 1992; Denver 1994; Fiorina 1981; Goemans 2000; Gorvin 1989; Lewis-Beck 1988; Miller and Shanks 1996; Nincic and Hinckley 1991; Pierce 1995). When the policies of the incumbent leadership have failed to achieve policy goals, the opposition can argue more effectively that the current leadership should be removed because of its track record of policy setbacks and incompetency. Furthermore, policy failures in one issue area can induce opposition against regime policies in other policy domains. For example, a regime's foreign policy failure can weaken its leader's political standing and his ability to secure favorable outcomes on domestic policies (e.g. Brace and Hinckley 1992). In sum, foreign policy setbacks can not only directly threaten a leader's tenure in office, but can also weaken his ability to pursue his broader policy agenda. However, it also follows that policy successes should have favorable political consequences. They may help to deter political opposition, strengthen a leader's hold on office, and increase the stock of political capital upon which leaders can draw to advance their broader policy agendas (see Brace and Hinckley 1992; Brody 1991; Edwards and Gallup 1990; Neustadt 1990).

A second implication of Premise 2 is that in territorial disputes the policy preferences of opposition elites and groups are characterized by what we term a pragmatic nationalist bias. That is, a policy of concessions and accommodation by state leaders in a territorial dispute is a policy that generally risks greater domestic political opposition than a policy of continued diplomatic stalemate. Political leaders are unlikely to encounter strong and consistent political pressures to avoid diplomatic and military conflict in favor of more moderate diplomatic and military policies intended to break a deadlock over disputed territory. While the threat or use of military force in support of territorial claims is likely to generate short-term domestic support, costly or failed attempts at military coercion will also mobilize domestic opposition (Huth 1996). Thus, state leaders must choose carefully when to seek territorial settlements by compromise or concessions, and when to escalate a territorial dispute by force of arms. The political risks to which leaders are most sensitive, then, are those associated with accommodative diplomatic policies or the failed use of military force. In this model political accountability influences leadership decisions not because opposition elites and mass publics generally have more dovish diplomatic and military policy preferences than incumbent leaders, but because they will seek to punish leaders who adopt controversial or failed foreign policies.[1]

[1] We have two reasons for theoretically focusing on the reactions of mass publics to governmental policies. First, we are not convinced that mass opinions are consistently anchored at dovish policy positions. Furthermore, we reject the idea that the foreign policy preferences we can identify in the mass public are consistently more dovish than the policy position of political elites and incumbents (e.g. Brace and Hinckley 1992; Chanley 1999; Gaubatz 1995; Herrmann, Tetlock, and Visser 1999; Holsti 1996; Jentleson and Britton 1998; Knopf 1998; Mueller 1994; Nincic 1992: ch. 2; Owen 1997; Page and Shapiro 1992; Russett 1990: ch. 4; Zimmerman 2002).

Premise 3: Differences in domestic political institutions are a source of variation in political accountability

The political accountability of state leaders varies both across and within political systems, as differences in political institutions affect the ability of opposition groups to contest government policies.

The political vulnerability of state leaders has three main components. Leaders are vulnerable because political opposition has the ability to: (a) block the policy programs favored by incumbent leaders, (b) bring about the downfall of a government, and (c) use or encourage violence in order to remove leaders from power and/or to punish them after removal from office. The presence or absence of democratic political institutions is one key factor that determines how accountable leaders are for their foreign policy decisions. Democratic institutions such as well-organized and independent political parties, regular competitive elections, and independent legislatures enable political opposition to challenge the government more effectively. As a result, political opposition is generally more capable of derailing policy programs and removing leaders from power in democratic regimes (see Bueno de Mesquita and Siverson 1995; Bueno de Mesquita, Siverson, and Woller 1992; Gelpi and Grieco 2001; Goemans 2000: ch. 3; Przeworski, Alvarez, Cheibub, and Limongi 2000: ch. 4), while opposition groups are more likely to use violence against incumbents in non-democratic regimes (Bienen and Van de Walle 1991).

The first implication of Premise 3 is that the strength and threat posed by political opposition forces can vary substantially both across different democratic countries, as well as within a particular country depending upon political conditions. For example, the threat of being removed through elections may be a very powerful political threat if presidential elections are coming up within a few months. However, if those elections are several years away, electoral defeat is a less pressing concern for the president. Similarly, in parliamentary systems where there is no fixed date for national elections, a prime minister is in a stronger position to determine the timing of the next election if his or her party commands a majority in the legislature. In contrast, a prime minister who depends upon a coalition of parties to form a working majority is more vulnerable to votes of no confidence, the break-up of coalition cabinets, and calls for early elections (e.g. Alt and King 1994; Laver and Schofield 1998; Lupia and Strom 1995; Powell 2000; Warwick 1994).

Presidents and prime ministers face similar types of constraints when they deal with legislatures regarding the ratification of international treaties (Lohmann and O'Halloran 1994; Martin 2000; Milner 1997; Milner and Rosendorff 1997; O'Halloran 1994; Putnam 1988). In cases where the executive's party commands majority support, opposition forces are less capable of blocking ratification. In minority or coalition governments, however, governing leaders face a more credible threat of legislative rejection of a treaty that is not favored by opposition parties. The general implication is that while democratic institutions provide greater opportunities for political opposition to exercise its influence, the degree of political accountability for democratic leaders depends significantly upon such factors as the proximity of elections and the strength of opposition parties in legislatures.

The second implication of Premise 3 is that among non-democratic political systems, the threat of violent coups and leadership removal varies substantially both across countries as well as over time within a single country (e.g. Bienen and Van de Walle 1991; Goemans 2000; Londregan and Poole 1990; O'Kane 1987; Wintrobe 1998; Zimmermann 1983: ch. 7). For non-democratic systems the personal risks to leaders of losing office (imprisonment, physical harm, and even death) are much higher, but can still vary within and across countries as political institutions change (e.g. Breslauer 1982; Dittmer 1990; Hough 1980; Huntington 1968; Lee 1991).

If we combine these two dimensions of political threat – effective strength of political opposition and personal risks if removed from office – into a simple 2×2 matrix, we find important differences among non-democratic leaders in their political vulnerability (see Figure 4.2). For example, leaders in the upper-left cell are quite vulnerable, while leaders in the lower-right cell face limited threats from political opposition. Thus, in some countries authoritarian governments fall frequently due to coups and political violence, while in other countries leaders remain in power for decades and choose their successors. The general implication is that authoritarian leaders who are politically vulnerable should be more attentive to the domestic political risks of foreign policy

Effective Strength of Political Opposition

		High	Low
Personal Risks to Incumbents if Removed from Office	High	High Vulnerability	Intermediate Vulnerability
	Low	Intermediate Vulnerability	Low Vulnerability

Figure 4.2 Political vulnerability of leaders in non-democratic systems

choices. In contrast, authoritarian leaders who are entrenched in office and face a weak and divided opposition should be less concerned with the response of political opposition to foreign policy initiatives.

Premise 4: The impact of political vulnerability on foreign policy

The greater the political vulnerability of leaders, the higher the political costs to them of foreign policy failures.

While policy setbacks and controversy over adopted policies are not welcomed by any incumbent leaders, the extent to which they pose a political threat depends considerably on whether political opponents of a regime are in a position to punish incumbents for pursuing such policies. Therefore, political leaders who face weak political opposition at home have greater flexibility regarding the diplomatic and military policies they can pursue in international disputes (e.g. Eyerman and Hart 1996; Fearon 1994b; Partell 1997; Partell and Palmer 1999; Schultz 1998, 1999, 2001a, 2001b).

An important implication of Premise 4 relates to bluffing and deception in international disputes. Bluffing is always a possibility in international negotiations and militarized disputes, and therefore state leaders try to judge whether their adversary is in fact bluffing. Leaders may bluff successfully in militarized disputes by building up military forces and even resorting to the limited use of force (thereby persuading an adversary that costly military conflict is likely) and then using the threat of war to induce concessions. The incentive to bluff in a round of negotiations follows a similar logic, as states adopt a very unyielding bargaining position in the hope that the other party will make concessions in order to break a stalemate and avoid the failure of negotiations. While in the abstract state leaders always have incentives to act tough in order to induce an adversary to retreat, there can be domestic costs to bluffing.[2] In particular, political opposition can charge the government with a major foreign policy reversal and retreat under pressure. Leaders who are not constrained by strong political opposition (i.e. who face limited domestic audience costs) should be willing to bluff since the domestic political risks of retreating from a clear and firm diplomatic or military policy are less extensive. It follows that threats of force or the adoption of firm bargaining positions by foreign policy leaders facing high domestic audience costs should be viewed as more credible by international adversaries, since such leaders

---

[2] International reputational costs are also of theoretical interest but are not considered because of this model's focus on domestic political accountability. Theoretical elaboration of international audience costs would fit well within the framework of the International Politics Model developed in Chapter 3, however.

are less likely to pursue a policy of bluffing (e.g. Fearon 1994b; Schultz 2001a).

Hypotheses

The hypotheses are divided into three general categories. We first make comparisons across different political systems, and then examine variation within both democratic and non-democratic political systems. We conclude by discussing propositions that focus on strategic interactions between pairs of states (dyads).

Comparisons across political systems

For the first hypothesis, Premise 3 provides the primary foundation for developing the proposition, but Premises 2 and 4 also provide supporting logic.

PA1i: The leaders of democratic states should be less willing to rely on military force to achieve territorial goals. As a result, democratic leaders should be:

a. less likely to initiate military threats as opposed to accepting the status quo, especially in situations of high military uncertainty, but are more likely to challenge the territorial status quo with a call for negotiations rather than a threat of military force,
b. more likely to make concessions in negotiations, and
c. less likely to resort to higher levels of escalation in military confrontations, especially in situations of higher levels of uncertainty and risk about military outcomes.

Since political opposition in authoritarian systems is less capable of contesting state policies, the Political Accountability Model predicts that political leaders from such countries are more willing to adopt conflictual policies in an attempt to overturn the status quo through coercive threats and pressure. Furthermore, these leaders can back away from threats with fewer domestic political risks if the target stands firm. We should therefore expect more frequent bluffs and military probes by non-democratic leaders to test the resolve of targets, including more frequent threats of force to bolster their bargaining position in negotiations (see our discussion of Premise 4). In contrast, democratic leaders should be more cautious about initiating such military actions since limited military probes and bluffs should carry a greater risk of political opponents charging the government with irresolution and a foreign policy setback (the first implication of Premise 2).

The differences between democratic and authoritarian leaders regarding the initiation and escalation of military force should be most apparent in situations where the risks of military conflict are greater. Thus, when the military balance is not favorable leaders should be less likely to initiate and escalate military confrontations. However, our argument is that democratic leaders should be particularly cautious under such conditions since the threat of domestic opposition challenging the government following a military setback or diplomatic retreat is greater in democratic systems. To initiate and then escalate with the large-scale use of force in such situations invites a higher risk of military defeat and the mobilization of political opposition. We recognize that political risks can be substantial for authoritarian leaders as well (e.g. Goemans 2000). Yet our claim is not that we should expect authoritarian leaders to resort frequently to military force under conditions of higher risk. Instead, the hypothesis is that such leaders should be more willing to gamble on a favorable military or diplomatic outcome given that they are in a stronger political position to counter or suppress political opposition in the event of a diplomatic or military setback.

The differences in the negotiating behavior of democratic and non-democratic leaders are more complex. On the one hand, if non-democratic leaders do decide to pursue negotiations, they are in a stronger political position (compared to democratic leaders) to counter or repress domestic opposition that might arise in response to concessions offered as part of a negotiated agreement. As a result, non-democratic negotiators might be expected to make concessions more frequently than their democratic counterparts since the domestic political risks are less severe. Democratic leaders, however, view military conflict as more risky than their non-democratic counterparts and generally should prefer a nonviolent settlement through negotiations. While concessions can be politically costly for democratic leaders, we believe that failed military initiatives are likely to be even more costly. In contrast, we expect non-democratic leaders to be more risk-acceptant in turning to military coercion as a way to achieve territorial claims. Put differently, while we do not expect democratic leaders often to make concessions in negotiations, they should offer limited concessions relatively more frequently as part of a negotiating strategy designed to reach an agreement based on mutual concessions than non-democratic leaders because the alternative of military coercion is generally less attractive to democratic leaders. This initial hypothesis on democratic behavior in negotiations is premised on the condition that the political costs of concession-making are not particularly high. When this condition no longer holds (see hypotheses **PA1iii**, **PA2i**, and **PA2ii** below), then we expect democratic negotiators to be highly sensitive to the costs of concessions and very unlikely to offer concessions.

PA1ii: Greater domestic political costs of retreating in the face of diplomatic and military pressure can provide an advantage to democratic states. As a result, we expect adversaries of democratic states to be:

a. less likely to challenge the status quo with military threats than with a call for negotiations,

b. more likely to offer concessions in negotiations when democratic leaders signal their resolve to stand firm, and

c. less likely to escalate to higher levels in military confrontations when democratic leaders signal their resolve to use military force.

The logic of **PA1ii** is that if adversaries know democratic leaders are constrained by domestic audience costs to avoid foreign policy retreats under diplomatic or military pressure, then they should prefer to target non-democratic leaders, who have greater domestic political flexibility to back down in the face of military threats and probes. Furthermore, the greater costs of backing down should help democratic leaders to send more credible signals of resolve in rounds of negotiations or in military confrontations. As a result, if democratic leaders clearly and publicly communicate their intention to stand firm in talks or to use force in a military confrontation, then their adversaries should believe that they face a resolved opponent. In a military confrontation this should help to deter escalation by the adversary of a democratic state. Similarly, during negotiations a signal of resolve by a democratic state should make it more likely that the adversary will understand that a deadlock can only be avoided by first offering (limited) concessions itself. Only then may democratic leaders be able to reciprocate concessions and to fend off domestic opposition to a negotiated agreement.

The next hypothesis builds on the general logic supporting **PA1i** but considers how state leaders respond to situations of stalemate in negotiations over disputed territory.

PA1iii: The bargaining strategies of non-democratic leaders in response to stalemates should be more variable and difficult to predict. In contrast, democratic leaders should pursue more consistent policies of:

a. responding to a deadlock in talks by continuing to seek further talks as opposed to turning to military coercion, and

b. avoiding a sharp reversal of policy in subsequent negotiations, in which intransigence is followed by concessions.

In non-democracies, the limited ability of political opposition to challenge incumbent leaders lessens the political risks for such leaders of either making concessions or turning to military coercion. Thus, non-democratic leaders should display more divergent patterns of diplomatic and military behavior in deciding how to respond to a seemingly resolved territorial adversary. On the one hand, they can refuse to make concessions, knowing that if talks end in stalemate, the subsequent use of military force to try to break that diplomatic deadlock also carries fewer domestic political risks. On the other hand, if the prospects of military coercion are not favorable, they can continue to rely on negotiations and then reverse policy by offering concessions to settle the dispute. This is because they have greater confidence that they can contain or repress any opposition that emerges to the negotiated settlement.

Democratic counterparts have less flexibility in their bargaining position since the making of significant concessions after negotiations have already ended in deadlock is potentially quite risky (see the second implication of Premise 2). This is because we expect both parties to blame the other side for the deadlock in talks. As a result, international negotiations in context of continued stalemate are likely to become a much more salient issue domestically for democratic leaders as opposition elites and segments of the general population express their opposition to offering concessions to a truculent adversary. At the same time, threats of military force and coercive bluffing are risky for democratic leaders, particularly given the heightened domestic attention to the territorial dispute. Limited military actions will most likely rally political support in the short term, but if such actions do not compel concessions from the adversary we then expect political opposition to arise. At this point democratic leaders face the difficult choice of whether or not to escalate to the large-scale use of force. As a result, democratic leaders are likely to be wary of either turning to military threats or offering concessions as a way to break the stalemate.

The next two hypotheses build on the logic of **PA1iii** and also draw upon Premises 2 and 3. The claim is that under certain conditions the greater accountability of democratic leaders can induce such leaders to adopt conflictual diplomatic and military policies.

PA2i: When democratic leaders view an international adversary as an enduring rival, they are more likely to adopt hard-line policies. In this situation, the diplomatic and military policies of democratic leaders should be quite similar, perhaps even more conflictual, than the policies adopted by non-democratic leaders. As a result, leaders from both states should be:
a. more likely to resort to military threats and the use of force in an attempt to change the status quo as opposed to relying on negotiations,
b. less likely to make concessions in negotiations, and
c. more likely to resort to higher levels of escalation in military confrontations.

PA2ii: When ethnic co-nationals populate disputed territory, democratic leaders will face even stronger domestic pressures than their non-democratic counterparts to adopt hard-line policies. As a result, democratic leaders should be:

a. more likely to challenge the status quo with calls for talks and military threats, and especially likely to resort to military threats as opposed to relying on negotiations,

b. less likely to make concessions in negotiations, and

c. more likely to resort to higher levels of escalation in military confrontations.

For **PA2i** the claim is that when the other state in a territorial dispute is an enduring rival,[3] democratic and non-democratic leaders are likely to engage in similar patterns of conflictual diplomatic and military behavior. As a result, this hypothesis emphasizes that under certain conditions differences in domestic political institutions should not produce strong differences in foreign policy choices by state leaders. Furthermore, democratic leaders may even have domestic political incentives to act tougher than their non-democratic counterparts.

When a democratic country faces an international opponent who in past conflicts has demonstrated the willingness to use military force and to oppose a negotiated settlement, this opponent is likely to be portrayed domestically as an enemy and a dangerous adversary by the political leadership of the democratic country (e.g. Huth 1996). An important implication is that foreign relations with this enduring rival will have a relatively high level of domestic political saliency within the democratic polity. In this context of heightened domestic political attention, accommodative diplomatic and military policies by the democratic leadership would be very likely to provoke political opposition. In fact, democratic leaders in this domestic setting should expect that tough diplomatic and military policies would be politically popular and quite defensible against opponents of the government. With this expectation, democratic leaders could use nationalist rhetoric as well as claims of threats to national security in order to justify more aggressive policies. Opposition groups and their leaders should also be more reluctant to criticize the regime for fear of being labeled as supporters of the enduring rival. Thus, the

[3] An enduring rival is broadly defined here as a state with whom another country has a protracted history of diplomatic and military conflict and in which a single primary issue or set of interrelated issues is the source of friction and competition. Critics of the enduring rivalry concept have focused their attention on two primary issues: (a) how to define an enduring rivalry, and (b) what are the theoretical explanations or causes of enduring rivalries? Critics do not reject the claim that enduring rivalries are an important subject to study. Instead, they question prevailing definitions of the term as well as theoretical arguments that might account for their emergence and evolution. For recent scholarly work on enduring international rivalries see Bennett (1996, 1997, 1998); Diehl (1998); Diehl and Goertz (2000); Gartzke and Simon (1999); Goertz and Diehl (1992, 1993); Thompson (1995).

democratic leadership should have the domestic political support to pursue a more confrontational foreign policy (pragmatic bias associated with Premise 2).

The logic of **PA2ii** extends this argument further and posits that greater political accountability will make democratic leaders even more conflictual than non-democratic leaders when ethnic co-nationals populate disputed territory. We begin by arguing that across all political systems incumbent governments are likely to secure domestic support for backing demands of greater political self-determination for ethnic co-nationals who are located across international borders (e.g. Carment and James 1997; Carment, James, and Rowlands 1997; Davis and Moore 1997; Huth 1996; Saideman 2001; also see Henderson 1997). However, we also expect that democratic leaders will face particularly powerful pressures from domestic opposition groups to take forceful initiatives in support of their ethnic co-nationals who claim mistreatment at the hands of a foreign government. We expect the defense of principles of political self-determination to have a high level of legitimacy in democratic systems and therefore opposition elites and groups in society will strongly criticize governments for failing to address effectively violations of such principles. As a result, for democratic leaders, the domestic political risks of diplomatic and military inaction are greater than for non-democratic leaders. Therefore, in this case democratic leaders are actually more likely to consider initiating and escalating military threats and to adopt an unyielding position in negotiations. In sum, we believe that support for political self-determination of ethnic co-nationals is a foreign policy issue with particularly high saliency for democratic leaders. Nationalist biases in favor of more aggressive and hard-line policies will induce democratic leaders to be much more risk-acceptant in pursuit of territorial claims than they generally would be.

Comparisons within political systems

The hypotheses in this section build upon and extend **PA1i** by drawing out the implications for intra-regime comparative analysis. The overriding theme of this section is that both democratic and non-democratic leaders should be more willing to adopt politically risky diplomatic and military policies as they become more secure from the threat of political opposition removing them from power. The testable implication is that when we make comparisons among democratic leaders or among non-democratic leaders, we should be able explain differences within each group by examining variation in the threat posed by political opposition under either broad regime category. We first make comparisons among democratic leaders, and then examine differences among non-democratic leaders.

Comparisons among democratic leaders

For democratic states the comparative analysis will focus on (a) the strength of opposition parties in national legislatures, and (b) the impact of competitive national elections. The first set of hypotheses makes comparisons among democratic state leaders by drawing on Premise 3 and its first implication, as well as on Premises 2 and 4.

PA3i: The presence of strong political opposition forces in legislatures and parliaments generally induces more conservative foreign policy choices by democratic leaders. Conversely, the lack of such political opposition should result in leaders considering more controversial foreign policy options. As a result, the stronger the ruling government's position in the legislature, the more likely political leaders are:

a. to challenge the territorial status quo through calls for talks and especially through threats of military force,

b. to make concessions in negotiations, and

c. to resort to higher levels of escalation in military confrontations.

PA3ii: Similarly, leaders also consider whether the leadership of a democratic territorial dispute adversary is in a position of domestic political strength or weakness. The leadership of the adversary is likely to be averse to political risks if it faces strong political opposition, but should be more willing to accept political risks if domestic opposition is relatively weak. As a result, when a state is engaged in a territorial dispute with a democratic adversary, as the ruling government in the adversary attains a stronger position in its legislature, the state facing the domestically secure adversary is:

a. less likely to challenge the territorial status quo by threats of military force but more likely to seek negotiations,

b. more likely to make concessions in negotiations, and

c. less likely to resort to higher levels of escalation in military confrontations.

The political influence of opposition parties in legislatures can stem from their ability to constrain executives in several ways, such as failing to support ratification of treaties, forcing the downfall of governments through votes of no confidence and the dissolution of coalition cabinets, and blocking the passage of legislation.[4] The political power of opposition parties should be stronger when the government is divided (Alesina and Rosenthal 1995; Binder 1999; Cox and Kernell 1991; Edwards, Barrett, and Peake 1997; Fiorina 1992; Lohmann and O'Halloran 1994; Mayhew

---

[4] These hypotheses focus on the constraining role of opposition parties in legislatures, but another avenue for theoretical analysis is to develop propositions about when opposition parties and legislatures can strengthen the bargaining position of executives in their pursuit of foreign policy goals. Two very good examples of this are Martin (2000) and Schultz (2001b).

1991; Milner and Rosendorff 1997; Warwick 1994; also see Bond and Fleisher 1990; Edwards 1989; Edwards and Wood 1999; Lindsay 1994; Peterson 1994; Wood and Peake 1998). By this we mean that the political party of the executive fails to achieve a position of majority strength in the legislature. As a result, a president or prime minister must depend upon one or more other political parties to form a working majority to pass legislation, and, in parliamentary systems, it may be necessary to bring opposition parties into the cabinet in order to form a government.

According to **PA3i**, divided government should push democratic leaders away from an active foreign policy and towards maintenance of the status quo in a territorial dispute. The lack of a cohesive majority in the legislature should make a president or prime minister wary of diplomatic or military initiatives. For example, the executive is likely to lack bargaining flexibility in international negotiations, and therefore stalemate is to be expected since only unilateral concessions by the other state (which are unlikely) can lead to a settlement. Knowing that deadlock is more likely, democratic leaders also have less of an incentive to pursue negotiations in the first place. That is, while refusing to make territorial concessions is generally not politically costly for democratic leaders, there may be some political risk associated with the failure to secure concessions from an adversary in repeated rounds of talks over disputed territory.

The same logic applies to decisions to initiate militarized disputes. The risks of a military setback or the failure to achieve diplomatic gains through the use of coercive pressure (military probes and bluffs) are generally higher in the face of strong political opposition. This is because opposition parties can exercise greater control within the legislature to ensure criticism of the policies and to more credibly threaten a vote of no confidence (for prime ministers). However, if these constrained leaders do challenge the status quo by initiating negotiations or military threats, they will seek to avoid the high political risks associated with either accommodative policies (substantial concessions in negotiations), or the loss of a war (military setback following escalation to high levels in a military confrontation).

In contrast, when the executive's party commands a majority position in the legislature, then opposition parties should be in a much weaker position to (a) veto the terms of international agreements they dislike, (b) ensure criticism through legislative debate and hearings, and (c) threaten removal in the event of a diplomatic or military retreat. As noted in the second implication of Premise 2, the general political problem for any executive is that territorial concessions are likely to be controversial. The concern is not that opposition parties in the legislature will pressure executives to be more accommodative but rather that they will reject concessions negotiated by the executive. The interesting theoretical question then becomes: when can executives secure ratification of agreements that contain territorial concessions? Executives generally encounter few problems with a policy of maintaining territorial claims and refusing to make concessions, since opposition parties are unlikely to take the lead in pressuring the executive to make territorial concessions. While concessions in a territorial dispute always entail some political risks for a democratic leader, those risks are not as great when the leader's political party has control of the legislature. Thus, when a territorial settlement agreement containing concessions comes before the legislature for approval, executive concerns about ratification failure should be reduced if the executive's party constitutes a strong majority in the legislature.

As a result, in **PA3ii** it is argued that secure democratic governments are more likely to be the targets of calls for talks based on the expectation that they can offer concessions and still secure domestic ratification. It follows then that adversaries will view secure democratic governments as more politically capable partners for trying to achieve a negotiated settlement. As we have already argued, concessions in negotiations are almost always controversial. One-sided agreements, in which leaders expect their territorial adversary to make a series of unilateral concessions, are therefore quite unlikely. As a result, the more important task for a country's leaders is to gauge the right time to put on the negotiating table offers of concessions that can be reciprocated by their negotiating partner. Leaders do not want to incur the political heat at home for offering concessions unless they believe that their negotiating partner can also withstand the same type of domestic political pressure and secure ratification of any agreement. Put differently, government leaders are unlikely to make the hard choices to offer concessions unless they expect that negotiations will produce an agreement that their adversary can secure support for at home. If leaders expect a negotiated agreement to unravel due to domestic opposition in the other country, then they have few incentives to expose themselves politically to charges of selling out from their own domestic opposition.[5]

According to **PA3i**, democratic leaders who have control of the legislature should be more willing to gamble with military probes and bluffs

---

[5] We agree with scholars such as Putnam (1988) and Schelling (1960) that negotiators will be sensitive to the strength of domestic opposition forces in both their own country and their bargaining adversary, and will attempt to use domestic constraints to their own advantage. At the same time, we agree with Milner (1997) and Milner and Rosendorff (1997), that such strategies can make reaching an international agreement more difficult, since policy differences between the two governments are likely to be larger on average, which makes it more difficult to reach an acceptable agreement. This risk is particularly high for territorial disputes given the second implication to Premise 2, which suggests that unilateral concessions are very risky. For an insightful recent formal analysis of this theoretical literature, see Tarar (2001).

(Premises 2 and 4), or even to escalate to high levels of force. Under such conditions leaders should be more confident of their ability to manage the political fallout from a failed policy of bluffing and limited escalation, or from an actual military setback following the large-scale use of force. Presidents and prime ministers should be able to work with their political allies in the legislature to limit censure and criticism of their failed military policies. Such leaders should also be able to minimize the risk that their legislative policy agendas might be strongly contested by opposition parties, who are disinclined to cooperate with an executive when he is politically weakened.

Because of this greater political flexibility, one might argue that secure democratic governments are more likely to be targets of threats and higher levels of escalation. The argument would be that since secure democratic leaders are better able to fight off domestic opposition following a military retreat or defeat, there should be incentives to contest secure democratic government with probes, bluffs, and even military escalation. While this logic is plausible, we do not find it fully persuasive. Risk-acceptant adversaries might be tempted consistently to gamble that secure democratic leaders in another country will back down under military pressure or accept a limited military defeat instead of standing firm and using force if challenged. However, we would expect risk-averse and risk-neutral leaders to be wary of such brinkmanship policies. Since we have no compelling reasons to believe that the population of political leaders is skewed towards risk-acceptant decision-makers, we expect adversaries in general to avoid military challenges against politically secure leaders. As a result, in **PA3ii** we hypothesize that governments are less likely to initiate and escalate military confrontations against secure democratic leaders.

The next set of hypotheses considers the political effects of elections on foreign policy choices.

PA4i: The more recently national elections for the executive have been held, the more likely are incumbent leaders:
a. to challenge the territorial status quo, especially through a threat of military action,
b. to make concessions in negotiations, and
c. to resort to higher levels of escalation in military confrontations.

PA4ii: The more recently national elections have been held in a democratic state, the more likely adversaries of that democratic state are:
a. to challenge the territorial status quo with calls for talks instead of military threats,
b. to make concessions in negotiations, and
c. to avoid higher levels of escalation in military confrontations.

Competitive elections and the threat of electoral defeat can be a powerful source of political accountability for democratic leaders. If voters use elections to express their judgements of the policy competency of incumbents (e.g. Aldrich, Sullivan, and Borgida 1989; Downs and Rocke 1995: ch. 3; Nincic and Hinckley 1991; Powell 2000; Smith 1998), then opposition parties and elites should draw upon controversial issues and setbacks in foreign policy to try to convince voters that incumbents should be removed. The second implication of Premise 2 suggests that international agreements containing territorial concessions or failed military initiatives to change the territorial status quo are the types of foreign policy issues that opposition groups should seize upon in an effort to discredit incumbents. Because leaders are aware of the electoral risks associated with such policies, we should expect a pattern to emerge between the timing of elections and the diplomatic and military policies pursued by leaders in territorial disputes. In **PA4i** the logic is that the accountability induced by elections should be greater when democratic leaders expect to face elections relatively soon.[6] In contrast, when elections are not expected for some time, then the threat of electoral defeat should have weaker political effects (Gaubatz 1991, 1999; Milner and Rosendorff 1997).

Our argument is that the democratic electorate has a relatively short time horizon for judging the competency of incumbent regimes and that recent policies weigh more heavily in forming the judgements of voters (see Frieden and Rogowski 1996; Garrett 1998; Lohmann 1997; Simmons 1994 for theoretical and empirical work on the concepts of political time horizons and discount rates). As a result, although a military setback is always damaging to a democratic leader, the damage is greater if the setback occurs three months before the next election as opposed to three years before such elections. Given sufficient time before the next election, the incumbent may be able to offset the initial policy setback with a subsequent record of favorable outcomes on other foreign policy issues, as well as through successful domestic policy programs. Therefore, the more recent national elections have been, the more willing incumbents should be to take the risk of adopting an active foreign policy in which they

---

[6] Of course, in presidential systems the time period between elections is fixed and thus known in advance. In parliamentary systems, elections must be held within a certain period of time but exactly when they are held is likely to be a function of a range of political conditions which incumbent, and to a lesser extent opposition, parties will seek to utilize to their strategic advantage. Despite the greater uncertainty facing leaders in such a situation, the general logic of the argument still holds. That is, once elections have occurred they are unlikely to be held again within a short period of time. This post-election period is politically important because the incumbent's political time horizon is not defined by the prospect of imminent elections.

seek negotiations or threaten the use of force in an attempt to change the status quo. Furthermore, democratic leaders should be more willing to make concessions in negotiations and resort to higher levels of escalation in military confrontations in the periods shortly after national elections.[7]

Precisely because democratic leaders are less constrained in the period shortly after elections and more capable of withstanding the political fallout of more accommodative policies, we argue in **PA4ii** that other states will recognize this and judge this to be a favorable time to seek a negotiated agreement or settlement. Following our logic developed in support of **PA3ii**, we argue that adversaries do not expect a negotiated agreement to be reached without some form of mutual concessions. As a result, it makes political sense for state leaders to offer concessions to democratic negotiating partners when they believe that democratic leaders are less constrained by the domestic political risks of concession-making (i.e. elections are not expected to be held soon). Conversely, when democratic leaders face elections soon they should shy away from territorial concessions in negotiations. Knowing this, adversaries should be less willing to offer concessions themselves. In short, with elections approaching, negotiations are more likely to end in deadlock.

When we consider the impact of recent elections in one's democratic adversary on the decision to initiate or escalate the use of military force, we encounter opposing arguments similar to those we discussed for **PA3ii**. Again, it seems possible that other states might be tempted to initiate and escalate military challenges against democratic governments that have recently held elections in an attempt to pressure secure leaders into making territorial concessions. As we argued above, only risk-acceptant leaders should consistently adopt such brinkmanship policies and therefore we argue that on average adversaries would be less likely to initiate and escalate military confrontations because they are worried that politically

---

[7] Another hypothesis that we derived from the model but did not test due to limited data was that when national elections are very proximate and democratic incumbents are facing possible defeat, they are:

a. more likely to initiate threats or the use of force instead of calling for negotiations or accepting the existing status quo,

b. less likely to make extensive concessions in negotiations over disputed territory, and

c. more likely to resort to higher levels of escalation in military confrontations.

When an incumbent president or prime minister faces a possible defeat in the election, an international crisis and military confrontation holds out the hope of producing rally-round-the-flag effects that could generate a short-term boost in the regime's political standing (Brace and Hinckley 1992; Brody 1991; Downs and Rocke 1995: ch. 3; Lian and Oneal 1993; Morgan and Bickers 1992; Mueller 1994; Page and Shapiro 1992; Russett 1990; Smith 1996, 1998). For such leaders, the domestic political need for a foreign policy victory could be so pressing that they become more risk-acceptant towards the use of force.

secure democratic leaders are more willing to risk a military conflict to defend their territorial claims.

Comparisons among non-democratic leaders

We now turn to the comparative analysis of non-democratic systems. The second implication of Premise 3 is the starting point for developing the next pair of hypotheses, with Premises 2 and 4 providing additional support.

PA5i: In non-democratic systems, incumbent leaders who feel secure from the threat of coups and political instability are more likely:

a. to challenge the territorial status quo, especially through the use of threats of military force,
b. to make concessions in negotiations, and
c. to escalate military confrontations to higher levels.

PA5ii: When adversaries face leaders in non-democratic systems who seem secure from the threat of coups and political instability, they are:

a. less likely to challenge the territorial status quo, especially through the use of threats of military force,
b. more likely to offer concessions in negotiations, and
c. less likely to escalate military confrontations to higher levels.

The underlying arguments for these two hypotheses are parallel to those for **PA3i–3ii** and **PA4i–4ii**. In a territorial dispute, politically secure non-democratic leaders should be more willing to pursue diplomatic and military policies that carry domestic political risks. Politically secure leaders have the domestic political flexibility to be either aggressive or accommodative. As a result, we should observe more activity and more variance in the policies adopted by such leaders, as well as more frequent policy reversals. In **PA5i** we argue that authoritarian leaders who face weak and divided opposition should be expected to initiate more diplomatic and military probes and bluffs to see if an adversary will retreat under pressure. They should also be more willing to reverse policy and offer concessions to avoid further escalation, or to choose the opposite policy and escalate to the large-scale use of force.

When authoritarian leaders face a domestic challenge to their authority or even their hold on office, the risks associated with a more active foreign policy should be more salient. As argued in the second implication of Premise 2, agreeing to territorial concessions will almost always carry some risk of being utilized by political opposition to discredit a regime. Thus, leaders already facing significant opposition should be particularly concerned with not providing further grounds for the opposition's challenge. As a result, the pursuit of negotiations is less likely during a period of political instability since the politically threatened leader has little opportunity for flexible bargaining. As argued already, the territorial dispute adversary should not be expected to make substantial unilateral concessions. Therefore the likely outcome of talks is a stalemate, and the prospect of a stalemate in negotiations should discourage initiatives to pursue talks. However, in the absence of an ongoing domestic crisis or challenge to a regime, political leaders should be more willing to make territorial concessions since they are in a stronger political position to withstand possible criticism and challenges from political opponents. Given that accommodation is a risky policy, the time to gamble on such a policy is when the political position of the leadership is stable and therefore the threat of coups is lower.

Following this logic, we argue in **PA5ii** that adversaries will calculate that the political security of the other country's leadership provides a favorable opportunity to pursue negotiations and reach agreements that contain mutual concessions. As argued earlier, adversaries should have greater confidence that politically secure non-democratic negotiating partners can withstand the domestic political opposition that will arise within their country to an agreement containing concessions. As a result, adversaries should be more willing to offer concessions as part of a bargaining strategy designed to achieve a mutually agreeable settlement that they expect will prove politically durable.

According to **PA5i**, military probes and bluffs should be less likely in times of political instability, since the failure to secure concessions after a threat or show of force is quite risky if political opposition already poses a threat to the regime.[8] Furthermore, the possible need to deploy the army for internal repression and regime maintenance raises questions about military resource constraints and the strategic disadvantages of dividing military forces between internal and external opponents. When a regime turns to the use of military force to repress internal unrest, leaders are more likely to confront a trade-off between internal and external coercive power. State leaders should recognize that if the armed forces of their country are either actively engaged in putting down domestic conflict, or

---

[8] Authoritarian leaders faced with domestic unrest and an increased threat of being removed from power may have political incentives to resort to the diversionary use of force. Our argument (see Huth and Lust-Okar 1998) is that diversionary incentives are likely only under a set of rather specific conditions which depend on whether (a) the government accommodates or rejects opposition policy demands, and (b) the opposition is part of or outside the political coalition supporting the regime. As a result, the diversionary use of force should not be expected to be the prevailing response of regimes to domestic unrest and instability. Unfortunately, we cannot test here hypotheses about the specific conditions under which the diversionary use of force is to be expected because it is not possible (given time and resource constraints) to gather sufficiently detailed information at the domestic level on such a large number of cases, which is required if the hypothesis is to be tested correctly.

may be called upon to do so, then the military forces that can be committed to an international dispute are reduced. As a result, authoritarian leaders facing domestic unrest should not favor high levels of escalation in territorial dispute confrontations. Instead, these leaders should seek a standoff short of armed conflict in which some limited escalatory actions are adopted and no concessions are offered. Such a policy may allow the leadership to benefit from some rally effects while avoiding riskier courses of action that might only worsen domestic political problems. It follows in **PA5ii** that adversaries would be more likely to target politically insecure non-democratic leaders due to the risks of challenging politically secure leaders. Not only is it quite risky to bluff secure non-democratic leaders into backing down under military pressure, but secure leaders are also less likely to have been compelled to commit their regular armed forces to missions of internal repression of armed opposition.

One of the important and common points of logic brought out by all of the hypotheses in this section is that states should seek negotiations with the political leaders of territorial dispute adversaries who are capable of countering domestic political opponents of accommodative territorial policies. As a result, states are more likely to be targets of diplomatic initiatives when their leaders are politically secure. For example, states should pursue more active diplomatic policies with democratic presidents or prime ministers when those leaders command majority support in the legislature, or when elections are not expected for some time. Along the same lines, challengers should be more likely to engage in negotiations and conflict resolution with non-democratic targets when the political leadership in the target is secure from threats of a military coup or political instability. In sum, challengers who recognize that politically viable territorial agreements will require mutual concessions are looking for target leaders who are able to fight and win the domestic political battle for a peaceful, but nevertheless controversial territorial settlement. If target leaders are politically secure, they have more room at the bargaining table to offer concessions. In contrast, governments that are very susceptible to a rebuke by the legislature, the electorate, or the military high command are more likely to settle for a stalemate in negotiations.

Comparisons among dyads

In this last section we examine the political institutions of both challengers and targets jointly, and consider how pairings of political institutions influence patterns of strategic interaction.

PA6: Lower levels of diplomatic and military conflict are expected in territorial disputes between two democratic states. As a result, state leaders in democratic dyads should be:

a. less likely to initiate military challenges and more likely to seek negotiations,
b. more likely to make concessions in negotiations over disputed territory, and
c. less likely to resort to higher levels of escalation in military conflicts over disputed territory.

This hypothesis converges with the conventional position in the democratic peace literature that disputes involving democratic dyads are more peaceful in comparison to disputes either among authoritarian states or between democratic and authoritarian states (see Chapter 1). The logic of **PA6** extends the reasoning presented in support of **PA1i** by considering the effects of high levels of political accountability in both challenger and target states. When foreign policy leaders in both states face political opposition forces that are in relatively strong positions to hold them responsible for controversial or failed policies, we should expect such decision-makers to be particularly wary of the political risks that are associated with diplomatic and military policies. As a result, democratic leaders should be more worried about the political dangers that crises and the large-scale use of military force entail (i.e. the audience costs to be borne for backing down or suffering high losses in a war) and should be less inclined to initiate military threats. Instead of relying on military threats and coercion, democratic leaders should turn to negotiations more frequently. Furthermore, democratic negotiators should favor mutual compromise with democratic counterparts as a way to try and secure domestic support for a territorial settlement, despite possible criticism from certain political opponents who will reject any territorial concessions.

The next hypothesis considers strategic interactions in territorial disputes between mixed dyads (i.e. disputes between a democratic and a non-democratic state).

PA7i: In mixed dyads military confrontations generally result from non-democratic challengers threatening democratic targets.

PA7ii: In mixed dyads the democratic state is more likely to adopt a position of intransigence in negotiations.

PA7iii: In mixed dyads the resort to high levels of escalation in a military confrontation is most likely by non-democratic leaders against democratic adversaries.

Hypotheses **PA7i** and **PA7iii** posit that in territorial disputes between democratic and non-democratic states, it is the decisions of non-democratic leaders that typically lead to military confrontations and higher levels of military escalation. The logic centers on the more limited political risks that non-democratic leaders face both in initiating military probes and bluffs and resorting to the large-scale use of force (Premises 3 and 4). The political risks faced by non-democratic leaders are limited fundamentally by the weakness of political opposition groups in such countries and their relative inability to hold leaders accountable for failed military policies. We do not believe that democratic states are typically targeted with military threats by non-democratic states because of a belief that democratic states are more likely to back down under the threat of an armed conflict in a crisis. Furthermore, if military conflict is frequent within mixed dyads, the primary explanation is not that democratic states often adopt aggressive policies, but that the more frequent military initiatives of non-democratic leaders cause democratic leaders to respond with force in kind. Nevertheless, it is important to emphasize that these two hypotheses do not preclude the aggressive use of threats and military force by democratic leaders. Indeed, several of the hypotheses already presented identify conditions under which democratic leaders are more willing to turn to the military option.

While **PA7i** and **PA7iii** argue that the decisions of non-democratic state leaders are central to understanding military conflict in mixed dyads, **PA7ii** claims that deadlock in negotiations rests on the shoulders of democratic leaders. As argued previously, democratic leaders should be very hesitant to offer concessions in talks due to concerns that opposition parties might hold the incumbent regime accountable for making unpopular or unsuccessful concessions. Democratic leaders should instead seek to shift the political risks of concessions on to their negotiating partner. In contrast, non-democratic states will be more likely to make concessions to break bargaining deadlocks since their greater political flexibility enables them to do this at less political risk.[9]

Operational measures for empirical testing

In this section we describe how each of the hypotheses from the Political Accountability Model is measured with operational indicators (see Table 4.1 for a summary listing of the hypotheses).

Measuring the accountability of democratic and
non-democratic leaders

To test **PA1i** we code the degree to which the political systems of challenger and target states are democratic as opposed to authoritarian. We utilize the *POLITY III* and *POLITY 98* data sets (see Jaggers and Gurr

---

[9] However, this does not mean that concessions from non-democratic leaders are very likely. As we have argued previously, stalemate is the most likely outcome under such conditions, but if a deadlock in talks is to be broken the initiative is more likely to come from the non-democratic country.

Table 4.1 *Summary of hypotheses to be tested from the Political Accountability Model*

	Predicted relationship in equations to be tested			
	Status quo stage		Negotiations stage	Escalation stage
Hypotheses regarding	Force	Talks		
Comparisons across political systems				
Democratic vs. non-democratic (**PA1i**)	−	+	+	−
Democracy and military risk (**PA1i**)	−	NA	NA	−
Democratic adversary and signaling (**PA1ii**)	−	NA	+	−
Democratic response to stalemate (**PA1iii**)	−	+	−	NA
Democracy and enduring rivalry (**PA2i**)	NS	NS	NS	NS
Democracy and ethnic ties (**PA2ii**)	+	+	−	+
Comparisons within political systems				
Legislative support for government (**PA3i**)	+	+	+	+
Adversary government legislative support (**PA3ii**)	−	+	+	−
Time since elections (**PA4i**)	−	−	−	−
Recent elections in adversary (**PA4ii**)	−	+	NA	NA
Time since elections in adversary (**PA4ii**)	NA	NA	−	+
Politically secure non-democratic leaders (**PA5i**)	+	+	+	+
Politically secure non-democratic leaders in adversary (**PA5ii**)	−	+	+	−
Comparisons among dyads				
Democratic dyads (**PA6**)	−	+	+	−
Non-democratic states in mixed dyads and military conflict (**PA7i & PA7iii**)	+	−	NA	+
Non-democratic states in mixed dyads and negotiations (**PA7ii**)	NA	NA	+	NA

Note: A positive sign (+) indicates that in the statistical tests the estimated coefficient should have a value greater than zero; a negative sign (−) indicates that in the statistical tests the estimated coefficient should have a value less than zero; NA indicates that there is no hypothesis to be tested, while NS indicates that the estimated coefficient should not be statistically significant.

1995) to create a net-democracy score variable, which ranges in value from −10 to +10. This 21-point net-democracy variable is created by subtracting each state's autocracy score (which ranges from 0 to 10) from its democracy score (which also ranges from 0 to 10). As values approach −10 the country is judged to be highly authoritarian, whereas scores approaching +10 indicate that a country is highly democratic. To aid in the interpretation of certain variables, at times we rescale the net-democracy variable so that all values are positive. In order to fill in cases of missing data, we consult various country-specific sources to find detailed information on political conditions for the countries and time periods for which there is no *POLITY* coding. In years when fundamental political changes resulted in shifts in the net-democracy score, we use these same sources to identify the month in which those political changes took place. We then assign different net-democracy scores for the periods prior to and after the political changes. Our classifications of a state's level of democracy, then, are accurate to a monthly degree of specificity.

We use this net-democracy variable to create an interaction term to test the **PA1i** hypotheses that democratic leaders are less likely to initiate and escalate military conflicts in situations of high military risk. We first determine the net-democracy level for each state using the coding rules described in the previous paragraph. Next we identify cases in which a state faces a situation of military risk or uncertainty.[10] A state faces a situation of military risk if its value for the short-term military balance is 0.4 or less (see Chapter 3).[11] The net-democracy and military risk variables are then multiplied together to create the final operational measure.

We create another interaction term to examine **PA1ii**, which claims that democratic targets send more credible signals of resolve than do non-democratic targets. We generate this interaction term by multiplying the net-democracy variable for the target (see above) and a dummy variable that indicates whether the target state signals resolve in its initial response to a challenger's threat of force or call for negotiations.[12] A signal of resolve in negotiations is coded as the refusal of the target negotiators to offer any concessions at the outset of talks. For military confrontations, a signal of resolve occurs when the target's initial response to the challenger's threat was to respond with an equal or greater level of force and to refuse any concessions. These two 21-point interaction terms are included in the relevant challenger equations for the Negotiations and Escalation Stages, respectively. To code these signaling variables, we relied on case-specific sources that provided detailed descriptions of

[10] We include this control variable for military risk in the statistical model so that we can properly test **PA1i**.

[11] We also create an alternative measure of military risk, with a particular emphasis on capturing the idea of possible uncertainty over the likely outcome of military conflicts. This military risk variable is coded with a one if a state's value on the short-term balance of capabilities variable lies in the range between 0.4 and 0.6. See Chapter 3 for the measurement of the short-term balance of forces variable.

[12] We include the appropriate target signal of resolve dummy variable in the statistical models for both the Negotiations and Escalation Stages. The inclusion of this variable serves as a control variable to allow for the comparison of democratic signals of resolve with non-democratic signals of resolve.

negotiations and military confrontations for each of the territorial disputes. These sources are listed in the case summaries and bibliographies for each territorial dispute in Appendices B–F.

To test hypothesis **PA1iii**, which posits that non-democratic leaders will respond to stalemates with more volatile and risky behavior, once again we use the net-democracy variable described earlier. In this case we create another dummy variable to identify situations in which a recent stalemate has occurred.[13] A prior stalemate in negotiations is measured with a dummy variable equal to one if a round of talks ended without any progress towards settlement. The stalemate is considered to be "recent" if it occurred within the past two years.[14] The concept of a stalemate is coded from the perspective of each state. A round of talks ends in stalemate if a given state offers only limited or no concessions, while its opponent offers no concessions at all. Secondary sources for each dispute were consulted in the coding of this variable (see the bibliography in Appendix for a listing of case-specific sources). We create the final operational measure by multiplying the net-democracy score by this recent stalemate dummy variable.

To test **PA2i** we create yet another interaction term to see whether democracies and non-democracies behave the same way when facing an enduring rival. As before, we utilize the net-democracy score described for **PA1i**. The next step is to create an enduring rivalry dummy variable, which reflects a high frequency of militarized conflict between challenger and target over the past few decades. To identify situations in which military conflict has occurred, we utilize the COW data sets on militarized disputes, international wars, and extra-systemic wars, as well as our own data on militarized disputes over territorial claims. Two states are considered to be enduring rivals if they have experienced military conflicts in five or more of the past twenty years.[15] We create the final operational measure by multiplying the net-democracy score by the enduring rivalry dummy variable.[16]

We create a final interaction term to examine the behavior of democracies when ethnic co-nationals are involved in the territorial dispute (**PA2ii**). As before, this term is created by multiplying the net-democracy

---

[13] We also include this recent stalemate control variable in the statistical model so that we can properly ascertain the impact of democracy following a recent stalemate.

[14] To check for robustness we create two additional measures based upon different time lags.Thus we also consider whether a country in a territorial dispute had experienced a stalemate within the past year or past five years.

[15] A second threshold for measuring enduring rivalry is constructed based on ten or more years with military disputes over the past twenty years.

[16] We also include this enduring rivalry dummy variable in the statistical model to allow for the proper test of **PA2i**.

variable (see above) by a dummy variable to indicate whether ethnic co-
nationals are located in the disputed territory.[17] To code for ethnic co-
nationals we relied upon Huth (1996) and the country-specific sources
listed in Appendices B–F.

Measuring accountability among democratic leaders
To test **PA3i** and **PA3ii** the first step is to identify all democratic countries
and then to collect data on the strength of the president or prime minister's party and its coalition allies.[18] For these two hypotheses, as well as
for all remaining Political Accountability Model hypotheses, a country is
considered democratic if its net-democracy score is greater than or equal
to +6 (on the −10 to +10 scale) and is considered non-democratic if
its net-democracy score is less than or equal to +5 (also on the −10 to
+10 scale). In presidential or mixed systems where the president was responsible for foreign policy decisions, we collect data on the percentage
of seats held by the president's party (and its coalition allies) in the lower
house of the legislature, as well as the corresponding percentage in the
upper house if the upper chamber had effective treaty ratification powers
(for use in the Negotiations Stage). In parliamentary or mixed systems
in which the prime minister was in charge of foreign policy, we assem-
ble data on the ruling coalition's percentage of seats in the lower house.
This data is drawn from general sources (*Annual Register*; Bidwell 1973;
Europa World Year Book; *Keesing's*; Mackie and Rose 1991; and *Political
Handbook of the World*) as well as country-specific works. In addition,
numerous country-specific sources on the political history of countries
are consulted when these basic sources do not contain all of the needed
information. We end up with four operational measures for the security
of democratic leaders. The first measure captures the percentage of legislative or parliamentary seats held by the ruling *party*. The second and
related indicator measures the percentage of legislative or parliamentary
seats held by the ruling *government*. The ruling government includes the
lead party, as well as its coalition partners. The final two measures are
dummy variables to indicate whether the ruling party and ruling government possess a majority of parliamentary or legislative seats.

---

[17] Once again, we also include in the statistical model a control dummy variable to indicate
the presence of ethnic co-nationals in disputed territory. The inclusion of this variable
allows us to isolate more correctly the impact of democracy when ethnic co-nationals
inhabit disputed territory.

[18] We include dummy variables in the statistical model to identify whether the challenger
and target are democratic. The inclusion of these control variables separates countries
into democracies and non-democracies and allows us to test the hypotheses of various
regimes.

To test the two hypotheses on elections (**PA4i–ii**), we collect information on the dates of all national elections either for presidents or for legislatures (depending upon the state's type of political system).[19] Our final operational measure is a count of the number of months since the last relevant national election. We count the number of months *since* the last election due to concerns with endogenous election timing in parliamentary democracies. At times we also employ a dummy variable to indicate that a national election has been held recently – that is, within the past year.

Measuring political security among non-democratic leaders

To test **PA5i** and **PA5ii** we derive four operational measures to indicate whether or not non-democratic leaders are politically secure. Keep in mind, however, that in the statistical analyses only one of the various operational measures is included in any given equation that is tested. In general, the set of findings reported by scholars studying domestic conflict and violence helps us to identify when authoritarian leaders are least likely to be politically at risk.

First, studies indicate (e.g. Auvinen 1997; Benson and Kugler 1998; Dudley and Miller 1998; Ellingsen 2000; Henderson and Singer 2000; Krain and Myers 1997; Muller and Weede 1994, 1999) that various forms of political unrest, ranging from protests to violent rebellion and civil wars, are less likely in more repressive authoritarian systems and more likely in less repressive authoritarian systems. Therefore, for our first measure we identify those non-democratic countries that could be considered the most authoritarian based upon their *POLITY III* or *POLITY 98* net-democracy scores. Regimes with a net-democracy score less than or equal to –5 (based on the –10 to +10 scale) are considered the most authoritarian and thus are given a value of one for this first measure of non-democratic political security.

Second, findings from cross-national studies of coups and the duration of tenure in power for non-democratic leaders (Bienen and Van de Walle 1991; Hanneman and Steinback 1990; Londregan and Poole 1990; Przeworski, Alvarez, Cheibub, and Limongi 2000; Zimmermann 1983: ch. 7) suggest that regimes that have come to power by means of a coup are particularly vulnerable to being removed by a coup. Another way of looking at the findings is that leaders who come to power by violence are generally at risk of being removed by violence. The threat of a coup, however, is greatest for the first several years after the coup and then drops off

---

[19] The same sources utilized to code for ruling party strength are relied upon to gather information on the dates of elections.

considerably. The critical question for new leaders is whether they can consolidate their political power base in the first year or two after coming to power and survive potential counter-coups. If regimes can survive this period, their chances of remaining in power increase substantially. A related finding in the coup literature is that failed coups and military revolts or uprisings are good predictors of future coup attempts in the short term. Thus, even if regimes have been in power for some time, the need to suppress attempted coups or military revolts indicates substantial discontent within the military and suggests that another coup attempt may be made soon. As a result, for this second measure we consider non-democratic leaders to be politically secure if they have not witnessed a coup or attempted coup in the past year.[20] Several sources were consulted to identify the dates of attempted and successful coups (Bueno de Mesquita and Siverson 1995; Calvert 1970; *Cross-Polity Data Set*; Dupuy and Dupuy 1993; *Europa World Year Book*; *Keesing's*; Thompson 1973; Vanhanen 1979: Appendix B).

Third, scholars argue that authoritarian leaders who take limited steps towards democratization are often entering a period of greater political risk and instability. Cross-national studies suggest that many transitions towards democracy fail and that periods marked by initial measures of political liberalization can be followed by political repression and military coups as the liberalization process collapses and reverts back to a more repressive political order (e.g. Anderson 1999; Bratton and van de Walle 1997; Crescenzi and Enterline 1999; Feng and Zak 1999; Higley and Gunther 1992; Linz and Stepan 1996; O'Donnel and Schmitter 1986; Power and Gasiorowski 1997; Przeworski 1991; Sutter 1995; Swaminathan 1999). Political vulnerability for incumbents can be high during this period of political change since some of the restrictive political institutions and practices of the past are lifted, which allows increased opportunities for political opposition to mobilize and express itself. This can lead to rising expectations of further political change and new policies for groups traditionally left outside the ruling coalition, which often pose an increased threat to those political forces who favor the status quo. As a result, a politically dangerous situation can arise in which supporters of the old political order fear further policy changes while opposition forces press for such changes with greater effectiveness. Therefore, our third measure for political security is a dummy variable coded with a value of

---

[20] Once again, we create two alternative measures for recent coup activity to check for robustness. The first alternate measure indicates whether a coup or attempted coup takes place during the current period of state interaction (see Chapter 2), while the second measure measures codes whether a coup or attempted coup has occurred in the past two years.

one if a non-democratic state had *not* undergone a period of significant political liberalization within the past year. A period of political liberalization is said to be taking place if a state's net-democracy score increases by at least two points from the previous year.[21] The beginning dates of all periods of political transition are established and cross-checked against other data sets on political change to confirm that political liberalization was not taking place during the period in question (Bratton and van de Walle 1997, *Europa World Year Book*, Gasiorowski 1996, Przeworski, Alvarez, Cheibub, and Limongi 2000: 59–76; Vanhanen 1979: Appendix B).

Fourth, in authoritarian political systems the resort to organized violent political rebellion by opposition groups outside of the military is a strong signal that the regime faces a critical problem of legitimacy among certain opposition groups who are highly resolved to overturn the political status quo. Given the high risks of repression and the consequences of failing to prevail in a violent confrontation with the regime, we should not expect organized and sustained rebellion unless opposition groups are willing to pay a high cost and believe that the regime is politically vulnerable (see Jackman 1993; Zimmermann 1983). Furthermore, as argued above, political turmoil and challenges to a government trigger military intervention against the regime when military leaders lose confidence in the incumbent's ability to control political opposition. Our final measure of political security, then, is a dummy variable coded with a value of one if a country has *not* experienced this type of violent political rebellion and challenges to the regime within the past year. The primary source for this information is the *Cross-Polity Data Set* of Arthur Banks, which contains annual information on rebellion and violent political challenges for the entire 1919–95 period. We use Banks' variables on revolutionary activity, insurgent movements, assassinations, riots, and violent demonstrations to code for the presence of violent political rebellion. Missing data on selected countries and time periods are collected from various other sources (*Annual Register*; *Europa World Year Book*, *Keesing's*; *London Times*; *New York Times*).

Measuring political vulnerability of states in dyads
To test **PA6** we create an operational measure to identify all territorial disputes in which both the challenger and target are democratic states. Following the coding rules described earlier, a democratic dyad is a dyad in which the net-democracy score for both the challenger and target is greater than or equal to +6 (on the −10 to +10 scale).

---

[21] In addition, a second dummy variable is constructed based on a two-year lag for identifying periods of political liberalization.

The final set of operational measures is developed to test hypotheses **PA7i–iii**. We first determine whether a dyad is a mixed dyad. Following the coding rules employed previously, a dyad is considered mixed if one state in the dispute (either the challenger or the target) has a net-democracy score greater than or equal to +6, while the other state has a net-democracy score less than or equal to +5. Following the logic contained in **PA7i** and **PA7iii**, we create a dummy variable equal to one to identify the non-democratic state in the mixed dyad.[22] The final operational measure used to test **PA7i**, **PA7ii**, and **PA7iii**, then, is an interactive dummy variable which identifies that a state is: (a) non-democratic, and (b) part of a mixed dyad. Since we include a mixed dyad control variable in the statistical model, this single interactive dummy variable effectively compares the behavior of non-democratic states in mixed dyads to the behavior of democratic states in mixed dyads. This allows us to examine **PA7ii** (a hypothesis about the behavior of democratic states in mixed dyads) as well as **PA7i** and **PA7iii** (hypotheses about the behavior of non-democratic states in mixed dyads) using a single interaction term.

Conclusion

In this chapter we presented the assumptions and underlying logic of the Political Accountability Model, from which a number of hypotheses were derived. The hypotheses associated with this model differ from those derived from the International Politics Model in the previous chapter. The International Politics Model did not explicitly address how differences in the domestic political institutions of states might influence the foreign policy choices of state leaders. Instead, in the International Politics Model, decision-maker choices among alternative diplomatic and military options are determined solely by assessments of the expected security gains or losses associated with those options, as well as the likely costs of employing military force. The Accountability Model expands this restricted conception of expected utility calculations by positing that political leaders include in their calculus the likely domestic political consequences of foreign policy choices. In particular, the Accountability Model proposes that incumbents select diplomatic and military policies with an eye towards avoiding policies that might mobilize strong political opposition. Conversely, they will favor policies that enhance their position in the domestic game of politics. Opposition elites and groups are likely to

---

[22] We also include a mixed dyad control variable in the statistical model. By including this variable we are able to make the proper comparison between democratic and non-democratic states in mixed dyads.

challenge their governments if incumbents make substantial territorial concessions or fail in efforts to change the status quo by the threat or use of military force. The theoretical foundation of the model is the strategic interplay between incumbent leaders and existing or potential political opposition forces. The effective threat posed by opposition groups depends not only on the outcomes of foreign policy initiatives by incumbents but also on the degree to which political institutions are open or closed. Theoretically, this produces many interesting situations in which leaders must calculate the political risks and rewards of pursuing claims to disputed territory.

While the International Politics Model views foreign policy leaders as competing solely in the game of international politics, the Accountability Model argues that an understanding of the game of domestic politics would improve our ability to explain inter-state relations. In this respect the Accountability Model offers new insights into the analysis of how diplomacy and force might be employed by state leaders in territorial disputes.

5   Domestic institutions and the Political
Norms Model

The Political Norms Model becomes the focus of our theory building efforts in this chapter. In the Political Accountability Model, competitive elections, independent legislative powers, and the threat of military coups are key sources of accountability for leadership decisions in foreign policy. In the Political Norms Model, analytical attention shifts to the principles that shape political elite beliefs about how to bargain and resolve political conflicts with domestic and international opponents. In the Accountability Model, state leaders are rational and self-interested politicians who strategically respond to a political environment in which institutions affect the ability of political opposition to reward and punish them for the policies they adopt. In the Norms Model, leaders from democratic and non-democratic states have different beliefs about the acceptability of compromising with and coercing political adversaries. The theoretical focus of the Norms Model therefore differs in comparison to the Accountability Model. In the Accountability Model, the analysis centers on state leaders as rational actors who desire to remain in power and therefore they are attentive to the domestic political implications of foreign policy choices. While there is no reason why the logic of the Norms Model would contest the idea that leaders are rational and strategic acting politicians, the theoretical focus is directed at explaining why political leaders develop varying beliefs about the legitimacy of different strategies of accommodation and coercion in political bargaining, and then explores the implications of such beliefs for foreign policy decision-making.

Political Norms Model

Figure 5.1 summarizes the logic of the Political Norms Model. The starting point is that the presence or absence of democratic political institutions is a source of variation in political elite norms regarding the use of violence and compromise with domestic political opponents. Elite norms of political bargaining in well-established democracies should differ in

Differences in Strength and Stability of Democratic Institutions Among States	Variation in Elite Norms Regarding Use of Violence and Compromise with Political Opponents at Domestic Level	Elite Norms of Domestic Conflict Resolution Influence Conflict Resolution in International Disputes	Variation in Domestic Norms Produces Different Choices by Executive Regarding Negotiations and Military Force in Territorial Disputes

Figure 5.1 Summary of logic in Political Norms Model

systematic ways from elite norms in stable and repressive non-democratic political systems. In particular, democratic norms of political bargaining emphasize the legitimacy of compromising with political opponents in a situation of political deadlock and restricting the threat or use of force in response to any coercion and violence that has been initiated by political opposition. The final step in the argument is that elite norms of domestic political bargaining shape leaders' beliefs about the appropriate way to combine diplomacy and military force in attempts to resolve international disputes.

Premises of the model

Three premises provide the foundation for building hypotheses about the relationship between political norms and foreign policy choices.

Premise 1: Norms are principles for political bargaining
Decisions by political actors regarding coercion and accommodation in situations of political conflict are influenced by norms, since norms help to establish the legitimacy of political bargaining strategies.

The use of the term "political norms" refers to principles or standards concerning which political actions and behaviors are seen as legitimate and desirable when engaging in political competition and seeking to resolve political conflict. We do not use the term "norms" to denote simply a common or typical pattern of political behavior, which is another common definition of the term.[1] Norms, however, can help to explain *why*

---

[1] It is necessary to clarify what is meant by the term "norms" since the term is commonly understood to refer to both of these meanings. For example, the *Oxford English Dictionary*, vol. x (1989: 515) defines a norm as: "A standard, model, pattern, type." See Gelpi (1997: 340) for a similar discussion in which the prescriptive and descriptive meanings of the term "norms" are presented. In addition to Gelpi's work, several other works by political scientists on the role of norms and ideas in international politics have been useful in developing this model (see Checkel 1999; Duffield 1992, 1995; Finnemore

individuals and groups engage in consistent patterns of political behavior. That is, if political norms are strongly held and widely shared among members of a political system, it is quite possible that certain patterns of behavior will emerge given the substantive content of those generally accepted principles. In any political system a recurring feature of political life is that conflicts of interest arise over state policies, as well as over which individuals will hold office. As a result, policy disagreements emerge and opposition groups seek to remove incumbents. If we believe that political norms influence patterns of political competition, one causal mechanism is through the principles accepted by political actors regarding the legitimacy of coercion and compromise with political opponents.

The distinction between viewing norms as principles or as a typical pattern of behavior (prescriptive versus descriptive) is important. If a compelling logical argument linking domestic norms to foreign policy choices is to be developed, such a theory will need to treat norms as legitimizing principles for political bargaining between groups that have conflicts of interest. This is particularly true of norms concerning political compromise and the threat or use of coercive force (see Premise 2 below for a fuller description of these components of political norms). If norms imply only recurring patterns of domestic political behavior, then the argument that these norms should also influence bargaining in international disputes seems quite questionable. Why should we expect that domestic patterns of political behavior will be replicated when international politics operates within a different strategic environment? The identification of a consistent pattern of domestic behavior in and of itself does not provide a clear logical basis for predicting similar patterns of political behavior in the context of international bargaining. If we are to argue that a domestic pattern of behavior should also emerge internationally, the key is to identify a cause of that domestic behavior which can also influence the decisions of foreign policy leaders.

An important implication of this first premise is that elite and non-elite political norms cannot be treated as necessarily the same. In fact, scholarship on elite and mass opinions and political culture suggests that there can be important differences between the two on issues relating to political tolerance, levels of knowledge, degree of partisanship, and other dimensions (e.g. Braumoeller 1997; Etzioni-Havley 1993; Holsti 1996; Kullberg and Zimmerman 1999; Murray 1996; Murray and Cowden 1999; Putnam 1976; Verba 1987; Zaller 1992; Zimmerman 2002). Since

1996; Finnemore and Sikkink 1998; Florini 1996; Goertz and Diehl 1992; Goldstein 1993; Goldstein and Keohane 1993; Katzenstein 1996; Klotz 1995; Kratochwil 1989; Legro 1995; Ruggie 1998; Shannon 2000; Weart 1998: chs. 4–5; Wendt 1999: ch. 6).

our analysis focuses on the foreign policy decisions of political leaders, we restrict the model to elite norms of political bargaining.

Premise 2: Domestic political institutions are a source of political norms

Domestic political institutions structure political conflict and help to induce political elites to resolve conflict in particular ways.

Stable and enduring domestic political institutions should contribute to the establishment of systematic patterns of political competition and conflict resolution. That is, durable institutions help to establish the prevailing "rules" for strategic interaction among political elites as well as between elites and the larger population (e.g. Lijphardt 1984; Mainwaring and Shugart 1997; O'Donnell and Schmitter 1986; Powell 1982, 2000; Przeworski, Alvarez, Cheibub, and Limongi 1996, 2000; Shugart and Carey 1992; Stepan and Skach 1993; Weaver and Rockman 1993). Politicians who disregard these rules face sanctions and risk political defeat, while those elites who skillfully use the rules to their advantage are rewarded with political success and advance to positions of leadership (e.g. Riker 1986; Weingast 1997). As a result, these rules regulating political competition gain acceptance among political elites as legitimate principles for how to bargain over policy differences and how to secure and maintain positions of political influence and power. If we think about the relationship between norms and institutions in a temporal sense, we can see the potential for positive reinforcement effects. Norms held among a limited set of elites may provide a rationale for the initial design of institutions, but as time passes and those institutions remain stable and help to produce consistent behavior, the norms themselves become more widely and fully accepted by actors within the political system (see Axelrod 1984, 1986 and Weingast 1997 on the evolution of norms).[2]

An implication of Premise 2 is that the differences between democratic and authoritarian political institutions should produce differences between elite political norms. As many comparative scholars have argued, norms of restrained competition and tolerance of political opposition are benchmarks of political elite beliefs in well-established democratic systems (e.g. Lijphardt 1984; Powell 1982; Przeworski, Alvarez, Cheibub, and Limongi 2000; Putnam 1976). Many studies also report that patterns

---

[2] Processes of political socialization contribute to this positive reinforcement since the general population is educated in numerous ways to understand and value the advantages of democratic rules of political competition and bargaining. In addition, findings from social psychology on the general desire of individuals to maintain social approval and self-esteem (e.g. Backman 1985; Cialdini and Trost 1998; Tetlock 1992) can further help to explain why norms can become stronger and more durable over time.

of violent political conflict, including rebellion, coups, ethnic warfare, mass killing, and civil war are all much less likely under well-established democratic regimes (e.g. Benson and Kugler 1998; Ellingsen 2000; Gurr 1993; Gurr and Lichbach 1986; Harff and Gurr 1988; Hegre, Ellingsen, Gates, and Gleditsch 2001; Henderson and Singer 2000; Krain 1997; Krain and Myers 1997; Lichbach and Gurr 1981; Muller and Weede 1994; Poe and Tate 1994; Rummel 1994, 1995b, 1997). Therefore, the more democratic the political order is, the more likely elites are:

a. to accept the principle of compromise with opposition over policy differences in a situation of political stalemate, and

b. to reject the threat or use of violence as a means to compel political opponents to concede on policy issues or to remove them from political office.[3]

It is important to discuss each of these components of democratic norms in greater detail in order to avoid confusion. The first component, the concept of political compromise, has two different levels of meaning. At the broadest level, political compromise refers to the willingness of elites to accept: (a) political opposition as a legitimate feature of politics, (b) unfavorable outcomes to political competition, and (c) limits on the policies that can be imposed by majorities and victors against minorities and defeated opposition. At this level of understanding, democratic elite norms include such critical features as acceptance of competing political parties and the necessity of sharing power with political opposition at times in order to form coalition governments. Political compromise also implies a willingness to accept political defeat in the sense that incumbents who lose elections permit political opponents to replace them in office. Similarly, incumbents do not suspend or abolish legislatures when political opposition is able to block the passage of legislation favored by the executive. Further, democratic norms of compromise imply that political opponents who lose elections are free to contest regime policies and to compete in fair elections in the future, and that minorities have certain rights that are respected by the majority (e.g. Alvarez, Cheibub, Limongi, and Przeworski 1996; Dahl 1998; Lijphardt 1984; Powell 1982,

---

[3] Some scholars (Bass 2000; Simmons 1999; Slaughter 1995) have argued that another component of democratic norms of political bargaining is a greater respect for legal principles and a greater reliance on the legal system to resolve disputes. This literature on democratic "legalism" represents a potentially fruitful area for further development of the Political Norms Model, but we leave it to future research. Incorporating this additional aspect of democratic norms into the model would raise interesting theoretical questions about issues such as (a) the willingness of states to turn to arbitration and adjudication of international disputes, (b) the compliance of states with legally based rulings and awards, and (c) the extent to which a state's diplomatic and military behavior is influenced by the strength of its legal claims regarding disputed issues.

2000; Przeworski, Alvarez, Cheibub, and Limongi 1996, 2000; Putnam 1976).[4]

At the more specific level of political bargaining and negotiation, political compromise refers to reciprocity in the exchange of policy concessions between political actors. As Robert Dahl states, "under a peaceful democratic process, settling political conflicts generally requires negotiation, conciliation, compromise."[5] Elites may directly trade concessions (to pass legislation for example) at a given point in time, or may exchange concessions over a longer period of time (see Keohane 1986). Elites bargain with political supporters and opponents in all political systems and therefore issue-specific logrolling is not unique to democratic systems. Our general claim is only that democratic leaders are more likely to accept the legitimacy of compromising with opponents as opposed to coercing them or changing political institutions so that opponents are less able to block decisions and policies favored by incumbents.

However, democratic norms of compromise do not imply that democratic leaders have a dominating preference for compromise outcomes in bargaining situations. Under the right political conditions, democratic leaders may not need to compromise with political opposition in pursuit of policies (e.g. the incumbent's party commands a strong majority in the legislature, or public opinion firmly favors its preferred policy position). In general, we can describe the outcomes to negotiations as follows: (a) the opposition concedes unilaterally on major issues, (b) the opposition concedes on major issues but requires limited concessions in return, (c) reciprocal compromise is needed to produce settlement, (d) the leader and his opposition reach stalemate without concessions, and (e) the opposition stands firm while the leader concedes on primary issues. If we think about the rank-ordering of preferences over these outcomes, it is clear that any political leader would prefer that the opposition concede. Therefore, there is no reason to expect democratic leaders to prefer the compromise outcomes "c" and "e" over outcomes "a" and "b." The difference that democratic norms might be expected to produce is that democratic elites would prefer outcome "c" over outcome "d", while non-democratic leaders would likely exhibit the reverse preference ordering. Put differently, democratic leaders would be more likely to seek mutual compromise to end political deadlock whereas non-democratic leaders would prefer coercive pressure rather than compromise as the way to break the deadlock.

---

[4] At this level of understanding, the norm of political compromise therefore has much in common with what other analysts refer to as principles of democratic liberalism (e.g. Doyle 1986; Owen 1997; Zakaria 1997).

[5] Dahl 1998: 150.

What is the logic behind democratic leaders turning to mutual concessions as the preferred response? The argument is that since the norms
of democratic political elites attach greater legitimacy to the existence
of political opposition and policy conflict as regular features of politics,
compromise with political opponents is more acceptable and even necessary to ensure that the political system operates effectively. Furthermore,
democratic principles of political equality imply that no group or individual can claim presumptive rights to define what is the best policy in a
situation of conflicting interests. This reinforces the acceptability of compromise, since neither party is retreating from a position of recognized
moral or political advantage (Dahl 1998: ch. 6; also see Gutmann 1980;
Gutmann and Thompson 1996). In contrast, if non-democratic elites are
less willing to accept opposition, debate, and challenges to government
policy as legitimate and enduring features of politics, then compromise
with political opponents is less desirable and may even be judged un-
acceptable. Compromise is also less necessary, since political deadlock
can be broken by coercing the opposition or by undermining the political institutions on which it relies. Democratic elites, however, are more
likely to question and reject the legitimacy of using coercion to break
political deadlock. In sum, there is a principle or norm of compromise
in democratic systems, but it must be understood in the context of political deadlock in which elites respond to political opposition that seems
unwilling to concede.

The other critical component of democratic norms is the disinclina-
tion to initiate or threaten violence to intimidate and remove political
opponents. Once again, the differences between elites in democratic and
non-democratic systems are most evident when policy disputes exist and
political opposition does not seem willing to concede. What is the political
response of incumbents at this stage? As argued above, democratic leaders should consistently reject violence as a means of settling disputes with
political adversaries because they accept democratic principles of political equality. However, in a political system where such principles are not
firmly accepted by elites, normative constraints on the use of coercion
against political opposition should be weaker. It is important to clarify,
however, that while democratic norms oppose aggressive coercion, they
do not imply an unwillingness to respond to or counter political violence.
In other words, a reluctance to initiate violence is compatible with the
normative belief that force is legitimate and may be necessary in defense
against political actors who resort to coercion themselves. Democratic
norms that favor the nonviolent resolution of domestic political conflicts
can coexist with norms that support the utility of force for purposes of
deterrence and the punishment of aggressive violent behavior.

Premise 3: Domestic norms influence bargaining in international disputes

Norms of political bargaining applied by leaders in dealing with domestic political opponents influence the bargaining strategies adopted by leaders in international disputes.

To build a theory of foreign policy choices based on domestic political norms, it is critical to demonstrate that the principles that influence choices in domestic policy also influence choices in international politics. If we find that norms are a determinant of strategies for bargaining and conflict resolution at the domestic level, do they remain an important causal factor when we shift our attention to international disputes?

Our argument is that well-established political norms can be understood as constituting fundamental components of a political elite's belief system about how to manage political conflict. Scholars studying the formation and content of individual belief systems have argued that normative principles and standards can be key components of such systems, and that these principles are reference points for judging what actions to take in a broad range of decision-making contexts (e.g. Kahnemann 1992). An implication of these findings is that norms regarding the legitimacy of compromise and the violent resolution of disputes are beliefs that political actors are likely to draw upon in a range of political settings. Furthermore, there is considerable evidence from scholarship in cognitive psychology that the core ideas and principles that define an individual's belief system are stable and resistant to change (e.g. Ajzen 1989; Fishbein and Ajzen 1975; Kruglanski, Baldwin, and Towson 1983). It follows then that basic principles or norms of coercion and accommodation in domestic political bargaining should continue to have causal effects even if the strategic environment of bargaining shifts to international disputes. This is not to claim that elites will ignore the new strategic environment and base their decisions solely on normative principles. Political leaders are rational and neither politically nor strategically naive. But within the constraints imposed by domestic political accountability or international political and military conditions, it is quite possible that the basic principles or normative elements of a leader's belief system continue to exert a causal impact on policy choices (e.g. Barnett 1998; Cronin 1999; Goldgeiger 1994; Murray, Cowden, and Russett 1999; Reus-Smit 1999; Risse-Kappen 1995; Shannon 2000; Wendt 1999: ch. 6).

Hypotheses

Comparing democratic and non-democratic political systems
The first two hypotheses are quite similar and draw on Premises 2 and 3.

PN1i: In a territorial dispute, leaders with strong nonviolent domestic political norms are:

a. more likely to rely on negotiations instead of military threats in an attempt to change the status quo,
b. more likely to make concessions in negotiations, and
c. less likely to resort to high levels of escalation in a military confrontation.

PN1ii: In response to a prior stalemate in negotiations over disputed territory, leaders with strong nonviolent domestic political norms should be:

a. more likely to favor continued negotiations instead of shifting to military threats and the use of force in an attempt to break the deadlock,
b. more likely to make concessions in negotiations in an attempt to break the deadlock, and
c. less likely to resort to high levels of escalation in a military confrontation.

The logic of **PN1i** is premised on the argument that leaders with strong nonviolent norms of domestic political bargaining should rely more heavily on negotiations to resolve disputes compared to their more violent and repressive non-democratic counterparts. Thus, while leaders with nonviolent norms should be active and seek changes in an unfavorable territorial status quo, they should not consistently initiate military threats and escalate confrontations in order to coerce concessions by threat of war or compel a change in the status quo by force of arms. Instead, they should turn to repeated rounds of talks and ultimately to limited concessions in an attempt to produce a negotiated settlement.

PN1ii extends this logic a bit further and posits that while all state leaders are likely to turn to negotiations initially in a territorial dispute and to withhold concessions in the early stages of negotiations, the differences in bargaining behavior between elites with strong versus weak democratic norms should be most evident after political deadlock has been established and leaders recognize that the opposition will not easily concede. If initial efforts at diplomacy prove unsuccessful, leaders with stronger nonviolent norms should be more likely: (a) to persist in further attempts at negotiations, and (b) to take the initiative in attempting to break the deadlock by offering concessions in subsequent negotiations that would be linked to similar concessions by the adversary.[6] Strong nonviolent norms should discourage political leaders from initiating military threats or resorting to the large-scale use of force in an attempt to

---

[6] A related hypothesis, which we do not attempt to test, would be that leaders with strong nonviolent norms are more likely to agree to either arbitration or adjudication of territorial disputes following stalemates in negotiations (see Simmons 1999 for a more extended discussion of this hypothesis; see also Dixon 1994; Raymond 1994).

break the stalemate through the use of coercive military pressure. Instead, democratic leaders should prefer the option of further negotiations and offer contingent concessions at this later stage of negotiations, with the expectation that the chances of reaching a negotiated agreement are limited unless some concessions are offered. In contrast, non-democratic leaders with violent norms should turn to the military option more frequently instead of agreeing to concessions to break the stalemate in negotiations. The reason is that using force is a more acceptable strategy for resolving political conflict in non-democratic systems than in democratic systems. As a result, these non-democratic leaders should initiate more military threats and then escalate to higher levels in an attempt to compel their adversary to concede disputed territory.[7]

Strong norms of non-violent bargaining imply that leaders should question the legitimacy of using force to compel adversaries to retreat and make concessions. We should expect leaders with stronger democratic norms to be reluctant to use escalating threats to apply greater military pressure; that is, to use the risk of war to induce concessions from another state's leadership. In short, aggressive brinkmanship strategies of escalating threats and the build-up of military forces should be more typical of more repressive and violent non-democratic leaders, who are more likely to believe that it is acceptable to threaten if not use force against political adversaries.

It is important to recognize that what distinguishes repressive non-democratic leaders from their democratic counterparts in their approach to changing the territorial status quo is their greater willingness to supplement diplomacy with coercive threats and force. The logic of normative constraints implies that leaders with strong democratic norms have a more limited set of policy options available to them as they press for change. In other words, the causal effects of democratic norms operate by shifting leaders' policy preferences away from the use of force and towards a greater reliance on negotiations to secure territorial claims. The difference centers on the acceptability of utilizing military force in an aggressive manner to secure territorial gains. In the abstract, all state leaders would generally prefer to achieve territorial goals without recourse to force. But in the absence of democratic norms of nonviolent conflict resolution, repressive authoritarian leaders should be more willing to turn to military force than should democratic leaders.

[7] This line of reasoning could be extended further to suggest that the willingness of such non-democratic leaders to shift policy and to make concessions would be likely only if prior military threats or the use of force had failed to coerce the adversary. For leaders operating under strong democratic norms, the shift to making concessions would not be a last resort after coercive force was ineffective; it would be a legitimate course of action in the first place.

The next hypothesis considers whether leaders with strong nonviolent domestic norms will take advantage of a position of relative strength to be more aggressive in their pursuit of territorial claims.

PN2: Strong nonviolent norms of bargaining should discourage leaders from relying on military force to secure territorial gains. As a result, even if countries enjoy a clear military advantage over their adversary, leaders with strong nonviolent norms should be less likely:

a. to initiate military threats or to favor force over negotiations as the means by which to challenge the status quo, or

b. to resort to high levels of escalation in a military confrontation.

The logic of this hypothesis is that if norms of nonviolent conflict resolution are well-established among political elites, then they should not be tempted by a military advantage to try and bully a weaker opponent. As a result, the increased likelihood of successfully coercing an opponent by force of arms should not induce democratic elites to shift policy away from a reliance on diplomacy and negotiations and towards initiating military threats and escalating confrontations by resorting to the large-scale use of military force. In contrast, elites with norms that sanction violence against opposition should be quite prepared to use force when they are confident that they possess superior force to coerce the opposition.

The last hypothesis in this section is derived from the argument, presented in support of Premise 2, that democratic norms do sanction the defensive use of force.

PN3: The differences in military behavior should be more evident when we compare democratic and authoritarian *challengers* than when we compare democratic and authoritarian *target* states. We should find that:

a. patterns of militarized dispute escalation differ significantly between leaders with strong versus weak nonviolent norms among challenger states. Leaders with more violent domestic norms are more likely to escalate military confrontations to high levels, whereas

b. patterns of militarized dispute escalation behavior are not significantly different between leaders with strong versus weak nonviolent norms among target states. All target states are expected to reciprocate the level of escalation by the challenger.

While challenger leaders with stronger nonviolent norms should be less likely to escalate militarized disputes to high levels, they should be quite willing as targets to respond forcefully to the military threats posed by other states. As argued in our discussion of Premise 2, nonviolent norms do not imply that political leaders should have strong dovish preferences. The *aggressive* threat or use of force would be inconsistent with strong nonviolent norms, but a policy of defending territory and responding to military threats would be compatible with such norms. Among challenger states we should observe a clear divergence in behavior in which authoritarian leaders with violent domestic norms more frequently escalate military confrontations. Among target states, however, we should expect leaders from both democratic and authoritarian states to reciprocate escalation consistently in defense of the territorial status quo.

Comparisons within political systems

The next hypothesis draws upon the argument associated with Premise 2 that the effects of domestic political norms on bargaining in international disputes are stronger for states in which domestic political institutions have been stable and there has been limited political change.

PN4: Relative to other democratic leaders, the leaders of recently established democratic regimes are:

a. more likely to resort to military force in an attempt to change the status quo instead of either negotiations or inaction,
b. less likely to make concessions in negotiations,
c. more likely to resort to high levels of escalation in military confrontations.

As argued in Premise 2, the development of strong political norms among elites may be time-dependent. If domestic norms of conflict resolution are produced (in part) by stable political institutions and the political behavior they promote, then the leaders of states where political institutions are newly democratic are not yet fully socialized with norms of compromise and nonviolent means of conflict resolution.[8]

While democratic institutions can be established through constitutional and electoral changes in relatively short periods of time, an elite political culture of democratic norms may require more time to become widely and deeply accepted (DiPalma 1991; Gibson 1996, 1998; Higley and Burton 1989; Higley and Gunther 1992; Higley, Kullberg, and Pakulski 1996; Linz and Stepan 1996; Remmer 1995; Zakaria 1997; Zimmerman 2002). This implies that the leaders of new democracies may retain the norms of the pre-democratic period and therefore be more willing to resort to aggressive military policies as opposed to seeking negotiated settlements of territorial disputes (e.g. Senese 1999; Snyder and Ballentine 1996).

The next hypothesis considers variation in elite norms among authoritarian systems:

---

[8] Another area for theoretical elaboration in the comparative analysis of democratic regimes lies in drawing on the work of scholars such as Arend Lijphart (e.g. 1984) to argue that differences in democratic institutions (multiparty vs. two-party systems, unicameral vs. bicameral legislatures, federal vs. unitary systems, etc.) might lead to differences in how strong norms of compromise are among democratic leaders. For example, we might posit that norms of compromise might be stronger in what Lijphart refers to as "consensus" as opposed to "majoritarian" governments in democracies.

PN5: Among non-democratic states, leaders who retain political power by resorting frequently to violence in the repression of political opposition are:

a. more likely to resort to military force in an attempt to change the territorial status quo instead of choosing either negotiations or inaction,
b. less likely to make concessions in negotiations, and
c. more likely to resort to high levels of escalation in military confrontations.

Among authoritarian states, the degree to which incumbent leaders rely upon force and violence to remain in power can vary substantially. In some states, political institutions evolve over time and the political system thus becomes less repressive and more open to limited forms of competition and less coercive forms of intra-elite bargaining (e.g. Breslauer 1982; Dittmer 1990; Hough 1980; Lee 1991). In other cases, however, the political order remains tightly closed to even limited forms of competition and political expression. It follows from Premise 2 that if significant differences exist in how repressive non-democratic political institutions are, then we should expect to find variation in the elite norms as well. Premise 3 leads us to expect that political leaders who have been consistently violent and ruthless in the repression of domestic opposition should have more intransigent and aggressive diplomatic and military policies in international disputes. Conversely, in authoritarian systems in which limited steps towards political liberalization have occurred, we should expect less violent and coercive elite norms to influence foreign policy choices.

Comparisons among dyads

The first two hypotheses consider the behavior of states in disputes where the leaders of both challenger and target share nonviolent political norms.

PN6i: Across all types of dyads in territorial disputes, the least conflictual disputes should be among states ruled by leaders with strong nonviolent political norms. As a result, when the leaders of both challenger and target governments share such nonviolent norms we should expect:

a. more frequent calls for talks and negotiations to change the status quo compared to inaction or the initiation of military threats,
b. more concessions in negotiations, and
c. lower levels of escalation in military confrontations.

This hypothesis extends the logic of **PN1i** and **PN1ii** to interactions between two states with democratic norms of political bargaining. If both parties prefer negotiations and mutual concessions as the way to resolve political conflict, then we should clearly expect that military confrontations should be quite infrequent and not escalate to war. Furthermore, negotiations should lead to concessions being exchanged within a few rounds of talks after it becomes clear that neither side will offer large unilateral concessions.

The next hypothesis extends the logic of **PN4** to the case where two recently established democratic governments are involved in a territorial dispute with each other.

PN6ii: Among democratic dyads, the most conflictual disputes are among new democracies. As a result, when the governments of both challenger and target are recently established democratic regimes we should expect:

a. more frequent initiations of military threats to change the status quo compared to efforts to pursue negotiations or decisions to maintain the status quo,
b. fewer concessions in negotiations, and
c. higher levels of escalation in military confrontations.[9]

One of the interesting implications of this hypothesis is that military confrontations and diplomatic stalemates can be expected in disputes among certain democratic dyads, whereas such courses of action should be avoided by other democratic dyads. Bargaining over disputed territory among leaders of recently established democracies should be more heavily influenced by prior prevailing non-democratic norms in which more coercive approaches to settling political conflicts were accepted. As a result, these democratic leaders should be more inclined to supplement diplomacy with force. In contrast, in territorial disputes among well-established democracies political leaders should bargain on the basis of strong norms that favor compromise and nonviolent conflict resolution. Therefore, military conflicts should be unlikely, whereas negotiated settlements should be more likely.

The next hypothesis draws out differences in behavior among non-democratic dyads.

PN7: Among non-democratic dyads, the most conflictual territorial disputes are between the most authoritarian and violent regimes. As a result, when the political systems of both challenger and target are highly repressive, we should expect:

a. more frequent initiations of military threats to change the status quo compared to efforts to pursue negotiations or decisions to accept the status quo,
b. fewer concessions in negotiations, and
c. higher levels of escalation in military confrontations.

---

[9] This last hypothesis regarding escalation in military confrontations will not be tested in Chapter 9 due to an insufficient number of cases.

It follows from the logic presented in support of **PN5** that the risks of military conflict and the inability to reach negotiated settlements are greatest when the leaders of two highly repressive political orders confront one another. In these territorial disputes both parties should be disinclined to offer concessions to break diplomatic deadlocks due to strong beliefs in the efficacy of force as a means to coerce concessions from the adversary. While it might be argued that these ruthless leaders would be able to signal a credible threat of force, this deterrent effect should be countered by their strong beliefs in the utility of force and a lack of confidence in their ability to secure concessions from the adversary without coercive force.[10] In this sense, the absence of a viable diplomatic option constrains these leaders to a reliance on force even though they expect the adversary to be resolved. The more interesting implication of this hypothesis is that high levels of diplomatic and military conflict would not be expected between two less repressive authoritarian regimes.

In the final hypothesis, we consider disputes between democratic and non-democratic adversaries.

PN8: In mixed dyads the party that consistently adopts more conflictual policies will be the state ruled by leaders with more violent and repressive political norms. Thus, relative to their more democratic counterparts, leaders from challengers and targets with more violent norms are:

a. more likely to resort to military force in an attempt to change the territorial status quo, as opposed to turning to negotiations or maintaining the status quo,
b. less likely to make concessions in negotiations, and
c. more likely to resort to high levels of escalation in military confrontations.

This hypothesis is consistent with the monadic approach to the democratic peace as described in Chapter 1. That is, leaders of states with stronger democratic norms should adopt consistent diplomatic and military policies in territorial disputes whether the adversary is democratic or not. Strong nonviolent political norms imply what we term a "firm-but-flexible" policy of bargaining in international disputes (Huth 1988). Leaders with stronger democratic norms are willing to make concessions to break a deadlock, but they require the other side to reciprocate with concessions. Furthermore, while the aggressive use of force by democratic leaders to compel an adversary into submission is not

---

[10] From the perspective of the Political Accountability Model, however, the entrenched leader's threat is not so clearly credible. As argued in the previous chapter, the lack of effective political opposition in many authoritarian systems allows leaders considerable flexibility to either escalate or back down.

expected, they should be prepared to deter military conflict or to defend against an attack. We should expect leaders with nonviolent norms to be fully capable of countering military threats and attacks with the build-up and use of force. As a result, we do not believe that a general policy of reciprocity in diplomacy and military preparedness places leaders with democratic norms at a disadvantage in negotiations (e.g. Druckman 1986; Druckman and Harris 1990; Stoll and McAndrew 1986), or in military confrontations with more repressive non-democratic states. Indeed, there is empirical evidence that such policies are relatively effective at protecting a state's security interests in international crises (e.g. Gelpi 1997; Huth 1988; Leng 1993).[11]

Hypothesis **PN8** differs from the arguments of some scholars (e.g. Dixon 1993, 1994; Doyle 1986; Owen 1997; Weart 1998) that democratic norms reduce armed conflict and promote settlements only in disputes with other democratic states. Based on the logic of the Norms Model as developed in this chapter, we do not see a strong theoretical foundation for arguing that leaders with democratic norms will attempt to ensure their security by adopting more inflexible and coercive policies when facing an adversary with non-democratic norms of bargaining. We would argue that the Political Norms Model implies that leaders with strong nonviolent norms do not view themselves as vulnerable. Furthermore, repressive authoritarian leaders should not believe that their more democratic counterparts can be bullied into unilateral concessions, nor that they will be reluctant to use force if attacked. It follows that in mixed dyads, the primary source for more aggressive and conflictual policies will be the decisions of repressive non-democratic leaders. The reason for this is not that more-democratic states are vulnerable to pressure, but that non-democratic elites with very violent norms are more willing to bargain in a more inflexible and coercive manner.[12]

The logic of **PN8**, however, does not contradict or reject the claim that in a democratic dyad the risk of war is low while the chances of a negotiated settlement are high. The argument advanced here is that such dyadic outcomes are based on a consistent pattern of behavior for democratic states in which democratic norms favor negotiations and mutual concessions if stalemate occurs, and reject the aggressive use of force. When both parties share these norms, military conflict is unlikely, while negotiated

---

[11] Furthermore, a number of studies have reported that democratic countries are quite successful in waging wars and emerging victorious, though it does appear that the advantages enjoyed by democracies diminish the longer the war persists (Bennett and Stam 1998; Lake 1992; Reiter and Stam 1998a, b, 2002; also see Larson 1996).

[12] These conclusions regarding mixed dyads parallel those presented in the previous chapter. The Political Norms and Political Accountability Models do not differ significantly on this question.

settlements are more likely because both parties will offer concessions to break a stalemate. If crises and war generally follow the failure of diplomacy and the inability to reach a negotiated settlement, then the opportunities for military conflict should be much fewer for disputes among democratic states. Furthermore, we should expect, even in those disputes where settlements have not been reached in the early stages of negotiations, that democratic leaders will consistently choose further diplomacy as opposed to coercive force.

Measurement of variables for empirical testing

In this section we describe the operational measures developed to test each of the hypotheses derived from the Political Norms Model (see Table 5.1 for a summary of the hypotheses).

Comparing states with non-violent vs. violent political norms

To test hypotheses **PN1i–PN3** a measure of elite norms of domestic political bargaining and conflict resolution must be developed. An operational measure of norms should tap both the propensity for political compromise as well as the use of violence and force by political elites. Therefore, we use two indicators to measure this norms variable: the level of democracy over time and the frequency of violent political conflict over time. The first indicator follows from the Norms Model's assumption that democratic institutions are associated with more bargaining and logrolling between elites (e.g. political relations between ruling and opposition parties/leaders as well as incumbent executives and legislatures) and less political violence. The second indicator focuses more directly on the use of violence and force as part of elite political culture. The purpose of using both components is to develop measures that are more sensitive to variation among both democratic and non-democratic regimes. Furthermore, we choose to examine both indicators over a twenty-year period. The time dimension captures the idea that norms develop through socialization and the legitimacy associated with consistent patterns of political behavior and practice. Stable political institutions help induce those behaviors and principles of legitimacy by means of the incentives and constraints they impose on political elites. For non-democracies the use of both indicators gauges the extent of violence and reflects the fact that authoritarian regimes can change over time with respect to the prevalence of violence and the degree of political freedoms. For democracies it is possible to measure not only the duration of democratic institutions but also the degree of violence in the recent (non-democratic) past.

Table 5.1 *Summary of hypotheses to be tested from the Political Norms Model*

	Predicted relationships in equations to be tested			
	Status quo stage		Negotiations	Escalation
Hypotheses regarding	Force	Talks	stage	stage
Comparisons across political systems				
Strong vs. weak nonviolent norms (**PN1i**)	−	+	+	−
Nonviolent norms and the response to stalemate (**PN1ii**)	−	+	+	−
Nonviolent norms and military advantage (**PN2**)	−	+	NA	−
Nonviolent vs. violent norms among challenger leaders (**PN3**)	NA	NA	NA	−
Nonviolent vs. violent norms among target leaders (**PN3**)	NA	NA	NA	NS
Comparisons within political systems				
Recently established democracies (**PN4**)	+	−	−	+
Highly repressive non-democracies (**PN5**)	+	−	−	+
Comparisons among dyads				
Dyads with nonviolent norms (**PN6i**)	−	+	+	−
Dyads of recently established democracies (**PN6ii**)	+	−	−	+
Dyads of highly repressive non-democratic leaders (**PN7**)	+	−	−	+
Leaders with stronger violent norms in mixed dyads (**PN8**)	+	−	−	+

Note: A positive sign (+) indicates that in the statistical tests the estimated coefficient should have a value greater than zero; a negative value (−) indicates that in the statistical tests the estimated coefficient should have a value less than zero; NA indicates that there is no hypothesis to test while NS indicates that in the statistical tests the estimated coefficient should not be statistically significant.

The first indicator measures the extent to which a state's political system has been democratic over the previous twenty-year period.[13] We turn

[13] Countries that were previously colonies during some portion of the twenty-year period are generally given a very low net-democracy score for all such years, and thus are coded as non-democratic for the overwhelming majority of pre-independence years. Also, in some cases the twenty-year lag cuts across periods in which countries experienced major political changes leading to their partial dissolution or enlargement and unification (e.g. Soviet Union, Yugoslavia, or Vietnam and Yemen). In cases of dissolution, we coded on the basis of the prior, larger state while in cases of enlargement we included data on the state that became the center of political power in the new unified country (e.g. North Vietnam and North Yemen).

to the *POLITY III* and *POLITY 98* net-democracy score to code a country as democratic or not (a value of +6 or greater on the –10 to +10 scale; see Chapter 4 for details on operationalization) for each of the past twenty years. We then compile a final operational measure (which ranges from 0 to 20) to indicate how many of the past twenty years the state had been democratic.

The second variable measures the frequency of political violence by governments against political opposition over the previous twenty-year period. In order to maintain consistency with the first indicator and to capture the wording of the hypotheses, the operational measure is coded as the number of the past twenty years in which the challenger (or target) did *not* experience violent political conflict (i.e. in which ruling elites did not employ violence against non-elites or against other high-level elites). Values closer to 0 indicate a high degree of elite-sponsored violence, while values closer to 20 indicate a relative lack of such violence. This measure attempts to capture the extent to which ruling elites use violence to hold on to power when challenged, and how frequently governments come to power and fall from power through violent political conflict. Data on violent leadership changes, military coups and coup attempts, military revolts, political purges by incumbent regimes, and civil wars are compiled from multiple sources (e.g. Bueno de Mesquita and Siverson 1995; *Cross-Polity Data Set*; Gasiorowski 1995; Small and Singer 1982; Thompson 1973; Vanhanen 1979).[14]

We use these two lagged measures of norms to create the interaction terms for **PN1ii** and **PN2**. To test **PN1ii** we multiply each lagged norms variable by a dummy variable equal to one if a stalemate has occurred in negotiations over disputed territory within the previous year.[15] Data on stalemates in prior negotiations came from the territorial dispute data set (see Appendices B–F) and a stalemate is coded according to the rules described in Chapter 4. The impact of nonviolent norms in response to stalemate, then, is measured with two alternative indicators, one which uses a lagged measure of democracy and another which uses a lagged measure of government-sponsored violence. Similarly, to test **PN2** we

---

[14] For countries that were colonies during some portion of the twenty-year period we collected data on the number of years during which there was violent conflict between the colonial government and the local population, including large-scale armed struggles for decolonization. Multiple historical sources were consulted as well as the COW Extra-Systemic War list (Small and Singer 1982), Tillema (1991), Clodfelter (1992), and various volumes of *Europa World Year Book*. Once again our coding of cases included countries in which political dissolution or unification took place and we followed a similar rule as noted in footnote 13.

[15] We also include this stalemate control variable in the statistical model to facilitate the testing of this interactive hypothesis (**PN1i**). Furthermore, we also employ a two-year and five-year lag for measuring prior stalemates.

create two parallel operational measures to capture the impact of nonviolent norms when a state possesses a military advantage. Both the lagged democracy and lagged violence terms are multiplied by a dummy variable that indicates that a state holds a military advantage over its territorial dispute adversary. A state is considered to possess such a military advantage if holds at least a 2 to 1 advantage in the short-term balance of forces (see Chapter 4 for operationalization of the short-term balance of forces variable).

Comparisons within political systems

To test **PN4** requires a measure that distinguishes between new and old democracies. We first create a simple dummy variable to indicate whether a country is currently democratic.[16] Once again, a state is considered democratic if its current net-democracy score (based on our supplemented *POLITY III* and *POLITY 98* data) is at least +6 on the −10 to +10 scale (see Chapter 4 for details). We next create a counter to track the number of years a country has been continuously democratic. For ease of interpretation, then, we create a series of dummy variables to indicate whether a state has become democratic within the past two years, past five years, or past ten years. As before, these three measures serve as alternative indicators of a "recent change" to democracy, and only one measure is employed in any given econometric model.

To test **PN5** it is necessary to create a relative measure of the degree to which an authoritarian regime is repressive and violent. We first create two parallel dummy variables to identify those regimes that can be considered authoritarian.[17] A country is considered to be authoritarian if its value for the twenty-year democracy lag and the twenty-year non-violence lag is less than or equal to fifteen. We then create two corresponding final measures to identify the most violent and repressive of these authoritarian regimes. For the first measure we begin by identifying the number of the past twenty years that a state has been very non-democratic; that is, in which its net-democracy score was −5 or less on the −10 to +10 scale. A state is then coded as possessing very strong repressive norms if it was very non-democratic for at least fifteen of the past twenty years. The second operational indicator is drawn from the government-sponsored violence measure used to test **PN1**. According to this second indicator, a

[16] We also include this current democracy dummy variable in the estimated model. The inclusion of this variable allows us to test the within democracies hypothesis (**PN4**).

[17] This authoritarian regime's dummy variable is included in the statistical model and the inclusion of this model allows us to test the within authoritarian regimes hypothesis (**PN5**),

state is considered to possess very violent norms if there was government-sponsored violence in at least ten of the past twenty years.[18]

Comparisons among dyads

To test **PN6i** we once again create two alternative measures to indicate whether or not a dyad can be considered democratic. The first measure utilizes the *POLITY*-based measure of lagged democracy described in the operationalization section for **PN1i**. According to this first measure, a dyad is democratic if both the challenger and target possessed net-democracy scores of +6 or higher (on the −10 to +10 scale) for at least sixteen of the past twenty years. Similarly, for the second measure, a dyad is democratic if both the challenger and target were free from government-sponsored violence for at least sixteen of the past twenty years (see the description for **PN1i** for more coding details).

To test **PN6ii** we create a dummy variable with a value of one if both challenger and target are currently democratic, and if both had first become democratic within the past two years (we also coded for five- and ten-year periods).[19] Once again, the data on net-democracy scores for each year is taken largely from the *POLITY III* and *POLITY 98* data sets. The threshold for democratic status is set at +6 on the −10 to +10 scale.

For **PN7** we utilized two alternative measures to indicate that both the challenger and target are among the most violent and repressive of all authoritarian regimes. These two indicators are simply the dyadic versions of the monadic measures described for **PN5**. According to the first measure, a dyad is considered highly repressive if both the challenger and target held net-democracy scores of −5 or less for at least fifteen of the past twenty years. For the second indicator, a pair of states is considered to possess highly violent norms if both the challenger and target experienced government-sponsored violence in ten or more of the past twenty years.

Finally, to test **PN8** we first identify all mixed dyads and then pin-point which of the states in the mixed dyad possesses the more violent political norms. Following convention, we create two alternative indicators. For the first operational measure, we first determine whether the dyad is mixed by examining the lagged net-democracy scores described earlier. The dyad is considered mixed if one state was democratic for at least sixteen or more of the past twenty years, while the other state was

---

[18] We also employ a fifteen-year threshold for government-sponsored violence as a robustness check.

[19] We also include in the statistical model a dummy variable for joint democratic status, which allows us to perform the proper test of **PN6ii**.

democratic for fifteen or fewer of those same twenty years.[20] To test **PN8**, then, we create a dummy variable to indicate which of the states in the mixed dyad is considered the non-democratic state. For the second operational measure of **PN8** we use the same general procedures described above to identify both mixed dyads, as well as the state in each dyad which possesses the more violent political norms. However, this time we use the twenty-year lagged measure of government violence. The threshold of sixteen of twenty years without government-sponsored violence is used to determine whether a state is considered democratic.

Conclusion

In this chapter we presented the logic and hypotheses of the Political Norms Model. Several differences can be identified between the hypotheses of the Political Norms Model and those of the International Politics and Political Accountability Models. First, the Norms Model argues that the duration and age of democratic institutions are important in shaping the decisions of incumbent political leaders. The Accountability Model, in contrast, centers on the existing balance of political power between competing parties within legislatures and the timing of elections. Furthermore, the Accountability Model attaches no theoretical significance to differences in the length of time democratic institutions have been in place in a given state; therefore divided government and recent elections should produce similar effects whether the state has been democratic for one year or twenty years.

Second, the Norms Model posits that leaders from very repressive political systems should be the most aggressive and intransigent adversaries in territorial disputes. The Accountability Model, however, argues that such leaders should have the political flexibility either to be aggressive, or to reverse policy by backing away from war or making major concessions in negotiations.

Third, in the International Politics and Political Accountability Models, state leaders are more likely to initiate and escalate the use of force when their state possesses a military advantage. For example, in terms of initiating force, democratic leaders may calculate that there are political payoffs to be gained by a challenge to the status quo that results in the diplomatic or military retreat of their weaker opponent. In contrast, the Norms Model holds that leaders with strong democratic norms are not more likely to engage in more aggressive military policies because of

---

[20] We also include this mixed dyad control variable in the statistical model so that we can compare the behavior of non-democracies and democracies in mixed dyads.

a military advantage. If democratic norms are well established, political leaders in challenger states should not shift to more coercive strategies in an attempt to overturn the status quo, but should instead continue to rely on negotiations.

Finally, the Norms Model hypothesizes that differences in diplomatic and military behavior should be more evident among democratic and non-democratic challenger states as opposed to among democratic and non-democratic targets. Neither the International Politics nor Political Accountability Models produces similar claims.

These types of differences in predicted relationships across the models will enable us to utilize the results of the empirical tests in Chapters 7 through 9 to assess the relative explanatory power of each model.

6   Domestic institutions and the Political Affinity Model

In this chapter we present the Political Affinity Model, our final theoretical approach for understanding how domestic political institutions can influence the foreign policy choices of state leaders. The theoretical insight offered by this model is that international bargaining over disputed territory should be examined within the broader context of the bilateral political relationship between challenger and target. Instead of elite norms or levels of political accountability playing a central explanatory role, in this model leader perceptions of shared political ties are of primary theoretical importance.

Political Affinity Model

The theoretical analysis centers on how domestic institutions shape decision-makers' assessments of whether other state leaders have common or divergent interests on fundamental issues of domestic and international security. Figure 6.1 presents the principal causal links in the model. The logical foundation is that common political institutions and ideologies between states produce shared political interests among those states' incumbent elites regarding whether preservation or change in the political status quo is desirable. Our argument is that leaders whose states share common political institutions and ideologies are less likely to adopt foreign policies that put each other's international and domestic security at risk. As a result, politically similar states should view each other as potential allies, while dissimilar states are likely to perceive one another as potential security threats. Incumbent leaders thus have stronger incentives to adopt more cooperative foreign policies towards political allies. As a result, the choices between negotiations and military force should vary in systematic ways depending on whether the other party in a territorial dispute is believed to be a potential political ally. That is, territorial disputes between politically similar states should be characterized by less military conflict and by more accommodative diplomacy and negotiations.

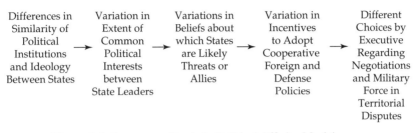

Figure 6.1 Summary of logic in Political Affinity Model

Premises of the model

Three premises provide the foundation for a number of hypotheses.

Premise 1: Foreign policy as a means of retaining political office

A primary goal of incumbents is to remain in office. Political leaders will therefore turn to foreign policy in an attempt to secure their hold on power against both internal political opposition as well as external threats.

Since retention in office is a central objective of incumbents, leaders are likely to view foreign policy as a potentially valuable means of securing their domestic political position. A similar assumption is part of the foundation for the Political Accountability Model, which considers how domestic opposition responds to different outcomes in foreign policy. In this model, however, we focus on different theoretical implications.

The first implication of Premise 1 is that state leaders may seek foreign support to bolster their domestic political standing and survival. That is, they may form alliances for purposes of domestic, as opposed to external, security (see Barnett 1992; Barnett and Levy 1991; David 1991; Levy and Barnett 1992). As we argue in the International Politics Model, however, external support most likely will require some form of political exchange in which one state adjusts its foreign policy in return for another state's support in preserving the domestic political status quo.[1] It follows that the value of allies abroad may be linked to whether they are expected to offer assistance in times of domestic political instability.

The second implication of this first premise is that the need for external allies should depend upon the degree to which a leader is threatened with losing office. A leader's demand for political allies will vary significantly

---

[1] A basic difference between this and the International Politics Model is that the International Politics Model views allies as potentially critical in bolstering solely the external security of states. It does not consider the ability of allies to enhance internal political security.

depending upon the stability and security of his hold on power. On the supply side, political allies should be most inclined to offer support when the threat confronting another state is not simply the loss of power for a particular foreign leader, but the actual collapse of the political order and its replacement with a different regime.

Premise 2: Group membership as a source of political identity formation

In politics, as in social life more generally, in-groups and out-groups are a central feature of political identity formation.

A fundamental aspect of identity formation in social life is whether individuals are considered to be members of, or outside of, a salient group. A variety of literatures in social psychology and political science (e.g. Brewer and Miller 1996; Cronin 1999; Gellner 1983; Hermann and Kegley 1995; Hobsbawm 1990; Horowitz 1985; Huntington 1996; Reus-Smit 1999; Ross 1986; Tajfel 1978, 1982; Tajfel and Turner 1979; Wendt 1999: chs. 5–6) converge on the conclusion that group social and political identities are defined simultaneously by the similarities among individuals, as well as the perceived differences compared to those outside the group. A fundamental tendency among groups is to draw distinctions and to categorize themselves into in-groups and out-groups. These literatures also conclude that the similarity of certain traits or characteristics can be an important source of group identity.

An implication of Premise 2 is that incumbent political leaders may form cross-national group identities based upon shared positions of leadership in similar political systems. Why should political elites draw upon common political institutions and ideologies when determining in-group and out-group membership? For one, certain political institutions and ideologies can be viewed as traits that are distinctive and identifiable across countries. For example, the differences between liberal democracies and traditional monarchies or one-party communist systems are quite clear and are well understood among political elites in different countries. Second, positions of political leadership and elite status are valued highly by most incumbents, and they risk a loss of political influence and standing if political institutions change in fundamental ways. Thus, political elite status at a given point in time is often linked to the preservation of the existing political order.[2] Whether political elites in different states are each trying to preserve the same type of regime at home is

---

[2] Of course, there are cases in which elites in the old political order are able to remain in positions of political influence and power despite fundamental changes in political institutions (e.g. consider Boris Yelstin and the fall of communist rule in the Soviet Union).

likely to be viewed as an important benchmark for assessing convergence or divergence in political interests.

Premise 3: Political conflict is greater between groups than within groups

Political relations among members of an in-group should be characterized by greater cooperation due to a heightened perception of common interests. Relations between different in-groups and out-groups, in contrast, should be more competitive and conflictual.

The logic underlying this assumption draws upon research in both political science and social psychology. First, while common interests are not a guarantee of success in resolving a bargaining problem or achieving cooperation (e.g. Fearon 1995, 1998b; Keohane 1984; Martin 1993; Milner 1997; Morrow 1994b; Stein 1990), the prospects for resolving disputes and securing stable agreements are improved if the divergence of interests between actors is more limited. Second, individuals should be more willing to make concessions within an in-group due to reduced concerns about reputational effects or relative gains. That is, individuals should be less concerned about the larger strategic implications of accommodation. Within in-groups, concessions generally are not offered under pressure, therefore the party making the concessions need not be concerned about sending a signal to potential adversaries that it can be coerced into backing down in a conflict.[3] Furthermore, we would expect the parties to be less concerned about compliance with agreements, or that the gains made by one side would be turned against the party making the concessions in the future (Cronin 1999; Downs and Rocke 1990; Downs, Rocke, and Barsoom, 1996; Fearon 1998b; Glaser 1994/95; Grieco 1988; Morrow 1999; Morrow, Siverson, and Tabares 1998, 1999; Powell 1991, 1994; Wendt 1999). Third, members of an in-group are more likely to empathize with each other and to acknowledge the legitimacy of competing claims and conflicting interests. Such empathy should increase their willingness to rely on negotiations instead of coercion to resolve disputes (e.g. Brewer and Miller 1996; Cronin 1999; Hewstone 1990; Keohane 1984; Martin 1993; Reus-Smit 1999; Stein 1990; Tajfel 1982; Tajfel, Billig, Bundy, and Flament 1971; Turner, Brown, and Tajfel 1979). Finally, members of an in-group are likely to engage in repeated interactions over time and therefore to view bargaining outcomes in the context of payoffs that can be achieved over a longer

---

[3] State leaders seem to worry a good deal about the reputational inferences other states draw about them even though it is not clear, theoretically or empirically, that other states do draw such strong inferences (see Huth 1997).

period of time (e.g. Axelrod 1984; Fearon 1998b; Keohane 1984; Lohmann 1997). This may help to maintain a continuing relationship by facilitating reciprocity in the exchange of concessions.

The first implication of Premise 3 is that members of an in-group are generally viewed as more reliable supporters and allies in situations of political conflict. Scholars have reported several findings that are consistent with this claim. For example, students of comparative politics have found that breakdowns of democracy are more likely to occur in states with fewer democratic neighbors, while successful, long-term transitions to democracy tend to occur in states with higher numbers of democratic neighbors (Gasiorowski 1995; Przeworski, Alvarez, Cheibub, and Limongi 1996; also see Huntington 1991; Lutz 1989; Starr 1991). Another study reports that in civil wars during the Cold War, Soviet or communist support for one side increased the chances of US intervention in support of the opposing side (Yoon 1997).

Recent empirical findings reported by international relations scholars are also of interest. Several studies find that politically similar states are more likely to intervene in support of each other in international crises, militarized disputes, and wars (Cronin 1999; Huth 1998; Kaw 1990; Kegley and Hermann 1997; Mousseau and Shi 1997; Raknerud and Hegre 1997; Werner and Lemke 1997).[4] A related finding is that politically dissimilar states are more likely to pursue hostile policies towards one another. For example, politically dissimilar states are more likely to become adversaries in military confrontations, and victorious states in wars are more likely to overthrow the regime of a defeated adversary if the defeated state is politically dissimilar (Werner 1996, 1999; also see Bueno de Mesquita and Siverson 1997; Leeds 1999; Mousseau 1998).

A second implication is that although a common group identity does not eliminate political competition and rivalry within the group, conflict with out-groups should reduce within-group competition. This implication is supported by the well-established finding within social psychology that the cohesion of a group increases when it is in conflict with outgroups (e.g. Coser 1956; Hogg 1992; Hogg and Abrams 1988; Sherif 1966; Simmel 1955; see Mercer [1995] for a careful review). It is bolstered further by findings about the generally strong (but short-term) "rally-round-the-flag" effect for US presidents in times of international crisis and war (e.g. Brace and Hinckley 1992; Brody 1991; Larson 1996; Mueller 1994; Russett 1990: ch. 2).

---

[4] There is a related debate among scholars whether military alliance ties are more likely between politically similar states (e.g. Emmons and Siverson 1991; Lai and Reiter 2000; Leeds 1999; Simon and Gartzke 1996).

Hypotheses

The first two hypotheses draw largely on Premise 3 for their supporting logic.

PAF1i: If countries share common political institutions and ideology, state leaders are:

a. less likely to resort to military threats and the use of force in an attempt to challenge the status quo as opposed to either seeking negotiations or accepting the status quo,

b. more likely to make concessions in negotiations, and

c. less likely to escalate military confrontations to higher levels.

The underlying logic of **PAF1i** is that leaders from politically similar states should generally have greater expected utility for cooperative (as opposed to conflictual) policies than should leaders from dissimilar states. One reason (derived from the first implication of Premise 3) is that high levels of diplomatic and military conflict put at risk the future support of a politically similar state. Since politically similar states are more reliable allies in times of domestic and international crisis, leaders have an incentive to moderate diplomatic and military conflict and to seek the resolution of territorial disputes. The risk is that continued conflict, particularly at high levels, will undermine the willingness of an ally to come to one's aid when needed in the future. As a result, larger concerns about damaging the reliability of allies should mitigate conflict. In contrast, for leaders from politically dissimilar states, the opportunity costs of pursuing more aggressive and conflictual policies should be weaker, since the adversary is not expected to be a potential ally due to the absence of common political ties and affinity. Furthermore, the use of coercive military pressure to prevail in a territorial dispute with a politically similar state could prove counterproductive in the longer term, since a military defeat for a political ally could increase the risk of one's own regime being overthrown (Bueno de Mesquita and Siverson 1995; Bueno de Mesquita, Siverson, and Woller 1992). Thus, a victory in the territorial dispute would come at the price of destabilizing a potential political ally.[5] Once again, these indirect costs associated with more aggressive policies should not exist for leaders from dissimilar states.

Finally, as suggested by Premise 3, concessions in negotiations should be more likely between politically similar states. Perhaps the most

---

[5] In addition, it might be the case that by creating political instability within their ally, political leaders increase the risk of challenges to their own tenure in power by encouraging opposition elites within their country to mobilize and seek political changes as well. This demonstration or diffusion effect might be particularly strong for contiguous states that are politically similar.

persuasive argument centers on reduced concerns about relative gains. That is, conceding territory to a state perceived to be a political ally should mitigate concerns that any economic or military gains associated with controlling the territory will be translated into future security threats.

The next hypothesis focuses on comparisons among politically similar states.

PAF1ii: Compared to countries that have been politically similar for a long period of time, countries which only recently have come to share common political institutions and ideology are more likely to experience conflictual relations. As a result, leaders of recently similar states are more likely:

a. to resort to military threats and the use of force in an attempt to challenge the status quo as opposed to either seeking negotiations or accepting the status quo,

b. to avoid making concessions in negotiations, and

c. to escalate military confrontations to higher levels.

The logic of this second hypothesis is that the strength of in-group identities is related to how long the members have been part of the same group. The intuition is that perceptions of shared interests and values solidify with time. Therefore, long-standing in-group members are likely to have more doubts and less confidence in new group members. As a result, more conflictual relations are to be expected since new group members are less likely to be viewed as reliable allies or committed to group values. This greater degree of mistrust or doubt then mitigates many of the features of in-group membership (see Premise 3), such as the promotion of less competitive approaches to bargaining and the de-legitimization of coercive strategies for resolving disputes.[6]

The next pair of related hypotheses focus on relations among politically similar states and draws on the second implication of Premise 1.

PAF2i: In territorial disputes among states that share common political institutions and ideology, international conflict is least likely when leaders face either internal or external threats to their political security. As a

---

[6] Another related hypothesis that focuses on political change is that regime transitions within states can be a cause of either more or less international conflict over disputed territory. When political change produces convergence between countries, less conflict is expected, and vice versa. We are not able to test this hypothesis here but it does have interesting implications for existing arguments on the relationship between democratization, revolutions, and war (e.g. Conge 1996; Enterline 1996, 1998; Gleditsch and Ward 2000; Mansfield and Snyder 1995; Snyder 2000; Thompson and Tucker 1997; Walt 1996; Ward and Gleditsch 1998). For example, a challenger's transition to democracy should heighten levels of conflict over disputed territory if both challenger and target were previously military juntas. Conversely, if the target is a democracy and the challenger shifts from a conservative monarchy to a democracy, then we would expect conflict to decrease after this transition.

result, politically threatened leaders in territorial disputes with similar adversaries are:

a. less likely to initiate military conflict compared to accepting the status quo or challenging the status quo by seeking negotiations,
b. more likely to make concessions in negotiations, and
c. less likely to resort to higher levels of escalation in military confrontations.

PAF2ii: State leaders whose politically similar territorial dispute adversary is facing an internal or external threat are:

a. less likely to initiate military conflict compared to accepting the status quo or challenging the status quo by seeking negotiations,
b. more likely to make concessions in negotiations, and
c. less likely to resort to higher levels of escalation in military confrontations.

As noted in the discussion of Premise 2, political conflict among members of an in-group is sometimes possible. For example, a potential countervailing consequence of political affinity could be competition and rivalry for a position of leadership within the group (e.g. the Sino-Soviet split in the 1960s). Conflict is most likely when the leaders of political allies are politically secure at home or do not face political threats from abroad. In a situation of political security, the demand or need for political allies should be weaker, and therefore concerns over ally reliability should carry less weight in foreign policy choices. Conversely, when incumbents face strong internal opposition or are involved in military conflicts with politically dissimilar states, then the demand for external support is greater (the second implication of Premise 1). Threatened leaders now have incentives to curry the favor of political allies. Leaders should also be hesitant to further destabilize leaders of potential allies, whose downfall may threaten the legitimacy of one's own regime. Furthermore, this potential ally may be needed to help bolster one's own domestic standing in times of future crisis or instability.

The final hypotheses consider the incentives of politically threatened leaders to be accommodative in the context of relations between dissimilar states.

PAF3i: In territorial disputes among states with dissimilar political institutions and ideologies, the incentives of threatened leaders to be accommodative are more contingent. Threatened leaders will be more conciliatory only when they face an outside threat from a state that shares common political ties with its territorial dispute adversary. In this situation leaders are:

a. less likely to initiate military conflict compared to accepting the status quo or challenging the status quo by seeking negotiations,

b. more likely to make concessions in negotiations, and
c. less likely to resort to higher levels of escalation in military confrontations.

PAF3ii: The logic of **PAF3i** also should apply to states engaged in a territorial dispute with an adversary that is threatened. In this scenario, if a state is politically similar to the country posing an external threat to its territorial dispute adversary, its leaders should now behave in a more confrontational manner in the territorial dispute. In particular, they should be:

a. more likely to initiate military conflict as opposed to seeking negotiations or accepting the territorial status quo,
b. less likely to make concessions in negotiations, and
c. more likely to resort to higher levels of escalation in military confrontations.

The argument for **PAF3i** is that threats to their political security drive leaders to adopt a defensive posture and to avoid a two-front conflict. The threatened party views the dissimilar state with suspicion to begin with (Premise 3) and therefore should be concerned that this dissimilar state will support or form a coalition with other states that could pose an additional security threat. However, this danger is closely linked to whether the territorial dispute adversary's political identity is similar to that of the threatening government. In the absence of such common political identities the danger of a larger coalition forming is not that likely. In contrast, if such common political ties do exist, the risk that a dangerous coalition will form is more credible. In this case leaders of a threatened state should be interested in securing the territorial dispute adversary's non-involvement in their existing conflict with another state. The price to be paid for such neutrality would be diplomatic accommodation and the avoidance of military conflict. As a result, the short-term security threats facing the threatened leadership induce it to adopt policies that it would generally oppose. When the threat of the dissimilar state forming a coalition with current threats is weak, however, there is no compelling incentive for the politically threatened leadership to appease the dissimilar state by adjusting its diplomatic or military policies in the territorial dispute.

For **PAF3ii** the logic is similar, yet works in a slightly different manner. Once again, states generally have incentives to limit their involvement in outside conflicts. However, if a state has a political ally who is currently threatening its territorial dispute adversary, the state now has an added incentive to behave more confrontationally in the territorial dispute. Since the outside party in this case is a political ally, it is a likely coalition partner in any initiative against the territorial dispute adversary. Therefore, a state

Table 6.1 *Summary of hypotheses to be tested from the Political Affinity Model*

Hypotheses regarding	Predicted relationships in equations to be tested			
	Status quo stage		Negotiations stage	Escalation stage
	Force	Talks		
Similar vs. dissimilar dyads (**PAF1i**)	−	+	+	−
Recent change to political similarity (**PAF1ii**)	+	−	−	+
Relations between similar states when a threat exists (**PAF2i**)	−	+	+	−
Relations between similar states when a threat to adversary exists (**PAF2ii**)	−	+	+	−
	−			
Relations between dissimilar states when a threat exists (**PAF3i**)	−	NA	+	−
Relations between dissimilar states when a threat to adversary exists (**PAF3ii**)	+	+	−	+

Note: A positive sign (+) indicates that in the statistical tests the estimated coefficient should have a value greater than zero; a negative sign (−) indicates that in the statistical tests the estimated coefficient should have a value less than zero.

in this new-found position of greater external support is more likely to threaten military force and to escalate to higher levels against its territorial dispute adversary since it is more confident of outside military support. In addition, state leaders should be less likely to make concessions in negotiations since the alternative policy option of using military force to break a stalemate in negotiations should be viewed as more attractive.

Measurement of variables

Once again, we develop a variety of operational measures to test the four hypotheses from the Political Affinity Model (see Table 6.1).

Similar and dissimilar political regimes

To test **PAF1i** we take a number of steps to determine whether the political regimes of the challenger and target can be classified as similar. Our final operational measure is a dummy variable equal to one if the two countries share the same regime type. We first classify all challenger and target states into different categories of regime type. Adapting the work of other scholars (e.g. Bratton and van de Walle 1997:77–78; Bueno de

Mesquita and Siverson 1997:183; Linz and Stepan 1996; Przeworski, Alvarez, Cheibub, and Limongi 2000), we identify the following types of political regimes:

1. Liberal democracies
2. Hereditary non-democratic monarchies
3. Collective rule by military junta
4. Single-party dominant fascist states
5. Single-party dominant communist states

In devising this list of regime types our goal is not to develop an inclusive typology of regimes so that all challengers and targets may be placed into one of the categories. Instead, we want to identify those regime types that have a coherent and distinct set of institutions and ideologies that are both general enough to be shared across countries yet distinctive enough to form a basis for common political interests. For example, we leave out what might be termed personalistic civilian dictatorships. Comparative scholars argue (e.g. Linz and Stepan 1996) that idiosyncratic traits are central features of such regimes and that these regimes often lack a clear political ideology (beyond the "cult of the leader") or set of political institutions.

With this list of regime types we then turn to the *POLITY III* data set to first identify all democratic states, utilizing the net-democracy score procedures we describe in Chapter 4. To classify the non-democratic states we then turn to the Banks *Cross-Polity* and *POLITY II* data sets to identify monarchies and military juntas. However, these two data sets do not readily separate and identify fascist and communist regimes, but instead produce a more general category of civilian authoritarian regimes. To identify fascist and communist regimes we conduct more detailed research with historical and country-specific sources, as well as general sources on regime change (e.g. *Africa Contemporary Record*; Gasiorowski 1995; Jelavich 1983; Seton-Watson 1962; Vanhanen 1979: Appendix B). Once we identify the regime type of both challenger and target, we construct the final operational variable for regime similarity.

Recent transitions to political similarity

To test **PAF1ii** we first identify all cases in which the challenger and target share common political institutions and ideology (based upon the coding rules for **PAF1i**). We then look to see how long the two countries have shared such political affinity. Finally, we create a dummy variable to indicate that the two states have only recently become politically similar; that is, they have shared common political ties for five or fewer years.[7]

---

[7] We also measure a recent change to similarity using both a two-year and a ten-year lag to check for the robustness of results.

Political insecurity and politically similar states

To operationalize **PAF2i** and **PAF2ii** we create an interactive dummy variable that indicates whether the challenger and target are similar, and whether either state faces a political threat. The political similarity of the challenger and target is determined by the coding procedures for **PAF1i**. A political threat exists if either a particular country (for **PAF2i**) or its opponent (for **PAF2ii**) faces an internal or external threat to its domestic political security.[8]

An internal threat exists when a state undergoes a period of domestic political unrest that threatens the incumbent leadership and the current regime. Domestic unrest events that threaten the leadership and the regime are defined as any one of the following: (a) an attempted coup or military revolt within the past year, (b) a successful coup within the past year, (c) political rebellion within the past year, or (d) ongoing civil war. Multiple sources were consulted for information on these types of political events (e.g. *Cross-Polity Data Set*; Dupuy and Dupuy 1993; Gasiorowski 1995; Thompson 1973; Vanhanen 1979).

An external threat is coded as present if a state is engaged in a separate territorial dispute with a politically dissimilar adversary that is both: (a) more powerful militarily, and (b) had been involved in prior militarized conflict over disputed territory within the past five years. A state is considered to possess a military advantage if it holds a majority (0.5 or greater) in the short-term balance of capabilities measure described in Chapter 3. We use the data set of territorial disputes listed in Appendices B–F to identify all adversaries who used force in a territorial dispute within the past five years. Once again, we rely on the coding procedures for **PAF1i** to determine if two adversaries are politically dissimilar.

Political insecurity and politically dissimilar states

The measures to test the final hypotheses, **PAF3i** and **PAF3ii**, are created through the use of several interactive dummy variables. The dummy variables for dissimilarity and the presence of an external threat are taken directly from the coding rules for **PA1i** and **PAF2i–ii**.[9] The only addition

---

[8] We include in the statistical model dummy variables to indicate whether the challenger and target are facing political threats. The inclusion of these control variables allows us to examine the impact of similarity when either state is threatened. For the Status Quo Stage we include variables for both internal and external threats, since we use internal threats to test **PAF2i** and **PAF2ii** and external threats to test **PAF3i** and **PAF3ii** in the Challenge the Status Quo Stage.

[9] For hypotheses **PA2i** and **PA2ii** we consider both internal and external threats. But for **PA3i** and **PA3ii** we only consider external threats due to the difficulty in ascertaining whether domestic groups share a common political ideology with the state's territorial dispute adversary.

is that we use the classification of regimes described earlier to determine whether the state posing the outside threat is similar to the territorial disputant (for **PAF3i**) or its dispute adversary (for **PAF3ii**).

Conclusion

The hypotheses of the Political Affinity Model are inherently dyadic in nature since political similarity or dissimilarity between states is the focus of theoretical analysis. One of the advantages of this model is its potential to explain variation in conflict within both democratic *and* non-democratic dyads. Much of the existing democratic peace literature focuses largely on behavior within democratic dyads. This model does not aggregate all non-democratic dyads into a single category, but instead recognizes several different types of non-democratic regimes. We attempt to draw out the theoretical implications of this variation in non-democratic regimes to understand political and military relations between non-democratic states. Another advantage of this model is that while it expects mixed dyads composed of politically dissimilar states to be generally more conflictual, it also attempts to identify when dissimilar states would have incentives to avoid diplomatic and military conflict.

One important difference between the Political Affinity Model and the International Politics Model is that political institutions abroad are critical in shaping incumbent leaders' assessments of external threats and likely allies. In the International Politics Model, political differences or similarities between states are not viewed as primary causes of alliance formation or threat perception.[10] The Affinity Model also differs from the Political Norms and Political Accountability Models in that it does not logically predict that democratic states should generally be less aggressive in mixed dyads. Thus, while the Norms Model posits that we should find a strong monadic effect for democracies in the empirical results, the Affinity Model clearly predicts only a dyadic effect for democracies.

At this point, three different models of domestic political institutions and foreign policy choices have been presented in tandem with a realist-type model of international politics. Most of the hypotheses derived

---

[10] In this respect the Political Affinity Model converges with arguments by constructivist scholars (e.g. Adler and Barnett 1998; Cronin 1999; Kivimaki 2001; Reus-Smit 1999; Wendt 1999) that shared identities across states can have far-reaching implications for achieving cooperative agreements, resolving conflicts, and avoiding military conflict. One difference, however, is that constructivists generally (Reus-Smit [1999] is clearly an exception, as is Cronin [1999] to a lesser extent) place greater emphasis on state interactions over time and the social learning resulting from such interactions as a source of identity formation. The Political Affinity Model, however, anchors identity formation in domestic political institutions.

from these three models are quite different from each other, and in all cases the operational measures for even similar hypotheses are notably different. As a result, the results produced by statistical tests of the various models should provide very useful information for evaluating the relative explanatory power of the hypotheses and their supporting logic.

7 Empirical results for decisions to challenge the status quo

In this and the next two chapters we assess the explanatory power of the international and domestic politics hypotheses we derived in the previous four chapters. In particular, we evaluate the relative ability of each of our four models – the International Politics Model, the Political Accountability Model, the Political Norms Model, and the Political Affinity Model – to explain the actions of state leaders in each of the three stages of territorial disputes laid out in Chapter 2. Once again, the three decisions we want to understand are: (1) the decision of challenger states regarding whether and how to challenge the territorial status quo, (2) the decisions of both challengers and targets to offer concessions during rounds of talks over disputed territory, and (3) the decisions of challengers and targets to escalate initial military confrontation by mobilizing or employing higher levels of force. In Chapter 7 we examine the decisions of challengers in the Challenge the Status Quo Stage, and then in Chapters 8 and 9 we examine the decisions of both states in the Negotiations and Escalation Stages, respectively. We test our slate of hypotheses through a series of quantitative tests using our data set on 348 territorial disputes that span the period 1919–1995 (as described in Chapter 2 and in Appendices B–E).

While we employ a different statistical model for the Status Quo Stage as opposed to the Negotiations and Military Escalation Stages, there are a few model estimation features common to all of our statistical tests. In each chapter we present the results of the statistical analysis sequentially, beginning with tests of the International Politics Model. As noted in Chapter 3, we treat this model as a starting point for theoretical analysis. After our initial presentation of results for the International Politics Model, we then consider each of the domestic-level models – the Political Accountability Model, the Political Norms Model, and the Political Affinity Model – as alternative approaches for explaining foreign policy choices. For each test of the domestic politics models we also include the set of variables from the International Politics Model. This consistent approach to model specification facilitates our assessment of empirical results across each of the domestic models and allows us to compare the relative explanatory power of the domestic and international politics models.

Furthermore, we estimate three separate equations to test the Political Accountability and Political Norms Models due to the number of hypotheses that comprise these two general models. Specifically, we estimate an "across regimes" equation, a "within regimes" equation, and a "dyadic" equation. Dividing the estimation in this manner is the most effective way to test such a wide range of arguments, and also makes the most sense conceptually. Another feature of model estimation is that we estimate all models using Huber or "robust" standard errors due to concerns with possible contemporaneous correlation and non-constant variances across the units of observation.[1] The primary trade-off of this decision is a slight loss of efficiency in our standard error estimates. Finally, we also run numerous auxiliary regressions to check for the presence of multicollinearity. In most cases the level of multicollinearity is relatively low (auxiliary r^2 <0.4) and there is little reason for concern. However, in the few instances in which multicollinearity is high, we discuss the nature of the multicollinearity and allay fears that such multicollinearity affects the validity of our results.

Moving to the presentation of results, we present our estimated results in a consistent fashion across all statistical models in all chapters. Most importantly, due to the non-linear nature of our models we always include a series of predicted probability results to provide a more substantive interpretation of variable effects. We estimate the impact of discrete changes in particular variables on the predicted probability of certain outcomes by holding all other variables constant. While the coefficient results for each econometric model typically provide a basic sense of the estimated direction and significance of hypothesized relationships, these predicted probability results are often more substantively meaningful. We then conclude each chapter with a summary discussion of the overall performance of each theoretical model and the implications for the literature on the democratic peace.

Estimation of the Challenge the Status Quo Stage

Before presenting the results of statistical tests for the Challenge the Status Quo Stage, it is useful to describe a few features of the data and

---

[1] Because the observations in our data set (particularly rounds of talks and militarized disputes) span different numbers of months, we are especially sensitive to concerns with heteroskedasticity.

the statistical models used to generate these results. As we discussed in Chapter 2, three choices are available to the leaders of states in the Challenge the Status Quo Stage (see Figure 2.2):

a. Refrain from initiatives and maintain the prevailing status quo.
b. Propose talks and rely on negotiations to secure changes in the status quo.
c. Resort to threats of military force in support of territorial claims.

Since these three choices are not ordered in any definitive way, we use a model that treats outcomes as nominal instead of ordered.[2] At first glance there may be a temptation to treat the three options of "doing nothing," "engaging in negotiations," and "threatening force" as ordered. One thought is that pursuing talks might constitute a middle-of-the-road or less costly way in which to advance a territorial claim short of threatening force. However, a strong case could also be made that engaging in talks is perhaps the least conflictual option, since doing nothing implies maintaining one's territorial claim whereas holding talks might signify an attempt to resolve the territorial issue cooperatively.[3] Nevertheless, if the "true" dependent variable is indeed ordered in some way, then a model for nominal dependent variables is simply inefficient compared to a model for ordered dependent variables. Yet this slight loss in efficiency is less pernicious than the effects of treating a variable that is truly nominal as if it were ordered, in which case the results might be severely biased (see Long 1997).[4] Furthermore, unlike models for ordered outcomes, models for nominal outcomes allow us to make pair-wise comparisons of any two choices, which is quite useful given the logic of many of our hypotheses.

As a result, we estimate a series of multinomial logit models to explain the decisions of leaders in the Challenge the Status Quo Stage.[5]

[2] Models for nominal outcomes are fairly rare in political science, but have become somewhat more popular recently. The relative scarcity of such models is likely due to data limitations, perceived difficulties in presenting the results of such models, as well as computational difficulties and software limitations. Nevertheless, the most popular and most statistically feasible of these models is the multinomial logit model, which is the model we employ in this chapter.

[3] In the first ordering a call for negotiations is construed as a form of challenge, whereas in the second ordering a call for negotiations is seen as a move towards accommodation or attempted resolution of the dispute.

[4] According to Long, "...when a method for ordinal variables is applied to a nominal dependent variable, the resulting estimates are biased or even nonsensical. If there is any question about the ordinality of the dependent variable, the potential loss of efficiency in using models for nominal outcomes is outweighed by avoiding potential bias" (1997: 149).

[5] Within the field of political science multinomial logit has been used to study voting in US elections (Whitten and Palmer 1996), voting in foreign elections (Domínguez and McCann 1996; Powers and Cox 1997), candidate strategies (Sellers 1998), and value orientations (Clarke et al. 1999). Within the subfield of international relations, Bennett and Nordstrom (2000) have used multinomial logit to study foreign policy substitutability.

Multinomial logit has the advantage of being the most straightforward and computationally feasible model for the estimation of equations in which the dependent variables have more than two outcomes that are not clearly ordered (Amemiya 1985; Greene 1997; Long 1997; Maddala 1983). We also consider a number of alternative models, yet none of these alternatives provides a better fit for our purposes than multinomial logit.[6] The primary drawback of multinomial logit is the fairly restrictive independence of irrelevant alternatives (IIA) assumption. The IIA assumption is met when an individual's preferences among alternatives remain consistent regardless of which choices are or are not available (McFadden 1978, 1981).[7] IIA is most likely to be a problem when any two outcome choices are clear substitutes. If the IIA assumption does not hold, then parameter estimates will be inconsistent. We employ the two best-known tests for the IIA assumption, the Hausman test (Hausman and McFadden 1984) and the Small–Hsiao test (Small and Hsiao 1985), and find no evidence to reject IIA in *any* of our models.[8] As has been

---

[6] We also considered the use of a multinomial probit model. Multinomial probit is more flexible than multinomial logit: it does not assume independence among alternative choices and allows for correlations across the disturbances of the choices. It does, however, require at least one parameter to be set to zero for identification purposes, which was conceptually difficult in our situation. Nevertheless, we attempted to estimate a series of multinomial probit models for the Challenge the Status Quo Game. In several cases we were unable to achieve convergence. When the models did converge, the results from the multinomial probit models were quite similar to those from the multinomial logit models. Yet in the end we chose mulitinomial logit, given the difficulties in estimating multinomial probit and since we have no reason to believe we have not met the assumptions for using multinomial logit.

[7] The classic example used to illustrate IIA is the red bus/blue bus example. Imagine an individual can choose between driving a car or taking a red bus to work. Assume the probability of each option is 0.5, thus the ratio between driving a car and choosing the red bus is 1:1. If a new bus company begins service, then the probability of driving a car to work might stay the same (0.5), but the probability of choosing the red bus might drop to 0.25 if half of the red bus riders switch to the blue bus. Now the ratio of those driving cars to those riding the red bus has risen to 2:1. Thus IIA has been violated. Within political science, for example, one is forced to assume that the probability of voting for Bill Clinton vs. George Bush in 1992 did not change with Ross Perot's addition to the race. Similarly, under the IIA assumption, the likelihood of voting for Al Gore vs. George W. Bush in 2000 would not be affected by Ralph Nader's entry into the race.

[8] The Hausman test, which is the most popular and best-known test, compares the multinomial logit estimator with an estimator that is considered to be consistent (Hausman and McFadden 1984). The somewhat lesser-known test, the Small–Hsiao test, amounts to a modified version of the standard likelihood ratio test (Small and Hsiao 1985). Both tests compare an unrestricted model containing all choices with a restricted model in which one choice is eliminated. In all cases we perform the tests after first eliminating the option of negotiations, and then eliminating the option of military force. The removal of either of the two forms of challenge is the most logical scenario in which IIA might be violated, since one might argue plausibly that these two choices could be seen as substitutes. At times we also witness a negative chi-square statistic for the Hausman test. Hausman and McFadden claim this should be interpreted as evidence that IIA has *not* been violated (Hausman and McFadden 1984: 1226).

noted by others, in the simple case with only three dependent variable choices, the multinomial logit model is essentially equivalent to estimating three separate binary logit models that compare *a* to *b*, then *a* to *c*, and ultimately *b* to *c* (Alvarez and Nagler 1998; Hausman and McFadden 1984). Yet the single multinomial logit model is more efficient than the three binary logit models.

As discussed in Chapter 1, our data set is not based upon dyad-year observations. Instead, each round of talks and each militarized dispute is included as an observation in our operational data set. We also include a series of non-challenge observations; that is, time periods or "episodes" in which a challenger state does not issue a formal challenge to dispute territory. Thus the data set used in the Challenge the Status Quo Stage consists of three types of cases: diplomatic initiatives to hold talks, militarized disputes, and periods of inactivity. For operational purposes, information on independent variables for the Challenge the Status Quo Stage is drawn from the beginning of each "play" of the Challenge the Status Quo Stage, or more precisely, from the month in which the challenger initiates a militarized confrontation or proposes that a round of talks begins.

Cases in which the challenger does not call for negotiations or initiate the use of force but rather accepts the status quo are more difficult to conceptualize and operationalize. We utilize a "twelve-month rule" to identify and create observations of "no challenge" to the territorial status quo. According to this selection rule, once twelve months have elapsed since a challenger state has threatened force or called for talks, it is considered not to have challenged the territorial status quo during that period of time. That period is then included in the data set as a case in which no challenge was made.[9] Each successive twelve months of activity is treated in the same way until the state once again calls for a new round of talks or threatens force. We also considered and employed a number of additional specifications for the decision to "do nothing."[10] We found the results for

---

[9] In this situation, we take the data at that moment in time (i.e. that month) and use this information to create the observation of "no challenge" in the Challenge the Status Quo data set.

[10] One option is to use a modified version of the twelve-month rule. In this case, periods of inactivity that are temporally distant from rounds of talks or militarized disputes are less relevant than periods of inactivity directly following or directly preceding observable activities. The logic is that states are more likely to actually consider the issue and to consciously decide to do nothing in periods when the territorial issue is salient as opposed to dormant. So the twelve-month rule is utilized for up to five years after some action and three or fewer years before some observable action. A final strategy is to randomly sample periods of inactivity from the months in which no action was taken. We included various numbers of random observations of inactivity as a control for "no action" and found only minor differences based upon the number of random observations included.

the Challenge the Status Quo Stage to be very stable regardless of the coding rule we employed for including observations of no challenge to the status quo.

Finally, the temporal structure of the data also raises some concerns about serial correlation. We draw on Beck, Katz, and Tucker (1998) and include a variable to count the number of months since the challenger last undertook some activity, whether it was a call for talks or threat of force (see also Beck 1998). This variable serves primarily as a control for the impact of time and past history on decisions to challenge the status quo.

We end up with 6,542 observations for the Challenge the Status Quo Stage. The most frequent choice of the challenger is to maintain the status quo and refrain from either diplomatic or military initiatives (approximately 67 percent of the observations). In contrast, the leaders of challenger states initiate talks about 27 percent (1,782 observations) of the time while resorting to military threats only 6 percent (390 observations) of the time.[11] The central question is how well each of the theoretical models can account for these empirical patterns, particularly decisions either to pursue negotiations or to adopt a more confrontational policy of coercion by threatening force.

On the whole, we find that the International Politics Model provides considerable insight into decisions to threaten force but is far less useful for understanding when leaders choose to rely on negotiations. Furthermore, the Political Accountability and Norms Models produce strong findings for decisions to seek negotiations and to threaten force. The Political Affinity Model, however, is only weakly supported by the statistical results. The findings in this chapter provide strong support for the conclusion that the diplomatic and military policies adopted by state leaders in international disputes are shaped systematically by domestic political institutions and norms as well as the international strategic context of political and military relations. As a result, the supportive findings for the Political Accountability and Norms Models in this chapter address a number of debates in the democratic peace literature and contribute to our understanding of how domestic politics influences international relations.

---

[11] These totals for rounds of talks and initiations of force are slightly higher than the numbers found in the analysis of the Negotiations and Escalation Stages in Chapters 8 and 9, as well as those reported in some tables in Chapter 2. In some of the disputes in which both states are considered challengers, it is impossible to determine which country actually initiated a round of talks or a military confrontation and thus we consider both countries to have issued a challenge. When we analyze the outcome of such talks or military confrontations, however, we eliminate one of these "joint" cases in order to avoid duplication. This explains why the number of "challenges" through talks or force is slightly higher than the actual number of rounds of talks or militarized disputes.

Table 7.1 *Multinomial logit results for International Politics Model: Status Quo Stage*

Variable	Decision to initiate talks vs. maintain status quo			Decision to threaten force vs. maintain status quo			Decision to threaten force vs. initiate talks		
	Coefficient	z	p-value	Coefficient	z	p-value	Coefficient	z	p-value
Military balance	−.020	−0.18	—	1.18	6.10	<.001	1.20	5.87	<.001
Strategic value of territory	.170	2.59	<.01	.350	3.03	<.01	.180	1.48	<.10
Common security interests	−.114	−1.85	<.05	−.572	−4.57	<.001	−.458	−3.51	<.001
Target involvement in other military dispute	−.031	−0.47	—	.364	2.86	<.01	.395	2.95	<.01
Challenger involvement in other military dispute	−.099	−1.34	<.10	.448	3.62	<.001*	.547	4.15	<.001*
Control for time since last challenge	−.008	−10.25	<.001	−.016	−6.04	<.001	−.009	−3.19	<.001

Hausman Test for IIA:
Drop Talks: χ^2 9.21 (7df), p = .24, do not reject IIA
Drop Force: χ^2 −.08 (7df), do not reject IIA
Small–Hsiao Test for IIA:
Drop Talks: χ^2 5.33 (7df), p = .62, do not reject IIA
Drop Force: χ^2 5.87 (7df), p = .56, do not reject IIA
N = 6542
Log Likelihood = −4871.70
Note: * = Two-tailed test of significance (all other p-values based on one-tailed tests).

Results of statistical tests

Before turning to a more detailed discussion of the results for each model, we want to explain how the statistical findings are reported in the tables below. Multinomial logit estimation requires one category to serve as the baseline category. The coefficient estimates for this option are thus set to zero for standardization purposes. For our purposes, the choice of "no challenge to the status quo" is the logical baseline category. The results for the remaining two choices – call for negotiations or initiate force – are presented in comparison to this baseline option of not issuing a challenge. But since we also care about the direct comparison of calling for talks versus threatening force, we simply re-estimate the model using "call for talks" as the baseline category. This is a straightforward transformation of the same model (Liao 1994).

As a result, for each estimated model in this chapter we present three sets of coefficient results (along with statistical significance) that directly compare the challenger's utility for each status quo stage option vis-à-vis the remaining two options. In particular, we present comparisons of the attractiveness of: (1) pursuing talks vs. maintaining the status quo, (2) initiating threats of force vs. maintaining the status quo, and (3) threatening force vs. initiating talks. These pairwise comparisons allow us to evaluate systematically the challenger's likelihood of choosing each option compared to any particular alternative. By examining the signs and statistical significance of these multinomial logit coefficients we can draw some conclusions about whether the various hypotheses are supported.

It is not possible, however, to assess directly the substantive impact of each variable based on the reported logit coefficients. As a result, we utilize predicted probability estimates to examine the substantive impact of a discrete change in a particular variable of interest (Long 1997). The general procedure is that we run a pair (or series) of estimations in which we hold the values of all but one variable in an equation constant, while changing the value for this one variable of interest from a starting value (typically zero or a low value) to a higher value. This allows us to better understand the impact any particular variable has on the probability of a challenger choosing among the options of maintaining the status quo or initiating talks or threats of force.

Results for the International Politics Model

The empirical results for the International Politics Model are reported in Table 7.1. Overall, the results of multinomial logit analysis are quite supportive of the model. Almost all of the coefficients for the hypotheses

Table 7.2 The impact of variables from the International Politics Model on decisions to challenge the status quo by threat of force

Variable	(a) Initial probability	(b) Probability after change in variable	(c) Change in probabilities (b−a)	(d) Percentage change in probabilities (c/a)
Military balance				
Change from 1:10 to 1:3	5.2%	6.3%	+1.1%	+21.2%
Change from 1:3 to 1:1	6.3%	8.3%	+2.0%	+31.7%
Change from 1:1 to 3:1	8.3%	10.8%	+2.5%	+30.1%
Change from 3:1 to 10:1	10.8%	12.8%	+2.0%	+18.5%
Total change from 1:10 to 10:1	5.2%	12.8%	+7.6%	+146.2%
Common security interests				
Change from 0 to 1	7.4%	4.5%	−2.9%	−39.2%
Strategic value of territory				
Changes from 0 to 1	5.6%	7.4%	+1.8%	+32.1%
Target involvement in other military dispute				
Changes from 0 to 1	7.4%	10.4%	+3.0%	+40.5%

Note: The probabilities represent the predicted probability of a challenge to the territorial status quo by a threat of force. The reported probabilities are calculated by holding each variable in Table 7.1 constant while changing the values of a single variable. In the baseline case, the territory is of strategic value to both states, the military balance is 3:2 in favor of the target, and the previous challenge to the status quo occurred 24 months ago. Meanwhile, common security ties, challenger involvement in another military dispute, and target involvement in another military dispute are held at zero.

tested have the correct signs, high levels of statistical significance, and meaningful substantive effects.[12] The overall picture that emerges from these results is that state leaders are strategic in deciding when to challenge the status quo, particularly with respect to threats of force. Questions of relative military strength, the opportune times at which to test the resolve of territorial adversaries, and the importance of the issues at stake in disputed territory all influence the policy choices of leaders in important ways.

The first conclusion to be drawn from Table 7.1 is that the multinomial logit results support four of the five hypotheses tested. That is, challenger states are more likely to seek negotiations and/or threaten force when: the disputed territory is of strategic value (hypothesis **IP3**), the challenger's relative military strength increases (hypothesis **IP2**), and the target state is engaged in a military conflict with another country (hypothesis **IP4ii**). In contrast, talks or military threats are less likely when challengers have common security interests with their territorial adversary (hypothesis **IP1**).

For example, when the target is involved in a military confrontation with another country, state leaders are particularly likely to challenge the status quo by threatening force. We see in Table 7.2 that target dispute involvement produces a 40 percent increase in the probability of the challenger threatening the target with force. While the military balance does not have a systematic impact on the choice to initiate talks vs. maintaining the status quo, challengers are more likely to threaten force vs. either maintaining the status quo or initiating talks as the military balance shifts to its advantage. In Table 7.2 we see that as the challenger's military position changes from one of considerable weakness (a ratio of 1:10) to one of decisive advantage (a ratio of 10:1), there is a steady increase in the probability of threatening force, which rises from just above 5 percent to nearly 13 percent. A good example of this pattern is the behavior of Somalia in its dispute with Kenya. From 1960–2, when Britain was still the colonial power, Somalia found itself at a great military disadvantage and refrained from initiating any threats against the British. Between 1963 and 1967, however, Somalia initiated four militarized confrontations against newly independent Kenya when the military balance had shifted to a position of rough parity. Finally, after 1967 Somalia's relative military position weakened and there were no new military conflicts initiated by Somalia. Another example that illustrates the role played by relative military strength is the behavior of Bolivia. In the period between

---

[12] There is very little multicollinearity exhibited in any of the International Politics Model tests (whether for the Status Quo, Negotiations, or Escalation Stages).

the two world wars Bolivia was involved in disputes with Paraguay and Chile. Bolivia initiated three military confrontations against Paraguay in the 1930s and in each case had a military advantage. In contrast, Bolivia found itself at a military disadvantage in its dispute with Chile and did not initiate a single military confrontation during the inter-war period.

The results in Table 7.1 also indicate that challenges to disputed territory are more likely when the disputed territory is of strategic value.[13] In fact, the likelihood of a military challenge increases by nearly one-third when the territory takes on some strategic value (see Table 7.2). Argentina, for example, was much more likely to initiate threats of force against Chile over the strategically located Beagle Channel Islands than it was in disputes with Paraguay or Uruguay over non-strategic territory. In Asia we find that China was also much more likely to initiate military confrontations over disputed territory with strategic value (e.g. disputes with Vietnam or India) compared to non-strategic territory (e.g. disputes with Burma, Nepal, or Bhutan).

The final supportive finding in Table 7.1 is that if the challenger and target currently share a common territorial dispute adversary, these shared security interests lead the challenger to be less active and confrontational in pursuing territorial claims against the target, as expected in hypothesis **IP1**. That is, the challenger is more likely to accept the prevailing status quo and refrain from either talks or threats of force.[14] Challengers are particularly unlikely to use coercive military means to challenge the prevailing territorial status quo when they share a common territorial dispute adversary with the target. In Table 7.2 we see that common security interests produce a 39 percent reduction in the predicted likelihood of threatening force. For example, if we return to the case of Bolivia's dispute with Paraguay in the inter-war period we find that Bolivia did not initiate any military confrontations when the two states shared a common adversary from 1919–27. However, Bolivia initiated three military

---

[13] A similar finding holds when we substitute into the equation the alternative operational measure for the value of disputed territory, the economic importance of territory. The logit coefficients are positive and statistically significant, particularly for the choices of initiating talks (z-statistic = 3.78, $p < 0.001$) or threatening force (z-statistic = 3.21, $p < 0.001$) vs. maintaining the status quo.

[14] As a robustness check we substitute into the equation alternative measures of common security interests. The first alternative measure is the presence of a military alliance between the challenger and target. The results we obtain using this indicator are not as strong. The coefficients are always negative, as expected, but the only coefficient that is clearly significant is for the choice between initiating talks vs. maintaining the status quo (z-statistic = -2.09, $p < 0.025$). The second alternative measure is involvement in a militarized dispute with a common adversary within the past two years. Here, once again, the findings are not supportive. The signs of the coefficients vary and are always insignificant, with z-statistics of less than 1.00.

confrontations during the period 1928–38 when the two states no longer shared a common adversary. The same pattern applies to the dispute between Ecuador and Peru in the inter-war period. Until 1930 the two states shared a common territorial dispute adversary and there were no military conflicts during this period. After 1930, however, a common adversary no longer existed and the two states experienced four military conflicts. Finally, in the Middle East we find that during North Yemen's long dispute with the British over South Yemen military confrontations were far more likely when North Yemen did not share a common territorial adversary with the British. For example, between 1919 and 1926 and then from 1935–59 a total of nine military confrontations were initiated by North Yemen when no common adversary existed. However, when Saudi Arabia becomes a common adversary of North Yemen and the UK from 1927–34, then North Yemen refrains from initiating any military confrontations against the British.

The second broad conclusion to draw from the findings in Table 7.1 is that variables from the International Politics Model are generally stronger in accounting for the decisions of state leaders to threaten force than they are in explaining decisions to initiate talks. For example, as noted above, the coefficient for the military balance variable is slightly negative but statistically insignificant as an explanation for the choice of challengers to initiate talks vs. maintain the status quo. The military balance variable, however, is positive and highly significant as an explanation for the choice of threatening force vs. either initiating talks or maintaining the status quo. A similar pattern applies to the variable for the involvement of the target in a military conflict with another country (**IP4ii**). Put differently, there are no variables in the International Politics Model that help to explain decisions to initiate talks but fail to say something about decisions to threaten force. The reverse pattern, however, is evident in several instances. The results in Table 7.3 reinforce this general point by showing that the substantive effects of variables on decisions to initiate talks are more modest, ranging from 4 percent to 9 percent changes in predicted probability levels (column d). The comparable changes in predicted probability values in Table 7.2, however, are much higher.

The only unexpected finding in Table 7.1 is that challengers actually seem more likely to issue military challenges in territorial disputes when they are simultaneously involved in military disputes with other countries, contrary to hypothesis **IP4i**. The logic of this original hypothesis was that if challengers were already engaged in military conflicts with other states, they would be less likely to initiate concurrently threats of force against their territorial adversary. The multinomial logit results, however, indicate that challengers are more likely to issue such threats vs. either

Table 7.3 *The impact of variables from the International Politics Model on decisions to challenge the status quo by initiating talks*

Variable	(a) Initial probability	(b) Probability after change in variable	(c) Change in probabilities (b−a)	(d) Percentage change in probabilities (c/a)
Common security interests Change from 0 to 1	34.9%	33.5%	−1.4%	−4.0%
Strategic value of territory Changes from 0 to 1	31.9%	34.9%	+3.0%	+9.4%
Challenger involvement in other military dispute Changes from 0 to 1	34.9%	31.4%	−3.5%	−10.0%

Note: The probabilities represent the predicted probability of a challenge to the territorial status quo through a call for negotiations. The reported probabilities are calculated by holding each variable in Table 7.1 constant while changing the values of a single variable. In the baseline case, the territory is of strategic value to both states, the military balance is 3:2 in favor of the target, and the previous challenge to the status quo occurred twenty-four months ago. Meanwhile, common security ties, challenger involvement in another military dispute, and target involvement in another military dispute are held at zero.

Table 7.4 *Examples of challengers initiating threats of force in territorial disputes despite involvement in militarized conflicts with other states*

Challenger	Year(s)	Target in territorial dispute
EUROPE		
Germany	1938–40	Austria, Belgium, Czechoslovakia, Lithuania, Poland
Hungary	1938–41	Czechoslovakia, Yugoslavia
Italy	1939–40	Albania
Russia	1919–20	Poland, Georgia
Russia	1939–46	Latvia, Lithuania, Estonia, Finland, Romania, Turkey
Yugoslavia	1919	Albania, Austria
ASIA		
China	1947–48	Mongolia
China	1955–62	India, Burma, Nepal
India	1954–61	Portugal
Japan	1932–41	China, France, Mongolia
MIDDLE EAST		
France	1919–20	Syria, Turkey
Great Britain	1920	Iraq
Great Britain	1953	Saudi Arabia
Iraq	1969–76	Kuwait
Israel	1953–66	Jordan

accepting the status quo or initiating talks. If the data set is examined more closely, we find a number of cases that seem to fit this pattern and list these examples in Table 7.4. While we do not have a clear explanation for this finding, what we see in Table 7.4 is that often the challenger is much more powerful than its adversary (e.g. Germany, Russia, and China vs. neighboring states), or the challenger threatens the target at an opportune time when the target is already confronted with military threats from other states (e.g. Hungary vs. Czechoslovakia and Yugoslavia, Japan vs. France, France vs. Turkey). This suggests that the possibility of a second military conflict was either not considered likely since the weak target would back down, or the challenger did not believe that a military conflict with the target would require a substantial diversion of forces from its other military confrontation.

It is also worth noting the impact of the control variable we included to take into account trends over time in how active the challenger was in pursuing its claim to disputed territory (*Time Since Last Challenge*). This variable measures the number of months since the challenger had most recently initiated talks or a threat of force. The negative and statistically significant relationship between this variable and any form of challenge to the status quo is quite intuitive (Table 7.1). The longer the period since

Table 7.5 Multinomial logit results for Political Accountability Model: hypotheses comparing regimes for Status Quo Stage

Variable	Decision to initiate talks vs. maintain status quo			Decision to threaten force vs. maintain status quo			Decision to threaten force vs. initiate talks		
	Coefficient	z	p-value	Coefficient	z	p-value	Coefficient	z	p-value
Challenger level of democracy	.022	3.01	<.01	-.054	-4.09	<.001	-.076	-5.42	<.001
Target level of democracy	.001	.30	—	.007	.86	—	.005	.67	—
Democracy * stalemate	-.002	-.17	—	-.014	-.75	—	-.012	-.65	—
Control for stalemate	.438	3.44	<.001	.305	1.44	<.10	-.133	-.61	—
Democracy * enduring rivalry	-.013	-1.22	<.10	.002	.11	—	.015	.79	—
Control for enduring rivalry	.183	1.44	<.10	.837	4.39	<.001	.655	3.22	<.001
Democracy * ethnic ties	.017	1.97	<.025	.039	2.28	<.025	.022	1.24	—
Control for ethnic ties	.112	1.12	—	.194	1.08	—	.081	.43	—
Democracy * military risk	-.005	-.57	—	.003	.18	—	.008	.43	—
Control for military risk	-.109	-.92	—	-.279	-1.23	—	-.169	-.71	—
INTERNATIONAL POLITICS MODEL									
Military balance	-.185	-.81	—	1.05	2.66	<.01	1.23	2.95	<.01
Strategic value of territory	.181	2.64	<.01	.226	1.79	<.05	.046	.35	—
Common security interests	-.046	-.71	—	-.446	-3.43	<.001	-.401	-2.96	<.01
Target other dispute involvement	-.026	-.38	—	.270	2.11	<.025	.296	2.21	<.025
Challenger other dispute involvement	-.102	-1.37	<.10	.467	3.67	<.001*	.570	4.23	<.001*
Control for time since last challenge	-.006	-8.79	<.001	-.016	-5.32	<.001	-.009	-3.18	<.001

Hausman Test for IIA:
  Drop Talks: χ^2 6.42 (17df), p=.99, do not reject IIA
  Drop Force: χ^2 -.34 (17df), do not reject IIA
Small-Hsiao Test for IIA:
  Drop Talks: χ^2 15.59 (17df), p=.55, do not reject IIA
  Drop Force: χ^2 20.56 (17df), p=.25, do not reject IIA
N = 6542
Log Likelihood = -4769.80
Note: * = Two-tailed test of significance (all other p-values based on one-tailed tests).

the last attempt to challenge the status quo, the less likely we should be to expect any current challenges to the status quo. This strong, negative relationship is evident in all models of the Challenge the Status Quo Stage.

We next turn our attention to the results for each of the domestic politics models. As noted above, we include the variables from the International Politics Model (as reported in Table 7.1) in all equations that test hypotheses from each domestic model. The results for the International Politics Model are robust and the coefficient estimates and significance levels of variables remain very stable across all of the multinomial logit analyses for the domestic models. As a result, we do not discuss these results further but instead focus on the new findings for each test of the domestic models.

Results for the Political Accountability Model

While the initial results for the International Politics Model help us to understand how the international context influences choices to challenge the status quo, we now turn to the central findings in this chapter concerning the role of domestic political variables. In Chapter 4 we classified hypotheses derived from the Political Accountability Model into three broad areas. The first were hypotheses that compared democratic and non-democratic systems, while the second and third sets of hypotheses related to comparisons within these two regime types and among dyads. In discussing the multinomial logit results, we follow this same set-up and present the findings sequentially for each of these categories of hypotheses.

The overall conclusion to be drawn from the logit results is that democratic leaders, compared to their non-democratic counterparts, are less likely to threaten military force to seek a change in the territorial status quo, but are more likely to rely on negotiations to push their territorial claims. This pattern holds true regardless of whether the adversary is democratic or not. As a result, there is clear evidence of monadic effects associated with democracy in reducing the threat of military confrontations in territorial disputes. At the same time, our results also show that democratic leaders can be quite aggressive when they anticipate that confrontational policies will generate political support at home.

Results for hypotheses that compare leaders of democratic and non-democratic states

The strongest result in Table 7.5 is that as challengers become more democratic, leaders are less likely to turn to military threats and to

Table 7.6 *The impact of the democracy and ethnic ties variables from the Political Accountability Model on decisions to challenge the status quo by threat of force*

Variable	(a) Initial probability	(b) Probability after change in variable	(c) Change in probabilities (b−a)	(d) Percentage change in probabilities (c/a)
Challenger level of democracy				
Change from −10 to −2	7.5%	4.7%	−2.8%	−37.3%
Change from −2 to 6	4.7%	3.0%	−1.7%	−36.2%
Change from 6 to 10	3.0%	2.3%	−.7%	−23.3%
Total change from −10 to 10	7.5%	2.3%	−5.2%	−69.3%
The impact of democracy when there are ethnic ties with territory				
Change from −10 to −2	6.3%	8.2%	+1.9%	+30.2%
Change from −2 to 6	5.2%	6.6%	+1.4%	+26.9%
Change from 6 to 10	4.1%	4.6%	+.5%	+12.2%
Change from −10 to 10	6.3%	11.7%	+5.4%	+85.7%

Note: The probabilities represent the predicted probability of a challenge to the territorial status quo by a threat of force. The reported probabilities are calculated by holding each variable in Table 7.5 constant while changing the values of a single term. In the baseline case, the territory is of strategic value to both states, the challenger net-democracy score is −2, the target net-democracy score is 2, the military balance is 3:2 in favor of the target, and the previous challenge to the status quo occurred twenty-four months ago. The impact of the *net-democracy * ethnic ties* term represents solely the impact of democracy when ethnic ties are present and does not capture the impact of democracy in any other way. All other variables are held at zero.

instead favor negotiations over threats of force.[15] All three coefficients for the *Challenger Level of Democracy* variable have the predicted signs and are statistically significant at the 0.01 level. Furthermore, in Table 7.6 we see that a change from being highly non-democratic to highly democratic (a change in the net-democracy score from -10 to $+10$) leads to a nearly 70 percent reduction in the probability of threatening force. In contrast, the same change in democracy levels leads to a 41 percent increase in the likelihood of seeking talks over disputed territory (see Table 7.7). These are strong results in support of hypothesis **PA1i**.[16] We should note that these results indicate that democratic challengers are not more willing to accept the territorial status quo; they simply choose to use negotiations instead of military coercion as the means by which to advance their claims. The behavior of Argentina nicely illustrates the impact of democracy on decisions to challenge the status quo. For example, five military confrontations were initiated against the British over the Falkland Islands but four of these took place (1976–82) when Argentina was highly undemocratic. Furthermore, Argentina initiated ten military confrontations against Chile in its long-standing dispute and all ten of these military confrontations were initiated when Argentina was non-democratic. In contrast, during each of the periods (often short-lived) of democratic rule in Argentina from 1919–95 there were no cases of military confrontations being initiated by Argentine leaders. The Argentine pattern is evident in other regions as well. In fact, if we put together a list of countries that initiated military confrontations most frequently, we find that all of them are non-democratic. For example, Cambodia initiated seven threats,

---

[15] We encounter a number of relatively high auxiliary r^2 values when checking for multicollinearity among the variables in this model. In particular, we obtain auxiliary r^2 values ranging from 0.5 to 0.75 when we regress the challenger democracy score variable, or any of the interaction terms containing this challenger democracy term, on all other independent variables in the model. We then re-run the model several times and test only one accountability model hypotheses each time, deleting the other variables from the accountability model that seem to be the source of the multicollinearity. In all cases, the original results from the full equation are upheld for the challenger democracy variable and each democracy-based interaction term being tested. The results for the international politics variables also remain unchanged.

[16] These reported effects for the *Challenger Level of Democracy* variable do not take into account the impact of the challenger's democracy level as it is funneled through the interaction terms with stalemate, ethnic ties, military weakness, and enduring rivalry. Therefore, this estimate for the impact of challenger democracy represents the "baseline" effect for challenger democracy, separate from the influence of challenger democracy under certain qualifying conditions (stalemate, ethnic ties, etc.). Therefore we re-estimate this model by deleting all interaction terms containing the challenger democracy level variable to see what changes, if any, occur to the estimates for *Challenger Level of Democracy* term. After re-estimation this *Challenger Level of Democracy* variable retains the exact same signs as before, and all three coefficient estimates for this variable maintain the same signs and are still significant at the 0.01 level.

Table 7.7 *The impact of the democracy and ethnic ties variables from the Political Accountability Model on decisions to challenge the status quo by initiating talks*

Variable	(a) Initial probability	(b) Probability after change in variable	(c) Change in probabilities (b−a)	(d) Percentage change in probabilities (c/a)
Challenger level of democracy				
Change from −10 to −2	26.9%	31.3%	+4.4%	+16.4%
Change from −2 to 6	31.3%	35.8%	+4.5%	+14.4%
Change from 6 to 10	35.8%	38.0%	+2.2%	+6.1%
Total change from −10 to 10	26.9%	38.0%	+11.1%	+41.3%
The impact of democracy when there are ethnic ties with territory				
Change from −10 to −2	26.2%	28.3%	+2.1%	+8.0%
Change from −2 to 6	32.9%	35.3%	+2.4%	+7.3%
Change from 6 to 10	40.3%	41.6%	+1.3%	+3.2%
Change from −10 to 10	26.2%	31.4%	+5.2%	+19.8%

Note: The probabilities represent the predicted probability of a challenge to the territorial status quo through a call for negotiations. The reported probabilities are calculated by holding each variable in Table 7.5 constant while changing the values of a single term. In the baseline case, the territory is of strategic value to both states, the challenger net-democracy score is −2, the target net-democracy score is −2, the military balance is 3:2 in favor of the target, and the previous challenge to the status quo occurred twenty-four months ago. The impact of the *net-democracy * ethnic ties* term represents solely the impact of democracy when ethnic ties are present and does not capture the impact of democracy in any other way. All other variables are held at zero.

Yugoslavia and Turkey initiated eight military conflicts, and North Yemen started fifteen military confrontations. There are also many examples of challengers becoming much more likely to initiate talks during periods of democratic rule compared to periods of authoritarian leadership. Once again, the case of Argentina is instructive. During periods of democratic rule, Argentina proposed talks in about 43 percent of Challenge the Status Quo Stage observations, while during periods of authoritarian rule this rate was only about 17 percent. Another example is Spain in its dispute with the British over Gibraltar. Spain turned to negotiations eleven times during the period of democratic rule from 1977–95, while only fifteen rounds of talks were initiated over the far longer period of non-democratic rule from 1919–75.

Greater political accountability can also induce political leaders to become confrontational if they expect that domestic audiences will rally behind such policies, as argued in hypotheses **PA2i** and **PA2ii**. The results in Table 7.5 are generally supportive of these two hypotheses. That is, democratic leaders are likely to be more active in pursuing territorial claims through both negotiations and threats of force when ethnic co-nationals populate disputed territory. In Tables 7.6 and 7.7 we see that when ethnic co-nationals are involved, highly democratic leaders are roughly 85 percent and 20 percent more likely than highly non-democratic leaders to threaten force and initiate talks, respectively. A good example of this pattern would include Poland's record of five military confrontations and eleven rounds of talks initiated in disputes with Czechoslovakia, Germany, Lithuania, and the Soviet Union during the short-lived period of Polish democratic rule between 1919 and 1924. In each case, Polish governments sought to incorporate territories populated by ethnic co-nationals. A similar pattern applies to Czech democratic leaders right after World War I when they proposed multiple rounds of talks and initiated a military confrontation in an attempt to extend their borders with Austria, Hungary, and Poland in order to include territories populated by Czech and Slovak populations.

Our next finding is that there is no discernible difference in the propensity of democratic leaders to turn to force against enduring rivals as compared to non-democratic leaders. While the enduring rivalry control variable is positive and statistically significant for the decisions to threaten force vs. maintain the status quo or initiate talks in Table 7.5, the interaction term for the variable *Democracy * Enduring Rivalry* is insignificant across all three outcomes on the dependent variable. This indicates that *all* states are more likely to challenge the status quo when the territorial claim is against an enduring rival and that democratic leaders are not systematically different in their behavior towards enduring rivals, as argued in **PA2i** (i.e. they are just as likely to threaten force).

Table 7.8 *Multinomial logit results for Political Accountability Model: hypotheses comparing differences within regimes for Status Quo Stage*

Variable	Decision to initiate talks vs. maintain status quo			Decision to threaten force vs. maintain status quo			Decision to threaten force vs. initiate talks		
	Coefficient	z	p-value	Coefficient	z	p-value	Coefficient	z	p-value
Legislative support for challenger government	-.001	-.35	—	.010	1.01	—	.011	1.12	—
Legislative support for target government	.001	.29	—	-.004	-.83	—	-.005	-.93	—
Time since elections in challenger	-.008	-2.79	<.01	-.011	-1.53	<.10	-.002	-.30	—
Recent elections in target	.219	2.38	<.01	-.006	-.03	—	-.224	-1.11	—
Secure non-democratic challenger	.095	1.33	<.10	.130	1.04	—	.035	.27	—
Secure non-democratic target	.014	.17	—	-.240	-1.67	<.05	-.254	-1.68	<.05
Control for challenger democracy	.699	3.40	<.001	-.922	-1.48	<.10	-1.62	-2.57	<.01
Control for target democracy	-.053	-.31	—	.105	.29	—	.158	.42	—
INTERNATIONAL POLITICS MODEL									
Military balance	-.059	-.47	—	1.30	6.04	<.001	1.36	5.93	<.001
Strategic value of territory	.156	2.36	<.01	.298	2.55	<.01	.141	1.15	—
Common security interests	-.101	-1.61	<.10	-.524	-4.14	<.001	-.423	-3.20	<.001
Target other dispute involvement	-.041	-.61	—	.371	2.88	<.01	.412	3.04	<.01
Challenger other dispute involvement	-.108	-1.47	<.10	.486	3.88	<.001*	.594	4.46	<.001*
Control for time since last challenge	-.007	-10.16	<.001	-.017	-6.24	<.001	-.010	-3.48	<.001

Hausman Test for IIA:
    Drop Talks: χ^2 7.83 (15df), p = .93, do not reject IIA
    Drop Force: χ^2 -.03 (15df), do not reject IIA
Small–Hsiao Test for IIA:
    Drop Talks: χ^2 17.52 (15df), p = .29, do not reject IIA
    Drop Force: χ^2 9.21 (15df), p = .87, do not reject IIA
N = 6542
Log Likelihood = -4827.460
Note: * = Two-tailed test of significance (all other p-values based on one-tailed tests).

The remaining results in Table 7.5 do not provide support for hypothesized differences in the behavior of democratic and non-democratic challengers. For example, it was expected that democratic leaders would be less likely to turn to military force in response to stalemates in negotiations than non-democratic leaders (hypothesis **PA1iii**). But the coefficients for the *Democracy* * *Stalemate* term are not statistically significant, though they do have the correct signs.[17] Similarly, it was expected that democratic leaders would be more hesitant to initiate military threats in a situation of military disadvantage (**PA1i**), but the coefficients for this variable, too, are not statistically significant.[18] Finally, challengers are not less likely to challenge democratic targets as hypothesized in **PA1ii**. The coefficients for the variable are actually positive, and once again do not reach standard levels of statistical significance.

In sum, if we look across these results, the hypotheses that posit basic differences or similarities in the behavior of democratic and non-democratic leaders are solidly supported. If we try to push the analysis further, however, with more fine-grained comparisons and hypotheses, the empirical evidence generally does not support the conclusion that the behavior of democratic leaders differs in systematic ways from that of non-democratic leaders.

Results for hypotheses that draw comparisons among leaders of democratic and non-democratic states

When we test hypotheses about differences in expected behavior among democratic leaders, we find that the timing of elections is quite important. In particular, among democratic challengers there seems to be an electoral cycle in which leaders are more willing to be active in pursuing territorial claims, including both talks and threats of forces, in periods shortly after national elections. This later finding is consistent with prior research that indicates that democracies are more likely to be involved in wars in periods shortly after national elections (Gaubatz 1999). As the time since the most recent national election increases, democratic leaders become more wary of diplomatic and military initiatives, as expected in **PA4i**. In Table 7.8 the coefficients for the challenger time since election variable are negative and statistically significant for decisions either

---

[17] In the results reported in Table 7.5 the stalemate variable is coded on the basis of a one-year lag. However, we also check the robustness of results using two- and five-year lags and find no important changes in the statistical results.

[18] We check for the robustness of results for this variable by adjusting the threshold that is used to code for a position of military weakness. The results always remain weak and never support the hypothesis.

Table 7.9 *The impact of the elections and secure non-democratic leadership variables from the Political Accountability Model on decisions to challenge the status quo by initiating talks*

Variable	(a) Initial probability	(b) Probability after change in variable	(c) Change in probabilities (b−a)	(d) Percentage change in probabilities (c/a)
Months since last election in challenger				
Change from 3 to 12	46.0%	44.3%	−1.7%	−3.7%
Change from 12 to 30	44.3%	41.0%	−3.3%	−7.4%
Change from 30 to 48	41.0%	37.6%	−3.4%	−8.3%
Total change from 3 to 48	46.0%	37.6%	−8.4%	−18.3%
Recent elections in target				
Change from 0 to 1	30.8%	35.7%	+4.9%	+15.9%
Secure non-democratic leader in challenger				
Change from 0 to 1	30.8%	32.5%	+1.7%	+5.5%

Note: The probabilities represent the predicted probability of a challenge to the territorial status quo through a call for negotiations. The reported probabilities are calculated by holding each term in Table 7.8 constant while changing the values of a single term. In the baseline case, the territory is of strategic value to both states, the military balance is 3:2 in favor of the target, and the previous challenge to the status quo occurred twenty-four months ago. The challenger and target democracy dummy variables are set at 1 for the challenger and target election timing comparisons, respectively. The challenger democracy dummy variable is set at 0 in order to make the comparison between secure and insecure non-democratic challengers. Unless indicated otherwise, all other variables are held at zero.

to initiate talks or threaten force vs. maintaining the status quo.[19] The substantive effects for this variable are presented in Tables 7.9 and 7.10. Challengers are 18 percent and 25 percent more likely to seek talks or threaten force, respectively, when elections were held just three months ago as opposed to if elections were held four years ago. For example, in all three of Greece's post-World War II disputes with Albania, Bulgaria, and Cyprus rounds of talks were only held in periods shortly after national elections had been held in Greece (not more than five months after an election). Another example is France's negotiating behavior in its three Middle East disputes with the British right after World War I. In early 1920 the French open up talks within a period of two to four months following national elections and in each dispute limited concessions are offered by the French over the borders with British-controlled Palestine, Jordan, and Iraq. There is also some evidence that challengers pay attention to the electoral cycle of democratic targets, as hypothesized in **PA4ii**. In Table 7.8 we see that challengers are more likely to seek talks over disputed territory within the first twelve months following national elections in the target. The coefficient for the *Recent Elections in Target* variable is positive and statistically significant for the decision to initiate talks vs. maintaining the status quo. In Table 7.9 we find that elections within the past year for the target produces a 16 percent increase in the probability that the challenger will propose talks. However, challenger decisions to initiate threats of force are not linked to the timing of elections in democratic targets, so the results provide only partial support for **PA4ii**.

The other hypothesis comparing democracies focuses on the strength of opposition parties in national legislatures (**PA3i** and **PA3ii**). In Table 7.8 we see that the results are generally weak. The coefficients on the challenger government legislative support variables are positive for the comparisons of force versus maintaining the status quo and force vs. initiating talks, but do not reach standard levels of statistical significance

---

[19] We again test for multi-collinearity among all of the explanatory variables and obtain a handful of high auxiliary r^2 values. Specifically, we obtain auxiliary r^2 values ranging from 0.85 to 0.90 when we regress both the challenger (and target) net-democracy and percentage seats variables on all other independent variables. These high values are not surprising given the nature of this model. It is logical that measures that make comparisons within democracies and within non-democracies should be correlated with a variable indicating whether or not a state is democratic. Nevertheless, we check for the stability of our original results by running separate regressions for democracies and then for non-democracies. In both cases all of the variables retain the same signs and in almost all cases the p-values do not change by more than 0.10. Furthermore, neither the signs nor statistical significance for the key variables of this model (challenger and target percentage of seats held by government, challenger and target election timing) change in any substantively meaningful way.

Table 7.10 *The impact of the election and secure non-democratic target variables from the Political Accountability Model on decisions to challenge the status quo by threatening force*

Variable	(a) Initial probability	(b) Probability after change in variable	(c) Change in probabilities (b−a)	(d) Percentage change in probabilities (c/a)
Months since last election in challenger				
Change from 3 to 12	4.8%	4.5%	−.3%	−6.3%
Change from 12 to 30	4.5%	4.0%	−.5%	−11.1%
Change from 30 to 48	4.0%	3.6%	−.4%	−10.0%
Total Change from 3 to 48	4.8%	3.6%	−1.2%	−25.0%
Politically secure non-democratic target				
Change from 0 to 1	8.8%	7.0%	−1.8%	−20.5%

Note: The probabilities represent the predicted probability of a challenge to the territorial status quo by a threat of force. The reported probabilities are calculated by holding each term in Table 7.8 constant while changing the values of a single term. In the baseline case, the territory is of strategic value to both states, the military balance is 3:2 in favor of the target, and the previous challenge to the status quo occurred twenty-four months ago. The challenger democracy dummy variable is set at 1 to ascertain the impact of the challenger months since election variable, and the target democracy dummy variable is set at 0 to make the comparison between secure and insecure non-democratic targets. Unless indicated otherwise, all other variables are held at zero.

(z-statistics of 1.01 and 1.12, respectively). Challengers also do not seem to be influenced by the strength or weakness of opposition parties in democratic targets. Once again the signs of the coefficients are in the predicted direction, but significance levels are very low.[20] The fact that the strength of opposition parties in both challenger and target legislatures did not seem to influence the choices of challengers to initiate talks or threats of force may be due to several reasons.

First, diplomatic initiatives often take place outside of public view. As a result, leaders may not be concerned about the influence of domestic political audiences at the early stages of initiatives, since the leaders of opposition parties may not even be aware of such actions. Democratic leaders may calculate that failures to make progress through preliminary talks do not carry much in the way of domestic political risks. This same type of logic can be applied to small-scale or limited military actions, which remain largely unknown if they do not lead to further escalatory actions. Empirically, we do not have systematic data on this question but our case knowledge leads us to believe that there are a good number of initiatives aimed at negotiations that are pursued in the initial stages without much publicity or knowledge by the general public or by opposition parties in the legislature. It is certainly true that if these initial talks continue and result in proposals for settlement that involve concessions of disputed territory, then these diplomatic developments will become well known and issues of ratification by the legislature are likely to loom much larger. However, it is important to recognize that in this chapter we are only focusing on the decision to seek talks and initiate negotiations. In the next chapter we focus on the outcomes of negotiations and do find that opposition party strength is important in explaining whether concessions are offered by democratic leaders.

Second, there are divergent incentives to initiate talks or threats of force that may mitigate the importance of potential legislative opposition to such foreign policy actions. For example, if talks are initiated with the desire of achieving a settlement in which territorial concessions may be necessary, then the threat of opposition parties criticizing the agreement and trying to block ratification should be important from the outset in the calculations of democratic presidents and prime ministers. If democratic leaders, however, propose talks without expectations of being able to reach a settlement or make progress towards a settlement, then talks

---

[20] Several alternative operational measures of opposition strength, such as minority government status, number of parties in the cabinet, or seats controlled by the ruling party, are substituted into the equation. In all cases, however, the results remain weak and do not vary from those reported in Table 7.8.

may nevertheless be pursued for other reasons. In particular, leaders may pursue talks in an attempt to shift blame for the failure of talks on to the shoulders of leaders in the other country, or to try and convince third parties of one's own commitment to negotiations and peaceful conflict resolution. In these latter situations, since expectations of negotiations leading to a possible settlement are low, concerns over ratification problems stemming from strong opposition in the legislature are not critical barriers to the leadership's decision to enter into talks.

Third, even if military threats do become publicly known there may be a nationalist bias that discourages opposition leaders in the legislature from quickly criticizing the government's actions. If there is a wait-and-see attitude among opposition elites and democratic leaders know this, they may conclude that they have some flexibility to take military initiatives and pull back if they conclude that escalation to high levels of force would be quite risky. Once again, when we focus the analysis on levels of escalation in Chapter 9, opposition strength in the legislature could prove more important than it does at the stage of initiating limited military probes or shows of force.

The final set of hypotheses focuses on non-democratic challengers. In **PA5i** it was argued that non-democratic leaders who were relatively secure (measured as the absence of any violent political rebellion within the past year) and therefore did not face a strong threat of a violent political opposition or military coups would be more willing to be active and take risks in pursuit of territorial claims. The estimated results are only partially supportive. For example, secure non-democratic challengers do seem to be somewhat more likely to propose talks vs. maintaining the status quo (see Table 7.8). However, the substantive change caused by this variable is relatively small, as secure non-democratic leaders are only 5.5 percent more likely to seek talks than insecure non-democratic leaders (see Table 7.9). Challengers, however, are less likely to threaten force against a secure non-democratic leader in the target state as argued in **PA5ii**. The coefficients for this variable in Table 7.8 are negative and marginally significant for the decisions to threaten force vs. either maintaining the status quo or initiating talks (p-values of less than 0.10 for both). The logic of **PA5ii** was that challengers would be concerned that secure leaders had the political flexibility to risk escalation and a military conflict and therefore challengers would be more cautious in initiating threats. In Table 7.10 we see a 20 percent reduction in the probability of challengers threatening force when they face a secure non-democratic political leader in the target state. A possible alternative argument was that challengers would be more likely to initiate threats in this situation, calculating that secure target leaders had the political strength to retreat in a crisis and survive politically. The results for this particular equation, however, clearly suggest that challengers were not inclined to gamble in this way.[21]

Results for hypotheses that compare across dyads

The final set of results to report for the Political Accountability Model centers on patterns of behavior among democratic dyads and in dyads consisting of democratic and non-democratic states (mixed dyads). In **PA6** we hypothesized that in territorial disputes between democratic states we should expect to find a greater reliance on talks and negotiations as opposed to threats of force. The results in Table 7.11 are very supportive, with all of the coefficients for the democratic dyad variable having the correct signs and achieving high levels of statistical significance. Furthermore, the substantive effects for this variable are large, which is indicated in Table 7.12. A challenger state that is part of a democratic dyad is over 40 percent more likely to pursue negotiations with its democratic territorial dispute adversary. On the other hand, the probability of a challenger state in a democratic dyad threatening force is just over 3 percent, compared to a figure of over 8 percent for a jointly non-democratic dyad (a reduction of over 63 percent). The comparisons in Table 7.13 confirm these same patterns. Challengers in democratic dyads initiate talks far more frequently than military threats. The ratio of talks to military threats in democratic dyads is greater than 13:1. The corresponding ratio for non-democratic dyads, however, is just over 3:1. Examples of the propensity of democratic dyads to hold talks would include the British proposing talks nine times with France in the dispute over the border of Syria and Iraq from 1919–32, or Ireland's twenty-eight rounds of talks with the British over Northern Ireland without once initiating a military confrontation. In the Americas we find that democratic El Salvador and Honduras in the 1980s and 1990s avoided any military confrontations and held repeated talks, and that democratic Argentina in the 1980s and 1990s initiated multiple rounds of talks but not a single military confrontation in disputes with democratic Chile and Great Britain. It is important to couple this dyadic effect of democracy with the earlier reported finding of a strong monadic effect for democracy. As we argued in Chapter 4, both monadic and dyadic effects are to be expected. The logic for dyadic effects, remember, follows from the general

---

[21] We substitute into the equation alternative operational measures of the political security of challenger and target leaders. These measures include coups within the past one or two years, and no movement towards political liberalization within the past one or two years. The results are generally weak with no clear pattern of results. The absence of violent rebellion within the past year therefore produces the most consistent set of results.

Table 7.11 *Multinomial logit results for Political Accountability Model: hypotheses comparing dyads for Status Quo Stage*

Variable	Decision to initiate talks vs. maintain status quo			Decision to threaten force vs. maintain status quo			Decision to threaten force vs. initiate talks		
	Coefficient	z	p-value	Coefficient	z	p-value	Coefficient	z	p-value
Democratic dyad	.477	5.10	<.001	−.876	−3.55	<.001	−1.35	−5.40	<.001
Non-democratic state in mixed dyad	−.304	−2.93	<.01	.426	1.98	<.025	.730	3.26	<.001
Control for mixed dyad	.322	3.48	<.001	−.467	−2.51	<.01	−.789	−4.09	<.001
INTERNATIONAL POLITICS MODEL									
Military balance	−.089	−.71	—	1.23	5.79	<.001	1.32	5.83	<.001
Strategic value of territory	.162	2.46	<.01	.328	2.82	<.01	.166	1.35	<.10
Common security interests	−.105	−1.69	<.01	−.550	−4.37	<.001	−.445	−3.37	<.001
Target other dispute involvement	−.038	−.56	—	.370	2.88	<.01	.408	3.01	<.01
Challenger other dispute involvement	−.110	−1.50	<.10	.479	3.87	<.001*	.590	4.47	<.001*
Control for time since last challenge	−.007	−10.13	<.001	−.017	−6.18	<.001	−.010	−3.45	<.001

Hausman Test for IIA:
  Drop Talks: χ^2 5.97 (10df), p=.82, do not reject IIA
  Drop Force: χ^2 −.19 (10df), do not reject IIA
Small–Hsiao Test for IIA:
  Drop Talks: χ^2 11.15 (10df), p=.35, do not reject IIA
  Drop Force: χ^2 7.13 (10df), p=.71, do not reject IIA
N = 6542
Log Likelihood = −4837.25
Note: * = Two-tailed test of significance (all other p-values based on one-tailed tests).

Table 7.12 *The impact of dyadic variables from the Political Accountability Model on decisions to challenge the status quo*

Variable	(a) Initial probability	(b) Probability after change in variable	(c) Change in probabilities (b−a)	(d) Percentage change in probabilities (c/a)
			I. Policy of initiating talks	
Democratic dyad				
Change from 0 to 1	32.1%	45.1%	+13.0%	+40.5%
Non-democratic state in mixed dyad				
Change from 0 to 1	40.7%	32.6%	−8.1%	−19.9%

Variable	(a) Initial probability	(b) Probability after change in variable	(c) Change in probabilities (b−a)	(d) Percentage change in probabilities (c/a)
			II. Policy of threatening force	
Democratic dyad				
Change from 0 to 1	8.4%	3.1%	−5.3%	−63.1%
Non-democratic state in mixed dyad				
Change from 0 to 1	4.8%	8.1%	+3.3%	+68.8%

Note: The probabilities represent the predicted probability of a challenge to the territorial status quo by a call for negotiations or threat of force, respectively. The reported probabilities are calculated by holding each term in Table 7.11 constant while changing the value of a single term. The predicted probabilities for a democratic dyad represent a comparison with a jointly non-democratic dyad. The non-democratic state in a mixed dyad is compared to a democratic state in a mixed dyad. The territory is of strategic value to both states, the military balance is 3:2 in favor of the target, and the previous challenge to the status quo occurred twenty-four months ago. Unless indicated otherwise, all other variables are held at zero.

Table 7.13 *The diplomatic and military behavior of democratic dyads in the Challenge the Status Quo Stage*

I. Democratic dyads				
Number of dyads	Number of observations	Number of rounds of talks	Number of military confrontations	Ratio of talks/ military conflicts
74	732	263	20	13:1
II. Non-democratic dyads				
Number of dyads	Number of observations	Number of rounds of talks	Number of military confrontations	Ratio of talks/ military conflicts
194	2826	708	207	3.4:1

logic of democratic leaders being more risk-averse to threatening force and favoring negotiations instead.

For mixed dyads the hypothesis is that non-democratic challengers should be the parties to more frequently initiate threats of force and to favor force over negotiations (**PA7i**). The results in Table 7.11 strongly support this hypothesis. Across all three policy options the coefficients are in the predicted direction and are statistically significant. In Table 7.12 the large substantive effects of this variable are reported. Non-democratic challengers in mixed dyads are nearly 20 percent less likely to propose talks than are democratic challengers in mixed dyads. Perhaps more importantly, these non-democratic challengers in mixed dyads are roughly 69 percent more likely to threaten force to advance a territorial claim than are democratic challengers in mixed dyads. These are important results that directly address the debate in the democratic peace literature as to whether conflict in mixed dyads is a result of equally aggressive behavior on the part of both democratic and non-democratic states. The findings presented here point firmly towards the non-democratic side as the party primarily responsible for initiating military conflicts in mixed dyads.

Several examples nicely illustrate these results. In the inter-war period non-democratic Turkey initiated two military confrontations against the British along the borders of Iraq between 1922 and 1926 and then in the late 1930s initiated four military confrontations along the borders of French-controlled Syria. China initiated multiple military probes along the border with India in the period 1955–62, while non-democratic Indonesia resorted to military threats and the use of force four times against the Netherlands from 1950–61 in the dispute over West Irian. The behavior of Argentina is also quite consistent with the logit results. That is, Argentina only initiated military confrontations against the British over the Falklands during periods of authoritarian rule.

Results for the Political Norms Model

We now turn to the results for the Political Norms Model. As with the Political Accountability Model, hypotheses for the Norms Model are directed at comparisons: of leaders from democratic and non-democratic political systems, among leaders of each type of political system, and then across dyads. The overall picture that emerges from the logit results is one of solid support for the Norms Model. Leaders with strong nonviolent norms of domestic political competition and conflict resolution are more likely to rely on negotiations and to shun the use of military force to challenge the status quo. These results are quite strong at both the dyadic and monadic levels, indicating that leaders with these nonviolent norms are less confrontational in disputes not only with other democratic states, but with non-democratic states as well. Furthermore, the leaders of newly established democracies and highly repressive countries are more aggressive. This points towards interesting differences in the strength and impact of norms among leaders in both democratic and non-democratic states. Finally, it follows from the strong monadic findings summarized above that in disputes between democratic and non-democratic states the outbreak of military confrontations is largely due to the decisions of non-democratic leaders to initiate threats of force.

Results for hypotheses that compare leaders with strong vs. weak nonviolent norms

The first finding to report from Table 7.14 is that as nonviolent political norms become more firmly established in political systems, political leaders are more likely to seek negotiations over disputed territory and to turn away from threats of force.[22] The coefficients for the *Strength of Nonviolent Norms* variable have the predicted signs and are highly statistically significant across all three policy choices, as hypothesized in **PN1i**. The substantive effects for this variable are quite powerful as well. Of the

---

[22] We encounter a handful of high r^2 values when we run auxiliary regressions on each of the independent variables in this model. Once again, the multicollinearity among independent variables is largely a consequence of the number of interaction terms in the model. We find the highest auxiliary r^2 value (0.88) when we regress all other independent variables on the recent stalemate control variable. This high value is primarily a result of the collinearity between the stalemate variable and the *non-violent norms * stalemate* interaction term. However, the coefficient estimates and standard errors for nearly all variables remain very stable when we re-estimate the model after deleting various independent variables from the model. Only the stalemate control variable and the *non-violent norms * stalemate* interaction term are affected when the other of these two terms is added or deleted from the model. Nevertheless, we stand by the decision to keep both terms in the model, since we are motivated by theoretical considerations to keep both in the model.

Table 7.14 *Multinomial logit results for Political Norms Model: hypotheses comparing regimes for Status Quo Stage*

Variable	Decision to initiate talks vs. maintain status quo			Decision to threaten force vs. maintain status quo			Decision to threaten force vs. initiate talks		
	Coefficient	z	p-value	Coefficient	z	p-value	Coefficient	z	p-value
Strength of nonviolent norms	.030	4.01	<.001	-.092	-7.47	<.001	-.121	-9.19	<.001
Nonviolent norms * military advantage	-.024	-2.91	<.025*	-.010	-.62	—	.013	.79	—
Nonviolent norms * stalemate	.023	1.43	<.10	-.028	-1.08	—	-.051	-1.92	<.05
Control for stalemate	.132	.61	—	.496	1.63	<.10	.363	1.13	—
INTERNATIONAL POLITICS MODEL									
Military balance	.325	2.04	<.025	1.43	4.94	<.001	1.11	3.05	<.01
Strategic value of territory	.167	2.49	<.01	.247	2.10	<.025	.080	.65	—
Common security interests	-.108	-1.73	<.05	-.522	-4.13	<.001	-.414	-3.14	<.001
Target other dispute involvement	-.013	-.20	—	.405	3.16	<.001	.419	3.03	<.01
Challenger other dispute involvement	-.067	-.90	—	.390	3.14	<.001*	.458	3.46	<.001*
Control for time since last challenge	-.007	-9.40	<.001	-.017	-5.54	<.001	-.010	-3.25	<.001

Hausman Test for IIA:
  Drop Talks: χ^2 .07 (11df), p = 1.00, do not reject IIA
  Drop Force: χ^2 −.40 (11df), do not reject IIA
Small–Hsiao Test for IIA:
  Drop Talks: χ^2 12.29 (11df), p = .34, do not reject IIA
  Drop Force: χ^2 6.88 (11df), p = .81, do not reject IIA
N = 6542
Log Likelihood = −4793.17
Note: * = Two-tailed test of significance (all other p-values based on one-tailed tests).

two operational indicators for nonviolent norms described in Chapter 5, we decided to employ the measure of the (in)frequency with which incumbent leaders resorted to violence against political opposition in their country over the past twenty years. This variable ranges in value from zero to twenty, with a score of zero indicating that political leaders resorted to violence for all twenty years and a score of twenty signifying that leaders were nonviolent for all twenty years.[23] In Table 7.15 we see that a change from highly repressive and violent norms (zero years of nonviolent behavior) to very peaceful norms of domestic conflict resolution (twenty years of nonviolent behavior) produces a 74 percent increase in the probability of proposing talks. On the other hand, this same change from highly violent norms to peaceful norms reduces the predicted probability of threatening force from 18 percent to less than 3 percent! These strong findings for nonviolent norms hold across a variety of model specifications.[24] Examples of disputes in which leaders with strong violent norms frequently initiated military confrontations include Argentina from 1951–82, Iraq from 1967–95, Saudi Arabia 1919–34, and Japan from 1919–45. In contrast, we find that no military confrontations are initiated when nonviolent norms are far stronger in Argentina during the period 1919–32 and when they re-emerge in the 1980s and 1990s. Interestingly, as violent norms become weaker among Saudi leaders in the post-World War II period there is a sharp drop in the number of military confrontations initiated compared to the pre-World War II period. Finally, another good

[23] It is important to note that this operational measure of norms is not highly correlated with our alternative measure of norms based on lagged values of *POLITY* net-democracy scores. The correlation between a *POLITY*-based, twenty-year lagged measure of democracy and our twenty-year lagged measure of nonviolent behavior is 0.43. While the two measures therefore tap somewhat different aspects of the concept of domestic political norms, they produce very similar results. When we substitute the *POLITY*-based twenty-year lagged measure of democracy into the equation all of the coefficients maintain the same signs and levels of statistical significance. It is also important to note that the lagged, violence-based measure of norms is not highly correlated with the Political Accountability Model measure of democracy, which is based on the current net-democracy score. The correlation between these two variables is only 0.38. The highest degree of correlation is between the *POLITY*-based, twenty-year lagged measure of democracy and the previously mentioned Accountability Model measure of democracy. Yet these measures are still distinct from one another, as the correlation is a moderately high 0.74. On the whole, then, the logit results for the Political Norms and Accountability Models reflect quite different operational measures and are clearly distinguishable from each other.

[24] Since we employ two interaction terms which also contain the *Strength of Nonviolent Norms* variable as a component term, the impact of nonviolent norms is channeled not only through the individual *Strength of Nonviolent Norms* term, but also through these two interaction terms. So we re-estimate the model by deleting these two interaction terms to examine the impact of the single nonviolent norms variable when it serves as the only measure of nonviolent norms in the equation. The coefficients on the *Strength of Nonviolent Norms* term retain the same signs and remain significant at the 0.001 level.

Table 7.15 *The impact of the nonviolent norms variable from the Political Norms Model on decisions to challenge the status quo*

I. Policy of initiating talks

Variable	(a) Initial probability	(b) Probability after change in variable	(c) Change in probabilities (b−a)	(d) Percentage change in probabilities (c/a)
Strength of nonviolent norms				
Change from 0 to 8 years	23.5%	30.7%	+7.2%	+30.6%
Change from 8 to 16 years	30.7%	37.6%	+6.9%	+22.5%
Change from 16 to 20 years	37.6%	40.9%	+3.3%	+8.8%
Total change from 0 to 20 years	23.5%	40.9%	+17.4%	+74.0%

II. Policy of threatening force

Variable	(a) Initial probability	(b) Probability after change in variable	(c) Change in probabilities (b−a)	(d) Percentage change in probabilities (c/a)
Strength of nonviolent norms				
Change from 0 to 8 years	18.0%	8.9%	−9.1%	−50.6%
Change from 8 to 16 years	8.9%	4.1%	−4.8%	−53.9%
Change from 16 to 20 years	4.1%	2.8%	−1.3%	−31.7%
Total change from 0 to 20 years	18.0%	2.8%	−15.2%	−84.4%

Note: The probabilities represent the predicted probability of a challenge to the territorial status quo by a call for negotiations or threat of force, respectively. The reported probabilities are calculated by holding each term in Table 7.14 constant while changing the value of the lagged government nonviolence term. Unless specified otherwise, the territory is of strategic value to both states, the military balance is 3:2 in favor of the target, and the previous challenge to the status quo occurred twenty-four months ago. All other variables are held at zero.

illustration is that of Peru. During the period 1919–31 nonviolent norms were fairly well established within the Peruvian political system and there were no cases of military confrontations being initiated in territorial disputes. As violent norms became stronger in the 1930s with more repressive regimes, five military confrontations were initiated from 1932–41.

Tests of the other two hypotheses produce more mixed results. We hypothesized that leaders with strong nonviolent norms would be less likely to respond to a stalemate in prior negotiations by turning to threats of force (**PN1ii**), and would not be tempted by a military advantage to resort frequently to military threats (**PN2**). In Table 7.14 we see some support for **PN1ii**. The coefficients for the *Nonviolent Norms * Stalemate* variable are all in the predicted direction, and two of the three coefficients (for the comparisons of initiating talks vs. status quo and threatening force vs. talks) are statistically significant. In Table 7.16 we see that leaders with strong nonviolent norms are nearly 55 percent more likely to respond to stalemates by continuing to seek further negotiations compared to leaders with very violent norms. On the other hand, leaders with strong nonviolent norms are 44 percent less likely to turn to military force to challenge a territorial claim.[25] While the results for **PN1ii** are generally supportive, the findings for **PN2** are weak, if not contradictory. We expected negative coefficients for the comparisons of the likelihood of threatening force compared to the remaining two options, but only one of the two coefficients is negative and it is not statistically significant. Furthermore, in Table 7.14 we see that leaders with strong nonviolent norms are actually less likely to initiate talks when their country enjoys a military advantage, which is the opposite of what we expected.[26]

Results for hypotheses that compare leaders among either democratic or non-democratic states

We report the results of this "within regimes" model in Table 7.17 and find support for both primary hypotheses. First, we find strong support for **PN4**. Among democratic states, the leaders of recently established democracies (within the last five years) are more likely to threaten force

---

[25] We test for the robustness of results by substituting into the equation alternative operational measures for the stalemate variable. We try two- and five-year lags for the recent stalemate variable instead of the one-year lag used in Table 7.14. The results are considerably weaker, with all of the coefficients becoming statistically insignificant at the 0.10 level (one-tailed).

[26] These results remain weak and insignificant when we substitute into the equation an alternative operational measure of military advantage in which the ratio of challenger to target capabilities is simply greater than 1:1 (as compared to our original threshold of a 2:1 advantage). Also, the contradictory finding reported in Table 7.14 that leaders with stronger democratic norms are less likely to seek talks is no longer supported by the results.

Table 7.16 *The impact of nonviolent norms on decisions to challenge the status quo when there has been a recent stalemate in talks*

I. Policy of initiating talks

Variable	(a) Initial probability	(b) Probability after change in variable	(c) Change in probabilities (b−a)	(d) Percentage change in probabilities (c/a)
Strength of nonviolent norms * stalemate				
Change from 0 to 8 years	23.4%	28.3%	+4.9%	+20.9%
Change from 8 to 16 years	37.0%	42.3%	+5.3%	+14.3%
Change from 16 to 20 years	49.9%	52.5%	+2.6%	+5.2%
Change from 0 to 20 years	23.4%	36.2%	+12.8%	+54.7%

II. Policy of threatening force

Variable	(a) Initial probability	(b) Probability after change in variable	(c) Change in probabilities (b−a)	(d) Percentage change in probabilities (c/a)
Strength of nonviolent norms * stalemate				
Change from 0 to 8 years	25.8%	20.7%	−5.1%	−19.8%
Change from 8 to 16 years	10.3%	7.8%	−2.5%	−24.3%
Change from 16 to 20 years	3.5%	3.0%	−.5%	−14.3%
Change from 0 to 20 years	25.8%	14.4%	−11.4%	−44.2%

Note: The probabilities represent the predicted probability of a challenge to the territorial status quo by a call for negotiations or threat of force, respectively. The reported probabilities are calculated by holding each term in Table 7.14 constant while changing the value of the *non-violent norms * stalemate* interaction term. The probabilities above represent solely the impact of nonviolent norms after a recent stalemate, and do not capture the impact of nonviolent norms in any other way. Unless specified otherwise, the territory is of strategic value to both states, the military balance is 3:2 in favor of the target, and the previous challenge to the status quo occurred twenty-four months ago. All other variables are held at zero.

Table 7.17 *Multinomial logit results for Political Norms Model: hypotheses comparing differences within regimes for Status Quo Stage*

Variable	Decision to initiate talks vs. maintain status quo			Decision to threaten force vs. maintain status quo			Decision to threaten force vs. initiate talks		
	Coefficient	z	p-value	Coefficient	z	p-value	Coefficient	z	p-value
Leaders in recently established democracies	.106	.77	—	.977	3.39	<.001	.870	2.96	<.01
Leaders with strongest violent norms	−.229	−3.22	<.01	.416	3.53	<.001	.646	5.12	<.001
Control for democratic status	.336	4.13	<.001	−.597	−2.72	<.01	−.933	−4.18	<.001
Control for nonviolent norms	−.061	−.80	—	−.994	−4.38	<.001	−.933	−4.04	<.001
INTERNATIONAL POLITICS MODEL									
Military balance	−.107	−.93	—	1.36	6.82	<.001	1.48	6.94	<.001
Strategic value of territory	.188	2.83	<.01	.273	2.33	<.01	.086	.69	—
Common security interests	−.114	−1.83	<.05	−.467	−3.70	<.001	−.353	−2.67	<.01
Target other dispute involvement	−.033	−.49	—	.377	2.97	<.01	.410	3.07	<.01
Challenger other dispute involvement	−.084	−1.13	—	.420	3.39	<.001 *	.504	3.80	<.001 *
Control for time since last challenge	−.007	−10.00	<.001	−.017	−6.13	<.001	−.009	−3.42	<.001

Hausman Test for IIA:
    Drop Talks: χ^2 −26.56 (11df), do not reject IIA
    Drop Force: χ^2 −.72 (11df), do not reject IIA
Small–Hsiao Test for IIA:
    Drop Talks: χ^2 11.90 (11df), p = .37, do not reject IIA
    Drop Force: χ^2 9.43 (11df), p = .58, do not reject IIA
N = 6542
Log Likelihood = −4792.28
Note: * = Two-tailed test of significance (all other p-values based on one–tailed tests).

Table 7.18 *The impact of the strong violent norms and recently established democracy variables from the Political Norms Model on decisions to challenge the status quo*

		I. Policy of initiating talks		
Variable	(a) Initial probability	(b) Probability after change in variable	(c) Change in probabilities (b−a)	(d) Percentage change in probabilities (c/a)
Leaders with strongest violent norms				
Change from 0 to 1	35.0%	28.9%	−6.1%	−17.4%

		II. Policy of threatening force		
Variable	(a) Initial probability	(b) Probability after change in variable	(c) Change in probabilities (b−a)	(d) Percentage change in probabilities (c/a)
Leaders from recently established democracies				
Change from 0 to 1	3.4%	8.2%	+4.8%	+141.2%
Leaders with strongest violent norms				
Change from 0 to 1	6.9%	10.9%	+4.0%	+58.0%

Note: The probabilities represent the predicted probability of a challenge to the territorial status quo by a call for negotiations or threat of force, respectively. The reported probabilities are calculated by holding each term in Table 7.17 constant while changing the values of a single term. The challenger democracy dummy variable is set at 0 for the comparison between a state with the strongest violent norms compared to a state with moderately violent norms. Conversely, the democracy dummy variable is set at 1 for the comparison between recently established democracies and long-standing democracies. Unless indicated otherwise, the territory is of strategic value to both states, the military balance is 3:2 in favor of the target, and the previous challenge to the status quo occurred twenty-four months ago. All other variables are held at zero.

vs. either maintaining the status quo or initiating talks than are leaders of long-standing democracies. The coefficients for both comparisons of the likelihood of force are positive and significant at the 0.01 level. In Table 7.18 we see that leaders of new democracies are more than twice as likely to threaten force than are leaders of older democracies, as the predicted probability of force rises from 3.4 percent to 8.2 percent.[27] In Table 7.19 we see that leaders in recently established democracies turn to military threats much more frequently than do leaders from established democracies. The ratio of military threats vs. calls for talks is less than 4:1 for new democratic leaders, but is 13:1 for established democracies. Good examples of leaders in recently established democracies threatening force include Somalia, Pakistan, Poland, and Syria, as listed in Table 7.19. For example, newly democratic Poland initiated a total of four military confrontations between 1919 and 1920, while Syria's transition to relatively democratic rule from 1955–61 was marked by five military confrontations initiated against Israel. For Pakistan we find that transitions to more democratic rule in the mid-1950s and early 1990s were associated with repeated military confrontations over bordering enclaves (1956–8), or along the disputed line of control in Kashmir (1990–2).

Second, among non-democratic challengers, those with the most violent norms are less likely to initiate talks vs. maintaining the status quo but are more likely to threaten force compared to either maintaining the status quo or initiating talks. The coefficients for all three of these policy choices are in the predicted direction, as hypothesized in **PN5**, and are significant at the 0.01 or 0.001 levels. The substantive effects of this variable are reported in Table 7.18. We see that non-democratic leaders with very violent domestic norms are 17 percent less likely to issue calls for negotiations, but are 58 percent more likely to threaten force. Strong supporting examples would include very high rates of military confrontations initiated by Argentina during the period 1958–82, Iraq from the late 1960s to early 1990s, Saudi Arabia in the 1920s and 1930s, and Syria from the mid-1960s to 1973.

Results for hypotheses that compare within and across dyads
Of the four dyadic norms hypotheses tested in this model, three receive solid support (see Table 7.20). In disputes where the leaders of both challenger and target share nonviolent norms we find that challengers are far less likely to turn to military threats in an attempt to overturn the status

---

[27] These results are not sensitive to the operational measure used to code how recently the country had become democratic. Instead of a five-year lag for "recent change" we also try two- and ten-year lags and the estimated results are very similar.

Table 7.19 *The diplomatic and military behavior of new and established democracies in the Challenge the Status Quo Stage*

	I. Policy of initiating talks			
	Number of observations	Number of rounds of talks	Number of military confrontations	Ratio of talks vs. military conflicts
Democratic within past 5 years	355	126	32	3.9:1
Democratic for more than 5 years	1142	390	30	13:1

II. Examples of new democracies threatening force

Recently established democratic challengers	Time period in which military confrontations initiated	Territorial adversaries
Somalia	1960–65	Ethiopia, Kenya
Ecuador	1981	Peru
Pakistan	1956–57, 1990–92	India
Czechoslovakia	1919	Hungary
Poland	1919–20	Lithuania, Soviet Russia
Syria	1955–59	Israel

Table 7.20 *Multinomial logit results for Political Norms Model: hypotheses comparing dyads for Status Quo Stage*

Variable	Decision to initiate talks vs. maintain status quo			Decision to threaten force vs. maintain status quo			Decision to threaten force vs. initiate talks		
	Coefficient	z	p-value	Coefficient	z	p-value	Coefficient	z	p-value
Dyads with strong nonviolent norms	-.312	-2.78	<.025*	-2.27	-4.24	<.001	-1.96	-3.62	<.001
Dyads of recently established democracies	.109	.52	—	1.08	2.14	<.025	.969	1.90	<.05
State in mixed dyad with strong violent norms	-.317	-3.25	<.001	.699	2.80	<.01	1.01	3.98	<.001
Dyads with strongest violent norms	-.182	-1.43	<.10	-.067	-.34	—	.115	.54	—
Control for current democratic dyad status	.469	4.51	<.001	-.838	-2.18	<.025	-1.31	-3.38	<.001
Control for mixed dyad	.218	2.50	<.01	-1.07	-4.67	<.001	-1.29	-5.51	<.001
INTERNATIONAL POLITICS MODEL									
Military balance	-.077	-.67	—	1.08	5.51	<.001	1.16	5.56	<.001
Strategic value of territory	.150	2.26	<.025	.351	2.98	<.01	.201	1.63	<.10
Common security interests	-.104	-1.67	<.05	-.493	-3.91	<.001	-.388	-2.95	<.001
Target other dispute involvement	-.024	-.36	—	.421	3.34	<.001	.445	3.36	<.001
Challenger other dispute involvement	-.085	-1.15	—	.460	3.76	<.001*	.545	4.18	<.001*
Control for time since last challenge	-.008	-10.35	<.001	-.016	-5.83	<.001	-.009	-3.08	<.001

Hausman Test for IIA:
  Drop Talks: χ^2 19.36 (13df), p = .11, do not reject IIA
  Drop Force: χ^2 −.10 (13df), do not reject IIA
Small–Hsiao Test for IIA:
  Drop Talks: χ^2 17.20 (13df), p =.19, do not reject IIA
  Drop Force: χ^2 18.45 (13df), p =.14, do not reject IIA

N = 6542

Log Likelihood = −4792.28

Note: * = Two-tailed test of significance (all other p-values based on one-tailed tests).

Table 7.21 *The impact of dyadic variables from the Political Norms Model on decisions to challenge the status quo by threatening force*

Variable	(a) Initial probability	(b) Probability after change in variable	(c) Change in probabilities (b−a)	(d) Percentage change in probabilities (c/a)
Dyad with strong nonviolent norms				
Change from 0 to 1	9.6%	.5%	−9.1%	−94.8%
Dyad of recently established democracies				
Change from 0 to 1	3.6%	9.5%	+5.9%	+163.9%
State in mixed dyad with strong violent norms				
Change from 0 to 1	3.2%	7.0%	+3.8%	+118.8%

Note: The probabilities represent the predicted probability of a challenge to the territorial status quo by a threat of force. The reported probabilities are calculated by holding each term in Table 7.20 constant while changing the values of a single term. The dyad with strong nonviolent norms is compared to a dyad with moderately violent norms. The recently democratic dyad (those with the weakest democratic norms) is compared to a long-standing democratic dyad (a dyad with strong democratic norms). The state with strong violent norms in a mixed dyad is compared to a state with nonviolent norms in a mixed dyad. Unless specified otherwise, the territory is of strategic value to both states, the military balance is 3:2 in favor of the target, and the previous challenge to the status quo occurred twenty-four months ago. All other variables are held at zero.

quo. As hypothesized in **PN6i**, the coefficients for the options of threatening force vs. either maintaining the status quo or initiating talks are negative and significant at the 0.001 level.[28] We see in Table 7.21 that the predicted probability of a military challenge to the territorial status quo is less than 1 percent for dyads with strong nonviolent norms. In contrast, dyads with moderately violent norms are nearly twenty times as likely to experience a military challenge! A number of disputes illustrate this pattern. For example, when Peru was a challenger in a non-democratic dyad it initiated military confrontations approximately 20 percent of the time (seven of thirty-six observations) but when it was a challenger in a democratic dyad it did not initiate any military confrontations (zero of thirteen observations). Similarly, when Italy was a challenger in a non-democratic dyad it initiated nine military confrontations but when it was a challenger in a democratic dyad it did not initiate any military confrontations. Finally, non-democratic Venezuela initiated three military conflicts against non-democratic Guyana between 1966 and 1981; however, when both countries become democratic from 1982–95 Venezuela did not threaten force once. The only puzzling finding for this variable is that challengers in these non-violent dyads are less likely to initiate talks as compared to accepting the status quo (Table 7.20).

[28] These results are very robust when we substitute into the equation the *POLITY*-based, twenty-year lagged measure of democratic norms.

Table 7.22 *The impact of dyadic variables from the Political Norms Model on decisions to challenge the status quo by initiating talks*

Variable	(a) Initial probability	(b) Probability after change in variable	(c) Change in probabilities (b−a)	(d) Percentage change in probabilities (c/a)
State in mixed dyad with strong violent norms				
Change from 0 to 1	40.4%	31.9%	−8.5%	−21.0%
Dyad with strongest violent norms				
Change from 0 to 1	33.0%	29.3%	−3.7%	−11.2%

Note: The probabilities represent the predicted probability of a challenge to the territorial status quo through a call for negotiations. The reported probabilities are calculated by holding each term in Table 7.20 constant while changing the value of a single term. The state with strong violent norms in a mixed dyad is compared to a state with nonviolent norms in a mixed dyad. The dyad with strong violent norms is compared to a dyad with moderately violent norms. Unless specified otherwise, the territory is of strategic value to both states, the military balance is 3:2 in favor of the target, and the previous challenge to the status quo occurred twenty-four months ago. All other variables are held at zero.

The second supported finding is that among democratic dyads, those involving recently established democracies are much more conflictual, as hypothesized in **PN6ii**. We see in Table 7.20 that leaders in such dyads are more likely to threaten force vs. either maintaining the status quo or initiating talks, and the substantive effects for this variable are very large. In Table 7.21 the results show that among democratic dyads with the weakest nonviolent norms there is an increase of over 160 percent in the likelihood of threatening force compared to democratic dyads with stronger nonviolent norms.[29]

In mixed dyads we hypothesized (**PN8**) that challengers with more violent norms should resort frequently to military threats and be less likely to rely on negotiations. The logit results are strongly supportive of this hypothesis, as all of the coefficients have the predicted signs and are significant at the 0.01 level. The state in a mixed dyad with stronger violent norms is more than twice as likely to threaten force than is the state with nonviolent norms (Table 7.21). Furthermore, this "non-democratic" state in a mixed dyad is 21 percent less likely to initiate talks as compared to the state with the more democratic or non-violent norms (Table 7.22). A number of disputes illustrate these general patterns. For example, in disputes where both sides were challengers to the status quo, the non-democratic party was far more likely to threaten force. In one

---

[29] These results are robust to changes in operational measures. We originally tested this variable in Table 7.20 with a measure of recently established democracies based on a five-year lag. When we substituted lags of two or ten years, the logit results are very similar to those reported in Table 7.20.

Table 7.23 *Multinomial logit results for Political Affinity Model: Status Quo Stage*

Variable	Decision to initiate talks vs. maintain status quo			Decision to threaten force vs. maintain status quo			Decision to threaten force vs. initiate talks		
	Coefficient	z	p-value	Coefficient	z	p-value	Coefficient	z	p-value
Political similarity	.266	2.57	<.025*	.870	3.83	<.001*	.604	2.57	<.025*
Recent change to political similarity	−.249	−1.66	<.05	.549	1.84	<.05	.798	2.59	<.01
Similarity * internal threat to challenger	.202	1.26	—	−.053	−.15	—	−.255	−.69	—
Control for internal threat to challenger	−.257	−3.79	<.001	−.316	−2.46	<.025*	−.059	−.43	—
Similarity * internal threat to target	.283	1.84	<.10*	−.160	−.50	—	−.440	−1.36	<.10
Control for internal threat to target	.120	1.71	<.10*	.539	4.30	<.001*	.419	3.17	<.01*
Dissimilarity * external threat to challenger	.099	1.12	—	1.14	7.69	<.001*	1.04	6.59	<.001*
Control for external threat to challenger	−.036	−.48	—	.601	3.78	<.001*	.637	3.87	<.001*
Dissimilarity * external threat to target	.194	2.02	<.025	.819	5.76	<.001	.625	4.02	<.001
Control for external threat to target	−.114	−1.69	<.10*	.724	5.18	<.001	.838	5.76	<.001
INTERNATIONAL POLITICS MODEL									
Military balance	−.014	−.11	—	1.31	5.62	<.001	1.32	5.35	<.001
Strategic value of territory	.165	2.50	<.01	.372	3.01	<.001	.207	1.60	<.10
Common security interests	−.122	−1.89	<.05	−.918	−6.93	<.001	−.796	−5.77	<.001
Target other dispute involvement	−.030	−.44	—	.458	3.51	<.001	.488	3.55	<.001
Challenger other dispute involvement	−.080	−1.08	—	.442	3.48	<.001*	.522	3.86	<.001*
Control for time since last challenge	−.007	−10.13	<.001	−.015	−5.62	<.001	−.007	−2.75	<.001

Hausman Test for IIA:
  Drop Talks: χ^2 2.18 (17df), p = 1.00, do not reject IIA
  Drop Force: χ^2 .11 (17df), p = 1.00, do not reject IIA
Small–Hsiao Test for IIA:
  Drop Talks: χ^2 8.60 (17df), p = .95, do not reject IIA
  Drop Force: χ^2 14.69 (17df), p = .62, do not reject IIA
N = 6542
Log Likelihood = −4792.28
Note: * = Two-tailed test of significance (all other p-values based on one-tailed tests).

notable case the Saudis initiated multiple military probes against the British in Kuwait, Jordan, and Iraq in the 1920s and 1930s, while the British did not initiate any military confrontations against the Saudis. Another example would be non-democratic Turkey initiating military confrontations along the borders of British controlled Iraq between 1922 and 1926 whereas the British did not initiate any such conflicts. Finally, non-democratic Peru initiated military confrontations in 1932 and 1934 against democratic Colombia, but Colombia did not threaten force over the disputed Leticia and Loreto regions.

The one hypothesis that did not receive much support from the logit results is **PN7**. We argued that the most conflict should be expected in territorial disputes in which strong violent norms are shared by the leaders of both states. The only partially supportive finding in Table 7.19 is that the coefficient for the decision to initiate talks vs. maintaining the status quo is negative and marginally significant. But the other two coefficients exhibit contradictory signs and are not statistically significant.

Results for the Political Affinity Model
Our final set of results are for tests of hypotheses derived from the Political Affinity Model. Compared to the other two domestic models, the results for the Affinity Model are much weaker. Only two of the six hypotheses tested are supported, while the remaining results are weak, inconclusive, or even contradictory to our expectations. Overall, the conclusion we draw is that there is only limited empirical support for the model.

We begin with the few positive results. There is empirical support for the hypothesis (**PAF1ii**) that among politically similar states conflict will be most frequent when such similarity has been established only recently (within the past five years). In Table 7.23 we see that all of the coefficients are in the predicted direction and are significant at the 0.05 level. These results indicate that leaders in situations of recent similarity with a territorial dispute adversary are more likely to threaten force when they challenge the status quo and to favor military threats over talks.[30] The substantive impact of this variable is quite large and is presented in Table 7.24. We see that a recent change to political similarity is associated with an 18 percent reduction in the probability of initiating talks and an 84 percent increase in the likelihood of a military threat. The other supportive finding is for hypothesis **PAF3ii**. In this hypothesis we argued that challengers would be more confrontational when their territorial dispute

---

[30] We check for the robustness of results by substituting alternative lags for determining how recently states had become politically similar. A ten-year lag produces very similar results but a lag of only three years produces much weaker results in which all of the coefficients are insignificant.

Table 7.24 *The Impact of variables from the Political Affinity Model on decisions to challenge the status quo*

	I. Policy of initiating talks			
	(a) Initial	(b) Probability after	(c) Change in	(d) Percentage change
Variable	probability	change in variable	probabilities (b−a)	in probabilities (c/a)
Recent change to political similarity				
Change from 0 to 1 40.3%		33.0%	−7.3%	−18.1%
Similarity * threat to target				
Change from 0 to 1 37.4%		44.5%	+7.1%	+19.0%
Dissimilarity * threat to target				
Change from 0 to 1 35.3%		40.3%	+4.9%	+13.8%
	I. Policy of threatening force			
	(a) Initial	(b) Probability after	(c) Change in	(d) Percentage change
Variable	probability	change in variable	probabilities (b−a)	in probabilities (c/a)
Recent change to political similarity				
Change from 0 to 1 5.5%		10.1%	+4.6%	+83.6%
Dissimilarity * threat to target				
Change from 0 to 1 11.3%		21.0%	+10.7%	+94.7%

Note: The probabilities represent the predicted probability of a challenge to the territorial status quo by a call for negotiations or threat of force, respectively. The reported probabilities are calculated by holding each term in Table 7.23 constant while changing the values of a single term. States which have recently become similar are compared to states which have been similar for more than five years. The probabilities for (dis)similarity in the presence of a threat to the target represent solely the impact of (dis)similarity when a threat to the target exists, and does not capture the impact of (dis)similarity more generally. Unless specified otherwise, the territory is of strategic value to both states, the military balance is 3:2 in favor of the target, and the previous challenge to the status quo occurred twenty-four months ago. All other variables are held at zero.

adversary was politically dissimilar and the adversary faced an external security threat from a state that was politically similar to the challenger. As expected, we see in Table 7.23 that the coefficients for the *Dissimilarity * External Threat to Target* variable are positive and statistically significant for all three comparisons. In fact, challengers in this situation are nearly twice as likely to challenge the status quo with a threat of force (see Table 7.24).

All of the remaining results in Table 7.23 either fail to support the hypotheses or seem to contradict our expectations. The most damaging result is for the general hypothesis of political affinity between states

(**PAF1i**), which is contradicted by the multinomial logit results. We expect to find that the coefficients for the decisions to threaten force vs. either maintaining the status quo or initiating talks would be negative and statistically significant. The actual results, however, are just the opposite. Political similarity is associated with challengers threatening force more frequently, and this finding is statistically significant at the .025 level (two-tailed).

Given these contradictory findings, we conduct some additional analyses in which we unpack the *Political Similarity* variable into a series of dummy variables for each affinity type (i.e. democratic, communist, military juntas, and monarchies). We then re-estimate the equations several times, including just one of the new dummy variables in each test. The results show that affinity between communist states and military juntas produce the contradictory findings of higher rates of military conflict, while affinity between monarchies produces insignificant results. Affinity between democratic states, however, is associated with a reduced risk of military threats. This final result is unsurprising, since we know already that similar results for a democratic dyad variable have been reported for the Political Accountability and Political Norms Models. The distinctive theoretical claim of **PAF1i** is that political similarity should be a general source of cooperative relations between all states and should therefore apply not only to democratic dyads, but also to other dyads composed of similar regime types. The contradictory findings for the *Political Similarity* variable in Table 7.23, therefore, constitute a powerful challenge to the underlying logic of the Political Affinity Model.

The other contradictory finding in Table 7.23 is for hypothesis **PAF3i**. We posited that challengers would be less confrontational when they faced an external security threat from a state that was politically similar to their territorial adversary (the challenger is thus dissimilar to both adversaries). The coefficients for the decisions to threaten force vs. either maintaining the status quo or initiating talks are expected to be negative and statistically significant. In Table 7.23, however, we see that these two coefficients are positive and significant at the 0.001 level. These results indicate, quite surprisingly, that challengers are more likely to be confrontational and threaten military force in such situations.

The final set of results in Table 7.23 are for hypotheses **PAF2i** and **PAF2ii**. The logic underlying these two hypotheses is that challengers should be more motivated to cooperate with politically similar territorial dispute adversaries when either they or their political ally faces domestic threats to their political security. The estimated results, however, are not very supportive. While all of the coefficients for the decisions to threaten force vs. either maintaining the status quo or initiating talks are negative (as expected), only one is significant at the 0.10 level.[31]

Conclusion

In this first empirical chapter we evaluated the power of four models to explain the decisions of leaders to initiate talks or threats of force in order to challenge the territorial status quo. We began with the International Politics Model and the statistical results were quite supportive of the hypotheses tested. In particular, this model was best at explaining decisions to threaten force, but was considerably less powerful in explaining the decision of state leaders to rely on talks and negotiations. The initial results for this model remained stable and robust once variables from the different domestic politics models were added to the equations tested. There is no question, then, that the international political-military setting figures centrally in decisions of challengers to initiate threats of force over disputed territory.

At the same time, two of the domestic politics models also provided additional explanatory insight into decisions by leaders to challenge the status quo by threats of force. Several hypotheses from both the Political Accountability and Political Norms Models were strongly supported and produced large substantive effects. We view these two domestic models as refining our understanding of why military confrontations emerge in several ways. First, the results of the Political Accountability Model indicate that the timing of military confrontations is linked to electoral cycles and that issues of self-determination for ethnic co-nationals are salient enough to democratic political leaders that the risks of military conflict will be accepted. The results of the Political Norms Models indicate that beliefs about the legitimacy of using force in settling domestic conflicts shapes the willingness of leaders to use force in international disputes. Leaders in stable and well-established democratic political systems are less inclined to initiate military threats and are disposed to favor negotiations over force as the approach to changing the territorial status quo. Finally, both of these domestic models provide evidence that the strategic calculations of challengers can change given an understanding of the domestic political conditions of its territorial adversary. The strong finding in both models that disputes between democratic states are far less likely to involve military confrontations and far more likely to involve frequent

---

[31] We substituted a measure of external threat in place of domestic threat to check for the robustness of results for each of these hypotheses. The logit results remained weak for **PAF2ii**. We even found contradictory results for **PAF2i**, which suggested that challengers might be more likely to threaten force in this situation.

negotiations supports the idea that democratic leaders have greater confidence in diplomacy and conflict resolution through negotiations when their opponent is also democratic. This channels disputes down a pathway of repeated talks and potentially towards a negotiated settlement.

This last point leads to what we view as the strongest contribution of the domestic models – their ability to explain why some territorial disputes follow the pathway of reliance on negotiations and potential conflict resolution through negotiated settlements. As we noted above, the results of the International Politics Model are quite powerful in explaining why disputes follow a pathway of military conflict. The limitation of this model, however, is that it cannot explain why the alternative choice of relying on negotiations is selected, or when leaders will shift policy and move towards negotiations following earlier military confrontations. The strength of the Accountability and Norms Models is that they not only help to explain why military confrontations emerge, but also tell us something about why state leaders sometimes pursue negotiations and refrain from using force as a means to pursue their territorial claims.

Another important conclusion we draw from the results of this chapter is that there are strong monadic effects associated with democracy. That is, even though we find strong support in both the Accountability and Norms Models for the conventional view that two democratic states are far less likely to become engulfed in military confrontations with each other, we also find equally strong evidence that democracies are less likely to turn to military force against all other types of adversaries, not just democratic opponents. The evidence on this question is strong and consistent across both the Accountability and Norms Models. We found no systematic evidence to support the conclusion that democratic states were generally as aggressive and confrontational as non-democratic states.

These findings do not contradict the empirical reality that democracies at times have been quite aggressive. As we argued in Chapters 4 and 5, and what we find strong evidence in support of in this chapter, is the conclusion that democratic norms and the greater accountability of democratic institutions generally make leaders of democracies less likely to turn to military force in disputes with other states. This is an important conclusion to draw about foreign policy behavior among democracies, but it should not be overstated either. Military force remains an option for foreign policy leaders in democratic countries and democratic leaders do choose that option in certain situations. What we think can be said with confidence about such decisions by democratic leaders is that they will be subjected to greater questioning as to their legitimacy and potential risks than would similar decisions made by non-democratic leaders.

Our final conclusion builds on this last point. The statistical results in this chapter are supportive of both the Political Accountability and Political Norms Models. It is difficult to argue that one model produces clearly stronger results than the other. The results of the next two chapters, then, will be central to determining whether on balance one model is more compelling. We do not believe that these two models need to be or should be viewed as incompatible with each other. One way of framing the results of this chapter is to argue that democratic leaders are influenced by normative beliefs to be less inclined to resort to threats as a way to seek policy goals in international disputes. This aversion to the aggressive use of force is often but not always reinforced by a sense of greater political risks associated with military conflicts. Put differently, political leaders can be influenced by normative beliefs about the role of diplomacy and force in international politics while remaining quite sensitive to the domestic political consequences of different foreign policy choices. Viewed in this way, the supportive results we find in this chapter for each of these models are not surprising. We do believe, however, that the empirical tests in the next two chapters will provide even more powerful results for evaluating these two models. The reason is that the analysis shifts to the outcomes of negotiations and military confrontations, and we believe that a focus on explaining these types of outcomes is a more demanding test of these models, since the decisions to concede territory or risk war with further military escalation are more consequential for state leaders.

8   Empirical results for decisions to offer concessions in negotiations

In this chapter we turn to the empirical analysis of decisions by leaders in both challenger and target states to offer concessions in negotiations over disputed territory. Our analysis of the Negotiations Stage in this chapter is designed to build on the initial decision of the challenger to seek talks in the Challenge the Status Quo Stage (Chapter 7). We now attempt to explain the *outcomes* of these diplomatic initiatives. As a result, in this chapter we take the cases from the Status Quo Stage in which the challenger proposed talks and use statistical analyses to test the ability of our four models to explain whether each state will offer territorial concessions during those rounds of negotiations.

We find that there are two general types of cases of "negotiations." The first type consists of those instances in which the challenger's initial call for talks leads to subsequent negotiations over a longer period of time. In the second case, however, the challenger's initiative does not lead to formal substantive talks, but the two parties do exchange proposals and discuss the possibility of opening up more extensive talks. Nevertheless, these initial talks quickly become stalemated at this preliminary stage of discussions. It is important to include this latter set of cases since they represent attempts to undertake more extensive negotiations, and the reasons why they do not advance beyond preliminary talks should be addressed by the theoretical models we are testing.

Estimation of the Negotiations Stage

Unlike the Challenge the Status Quo Stage, here we consider decisions made by both the challenger and the target. However, we do not analyze rounds of talks dyadically and do not attempt to code a "joint" level of concessions outcome for a pair of states. Instead, we code two separate outcomes to indicate the degree of concessions made by each state. This allows us to understand how particular variables affect the decision-making calculus of the leadership in each state. The task is to find a way to consider challenger and target decisions separately, while also incorporating the fact that the two states' decisions are interrelated (Smith 1999). The use of "directed-dyads" is one way to consider the behavior of two states in a dispute, yet a major drawback to this approach is that the two directional observations of the same dyad are not independent.[1] As a result, the disturbances across these two directional observations are likely to be correlated.[2]

We believe that a bivariate probit model provides a promising way to capture the interrelatedness of two separate state decisions while also attempting to maintain econometric assumptions.[3] The bivariate probit model estimates a separate set of results for both the challenger and target, yet incorporates the correlation between the disturbances of the two states' equations and provides an estimate of the magnitude of this relationship. The parameter rho (ρ), which ranges from -1 to 1, represents the estimated correlation of the errors between the two equations. A statistically significant and positive rho indicates that the unmeasured factors that affect the outcome of the challenger equation also affect the outcome of the target equation in a similar way. A statistically significant and negative rho, on the other hand, indicates that common unmeasured factors affect the outcomes of the two equations in an opposite manner. For most social science processes, a positive rho is more likely than a negative one.

Bivariate probit and related models are often used as a method for addressing concerns about non-random samples in which the researcher estimates a model for two potentially interrelated decisions *of the same actor* (Berinsky 1999; Reed 2000).[4] Yet bivariate probit works just as well, if not better, for modeling the related actions of two separate actors.[5] In our case we are able to examine the behavior of both challengers and targets

[1] See Bennett and Stam (2000) for a comparison of dyadic and directed-dyad estimates of the same model.

[2] By using directed-dyads, the researcher is in effect overstating the amount of new, independent information contained in the data set. The directed-dyad structure leads to a violation of the assumption that residuals are not correlated across observations. The stochastic part of the A vs. B observation is likely related to the stochastic component of the B vs. A observation. In other words, the important factors omitted from one directed-dyad observation are likely to be the same factors omitted from the other directed-dyad observation.

[3] See Greene (1997: 906–11) for a general discussion of bivariate probit and Smith (1999) for a specific discussion of bivariate models and the interrelatedness of state decisions.

[4] The rationale is that some final sample of interest might be non-random. For instance, an actor considers whether to initiate, take part, or participate in some action, yet at the same time is forward-looking and simultaneously considers how he plans to behave once he has "opted in" to some course of action. Thus any investigation of a final outcome must consider both a "selection" decision and an "outcome" decision.

[5] For example, Zorn (2002) utilizes bivariate probit to examine Department of Justice and Office of the Solicitor General decisions to appeal lower court decisions that have gone against the United States federal government.

during a round of negotiations. In this chapter, then, we estimate a series of bivariate probit models to explain decisions by leaders in challenger and target states to offer or withhold concessions in rounds of talks. One important point is that the analysis of outcomes of rounds of talks raises possible concerns with selection bias, since a challenger's decision to offer concessions could be linked to its initial decision to enter into negotiations. As a result, along with each bivariate probit model in this chapter we also estimate a Heckman or "censored" probit model for the challenger to examine whether factors that affect a challenger's decision to call for talks are linked to its subsequent decision regarding whether to make concessions (Heckman 1979).[6] In nearly all cases there is no clear evidence that a selection model is needed.[7] Nevertheless, we do note a few instances in which the impact of particular variables on challenger concession decisions is affected somewhat once we account for the impact of such variables on the "selection" equation. The censored probit model is somewhat limited because it only provides estimates for the behavior of the challenger. Nevertheless, we consider the challenger results to be more insightful, since the challenger is typically the driving force behind any territorial dispute activity while the target is often more reactive as opposed to proactive. We should note, however, that we view the results of the censored probit models with some skepticism, since they do not account for the interdependence between the challenger and target decisions.[8]

---

[6] Since the selection equation requires a dichotomous dependent variable, we are forced to modify the trichotomous dependent variable we use for the Challenge the Status Quo Stage in Chapter 7. We first assign a value of "1" to all observations in which the challenger initiates a round of talks. We then take all cases in which no challenge was made or in which a threat of military force was issued and assign a value of "0" to these two types of cases. While giving these two seemingly disparate outcomes the same value may seem strange, keep in mind that the primary purpose of the selection equation is to explain why the challenger initially chose to pursue negotiations over the other two options. We simply want to know what factors compel challengers to head down this road of diplomatic activity. Furthermore, the fact that the original trichotomous dependent variable is nominal (and not ordered) and that we meet the IIA assumption makes the decision to code the selection model equation dependent variable in this way a logical one.

[7] Similar to the bivariate probit, the Heckman probit model also provides an estimate (rho) of the correlation between the selection and outcome equations. For our purposes, the Heckman rho estimate indicates the degree to which the disturbances from the Challenge the Status Quo equation are correlated with the disturbances from the Negotiations Stage equation. Across the models in this chapter the estimated rho for these Heckman models varies tremendously, from very low levels in most cases up to levels approaching 0.6. However, in all cases this estimate of rho does not come close to approaching standard levels of statistical significance, which allays our fears about the need to systematically address concerns with selection bias.

[8] Ideally, we also would have liked to combine the bivariate probit model with a selection model that accounts for the decision of the challenger in the Status Quo Stage to seek negotiations. Unfortunately, such a statistical model is beyond current capabilities.

We should also note a final issue regarding the operationalization and estimation of the Negotiations Stage. Since conditions may change during the course of a lengthy round of negotiations and new information may be revealed during this period of time, the data used in the estimation of this period of interaction are drawn from the last month of each round of talks.[9] This serves to update any changes that might have occurred from the beginning of any negotiations until the final point at which concessions are or are not put on the table.

Results of statistical tests

In total, there are 1,528 rounds of negotiations in our data set of 348 territorial disputes from 1919–95.[10] The dependent variable for both challengers and targets is a dichotomous variable that indicates whether the leaders of each state make any type of concessions in a given round of talks over disputed territory. For operational purposes a state is considered to have made concessions if it offered either: (a) limited concessions, or (b) major concessions.[11] Nevertheless, the prevailing policy of both challengers and targets is to refrain from offering concessions in a given round of talks. Challengers offer concessions in 37 percent of the cases (568/1528), while targets offer concessions about 36 percent of the time (545/1528). In the empirical analyses, then, we are therefore particularly interested in whether each of the models tested can account for decisions by leaders to offer concessions.

This chapter is structured along lines similar to the previous chapter. We first present the statistical results for each of the four models tested, beginning with the International Politics Model and ending with the Political Affinity Model. For each model we present estimates of coefficients and their statistical significance. We also note the estimated rho for each model, which indicates the degree to which the challenger and target

---

[9] Recall that the data used to predict challenger decisions to challenge the status quo are taken from the beginning month of the round of talks, when the actual call for talks is first made.

[10] The number of observations for the Negotiations Stage is slightly lower than the corresponding number of calls for talks found in the Challenge the Status Quo Stage (Chapter 7) and in some tables presented earlier in the book (Chapter 2). This can be attributed to the fact that in some disputes both states have territorial claims and both can be considered challengers. From the available data it seems that in a small percentage of these dual-challenger disputes both sides brought forward initiatives to hold talks and therefore it was not possible simply to code one party as the initiator. However, in this chapter we cannot include both challenger cases in the data set, since in these instances we would be analyzing the same round of talks twice. For the Negotiations Stage analysis, then, one of these two observations is randomly dropped from the data set.

[11] See Chapter 2 for a discussion of how the outcomes of negotiations are conceptualized.

decisions are related. Across all models in this chapter the estimated rho ranges from 0.84 to 0.86 and is statistically significant in all cases. This provides strong evidence for the use of the bivariate probit model as opposed to the use of two separate, unrelated probit equations for each state.[12]

In our discussion of the results we once again devote particular attention to the substantive impact of variables. As a result, we follow a procedure similar to the previous chapter in which we present a series of additional tables that show what impact a variable has on the probability of a challenger or target offering concessions. The probabilities are generated by taking the probit coefficients reported in the equations and running simulations in which the values of all but one variable are held constant. The changes in the predicted probabilities allow us to assess what impact a change in a single variable has on the probability of leaders choosing to offer concessions. We conclude with a summary of the performance of each of the models tested and consider the implications for the literature on the democratic peace.

The results in this chapter indicate that the Political Accountability Model provides the most explanatory power for understanding state behavior in the Negotiations Stage. We also find supportive but not strong results for the Political Norms Model. Thus, while the Accountability and Norms Models both do well in explaining the initiation of talks, the Accountability Model is stronger in explaining when and why concessions are offered. We also find that the International Politics Model does poorly in explaining decisions to offer concessions, as does the Political Affinity Model. These overall results build on the findings of the previous chapter that domestic models which focus on institutional accountability and norms of political bargaining and conflict resolution are quite useful in understanding the choices of state leaders to pursue talks and to then offer concessions. One of the most important insights provided by the Accountability Model in this chapter centers on how the domestic political costs of concession-making often constrain democratic leaders to be quite tough and unyielding in international negotiations. On the other hand, the overall finding that the International Politics Model does not provide strong insights into the outcomes of negotiations is quite consistent with the results of the Status Quo Stage, where we found this model to fare quite poorly in explaining choices to pursue talks. We will see, however, in the next chapter, where the analysis shifts to the outcomes

[12] Nevertheless, we also estimate a pair of probit models for both the challenger and target as a robustness check. In most cases the results are relatively similar to the results generated by the bivariate probit models, but the degree of similarity varies considerably. However, due to the large and statistically significant rho found in the bivariate probit models we choose to focus exclusively on the bivariate probit results.

Table 8.1 *Bivariate probit results for International Politics Model:*
Negotiations Stage

Variable	Challenger decision to offer concessions			Target decision to offer concessions		
	Coefficient	z	p-value	Coefficient	z	p-value
Military balance	.718	5.41	<.001*	−.571	−4.31	<.001
Strategic value of territory	.035	.25	—	−.034	−.55	—
Common security interests	.196	2.45	<.01	.194	2.37	<.01
Target involvement in other military dispute	−.021	−.27	—	.103	1.34	<.10
Challenger involvement in other military dispute	−.064	−.75	—	.044	.52	—
Constant	−.622	−8.72	<.001*	−.076	−.80	—

	Estimate	Std Err	Test Statistic	p-value
Rho $\varepsilon_1\varepsilon_2$	.855	.016	χ^2 (1df) 431.35	.000

N = 1528
Log-Likelihood = −1644.02
Note: * = Two-tailed test of significance (all other tests are one-tailed unless indicated otherwise).

of military confrontations, that the International Politics Model is much more powerful in explaining leader choices than either the Accountability or Norms Models.

Results for the International Politics Model

The empirical results for the International Politics Model are reported in Table 8.1. Overall, the results are quite striking in that only one of the five hypotheses tested is clearly supported by the statistical findings. The general conclusion to draw from these results is that the International Politics Model provides only limited insights into the decisions of state leaders in the Negotiations Stage. As noted above, this set of results parallels what we found in our analysis of the Status Quo Stage in Chapter 7. There we found that the International Politics Model was powerful in explaining choices to threaten force, but was much weaker in explaining decisions to pursue talks. Given these prior results, it is not surprising that the International Politics Model is quite weak as an explanation for the outcomes of negotiations.

The strongest results are for hypothesis **IP1**, which posits that challengers and targets should be more likely to offer concessions when they share common security interests. In Table 8.1 we see that the coefficients for this variable are positive and highly significant for both the challenger and the target. In particular, when the challenger and target share a military alliance they are more likely to concede territory to each other.[13] In Tables 8.2 and 8.3 we see that a common alliance produces predicted increases of 20 percent and 22 percent in the probability of challengers and targets offering concessions.[14] For example, prior to World War II the Netherlands did not offer any concessions in negotiations with Belgium, a non-ally, over small enclaves along the border. After World War II both states became members of NATO and in the mid-to-late 1950s the Netherlands made a series of concessions to help settle its dispute with Belgium. Morocco refused to offer concessions to Spain in either its disputes over the Spanish Sahara (1956–75) or enclaves and offshore islands (1956–95), but was willing to offer concessions to Arab League allies such as Mauritania and Algeria in the 1960s and early 1970s.

Another finding that is partially supported is for the military balance variable. The intuitive hypothesis is that the greater the relative military strength of a state, the less likely its leaders would be to offer concessions in negotiations **(IP2)**. The results for the target in Table 8.1 provide strong support for this hypothesis, as the coefficient is negative and statistically significant as expected. Substantively, we see in Table 8.3 that as the target's military position changes from one of weakness (a ratio of 1:10) to one of clear advantage (a ratio of 10:1), the target becomes 39 percent less likely to offer territorial concessions. What is surprising, however, are the results for the challenger. We find that as challengers become stronger, they are *more* likely to offer concessions. The coefficient is positive and statistically significant, contrary to the predictions of **IP2**.[15] What may be contributing to this finding is that very strong challengers may offer concessions to weak adversaries in part because a great disparity in relative capabilities indicates that the security consequences of conceding territory are quite minimal. For example, in the data set we find China making concessions to Bhutan, Afghanistan, and Burma; the British conceding territory in Africa to Ethiopia and Portugal; and Saudi Arabia making concessions to Oman and Qatar.

---

[13] These results are robust when we consider possible selection effects that might bias the results for the challenger. When we run a Heckman selection model that accounts for the decision of the challenger to initiate talks, we still find that the alliance variable has a positive and significant impact on challenger decisions to offer concessions.

[14] We also substitute alternative measures for common security interests into the equation. We find that a common adversary in militarized disputes within the past five years produces positive and significant results for both states. However, the coefficient for the common territorial dispute adversary indicator, while positive, is not statistically significant for either the challenger or target.

[15] These surprising results are not due to problems of selection bias. We run a Heckman selection model for the challenger in which the decision to initiate talks is explicitly modeled and the coefficient for the military balance variable remains positive and statistically significant in the second equation for explaining concessions.

Table 8.2 *The impact of variables from the International Politics Model on challenger decisions to offer concessions*

Variable	(a) Initial probability	(b) Probability after change in variable	(c) Change in probabilities (b−a)	(d) Percentage change in probabilities (c/a)
Common security interests based on military alliance ties				
Change from 0 to 1	38.2%	45.9%	+7.7%	+20.2%

Note: The probabilities represent the marginal probability of challenger concessions, regardless of whether the target also offers concessions. The reported probabilities are calculated by holding each of the variables in Table 8.1 constant while changing the values of the military alliance variable. Unless specified otherwise, the territory is considered to be of strategic value to both states and the military balance is 3:2 in favor of the target. Meanwhile, common security ties, challenger involvement in another military dispute, and target involvement in another military dispute are held at zero.

Table 8.3 *The impact of variables from the International Politics Model on target decisions to offer concessions*

Variable	(a) Initial probability	(b) Probability after change in variable	(c) Change in probabilities (b−a)	(d) Percentage change in probabilities (c/a)
Military balance				
Change from 1:10 to 1:3	43.6%	40.1%	−3.5%	−8.0%
Change from 1:3 to 1:1	40.1%	34.7%	−5.4%	−13.5%
Change from 1:1 to 3:1	34.7%	29.5%	−5.2%	−14.9%
Change from 3:1 to 10:1	29.5%	26.5%	−3.0%	−10.1%
Total change from 1:10 to 10:1	43.6%	26.5%	−17.1%	−39.2%
Common security interests based on military alliance ties				
Change from 0 to 1	32.6%	39.8%	+7.2%	+22.1%
Target involvement in military dispute				
Change from 0 to 1	32.6%	36.4%	+3.8%	+11.7%

Note: The probabilities represent the marginal probability of target concessions, regardless of whether the challenger also offers concessions. The reported probabilities are calculated by holding each of the variables in Table 8.1 constant while changing the values of a single variable. Unless specified otherwise, the territory is considered to be of strategic value to both states, the military balance is 3:2 in favor of the target, and common security ties, challenger involvement in another military dispute, and target involvement in another military dispute are held at zero.

The remaining hypotheses from the International Politics Model generally are not supported by the results in Table 8.1. First of all, leaders in challenger and target states are not less likely to offer concessions in negotiations when disputed territory is of strategic value to each side (hypothesis **IP3**). We expected to find a negative relationship between strategic value of territory and concessions, but the somewhat contradictory coefficient estimates for the challenger and target are not statistically significant (z-scores of 0.25 and -0.55 respectively).[16] Finally, the involvement of either the challenger or target in militarized disputes with other states does not have any strong and consistent impact on negotiations, contrary to hypotheses **IP4i** and **IP4ii**. The only somewhat supportive finding is that targets are more likely to offer concessions when they are involved in other disputes, but the level of statistical significance is somewhat marginal ($p < 0.10$). In Table 8.3 we see that targets who are engaged in military conflicts with other states are only 12 percent more likely to offer concessions in territorial disputes.

We now turn to the statistical findings for each of the domestic-level models. As we explained in Chapter 7, we include the variables from the International Politics Model (as reported in Table 8.1) in each of the domestic politics model equations. In all of these subsequent equations, the findings for the International Politics Model remain stable and only the *Common Security Interests* and target *Military Balance* coefficient estimates are statistically significant. For the remainder of this chapter we do not discuss these consistent, but generally weak, results for the International Politics Model any further.

Results for Political Accountability Model

As we discussed in Chapter 7, we test the hypotheses from the Political Accountability Model (and Political Norms Model) in three stages that correspond to the logic of hypotheses derived from the model. We begin with findings for hypotheses that compare democratic and nondemocratic systems, and then we turn to results for hypotheses that compare within these two regime types and among dyads.

Overall, a number of hypotheses are supported by the bivariate probit results. It is also worth noting that the results are generally stronger for the challenger than for the target. Nevertheless, there is strong evidence that democratic leaders typically are more likely to offer concessions when the issues at stake in negotiations over disputed territory are not highly salient

---

[16] Similarly weak findings are produced when we substitute into the equation the alternative operational measure for the value of disputed territory, the economic importance of territory. The probit coefficients are positive but very insignificant, with z-statistics of 0.24 and 0.15 for the challenger and target, respectively.

or controversial to domestic audiences. However, democratic leaders are far less likely to offer concessions when they expect the domestic political costs of concessions to be high. There also seems to be an electoral cycle associated with democratic states in which the prospects for progress in talks are much greater shortly after elections, whereas stalemate in negotiations is more likely as elections approach. Furthermore, democratic leaders worry about the prospects for ratification of territorial treaties and thus are more likely to offer concessions when their ruling coalition controls a majority of seats in the legislature. Finally, there is clear evidence that in democratic dyads leaders of both states are more likely to offer concessions.

Results for hypotheses that compare leaders of democratic and non-democratic states

The results in Table 8.4 suggest a more complex pattern of negotiating behavior when comparing democratic and non-democratic leaders than is commonly found in the democratic peace literature.[17] First, we hypothesize in **PA1i** that democratic leaders should be more inclined to offer concessions in negotiations in the baseline case where the political costs are expected to be limited. We argue that given the greater aversion to the risks of military conflict for democratic leaders, they should prefer to rely on negotiations to settle disputes. At least for territorial dispute targets, the bivariate probit results provide strong support for this hypothesis about the propensity of democratic leaders to make concessions in negotiations.[18] The coefficient estimate for the *Target Level of Democracy*

---

[17] We find little evidence to be worried about multicollinearity among the independent variables in the model displayed in Table 8.4. We encounter a moderate yet acceptable auxiliary r-squared value of 0.54 when we regress the *challenger democracy * ethnic ties* interaction term on all remaining independent variables, but all other auxiliary r-squared values are less than 0.4. Furthermore, we also find no evidence to be worried about potential selection bias affecting the results for the challenger concession decision. The Heckman probit model, which incorporates the challenger's decision to call for talks into the analysis of the challenger's decision on whether to offer concessions, returns a rho of only 0.18, which is not statistically significant (p-value = 0.45). The signs and statistical significance of all Political Accountability Model variables of interest remain unaffected as well.

[18] Since the impact of target democracy (on the target decision to offer concessions) is channeled through the individual target *Level of Democracy* term, as well as through three interaction terms, we also re-estimate the model after we delete those three interaction terms. This allows us to ascertain the aggregate impact of target democracy simply by examining the new coefficient results for the target *Level of Democracy* term. Even after this re-estimation the target *Level of Democracy* variable retains its positive sign and is statistically significant near the 0.05 level. This strengthens our conclusion that, on the whole, democratic targets are more likely to offer concessions than are non-democratic targets. We do the same thing for the challenger net-democracy variable, but find no evidence to suggest that democratic challengers are more or less likely to offer concessions.

Table 8.4 *Bivariate probit results for the Political Accountability Model: hypotheses comparing regimes for the Negotiations Stage*

Variable	Challenger decision to offer concessions			Target decision to offer concessions		
	Coefficient	z	p-value	Coefficient	z	p-value
Challenger level of democracy	.004	.75	—	.023	4.03	<.001
Target level of democracy	-.003	-.40	—	-.014	-1.96	<.025
Democracy * stalemate	-.075	-1.11	—	.022	.31	—
Control for stalemate	-.010	-1.12	—	-.007	-.78	—
Democracy * enduring rivalry	-.342	-4.00	<.001	-.210	-2.43	<.01
Control for enduring rivalry	-.013	-1.85	<.05	-.012	-1.67	<.05
Democracy * ethnic ties	-.070	-1.21	—	-.021	-.35	—
Control for ethnic ties						
Target signal of resolve * target level of democracy	.012	2.47	<.01			
Target signal of resolve	.041	.54	—			
INTERNATIONAL POLITICS MODEL						
Military balance	.824	5.85	<.001*	-.751	-5.28	<.001
Strategic value of territory	.065	1.02	—	-.042	-.68	—
Common security interests	.168	2.08	<.025	.179	2.16	<.025
Target involvement in other military dispute	-.028	-.36	—	.077	.99	—
Challenger involvement in other military dispute	-.070	-.80	—	.036	.42	—
Constant	-.590	-5.66	<.001*	.064	.61	—
	Estimate	Std Err	Test Statistic	p-value		
Rho $\varepsilon_1\varepsilon_2$	.867	.020	χ^2 (1df) 273.78	.000		

N=1528

Log-Likelihood = -1620.22

Note: * = Two-tailed test of significance (all other tests are one-tailed unless indicated otherwise).

variable is positive and significant at the 0.001 level. In Table 8.6 we see that the change from a highly undemocratic leader to a highly democratic leader produces a 65 percent increase in the likelihood that concessions will be offered by the target. The coefficient for the *Challenger Level of Democracy* variable, however, is positive but not statistically significant. We therefore conclude that **PA1i** is only partially supported.

The remaining results in Table 8.4 make it clear, however, that once the domestic political costs of making concessions rise for leaders, then we should expect democratic leaders to be quite reluctant to offer concessions and potentially even less willing to concede than their non-democratic counterparts. In short, greater accountability can induce democratic leaders to be quite tough and intransigent in negotiations. For example, as argued in **PA2ii**, democratic leaders in both challenger and target states are indeed less likely to make concessions when disputed territory is populated by ethnic co-nationals. For both challenger and target states the coefficients on the *Democracy * Ethnic Ties* variables are negative and statistically significant, and the substantive effects are quite similar across the two states. In Tables 8.5 and 8.6 challengers and targets are 23 percent and 27 percent less likely to make concessions, respectively, when highly democratic leaders are negotiating to protect ethnic co-nationals in disputed territory. One example is the unwillingness of democratic Turkey and democratic Cyprus after 1974 to offer concessions to break the deadlock over Turkish control of northern Cyprus. Another example is Pakistani negotiating behavior with India over the disputed Kashmir region. While Pakistan has held twenty-three rounds of talks since 1949, it has only offered limited concessions on three occasions and in each case this was during a period of only semi-democratic rule (1952, 1955, and 1972). When talks have been held during the periods of strongest democratic rule in Pakistan (1958, 1989–90, 1993–5), no concessions have been offered in six rounds of talks.

A related finding is that democratic leaders, like their non-democratic counterparts, are less likely to make concessions when their adversary is an enduring rival (**PA2i**). The enduring rivalry control variable is negative and statistically significant (see Table 8.4), yet the interaction term for the variable *Democracy * Enduring Rivalry* is not statistically significant for either the challenger or target. This pair of results indicates that democratic leaders are equally as unlikely to offer concessions when negotiating with a long-term adversary. Finally, we argued in **PA1iii** that democratic leaders would be less likely to offer concessions in the more politicized context of negotiations that have failed in the past and ended in deadlock. The bivariate probit results for the target are strongly supportive. We find that the target coefficient for the variable *Democracy * Stalemate* is

Table 8.5 *The impact of the democracy and ethnic ties interaction term and the democracy signaling variable from the Political Accountability Model on challenger decisions to offer concessions*

Variable	(a) Initial probability	(b) Probability after change in variable	(c) Change in probabilities (b−a)	(d) Percentage change in probabilities (c/a)
The impact of democracy when there are ethnic ties with territory				
Change from −10 to −2	43.1%	39.0%	−4.1%	−9.5%
Change from −2 to 6	40.2%	36.3%	−3.9%	−9.7%
Change from 6 to 10	37.5%	35.5%	−2.0%	−5.3%
Change from −10 to 10	43.1%	33.2%	−9.9%	−23.0%
Signals of resolve sent by targets of varying democracy levels				
Change from −10 to −2	39.0%	42.7%	+3.7%	+9.5%
Change from −2 to 6	42.7%	46.4%	+3.7%	+8.7%
Change from 6 to 10	46.4%	48.3%	+1.9%	+4.1%
Total change from −10 to 10	39.0%	48.3%	+9.3%	+23.8%

Note: The probabilities represent the predicted probability of challenger concessions, regardless of whether the target also offers concessions. The reported probabilities are calculated by holding each of the variables in Table 8.4 constant while changing the values of a single term. The probabilities represent the impact of democracy solely when ethnic ties exist and when coupled with a signal of resolve, and do not measure the impact of democracy in any other way. The ethnic ties and signal of resolve dummy variables are set at one in order to test the impact of the two interaction terms. Unless specified otherwise, the territory is considered to be of strategic value to both states and the military balance is 3:2 in favor of the target. All other variables are held at their median values.

Table 8.6 *The impact of variables from the Political Accountability Model comparing across regimes on target decisions to offer concessions*

Variable	(a) Initial probability	(b) Probability after change in variable	(c) Change in probabilities (b–a)	(d) Percentage change in probabilities (c/a)
Target level of democracy				
Change from –10 to –2	25.5%	31.7%	+6.2%	+24.3%
Change from –2 to 6	31.7%	38.5%	+6.8%	+21.4%
Change from 6 to 10	38.5%	42.1%	+3.6%	+9.4%
Total change from –10 to 10	25.5%	42.1%	+16.6%	+65.1%
The impact of democracy when there are ethnic ties with territory				
Change from –10 to –2	28.9%	25.6%	–3.3%	–11.4%
Change from –2 to 6	31.9%	28.4%	–3.5%	–11.0%
Change from 6 to 10	35.0%	33.2%	–1.8%	–5.1%
Change from –10 to 10	28.9%	21.1%	–7.8%	–27.0%
The impact of democracy when there has been a recent stalemate				
Change from –10 to –2	31.0%	27.1%	–3.9%	–12.6%
Change from –2 to 6	33.5%	29.5%	–4.0%	–11.9%
Change from 6 to 10	36.2%	34.1%	–2.1%	–5.8%
Change from –10 to 10	31.0%	21.8%	–10.7%	–34.5%

Note: The probabilities represent the predicted probability of target concessions, regardless of whether the challenger also offers concessions. The reported probabilities are calculated by holding each of the variables in Table 8.4 constant while changing the values of a single term. The predicted probabilities associated with changes in the *democracy * ethnic ties* and *democracy * stalemate* interaction terms represent the impact of democracy solely when ethnic ties exist and after a stalemate, and do not measure the impact of democracy in any other way. The ethnic ties and stalemate dummy variables are set at one in order to test the impact of the two interaction terms, respectively. Unless specified otherwise, the territory is considered to be of strategic value to both states and the military balance is 3:2 in favor of the target. All other variables are held at their median values.

Table 8.7 *Bivariate probit results for the Political Accountability Model: hypotheses comparing differences within regimes for the Negotiations Stage*

Variable	Challenger decision to offer concessions			Target decision to offer concessions		
	Coefficient	z	p-value	Coefficient	z	p-value
Legislative support for challenger government	.012	3.09	<.001	.009	2.49	<.01
Legislative support for target government	−.001	−.39	—	.001	.30	—
Time since elections in challenger	−.007	−2.14	<.025	−.003	−.87	—
Time since elections in target	−.005	−1.68	<.05	−.003	−1.11	—
Secure non-democratic challenger	−.030	−.27	—	.158	1.39	<.10
Secure non-democratic target	.072	.49	—	.013	.09	—
Control for challenger democracy status	−.601	−2.32	<.01	−.329	−1.31	<.10
Control for target democracy status	.455	1.95	<.10*	.271	1.15	—
INTERNATIONAL POLITICS MODEL						
Military balance	.750	5.25	<.001*	−.618	−4.31	<.001
Strategic value of territory	.036	.57	—	−.012	−.19	—
Common security interests	.163	1.98	<.025	.229	2.77	<.01
Target involvement in other military dispute	−.131	−1.67	<.05	.033	.43	—
Challenger involvement in other military dispute	−.080	−.91	—	.084	.98	—
Constant	−.718	−3.97	<.001*	−.314	−1.71	<.10*

	Estimate	Std Err	Test Statistic	p-value
Rho $\varepsilon_1\varepsilon_2$	.859	.016	χ^2 (1df) 428.73	.000

N = 1528

Log-Likelihood = −1627.93

Note: * = Two-tailed test of significance (all other tests are one-tailed unless indicated otherwise).

negative and statistically significant at the 0.025 level. In Table 8.6 we see a nearly 35 percent reduction in the likelihood of democratic leaders of target states offering concessions when they are in negotiations following a recent stalemate in talks.[19]

The final result in Table 8.4 builds nicely on the above findings that once democratic leaders believe that there are domestic political risks associated with being accommodative, they shift to quite unyielding negotiating positions. In **PA1ii** we hypothesized that the greater potential audience costs for democratic leaders could make signals of their intentions to withhold concessions in negotiations more credible to their adversary. The results presented in Table 8.4 are supportive of this hypothesis. We see that the coefficient estimate for the interaction term *Target Signal of Resolve * Target Level of Democracy* is positive and statistically significant as expected. That is, challengers are more likely to offer concessions in negotiations when democratic targets signal early on in negotiations that they do not intend to offer concessions. We see in Table 8.5, in fact, that leaders are 24 percent more likely to make territorial concessions when a democratic territorial dispute adversary signals its initial unwillingness to make concessions as opposed to when such signals of intransigence are sent by very non-democratic leaders. A number of examples illustrate these findings. For example, China has held thirty-one rounds of talks in the post-World War II period in which adversaries signaled their intention to offer concessions. China did not offer concessions to any of the twenty-two non-democratic states that signaled their resolve (e.g. Vietnam, Soviet Union, and Nepal) but did offer concessions in six of nine cases involving democratic states signaling their resolve (Britain, India, and Japan). Another case is Yugoslavia, which offers concessions to seemingly resolved non-democratic targets such as Albania and Bulgaria in only one of seven rounds of talks. However, Yugoslavia offers concessions in eight of ten rounds of talks to resolved democratic adversaries including Austria, Greece, and Italy.

Results for hypotheses that draw comparisons among leaders
of democratic and non-democratic States
We begin by presenting results for hypotheses about differences in expected behavior among democratic state leaders and then discuss findings for non-democratic leaders.[20] The first finding in Table 8.7 is that leaders

---

[19] In the equation reported the stalemate variable was coded on the basis of a one-year lag but we also checked for two- and five-year lags with no important changes in the statistical results.

[20] We also estimate the model from Table 8.7 using a Heckman selection model. The results of the Heckman model indicate little reason to worry about selection bias broadly. The

Table 8.8 *The impact of the elections and secure leadership variables from the Political Accountability Model on challenger decisions to offer concessions*

Variable	(a) Initial probability	(b) Probability after change in variable	(c) Change in probabilities (b–a)	(d) Percentage change in probabilities (c/a)
Percentage of legislative seats held by ruling government in challenger				
Change from 40% to 50%	24.7%	28.6%	+3.9%	+14.6%
Change from 50% to 60%	28.6%	32.7%	+4.1%	+14.3%
Change from 60% to 70%	32.7%	37.1%	+4.4%	+13.4%
Change from 70% to 80%	37.1%	41.7%	+4.6%	+12.4%
Total change from 40% to 80%	24.7%	41.7%	+17.0%	+68.8%
Months since last election in challenger state				
Change from 3 to 12	36.3%	33.8%	−2.5%	−6.9%
Change from 12 to 30	33.8%	29.1%	−4.7%	−13.9%
Change from 30 to 48	29.1%	24.7%	−4.4%	−15.1%
Total change from 3 to 48	36.3%	24.7%	−11.6%	−32.0%
Months since last election in target state				
Change from 3 to 12	49.8%	48.1%	−1.7%	−3.4%
Change from 12 to 30	48.1%	44.9%	−3.2%	−6.6%
Change from 30 to 48	44.9%	41.7%	−3.2%	−7.1%
Total change from 3 to 48	49.8%	41.7%	−8.1%	−16.3%

Note: The probabilities represent the marginal probability of challenger concessions, regardless of whether the target also offers concessions. The reported probabilities are calculated by holding each of the variables in Table 8.7 constant while changing the values of a single variable. The baseline case is a democratic challenger state in which the ruling government holds 55% of legislative seats and in which an election was held twenty-four months ago. Unless specified otherwise, the territory is considered to be of strategic value to both states and the military balance is 3:2 in favor of the target. All other variables are held at their median values.

in challenger states are more willing to make concessions as their ruling coalition controls more seats in the legislature. The coefficient is positive and statistically significant as predicted by **PA3i**. Similarly, leaders in target states are more likely to offer concessions when the ruling coalition of democratic leaders in the challenger state controls more seats in the legislature, as hypothesized in **PA3ii**. According to Table 8.8, democratic leaders in challenger states are nearly 69 percent more likely to offer concessions when their ruling coalition in the legislature shifts from controlling 40 percent to 80 percent of the seats. For example, Ecuador does not offer any concessions to Peru in five rounds of talks held between 1982 and 1994, and during this period the ruling coalition in Ecuador controls a minority of legislative seats on four of five occasions (it holds a mere 54 percent in the other case). In contrast, during the period 1919–35 Belgian governments offer concessions in five rounds of talks in three different disputes, and in each case the governing coalition in Belgium controls over 90 percent of the seats in parliament.

Similarly, we see in Table 8.9 that target leaders are about 54 percent more likely to offer concessions to democratic presidents or prime ministers in challenger states when those democratic leaders are in a strong position to secure domestic support and ratification for any negotiated agreement.[21] The negotiating behavior of British territorial dispute adversaries provides a nice illustration of this pattern. Only on four occasions,

selection (Challenge the Status Quo Stage) and outcome (Negotiations Stage) equations are correlated only by a factor of 0.17, and the estimate of rho is not statistically significant ($p = 0.39$). However, we once again perform checks for multicollinearity and this time we find high auxiliary r-squared values in certain cases. In particular, we encounter auxiliary r-squared values of up to 0.91 when we regress the challenger (or target) democracy dummy variable or the challenger (or target) legislative support variable on the remaining independent variables. The multicollinearity is largely a result of the fact that the two measures which compare within democratic regimes (challenger [target] government legislative support and challenger [target] time since elections) are correlated both with one another, and with the democracy dummy variable. We re-run the model in two different ways. First, we estimate the model by dropping one of the two "within democracy" variables, either the challenger (target) legislative support variable or the challenger (target) time since election variable. Next, we conduct probit analysis first on just the democratic challengers (and then targets) and then on the non-democratic challengers (and then targets). In all cases our primary results from Table 8.7 – namely the impact of the challenger ruling coalition on both states' decisions and the impact of election timing in both states on the challenger decision – hold across these different specifications.

[21] We also run a Heckman selection model for the challenger in which the decision to initiate talks was explicitly modeled and the coefficient for the *Legislative Support for Challenger Government* variable remains positive and statistically significant in the second equation for explaining concessions. However, several alternative operational measures of opposition strength, such as minority government status and percentage seats controlled by the ruling party, are substituted into the equation and the results then become much weaker.

Table 8.9 *The impact of the elections and secure leadership variables from the Political Accountability Model on target decisions to offer concessions*

Variable	(a) Initial probability	(b) Probability after change in variable	(c) Change in probabilities (b–a)	(d) Percentage change in probabilities (c/a)
Percentage of legislative seats held by ruling government in target				
Change from 40% to 50%	23.4%	26.2%	+2.8%	+12.0%
Change from 50% to 60%	26.2%	29.4%	+3.2%	+12.2%
Change from 60% to 70%	29.4%	32.6%	+3.2%	+10.9%
Change from 70% to 80%	32.6%	36.0%	+3.4%	+10.4%
Total change from 40% to 80%	23.4%	36.0%	+12.6%	+53.8%
Secure non-democratic leader in challenger				
Change from 0 to 1	24.3%	29.5%	+5.2%	+21.4%

Note: The probabilities represent the marginal probability of target concessions, regardless of whether the challenger also offers concessions. The reported probabilities are calculated by holding each of the variables in Table 8.7 constant while changing the values of a single variable. The months since election variable is fixed at twenty-four months for the percentage seats held by the ruling government comparisons. Secure non-democratic challengers are compared to insecure non-democratic challengers. Unless specified otherwise, the territory is considered to be of strategic value to both states and the military balance is 3:2 in favor of the target. All other variables are held at their median values.

all in the 1920s and early 1930s, is there a minority government in power in Britain. Yet in all four rounds of talks the Labour-led government of Ramsay MacDonald is unable to secure concessions from the negotiating adversary. Taking this pattern a bit further, we see that British governments with slim majorities also find it difficult to secure concessions from a territorial dispute adversary. British governments with less than 60 percent of support in parliament have garnered concessions only 33 percent of the time (in seven of twenty-one rounds of talks). Meanwhile, British governments with strong majorities of 70 percent or more of the seats in parliament have secured concessions 68 percent of the time (seventeen of twenty-five rounds of talks).

While these are strong findings, challengers do not seem that sensitive to the legislative strength of the ruling government in the target (z-statistic $= -0.39$). Furthermore, democratic leaders in targets also are not influenced by the strength of ruling coalition support in their own legislature.[22] One possible interpretation of these findings is that democratic leaders in target states almost always expect to encounter domestic political opposition to concession-making since the status quo favors them. As a result, they are particularly concerned to only make concessions to democratic adversaries when they expect that their democratic counterpart can win the political battle at home for support of a negotiated agreement. Put differently, democratic leaders in target states do not want to put themselves through the political struggle of defending an agreement that contains concessions unless they are confident that their negotiating partner can reciprocate concessions and still survive politically when the controversial agreement is brought back home for approval and ratification.

The results in Table 8.7 also indicate that the timing of elections is quite important to democratic leaders in challenger states. For example, among democratic challengers there seems to be an electoral cycle in which leaders are more willing to make concessions in negotiations in periods shortly after national elections, but as time passes and new national elections approach, democratic leaders become more reluctant to make concessions (see **PA4i**). In Table 8.7 the challenger time since election variable is statistically significant as an explanation for the challenger's decisions to withhold making concessions to the target. The substantive

---

[22] Several alternative operational measures of opposition strength, such as minority government status and the percentage of seats controlled by the ruling party, are substituted into the equation, but the results remain weak. We also run a Heckman selection model for the challenger in which the decision to initiate talks is modeled explicitly. Nevertheless, the coefficient for the variable *Legislative Support for Target Government* remains insignificant in the second equation for explaining concessions.

effects for this variable are presented in Table 8.8, where we find that challengers are 32 percent more likely to offer concessions three months after their most recent election as compared to when the last national election was held four years ago. For example, the behavior of democratic Greece is quite instructive. Greece offers concession in talks with Italy in 1928, Bulgaria in 1947, and Cyprus in 1982, and in each case the negotiations had been initiated within three months after a Greek national election. The same pattern holds true for French concessions to the British in negotiations over the disputed borders of Middle East mandates in 1920. In each of three cases, French concessions followed negotiations that had been initiated within two to four months of the most recent national election.

The bivariate probit results also suggest that challengers pay attention to the electoral cycle of democratic targets, as hypothesized in **PA4ii**. In Table 8.7 we see that challengers are less likely to offer concessions over disputed territory as the democratic target moves closer to holding national elections. The coefficient for this variable is also negative and statistically significant. In Table 8.8 we find that as the time since the most recent election for the target increases there is a 16 percent reduction in the probability of a challenger offering concessions.[23] For example, Dutch concessions to Belgium in three of four cases in the 1950s are offered within twelve months of Belgian national elections. Also, Great Britain settles its dispute with France over the border between Syria and Iraq right after the French national election in 1932. In another series of talks, Egypt, in its dispute with Great Britain over military base rights, offers concessions in five different rounds of talks and in four cases these concessions were offered to British governments that had held elections within the last twelve months. Finally, China and Great Britain reach an agreement through mutual concessions in early 1984 to end the dispute over Hong Kong shortly after the victory of the Thatcher government in the British elections of 1983. Target decisions to offer concessions, however, do not seem to be linked to the timing of elections either in their own country, or in democratic challengers. While the coefficients are negative as expected in Table 8.7, they do not quite reach standard levels of statistical significance. In sum, while recent elections in either state do seem to increase the likelihood of concessions being made, the timing of elections seems to exert a considerably larger influence on the leaders of challenger states as opposed to the leaders of target states.

---

[23] These results are robust when we run a Heckman selection model for the challenger in which the decision to initiate talks is modeled explicitly. The coefficients for both the challenger and target election timing variables remain negative and statistically significant in the second equation for explaining concessions.

The final set of hypotheses tested focuses on non-democratic challengers and here the results are generally weak. There does not seem to be much difference between the negotiating behavior of politically secure non-democratic leaders and the negotiating behavior of politically insecure non-democratic leaders. We had expected that secure leaders would be more likely to make concessions (**PA5i**), but the bivariate probit coefficients for secure leaders in the challenger and target equations are not statistically significant. Furthermore, challengers are not more likely to offer concessions to politically secure non-democratic leaders in target states, as hypothesized in **PA5ii**. The one supportive finding, however, is that targets are more likely to offer concessions to secure non-democratic leaders in challenger states. The coefficient is positive and marginally significant ($p < 0.10$). In Table 8.9 we see that targets are 21 percent more likely to make concessions when negotiating with secure non-democratic challengers.

Results for hypotheses that compare across dyads
In this last section of results for the Political Accountability Model we look at hypotheses about democratic dyads and mixed dyads. In **PA6** we posit that in negotiations among democratic states we should expect both parties to offer concessions more frequently. The bivariate probit results in Table 8.10 support this hypothesis, as both challengers and targets in democratic dyads are more likely to offer concessions in negotiations over disputed territory. In Table 8.11 we see that challengers and targets in a democratic dyad are 17 percent and 30 percent more likely, respectively, to offer concessions than states in non-democratic dyads. For example, in the dispute between Honduras and El Salvador negotiations are infrequent and inconclusive during the period from 1919–83, when the two states are never jointly democratic. Once both states become more democratic in the mid-1980s talks are held frequently, with mutual concessions effectively ending the dispute in 1992. A similar pattern can be seen in the dispute between Argentina and Chile. Prior to the 1990s the two states were never jointly democratic and concessions in negotiations were rare. In the 1990s, however, four rounds of talks were held between the two democratic states and concessions were offered by one or both sides in all four rounds of talks.

The second dyadic result is for hypothesis **PA7ii**, which focuses on the behavior of states in mixed dyads. We find that non-democratic challengers in mixed dyads are considerably more likely to offer concessions in negotiations than are democratic challengers in mixed dyads (see Table 8.10). In fact, non-democratic challengers in these mixed dyad situations are over 38 percent more likely to make concessions than are

Table 8.10 *Bivariate probit results for Political Accountability Model: hypotheses comparing dyads for the Negotiations Stage*

Variable	Challenger decision to offer concessions			Target decision to offer concessions		
	Coefficient	z	p-value	Coefficient	z	p-value
Democratic dyad	.156	1.53	<.10	.246	2.42	<.01
Non-democratic state in mixed dyad	.319	2.83	<.01	-.333	-2.93	<.01*
Control for mixed dyad	-.127	-1.20	—	.196	2.31	<.025*
INTERNATIONAL POLITICS MODEL						
Military balance	.872	6.13	<.001*	-.733	-5.16	<.001
Strategic value of territory	.039	.61	—	-.030	-.49	—
Common security interests	.184	2.26	<.025	.182	2.21	<.025
Target involvement in other military dispute	-.055	-.70	—	.065	.85	—
Challenger involvement in other military dispute	-.072	-.84	—	.034	.40	—
Constant	-.737	-8.08	<.001*	-.046	-.45	—
	Estimate	Std Err	Test Statistic	p-value		
Rho $\varepsilon_1\varepsilon_2$	.854	.017	χ^2 (1df) 427.12	.000		

N = 1528

Log-Likelihood = −1636.20

Note: * = Two-tailed test of significance (all other tests are one-tailed unless indicated otherwise).

Table 8.11 *The impact of dyadic variables from the Political Accountability Model on challenger and target decisions to offer concessions*

	Probability of challenger concessions			
Variable	(a) Initial probability	(b) Probability after change in variable	(c) Change in probabilities (b–a)	(d) Percentage change in probabilities (c/a)
Democratic dyad				
Change from 0 to 1	36.3%	42.3%	+6.0%	+16.5%
Non-democratic state in mixed dyad				
Change from 0 to 1	31.6%	43.7%	+12.1%	+38.3%

	Probability of target concessions			
Variable	(a) Initial probability	(b) Probability after change in variable	(c) Change in probabilities (b–a)	(d) Percentage change in probabilities (c/a)
Democratic dyad				
Change from 0 to 1	30.3%	39.3%	+9.0%	+29.7%

Note: The probabilities represent the marginal probability of challenger and target concessions, respectively, regardless of whether the other state also offers concessions. The reported probabilities are calculated by holding each of the variables in Table 8.10 constant while changing the values of a single variable. The change to a democratic dyad represents a change from a jointly non-democratic dyad to a democratic dyad. The non-democratic state in a mixed dyad is compared to a democratic state in a mixed dyad. Unless specified otherwise, the territory is considered to be of strategic value to both states and the military balance is 3:2 in favor of the target. All other variables are held at their median values.

democratic challengers in mixed dyads. This finding is consistent with the earlier results we reported concerning the greater unwillingness of democratic leaders to offer concessions when the political costs for accommodative policies were high. Our argument for **PA7ii** is that oftentimes non-democratic leaders would have to take the initiative in negotiations with constrained democratic leaders by offering limited concessions in order to break a stalemate. This offer of concessions could then be used by democratic leaders to justify to their own domestic opposition the need to respond with concessions. However, when we look at target behavior we see that non-democratic targets in mixed dyads are less likely to offer concessions, contrary to **PA7ii**. Overall, then, the results for **PA7ii** are somewhat mixed, though we give greater weight to the findings for the challenger since we believe that concession-making in negotiations is driven largely by the initiatives of the challenger. This is because the target is generally reactive, as it will often respond to such offers of concessions but will rarely put concessions on the table before the challenger does.

These are interesting results that contrast somewhat with our findings in Chapter 7 that non-democratic states are consistently the more aggressive party when it comes to initiating military threats in mixed dyads. As we argued in Chapter 4, while democratic states should not be aggressive in threatening force against non-democratic states, we do expect that greater political accountability will often make democratic leaders more hesitant to offer concessions in negotiations. The results across Chapters 7 and 8 fit this pattern quite well.

Results for the Political Norms Model

The Political Norms Model produces much weaker results for the Negotiations Stage than it did for the Challenge the Status Quo Stage. In the previous chapter we found that strong nonviolent norms produced monadic as well as dyadic effects. Leaders with nonviolent domestic norms of political competition and conflict resolution were much more likely to rely on negotiations as opposed to military force to challenge the status quo. In addition, we found evidence of variation in diplomatic and military behavior among both democratic and non-democratic leaders. In this chapter, however, the statistical findings suggest that once leaders with stronger democratic norms enter into negotiations, their bargaining behavior does not differ in strong and systematic ways from that of non-democratic leaders (i.e. monadic-level effects are not that powerful). The strongest finding is that in disputes where challenger and target leaders share strong nonviolent norms both are more likely to offer concessions. We also find some evidence to suggest that concessions are less likely to be offered in disputes between two highly undemocratic states with violent norms.

Results for hypotheses that compare leaders with strong vs. weak nonviolent norms

We first test hypothesis **PN1i**, which posits that political leaders will be more likely to offer concessions in negotiations as nonviolent norms become more firmly established in political systems.[24] In Table 8.12 the coefficients for the *Strength of Nonviolent Norms* variable are in the predicted positive direction for both challengers and targets, yet the estimate is only marginally significant for the target ($p < 0.10$) and is insignificant for the challenger.[25] The substantive impact of the norms variable is reported in Table 8.13. As norms of nonviolent domestic political bargaining become stronger, target leaders are 23 percent more likely to offer territorial concessions.

While the bivariate probit results provide only modest support for **PN1i**, we are hesitant to conclude with confidence that the statistical evidence for this hypothesis is weak due to concerns with selection effects. When we re-run the analysis as a two-stage Heckman selection model – in which the challenger's decision to initiate talks is explicitly modeled along with the challenger's decision to offer concessions – we find stronger support for the proposition that strong nonviolent norms are associated with offering concessions.[26] In the Heckman model, the challenger nonviolent norms variable does have a positive impact on challenger concessions and is statistically significant at the 0.05 level. This is one of the very few instances in which the results of the bivariate probit model differ from those we obtain using a Heckman selection model. Due to these conflicting findings the conclusion we feel safer in drawing is that there may be monadic effects associated with democratic norms and offering concessions in negotiations, but they are not likely to be strong

[24] We test for levels of multicollinearity among all of the explanatory variables and find relatively high multicollinearity (between 0.85 and 0.90) when we perform auxillary regressions on the stalemate variable and the *nonviolent norms * stalemate* term. Nevertheless, the results contained in Table 8.12 remain robust under a variety of specifications, in particular when we delete the variables that seem to exhibit high multicollinearity.

[25] Similarly weak results are produced when we substitute into the equation the *POLITY*-based lagged measure of democratic norms.

[26] We do not, however, find evidence of selection bias broadly. The estimated rho of the Heckman model is -0.04, and the p-value for this estimate is 0.79. In other words, we only focus on possible selection bias as it might affect coefficient estimates for the nonviolent norms variable.

Table 8.12 *Bivariate probit results for the Political Norms Model: hypotheses comparing across regimes for the Negotiations Stage*

Variable	Challenger decision to offer concessions			Target decision to offer concessions		
	Coefficient	z	p-value	Coefficient	z	p-value
Strength of nonviolent norms	.006	.96	—	.009	1.41	<.10
Nonviolent norms * stalemate	.012	.74	—	.012	.67	—
Control for stalemate	-.322	-1.35	<.10	-.276	-1.02	—
INTERNATIONAL POLITICS MODEL						
Military balance	.702	5.25	<.001*	-.600	-4.41	<.001
Strategic value of territory	.041	.64	—	-.031	-.51	—
Common security interests	.199	2.44	<.01	.181	2.20	<.025
Target involvement in other military dispute	-.026	-.34	—	.092	1.20	—
Challenger involvement in other military dispute	-.057	-.66	—	.049	.57	—
Constant	-.668	-6.30	<.001*	-.166	-1.38	—
	Estimate	Std Err	Test Statistic	p-value		
Rho $\varepsilon_1\varepsilon_2$	.845	.018	χ^2 (1df) 403.76	.000		

N = 1528
Log-Likelihood = -1639.37
Note: * = Two-tailed test of significance (all other tests are one-tailed unless indicated otherwise).

Table 8.13 *The impact of nonviolent norms on target decisions to offer concessions*

	(a) Initial probability	(b) Probability after change in variable	(c) Change in probabilities (b–a)	(d) Percentage change in probabilities (c/a)
Variable				
Target strength of nonviolent norms				
Change from 0 to 8 years	28.9%	31.5%	+2.6%	+9.0%
Change from 8 to 16 years	31.5%	34.2%	+2.7%	+8.6%
Change from 16 to 20 years	34.2%	35.6%	+1.4%	+4.1%
Total change from 0 to 20 years	28.9%	35.6%	+6.7%	+23.2%

Note: The probabilities represent the marginal probability of target concessions, regardless of whether the challenger also offers concessions. The reported probabilities are calculated by holding each of the variables in Table 8.12 constant while changing the value of the twenty-year lagged nonviolence variable. The territory is considered to be of strategic value to both states and the military balance is 3:2 in favor of the target. All other variables are held at their median values.

given our mixed results.[27] This qualified conclusion contrasts somewhat with the findings in the Status Quo Stage, where leaders with strong nonviolent norms clearly favored negotiations as the approach to pursuing territorial claims. We believe that this pattern of results indicates that while nonviolent norms do influence leader choices to rely on negotiations and to consider concessions, the political costs of concessions, as highlighted by the Political Accountability Model, are salient enough to democratic negotiators that there is no strong pattern of them offering concessions more frequently than their non-democratic counterparts.

Next we examine the hypothesis that leaders with strong nonviolent norms should be more likely to respond to a stalemate in prior negotiations by offering limited concessions in subsequent rounds of talks as a way to try and break the deadlock (**PN1ii**). We find no support for this

[27] We also re-estimate this model by deleting the *nonviolent norms * stalemate* interaction term, thereby leaving the challenger (target) nonviolent norms term as the sole measure of nonviolent norms in the model. The results of this re-estimation provide a bit of further evidence in support of the claim that nonviolent norms are related to concessions. The challenger nonviolent norms variable now becomes positive and marginally significant (p-value = 0.103) and the target nonviolent norms variable remains positive and statistically significant (p < 0.05).

Table 8.14 *Bivariate probit results for the Political Norms Model: hypotheses comparing differences within regimes for the Negotiations Stage*

Variable	Challenger decision to offer concessions			Target decision to offer concessions		
	Coefficient	z	p-value	Coefficient	z	p-value
Leaders in recently established democracies	−.026	−.23	—	.200	2.03	<.05*
Leaders with strongest violent norms	−.043	−.68	—	−.007	−.10	—
Control for present democratic status	−.063	−.92	—	.027	.39	—
Control for nonviolent norms	.076	1.16	—	.089	1.38	<.10
INTERNATIONAL POLITICS MODEL						
Military balance	.732	5.48	<.001*	−.596	−4.30	<.001
Strategic value of territory	.047	.75	—	−.040	−.66	—
Common security interests	.203	2.50	<.01	.195	2.39	<.01
Target involvement in other military dispute	−.024	−.31	—	.089	1.15	—
Challenger involvement in other military dispute	−.063	−.74	—	.038	.45	—
Constant	−.620	−8.17	<.001*	−.112	−1.15	—
	Estimate	Std Err	Test Statistic			p-value
Rho $\varepsilon_1\varepsilon_2$	.855	.017	χ^2 (1 df) 422.52			.000

N = 1528

Log-Likelihood = −1638.01

Note: * = Two-tailed test of significance (all other tests are one-tailed unless indicated otherwise).

hypothesis, as the coefficients for the *Nonviolent Norms* * *Stalemate* term are insignificant in both the challenger and target equations (see Table 8.12).[28] Once again, the comparison with the earlier results in this chapter for the Political Accountability Model are instructive. For the Accountability Model, we argued that a prior stalemate is expected to increase the attention and controversy surrounding negotiations and should make democratic leaders less likely to offer concessions due to increased domestic audience costs. The empirical findings are much stronger in favor of this Accountability Model hypothesis. It seems as if domestic political constraints exert a conservative influence on democratic bargaining behavior; that is, they push leaders away from the granting of concessions when they are expected to be controversial.

Results for hypotheses that compare leaders among either democratic or non-democratic states

The results from tests of the two within regimes hypotheses are presented in Table 8.14, and we find little to no support for either of these hypotheses.[29] The first hypothesis tested is the argument that among democratic states, the leaders of recently established democracies should be less likely to offer concessions (**PN4**). However, in Table 8.14 we see that the challenger coefficient is negative but not statistically significant, while the coefficient for the target is actually positive and significant at the 0.05 level. The negotiating behavior for recently democratic targets, then, does not correspond to what was expected.[30]

The second hypothesis maintains that among non-democratic leaders, those with the most violent norms are less likely to offer concessions in negotiations over disputed territory (**PN5**). Once again, we expect to find negative coefficients for the indicators of strongest violent norms. But in Table 8.14 we see that while the coefficients are negative as expected, both the challenger and target estimates fail to reach standard levels of

---

[28] We test for the robustness of these results by substituting into the equations alternative lags for the stalemate variable (two and five years) and the findings remain weak and insignificant.

[29] We test for levels of multicollinearity among all of the explanatory variables in this model and find the auxillary r-squared values to be low, ranging from 0.15 to 0.47.

[30] These results for the challenger and target are not highly sensitive to the operational measure used to code how recently the country had become democratic. Alternative lags of two and ten years are also considered, but the results remain quite similar for the challenger. The target results hold when we use the two-year lag, but become insignificant when we employ a ten-year lag. We also find no difference in the challenger estimate for recently established democracies when we estimate a Heckman selection model.

Table 8.15 *Bivariate probit results for Political Norms Model: hypotheses comparing dyads for the Negotiations Stage*

Variable	Challenger decision to offer concessions			Target decision to offer concessions		
	Coefficient	z	p-value	Coefficient	z	p-value
Dyad with strong nonviolent norms	.293	2.41	<.01	.389	3.20	<.001
Dyad with recently established democracies	.279	1.33	—	.480	2.23	<.05*
State in mixed dyad with strong violent norms	-.083	-.76	—	-.003	-.03	—
Dyads with strongest violent norms	-.235	-1.60	<.10	-.178	-1.21	—
Control for current democratic dyad status	-.037	-.35	—	-.003	-.03	—
Control for mixed dyad	.101	1.03	—	.044	.50	—
INTERNATIONAL POLITICS MODEL						
Military balance	.738	5.42	<.001*	-.604	-4.46	<.001
Strategic value of territory	.036	.56	—	-.030	-.48	—
Common security interests	.200	2.47	<.01	.189	2.28	<.025
Target involvement in other military dispute	-.027	-.35	—	.090	1.16	—
Challenger involvement in other military dispute	-.070	-.81	—	.028	.33	—
Constant	-.667	-7.98	<.001*	-.109	-1.10	—
	Estimate	Std Err	Test Statistic	p-value		
Rho $\varepsilon_1 \varepsilon_2$	.854	.017	χ^2 (1df) 426.50	.000		

N = 1528
Log-Likelihood = −1632.40
Note: * = Two-tailed test of significance (all other tests are one-tailed unless indicated otherwise).

statistical significance.[31] In sum, the results for these two hypotheses that look for variation in behavior among democratic and non-democratic leaders are weak, with only very limited evidence of consistent and important differences in behavior.

Results for hypotheses that compare within and across dyads
We test four different dyadic hypotheses, but find strong support for only one of these hypotheses (see Table 8.15).[32] The lone supported hypothesis is **PN6i**, which maintains that concessions are more likely in disputes where the leaders of both states share nonviolent norms. The coefficients for the *Dyad with Strong Nonviolent Norms* variable are positive and significant at the 0.01 level for both challengers and targets (Table 8.15).[33] We see in Table 8.16 that dyads with nonviolent, democratic norms are associated with 31 percent and 48 percent increases in the predicted likelihood of challengers and targets offering concessions, respectively.

The second hypothesis maintains that among dyads with democratic norms, we should expect less frequent concessions by challenger and targets when both states have only recently become democratic (**PN6ii**). We expected to find negative coefficient results, but instead we find weak and even contradictory results. The signs on the coefficients for democratic dyads with the weakest norms are not only positive, but the target coefficient is statistically significant at the 0.05 level. The lack of support for **PN6ii** in the Negotiations Stage contrasts with our earlier findings for the Status Quo Stage, in which we find strong support for the claim that challenger leaders in recently established democratic dyads are more likely to threaten force to advance territorial claims.[34]

---

[31] These results for challenger and target are not sensitive to the operational measure used to code how strong violent norms are among non-democratic leaders. We substitute an alternative norms measure based on *POLITY* data and find no important differences. We also check for possible selection bias in the estimation of the challenger coefficient. This time the Heckman model does produce somewhat stronger results for the challenger in the equation for explaining concessions. The coefficient for strong violent norms is negative, as expected, and now reaches marginal levels of statistical significance ($p < 0.10$).

[32] Once again we examine the possibility for multicollinearity among the variables in this model (see Table 8.15), but find most auxiliary r-squared values to be below 0.2, with 0.54 being the highest value we find.

[33] These strong results are very robust when we check for selection bias with a Heckman model for the challenger. This dyadic result for the target, however, is not as robust when we substitute into the equation the *POLITY*-based measure of norms. While the challenger results are robust, the coefficient for the target remains positive but is no longer statistically significant.

[34] These weak results are not sensitive to changes in the operational measure for coding recently established democracies. We substituted a five-year lag for the original ten-year lag and obtained similar results. We did not try a two-year lag due to the lack of a sufficient number of cases.

Table 8.16 *The impact of dyadic variables from the Political Norms Model on challenger and target decisions to offer concessions*

		Probability of challenger concessions		
Variable	(a) Initial probability	(b) Probability after change in variable	(c) Change in probabilities (b–a)	(d) Percentage change in probabilities (c/a)
Dyad with strong nonviolent norms				
Change from 0 to 1	36.8%	48.3%	+11.5%	+31.2%
Dyad with strongest violent norms				
Change from 0 to 1	36.8%	28.4%	−8.4%	−22.8%

		Probability of target concessions		
Variable	(a) Initial probability	(b) Probability after change in variable	(c) Change in probabilities (b–a)	(d) Percentage change in probabilities (c/a)
Dyad with strong nonviolent norms				
Change from 0 to 1	30.8%	45.5%	+14.7%	+47.7%

Note: The probabilities represent the marginal probability of challenger and target concessions, respectively, regardless of whether the other state also offers concessions. The reported probabilities are calculated by holding each of the variables in Table 8.15 constant while changing the values of a single variable. The baseline dyad for all comparisons is a dyad with moderately violent norms. In all scenarios above the territory is considered to be of strategic value to both states and the military balance is 3:2 in favor of the target. All other variables are held at their median values.

Turning to mixed dyads, recall that we hypothesized (**PN8**) that leaders with violent, non-democratic norms should be less likely to offer concessions. Once again, our bivariate probit results provide no support for this hypothesis. The coefficients for the variable are negative as expected in both the challenger and target equations, but neither estimate is statistically significant. Once again, the weak findings here contrast with the much stronger results in the Status Quo Stage, where we found that non-democratic challengers in mixed dyads were more likely to threaten force and less likely to initiate talks. The final set of results is for hypothesis **PN7**. The hypothesis is that concessions should be least likely in territorial disputes in which both the challenger and target leaders hold very strong violent norms. We see in Table 8.15 that leaders in these violent-norms dyads are somewhat less likely to make concessions, but only the coefficient for the challenger is statistically significant.[35] Nevertheless, in Table 8.16 we see a 23 percent reduction in the probability of challenger concessions when both states are characterized by very violent norms.

Results for the Political Affinity Model

The final set of bivariate probit results is for the Political Affinity Model. As was the case for the Status Quo Stage, the Affinity Model provides a much weaker set of results for the Negotiations Stage than the other two domestic models, especially the Political Accountability Model. The bivariate probit results support only two of the six hypotheses in question.[36]

The first positive finding is for hypothesis **PAF1ii**. We argue that among politically similar states, we should expect fewer concessions when similarity had been established recently. In Table 8.17 we see that the challenger and target coefficients for this variable are negative and significant as expected.[37] The substantive impact of this recent change is reported in Tables 8.18 and 8.19. We find that a change to political similarity within the past five years is associated with 34 percent and 51 percent reductions

---

[35] The *POLITY*-based measure of norms produces somewhat different results. Using this measure of violent norms we once again obtain negative signs on the coefficients, but this time it is the target estimate that is statistically significant.

[36] We perform a series of auxiliary regressions and find little reason to be concerned with multicollinearity among the variables in Table 8.17. The highest r-squared value found in any of these regressions is 0.64. We also find little support for the existence of selection bias broadly. The estimated rho of the Heckman model is only 0.21, and this estimate is not statistically significant (p-value of 0.27).

[37] We check for the robustness of results by substituting alternative lags for determining how recently states had become politically similar. Three- and ten-year lags produce very similar results for both the challenger and target. In addition, these results are stable when we check for potential selection bias in the challenger equation with a Heckman model. The coefficient remains negative and significant.

Table 8.17 *Bivariate probit results for the Political Affinity Model: Negotiations Stage*

Variable	Challenger decision to offer concessions			Target decision to offer concessions		
	Coefficient	z	p-value	Coefficient	z	p-value
Political similarity	-.051	-.44	—	.084	.73	—
Recent change to similarity	-.346	-2.00	<.025	-.559	-3.18	<.001
Political similarity * external threat to challenger	.442	2.25	<.025	.327	1.67	<.05
Political similarity * external threat to target	.133	.71	—	-.025	-.14	—
Dissimilarity * external threat to challenger	-.053	-.46	—	-.101	-.86	—
Dissimilarity * external threat to target	.135	1.15	—	.081	.69	—
Control for challenger external threat	.061	.55	—	.026	.23	—
Control for target external threat	.012	.13	—	.009	.10	—
INTERNATIONAL POLITICS MODEL						
Military balance	.635	4.32	<.001*	-.472	-3.19	<.001
Strategic value of territory	.042	.66	—	-.033	-.52	—
Common security interests	.211	2.56	<.01	.212	2.52	<.01
Target involvement in other military dispute	-.016	-.21	—	.095	1.23	—
Challenger involvement in other military dispute	-.082	-.93	—	.048	.55	—
Constant	-.643	-6.97	<.001*	-.151	-1.27	—
	Estimate	Std Err	Test Statistic	p-value		
Rho $\varepsilon_1 \varepsilon_2$	.856	.017	χ^2 (1df) 425.94	.000		

N = 1528
Log-Likelihood = -1630.06
Note: * = Two-tailed test of significance (all other tests are one-tailed unless indicated otherwise).

in the predicted probability that challengers and targets, respectively, will offer concessions.

The second supportive finding is for hypotheses **PAF2i** and **PAF2ii**. The logic of this hypothesis is that states should be more likely to offer concessions to politically similar territorial dispute adversaries when they or their political ally are confronted with an external threat to their security. We see in Table 8.17 that both the challenger and target equation estimates of the *Political Similarity* * *External Threat to Challenger* term are positive and statistically significant, as expected. In Tables 8.18 and 8.19 we see that threatened challenger states are 45 percent more likely to offer concessions to politically similar target states, whereas targets are now 38 percent more likely to offer concessions to the leadership of these politically similar and vulnerable challenger states. However, the bivariate probit results are not fully supportive of these two hypotheses because similar results do not hold when the target state is facing an external threat. Neither the challenger nor the target estimate for the *Political Similarity* * *External Threat to Target* term is statistically significant. That is, challengers do not respond to the external threats facing the target by being more accommodative in negotiations, and leaders within target states do not offer concessions more frequently when they face external security threats.[38]

The remaining bivariate probit results do not lend support to the Political Affinity Model. As with the Status Quo Stage, the general hypothesis that political affinity between states should be associated with a higher likelihood of concessions (**PAF1i**) is not borne out by the empirical evidence. We expect all pairings of similar states to be more likely to offer concessions to one another, but this is not what we find. The coefficient on the political similarity variable actually has a negative sign in the challenger equation (but is not statistically significant). While the target coefficient has the correct sign, it too is not statistically significant. As we did in Chapter 7, we once again perform some additional analyses to determine whether the weak results for the affinity variable apply to each of the four similar regime types (democratic, communist, military juntas, and monarchies). These supplementary analyses are quite instructive. Only states in democratic dyads are more likely to offer concessions to one another, which is consistent with our findings earlier in this chapter in the context of the Accountability and Norms Models. In contrast,

---

[38] Selection bias does not seem to be a problem for this variable. The strong findings in Table 8.17 for the challenger remain stable when we run a Heckman probit model. However, we find that the results are much weaker – with all of the coefficients statistically insignificant across the challenger and target equations – when we substitute a measure of domestic threat in place of external threat to check for the robustness of results.

Table 8.18 *The impact of the recent change to similarity and similarity in the presence of an external threat terms from the Political Affinity Model on challenger decisions to offer concessions*

Variable	(a) Initial probability	(b) Probability after change in variable	(c) Change in probabilities (b–a)	(d) Percentage change in probabilities (c/a)
Change to political similarity within the past 5 years				
Change from 0 to 1	34.5%	22.9%	−11.6%	−33.6%
Political similarity when an external threat to challenger exists				
Change from 0 to 1	38.8%	56.2%	+17.4%	+44.8%

Note: The probabilities represent the marginal probability of challenger concessions, regardless of whether the target also offers concessions. The reported probabilities are calculated by examining the change in a single variable or interaction term in Table 8.17 while holding all other variables constant. The political similarity variable is held at one for both comparisons above. States which have become similar within the past five years are compared to states which have been similar for more than five years. The probabilities for similarity in the presence of a threat to the target represent solely the impact of similarity when a threat to the target exists, and do not capture the impact of similarity more generally. The territory is considered to be of strategic value to both states and the military balance is 3:2 in favor of the target. All other variables are held at their median values.

Table 8.19 *The impact of the recent change to similarity and similarity in the presence of an external threat to your adversary terms from the Political Affinity Model on target decisions to offer concessions*

Variable	(a) Initial probability	(b) Probability after change in variable	(c) Change in probabilities (b–a)	(d) Percentage change in probabilities (c/a)
Change to similarity within the past 5 years				
Change from 0 to 1	35.1%	17.3%	–17.8%	–50.7%
Political similarity when an external threat to challenger exists				
Change from 0 to 1	32.9%	45.4%	+12.5%	+38.0%

Note: The probabilities represent the marginal probability of target concessions, regardless of whether the challenger also offers concessions. The reported probabilities are calculated by examining the change in a single variable or interaction term in Table 8.17 while holding all other variables constant. States which have become similar within the past five years are compared to states which have been similar for more than five years. The probabilities for similarity in the presence of a threat to the target represent solely the impact of similarity when a threat to the target exists, and do not capture the impact of similarity more generally. In all cases the territory is considered to be of strategic value to both states and the military balance is 3:2 in favor of the target. All other variables are held at their median values.

communist states are less likely to offer concessions to one another, while no clear pattern emerges in negotiations among either military juntas or monarchies. As a result, we find no evidence that political similarity broadly makes states more likely to offer territorial concessions.

The final weak set of results is for hypotheses **PAF3i** and **PAF3ii**. For **PAF3i** we expect to find that both dissimilar challengers and targets will be more likely to make concessions when they face an outside threat and the state posing this external threat shares political affinity with its territorial dispute adversary. The coefficient for the *Dissimilarity * External Threat to Target* term does have a positive sign in the target equation, but this estimate is not statistically significant. The parallel estimate for the challenger (*Dissimilarity * External Threat to Challenger*), however, has a negative sign in the challenger equation and is not statistically significant. For hypothesis **PAF3ii** we posit that states should be less likely to offer concessions when a state with whom they are politically similar is posing an outside threat to their politically dissimilar territorial dispute adversary. In Table 8.17, however, the coefficients for the two relevant variables measuring dissimilarity and a threat to the adversary have mixed signs and neither is statistically significant at conventional levels (challenger z-statistic = 1.15, target z-statistic = −0.86).

Conclusion

In this second empirical chapter we tested how well each of the four models accounted for decisions by leaders to offer concessions in negotiations. The results for the International Politics Model were quite weak, which is consistent with the earlier results for this model in the Status Quo Stage. In Chapter 7 we found that international political-military variables were powerful in explaining decisions to threaten force, but were rather weak in explaining the decisions of state leaders to initiate talks. Across the Status Quo and Negotiations Stages, then, the International Politics Model does poorly at explaining: (a) why leaders in territorial disputes follow a nonviolent path of reliance on negotiations, and (b) when they are likely to seek peaceful settlements through concessions in negotiations. The Political Affinity Model also produced weak results, and this follows a pattern similar to what we observed for the Status Quo Stage. As a result, we conclude that the Affinity Model seems to offer few insights into the initiation or outcome of negotiations over disputed territory.

To understand when and why territorial concessions are offered by state leaders in negotiations we must turn to domestic-level models, particularly the Political Accountability Model. Five main findings emerge from the statistical tests for the Political Accountability Model. First, democratic leaders in challenger states are quite sensitive to electoral cycles and prefer to offer concessions in periods shortly after national elections have been held in their own country as well as in democratic targets. As elections approach, international negotiations are less likely to produce settlement agreements. Second, democratic leaders in challenger states are also keenly aware of the domestic politics of treaty ratification and therefore are unlikely to bring back home territorial agreements containing concessions unless they command strong party support in their legislature. Third, democratic leaders often avoid accommodation in negotiations because they are constrained by the expectation of domestic opposition to territorial concessions. Instead, these leaders count on the political payoffs associated with adopting hard-line bargaining positions. As a result, democratic politics can often serve to make compromise more difficult and prolong the period of time needed to negotiate the settlement of a territorial dispute. Fourth, target leaders are unlikely to put concessions on the table unless they are confident that their negotiating partner (democratic or non-democratic) is in a secure position politically to reciprocate with concessions and still survive the political battle at home over ratification of any negotiated agreement. Put differently, claims by challenger leaders that their hands are tied by strong domestic opposition do not induce concessions by targets. Instead, political strength and the freedom to prevail over domestic opposition are what targets look for in the political leadership of challenger states. Fifth, leaders of democratic states are more likely to offer concessions to other democratic leaders. As a result, one reason why democratic dyads avoid war with each other over disputed territory is because they are more likely to settle disputes through mutual concessions in negotiated agreements.

Meanwhile, the Political Norms Model is considerably weaker as an explanation for negotiation outcomes than it was as an explanation for Status Quo Stage decisions. The only clear finding in this chapter is that both sides seem to be more willing to offer concessions when the leaders of both states hold strong nonviolent democratic norms. Thus, as with the Accountability Model, there seems to be a strong democratic dyad effect associated with mutual concessions in negotiations. The remaining hypotheses for the Norms Model, however, were not strongly supported. We believe the primary reason for the weaker overall performance of the Norms Model is that this model does not capture the domestic political costs of concession-making for incumbents very well, particularly for democratic leaders. This is one of the strengths of the Political Accountability Model and that is why we think the Accountability Model performs much better in this chapter compared to the Norms Model.

One interesting finding in this chapter is that the monadic effects associated with democracy are much weaker than they were in the previous chapter. That is, in the Status Quo Stage we found strong evidence in both the Accountability and Norms Models that democracies in general were less likely to turn to military force and instead to favor negotiations in disputes with all adversaries, not just democracies. The evidence in this chapter, however, indicates that once they are engaged in talks the negotiating behavior of democratic states is not that different from that of their non-democratic counterparts. In both the Accountability and Norms Models there is only slight evidence to indicate that democratic leaders may be somewhat more likely to offer concessions. But once again, these monadic results are far weaker than those associated with the Status Quo Stage.

Our final conclusion is that the statistical results in this chapter are much more supportive of the Political Accountability Model when compared to the Political Norms Model. While we found it difficult to argue that one model produced clearly stronger results than the other for the Status Quo Stage, there is no such uncertainty when assessing the two models for the Negotiations Stage.

We now turn to the final empirical chapter in which we analyze the decisions of state leaders to escalate military confrontations to high levels and risk war. The decision to risk war over disputed territory is certainly one of the most consequential policy choices that political leaders can confront. For this very reason, the performance of each theoretical model in explaining military escalation is of central importance to our efforts to draw conclusions about the extent to which domestic and international conditions influence the foreign policy choices of state leaders.

9 Empirical results for decisions to escalate with military force

In this final empirical chapter we analyze the decisions of leaders in challenger and target states to risk war by escalating military confrontations in territorial disputes. The military confrontations we examine in this chapter are those initiated by the challenger either through threats of force, military movements and deployments, or the limited use of force in disputed territory (see Chapter 7). Once again, we test the hypotheses derived from our four models to determine which international politico-military and domestic political conditions influence policy choices in this Escalation Stage.

Estimation of the Escalation Stage

We estimate the Military Escalation Stage in a manner that parallels our estimation of the Negotiations Stage in Chapter 8. However, instead of explaining whether state leaders make concessions once they have entered into a round of talks, our focus now shifts to an examination of whether the challenger or target escalates the use of military force now that the two states are engaged in a military confrontation. We once again employ a bivariate probit model to examine the escalation decisions of both the challenger and the target.[1] As we discussed in the previous chapter, bivariate probit models take into account many of the strategic dynamics inherent to the Military Escalation Stage, yet still allow us to test separate sets of hypotheses for each of the two states embroiled in a militarized dispute. Furthermore, we find particularly strong evidence to justify the use of a bivariate model to test the Escalation Stage hypotheses. In this chapter our estimates of rho – the correlation across the disturbances of the challenger and target equations – range from approximately 0.92 to 0.95 and are statistically significant in all cases. Nevertheless, we also estimate a Heckman probit model along with each bivariate probit model to check

---

[1] See Chapter 8 for a discussion of bivariate probit and its applicability to these types of "joint" decisions in international relations.

for the robustness of challenger results.[2] The rationale behind checking our results through the use of the Heckman model is that the factors which affect whether challengers initiate military confrontations might also affect whether they ultimately escalate force in these confrontations. We simply want to make sure that our bivariate probit estimates (for the challenger) do not seem to be affected by selection bias. Finally, as was the case for the data used in the previous chapter, the data contained in the observations for the Escalation Stage analysis are taken from the last month of each militarized confrontation, when both states seemingly make some final decision about the level of escalation each is willing to employ.[3] Taking the data from the end of each militarized episode also captures the fact that conditions may have changed since the initial threat of force was made by the challenger and that new information might have been revealed to either or both parties during the course of the confrontation.

Results of statistical tests

The data set we analyze in this chapter consists of 374 military confrontations from 1919–95 that were initiated by challenger states.[4] The dependent variable for both challengers and targets is a dichotomous variable that indicates whether the leaders of each state escalate the initial military confrontation to: (a) high levels, in which either large-scale force is employed or mobilized for an attack, or (b) low or very limited levels of military escalation (see Chapter 2 for a discussion of how escalation levels are coded). For both parties the decision to risk war by engaging in high levels of escalation is relatively rare. Challengers escalate to high levels in

---

[2] Also see Chapter 8 for a more detailed discussion of the Heckman probit model.

[3] Recall once again that the data used in the Challenge the Status Quo Stage – to predict the initiation of force by the challenger – is taken from the initial month of each militarized confrontation, when the threat or initial mobilization of force first occurs.

[4] While there were 390 cases of challengers initiating military confrontations in the data set for the Status Quo Stage in Chapter 7, we now drop sixteen cases to avoid the double-counting of some confrontations. This is because there are sixteen instances in the Status Quo Stage – each of which stems from the relatively small number of disputes in which both sides are considered challengers – in which we code both sides as initiating military threats at the same time. We code these sixteen cases in this way due to the fact that available data did not allow us to determine with confidence whether one party clearly initiated military actions before the other. Instead, the data seem to indicate that both sides reached decisions to initiate threats of force at the same time. As a result, we code both states as initiators in these few cases. However, now that we are examining the outcomes of military confrontations, we need to drop one of these "dual challenge" cases for our Escalation Stage analysis so that we do not analyze these sixteen cases twice. Thus we randomly select one of the two cases for inclusion in the data set that we analyze in this chapter.

about 24 percent of the military confrontations (89/374), while targets escalate to such levels in an even lower 18 percent of cases (67/374). Mutual decisions to escalate to high levels occur in 40 cases in which a war is fought over disputed territory (see Table 1.3 in Chapter 1). Based upon these data, then, in the empirical analyses we are particularly interested in whether each of the four theoretical models can account for decisions by either state to escalate to high levels of force.

This chapter is organized similarly to the previous two empirical chapters. In the body of the chapter we report the statistical results for each of the four models tested, beginning once again with the International Politics Model and then covering each of the domestic politics models. In our discussion we continue to emphasize the substantive importance of the findings by presenting sets of predicted probabilities. We conclude the chapter with an overall assessment of the explanatory power of each model tested and relate this to the larger literature on the democratic peace.

The results in this chapter follow a clear pattern that builds on the results from the Status Quo and Negotiations Stages. Specifically, we find that the International Politics Model provides the most explanatory power for understanding escalation decisions. This finding parallels the conclusions drawn previously that this model provides considerable insight into the initiation of military confrontations, but is far less powerful in accounting for the initiation and outcome of negotiations. The results in this chapter for the Political Accountability and Norms Models are supportive, but not strongly so. This pattern of results is also consistent with our earlier findings for the Status Quo and Negotiations Stages. These two domestic models are best at explaining why disputes follow a pathway of negotiations and peaceful settlements, and at times provide valuable additional insights into the initiation and escalation of military confrontations.Finally,the results for the Political Affinity Model remain quite weak, as they have been for the previous two chapters. As a result, we conclude that this model is undoubtedly the weakest of our four models in accounting for overall patterns of diplomatic and military behavior in territorial disputes.

Results for the International Politics Model

The empirical results for the International Politics Model are reported in Table 9.1. The results are quite strong, and contrast sharply with the weak results reported for this model in the analysis of the Negotiations Stage in Chapter 8. In particular, the results in this chapter consistently support hypotheses about the escalation behavior of the challenger state,

Table 9.1 *Bivariate probit results for International Politics Model: Escalation Stage*

Variable	Challenger decision to escalate with force			Target decision to escalate with force		
	Coefficient	z	p-value	Coefficient	z	p-value
Military balance	.878	2.93	<.01	−.246	−.86	—
Local balance of forces advantage	.544	3.75	<.001	.092	.52	—
Strategic value of territory	.533	3.81	<.001	.331	2.43	<.01
Common security interests	−.407	−2.15	<.025	−.109	−.62	—
Target involvement in other military dispute	.376	2.22	<.025	.414	2.59	<.01*
Challenger involvement in other military dispute	.297	1.79	<.10*	.142	.87	—
Constant	−1.76	−8.68	<.001*	−1.13	−5.47	<.001*
	Estimate	Std Err	Test Statistic	p-value		
Rho $\varepsilon_1 \varepsilon_2$	.924	.027	$\chi^2(1\text{df})$ 75.71	.000		

N=374
Log-Likelihood = −260.90
Note: * = Two-tailed test of significance (all other tests are one-tailed unless indicated otherwise).

yet provide a weaker explanation for the escalatory behavior of the target. This pattern of stronger findings for the challenger is true of the bivariate results for all models across both this chapter and the previous chapter. As we argued in Chapter 8, we think this pattern largely reflects the fact that to a considerable extent targets follow a policy of reciprocating the diplomatic and military behavior of the challenger. As a result, many of the individual explanatory variables in the target equations do not produce strong results since the target's principle of strategic reciprocation is captured nicely in the bivariate analysis by the estimated rho parameter (which is large and statistically significant in all equations).

Of the six International Politics Model hypotheses tested, five receive clear support for the challenger while only two receive support for the target. For example, the balance of relative military strength is quite important in explaining challenger decisions to escalate, as posited in **IP2**. For the challenger, the coefficients for both the general military balance and local balances of forces variables are positive and statistically significant. In Table 9.2 we see that these two variables have powerful substantive effects. A shift in the general military balance from one of clear weakness to one of overwhelming advantage for the challenger produces a 165 percent increase in the probability of challenger escalation. Similarly, the challenger is nearly twice as likely to escalate to high levels of force if it enjoys an advantage in the local balance of forces (see Table 9.2).[5] A number of examples illustrate the importance of the local balance of forces. In the 1930s and the early stages of World War II, Germany, Italy, and the Soviet Union initiated and escalated a series of military confrontations to secure control of disputed territory and in almost every single case these three states enjoyed a sizeable advantage in the balance of local forces. For Germany the weak targets included Lithuania, Austria, Czechoslovakia, and Poland, while Italy escalated against weaker adversaries such as Ethiopia, Albania, and Greece. Meanwhile, the Soviets targeted the Baltic states, Romania, and Finland to annex territory lost after World War I and to secure military base positions in strategically located areas. Furthermore, China initiated a series of military probes and confrontations with India along their disputed border between 1955 and 1962 but

---

[5] An interesting finding is that the general balance of forces variable becomes much weaker when a Heckman selection model is estimated for the challenger. In the Heckman model the general balance of forces is a powerful variable in explaining whether challengers *initiate* threats, but the local balance of forces is what determines whether the challenger will escalate to high levels. This is a quite intuitive result since the local balance of forces is a more accurate measure of what capabilities challengers have mobilized and positioned for an attack whereas the general balance of forces variable better captures available potential military strength.

Table 9.2 *The impact of variables from the International Politics Model on challenger decisions to escalate with force*

Variable	(a) Initial probability	(b) Probability after change in variable	(c) Change in probabilities (b–a)	(d) Percentage change in probabilities (c/a)
Military balance				
Change from 1:10 to 1:3	12.6%	15.7%	+3.1%	+24.6%
Change from 1:3 to 1:1	15.7%	21.6%	+5.9%	+37.6%
Change from 1:1 to 3:1	21.6%	28.5%	+6.9%	+31.9%
Change from 3:1 to 10:1	28.5%	33.4%	+4.9%	+17.2%
Total Change from 1:10 to 10:1	12.6%	33.4%	+20.8%	+165.1%
Local balance of forces advantage	19.1%	37.1%	+18.0%	+94.2%
Change from 0 to 1				
Strategic value of territory	8.0%	19.1%	+11.1%	+138.8%
Change from 0 to 1				
Common security interests	19.1%	10.0%	−9.1%	−47.6%
Change from 0 to 1				
Target involvement in other military dispute	19.1%	30.9%	+10.8%	+56.5%
Change from 0 to 1				

Note: The probabilities represent the marginal probability of challenger escalation, regardless of whether the target also escalates. The reported probabilities are calculated by holding each of the variables in Table 9.1 constant while changing the values of a single variable. Unless specified otherwise, the territory is considered to be of strategic value to both states, the military balance is 3:2 in favor of the target, and common security ties, challenger involvement in another military dispute, and target involvement in another military dispute are held at zero.

did not escalate any of them to war until 1962 when it enjoyed a strong advantage in the local balances of forces.

Interestingly, these two variables measuring the local and general balance of forces are not statistically significant in the target equation. We would argue that these far weaker results reflect a two-fold pattern: (a) weak targets often respond with force to defend territory when attacked (e.g. Italy vs. Ethiopia in 1935 or the Soviet Union vs. Finland in 1939), and (b) strong targets rarely escalate to high levels if weaker challengers do not first escalate (Syrian border clashes with Israel in the 1950s and early 1960s or North Yemen and Saudi border incursions against British territories in the Persian Gulf in the 1920s and 1930s).

Another strong finding is that both challengers and targets are more likely to escalate military confrontations if disputed territory is of strategic value to their leaders. In Table 9.1 we see that the coefficients for both actors are positive and very statistically significant as hypothesized in **IP3**.[6] Furthermore, the substantive effects for this variable are considerable. According to the results in Tables 9.2 and 9.3, challengers and targets are 139 percent and 70 percent more likely to escalate to higher levels, respectively, when strategic territory is disputed. One way to illustrate these findings is to look at regional differences. For example, relatively few disputes in the Americas centered on strategically valuable territory and the percentage of military confrontations that escalated to high levels in this region was very low. In fact, in the Americas only about 8 percent of military conflicts escalated to such levels. In contrast, in the Middle East, Asia, and Europe a much greater percentage of the disputes centered on territory with strategic value and the escalation of military confrontations to high levels was therefore much more frequent. In the Middle East and Asia, 20 percent and 24 percent of military confrontations escalated to high levels of force, respectively, while in Europe 50 percent of military conflicts escalated.

A third supportive finding in Table 9.1 is that when the challenger shares common security ties (a common territorial dispute adversary) with the target, the challenger is less likely to escalate to high levels. As predicted by **IP1**, the coefficient for this variable is negative and significant at the 0.025 level. In Table 9.2 we see that the likelihood of challenger escalation in this case drops by nearly half, from just over 19 percent to 10 percent. China, for example, only escalated to high levels in one of fourteen confrontations when it shared a common adversary with

---

[6] Similar, but slightly less strong, findings are produced when we substitute into the equation the alternative operational measure for the value of disputed territory, the economic importance of territory. In this case the bivariate probit coefficients are positive and significant for both challenger ($p < 0.05$) and target ($p < 0.10$).

Table 9.3 *The impact of variables from the International Politics Model on target decisions to escalate with force*

Variable	(a) Initial probability	(b) Probability after change in variable	(c) Change in probabilities (b–a)	(d) Percentage change in probabilities (c/a)
Strategic value of territory Change from 0 to 1	10.1%	17.2%	+7.1%	+70.3%

Note: The probabilities represent the marginal probability of target escalation, regardless of whether the challenger also escalates. The reported probabilities are calculated by holding each of the variables in Table 9.1 constant while changing value of territory variable. The military balance is 3:2 in favor of the target, and common security ties, challenger involvement in another military dispute, and target involvement in another military dispute are held at zero.

its territorial dispute opponent, and Iraq did not escalate a single military confrontation to high levels when it shared a common adversary with its opponent in the current military crisis. Similarly, Iran did not escalate military confrontations against Iraq in the 1950s and early 1960s when they shared a common adversary but did escalate to high levels in late 1960s and early 1970s when they no longer shared a common adversary.

Nevertheless, target decisions to escalate do not seem to be systematically influenced by common security ties. The coefficient for the target is negative, but is not statistically significant (z-statistic $= -0.62$).[7] The final supportive finding is that challengers take advantage of the target's involvement in militarized disputes with other states to escalate to higher levels against the target, as hypothesized in **IP4ii**. In Table 9.1 the coefficient for this variable is positive and statistically significant, and a change in this variable produces a nearly 58 percent increase in the probability of challenger escalation according to the results of Table 9.2. Overall, these supportive results for the challenger are highly consistent with the statistical results for the International Politics Model in the Status Quo Stage. The same set of variables seems to explain both the decision to initiate force, as well as the decision to escalate force.[8]

The only weak results are for the hypothesis that states should be less likely to escalate if they are currently involved in another militarized dispute. Instead, the probit results indicate that challengers and targets are *more* likely to escalate despite their involvement in other military confrontations, contrary to hypothesis **IP4i**. The coefficients are positive and strongly significant for the target (p < 0.01), and marginally so for the challenger (p < 0.10). A similar finding is reported for the challenger in the analysis of the Status Quo Stage in Chapter 7. There we argued that what might explain this unexpected finding is that challengers who did

---

[7] When we substitute alternative measures for common security interests into the equation, we find that a common adversary in militarized disputes within the past two or five years produces significant results for the target. The coefficient for the common military alliance indicator, while negative, is not significant for either the challenger or target.

[8] These bivariate results for the military balance, strategic value of territory, common security interests, and target dispute involvement remain fairly robust when we consider possible selection effects that might bias the results for the challenger. We run a Heckman selection model that accounts for the decision of the challenger to initiate a military threat in the Status Quo Stage and find that the common security ties and general balance of forces variables weaken somewhat in terms of statistical significance in the escalation equation (the local balance of forces remains very significant, as does the strategic value of territory). This may be due to the fact that both the common security ties and general balance of forces variables produce very strong results in the selection equation (i.e. the Challenge the Status Quo Stage). As a result, the direct impact of these two variables on escalation outcomes may be reduced, since the strong effect for these variables is associated strongly with the challenger's choice at the initial stage regarding whether or not to threaten force in the Challenge the Status Quo Stage.

Table 9.4 Bivariate probit results for Political Accountability Model: hypotheses comparing regimes for the Escalation Stage

Variable	Challenger decision to escalate with force			Target decision to escalate with force		
	Coefficient	z	p-value	Coefficient	z	p-value
Challenger level of democracy	-.004	-.26	—	.006	.33	—
Target level of democracy				-.008	-.43	—
Democracy * stalemate	-.030	-1.31	-.10	-.421	-2.63	<.01*
Control for stalemate	-.418	-2.18	<.05*	-.016	-1.14	—
Democracy * enduring rivalry	-.000	-.03	—	.233	1.47	<.10
Control for enduring rivalry	.106	.62	—	.005	.32	—
Democracy * ethnic ties	-.014	-.77	—	.053	.43	—
Control for ethnic ties	.400	2.80	<.01	-.026	-1.60	<.10
Democracy * military risk	.010	.47	—	.066	.29	—
Control for military risk	-.141	-.71	—			
Target signal of resolve * target democracy level	-.036	-2.62	<.01			
Target signal of resolve	-.052	-.44	—			
INTERNATIONAL POLITICS MODEL						
Military balance	.931	3.09	<.001	-.062	-.14	—
Local balance of forces advantage	.440	3.05	<.01	.026	.14	—
Strategic value of territory	.559	3.77	<.001	.334	2.36	<.01
Common security interests	-.432	-2.35	<.025	-.128	-.73	—
Target involvement in other military dispute	.300	1.78	<.05	.360	2.22	<.05*
Challenger involvement in other military dispute	.351	2.14	<.025*	.135	.82	—
Constant	-1.92	-7.24	<.001*	-1.24	-5.38	<.001*
	Estimate	Std Err	Test Statistic	p-value		
Rho $\varepsilon_1 \varepsilon_2$	.956	.021	χ^2(1df) 61.56	.000		

N = 374

Log-Likelihood = −243.06

Note: * = Two-tailed test of significance (all other tests are one-tailed unless indicated otherwise).

threaten force often did so against weaker territorial adversaries and, as a result, the potential for becoming engulfed in a second military conflict that would require large numbers of forces was not that great. This same line of reasoning might also help to explain why challengers and targets might escalate to higher levels despite involvement in other militarized disputes.[9]

We now turn to the statistical findings for each of the domestic-level models. We follow the same procedure we used in Chapters 7 and 8 and include the variables from the International Politics Model (as reported in Table 9.1) in all of the domestic model equations. In all of the subsequent equations the findings for the International Politics Model remain very stable. Therefore we do not address these consistent results when analyzing the new findings for each of the domestic models.

Results for the Political Accountability Model

The overall conclusion we reach is that the bivariate probit results provide only moderate support for the hypotheses derived from the Political Accountability Model. The strongest finding is that escalation to high levels is very unlikely among democratic dyads. This result converges with the conventional wisdom in the democratic peace literature that democracies rarely, if ever, go to war against each other. On the other hand, the results in this chapter indicate that the monadic-level impact of democracy on military escalation is much weaker. These monadic-level findings on escalation contrast with our results in Chapter 7, where we found that democracy had a very strong monadic effect associated with reducing the probability that states would initiate military threats. What we find in this chapter is that once democratic leaders find themselves in military confrontations they are often neither more nor less likely to escalate than non-democratic leaders. That is, once democratic states are involved in a militarized dispute, they are no longer averse to the use of force.

Results for hypotheses that compare leaders of democratic and non-democratic states

There are three findings in Table 9.4 that support hypotheses about the decisions of challenger states to escalate military confrontations and two

---

[9] These surprising results for the challenger also may be related to problems of selection bias. We run a Heckman selection model for the challenger in which the initial decision to threaten force is also modeled (along with the challenger's escalation decision) and the coefficient for the challenger other dispute involvement variable is positive but not statistically significant (z-statistic $= 0.96$) in the second equation for explaining escalation levels.

findings that support hypothesized target behavior. Otherwise the bivariate probit results are quite weak for both states.[10] One of the strongest results for challengers is that when democratic leaders in target states signal their resolve to use force early on in a military confrontation, challengers are less likely to escalate to high levels. The coefficient for the *Target Signal of Resolve* * *Target Democracy* interaction term is negative, as hypothesized in **PA1ii**, and is statistically significant at the 0.01 level. This finding supports the argument that the higher domestic costs of retreating in a military crisis for democratic leaders can bolster the credibility of deterrent threats that they issue (e.g. Fearon 1994b; Gelpi and Griesdorf 2001; Schultz 2001a).[11] In Table 9.5 we see that when we compare the deterrent impact of signals sent by highly non-democratic vs. highly democratic leaders, we find that challengers are much less likely to escalate against democratic adversaries who signal a willingness to escalate to higher levels. In fact, democratic governments who send signals of resolve are three times less likely to be the target of further escalation than are non-democratic governments who send such signals. In this situation target democracy reduces the predicted probability of challenger escalation from 25 percent to just over 8 percent. If we look at the case evidence more closely the same patterns are quite evident. For example, there were 43 military confrontations in which the leaders of highly democratic target states (+10 on the *POLITY* scale) signaled resolve and in only five cases did the challenger escalate (about 12 percent of cases). A nice example is that when Argentina undertook limited naval military actions near the Falkland Islands in 1948 and 1976 the British countered with warnings and naval actions and no further escalation took place. However, in 1982 threatening military actions by Argentina did not prompt a strong deterrent signal from the British and this time Argentina did launch an attack to seize the islands. In contrast, there were

[10] We perform a series of regressions to check for the presence of multicollinearity among all of the explanatory variables. We obtain our highest auxiliary r-squared value of 0.73 when we regress the challenger democracy term on all other variables in the challenger model. Nevertheless, a series of additional checks indicate that multicollinearity does not pose a serious problem for the model in Table 9.4. All other auxiliary regressions return r-squared values below 0.55. Furthermore, we also run a Heckman probit model to check for the broad presence of selection effects in the Escalation Game model reported in Table 9.4. The resulting rho from this Heckman model is -0.55, but this estimate is not statistically significant at conventional levels.

[11] These results are robust when we check for problems of selection bias. This time we run a Heckman selection model for the challenger in which we explicitly model whether challengers are likely to initiate threats of force against democratic targets. Even after accounting for this selection decision, the coefficient on the *Target Signal of Resolve* * *Target Democracy* term remains negative and statistically significant in the second equation for explaining levels of escalation.

87 military confrontations in which the leaders of very authoritarian regimes (-3 to -9 on the Polity scale) signaled resolve, but challengers nevertheless escalated to high levels in a much larger 44 percent of the cases (38/87).

The second supportive finding for challengers is that compared to their non-democratic counterparts, democratic leaders are less likely to escalate to high levels in the context of a prior stalemate in recent talks. The coefficient for the *Democracy * Stalemate* term is negative and marginally significant (z-statistic $= -1.31$, $p < 0.10$). This finding supports the argument of hypothesis **PA1iii** that democratic leaders are generally more wary of turning to military force to secure territorial claims following the failure of recent negotiations given the greater domestic political risks associated with war. In Table 9.5 we find that highly democratic states are less than one-third as likely (4.8 percent vs. 14.5 percent) to escalate with force in response to a prior stalemate in negotiations than are highly non-democratic states.

The next supportive finding applies to both the challenger and target. For hypothesis **PA2i** we argued that democratic leaders should be like their non-democratic counterparts in their willingness to escalate military conflicts to high levels when their territorial adversary is an enduring rival. As a result, the *Democracy * Enduring Rivalry* interaction term is expected to be insignificant for both the challenger and target. This is indeed what we find in Table 9.4. The results indicate that democratic leaders are not systematically different in their escalatory behavior towards enduring rivals. Furthermore, there is only partial support for our logic concerning the propensity of all states to escalate against an enduring rival. The coefficient on the enduring rivalry dummy variable, while positive for both challengers and targets, is only (marginally) statistically significant for the target ($p < 0.10$). As a result, while democracies are no different from non-democracies in the context of enduring rivalry, states in general do not seem to escalate force against enduring rivals as frequently as we had expected.

The final relatively supportive finding in Table 9.4 is that democratic leaders in target states are more hesitant to escalate to high levels when the balance of military forces is unfavorable, as hypothesized in **PA1i**. The coefficient for the *Democracy * Military Risk* interaction term is negative and of marginal significance ($p < 0.10$) in the target equation. The substantive effects for this variable, however, are quite large. In Table 9.6 we see that democracies are less than half as likely to escalate under conditions of military risk. The predicted probability of a democracy escalating in this case drops from over 25 percent (for a very non-democratic state) to just under 12 percent (for a very democratic state).

Table 9.5 *The impact of the democracy and stalemate and democracy and signal of resolve interaction terms from the Political Accountability Model on challenger decisions to escalate with force*

Variable	(a) Initial probability	(b) Probability after change in variable	(c) Change in probabilities (b–a)	(d) Percentage change in probabilities (c/a)
The impact of democracy when there has been a recent stalemate				
Change from −10 to −2	14.5%	9.7%	−4.8%	−33.1%
Change from −2 to 6	9.1%	5.8%	−3.3%	−36.3%
Change from 6 to 10	5.4%	4.2%	−1.2%	−22.2%
Change from −10 to 10	14.5%	4.8%	−9.7%	−66.9%
Signals of resolve sent by targets of varying democracy levels				
Change from −10 to −2	25.2%	17.0%	−8.2%	−32.5%
Change from −2 to 6	17.0%	10.7%	−6.3%	−37.1%
Change from 6 to 10	10.7%	8.3%	−2.4%	−22.4%
Change from −10 to 10	25.2%	8.3%	−16.9%	−67.1%

Note: The probabilities represent the marginal probability of challenger escalation, regardless of whether the target also escalates. The reported probabilities are calculated by holding each of the variables in Table 9.4 constant while changing the values of a single term. The probabilities represent the impact of democracy solely after a recent stalemate and when coupled with a signal of resolve, and do not measure the impact of democracy in any other way. The stalemate and signal of resolve dummy variables are set at one in order to test the impact of the two interaction terms. Unless specified otherwise, the territory is considered to be of strategic value to both states and the military balance is 3:2 in favor of the target. The challenger and target net-democracy scores are set to −2 and 0, respectively. All other variables are held at their median values.

Table 9.6 *The impact of the democracy and military risk interaction term from the Political Accountability Model on target decisions to escalate with force*

Variable	(a) Initial probability	(b) Probability after change in variable	(c) Change in probabilities (b–a)	(d) Percentage change in probabilities (c/a)
The impact of democracy under conditions of military risk				
Change from −10 to −2	25.1%	19.0%	−6.1%	−24.3%
Change from −2 to 6	20.2%	14.9%	−5.3%	−26.2%
Change from 6 to 10	16.0%	13.6%	−2.4%	−15.0%
Change from −10 to 10	25.1%	11.8%	−13.3%	−53.0%

Note: The probabilities represent the marginal probability of target escalation, regardless of whether the challenger also escalates. The reported probabilities are calculated by holding each of the variables in Table 9.4 constant while changing the value of the *democracy * military risk* term. The impact of the *democracy* * *military risk* interaction term represents solely the impact of democracy under conditions of military risk, and does not capture the impact of democracy in any other way. In all scenarios the military risk parent variable is set at 1. Unless specified otherwise, the territory is considered to be of strategic value to both states and the military balance is 3:2 in favor of the target. The challenger and target net democracy scores are set to −2 and 0 respectively. All other variables are held at their median values.

The remaining results in Table 9.4 do not lend much support to the hypotheses tested. For example, the broad monadic-level hypothesis (**PA1i**) that democratic leaders should generally be more cautious in escalating to high levels is not consistently supported. While there is some limited evidence that democracies are less likely to escalate after recent stalemates or in situations of military uncertainty, for both the challenger and target the more general test of **PA1i** based on the *Level of Democracy* variables produces inconclusive and insignificant probit coefficients. These weak findings at the monadic level do not imply that democracies are very aggressive and often escalate to high levels.[12] These results simply indicate that, on average, when engaged in military conflicts democracies are not particularly reluctant to escalate levels of force.

However, if we look at the data for challengers, we find that there are not many cases in which a democracy has initiated force to begin with (56 cases out of 374). This highlights the strong monadic effect of democracy reported in the Status Quo Stage, where we found that democracies are far less likely to initiate military confrontations than non-democracies. Our second and related point, then, is that the basic rate of democratic escalation is quite similar to the corresponding rate of non-democratic escalation. Of those 56 cases of initiation by democracies, in only 11 cases (roughly 20 percent) does a democratic challenger escalate to high levels. However, non-democratic challengers are nearly as unlikely to escalate force themselves, as they only escalate about 24 percent of the time (78 out of 318 cases). Based upon all of this evidence, we conclude that the differences in escalatory behavior simply are not that significant.

The other weak, yet noteworthy, finding in Table 9.4 relates to hypothesis **PA2ii**, which posits that democratic leaders are more likely than their non-democratic counterparts to escalate military conflicts to high levels when disputed territory is populated by ethnic co-nationals and when questions of political self-determination are at stake. While the coefficients for the *Democracy * Ethnic Ties* term are not statistically significant for either the challenger or target, the *Ethnic Ties* control variable is

---

[12] We also examine the results of a Heckman selection model to see if the impact of challenger democracy on escalation outcomes is affected once we account for the pacifying impact of democracy on the challenge the status quo decision. The Heckman model indicates that once we account for selection processes, democratic challengers may actually be slightly *more* likely to escalate with force than non-democracies. While the challenger democracy coefficient is insignificant and has a negative sign in our original estimate in Table 9.4, in the Heckman model the challenger democracy coefficient is positive and marginally significant ($p < 0.10$) as an explanation for challenger escalation decisions. We simply take this new information as strong evidence that democracies are not less willing to use force once a militarized dispute has erupted.

positive and statistically significant (at the 0.01 level) for the challenger.[13] This indicates, then, that both democratic and non-democratic challengers are more likely to escalate to high levels in support of ethnic co-nationals.

Results for hypotheses that draw comparisons among leaders
of democratic and non-democratic states

On the whole the bivariate results for this second set of tests are relatively weak across the hypotheses tested.[14] For comparisons among democratic states the only strong finding is that challengers are less likely to escalate against politically secure democratic targets. In Table 9.7 the coefficient on the *Legislative Support for Target Government* variable in the challenger equation is negative and significant at the 0.01 level. This result supports **PA3ii** and indicates that challengers seem to give greater weight to the possibility that political security for democratic leaders in target states will make such leaders more willing to risk a war and to escalate to high levels.[15] As we noted in Chapter 4, an alternative argument is that political security would allow democratic leaders to back down in a crisis. Knowing this, adversaries might be tempted to escalate against secure democratic leaders expecting that these secure leaders could be coerced into a retreat under the threat of war. The results in Table 9.7, however, do not support this alternative argument. In Table 9.8 we see that when a democratic target government controls a majority of seats in the legislature, the likelihood that a challenger will escalate force against this target drops by more than half, from 22 percent to 9 percent. There is also some evidence that targets respond to politically secure democratic challengers in the same way. In Table 9.7 we see that in the target equation the *Legislative Support for Challenger Government* variable has

---

[13] These weak results for the *Democracy * Ethnic Ties* term are not due to problems of selection bias. We run a Heckman selection model for the challenger and find that this democracy and ethnic ties interaction term remains insignificant in the second equation for explaining escalation levels.

[14] We find a moderate degree of multicollinearity in this version of the Political Accountability Model. We obtain auxiliary r-squared values between 0.75 and 0.77 when we regress the democracy control variables and challenger (target) strength of government variables on all remaining variables. We run a series of additional models in which we typically delete one variable that seems to exhibit multicollinearity. Our results are largely unchanged, and typically remain quite weak. There is also no conclusive evidence of widespread selection bias in this model, either. The estimated rho from a Heckman model is −0.48, but once again this estimate is not statistically significant.

[15] These results remain robust when we check for selection bias. The coefficient for the *Legislative Support for Target Government* variable remains negative and statistically significant in the Heckman equation for explaining escalation levels.

Table 9.7 *Bivariate probit results for Political Accountability Model: hypotheses comparing differences within regimes for the Escalation Stage*

Variable	Challenger decision to escalate with force			Target decision to escalate with force		
	Coefficient	z	p-value	Coefficient	z	p-value
Legislative support for challenger government	.118	.36	—	-.373	-1.23	—
Legislative support for target government	-.566	-2.33	<.01	-.043	-.18	—
Time since elections in challenger	.007	.65	—	.004	.37	—
Time since elections in target	.014	2.00	<.025	.000	.02	—
Secure non-democratic challenger	-.083	-.47	—	-.399	-2.34	<.01
Secure non-democratic target	.171	.87	—	.245	1.26	<.10
Control for challenger democracy status	-.453	-1.05	—	-.095	-.26	—
Control for target democracy status	-.346	-1.32	—	-.427	-1.26	—
INTERNATIONAL POLITICS MODEL						
Military balance	.745	2.49	<.01	-.038	-.13	—
Local balance of forces advantage	.490	3.52	<.001	.117	.70	—
Strategic value of territory	.554	4.12	<.001	.479	3.47	<.001
Common security interests	-.436	-2.37	<.01	-.099	-.57	—
Target involvement in other military dispute	.373	2.06	<.05	.517	3.06	<.01*
Challenger involvement in other military dispute	.310	1.84	<.10*	.087	.52	—
Constant	-1.61	-7.16	<.001*	-1.15	-5.46	<.001*
	Estimate	Std Err	p-value	Test statistic		p-value
Rho $\varepsilon_1\varepsilon_2$	.954	.020		χ^2(1df) 66.04		.000

N = 374

Log-Likelihood = -248.76

Note: * = Two-tailed test of significance (all other tests are one-tailed unless indicated otherwise).

Table 9.8 *The impact of target government strength and election timing on challenger decisions to escalate with force*

Variable	(a) Initial probability	(b) Probability after change in variable	(c) Change in probabilities (b–a)	(d) Percentage change in probabilities (c/a)
Ruling government in target is a majority government				
Change from 0 to 1	22.0%	9.0%	–13.0%	–59.1%
Months since last election in target state				
Change from 3 to 12	5.2%	6.6%	+1.4%	+26.9%
Change from 12 to 30	6.6%	10.5%	+3.9%	+59.1%
Change from 30 to 48	10.5%	15.8%	+5.3%	+50.5%
Total change from 3 to 48	5.2%	15.8%	+10.6%	+203.8%

Note: The probabilities represent the marginal probability of challenger escalation, regardless of whether the target also escalates. The reported probabilities are calculated by holding each of the variables in Table 9.7 constant while changing the value of a single variable. The target months since election variable is fixed at twenty-four months for the target majority versus minority government comparison, and the target majority government variable is set at 1 for the months since target election comparisons. In both cases the target democracy dummy variable is set at 1. Unless specified otherwise, the territory is considered to be of strategic value to both states and the military balance is 3:2 in favor of the target. All other variables are held at their median values.

a negative coefficient and is close to marginal levels of significance (z-statistic $= -1.23$). On the whole, then, state leaders are hesitant to escalate force against democratic leaders who have strong party support in their legislature.

While the timing of elections is important for understanding when democratic leaders initiate military threats (see Chapter 7), there does not seem to be strong and consistent support for the argument that decisions regarding escalation are influenced by the timing of elections. The first hypothesis tested (**PA4i**) is that democratic leaders should be more likely to escalate following a recent election in their country and, conversely, less likely to escalate as new elections approach. The coefficients for the time since last election variable in the challenger and target equations, however, are weak and insignificant.

Nevertheless, there is support for the logic just described when extended to the responses of states to the timing of elections in other countries. Since democratic leaders in most cases should become wary of involvement in military conflicts as elections approach, this should lead adversaries to think that they should escalate against democratic states when democratic adversary governments are late in the electoral cycle (**PA4ii**). Again, as we noted in Chapter 4, there is an alternative argument that while democratic leaders would prefer to avoid the risks of a military conflict as elections approach, they also would not want to appear as weak and be charged with a retreat in a military confrontation near election time. The results in Table 9.7 provide much stronger support for the first argument. The coefficient for the *Time Since Elections in Target* variable is positive and statistically significant in the challenger equation.[16] In Table 9.8 we see that as the time since the last national election in the target increases from just three months to forty-eight months, the challenger now becomes more than three times as likely to escalate force to high levels against the target.

The bivariate probit results are quite weak for the hypothesis that among democratic governments, leaders should be more likely to escalate to high levels if they have strong party support in their own legislature (**PA3i**). In Table 9.7 we see that the coefficients for this variable are insignificant in both the challenger and target equations. This suggests that democratic leaders are neither more nor less likely to escalate if their governing coalition commands majority support.

---

[16] This result is fairly robust when we check for selection bias. We run a Heckman selection model for the challenger in which the decision to threaten force is also modeled and the coefficient for the *Time Since Elections in Target* variable remains positive and significant (but the z-statistic does drop to 1.43, $p < 0.10$) in the second equation for explaining escalation levels.

The last set of results to report focus on hypotheses comparing non-democratic states. In **PA5i** it was argued that leaders who are relatively secure (measured as the absence of any violent political rebellion within the past year) should be more willing to risk a military conflict and therefore to escalate to high levels. The probit results, however, are mixed. The results for the challenger are not statistically significant, but there is some support for **PA5i** in the target equation. We find that the coefficient for secure non-democratic target leaders is positive and marginally significant ($p < 0.10$). In Table 9.9 we see that secure non-democratic target leaders are about 33 percent more likely to escalate to high levels of force than are less secure non-democratic leaders. There is also support in Table 9.7 for the hypothesis (**PA5ii**) that targets are less likely to escalate to high levels when there is a secure non-democratic leader in the challenger state. In the target equation we see that the variable for a secure non-democratic challenger has a negative and statistically significant coefficient that produces a 43 percent reduction in the probability of target escalation (see Table 9.9).[17]

Results for hypotheses that compare across dyads
The last set of results to report for the Political Accountability Model are for hypotheses on democratic dyads and mixed dyads.[18] In **PA6** we hypothesized that for democratic dyads we should expect leaders of both challenger and target states to be less likely to escalate to high levels. The results in Table 9.10 are supportive of the hypothesis. In both equations the coefficients for the democratic dyad variables are negative and statistically significant, and the results are particularly strong for the challenger. The substantive effects on both states in the democratic dyad are also large (see Table 9.11). The predicted probability of targets in democratic dyads escalating to high levels of force is less than one-quarter the predicted probability of targets in non-democratic dyads escalating to high levels (21 percent vs. 5 percent). But the most telling results can be found simply by examining the raw number of cases of democratic dyad escalation. Of the small number of democratic dyads involved in military confrontations (sixteen cases), there are no cases of mutual decisions to escalate to high levels! In fact, territorial dispute challengers in democratic dyads

---

[17] We substitute alternative operational measures of the political security of the challenger into the equation to check for robustness. These measures include coups within the past one or two years, or no movement towards political liberalization within the past one or two years. The results for these indicators are generally weak. Therefore, the absence of violent rebellion within the past year seems to produce the strongest set of results in support of **PA5ii**.

[18] Auxiliary regressions reveal little multicollinearity among the independent variables in this dyadic model.

Table 9.9 *The impact of secure non-democratic governments on target decisions to escalate with force*

Variable	(a) Initial probability	(b) Probability after change in variable	(c) Change in probabilities (b−a)	(d) Percentage change in probabilities (c/a)
Secure non-democratic government in challenger Change from 0 to 1	25.8%	14.7%	−11.1%	−43.0%
Secure non-democratic government in target Change from 0 to 1	25.8%	34.3%	+8.5%	+32.9%

Note: The probabilities represent the marginal probability of target escalation, regardless of whether the challenger also escalates. The reported probabilities are calculated by holding each of the variables in Table 9.7 constant and comparing secure non-democratic governments to insecure non-democratic governments. Unless specified otherwise, the territory is considered to be of strategic value to both states and the military balance is 3:2 in favor of the target. All other variables are held at their median values.

Table 9.10 *Bivariate probit results for Political Accountability Model: hypotheses comparing dyads for the Escalation Stage*

Variable	Challenger decision to escalate with force			Target decision to escalate with force		
	Coefficient	z	p-value	Coefficient	z	p-value
Democratic dyad	−6.59	−40.00	<.001	−.857	−1.45	<.10
Non-democratic state in mixed dyad	−.099	−.35	—	.552	1.95	<.05
Control for mixed dyad	−.016	−.06	—	−.351	−1.82	<.10*
INTERNATIONAL POLITICS MODEL						
Military balance	.753	2.51	<.01	−.061	−.20	—
Local balance of forces advantage	.550	3.85	<.001	.087	.53	—
Strategic value of territory	.543	3.74	<.001	.405	2.81	<.01
Common security interests	−.404	−2.18	<.025	−.153	−.87	—
Target involvement in other military dispute	.392	2.22	<.025	.498	2.97	<.01*
Challenger involvement in other military dispute	.288	1.75	<.10*	.111	.68	—
Constant	−1.64	−7.50	<.001*	−1.16	−5.61	<.001*
	Estimate	Std Err	Test Statistic	p-value		
Rho $\varepsilon_1\varepsilon_2$	.935	.025	χ^2 (1df) 73.91	.000		

N = 374
Log-Likelihood = −255.27
Note: * = Two-tailed test of significance (all other tests are one-tailed unless indicated otherwise).

Table 9.11 *The impact of dyadic variables from the Political Accountability Model on challenger and target decisions to escalate with force*

| | | Probability of challenger escalation | | |
Variable	(a) Initial probability	(b) Probability after change in variable	(c) Change in probabilities (b–a)	(d) Percentage change in probabilities (c/a)
Democratic dyad				
Change from 0 to 1	21.5%	0%	−21.5%	−100%

| | | Probability of target escalation | | |
Variable	(a) Initial probability	(b) Probability after change in variable	(c) Change in probabilities (b–a)	(d) Percentage change in probabilities (c/a)
Democratic dyad				
Change from 0 to 1	21.4%	5.0%	−16.4%	−76.6%
Non-democratic state in mixed dyad				
Change from 0 to 1	12.6%	27.8%	+15.2%	+120.6%

Note: The probabilities represent the marginal probability of challenger and target escalation, respectively, regardless of whether the other state also escalates. The reported probabilities are calculated by holding each of the variables in Table 9.10 constant while changing the values of a single variable. The change to a democratic dyad represents a change from a jointly non-democratic dyad. A non-democratic state in a mixed dyad is compared to a democratic state in a mixed dyad. Unless specified otherwise, the territory is considered to be of strategic value to both states and the military balance is 3:2 in favor of the target. All other variables are held at their median values. The predicted probability of 0% for the challenger reflects the fact that there are no cases in which a democratic challenger escalates force against a democratic target.

Table 9.12 *The Political Accountability Model and the escalation behavior of democratic dyads*

Challenger	Target	Year	High level of escalation by challenger	High level of escalation by target
EUROPE				
Poland	Czechoslovakia	1919	No	No
ASIA				
India	Pakistan	1956	No	No
India	Pakistan	1957	No	No
Pakistan	India	1956	No	No
Pakistan	India	1957	No	No
Pakistan	India	1990	No	No
Pakistan	India	1991	No	No
Pakistan	India	1992	No	No
MIDDLE EAST				
Syria	Israel	1955	No	No
Syria	Israel	1956	No	No
Syria	Israel	1957	No	No
Syria	Israel	1958	No	No
Syria	Israel	1959	No	No
Syria	Israel	1960	No	No
AMERICAS				
Argentina	UK	1976	No	No
Ecuador	Peru	1981	No	Yes

never escalate to high levels of force and only one democratic target state escalates to high levels of force in a military confrontation with a fellow democracy (see Table 9.12).

For mixed dyads the hypothesis is that non-democratic states in mixed dyads should be more likely to escalate military confrontations as compared to democratic states in mixed dyads (**PA7i**). However, the results in Table 9.10 are only partially supportive of this hypothesis. This mixed dyad hypothesis receives support in the target equation ($p < 0.05$), yet receives no support in the challenger equation. In Table 9.11 we see that non-democratic targets in mixed dyads are more than twice as likely to escalate force than democratic targets in mixed dyads. However, the insignificant results for the challenger state differ markedly from our findings for the Status Quo Stage in Chapter 7. There we found that non-democratic challenger states in mixed dyads were much more likely to initiate military threats than democratic challengers in mixed dyads. In the Escalation Stage, however, there is no clear difference in

Table 9.13 Bivariate probit results for the Political Norms Model: hypotheses comparing across regimes for the Escalation Stage

Variable	Challenger decision to escalate with force			Target decision to escalate with force		
	Coefficient	z	p-value	Coefficient	z	p-value
Strength of nonviolent norms	−.008	−.42	—	−.020	−1.08	—
Nonviolent norms * military advantage	−.016	−.93	—	−.016	−1.15	—
Nonviolent norms * stalemate	.005	.13	—	.007	.16	—
Control for stalemate	−.345	−.80	—	−.425	−.84	—
INTERNATIONAL POLITICS MODEL						
Military balance	1.20	3.19	<.001	.057	.15	—
Local balance of forces advantage	.535	3.52	<.001	.085	.49	—
Strategic value of territory	.485	3.36	<.001	.353	2.46	<.01
Common security interests	−.404	−2.13	<.025	−.136	−.77	—
Target involvement in other military dispute	.404	2.42	<.01	.408	2.51	<.025*
Challenger involvement in other military dispute	.273	1.65	<.10*	.099	.60	—
Constant	−1.71	−5.23	<.001*	−.917	−3.06	<.01*
	Estimate	Std Err	p-value			p-value
Rho $\varepsilon_1\varepsilon_2$	.924	.027	Test Statistic x^2(1df) 78.25			.000

N = 374

Log-Likelihood = −255.78

Note: * = Two-tailed test of significance (all other tests are one-tailed unless indicated otherwise).

the escalatory behavior of such democratic and non-democratic challenger states. In this chapter, then, we must conclude that the evidence
for non-democratic bellicosity in mixed dyad situations is far less clear-
cut. While non-democratic targets are more aggressive than democratic
targets, among challengers non-democratic states are no more likely than
democratic states to escalate military conflicts to high levels in these mixed
dyad military confrontations.

Results for the Political Norms Model

We now turn to the bivariate probit results for the Political Norms Model.
The general conclusion we draw from the statistical findings is one of partial support for the model. We do not find strong evidence to support the
monadic hypothesis that norms of nonviolent political bargaining discourage leaders from escalating military confrontations to high levels.
These weak results contrast with the quite strong monadic-level findings
from the Status Quo Stage, where we found that leaders with democratic,
nonviolent norms favored negotiations over military threats in disputes
with all types of adversaries. The dyadic-level findings in this chapter,
however, are strong for both target and challenger and lend support to
the conventional wisdom that democratic dyads are more peaceful. Leaders with strong domestic norms of nonviolent bargaining do not escalate
to high levels against other states in which leaders share similarly peaceful norms. We also find support for hypotheses that focus on comparisons among democratic or non-democratic leaders. For example, among
democratic states the leaders of newly established democracies seem to
be more aggressive; that is, they escalate military confrontations to high
levels more frequently than long-standing democracies. Turning to comparisons among non-democracies, disputes between states in which both
sides share quite violent domestic norms of political behavior also seem
to be more likely to escalate to high levels. In sum, the statistical results provide modest support for arguments that the military choices of
democratic and non-democratic leaders vary in systematic ways due to
differences in domestic norms.

Results for hypotheses that compare leaders with strong vs. weak nonviolent norms

The first finding to report in Table 9.13 is for hypothesis **PN1i**, in which
we posit that as nonviolent norms become more firmly established in political systems, political leaders should be less likely to escalate military
confrontations over disputed territory.[19] The bivariate probit estimates

---

[19] In our tests for multicollinearity we find auxiliary r-squared values ranging from 0.85
    to 0.89 for regressions on three variables: *Strength of Nonviolent norms, Nonviolent*

in Table 9.13 show that the coefficients on the *Strength of Nonviolent Norms* variable are negative but not statistically significant for both the challenger and target, although the target estimate approaches marginal levels of significance. However, further exploration reveals a number of additional qualifications to these results in Table 9.13. First, if we address problems of possible multicollinearity and delete all norms model variables but the standard twenty-year lagged measure of nonviolent norms, we now find some support for **PN1i**. In this case the coefficient on the *Strength of Nonviolent Norms* term becomes negative and statistically significant for the target ($p < 0.10$) and negative and suggestively significant (p-value of 0.18, one-tailed) for the challenger. We also find very similar results when we examine the full model (from Table 9.13) using the alternative measure for democratic norms, the *POLITY*-based twenty-year democracy lag.[20]

However, if we consider the possibility for selection bias and examine a Heckman probit model, we obtain quite different results.[21] After accounting for the fact that challengers with nonviolent norms rarely initiate military confrontations, we now find that such challengers might be *more* likely to escalate to higher levels of force given that they are in a military confrontation. In the Heckman model equation for challenger escalation, the nonviolent norms coefficient is now positive and is statistically significant at conventional levels. One possible explanation for this last finding is that those democratic challengers that do initiate threats are quite atypical. Therefore their escalatory behavior reflects the impact of those factors that influenced the (unusual) decision to initiate threats to begin with. In any event, we notice that we obtain different and seemingly contradictory results based on the type of model we employ.

Given the uncertainty surrounding these results, it is difficult to identify any definitive patterns for the impact of nonviolent norms on decisions to escalate with the large-scale use of force. Nevertheless, based upon the totality of our statistical findings for **PN1i** we do feel comfortable

---

*Norms * Stalemate*, and the *Stalemate* control variable. Some of our estimates of the model in Table 9.13 therefore do change when we run alternative specifications of this model. We note these changes in the text and in future footnotes.

[20] Specifically, when we use the twenty-year lag of POLITY scores, the coefficient for target democratic norms is negative and statistically significant and the coefficient for challenger democratic norms is negative but not statistically significant.

[21] This is the only case in the entire book where we find evidence of widespread selection bias, and in which individual coefficient estimates seem to change dramatically when we account for the challenger selection equation in the examination of escalation decisions. The estimated rho for this Heckman model for across-regimes comparisons of norms is -0.51, and this estimate is significant at the 0.10 level. We further discuss the impact of possible selection bias on individual hypotheses in the remainder of this section, as appropriate.

making the claim that there is not clear evidence to support the theory that nonviolent norms of conflict resolution constrain leaders from escalating to higher levels of force. As noted above, these findings differ from our conclusions about democratic norms drawn from the Status Quo Stage. There we found that leaders with strong nonviolent norms were far less likely to turn to military threats. Across these two stages of a territorial dispute our aggregate results indicate that while strong nonviolent and democratic norms do channel disputes down a path of negotiations instead of military confrontations, these same norms seem to have less impact on policy choices when leaders face the decision of whether to escalate military confrontations. At this latter stage, variables from the International Politics Model as well as the Accountability Model seem to be more influential.

Neither of the two remaining norms hypotheses is strongly supported by the bivariate probit results reported in Table 9.13, but once again further analyses modify this conclusion somewhat. First, in **PN1ii** we argued that leaders with strong nonviolent norms would be less likely to respond to a stalemate in prior negotiations by escalating military confrontations to high levels. Neither the challenger nor the target coefficients for this interaction term approach conventional levels of statistical significance.[22] Second, in **PN2** we hypothesize that leaders with strong nonviolent norms would not be tempted by a military advantage to escalate to high levels. Yet we find little support for **PN2** based upon the bivariate probit results reported in Table 9.13. The coefficients are negative for both challengers and targets, as expected, but they are insignificant in both equations.[23]

However, a variety of additional tests provide some support for **PN2**. First of all, when we re-estimate the model in Table 9.13 after dropping all norms model variables other than the *Nonviolent Norms * Military Advantage* term, we now obtain a negative and statistically significant (p < 0.10) coefficient result for this interaction term in the target equation. Furthermore, we obtain similar results for the target when we add a military advantage control variable to the full model (as in Table 9.13).[24] We

---

[22] Even weaker results are produced when we substitute into the equation alternative measures for stalemate based on two- and five-year lags instead of the one-year lag we employ initially.

[23] We test for the robustness of results by substituting into the equation an alternative operational measure for military advantage. A dummy variable with a value of one is now included whenever a state enjoys a simple majority military balance advantage. The bivariate probit results remain very similar, though just a bit stronger, for both challenger and target. For the target, the negative coefficient is marginally significant (z-statistic = −1.35, p < 0.10).

[24] In this case the *Nonviolent Norms * Military Advantage* term is negative and significant at the 0.10 level in the target equation. We originally chose to leave out this military advantage control variable due to concerns with high multicollinearity.

Table 9.14 Bivariate probit results for the Political Norms Model: hypotheses comparing differences within regimes for the Escalation Stage

Variable	Challenger decision to escalate with force			Target decision to escalate with force		
	Coefficient	z	p-value	Coefficient	z	p-value
Leaders in recently established democracies	.406	1.44	<.10	.939	3.43	<.001
Leaders with strongest violent norms	−.010	−.08	—	−.097	−.67	—
Control for nonviolent norms	.014	.07	—	.210	1.05	—
Control for present democratic status	−.427	−1.64	<.05	−.632	−2.89	<.01
INTERNATIONAL POLITICS MODEL						
Military balance	.983	3.30	<.001	−.056	−.19	—
Local balance of forces advantage	.528	3.75	<.001	.105	.67	—
Strategic value of territory	.468	3.29	<.001	.364	2.55	<.01
Common security interests	−.371	−2.01	<.025	−.114	−.65	—
Target involvement in other military dispute	.394	2.41	<.01	.532	3.17	<.01*
Challenger involvement in other military dispute	.320	1.94	<.10*	.037	.23	—
Constant	−1.76	−8.27	<.001*	−1.12	−5.13	<.001*
	Estimate	Std Err	Test Statistic χ^2(1df) 75.22	p-value		
Rho $\varepsilon_1\varepsilon_2$	.956	.019	p-value	.000		

N = 374
Log-Likelihood = −251.53
Note: * = Two-tailed test of significance (all other tests are one-tailed unless indicated otherwise).

run some predicted probability simulations and typically find that target leaders with strong nonviolent norms are roughly 40 percent less likely to escalate when they have a military advantage compared to target leaders who hold very violent norms.

Finally, we actually obtain a negative and statistically significant coefficient estimate on this interaction term for the challenger when we examine the results of a Heckman probit model (see note 21). With the Heckman model, the coefficient on the *Nonviolent Norms * Military Advantage* interaction term in the challenger equation has a negative coefficient that is statistically significant (p-value = 0.06). So in the end, we find some support for the idea that nonviolent norms of conflict resolution exert a pacifying influence in situations of military strength.

The final hypothesis is that differences in the strength of democratic norms should influence the escalation choices of challengers more than those of targets (**PN3**). This hypothesis cannot be directly tested with a single variable in a bivariate probit equation. Instead we look to see if the results in Table 9.13 are notably stronger for the challenger than for the target. In one sense the behavior of targets does support the hypothesis due to the fact that the strength or weakness of nonviolent norms of conflict resolution does not seem to affect the escalation decisions of leaders of target states. The evidence for challengers, however, is not supportive of the hypothesis. We should find that among leaders of challenger states those with stronger nonviolent norms are less likely to escalate to high levels of force. However, as discussed for **PN1i** above, the challenger state findings for the *Strength of Nonviolent Norms* variable are inconclusive, if not in direct contradiction of this claim. As a result, we fail to find strong support for **PN3**.

Results for hypotheses that compare leaders among either democratic or non-democratic states

In Table 9.14 we report the results for the two within regimes hypotheses that were tested.[25] First, among democratic states we observe that the leaders of recently established democracies (within the last five years) are more likely to escalate military confrontations to high levels. For both the challenger and target the coefficients are positive and statistically significant as hypothesized in **PN4**. The findings for target states are particularly strong, while the findings for the challenger are slightly less convincing. In

---

[25] Auxiliary regression results reveal no significant problem with multicollinearity. The highest auxiliary r-squared value for any challenger equation variable is 0.55, while the highest corresponding value for the target is 0.45. The Heckman probit results provide no reason to suspect substantial selection bias. The estimated rho is −0.32, but the p-value for this estimate is only 0.35.

Table 9.15 *The impact of the recent transition to democracy variable from the Political Norms Model on challenger and target decisions to escalate with force*

	Probability of challenger escalation			
Variable	(a) Initial probability	(b) Probability after change in variable	(c) Change in probabilities (b−a)	(d) Percentage change in probabilities (c/a)
Challenger has become democratic within the past five years				
Change from 0 to 1	9.0%	17.5%	+8.5%	+94.4%

	Probability of target escalation			
Variable	(a) Initial probability	(b) Probability after change in variable	(c) Change in probabilities (b−a)	(d) Percentage change in probabilities (c/a)
Target has become democratic within the past five years				
Change from 0 to 1	7.7%	31.3%	+23.6%	+306.5%

Note: The probabilities represent the marginal probability of challenger and target escalation, respectively, regardless of whether the other state also escalates. The reported probabilities are calculated by holding each of the variables in Table 9.14 constant while changing the value of the democracy within five years variable. The current democracy control variable is set to 1 for both the challenger comparison and target comparisons. The democratic norms control variable is set to 0, which is consistent with the idea of a recent change to democracy. The territory is considered to be of strategic value to both states and the military balance is 3:2 in favor of the target. All other variables are held at their median values.

Table 9.15 we see that newly democratic challenger states are nearly twice as likely as more established democracies to escalate to the large-scale use of force, while newly democratic targets are more than four times as likely to escalate to high levels.[26] Examples of recently established democratic challengers that escalated to high levels include Polish attempts to extend its border eastward against Soviet Russia in 1919 and 1920, the Czech attack against politically unstable Hungary in 1919, and the large-scale Indian military operation to secure control over much of disputed Kashmir in 1947–8. Forceful military responses by new democratic target states include the strong counter-attacks and successes of Israeli military forces in 1948–9 following the Arab invasion and Peruvian escalation to the brink of war in 1981 following Ecuadorian military incursions along their disputed border.

Second, we test the hypothesis (**PN5**) that among non-democratic challengers, those with the most violent norms are more likely to escalate military confrontations to high levels. We expect to find positive coefficients for this variable in Table 9.14, but instead we see that the coefficients for both challenger and target are negative and not statistically significant. As a result, the bivariate probit results are not supportive of **PN5**.[27]

Results for hypotheses that compare within and across dyads

We test three hypotheses in this final, dyadic version of the Norms Model. The bivariate results reported in Table 9.16 are generally supportive of the hypotheses.[28] The first finding is that in disputes where both challenger and target leaders share nonviolent norms it is unlikely that either party will escalate force to high levels. The coefficients for both states are negative and significant at the 0.001 level, as predicted by hypothesis **PN6i**. In fact, Tables 9.17 and 9.18 reveal that the predicted probability of escalation is actually 0 percent in these dyadic, nonviolent norms cases! This

---

[26] These results for the target are not sensitive to the operational measure used to code how recently the country had become democratic. We also substitute two- and ten-year lags in place of a five-year lag and achieve quite similar results. We are less confident about the robustness of results for the challenger, however. When we substitute these same alternative measures into the challenger equation we find that the coefficient remains positive, but drops below standard levels of significance (z-statistics are less than 1.00). Furthermore, the coefficient estimate for newly democratic challenger states in the Heckman model (escalation decision), while still exhibiting a positive sign, is no longer statistically significant. This is likely due to the fact that newly democratic challengers are particularly likely to initiate force in the Challenge the Status Quo Stage and the bivariate probit results for the Escalation Stage (see Table 9.14) are picking up some of this effect.

[27] These results remain weak and do not support **PN5** when the alternative operational measures based on POLITY scores are used to code non-democratic norms.

[28] We test for levels of multicollinearity among all of the explanatory variables and find the auxiliary r-squared values to range from low to moderate values between 0.31 and 0.75.

Table 9.16 Bivariate probit results for the Political Norms Model: hypotheses comparing dyads for the Escalation Stage

Variable	Challenger decision to escalate with force			Target decision to escalate with force		
	Coefficient	z	p-value	Coefficient	z	p-value
Dyad with strong nonviolent norms	-5.96	-29.89	<.001	-5.60	-35.12	<.001
State in mixed dyad with stronger violent norms	-.356	-.96	—	.763	2.09	<.025
Dyads with strongest violent norms	.583	2.24	<.025	.363	1.45	<.10
Control for mixed dyad	.367	1.08	—	-.115	-.57	—
INTERNATIONAL POLITICS MODEL						
Military balance	.871	2.69	<.01	-.166	-.54	—
Local balance of forces advantage	.565	3.79	<.001	.060	.35	—
Strategic value of territory	.514	3.66	<.001	.356	2.48	<.01
Common security interests	-.470	-2.47	<.01	-.176	-.98	—
Target involvement in other military dispute	.383	2.20	<.025	.424	2.60	<.01*
Challenger involvement in other military dispute	.223	1.31	—	.099	.59	—
Constant	-1.79	-7.99	<.001*	-1.20	-5.56	<.01*
	Estimate	Std Err	Test Statistic	p-value		
Rho $\varepsilon_1\varepsilon_2$	.923	.028	χ^2(1df) 72.85	.000		

N = 374
Log-Likelihood = -254.59
Note: * = Two-tailed test of significance (all other tests are one-tailed unless indicated otherwise).

Table 9.17 *The impact of dyadic variables from the Political Norms Model on challenger decisions to escalate with force*

		Probability of challenger escalation		
Variable	(a) Initial probability	(b) Probability after change in variable	(c) Change in probabilities (b−a)	(d) Percentage change in probabilities (c/a)
Dyad with strong nonviolent norms Change from 0 to 1	17.7%	0%	−17.7%	−100%
Dyad with strongest violent norms Change from 0 to 1	17.7%	36.5%	+18.8%	+106.2%

Note: The probabilities represent the marginal probability of challenger escalation, regardless of whether the target also escalates. The reported probabilities are calculated by holding each of the variables in Table 9.16 constant while changing the values of a single variable. The probability of escalation for the challenger in a dyad with strong nonviolent norms is compared to the probability of escalation for a challenger in a dyad with strong violent norms. The probability of escalation for a challenger in a dyad with strong nonviolent norms is compared to the probability of escalation for a challenger in a dyad with weaker violent norms. The territory is considered to be of strategic value to both states and the military balance is 3:2 in favor of the target. All other variables are held at their median values. The predicted probability of 0% for the challenger with strong nonviolent norms reflects the fact that there are no cases in which a challenger with strong nonviolent norms escalates force against a target which also shares strong nonviolent norms.

Table 9.18 *The impact of dyadic variables from the Political Norms Model on target decisions to escalate with force*

	(a) Initial probability	(b) Probability after change in variable	(c) Change in probabilities (b−a)	(d) Percentage change in probabilities (c/a)
			Probability of challenger escalation	
Variable				
Dyad with strong nonviolent norms				
Change from 0 to 1	17.1%	0%	−17.1%	−100%
State in mixed dyad with stronger violent norms				
Change from 0 to 1	14.4%	38.2%	+23.8%	+165.3%
Dyad with strongest violent norms				
Change from 0 to 1	17.1%	27.9%	+10.8%	+63.2%

Note: The probabilities represent the marginal probability of target escalation, regardless of whether the challenger also escalates. The reported probabilities are calculated by holding each of the variables in Table 9.16 constant while changing the values of a single variable. The probability of escalation for the target in a dyad with strong nonviolent norms is compared to the probability of escalation for a target in a dyad with strong violent norms. The probability of escalation for a target with violent norms in a mixed dyad is compared to the probability of escalation for a target with nonviolent norms in a mixed dyad. Finally, the probability of escalation for a target in a dyad with strong violent norms is compared to the probability of escalation for a target in a dyad with weaker violent norms. In all cases the territory is considered to be of strategic value to both states and the military balance is 3:2 in favor of the target. All other variables are held at their median values. The predicted probability of 0% for the challenger with strong nonviolent norms reflects the fact that there are no cases in which a target with strong nonviolent norms escalates force against a challenger which also shares strong nonviolent norms.

reflects the fact that in our data set there are no cases in which dyads characterized by joint nonviolent norms escalate to high levels of force! It is important to recognize, however, that there are only four cases of such dyads being involved in military confrontations to begin with. This very small number of cases reflects the powerful findings in the Status Quo Stage that challengers with strong nonviolent norms are very unlikely to initiate military threats against target states who share similar nonviolent norms. A very important point about the democratic peace follows from these data. The absence of war among democratic dyads over disputed territory across the 1919–95 period is due largely to the fact that in these disputes challengers rarely threatened force to begin with and instead relied on negotiations. While leaders in democratic dyads did not escalate to high levels in the military confrontations they were involved in, the limited number of such military confrontations (four in total) suggests that no strong conclusions should be drawn about the superior crisis management policies of leaders with strong nonviolent norms. Instead, the key to avoiding war seems to be the strong preference of leaders with nonviolent norms to favor peaceful diplomacy and to engage in repeated negotiations with their more democratic counterparts until a settlement is reached.

The second hypothesis we test is the claim that in mixed dyads non-democratic leaders with violent norms are more likely to escalate to high levels of force than democratic leaders in such dyads (**PN8**). However, the bivariate probit results in Table 9.16 are somewhat mixed. The coefficient for the target is positive and statistically significant as expected, but the results for the challenger are weak and insignificant. In Table 9.18 we see the large substantive effects of regime type (in mixed dyads) on the likelihood of target escalation. Democratic targets in mixed dyads have a predicted probability of escalation of 14 percent, while non-democratic targets in mixed dyads are expected to escalate 38 percent of the time. The weak findings for the challenger, however, contrast with the strong finding in the Status Quo Stage that non-democratic challenger leaders with violent norms are typically the more aggressive party in mixed dyads.

The final dyadic hypothesis we examine is **PN7**. Our claim is that high levels of escalation should be most common in military confrontations between states in which strong violent norms are held by the leaders of both states. As a result, the coefficients for the challenger and target should be positive and significant in Table 9.16. This is indeed what we find, though the findings do seem stronger for the challenger as opposed to the target ($p < 0.025$ vs. $p < 0.10$ for challenger and target, respectively). In Tables 9.17 and 9.18 the substantive impact of this variable is reported and the effects are sizeable. The predicted probability of escalation for challengers

Table 9.19 *Bivariate probit results for the Political Affinity Model: hypotheses comparing differences between similar and dissimilar regimes for the Escalation Stage*

Variable	Challenger decision to escalate with force			Target decision to escalate with force		
	Coefficient	z	p-value	Coefficient	z	p-value
Political similarity	.333	1.23	—	.219	.87	—
Recent change to political similarity	−1.63	−3.26	<.001*	−.637	−1.34	—
INTERNATIONAL POLITICS MODEL						
Military balance	.920	3.08	<.025	−.292	−1.02	—
Local balance of forces advantage	.571	3.87	<.001	.081	.46	—
Strategic value of territory	.544	3.85	<.001	.342	2.45	<.01
Common security interests	−.478	−2.47	<.01	−.131	−.73	—
Target involvement in other military dispute	.354	2.10	<.025	.397	2.50	<.025
Challenger involvement in other military dispute	.293	1.73	<.10*	.150	.90	—
Constant	−1.93	−6.11	<.001*	−1.11	−5.24	<.001*
	Estimate	Std Err	Test Statistic	p-value		
Rho $\varepsilon_1\varepsilon_2$	.925	.027	χ^2(1df) 73.68	.000		

N = 374
Log-Likelihood = −256.37
Note: * = Two-tailed test of significance (all other tests are one-tailed unless indicated otherwise).

in these situations of dual violent norms more than doubles – from 18 percent to over 36 percent – compared to a situation in which leaders in both non-democratic regimes hold less violent norms. Similarly, the likelihood that targets in similar situations of joint violent norms will escalate is nearly 28 percent, which is 63 percent higher than the predicted likelihood of escalation for targets in dyads characterized by less violent norms. A good example of a territorial dispute between authoritarian and repressive regimes is the conflict between Japan and China over Manchuria. Japan pursues a consistent policy from 1932 onwards of first establishing and then trying to extend its occupation and control over the region. Between 1934 and 1937 six military confrontations take place and both sides escalate to the brink of another war several times. War finally does break out in 1937, and lasts until 1945. Another example in the 1930s was the border dispute between Japanese-controlled Manchukuo and the Far Eastern sector of the Soviet border. Japanese and Soviet military confrontations took place along the disputed border and a limited war was fought over Changkufeng in 1938. Then in the following year Japan launched an attack that led to the short but very deadly Nomohan War.

Results for the Political Affinity Model

The final set of results we discuss is for the Political Affinity Model. We once again find that compared to the other two domestic models, the empirical evidence provides much less support for the Affinity Model. There are supportive results for two of the hypotheses tested, but otherwise the bivariate probit results are either weak or contradict the remaining four hypotheses tested.[29] One additional note is that this time we split our analysis of the Political Affinity Model and estimate two statistical models as opposed to one all-inclusive model. We are forced to divide the Political Affinity hypotheses due to the relatively low number of cases in the Escalation Stage, coupled with the potential for high multicollinearity given the number of interaction terms in the Affinity Model. We examine hypotheses **PAF1i** and **PAF1ii** in the first bivariate probit model, and then test the remaining hypotheses in the second bivariate probit model.

The first set of findings is for hypotheses **PAF1i** and **PAF1ii**. Our first and most overarching hypothesis is that political affinity should reduce the likelihood of escalation in military confrontations. Once again, the results in Table 9.19 clearly indicate that **PAF1i** is not supported by the

[29] Yet again we test for levels of multicollinearity among all of the explanatory variables in this model and find the auxiliary r-squared values to be very low.

Table 9.20 *Bivariate probit results for the Political Affinity Model: hypotheses comparing the impact of affinity in the presence of external threats for the Escalation Stage*

Variable	Challenger decision to escalate with force			Target decision to escalate with force		
	Coefficient	z	p-value	Coefficient	z	p-value
Political similarity * external threat to challenger	-.511	-1.03	—	-.748	-1.56	<.10
Political similarity * external threat to target	-.795	-1.40	<.10	-1.54	-2.86	<.01
Dissimilarity * external threat to challenger	-.290	-1.21	—	-.204	-.78	—
Dissimilarity * external threat to target	-.565	-2.06	<.05*	-.720	-2.53	<.025*
Control for political similarity	.517	1.17	—	.918	2.14	<.05*
Control for challenger external threat	.059	.25	—	.066	.26	—
Control for target external threat	.999	2.96	<.01*	1.06	3.67	<.001*
INTERNATIONAL POLITICS MODEL						
Military balance	.882	1.92	<.05	-.552	-1.26	—
Local balance of forces advantage	.598	4.05	<.001	.111	.64	—
Strategic value of territory	.537	3.83	<.001	.382	2.60	<.01
Common security interests	-.428	-2.08	<.025	-.087	-.45	—
Target involvement in other military dispute	.409	2.36	<.025	.476	2.96	<.01*
Challenger involvement in other military dispute	.269	1.54	—	.079	.46	—
Constant	-2.22	-5.41	<.001*	-1.51	-3.64	<.001*
	Estimate	Std Err	Test Statistic	p-value		
Rho $\varepsilon_1\varepsilon_2$	.925	.027	χ^2(1df) 73.15	.000		

N = 374
Log-Likelihood = -246.47
Note: * = Two-tailed test of significance (all other tests are one-tailed unless indicated otherwise).

estimated results. The coefficients for the *Polity Similarity* variable are actually positive, yet not quite statistically significant, for both challengers and targets. As we have done in the face of similar results in previous chapters, we probe this finding further by disaggregating the affinity variable into each of the four types of similar regimes. Yet again, we find that the results are not uniform across each regime pairing. In particular, we find a consistent pattern – similar to what we found in Chapters 7 and 8 – in which democratic pairs of states behave very differently than other similar dyads. For the Escalation Stage, we find that democratic dyads are less likely to escalate to high levels. On the other hand, monarchies are more likely to escalate, while there is no discernible pattern of escalation for communist or military junta dyads. These consistent and weak results for the *Political Similarity* variable across all three stages strongly suggest that political similarity by itself is not a powerful reason for state leaders to be more cooperative and to avoid military conflict.

The second hypothesis focuses on pairs of states that have recently become politically similar (**PAF1ii**). We argue that compared to other cases of political similarity, states that have been politically similar for only a short period of time (within the past five years) are more likely to escalate to high levels of force. We expect to observe positive coefficients for this variable in Table 9.19, but in fact we see that recent affinity makes states particularly unlikely to escalate to higher levels of force. The sign on the challenger *Recent Change to Political Similarity* variable is not only negative, but is also significant at the 0.001 level.[30] This is a surprising finding given that the same variable was associated with a higher probability of challengers initiating military confrontations in the Status Quo Stage.

In Table 9.20 we report the bivariate probit results for the remaining four Affinity Model hypotheses. Our first conclusion is that we do find generally supportive results for hypotheses **PAF2i** and **PAF2ii**. The predictions of these two hypotheses are that states should be less likely to escalate to high levels against politically similar territorial dispute adversaries when either they or their politically similar adversary face threats to their political security. As a result, we expect to find negative coefficients on all of the *Political Similarity* * *External Threat* interaction terms in Table 9.20. Indeed, all four relevant coefficients are negative and three of them achieve standard levels of statistical significance.[31] In

---

[30] We check for the robustness of this unexpected finding by substituting alternative lags for determining how recently states had become politically similar. Both ten- and three-year lags produce very similar results for the challenger and target.

[31] These results weaken somewhat when we substitute a measure of domestic threat in place of external threat to check for the robustness of the findings. Yet two of the four coefficients remain statistically significant with negative coefficients.

Table 9.21 *The impact of the external threat to similar adversary interaction term from the Political Affinity Model on challenger decisions to escalate with force*

Variable	(a) Initial probability	(b) Probability after change in variable	(c) Change in probabilities (b–a)	(d) Percentage change in probabilities (c/a)
Political similarity when an external threat to target exists				
Change from 0 to 1	39.2%	14.2%	−25.0%	−63.8%

Note: The probabilities represent the marginal probability of challenger escalation, regardless of whether the target also escalates. The reported probabilities are calculated by examining a change in the interaction term above, while holding the external threat variable at 1 and holding all other variables constant. The above probabilities reflect the impact of challenger and target similarity only when the target faces an external threat, and do not capture the impact of challenger and target similarity in any other way. The territory is considered to be of strategic value to both states and the military balance is 3:2 in favor of the target. All other variables are held at their median values.

Table 9.21 we see that challenger states who are politically similar to their territorial adversary are 64 percent less likely to escalate force against this threatened adversary than are leaders who do not share political affinity with a threatened adversary. The substantive impact on targets mirrors this impact. Leaders of target states are 62 percent less likely to escalate force when facing a politically similar and threatened adversary as opposed to when they face a threatened, yet dissimilar adversary. Furthermore, if the target itself is confronted with an external security threat, it is ten times less likely to escalate to higher levels of force if its territorial dispute adversary is politically similar as opposed to politically dissimilar (see Table 9.22).

The last set of results is for the paired hypotheses **PAF3i** and **PAF3ii**. The bivariate probit results support the first hypothesis but not the second. For **PAF3i** we posit that states should be less likely to escalate to high levels when facing an external threat from a state that shares political affinity with its territorial dispute adversary. As a result, the *Dissimilarity* * *External Threat to Challenger* variable should have a negative coefficient in the challenger equation, while the *Dissimilarity* * *External Threat to Target* variable should have a negative coefficient in the target equation. Both of these coefficients are in fact negative. The target coefficient is statistically significant ($p < 0.025$), while the challenger coefficient is just short of standard significance levels (z-statistic $= -1.21$). Substantively, target states are 38 percent less likely to escalate force when the challenger is politically aligned with the state that is threatening the target (Table 9.22).

For **PAF3ii** we put forward the reverse argument that a state should be more likely to escalate to high levels against a politically dissimilar territorial dispute adversary when a third state with which it shares political similarity is currently posing a threat to that dissimilar territorial dispute opponent. However, the bivariate probit results do not support this hypothesis. In Table 9.20 the coefficient for the *Dissimilarity* * *Threat to Target* variable in the challenger equation should be positive, but in reality it is negative and statistically significant. In the target equation the coefficient for the *Dissimilarity* * *Threat to Challenger* variable is also surprisingly negative, though it is not statistically significant.

Conclusion

In this final empirical chapter we evaluated the power of our four models to explain the decisions of leaders to escalate military confrontations over disputed territory to high levels and risk war. The results for the International Politics Model are consistently strong, indicating that leaders are influenced by variables such as relative military power, the strategic value

Table 9.22 *The impact of variables concerning external threats to similar and dissimilar adversaries from the Political Affinity Model on target decisions to escalate with force*

Variable	(a) Initial probability	(b) Probability after change in variable	(c) Change in probabilities (b−a)	(d) Percentage change in probabilities (c/a)
Political similarity when an external threat to target exists				
Change from 0 to 1	37.1%	3.1%	−34.0%	−91.6%
Political similarity when an external threat to challenger exists				
Change from 0 to 1	37.1%	14.1%	−23.0%	−62.0%
Political dissimilarity when there is political similarity between the challenger and the source of the target external threat				
Change from 0 to 1	72.2%	44.8%	−27.4%	−38%

Note: The probabilities represent the marginal probability of target escalation, regardless of whether the challenger also escalates. For the first two interaction terms, the external threat variable is held at 1. These two sets of probabilities reflect the impact of challenger and target similarity when the target (challenger) faces an external threat, and do not incorporate the impact of political similarity in any other way. The third set of probabilities reflects the impact of challenger and target dissimilarity on target behavior solely when the target is threatened by a third state and that third state and the challenger share regime similarity. In all cases, the territory is considered to be of strategic value to both states and the military balance is 3:2 in favor of the target. All other variables are held at their median values.

of disputed territory, and common security ties when contemplating decisions to escalate with high levels of force. These strong findings for the Escalation Stage closely match the results for the Status Quo Stage, where we found this model was best at explaining decisions to threaten force. When we combine our results across these two stages of a territorial dispute, a clear picture emerges in which international political and military conditions are central to explaining decisions by states to initiate and escalate threats of military force over disputed territory.

Domestic-level variables, however, also have an impact on the escalation of military confrontations. While we think that international political-military variables are of central importance, we also believe that the Accountability and Norms Models provide further insights into state behavior in confrontations that could escalate to war. The most powerful finding for both models is that escalation to war never took place in disputes between pairs of states with strong democratic institutions or strong norms of nonviolent bargaining. We also noted that for both models, the number of such democratic dyads involved in military confrontations is quite low. In the Accountability Model there are only sixteen democratic dyads engaged in military confrontations while there are just four such cases for the Norms Model. We think this is a very telling point that is central to understanding the absence of war among democratic states. While the avoidance of war in twenty cases of democratic dyad confrontations is an important finding, we think a far more crucial point to appreciate is how infrequently states with democratic institutions or norms end up in military crises with each other in the first place. In our judgement, the key to avoiding war in democratic dyads is the initial decision of democratic challenger states to direct disputes down a pathway of peaceful diplomacy and reliance on repeated talks to eventually produce negotiated settlements. While we do believe that democratic accountability and norms generally do contribute to the avoidance of war in military confrontations, we are even more impressed by the fact that these domestic influences are so powerful at earlier stages in a dispute that democratic leaders rarely find themselves having to manage military crises with democratic adversaries.

The Accountability Model also refines our understanding of military escalation decisions with the finding that state leaders are generally wary of risking war against other countries when the adversary's leadership is politically secure from domestic political opposition. The evidence supports the argument that leaders fear an adversary's greater political security will allow this adversary to risk war and counter any escalatory moves they might initiate. The other interesting finding for the Accountability Model is that democratic leaders can bolster the credibility of their deterrent policies by signaling earlier on in a crisis their intention to escalate if necessary. This finding supports arguments that the greater domestic political costs of retreating in a crisis for democratic leaders can be used to their strategic advantage, since adversaries recognize that the political costs of inaction for democratic leaders can be a motivating force for such leaders to stand firm and risk war.

The final conclusion we draw from the statistical findings in this chapter is that the moderating effects of democracy at the monadic level are much weaker for both the Accountability and Norms Models once democratic leaders find themselves making decisions in a military confrontation. We found strong monadic effects associated with democracy for both models in the Status Quo Stage, where democratic leaders were less likely to turn to military force against all other types of adversaries. We believe that the weaker monadic results in the Escalation Stage for both domestic models reflect two general influences. First, at times the political payoffs of more aggressive and escalatory policies for democratic leaders are more salient than the constraining effects of nonviolent norms. As a result, when the incentives to escalate diverge between the Accountability and Norms Models, we think that the short-term political calculations suggested by the Accountability Model prevail more frequently. Furthermore, we believe the greater domestic costs democratic leaders face for retreating in a crisis push democratic leaders towards escalation frequently enough to eliminate any sharp differences in patterns of escalation when comparing democratic and non-democratic states. Second, the strong tendency for all target states to defend disputed territory when attacked or threatened with war means that there is limited variance in the military behavior of such states that can be accounted for by either model.

10   What have we learned about the democratic peace?

In the opening chapter to this book we argued that while scholarship over the past decade has made substantial contributions to our understanding of how domestic political institutions influence patterns of international conflict, opportunities remain for continuing research to make important new advances in our understanding of the democratic peace. In particular, we claimed that the deductive logic of different models of the democratic peace could be developed more fully, thus producing a broader range of hypotheses to explain the diplomatic and military policies that state leaders adopt in international disputes. We also argued in favor of new statistical tests of theoretical models of the democratic peace, and claimed that such tests should focus on the evolution of territorial disputes into different stages and the choices made by state leaders at these various stages.

It is now time to step back from the extended and detailed discussion of theoretical models, hypotheses, and statistical results. In this concluding chapter we pull together our research findings and summarize the contributions we have made on both the theoretical and empirical fronts and also discuss some of the policy implications of our research. We begin by reviewing the empirical results for each of the models tested and drawing conclusions about the performance of each model. We follow our summary of results by considering how our findings address central debates and research puzzles in the democratic peace literature and the study of international conflict more broadly. We then turn to a discussion of the policy relevance of our findings. In the final section we draw upon the key insights of our work and explore some possible directions for future research.

Review of empirical findings

While we suspect many readers hope never again to look at another table containing statistical results after working their way through Chapters 7

Table 10.1 *Empirical support for hypotheses tested from the International Politics Model*

	Predicted relationships in equation to be tested			
	Status quo stage			
Hypotheses regarding	Force	Talks	Negotiations stage	Escalation stage
Common security ties (**IP1**)	−(S)	−(S)	+(S)	−(M)
Military balance (**IP2**)	+(S)	+(W)	−(M)	+(M)
Strategic value of territory (**IP3**)	+(S)	+(S)	−(W)	+(S)
Involvement of state in another dispute (**IP4i**)	−(W)	−(M)	+(M)	−(W)
Adversary's involvement in another dispute (**IP4ii**)	+(S)	+(W)	−(W)	+(M)

Note: A positive sign (+) indicates that in the statistical tests the estimated coefficient should have a value greater than zero; a negative sign (−) indicates that in the statistical tests the estimated coefficient should have a value less than zero. "S" indicates that the statistical findings provide strong support for the hypothesis; "M" indicates that the statistical findings provide moderate support for the hypothesis; "W" indicates that the statistical findings provide weak or no support for the hypothesis.

to 9, we think it is helpful to organize our reviews of each model with a series of summary tables (Tables 10.1–10.4).

We start with the results for the International Politics Model (see Table 10.1). The five independent variables that comprise the International Politics Model generate mixed, yet systematic results. The strongest findings were produced for the Status Quo and Escalation Stages, while much weaker results were associated with the Negotiations Stage. This pattern of results indicates that the International Politics Model is far better at explaining the decisions of state leaders to initiate and escalate military confrontations over disputed territory than accounting for decisions to pursue negotiations and to offer territorial concessions. For example, the strategic value of territory, the relative balance of military strength, and the adversary's involvement in other military conflicts all figured centrally in decisions to threaten and use military force (**IP3, IP2,** and **IP4ii**). The estimated coefficients for these three variables were consistently in the predicted direction and statistically significant, and changes in these three variables always produced substantively large effects. The lone variable that did help to explain diplomatic patterns of dispute settlement was the presence of common security ties between challenger and target states (**IP1**). If the leaders of challenger and target states shared a common territorial dispute adversary or military alliance, they were both more likely to offer concessions to one another if they entered into negotiations. In sum, the International Politics Model offers considerable explanatory insights into the causes of crises and wars over disputed territory in this past century. The primary limitation of the model is that it does not account for the alternative policies of addressing territorial claims through negotiations and settling disputes through negotiated agreements.

The most elaborate model we tested was the Political Accountability Model (see Table 10.2). A total of fifteen hypotheses were tested, providing for an extensive assessment of the causal impact of institutional accountability on leadership decisions in foreign policy. We found the Political Accountability Model to be particularly strong precisely where the International Politics Model was weak. Overall, the strongest results for the Accountability Model were associated with decisions to initiate talks in the Status Quo Stage and to offer concessions in the Negotiations Stage. For example, we determined that the initiation of talks and the decision to put concessions on the table were linked to the electoral cycle of democratic countries (**PA4i–ii**). In particular, we found that the beginning of negotiations and their conclusion with concessions were most likely in periods shortly after national elections. In contrast, diplomatic initiatives to start talks and to reach agreements based on mutual concessions were far less likely as new elections approached. Democratic leaders were also strategic in deciding when to engage in domestic political struggles over the ratification of territorial treaties. For example, concessions were more likely by democratic leaders when the president or prime minister's ruling party or coalition controlled a majority of seats in the legislature or parliament (**PA3i**). A similar finding held when we considered the political standing of democratic leaders in adversary states. That is, the political strength and security of a democratic adversary government (**PA3ii**) was often viewed as a favorable opportunity for states to try and reach a negotiated territorial agreement based on mutual concessions. Finally, while democratic leaders favored negotiations over threats of force to challenge the territorial status quo (**PA1i**), they were often quite hesitant to offer concessions in negotiations when domestic opposition and controversy was expected in the wake of more accommodative policies (**PA1iii, PA2i–ii**). In the absence of high political costs for offering concessions, democratic leaders do seem inclined to seek a settlement through reciprocal concessions, but standing firm and accepting stalemated talks is preferable to democratic leaders when public and elite opinion is deeply divided or anchored at more hawkish policy positions.

The Accountability Model also provided insights into the initiation and escalation of military confrontations. One consistent finding was

Table 10.2 *Empirical support for hypotheses tested from the Political Accountability Model*

	Predicted relationship in equations to be tested			
	Status quo stage		Negotiations	Escalation
Hypotheses regarding	Force	Talks	stage	stage
Comparisons across political systems				
Democratic vs. non-democratic (**PA1i**)	−(S)	+(S)	+(M)	−(W)
Democracy and military risk (**PA1i**)	−(W)	NA	NA	−(M)
Democratic adversary and signaling (**PA1ii**)	−(W)	NA	+(S)	−(S)
Democratic response to stalemate (**PA1iii**)	−(W)	+(W)	−(M)	NA
Democracy and enduring rivalry (**PA2i**)	NS(S)	NS(S)	NS(S)	NS(S)
Democracy and ethnic ties (**PA2ii**)	+(S)	+(S)	−(S)	+(W)
Comparisons within political systems				
Legislative support for government (**PA3i**)	+(W)	+(W)	+(S)	+(W)
Adversary government legislative support (**PA3ii**)	−(W)	+(W)	+(M)	−(M)
Time since elections (**PA4i**)	−(M)	−(S)	−(M)	−(W)
Recent elections in adversary (**PA4ii**)	−(W)	+(S)	NA	NA
Time since elections in adversary (**PA4ii**)	NA	NA	−(M)	+(M)
Politically secure non-democratic leaders (**PA5i**)	+(W)	+(M)	+(W)	+(M)
Politically secure non-democratic leaders in adversary (**PA5ii**)	−(S)	+(W)	+(M)	−(M)
Comparisons among dyads				
Democratic dyads (**PA6**)	−(S)	+(S)	+(S)	−(S)
Non-democratic states in mixed dyads and military conflict (**PA7i & PA7iii**)	+(S)	−(S)	NA	+(M)
Non-democratic states in mixed dyads and negotiations (**PA7ii**)	NA	NA	+(M)	NA

Note: A positive sign (+) indicates that in the statistical tests the estimated coefficient should have a value greater than zero; a negative sign (−) indicates that in the statistical tests the estimated coefficient should have a value less than zero. "NA" indicates that there is no hypothesis to be tested, while "NS" indicates that the estimated coefficient should not be statistically significant. "S" indicates that the statistical findings provide strong support for the hypothesis; "M" indicates that the statistical findings provide moderate support for the hypothesis; "W" indicates that the statistical findings provide weak or no support for the hypothesis.

that leaders were reluctant to escalate military confrontations to high levels when the adversary's leadership was politically secure and thus more capable of withstanding any domestic opposition that might arise in the event of an armed conflict (**PA3ii, PA4ii, PA5ii**). Another supportive finding was that democratic leaders were able to signal their resolve to use force in military confrontations more effectively than their non-democratic counterparts (**PA1ii**). When democratic leaders in target states signaled their intention to use force at the outset of a military confrontation, challengers were less likely to escalate and risk war. We also found that democratic dyads were far less likely to become embroiled in military confrontations and that democratic leaders were unlikely to escalate those confrontations to higher levels of force (**PA6**). In fact, there were no cases of democratic challengers and targets waging war against each other over disputed territory. Finally, in disputes between democratic and non-democratic states, military conflict generally resulted from the more aggressive policies of non-democratic leaders (**PN7i, PN7iii**). Compared to democratic leaders in mixed dyads, non-democratic leaders were more likely to initiate military threats and to escalate them to high levels.

The results for the Political Norms Model were quite strong for the Status Quo Stage but weaker for the subsequent Negotiations and Escalation Stages (see Table 10.3). For example, leaders with strong nonviolent norms were far less likely to rely on military threats and to instead favor negotiations in pursuit of territorial claims in the Status Quo Stage (**PN1i**). However, these same leaders were only somewhat more likely to offer concessions in negotiations and there was no systematic evidence that they were less likely to escalate military confrontations to high levels. Similarly, among authoritarian regimes, leaders with particularly violent norms were more likely to initiate military threats as opposed to seeking negotiations in the Status Quo Stage (**PN5**). In the Negotiations and Escalation Stages, however, there was only weak support for the hypothesis that these same leaders would be less likely to offer concessions yet more willing to escalate to high levels of force. However, when the leaders of both challenger and target states shared very violent domestic norms (**PN7**), then neither party was likely to offer concessions in negotiations, while both sides were more likely to escalate military confrontations to high levels.

Another finding was that the leaders of new democracies were more conflictual than leaders from well-established democratic countries (**PN4**). For example, leaders of newly democratic countries were clearly more likely to initiate and escalate military confrontations and somewhat less likely to offer concessions in negotiations. The Norms Model

Table 10.3 *Empirical support for hypotheses tested from the Political Norms Model*

| | Predicted relationship in equations to be tested | | | |
| | Status quo stage | | Negotiations stage | Escalation stage |
Hypotheses regarding	Force	Talks		
Comparisons across political systems				
Strong vs. weak nonviolent norms (PN1i)	−(S)	+(S)	+(M)	−(W)
Nonviolent norms and the response to stalemate (PN1ii)	−(M)	+(M)	+(W)	−(W)
Nonviolent norms and military advantage (PN2)	−(W)	+(W)	NA	−(W)
Nonviolent vs. violent norms among challenger leaders (PN3)	NA	NA	NA	−(W)
Nonviolent vs. violent norms among target leaders (PN3)	NA	NA	NA	NS(S)
Comparisons within political systems				
Recently established democracies (PN4)	+(S)	−(W)	−(W)	+(S)
Highly repressive non-democracies (PN5)	+(S)	−(S)	−(W)	+(W)
Comparisons among dyads				
Dyads with nonviolent norms (PN6i)	−(S)	+(W)	+(S)	−(S)
Dyads of recently established democracies (PN6ii)	+(S)	−(W)	−(W)	+(NT)
Dyads of highly repressive non-democratic leaders (PN7)	+(W)	−(M)	−(M)	+(S)
Leaders with strongest violent norms in mixed dyads (PN8)	+(S)	−(S)	−(W)	+(M)

Note: A positive sign (+) indicates that in the statistical tests the estimated coefficient should have a value greater than zero; a negative sign (−) indicates that in the statistical tests the estimated coefficient should have a value less than zero. "NA" indicates that there is no hypothesis to be tested; "NS" indicates that the estimated coefficient should not be statistically significant. "S" indicates that the statistical findings provide strong support for the hypothesis; "M" indicates that the statistical findings provide moderate support for the hypothesis; "W" indicates that the statistical findings provide weak or no support for the hypothesis; "NT" indicates that the hypothesis could not be tested due to insufficient data.

also produced fairly strong results when we examined the diplomatic and military interactions of states with strong nonviolent democratic norms (**PN6i**). In such dyads the initiation and escalation of military conflicts were far less likely and, in fact, there were no cases of war being fought

Table 10.4 *Empirical support for hypotheses tested from the Political Affinity Model*

	Predicted relationships in equations to be tested			
	Status quo stage		Negotiations stage	Escalation stage
Hypotheses regarding	Force	Talks		
Similar vs. dissimilar dyads (**PAF1i**)	−(W)	+(W)	+(W)	−(W)
Recent change to political similarity (**PAF1ii**)	+(S)	−(S)	−(S)	+(W)
Relations between similar states when a threat exists (**PAF2i**)	−(W)	+(W)	+(M)	−(M)
Relations between similar states when a threat to adversary exists (**PAF2ii**)	−(M)	+(W)	+(M)	−(S)
Relations between dissimilar states when a threat exists (**PAF3i**)	−(W)	NA	+(W)	−(M)
Relations between dissimilar states when a threat to adversary exists (**PAF3ii**)	+(S)	+(S)	−(W)	+(W)

Note: A positive sign (+) indicates that in the statistical tests the estimated coefficient should have a value greater than zero; a negative sign (−) indicates that in the statistical tests the estimated coefficient should have a value less than zero; "NA" indicates that there is no hypothesis to be tested. "S" indicates that the statistical findings provide strong support for the hypothesis; "M" indicates that the statistical findings provide moderate support for the hypothesis; "W" indicates that the statistical findings provide weak or no support for the hypothesis.

between states in which both leaders shared strong domestic norms of nonviolent bargaining. Furthermore, these same leaders were more likely to offer concessions in negotiations compared to leaders with more violent, non-democratic norms. An interesting finding regarding democratic dyads was that military conflicts were more likely in disputes between two newly democratic states compared to disputes between two well-established democracies (**PN6ii**). Finally, in mixed dyads military conflict was due largely to the more aggressive policies of leaders with stronger violent norms (**PN8**). Leaders with such violent norms were more likely to initiate military threats and to escalate these military confrontations to high levels.

The last set of results to review is for the Political Affinity Model (see Table 10.4). Of the three domestic models tested, the Affinity Model produced the weakest results. Across each of the three stages of territorial disputes tested weak results were generally more common than supportive results, and no single hypothesis received consistently strong support. As a result, we conclude that the similarity of political institutions between states and the corresponding incentives to cooperate with potential political allies is not a strong and consistent motivating force that limits diplomatic and military conflict between states.

The best set of results was for the hypothesis that states would be more conflictual with a political ally when the two states had only recently become politically similar (**PAF1ii**). In the Status Quo Stage challenger states were more likely to issue threats and to avoid negotiating with new political allies. In the Negotiations Stage both challengers and targets were less likely to offer concessions to new political allies. There were also supportive findings for the claim that when state leaders were threatened by security threats, they were more likely to accommodate their political allies (**PAF2i**). For example, threatened leaders were more likely to offer concessions while less likely to escalate military confrontations against politically similar territorial dispute adversaries. A related supportive finding was that if a political ally was threatened, state leaders were less likely to initiate military conflicts or escalate them to high levels against the threatened ally (**PAF2ii**).

Contributions to the democratic peace literature

In discussing the contributions of our research, we want to return to a number of questions we raised in our review of the democratic peace literature in Chapter 1. In that review we identified six areas in which we believed our research could advance scholarship on the democratic peace. We now reconsider these six areas and discuss how our results have added to scholarly knowledge in these areas.

The payoffs of adopting an alternative research design

We want to begin by arguing that our decision to replace the dyad-year as the unit of analysis with state-level choices at each stage of a territorial dispute provides a number of advantages. When disputes are broken down into three related but sequential stages we believe that theoretical analysis is improved since a more complete set of policy choices requires explanation. Instead of theorizing about the "conflict involvement" of dyads, the researcher is pressed to account for more precise policy choices regarding the initiation of talks or military confrontations, as well as the outcomes of negotiations or military crises. Furthermore, the decisions of both challenger and target states are analyzed explicitly, enabling the analyst to try and account for patterns of initiation and response in their strategic interactions over disputed territory. The result is that multiple dependent variables require theoretical explanation and the opportunity arises for analysts to think carefully about the logical implications of models of domestic institutions for explaining the various outcomes to each stage of a territorial dispute. In sum, we believe this type of theoretical and empirical research nicely captures some of the essential dynamics of international disputes that theories of the democratic peace should seek to explain.

One important advantage of this research design for our purposes is that the results of empirical tests can be compared across the different stages. As a result, we were able to determine that the International Politics Model was quite powerful at explaining decisions to threaten and then escalate military confrontations but quite weak at explaining the linked decisions to initiate talks and to offer concessions in negotiations. In contrast, we found that domestic-level models were better at accounting for the initiation and outcome of negotiations as opposed to the initiation and escalation of force. These are new findings that we do not believe have been identified in prior research.

By focusing on states as the unit of analysis we were able to clarify and sharpen our understanding of the monadic version of the democratic peace. For example, one interesting finding is that the monadic results for the Accountability and Norms Models are quite similar. The results from tests of both models show that the monadic effects of democracy are strongest in the initial period of the Status Quo Stage. Democratic leaders are far more likely to favor negotiations over threats of force compared to their non-democratic counterparts. However, once we turn to the Negotiations and Escalation Stages, we find that democratic leaders are not that different in their decisions to offer concessions or escalate military force. An additional advantage of our design is that we can test specific "directional" hypotheses and pinpoint more precise causal mechanisms. For instance, as mentioned earlier, we found a series of consistent results for the impact of domestic political strength. Our results demonstrate more precisely that military confrontations often do not escalate to higher levels of force because state leaders fear that a domestically secure adversary will be able to bear the political costs of fighting a war.

An added benefit of our research design is that we can still test important dyadic hypotheses while also testing a number of monadic hypotheses that the dyad-year design cannot accommodate. Furthermore, we add to the richness of previous dyadic findings of a democratic peace by testing dyadic propositions across different conflict stages. For example, we see that the absence of war between democratic dyads is due largely to the fact that democratic states rarely initiate military confrontations against each other in the Status Quo Stage and instead are much more likely to rely on negotiations. As a result, democratic states generally settle their disputes through negotiations and avoid altogether the risks and dangers associated with escalation in military crises. In conclusion, we think that empirical patterns of conflict and cooperation become more transparent to the researcher when disputes are explicitly broken down into a series of state decisions at different stages. This greater transparency then helps the researcher to generalize with greater accuracy and precision.

Comparing the explanatory power of Political Norms vs. Political Accountability Models

A common position in the literature is that democratic norms and institutions are complementary causes of the democratic peace and that it is difficult to separate out the causal effects of each model in empirical tests (see the literature reviews in Maoz 1997, 1998, and Ray 1995). In this book, however, we have argued that theories of political norms and institutional accountability do not consistently predict the same pattern of diplomatic and military behavior. In particular, we identified divergent hypotheses regarding comparisons of democratic vs. non-democratic states. The clear prediction that emerges from the Norms Model in Chapter 5 is that leaders with strong nonviolent democratic norms should adopt less aggressive and conflictual policies than their non-democratic counterparts. However, the logic of the Political Accountability Model in Chapter 4 suggests that at times domestic political incentives can push democratic leaders towards policies that are equally, if not more, conflictual than those expected of non-democratic leaders.

These are points of clear divergence between the two models. We found that the empirical evidence generally supported the expectations of the Accountability Model. For example, our results show that democratic leaders find it quite difficult to offer concessions in certain situations: to enduring rivals, in the aftermath of recent stalemated talks, and when issues of political self-determination for ethnic co-nationals are at stake. Furthermore, democratic leaders are no different than non-democratic leaders in their willingness to threaten force against enduring rivals, and they are actually more likely to initiate military threats in support of ethnic co-nationals seeking self-determination.

In short, the primary weakness of the Norms Model when drawing comparisons across political systems is twofold: (a) the failure to account adequately for democratic intransigence in negotiations, and (b) the difficulty of explaining why at times democratic leaders become as aggressive, if not more so, than non-democratic leaders. We believe that the basic logic of the Political Accountability Model can be used to explain this pattern of more aggressive democratic behavior. That is, when norms-based incentives to pursue more cooperative policies conflict with domestic political pressures to act more aggressively, the latter should have a stronger impact since they are more directly linked to the political survival of incumbent leaders. Put differently, democratic norms of conflict resolution may lose out to nationalism and expectations of political support for tougher hard-line policies when adversaries are long-term rivals, or are denying rights of self-determination to ethnic co-nationals in disputed territory.

The puzzle of variation in the conflict behavior of democratic and non-democratic states

We noted in Chapter 1 that an underdeveloped area of theoretical analysis in the democratic peace literature was the substantial variation in the conflict behavior of both democratic and non-democratic states. As a result, in the development of both the Political Norms and Accountability Models we devised hypotheses that attempted to explain intra-regime differences in diplomatic and military behavior. The intra-regime comparisons in the Norms Model focus on how long democratic institutions have been in place, or how violent and repressive leaders in non-democratic systems have been. The Accountability Model argues that the political security of incumbent leaders is central to understanding their diplomatic and military behavior. Among democratic leaders, the timing of elections and the strength of opposition parties are key differences, while in non-democratic systems the presence or absence of violent rebellion and recent military coup attempts are critical. Empirically, the statistical results in Chapters 7 to 9 provide considerable support for a number of within-regimes hypotheses from both the Norms and Accountability Models. For example, as noted earlier, hypotheses from the Norms Model that leaders from recently established democracies should engage in more conflictual behavior were supported by the results of the statistical tests (also see Senese 1999). This pattern was true at the individual state level as well as at the dyadic level. Similarly, among non-democratic states we found evidence at both the monadic and dyadic levels to indicate that leaders with the most violent domestic norms were more likely to challenge the status quo with military threats and to escalate military confrontations to high levels.

The empirical findings for the Accountability Model were also supportive. Among democracies, differences in the electoral cycle were central to understanding whether negotiations would be pursued and if concessions would be offered in rounds of talks. In addition, there was some support for the hypothesis that democratic leaders were more likely to initiate military threats early in their own electoral cycle or in the electoral cycle of democratic adversaries. The strength of opposition parties was also important in understanding whether democratic leaders would offer concessions in negotiations or adopt more inflexible positions. Among non-democratic states, the strongest findings were that adversaries were less likely to initiate and escalate military threats against well-entrenched leaders, but there was not strong evidence that such leaders were more likely to turn to military force themselves.

Overall, we believe these findings from the Norms and Accountability Models contribute to a more nuanced understanding of the complex pattern of conflictual and cooperative foreign policy behaviors pursued by both democratic and non-democratic leaders.

The debate over audience costs and democratic institutions

In Chapter 1 we noted that two different lines of argument have emerged regarding the impact of domestic audience costs on foreign policy decisions. In one line of analysis, attention is focused on the potential response of opposition elites and the public to the use of force and high levels of escalation. The general conclusion drawn is that democratic leaders should be cautious about the use of military force in international disputes because democratic institutions provide greater opportunities for political opposition to contest and even to remove leaders for pursuing costly or failed policies of military conflict (e.g. Bueno de Mesquita and Lalman 1992: ch. 5; Maoz and Russett 1993; Morgan and Campbell 1991). Another line of argument, however, has shifted the analysis of democratic accountability to focus on the political costs that democratic leaders risk when they back away from higher levels of conflict in a crisis or international dispute (Fearon 1994b; Schultz 1998, 2001a, 2001b). The central claim is that threats of military force by democratic leaders are actually quite credible because such leaders know that a failure to follow through on such threats will be used by political opponents to charge the political leadership with weakness and ineffectiveness. In contrast, non-democratic leaders can issue strong threats and then decide to back down, since the political risks of retreating or bluffing are less threatening because domestic political opposition is in a much weaker position. High domestic audience costs for accommodative policies, then, can provide incentives for democratic leaders to prefer conflictual over more accommodating policies.

Theoretically, the position we have taken in this debate is that democratic leaders should be attentive to both types of domestic audience costs.

In that sense, we do not believe the models and arguments of scholars that focus on different types of audience costs should necessarily be viewed as rival approaches. Instead, scholars can and should focus on the different ways in which political accountability influences foreign policy decisions. We see no logical reason to argue that democratic leaders who are worried about the political costs of retreating in a crisis would not also be worried about the domestic political response to becoming involved in a large-scale military confrontation. As a result, we expect both types of audience costs to be important and our empirical findings support this conclusion. For example, the signaling hypothesis (**PA1ii**) associated with arguments concerning the costs of retreat and more accommodative policies for democratic leaders was strongly supported in the Negotiations and Escalation Stages. The signals of resolve sent by democratic leaders did indeed seem to be viewed as more credible by adversaries. We also found that democratic leaders were less likely to offer concessions in negotiations over disputed territory when they expected more accommodative policies to be particularly controversial and open to domestic criticism. On the other hand, the strong monadic effect of democracy in the Status Quo Stage (to not initiate military confrontations) is consistent with arguments about the generally higher risks of using force in international disputes for democratic leaders. Furthermore, another finding we report that is consistent with claims about the higher political costs of using force for democracies is that the absence of strong opposition parties in democratic legislatures and parliaments deters military escalation by outside parties. That is, states are deterred from attacking democratic adversaries whose leaders face weak political opposition because these politically secure democratic leaders can now escalate militarily, knowing that political opposition within the legislature is less capable of holding leaders accountable for military setbacks.

Overall, our empirical findings do not provide clear and consistent support for the influence of only one type of domestic audience cost. Instead, we found supporting evidence for both types of costs. Nevertheless, not all of the hypotheses received strong support. For example, democratic states were neither more nor less likely to be the targets of military threats in the Status Quo Stage. Arguments emphasizing the costs of escalation for democratic leaders might expect democratic leaders to be more frequent targets, while a theoretical focus on the higher costs of retreat for democratic leaders might lead to the expectation that democratic states would be targeted less frequently. While it is very useful to specify the different hypotheses associated with each type of audience cost (as we attempted in Chapter 4), the larger common theoretical link remains: democratic political leaders are very likely to be concerned about the political risks of either accommodative or confrontational foreign policies in many international disputes. In sum, instead of viewing the more recent work on the domestic audience costs of retreat for democratic leaders as posing a theoretical challenge to earlier work, we think it is better to view such work as highlighting aspects of democratic accountability that had been neglected in earlier work on the democratic peace.

The debate over the strategic behavior of democratic states in disputes with non-democratic states

As we argued in Chapter 1, dyadic and monadic versions of the democratic peace are typically based on quite different views about how democratic state leaders will bargain in disputes with non-democratic opponents. The theoretical debate centers on whether democratic leaders should be expected to adopt more intransigent and aggressive policies towards non-democracies. Proponents of the dyadic approach argue that democratic leaders will consistently prefer negotiations to the use of force only in disputes with other democracies, whereas they will be intransigent and aggressive in their policies towards non-democracies. In Chapters 4 and 5 we argued against this common position in the literature and instead hypothesized that military conflict in mixed dyads should generally result from the more risk-acceptant and aggressive policies of non-democratic leaders. The empirical results we report in Chapters 7 and 9 provide consistent support for our hypotheses. As a result, we find little systematic evidence to support the conclusion that military conflict in disputes between democratic and non-democratic states is often driven by the more aggressive policies of democratic leaders. Instead, we find that high levels of military conflict involvement for democratic states in mixed dyads is more often a reflection of democratic states responding to the initial military threats or escalatory policies of non-democratic states.

The debate over international-level vs. domestic-level explanations of foreign policy behavior

Back in Chapter 1 we argued that the democratic peace literature has been an integral part of the theoretical and empirical debate concerning the importance of domestic political factors in explaining military conflict and war. The starting point for our theoretical analysis in this book was that realist critics had failed to present a compelling logical case for why domestic-level variables should not be expected to shape the foreign policy choices of state leaders in systematic ways. At the same time, we also noted that we think the diplomatic and military policies of states are quite responsive to the international strategic and military environment within which policy-makers must operate. As a result, we find ourselves holding the middle ground. We argue that both domestic- and international-level variables logically should be expected to affect state policy in international disputes. Furthermore, we think less effort should be devoted to drawing strong distinctions between the two levels of analysis. Instead, we think a more compelling theoretical orientation is to consider foreign policy choices over war and peace as reflecting the interplay of domestic and international conditions.

Empirically, the broad and diverse set of supportive findings we report for the Political Accountability and Political Norms Models indicates clearly that domestic political conditions are essential to understanding how international disputes evolve over time. This does not imply that international political and military conditions provide limited insights into the dynamics of international disputes. As we have already discussed, the International Politics Model produced strong results for the initiation and escalation of military confrontations over disputed territory. Nevertheless, the Accountability and Norms Models also produced a number of strong findings that helped us to further explain and refine our understanding of when military conflicts will be initiated and when such conflicts will escalate to higher levels. The limitations of adopting a theoretical approach that focuses exclusively on international-level variables is most evident when trying to explain when and why state leaders will seek negotiations and the peaceful settlement of international disputes. The weakest results for the International Politics Model are associated with explaining efforts by state leaders to open up negotiations and whether they will offer concessions over disputed territory. In contrast, some of the strongest findings for the Accountability and Norms Models center on understanding why state leaders will turn to negotiations and peaceful dispute settlement. While we value and recognize the intellectual attractiveness of highly parsimonious theories, we believe that critical decisions in foreign policy over war and peace will rarely reflect the dominating influence of a very small number of factors that reside at either the domestic or international levels. The great challenge for scholars is to develop rigorous theory that combines both levels of analysis while retaining as much parsimony as possible.

Policy implications

In this section we draw some connections between the results of our research and their policy implications. In Chapter 1 we identified several areas in which we argued that our research could prove policy-relevant.

We now return to each of these areas and consider how our findings might contribute to better policy.

Is democracy an asset or liability for foreign policy-makers?

We believe that the empirical evidence supports the conclusion that democratic norms and accountability are, on balance, an asset that can be used by democratic leaders to protect and advance their country's interests in international disputes. Specifically, five findings are the basis for drawing this conclusion. First, democratic states were not singled out as targets of military threats and probes in the Status Quo Stage. As a result, there is no systematic evidence to suggest that the leaders of non-democratic states believe that democratic leaders are vulnerable to coercive pressure and therefore more willing to offer territorial concessions in order to avoid military confrontations. Second, in the Escalation Stage the deterrent policies of democratic leaders were more effective in preventing escalation than those of non-democratic leaders. This indicates that adversaries recognize that once democratic leaders take a strong and public position in a crisis they are unlikely to back down due to the domestic political costs of a retreat. As a result, greater political accountability enhances the credibility of deterrent threats by democratic leaders. Third, in the Negotiations Stage it was found that states were more likely to offer concessions when their democratic negotiating adversary enjoyed strong political support in the legislature or parliament. This is because presidents and prime ministers, when backed by majority support from political parties back home, come to the negotiating table with the credible power to make deals that could be ratified. As a result, states are more willing to put concessions on the table because they expect any agreement reached will remain in place when taken back home by their democratic counterpart. Once again, greater political accountability can strengthen the bargaining position of democratic leaders. Fourth, in the Negotiations Stage signals of resolve by democratic leaders were more effective in securing concessions from negotiating adversaries than were signals of resolve by non-democratic states. This finding suggests that democratic states can be quite effective in bargaining with non-democratic states and that democratic leaders are quite capable of sending credible signals of resolve in rounds of talks. Fifth, in the Negotiations Stage there was no systematic evidence that democratic states were more likely to concede in the wake of previously stalemated talks. The evidence, in fact, suggests the opposite is more likely to be true. That is, non-democratic leaders are more likely to make concessions in the wake of previously stalemated talks than are democratic leaders. This indicates that democratic norms do not lead democratic negotiators to concede first in difficult negotiations and it also suggests that non-democratic negotiators do not rely upon concessions from democratic states to break stalemates in negotiations.

The broad policy implications that follow from these findings are that democratic leaders should be able to effectively manage disputes with non-democratic states. When democratic leaders have strong support in the legislature or parliament they should push for talks and concessions from their non-democratic adversary. Furthermore, democratic leaders should be prepared to stake out firm negotiating positions early on in talks. If a military confrontation does emerge, then deterrent policies can be quite effective as long as democratic leaders take the initiative and signal their resolve and communicate this resolve early on in a crisis.

Promoting the resolution of international disputes

There are two findings from our research that have useful policy implications in terms of the conditions under which disputes are most likely to be resolved through negotiations. First, there is strong evidence that democratic leaders are more inclined to pursue talks and offer concessions in periods shortly after national elections. As a result, this suggests that states should seize the opportunity after elections to push for talks and to try and make relatively rapid progress in the negotiations if the goal is to conclude an agreement. For one, the later the talks begin and the longer they last, the lower the prospects of securing concessions from the democratic negotiating partner. A related implication is that state leaders may want to downplay the resumption of negotiations or try to generate strong expectations of progress in ongoing or forthcoming talks if they know that their democratic negotiating partner is entering into the later stages of the electoral cycle. In this situation, it might be preferable to defer talks or to accept the fact that the goal of talks at this time should not be to reach any formal agreement but rather to lay the groundwork for more serious talks after elections have been held.

A second finding with policy relevance is that states are more likely to concede in negotiations when the ruling coalition of the president or prime minister controls a significant majority of the seats in the legislature or parliament. One implication is that democratic leaders should be strategic and use this situation of domestic strength to their advantage in negotiations. For example, an opportune time for democratic leaders to press adversaries to make concessions is when democratic leaders have strong legislative or parliamentary support. Conversely, democratic leaders should understand that they are less likely to secure concessions when they lack such political backing. This point leads directly to the second implication that the bargaining tactic of using political weakness at home to gain greater concessions at the international negotiating table is unlikely to be very effective. The empirical evidence suggests that state leaders are more impressed with the political security of their negotiating partners. While it may be an appealing policy to try and use political weakness to strengthen one's bargaining position, the hard reality is that states are more likely to offer concessions to politically secure negotiating partners because they view commitments to reciprocate concessions and then ratify agreements as more credible from leaders with strong backing at home.

Third-party efforts at mediation and extended deterrence

Two additional findings are of practical value to policy-makers who seek to protect an ally involved in a territorial dispute. First, challengers take advantage of an adversary's involvement in military confrontations with other states to initiate threats and to probe the resolve and military capabilities of the potentially distracted adversary. As a result, for those states seeking to deter military threats to their allies, they should recognize this situation as a vulnerable time for their ally and therefore be prepared to warn challengers that they are committed to their ally's security. Concrete policy actions could include public and repeated statements by high-level officials of their country's extended deterrent commitments as well as military exercises and deployments that demonstrate the ability to project military forces. Second, once military threats have been issued, further escalation by challengers is strongly influenced by the local balance of conventional forces. For states worried about attacks against allies, their short-term threats and military actions will fail to achieve strong deterrent effects unless they can concretely contribute to denying the challenger a local military advantage. As a result, the defending state often will need to undertake substantial military actions on short notice.

If we turn to the role of third parties as mediators in negotiations over disputed territory, we believe that several findings from the Status Quo and Negotiations Stages are of policy relevance. For example, the previously discussed findings on the importance of the electoral cycle for the initiation and outcome of negotiations suggests that a "ripe" time for mediators to push democratic leaders to open up talks and offer concessions is shortly after national elections. Therefore, if democratic leaders enjoy strong party support, then mediators should press negotiating partners of the democratic state that the time is favorable for negotiating mutual concessions and securing treaty ratification. Finally, we found considerable evidence that democratic leaders can be quite sensitive to the domestic political costs of offering concessions. As a result, third parties should be very attentive to designing initiatives and crafting agreement terms so that any substantial territorial concessions made by the democratic side are offset by side payments back to the democratic side in the form of non-territorial gains.

Directions for future research

In this final section we would like to discuss some preliminary ideas for further research that build on the theoretical and empirical work we have presented in this book.

The Political Norms Model

We think one area within the Norms Model that holds promise is to develop and test hypotheses that focus more directly on the norms of individual leaders. In our analyses we focused on broader patterns of domestic political conflict and bargaining within which political elites operated and argued that elite norms of conflict resolution would be reflective of this domestic environment. Of course, individual political leaders may respond differently to this same domestic political environment, and as a result, political norms may vary among political leaders despite a common political setting. In particular, we think it would be fruitful to try and develop general arguments to explain why some political leaders adopt more nonviolent norms in international disputes despite frequent political violence and repression of opposition groups at home.

Another topic to explore would be the strength of domestic legal systems as an important aspect of democratic norms. It would be particularly useful to know whether domestic political conflicts are commonly subject to legal adjudication. This type of theoretical approach would facilitate comparisons across different political systems as well as comparisons among democratic regimes. For example, researchers could look for cross-national patterns of recourse to arbitration and legal adjudication as a means of settling international disputes. Another related area of inquiry would be to examine the impact of international law on diplomatic and military behavior.

A third area to consider would be the impact of democratic norms in wartime situations (civil and interstate), with particular attention directed at questions of targeting and killing civilians. Among the important issues within this area would be state compliance with the laws of war and the conditions under which civilians are at greatest risk of being attacked and punished by democratic leaders. Put differently, we might want to understand when and why democratic leaders sometimes disregard legal and moral constraints on protecting civilians in wartime.

The Political Accountability Model

We think continued empirical research on the domestic audience costs of retreating for democratic leaders is important to pursue. A limitation of existing empirical tests (including our own efforts) is that the extent of public or opposition elite knowledge is not carefully coded. While it may seem intuitive to think that military confrontations are very public events involving threats and shows of force, we actually think there may be considerable variation in public and elite awareness regarding the military actions that have happened or are currently happening between governments. The political costs to democratic leaders of not escalating further or failing to secure any gains could be minimal if domestic audiences are not aware that a military confrontation is taking place. More compelling tests of these audience costs arguments therefore should try to include data on the public versus hidden nature of military confrontations and short-term periods of international conflict.

We also believe that the Accountability Model could address questions of legal adjudication and compliance with international law in international disputes. We think that the causal arguments of the Norms and Accountability Models may differ on these questions. For example, we would expect accountability-based arguments to focus on the attitudes of domestic political opposition towards third-party involvement. Domestic audiences, however, may or may not accept this type of outside involvement. While it could be argued that democratic leaders might turn to legal principles and adjudication as a way to justify concessions in an international dispute, it does not seem clear that this is a fully persuasive argument. Democratic leaders might also be leery of the possible domestic costs associated with losing an international adjudicative ruling or the international costs associated with failing to comply with international directives. Our initial reaction is that democratic leaders would only be willing to seek out third-party dispute resolution when (a) an international dispute does not attract that much domestic attention, or (b) domestic audiences have confidence in and respect for third-party institutions (US policy towards the newly created International Criminal Court?). In contrast, we would think that the Norms Model would lead to less contingent or qualified claims about the willingness of democratic leaders to accept legal principles in the resolution of international disputes.

As with the Norms Model we also see promise in developing the theoretical implications of the Accountability Model for the wartime behavior of governments. For example, how does democratic accountability influence decisions to target civilians or to adopt different strategies of attack and defense? What role has domestic political opposition to the costs of war played in decisions by democratic leaders to negotiate over the termination of wars (e.g. Reiter and Stam 2002: ch. 7)? With these and other questions we see the opportunity to develop and compare hypotheses from both models and to devise new empirical tests.

General research design for studying international disputes

We believe that the general logic of thinking about international disputes as evolving over time into different stages is a very useful approach to structuring theoretical and empirical research. While we have focused on state behavior in territorial disputes, we certainly believe that other types of international disputes could be fruitfully understood within this general framework. For example, we think international trade disputes can be viewed as involving various stages centering around a series of decisions regarding when to: (a) raise complaints, (b) rely on bilateral negotiations to try and resolve differences, or (c) submit unsettled disputes to legal adjudication by bodies such as the World Trade Organization. We also think that issues of state compliance with international agreements and treaties could be modeled as a multi-stage game in which critical choices are made regarding questions such as: when to challenge agreements, by what means to challenge agreements, and how outside parties should respond to challenges.

In writing this book we hoped to make useful contributions to the specific topic of the democratic peace. In particular, we felt it was important to develop and push further the basic logic of models of domestic political institutions and to devise empirical tests that were more closely matched to the strategic choices of state leaders at different stages of international disputes. In so doing, however, we also sought to develop more general theoretical models that would provide a framework for thinking systematically about the connections between domestic and international politics. On the empirical side, we also sought to develop a general research design strategy that could be applied more broadly by scholars who seek to test theoretical models and hypotheses about state behavior in international disputes. While we urged our readers to be patient at the outset of this book, we hope those readers who followed our advice and read yet another book on the democratic peace were not disappointed.

Appendix A
The territorial dispute data set, 1919–1995

This appendix is divided into two sections. In the first section we discuss the concept of a territorial dispute in international politics. The second section concerns coding issues that we addressed in our efforts to create a data set of territorial disputes.

Territorial conflict in the international system

In the twentieth century territorial conflict has centered upon six types of disputes:

1. *Disputes between two states over competing claims to their homeland territory.* These are typically disputes between neighboring states who disagree over the location of land or river borders, the sovereignty of offshore islands, or whether the very sovereignty and independence of neighbors should be recognized.

2. *Disputes between two states with competing claims to the homeland territory of one state and the overseas territory of the other state.* These disputes often have involved major powers establishing spheres of influence and colonial empires abroad, in which territorial conflict with local states emerged over the location of borders, the sovereignty of islands, and rights to military bases. For example, in the first half of the twentieth century, China raised the issue of leased territories with Britain and France and disputed its border with the British Empire in India. Other examples include Thailand's border with French Indochina, Ethiopia's borders with Italian and British colonies, and Liberia's borders with French colonies.

3. *Disputes between two states whose competing claims involve the overseas territory of both states.* These disputes arise when two colonial empires come into direct territorial contact with each other and the borders and rights to offshore islands need to be established. Good examples include border disputes among the European colonial empires in

Africa and in the Middle East from the turn of the century to the end of World War II.

4. *Disputes between an existing state and an aspiring new state that seeks to establish its independence by seceding from the homeland territory of the existing state.* These disputes arise from the political and military weakness of central governments that are typically unable to exert effective administrative and military control of territory along their existing borders. Examples include the formation of independent states in European Russia and Central Asia following the collapse of the Tsarist regime during World War I and then again in the 1990s, the bid for independence by Tibet and Outer Mongolia from China prior to World War II, and more recently Eritrea's struggle for independence from Ethiopia.

5. *Disputes in which political units within the colonial overseas empire of a state seek to establish and be recognized as independent states.* These disputes comprise the history of decolonization across all regions of the international system as emerging states pressured British, French, Dutch, Spanish, Portuguese, Belgian, US, and Japanese governments to relinquish control of colonial and overseas territories.

6. *Disputes between states which center on claims to territorial rights to waters or land along the seabed.* These disputes concern the extension of territorial water rights off coastlines and islands, the seabeds located beneath territorial waters, and the location of continental shelves off the coastlines of states.

The first five categories of territorial disputes all focus on competing claims to land-based territory, while the sixth category focuses on claims which extend into and along the bottom of seas and oceans. The territorial dispute data set used for empirical tests in this book falls into the first three categories. The data set therefore does not generally include cases that stemmed from the break-up of existing states, typically during periods of civil war or revolution; the decolonization of colonial empires; or maritime disputes.

One borderline type of territorial dispute, which may be assigned to either category 1 or category 4, should be discussed. We included in category 1 disputes in which a central government did recognize the independence of a recently seceded new state but then subsequently reversed that policy. Thus, our data set includes several disputes that resulted from the collapse of Tsarist Russia following World War I because the new Soviet regime did explicitly recognize by treaty and/or public statements the independence of some former Russian republics and territories, but then changed that policy and reintegrated them into the newly established Soviet Union. In contrast, if the central government never recognized or accepted proclamations of self-determination and territorial independence, then we assigned the dispute to category 4 (e.g. several cases involving Serbia and the collapse of Yugoslavia in the early 1990s).

In addition, the six categories listed above do not include (a) the initial process of state formation and the many territorial conflicts which arose as smaller political-territorial units were merged into larger units, or (b) the process of colonization and empire-building by states. For the territorial disputes we studied, these historical processes had already taken place. We focused on the resulting territorial interactions between states and their colonial possessions in the twentieth century.

A complete history and analysis of territorial conflict in the international system would cover:

1. Competition between non-state territorial units that results in state formation.
2. Imperial expansion of states to include control of territory beyond homeland territory.
3. Conflict over territorial rights between state actors over homeland and/or empire territory.
4. Resistance of political-territorial units within colonial empires and homeland territories against the sovereign powers of colonial or national governments and the struggle for political-territorial independence.

These four stages of territorial conflict do not progress in a sequential order but overlap and occur simultaneously in the international system across various regions. In this book and previous research (Huth 1996) we have attempted to study only stage 3, and even within it we do not attempt to study all types of territorial disputes (maritime disputes are excluded).

In the territorial dispute data set from 1919–95 that we relied upon in this book (see Appendices B–F), disputes are broadly defined as disagreements between governments over (a) the location of existing international boundaries in particular sectors or along the length of their common border, (b) the refusal of one government to recognize another's claim of sovereign rights over islands, claiming sovereignty for itself instead, or (c) the refusal of one government to recognize another state as a sovereign political-territorial unit, laying claim to the territory of that state. A more complete and specific definition is presented in Huth (1996: ch. 2).[1]

---

[1] A short explanation is required on how cases of military occupation were coded. We included as territorial disputes cases where a state's occupation of foreign territory is

Coding issues

A number of coding issues arose in our efforts to compile a data set of territorial disputes. In creating this data set we collected the following information for each territorial dispute:

1. The states that seek to change the status quo (challenger states) by gaining territory and those that desire to preserve the status quo (target states).[2]
2. The beginning and end dates of each dispute.
3. The outcome of each dispute in terms of changes, if any, in the territorial status quo.
4. The dates of any militarized disputes initiated by challenger states in an attempt to overturn the status quo, and the outcome of such military confrontations.
5. The dates of any talks or negotiations held over disputed territory involving the challenger and target, and the outcomes of such talks.

In the bibliographies located at the end of Appendices B–F we list, for all of the territorial disputes in a region, the sources we used to collect information on the diplomatic and military actions of the states involved.

Some of the most important coding issues were as follows.

How to code disputes pursued intermittently

Sometimes a challenger pursued a claim to a territory, desisted, and then tried again after a hiatus of many years. Should this be considered one dispute or two? Similarly, suppose the first period of conflict ended in some form of settlement or agreement, but some years later the challenger renewed its claim despite the earlier resolution. Is this the same dispute? We coded these instances as multiple cases even though they involve the same challenger pressing similar territorial claims. The issues in dispute did not change over time, but given the earlier resolution of the dispute, we think it is appropriate to code the renewal of the claim as the beginning of a dispute. We could call these renewals a second phase to the dispute. The critical factor for us was that the challenger in an earlier period had

linked to an interest in annexing the territory. In other words, there must be evidence that the occupation is connected to territorial goals for the occupying state (e.g. Japanese policy in Manchuria 1931–2, Israeli occupation of the Golan Heights after the Six-Day War). In contrast, we exclude all cases of occupation that are unconnected to territorial goals and are largely political in nature (e.g. US interventions in Central America in the 1920s and 1930s, Soviet forces in Austria after World War II).

[2] In some disputes both states have claims to territory controlled by the other state or the existing border is very poorly established by prior agreements. In both situations, each state is listed as a challenger in Appendices B–F.

reached some agreement on the issue in dispute, and thus the dispute had ended. Without such an agreement we would not code multiple cases; instead we would argue that the dispute was not actively pursued for some period and then at a later date the challenger put the dispute back on the agenda of bilateral relations. Disputes often lapsed into periods in which no diplomatic activity or pursuit of a claim occurred, but such inactivity is different from a case where the challenger actually signed an agreement or acknowledged the resolution of the dispute at a previous point in time.

How to label challenger and target

The coding of challenger status in some cases had to be considered carefully. In particular, cases in which the challenger occupied disputed territory and attained *de facto* control over it while the target state refused to recognize the challenger's gains could be coded in two possible ways. Either way is plausible, and our concern was to code these cases consistently without shifting between these two approaches.

One approach (which we ultimately adopted for the cases listed in Appendices B–F) is that once the challenger has *de facto* control of disputed territory, then the erstwhile challenger should be coded as the target and the former target should be coded as the new challenger. The reason is that the original challenger had gained what it sought and therefore no longer desired to overturn the territorial status quo, but in fact sought recognition and acceptance of the new status quo. In contrast, the former target was now seeking to overturn this new status quo and therefore can be labeled the challenger. Underlying this change in labels is the notion that effective control and occupation of territory is critical to determining the status of challenger vs. target.

Another approach is to argue that the status quo is defined by the formal or legal status of the territory. Thus, the original challenger would retain its label until there is some agreement or treaty legitimizing a change in the territorial status quo. If the latter approach is adopted, then the challenger should be coded as occupying by military force the disputed territory until such time as the target reaches some agreement with the challenger.

How to code multiple claims between the same parties

In some disputes, a challenger sought to gain control over several distinct territories currently controlled by a single target. Should each claim be coded as a dispute, or should they be combined into a single dispute? We combined multiple claims into a single dispute when the challenger and target discussed and treated the multiple claims as a single set or package of territorial issues. In contrast, if the parties generally separated the claims in talks then we coded multiple disputes. Most cases of this type were handled as single separate disputes by the opposing parties and were coded as such.

How to determine whether a claim exists

Another issue in some cases was how to code whether the challenger had a claim to territory. This question could be difficult to answer for two possible reasons: (a) the legislative branch and the executive branch took contradictory courses of action, or (b) the executive branch's declaratory policy was inconsistent with operational policy.

In the first case, we always sided with the actions and policy of the executive branch in assessing whether a dispute existed and what the claims were. We frequently found evidence of political parties, individual legislators, and even legislatures as a body issuing claims where the governments in power did not. However, if an agreement or treaty signed by the executive stipulated that the legislature must ratify the agreement, then the rejection of the agreement by the legislature meant that the dispute persisted and that the executive branch had to renew talks if a lasting settlement were to be attained.

In the second case we relied on official declaratory policy in order to minimize the need to infer intentions and motives of policy-makers. In some cases the problem arose because the executive branch lacked full control over its foreign policy apparatus and, as a result, individual military or political officials pursued independent policies. In a small number of cases the issue was that the president or prime minister announced one policy but seemed to be pursuing another. Perhaps the best example was Armenia vs. Azerbaijan in the 1990s, as the Armenian government had on several occasions disavowed any direct territorial claims but its military support for ethnic Armenians in Nagorno-Karabakh suggested otherwise.

Coding by delimitation vs. demarcation

In coding the existence and duration of a territorial dispute it was repeatedly important to distinguish between the processes of delimitation and demarcation of a border or boundary. Delimitation refers to determining the location of a border in a treaty or written document, usually with respect to an attached map. Demarcation refers to the practice of actually placing on the ground physical markers to indicate the exact location of the boundary between two states. Demarcation presumes an agreement on delimitation, whether in very specific or in general terms. It is common, however, for a team of demarcation experts to have to make decisions on the ground about boundary markers since treaties and maps may not be detailed enough to provide precise guidance. Thus, treaties and agreements often recognize that the process of demarcation may lead to border adjustments and that minor changes can be expected.

In our research we generally excluded the demarcation process from the domain of territorial disputes. Only when problems of demarcation are so serious that they lead one or both states to reject, disavow, or seek modification of an existing treaty or agreement did we consider this a territorial dispute. Furthermore, we did not code the absence of demarcation as evidence of a territorial dispute. It is not unusual for countries to agree on delimitation in a treaty but then not carry out demarcation for an extended period of time. We coded disputes as ending when the treaty of delimitation was signed regardless of when demarcation was completed or even attempted.

How to code latent disputes

A final issue to consider is what might be labeled "latent" disputes. The most interesting and difficult cases to code are those in which governments seemed to recognize that there was no commonly accepted definition of a border in some area, yet they did not seem to press their interpretation of where the border should be located. From the available sources it can be difficult to determine whether the parties made official claims but agreed (perhaps tacitly) not to pursue the issue, or whether they never actually communicated a claim but did understand that a difference of opinion existed. As a general coding rule we did not code a territorial dispute as existing in these cases unless we found consistent evidence from at least two sources that one or both states had actually communicated a claim to territory and the target of that claim responded by disputing the claim.

Appendix B
Territorial disputes in Europe, 1919–1995

List of dispute cases

In this first section a summary list of territorial disputes in Europe is presented. For each dispute the following information is provided: (a) the first state listed is the challenger and the second is the target, (b) the first and last year of the dispute, and (c) a brief description of the territorial claims of the challenger. For those disputes marked with an asterisk both states are challengers and therefore the dispute is listed a second time with the identity of challenger and target reversed.

1. Albania vs. Greece* 1919–21: Claims to Epirus which extend beyond borders established in 1913
2. Albania vs. Yugoslavia* 1919–21: Claims to territories that extended beyond borders established in 1913
3. Austria vs. Hungary* 1919: Claims to Burgenland
4. Austria vs. Italy 1945–6: Claims in South Tyrol including Bolzano and sections of Trentino
5. Belgium vs. Germany 1919: Claims to Eupen and Malmedy
6. Britain vs. France* 1919–53: Claims to islands of Minquiers and Ecrehos off the French coast in the English Channel
7. Bulgaria vs. Greece 1922–3: Claims to Greek Thrace
8. Bulgaria vs. Greece* 1945–7: Claims to Greek Thrace
9. Bulgaria vs. Romania 1940: Claims to Southern Dobroju
10. Croatia vs. Slovenia* 1993–5: Claims to sections of newly established international border
11. Cyprus vs. Turkey 1974–95: Opposition to the Turkish partition of Cyprus and the formation of a Turkish Cypriot state
12. Czech Republic vs. Slovakia* 1993–4: Claims to several small sections of newly established border
13. Czechoslovakia vs. Austria 1919: Claims to Bohemia, Moravia, Gmund, and Themenau
14. Czechoslovakia vs. Hungary 1919–20: Claims to Slovakia, Bohemia, Moravia, and Silesia

15. Czechoslovakia vs. Hungary 1946–7: Claims to small areas located in Bratislava
16. Czechoslovakia vs. Poland* 1919–20: Claims to Teshen, Spiza, and Oriva
17. Denmark vs. Germany 1919–20: Claims to Schleswig
18. Denmark vs. Norway 1921–33: Claims to extend sovereign rights over Greenland along eastern coast
19. East Germany/Soviet Union vs. US/West Germany/France/UK 1948–71: Claims to West Berlin as part of East German territory and desire to terminate Western occupation rights
20. Estonia vs. Latvia* 1919–20: Claims to Hainasion in Gulf of Riga, island of Ruhnu, and town of Valga
21. Estonia vs. Russia 1992–5: Claims to bordering territory of Petseri and eastern bank of the River Narva annexed by the Soviet Union during World War II
22. Finland vs. Soviet Union* 1919–20: Claims to Petsamo, East Karelia, and other sections along the border
23. Finland vs. Soviet Union 1941–7: Claims to all territory gained by the Soviets in Winter War of 1939–40 as well as additional territory in eastern Karelia
24. France vs. Britain* 1919–53: Claims to islands of Minquiers and Ecrehos off the French coast in the English Channel
25. France vs. Germany 1919: Claims to Alsace-Lorraine, Rhineland, and Saar
26. France vs. Italy 1945–6: Claims to small sections of territory in the Po Valley
27. Germany vs. Austria 1938: Call for union with Austria
28. Germany vs. Belgium 1925–40: Claims to Eupen and Malmedy
29. Germany vs. Czechoslovakia 1938–9: Claims to Sudetenland and Silesia
30. Germany vs. France 1922–36: Claims to re-establish full sovereign control over territories of the Rhineland and Saar
31. Germany vs. Lithuania 1938–9: Claims to Memel
32. Germany vs. Poland 1938–9: Claims to revision of border and Danzig
33. Greece vs. Albania* 1919–24: Claims to revise borders established in 1913
34. Greece vs. Albania 1945–71: Claims to Northern Epirus
35. Greece vs. Bulgaria 1919: Claims to Thrace
36. Greece vs. Bulgaria* 1945–7: Claims to Thrace beyond pre-World War II borders
37. Greece vs. Cyprus 1969–82: Calls for incorporating Cyprus as part of Greece (enosis)

38. Greece vs. Italy 1919–28: Claims to the Dodecanese Islands
39. Greece vs. Turkey 1919–23: Claims to Epirus, Smyrna, Thrace, and Aegean islands.
40. Greece vs. Britain 1951–9: Desire to incorporate Cyprus as part of Greece (enosis)
41. Hungary vs. Austria* 1919–21: Claims to Burgenland
42. Hungary vs. Czechoslovakia 1938–9: Claims to Subcarpathia
43. Hungary vs. Romania 1939–40: Claims to Transylvania
44. Hungary vs. Yugoslavia 1940–1: Claims to territory lost in 1920 Peace Treaty
45. Ireland vs. Britain 1922–95: Claims to Northern Ireland
46. Italy vs. Albania 1919–20: Claims to Port of Valona and Sasseno Island as well as protectorate rights
47. Italy vs. Albania 1939: Demanding right to establish military bases on national territory and occupy islands
48. Italy vs. Austria 1919: Claims to Brenner Pass, South Tyrol, Istrian Peninsula
49. Italy vs. Greece 1940–1: Claims to Corfu and other islands along with Northern Epirus
50. Italy vs. Yugoslavia* 1919–24: Claims to Istrian Peninsula, Fiume, Dalmatian Coast, and offshore islands
51. Italy vs. Yugoslavia* 1945–75: Claims to Trieste
52. Latvia vs. Estonia* 1919–20: Claims to Hainasion in Gulf of Riga, island of Ruhnu, and town of Valga
53. Latvia vs. Lithuania* 1919–21: Claims along length of border
54. Latvia vs. Russia 1994–5: Claims to Abrene and adjacent territory which were annexed by Soviet Union during World War II
55. Lithuania vs. Germany 1919: Claims to Memel
56. Lithuania vs. Latvia* 1919–21: Claims along length of common border
57. Lithuania vs. Poland* 1919–38: Claims to Vilna
58. Netherlands vs. Belgium 1922–59: Claims to several small enclaves along border
59. Netherlands vs. West Germany* 1955–60: Claims to several small sections along border
60. Poland vs. Czechoslovakia* 1919–24: Claims to Teshen, Spiza, and Oriva and then small border adjustment near Jaworzina
61. Poland vs. Czechoslovakia 1938: Claims to Teshen and Silesia
62. Poland vs. Germany 1919–22: Claims to Danzig, Prussia, and Upper Silesia
63. Poland vs. Lithuania* 1919–23: Claims to Vilna
64. Poland vs. Soviet Russia* 1919–21: Claims to large sections of Ukraine and Belarus

65. Romania vs. Hungary 1919–20: Claims to Transylvania, Banat, and Hungarian Plain
66. Romania vs. Hungary 1945–7: Claims to all of Transylvanian territory lost to Hungary in 1939–40
67. Romania vs. Soviet Russia 1919–20: Claims to Bessarabia
68. Romania vs. Yugoslavia 1919–22: Claims to Banat and territory awarded to Yugoslavia at Versailles
69. Russia vs. Ukraine 1992–5: Call for exclusive naval base rights at Sevastopol
70. Slovakia vs. Czech Republic* 1993–4: Claims to several small sections of newly established border
71. Slovenia vs. Croatia* 1993–5: Claims to territory inland of Piran Bay as well as several small sections along length of border
72. Soviet Russia vs. Finland* 1919–20: Claims to Petsamo and areas along border
73. Soviet Russia vs. Poland* 1919–21: Claims to territory along borders of Ukraine and Belarus with Poland
74. Soviet Russia/Union vs. Romania 1920–40: Claims to Bessarabia and then Bukavina and Herta
75. Soviet Union vs. Romania 1941–4: Claims to Bessarabia, Bukovina, and Herta which the Soviets had annexed in 1940 but Romania took back in June and July 1941
76. Soviet Union vs. Estonia 1939–40: Claims of right to occupy territory, establish military bases, and annex border territories/ islands
77. Soviet Union vs. Finland 1938–41: Claims to sovereignty/right to establish naval bases on islands in the Gulf of Finland and at Porkkala and claims to bordering territory of Petsamo, Karelia, Sallo, and Kuusamo
78. Soviet Union vs. Latvia 1939–40: Claims of right to occupy territory and establish military bases
79. Soviet Union vs. Lithuania 1939–40: Claims of right to occupy territory and establish military bases
80. Spain vs. Britain 1919–95: Claim to sovereignty over the British naval base at Gibraltar
81. Sweden vs. Finland 1920–1: Claims to sovereign rights over Aaland Islands
82. Turkey vs. Britain 1955–9: Desire to annex or partition Cyprus prior to its independence
83. West Germany vs. Czechoslovakia 1955–73: Refusal to accept Czech re-incorporation of Sudetenland territory following World War II and claim to Sudetenland as German territory

84. West Germany vs. East Germany 1955–72: Refusal to accept sovereignty of East Germany and claim to East Germany as part of a reunified Germany
85. West Germany vs. France 1955–6: Claims to Saar region
86. West Germany vs. Poland 1955–70: Refusal to recognize post-World War II western Polish borders (the Oder–Neisse Line) and claim to these bordering areas as German territory
87. West Germany vs. Netherlands* 1955–60: Claims to several small sections along border
88. Yugoslavia vs. Albania* 1919–25: Claims along border near Lake Ochrida
89. Yugoslavia vs. Austria 1919–20: Claim to Klagenfurt Basin
90. Yugoslavia vs. Bulgaria 1919: Claims to Strumica Valley in Macedonia
91. Yugoslavia vs. Greece 1925–9: Claims to Port of Salonica
92. Yugoslavia vs. Greece 1945–6: Claims to Port of Salonica
93. Yugoslavia vs. Hungary 1919–20: Claims to Croatia-Slavonia and Banat
94. Yugoslavia vs. Italy* 1919–24: Claims to Istrian Peninsula, Fiume, Dalmatian Coast, and offshore islands
95. Yugoslavia vs. Italy* 1945–75: Claims to Trieste

Case summaries of territorial disputes in Europe, 1919–1995

In this section a short summary is provided for each of the territorial disputes listed in section one. In each summary a description of the disputed territory is provided along with the outcome of the dispute. Sources are listed at the end of each case summary and the complete citation for the sources can be found in the bibliography in section three.

Dispute Number: 1, 33
Countries: Albania vs. Greece and vice versa.
Years of Dispute: 1919–24
Disputed Territory: Both countries sought to extend their borders beyond the boundary established by the 1913 Greco-Albanian Protocol of Florence. Albania claimed additional territories in the Epirus region while Greece focused its claims on the districts of Argyro-Castro and Koriza. For Greece gaining territory in the Koriza region was important because it would help to secure communication and supply lines between Greek Macedonia and Epirus.

Outcome of Dispute: In November 1921 the League of Nations decided to uphold the borders established in the 1913 Protocol with only minor modifications. Albania accepted this decision but Greece did not. After more than two years of negotiations Greece in October 1924 agreed to comply with the final recommendations of a border commission appointed by the League. As a result, Greek forces withdrew from disputed areas and accepted the new boundary lines.

Sources: *A History of the Peace Conference of Paris* (vol. 4); Biger 1995; Destani 1999; *International Boundary Study* (#113); Kondis n.d.; *League of Nations Official Journal, July–December 1921, October–November 1924*; Stickney 1926; Sula 1967; *Survey of International Affairs 1925* (vol. 2); Vickers 1995.

Dispute Number: 2, 88
Countries: Albania vs. Yugoslavia and vice versa
Years of Dispute: 1919–25
Disputed Territory: Yugoslavia asserted claims to northern areas near Lake Ochrida, while Albania sought to extend its borders beyond those established in 1913.

Outcome of Dispute: In November 1921 the Conference of Ambassadors called for preserving the 1913 borders with only slight modifications in favor of Yugoslavia. Albania accepted this decision but Yugoslavia did not. It was not until the fall of 1925 that a final settlement was achieved. In an agreement reached in October 1925 Yugoslavia gained small sections of territory in Sveti Naum and Vermosha in return for accepting the League's decision of 1921.

Sources: *A History of the Peace Conference of Paris* (vol. 4); Biger 1995; Destani 1999; *International Boundary Study* (#116); Kondis n.d.; *League of Nations Official Journal, July–December 1921, July–October 1924*; Stickney 1926; Sula 1967; *Survey of International Affairs 1920–1923, 1925* (vol. 2); Vickers 1995.

Dispute Number: 3, 41
Countries: Austria vs. Hungary and vice versa
Years of Dispute: 1919–21
Disputed Territory: Austria and Hungary both asserted claims to the Burgenland region.

Outcome of Dispute: Although both sides agreed to a plebiscite, the formation of a Bolshevik government in Hungary convinced the Allies in 1919 to award the area to Austria without a plebiscite. Hungary protested and the plebiscite was finally held in December 1921. A clear majority favored ties with Hungary and therefore the disputed territory in large part was transferred to Hungary.

Sources: Biger 1995; Deak 1942; Macartney 1937; Sharp 1991; *Survey of International Affairs 1920–1923*; Wambaugh 1933.

Dispute Number: 4
Countries: Austria vs. Italy
Years of Dispute: 1945–6
Disputed Territory: Austria asserted claims to South Tyrol, including all of Bolzano, parts of Trentino, Pusterthal, and the Brenner Pass.
Outcome of Dispute: In September 1946 an agreement was reached in which Austria recognized Italian sovereignty over the disputed areas but Italy pledged to support regional autonomy in South Tyrol and to guarantee political and social rights of the German-speaking population.
Sources: *International Boundary Study* (#58); Leiss 1954; *Making the Peace Treaties 1941–1947*; Opie 1951; *Paris Peace Conference 1946*; *Survey of International Affairs 1939–1946.*

Dispute Number: 5
Countries: Belgium vs. Germany
Year of Dispute: 1919
Disputed Territory: At the Paris Peace Conference Belgium presented claims to the territories of Eupen and Malmedy.
Outcome of Dispute: In the Peace Treaty signed in June 1919 Germany cedes the territories to Belgium. It is worth noting that a provision in the treaty allowed Germany to request a vote by the populations in the disputed areas and in the fall of 1919 such a request was made by Germany. The vote was held in July 1920 and favored Belgium.
Sources: *A History of the Peace Conference of Paris* (vol. 2); Biger 1995; *International Boundary Study* (#7); Wambaugh 1933.

Dispute Number: 6, 24
Countries: Great Britain vs. France and vice versa.
Years of Dispute: 1919–53
Disputed Territory: Both states claimed the Channel Islands of Minquiers and Ecrehos.
Outcome of Dispute: In November of 1953 the ICJ issued a ruling favoring the UK and France accepted the ruling.
Sources: *Great Britain Foreign Office Archives 1945–50*; *Keesing's 1945–53*; Johnson 1954.

Dispute Number: 7, 35
Countries: Bulgaria vs. Greece and vice versa
Years of Dispute: 1919–23
Disputed Territory: At the Paris Peace Conference Greece claimed Bulgarian territory in Thrace which would cut off Bulgaria's access to the Aegean. In 1922 Bulgaria attempted to regain territory in Thrace that it had lost in the 1919 Peace Treaty.
Outcome of Dispute: In the Treaty of Neuilly signed in November 1919 Greece secured control over Thrace from Bulgaria. At the Lausanne Peace Conference in 1923 Bulgaria's claims to Thrace were rejected and Bulgaria accepted this outcome.
Sources: A History of the Peace Conference of Paris (vol. 4); Biger 1995; International Boundary Study (#56); Survey of International Affairs 1920–23.

Dispute Number: 8, 36
Countries: Bulgaria vs. Greece and vice versa
Years of Dispute: 1945–7
Disputed Territory: Bulgaria asserted her claims to Western Thrace (as well as Eastern Macedonia up to the Struna river, including the island of Thasos) primarily to gain access to Aegean Sea, while Greece sought territory in Thrace beyond its pre-World War II borders.
Outcome of Dispute: At the Paris Peace Conference the claims of both countries were rejected. The Bulgarian Peace Treaty is signed without Bulgaria securing gains in Thrace and Greece's pre-World War II borders are restored and agreed upon in December of 1946. These terms are formalized in the February 1947 Peace Treaty which establishes the border as following the 1940 boundary lines.
Sources: Biger 1995; Crampton 1987; International Boundary Study (#56); Kousoulas 1953; O'Ballance 1966; Pundeff 1994; Roucek 1948; Survey of International Affairs 1939–1946.

Dispute Number: 9
Countries: Bulgaria vs. Romania
Year of Dispute: 1940
Disputed Territory: Bulgaria asserted claims to territories in South Dobroju which had been lost in the 1913 Balkan Wars.

Outcome of Dispute: Romania conceded the disputed territory to Bulgaria in September 1940.

Sources: Biger 1995; *International Boundary Study* (#53); Roucek 1948.

Dispute Number: 10, 71

Countries: Croatia vs. Slovenia and vice versa.

Years of Dispute: 1993–5

Disputed Territory: Both countries asserted claims to small sections of territory along the length of the border, but the dispute centered along the boundary inland of the Bay of Piran.

Outcome of Dispute: By the end of 1995 many of the small disputed areas along the border had been settled by mutual concessions. However, there was no resolution of conflicting claims in the Piran Bay.

Sources: *Boundary and Security Bulletin 1993–95*; *Keesing's 1993–95*.

Dispute Number: 11

Countries: Cyprus vs. Turkey

Years of Dispute: 1974–95

Disputed Territory: Following the 1974 invasion by Turkey, Cyprus has called for the withdrawal and end of Turkish military occupation in northern Cyprus and Turkish support for establishing a Turkish Cypriot state (about 30 percent of the island's territory).

Outcome of Dispute: Turkish forces remain in northern Cyprus and Turkish governments have supported the establishment of a Turkish Cypriot state which Cyprus has refused to accept.

Sources: Allcock 1992; *Boundary and Security Bulletin 1993–95*; Ertekun 1984; *Keesing's 1974–95*; Levie 1989; Necatigil 1985, 1989; Polyviou 1980.

Dispute Number: 12, 70

Countries: Czech Republic vs. Slovakia and vice versa

Years of Dispute: 1993–4

Disputed Territory: The two states disputed four small sections of the border, including Sidonia, Kasarna, Vrbovce, and along the Moraver river.

Outcome of Dispute: By November 1994 an agreement was reached that settled the dispute through mutual concessions.

Sources: *Boundary and Security Bulletin 1993–95*; *Keesing's 1993–94*.

Dispute Number: 13
Countries: Czechoslovakia vs. Austria
Year of Dispute: 1919
Disputed Territory: Czechoslovakia claimed territories in Bohemia, Moravia, Silesia, Gmund, and Themenau.
Outcome of Dispute: In the Treaty of Saint-Germain signed in September 1919 almost all the disputed territory was given to Czechoslovakia.
Sources: *A History of the Peace Conference of Paris* (vol. 4); Biger 1995; Sharp 1991.

Dispute Number: 14
Countries: Czechoslovakia vs. Hungary
Years of Dispute: 1919–20
Disputed Territory: Czechoslovakia claimed territories in Slovakia, Ruthenia, Bohemia, Moravia, and parts of Silesia.
Outcome of Dispute: The Czechs gained control of almost all the disputed territories in the Hungarian Peace Treaty signed in June 1920.
Sources: *A History of the Peace Conference of Paris* (vols. 1, 4); Biger 1995; Deak 1942; *International Boundary Study* (#66); Sharp 1991; *Survey of International Affairs 1920–1923*.

Dispute Number: 15
Countries: Czechoslovakia vs. Hungary
Years of Dispute: 1946–7
Disputed Territory: Czechoslovakia claimed small sections near Bratislava, including several villages.
Outcome of Dispute: A compromise proposal in August 1946 awarded about half of the disputed territory to Czechoslovakia and in the February 1947 Peace Treaty Hungary formally accepted a settlement on these terms.
Sources: Biger 1995; *International Boundary Study* (#66); Kertesz 1985; Leiss 1954; Opie 1951; *Survey of International Affairs 1939–1946*.

Dispute Number: 16, 60
Countries: Czechoslovakia vs. Poland and vice versa
Years of Dispute: 1919–24
Disputed Territory: In 1919 both states presented claims to Teshen, Spiza, and Oriva. Also, Poland sought small border adjustments near Jaworzina beginning in the fall of 1920.

Outcome of Dispute: In an award announced by the Conference of Ambassadors in July 1920 the disputed territories were divided between the two states on terms favorable to the Czechs. While Czechoslovakia accepted the decision, Poland contested the award in the area near Jaworzina. This limited dispute was settled through arbitration by the ICJ. In December 1923 the ICJ upheld the initial frontier set at the Conference of Ambassadors in 1920 and thereby rejected Poland's claim to adjusting the boundary near Jaworzina.

Sources: *A History of the Peace Conference of Paris* (vol. 4); Biger 1995; *Survey of International Affairs 1920–24*; Wambaugh 1933.

Dispute Number: 17
Countries: Denmark vs. Germany
Years of Dispute: 1919–20
Disputed Territory: Denmark claimed large sections of German controlled territories in Schleswig.

Outcome of Dispute: The two countries agreed to plebiscites within two zones (North Schleswig and Central Schleswig) which were held between February and March 1920. The results favored Denmark in the northern sections while favoring Germany in the central sectors. The territories were then divided according to these results.

Sources: *A History of the Peace Conference of Paris* (vol. 2); Biger 1995; *International Boundary Study* (#81); Wambaugh 1933.

Dispute Number: 18
Countries: Denmark vs. Norway
Years of Dispute: 1921–33
Disputed Territory: Denmark asserted a claim to all of Greenland along its eastern coastline.

Outcome of Dispute: In April 1933 the ICJ ruled in favor of Denmark and Norway accepted the ruling.

Sources: *Legal Status of Eastern Greenland*; Preuss 1932; *Survey of International Affairs 1920–24*.

Dispute Number: 19
Countries: East Germany/Soviet Union vs. United States/West Germany/France/UK
Years of Dispute: 1948–71
Disputed Territory: East Germany with the support of the USSR claimed West Berlin as part of East German territory

and sought to terminate Western occupation rights in West Berlin.

Outcome of Dispute: In September 1971 the Quadripartite Berlin Agreement was signed which settled the dispute. In the agreement East Germany and the USSR accepted the prevailing status quo. East Germany and the USSR acknowledged Western rights in Berlin and pledged to not restrict Western access to and transit from West Berlin.

Sources: Brecher and Wilkenfeld 1997; Charles 1959; Davison 1958; Griffith 1978; Hanrieder 1967, 1989; *Keesing's 1948–71*; McAdams 1993; McGhee 1989; Slusser 1973; Whetten 1980.

Dispute Number: 20, 52
Countries: Estonia vs. Latvia and vice versa
Years of Dispute: 1919–20
Disputed Territory: Estonia and Latvia both asserted competing claims to Hainasion in the Gulf of Riga, the island of Ruhnu, and the bordering town of Valga.

Outcome of Dispute: In March 1920 a compromise settlement was reached in which Hainasion was awarded to Latvia, Ruhnu to Estonia, while control over Valga was divided between the two states.

Sources: Biger 1995; *British Documents on Foreign Affairs, Part II, Series A* (vol. 3); Rauch 1974.

Dispute Number: 21
Countries: Estonia vs. Russia
Years of Dispute: 1992–5
Disputed Territory: Estonia claimed territory in the Pechory District of the Pskov region along the border with Russia.

Outcome of Dispute: No settlement was reached by the end of 1995 but a final agreement was reached in March 1999. The agreement called for an exchange of small parcels of land totaling about thirty square kilometers.

Sources: *Boundary and Security Bulletin 1993–95*; *Foreign Broadcast Information Service: Daily Reports Central Eurasia 1992–95*; Jaats 1995; *Kessing's 1993–95*.

Dispute Number: 22, 72
Countries: Finland vs. Soviet Russia and vice versa
Years of Dispute: 1919–20
Disputed Territory: Finland sought territory in East Karelia while the Soviets presented claims to Petsamo and several other small border adjustments.

Outcome of Dispute: In the Treaty of Dorpat signed in October 1920 Soviet Russia recognized Finnish sovereignty over Petsamo but Finland dropped claims to East Karelia and several bordering towns.

Sources: *A History of the Peace Conference of Paris* (vol. 6); Biger 1995; *British Documents on Foreign Affairs, Part II, Series A* (vol. 5); *International Boundary Study* (#74); Kirby 1979; Puntila 1974; *Survey of International Affairs 1920–1923*.

Dispute Number: 23
Countries: Finland vs. Soviet Union
Years of Dispute: 1941–7
Disputed Territory: Finland sought to regain those territories lost to the Soviets during the Winter War of 1939–40.
Outcome of Dispute: In the 1947 Paris Peace Treaty Finland made a number of unilateral concessions by accepting the 1940 borders, ceding Petsamo, and leasing the Porkkala Peninsula as a naval base for fifty years.
Sources: Biger 1995; Forsberg 1995; *International Boundary Study* (#74); Jakobson 1968.

Dispute Number: 25
Countries: France vs. Germany
Year of Dispute: 1919
Disputed Territory: France claimed the territories of Alsace-Lorraine, Rhineland, and the Saar.
Outcome of Dispute: In the Peace Treaty signed by Germany in June 1919 France gained control over Alsace-Lorraine, the right to occupy and demilitarize the Rhineland until 1935, and to occupy the Saar until 1935 by which time a plebiscite would be held to determine its final status.
Sources: *A History of the Peace Conference of Paris* (vol. 2); Biger 1995; Sharp 1991.

Dispute Number: 26
Countries: France vs. Italy
Years of Dispute: 1945–6
Disputed Territory: France claimed several small sections of the border in the Po Valley, including Little Saint Bernard Pass, the Mont Thabor-Chaberton district, the Mont Cenis plateau, Tenda, and Briga.
Outcome of Dispute: All of the territories were given to France in the Italian Peace Treaty signed in October of 1946.

Sources: *International Boundary Study* (#4); Leiss 1954; *Survey of International Affairs 1939–1946.*

Dispute Number: 27
Countries: Germany vs. Austria
Year of Dispute: 1938
Disputed Territory: Germany called for the incorporation of Austria into a larger Germany.
Outcome of Dispute: Under the threat of an invasion Austria agreed to a union with Germany in March 1938.
Sources: Brecher and Wilkenfeld 1997; Bullock 1962; Gehl 1963; Weinberg 1980.

Dispute Number: 28
Countries: Germany vs. Belgium
Years of Dispute: 1925–40
Disputed Territory: Germany called for the return of Eupen and Malmedy (areas with a German majority population and strategic railway lines) which had been ceded to Belgium in 1919.
Outcome of Dispute: In May 1940 Germany successfully invaded Belgium and reclaimed the territories. After World War II the territories were returned to Belgium without any dispute from West Germany.
Sources: Biger 1995; *International Boundary Study* (#7); *Survey of International Affairs 1925–1938.*

Dispute Number: 29
Countries: Germany vs. Czechoslovakia
Years of Dispute: 1938–9
Disputed Territory: Germany claimed territories in the Sudetenland and Silesia
Outcome of Dispute: Czechoslovakia ceded the Sudetenland to Germany in the fall of 1938 and by March 1939 Germany had occupied all of Czechoslovakia.
Sources: Biger 1995; Brecher and Wilkenfeld 1997; Bullock 1962; Huth 1988; Olivova 1972; Seton-Watson 1962.

Dispute Number: 30
Countries: Germany vs. France
Years of Dispute: 1922–36
Disputed Territory: Germany sought the early withdrawal of French forces from the Rhineland and Saar and the restoration

of sovereignty over the territories which had been lost as a result of the Peace Treaty signed in 1919 (see dispute #25).

Outcome of Dispute: In January 1935 a plebiscite was held in the Saar and the population voted overwhelmingly in favor of reunion with Germany. By March that year German control of the Saar was re-established. In the Rhineland an agreement was signed in August 1929 for the French to withdraw by June 1930. Complete German control and remilitarization of the Rhineland was achieved by the spring of 1936.

Sources: Brecher and Wilkenfeld 1997; Emmerson 1977; *Survey of International Affairs 1925–36*; Weinberg 1970.

Dispute Number: 31
Countries: Germany vs. Lithuania
Years of Dispute: 1938–9
Disputed Territory: Germany demanded the return of the city of Memel and surrounding territories.
Outcome of Dispute: In March 1939, under threat of invasion, Lithuania ceded Memel to Germany.
Sources: Brecher and Wilkenfeld 1997; Rauch 1974.

Dispute Number: 32
Countries: Germany vs. Poland
Years of Dispute: 1938–9
Disputed Territory: In the fall of 1938 Germany called for a revision of its border with Poland along the corridor and the return of Danzig.
Outcome of Dispute: In September 1939 German troops successfully invaded Poland and took control of all the disputed territories.
Sources: Debicki 1962; Huth 1988; Levine 1973.

Dispute Number: 34
Countries: Greece vs. Albania
Years of Dispute: 1945–71
Disputed Territory: Greece laid claims to Northern Epirus.
Outcome of Dispute: In the negotiations leading to the treaties signed at the Paris Peace Conference Greece failed to secure support for its territorial goals but refused to renounce its territory claims against Albania. It was not until May 1971 when Greece signed a treaty with Albania that normalized relations that it recognized (tacitly) the post-World War II borders of Albania.

Sources: Day 1982; Destani 1999; *Keesing's 1960–71*; Roucek 1948; *Survey of International Affairs 1946*.

Dispute Number: 37
Countries: Greece vs. Cyprus
Years of Dispute: 1969–82
Disputed Territory: Greece sought to incorporate Cyprus through its policy of enosis.
Outcome of Dispute: The long-standing Greek policy of enosis was repudiated when the Greek Prime Minister Papandreou in February 1982 tacitly renounced the policy in several speeches and explicitly affirmed Greece's support for the independence and sovereignty of Cyprus.
Sources: Bahcheli 1990; Day 1982; *Keesing's 1969–82*; Polyviou 1980.

Dispute Number: 38
Countries: Greece vs. Italy
Years of Dispute: 1919–28
Disputed Territory: Greece claimed the Dodecanese Islands in the Aegean.
Outcome of Dispute: Between 1919 and 1923 several provisional agreements by Italy to cede the islands to Greece unraveled and in the 1928 Treaty of Friendship between the two countries Greece renounced all claims to the islands.
Sources: Albrecht-Carrie 1966; Cassels 1970; Helmreich 1974; MacCartney 1938; *Survey of International Affairs 1924, 1928*.

Dispute Number: 39
Countries: Greece vs. Turkey
Years of Dispute: 1919–23
Disputed Territory: In February 1919 Greece laid claims to Epirus, Thrace, Smyrna, and a number of offshore islands.
Outcome of Dispute: By 1922 Greece was badly defeated in its war with Turkey and therefore Greek claims to Turkish territories were no longer tenable. In the Lausanne Peace Treaty signed in July 1923 Turkey retained control over almost all of the territories originally claimed and occupied by Greece.
Sources: *A History of the Peace Conference of Paris* (vol. 6); Beeley 1978; Biger 1995; *British Documents on Foreign Affairs, Part II, Series B* (vol. 30); *International Boundary Study* (#41); Sachar 1969; Sonyel 1975.

Dispute Number: 40
Countries: Greece vs. Great Britain
Years of Dispute: 1951–9
Disputed Territory: Greece sought enosis (the union of Cyprus with Greece) but Great Britain favored independence for the island (also see dispute number 82 for a summary of Turkish territorial claims in the 1950s).
Outcome of Dispute: In February 1959 the London–Zurich Accords were signed which provided for the establishment of an independent Cypriot State with provisions for: (1) a Greek-Cypriot President and Turkish-Cypriot Vice-President; (2) a defense alliance between Greece, Turkey, and Cyprus; (3) the retention of two British military bases along the southern coast of Cyprus; and (4) a guarantee of Cypriot independence by Greece, Turkey, and Britain.
Sources: Alastos 1955; Alford 1984; Averoff-Tossizza 1986; Bahcheli 1990; Bitsios 1975; Ehrlich 1974; Ertekun 1984; *Keesing's 1951–59*; Purcell 1969; Stephens 1966; Sonyel 1985.

Dispute Number: 42
Countries: Hungary vs. Czechoslovakia
Years of Dispute: 1938–9
Disputed Territory: The Hungarians laid claim to areas of Slovakia, Ruthenia, and Subcarpathia.
Outcome of Dispute: In a military confrontation threatening war in the fall of 1938 Hungary compelled concessions from the Czechs in Slovakia with the support of Germany. In March 1939 Hungarian troops invaded the remaining disputed areas and occupied them with limited resistance from Czech forces.
Sources: Biger 1995; *International Boundary Study* (#66); Macartney 1956; Seton-Watson 1962.

Dispute Number: 43
Countries: Hungary vs. Romania
Years of Dispute: 1939–40
Disputed Territory: Hungary claimed territories in Transylvania.
Outcome of Dispute: A crisis threatened war in the fall of 1939 but Romania was unwilling to concede any territory. A second crisis emerged in the spring of 1940 and in the negotiations that followed an agreement was reached in August with Romania facing pressure from both Germany and the Soviet Union to concede territory. The Vienna Award gave Hungary nearly

45,000 kilometers of Transylvanian territory (about 40 percent of what Hungary had claimed) from the Romanians.

Sources: Biger 1995; *International Boundary Study* (#47); Macartney 1956; Seton-Watson 1962.

Dispute Number: 44
Countries: Hungary vs. Yugoslavia
Years of Dispute: 1940–1
Disputed Territory: Hungary laid claims to areas lost to Yugoslavia in the 1920 Peace Treaty, particularly in the Banat region (see dispute number 93).
Outcome of Dispute: The Yugoslav government collapsed in March 1941 and the new government that was formed was deemed unreliable by Hitler. German armed forces invaded Yugoslavia in April, and Hungary, seizing a favorable opportunity, also attacked and took control of the disputed territories.
Sources: Biger 1995, Macartney 1956, 1957; Seton-Watson 1962.

Dispute Number: 45
Countries: Ireland vs. Great Britain
Years of Dispute: 1922–95
Disputed Territory: Following its independence in 1922 a limited dispute emerged over the boundaries between Ireland and Northern Ireland but the larger conflict has centered on Irish claims to all of Northern Ireland.
Outcome of Dispute: In a boundary agreement signed in November 1925 Ireland accepted the provisional boundary that had been established in 1922 but the larger dispute over the status of Northern Ireland has remained unresolved.
Sources: Allcock 1992; *Annual Register 1922–40*; *Boundary and Security Bulletin 1993–95*; Canning 1985; *Keesing's 1950–95*; Lee 1989; *Report of the Irish Boundary Commission*.

Dispute Number: 46
Countries: Italy vs. Albania
Years of Dispute: 1919–20
Disputed Territory: Following World War I at the Paris Peace Conference Italy presented claims to the Albanian island of Sasseno and Port Valona and also sought to establish mandate rights over the remainder of Albania.
Outcome of Dispute: In an agreement reached in August 1920 Italy secured the island of Sasseno but dropped claims to Valona or to seek mandate rights.

Sources: A History of the Peace Conference of Paris (vol. 4); Currey 1932; Destani 1999; Vickers 1995.

Dispute Number: 47
Countries: Italy vs. Albania
Year of Dispute: 1939
Disputed Territory: In March 1939 the Albanians were issued an ultimatum by Italy demanding that Italian troops be permitted to occupy Albanian territory and to militarize the islands which lay off the coast of Albania.
Outcome of Dispute: Albania rejected the Italian ultimatum and refused to allow Italian troops on its territory. Italy responded in April by invading then annexing all of Albania.
Sources: Brecher and Wilkenfeld 1997; Knox 1982.

Dispute Number: 48
Countries: Italy vs. Austria
Year of Dispute: 1919
Disputed Territory: Based on the Treaty of London secretly signed in 1915, Italy at the Paris Peace Conference presented claims to the Brenner Pass, South Tyrol, and the Istrian Peninsula.
Outcome of Dispute: In the Treaty of St. Germain signed in 1919 Italy's boundary was moved northward to the Brenner Pass and as a result Italy secured control over about half of the territory it claimed.
Sources: A History of the Peace Conference of Paris (vol. 4); Currey 1932; International Boundary Study (#58).

Dispute Number: 49
Countries: Italy vs. Greece
Years of Dispute: 1940–1
Disputed Territory: Italy demanded that Greece cede a number of islands, including Corfu and that Northern Epirus be annexed to Italian-occupied Albania.
Outcome of Dispute: Greece rejected all of the Italian demands with the result that Italy launched an invasion and eventually took control of the islands and Epirus with German support.
Sources: Brecher and Wilkenfeld 1997; Survey of International Affairs 1939–46; Van Creveld 1973.

Dispute Number: 50, 94
Countries: Italy vs. Yugoslavia and vice versa
Years of Dispute: 1919–24

Disputed Territory: Both parties asserted overlapping territorial claims to the Istrian Peninsula, Fiume, the Dalmatian coastline, and offshore islands.

Outcome of Dispute: The Rapallo Agreement signed in November 1920 settled the dispute through mutual concessions with Italy gaining more territory along the Istrian Peninsula and control of offshore islands while Yugoslavia gained more along the Dalmatian coastline. Claims over Fiume remained unsettled as both parties could not agree on the exact boundary lines around the area. In an agreement reached in January 1924 the dispute over Fiume was settled on terms generally favored by Italy. Both sides made reciprocal concessions under the agreement – much of Fiume was given to Italy but Yugoslavia gained additional territory along the Dalmatian coastline, a fifty-year lease on the Fiume port, and the contraction of Italy's coastal access to Fiume.

Sources: *A History of the Peace Conference of Paris 1920* (vol. 4); Albrecht-Carrie 1950; Cassels 1970; Currey 1932; Macartney 1938; Shorrock 1988.

Dispute Number: 51, 95
Countries: Italy vs. Yugoslavia and vice versa
Years of Dispute: 1945–75
Disputed Territory: With the end of World War II a dispute emerged between the two states over conflicting claims to Trieste and adjoining territories.

Outcome of Dispute: A temporary agreement for the administration of the disputed territories was established at the end of the war with Allied forces in control of Trieste and the surrounding areas. In October 1954 an agreement was reached on administration of the disputed areas with Italy securing control over a northern zone, including the city of Trieste, while the southern zone was put under Yugoslav administrative control. The agreement, however, did not settle the question of sovereign rights to the disputed territories. It was not until October 1975 that an agreement was reached which formalized the division of territory between the two states.

Sources: Bogdan 1970; Day 1982; *Keesing's 1948–75*; Rabel 1988; *Survey of International Affairs 1939–48*.

Dispute Number: 53, 56
Countries: Latvia vs. Lithuania and vice versa
Years of Dispute: 1919–21

Disputed Territory: Latvia and Lithuania both asserted claims to the town of Daugavpils and several small sections of territory along the length of the border.

Outcome of Dispute: In March 1921 British arbitration produced a compromise settlement. Lithuania was given a narrow strip of coastal territory in Courland, while Latvia was compensated by border adjustments in the vicinity of Oknist and to the south of Autz.

Sources: Biger 1995; *British Documents on Foreign Affairs, Part II, Series A* (vols. 2–3); Rauch 1974.

Dispute Number: 54
Countries: Latvia vs. Russia
Years of Dispute: 1994–5
Disputed Territory: Latvia asserted claims to Abrene which had been annexed by the Soviet Union in 1944.
Outcome of Dispute: Despite negotiations there was no resolution of the dispute.
Sources: *Boundary and Security Bulletin 1993–95; Foreign Broadcast Information Service: Daily Reports Central Eurasia 1994–95*; Dauksts and Puga 1995; *Keesing's 1994–95*.

Dispute Number: 55
Countries: Lithuania vs. Germany
Year of Dispute: 1919
Disputed Territory: Lithuania seeks to incorporate Memel.
Outcome of Dispute: In the Peace Treaty of June 1919 Germany ceded sovereign rights to Memel though those sovereign rights were not transferred to Lithuania (in 1928 Germany formally recognized Lithuanian sovereignty over Memel). After 1919 the dispute over Memel is between Lithuania and the League of Nations.
Sources: *A History of the Peace Conference of Paris* (vol. 2); Rauch 1974; *Survey of International Affairs 1920–1923*.

Dispute Number: 57, 63
Countries: Lithuania vs. Poland and vice versa
Years of Dispute: 1919–38
Disputed Territory: Both countries assert claims to the city of Vilna and surrounding territories.
Outcome of Dispute: In October 1920 Polish irregular forces took control of Vilna and by March 1923 the Conference of Ambassadors recognized Polish control of Vilna. Lithuania, however,

refused to recognize Polish control for many years but in 1938 Poland, under a threat of force, compelled Lithuania to recognize Polish sovereignty.

Sources: Rauch 1974; *Survey of International Affairs 1920–1938*.

Dispute Number: 58
Countries: Netherlands vs. Belgium
Years of Dispute: 1922–59
Disputed Territory: Netherlands asserted claims to small enclaves along the border.
Outcome of Dispute: After some discussion both sides agreed to submit the dispute to the ICJ in November of 1957. In a ruling issued in June 1959, the ICJ awards the disputed territory to Belgium.
Sources: Biger 1995; *Case Concerning Sovereignty over Certain Frontier Lands*.

Dispute Number: 59, 87
Countries: Netherlands vs. West Germany and vice versa
Years of Dispute: 1955–60
Disputed Territory: Each country asserted claims to several small sections along the border, including the boundaries in rivers and access to and use of ports.
Outcome of Dispute: In the April 1960 agreement the pre-World War II border is largely re-established with minor modifications along the provisions that three villages (hamlets of Elten and Dinxperlo, and Tudderen) were to be returned to Germany in exchange for a forest near Elten and rights to operate coal mines near Hillenberg and Wehr. Also, both countries retained access to the sea via the Dollard-Ems Estuary.
Sources: Biger 1995; *International Boundary Study* (#31); *Keesing's 1955–60*.

Dispute Number: 61
Countries: Poland vs. Czechoslovakia
Year of Dispute: 1938
Disputed Territory: Poland asserted claims to Teschen and Silesia.
Outcome of Dispute: The Czechs conceded Teschen and Silesia in the fall of 1938 under the threat of a Polish attack.
Sources: Debicki 1962; Macartney 1956; Seton-Watson 1962.

Dispute Number: 62
Countries: Poland vs. Germany
Years of Dispute: 1919–22

Disputed Territory: Poland claimed Danzig, areas of East and West Prussia, and much of Upper Silesia.

Outcome of Dispute: In 1919 the Allied countries make Danzig a free city while a Polish corridor to the Baltic Sea is established in Prussia and plebiscites are called for in Silesia and East Prussia. In July 1920 and March 1921 plebiscites were held in Allenstein, Marienwerder, and Upper Silasia and from August to October 1921 negotiations were held over the disputed territories. In the negotiations mutual concessions were exchanged with Germany remaining in control of much of Marienwerder but losing more territory in Upper Silesia.

Sources: *A History of the Peace Conference of Paris* (vol. 2); Debicki 1962; Sharp 1991; *Survey of International Affairs 1920–23*; Wambaugh 1933.

Dispute Number: 64, 73
Countries: Poland vs. Soviet Russia and vice versa
Years of Dispute: 1919–21
Disputed Territory: Poland sought to extend its border (the Curzon Line) into Belarus and the Ukraine while Soviet Russia sought to reduce the size of the new Polish state.

Outcome of Dispute: The Treaty of Riga signed in October 1920 ends the war with provisional reciprocal concessions on territorial claims. The Poles secured less than they sought but more than the Curzon Line while the Soviets were willing to accept a border west of the Curzon Line (the status quo position before the war). These preliminary agreements were formalized in a treaty signed in March 1921.

Sources: *A History of the Peace Conference of Paris* (vol. 6); *British Documents on Foreign Affairs, Part II, Series A* (vol. 3); Davies 1972; Debicki 1962.

Dispute Number: 65
Countries: Romania vs. Hungary
Years of Dispute: 1919–20
Disputed Territory: Romania asserted claims to Transylvania, all of Banat, and parts of the Hungarian Plain.

Outcome of Dispute: In the Treaty of Trianon signed in June 1920 Hungary concedes almost all of the disputed territories to Romania. The only exception is a section of the Banat which is divided between Yugoslavia and Hungary.

Sources: *A History of the Peace Conference of Paris* (vol. 4); Deak 1942; *International Boundary Study* (#47); Sharp 1991; *Survey of International Affairs 1920–1923*.

Dispute Number: 66
Countries: Romania vs. Hungary
Years of Dispute: 1945–7
Disputed Territory: Romania claimed sovereignty over all of Transylvanian territory lost to Hungary in 1940 (see dispute number 43).
Outcome of Dispute: At the Paris peace negotiations all of the territory gained by Hungary in 1940 was returned to Romania in the Peace Treaty signed in February 1947.
Sources: *International Boundary Study* (#47); Leis 1954; Opie 1951.

Dispute Number: 67, 74
Countries: Romania vs. Soviet Union and vice versa
Years of Dispute: 1919–40
Disputed Territory: Following World War I Romania sought to annex the territory of Bessarabia which it had occupied by the end of the war. The annexation of Bessarabia by Romania was formalized in an October 1920 treaty between Romania and the allied powers but the Soviets refused to recognize the annexation. In 1940, USSR asserted her claims to Bessarabia and Northern Bukovinia.
Outcome of Dispute: Under threat of an armed conflict Romania made unilateral concessions, agreeing to cede all of disputed areas of Bessarabia (and Northern Bukovinia) to the USSR in June 1940.
Sources: Biger 1995; Brecher and Wilkenfeld 1997; Chiper 1995; *International Boundary Study* (#43); *Keesing's 1940*; *Survey of International Affairs 1920–32*.

Dispute Number: 68
Countries: Romania vs. Yugoslavia
Years of Dispute: 1919–22
Disputed Territory: Romania sought to gain control over all of the territory of Banat. Romania secures much of the Banat in negotiations with Hungary (see dispute number 65) but also seeks to gain sections of the Banat that were awarded to Yugoslavia (see dispute number 93).
Outcome of Dispute: In an agreement reached in February 1922 Romania gained minor adjustments in the Banet compared to the terms of the 1920 treaty negotiated with Hungary.
Sources: Biger 1995; Sharp 1991; *Survey of International Affairs 1920–1923*.

Dispute Number: 69
Countries: Russia vs. Ukraine
Years of Dispute: 1992–5
Disputed Territory: Russia sought to secure exclusive military base rights for its Black Sea fleet at Sevastopol and surrounding territory.
Outcome of Dispute: No final agreement was reached by the end of 1995 despite repeated negotiations and progress towards a settlement. In May 1997 the conflict over base rights was resolved with an agreement in which Russia was allowed to rent bases at Sevastopol for a twenty-year period at an annual amount of $500 million.
Sources: *Boundary and Security Bulletin 1993–1995*; Drohobycky 1995; *Keesing's 1992–95*; Savchenko 1997.

Dispute Number: 75
Countries: Soviet Union vs. Romania
Years of Dispute: 1941–4
Disputed Territory: In 1941 Romanian and German forces invaded the Soviet Union and took control of Bessarabia, Northern Bukovina, and the Herta District and reintegrated these territories back into Romania. The Soviets, however, refused to recognize the annexation by Romania.
Outcome of Dispute: In the September 1944 armistice agreement, Romania agreed to return all of the territories taken in 1941 (after the war the peace treaty signed in 1947 formalized the transfer of territories).
Sources: Brecher and Wilkenfeld 1997; Chiper 1995; Day 1982; *International Boundary Study* (#43).

Dispute Number: 76
Countries: Soviet Union vs. Estonia
Years of Dispute: 1939–40
Disputed Territory: USSR demanded the right to occupy Estonian territory, establish military bases, and to annex border territories, including the Petseri district and part of Virumoa.
Outcome of Dispute: Under the threat of invasion Estonia permits the Soviets in September of 1939 to establish military bases and then in June 1940 the Soviets occupy additional bases and territory. By August 1940 the Soviets annex all of Estonia.
Sources: Brecher and Wilkenfeld 1997; Rauch 1974.

Dispute Number: 77
Countries: Soviet Union vs. Finland
Years of Dispute: 1938–41
Disputed Territory: The Soviets sought the right to occupy a number of Finnish islands (especially Hango) in order to establish naval bases and also called for frontier adjustments to extend defenses around Leningrad.
Outcome of Dispute: In the March 1940 armistice agreement Finland conceded almost all of the disputed territories but Petsamo remained an area of contention until the spring of 1941 when the Soviets dropped their demands for additional territory.
Sources: Brecher and Wilkenfeld 1997; Carlgren 1977; Huth 1988; *International Boundary Study* (#74); Nevakivi 1976; *Survey of International Affairs 1939–1946*; Upton 1974.

Dispute Number: 78
Countries: Soviet Union vs. Latvia
Years of Dispute: 1939–40
Disputed Territory: The Soviets demanded rights to establish military bases and to occupy territory in Latvia – especially the territories conceded in the 1920 Peace Treaty with Latvia.
Outcome of Dispute: Under the threat of invasion Latvia in October 1939 acquiesced to USSR's demand for the right to establish military bases and occupy territory. In June 1940 Latvia was compelled to allow the Soviets to take control of additional bases and territories and in August of that year the Soviets annexed all of Latvia.
Sources: Brecher and Wilkenfeld 1997; Rauch 1974.

Dispute Number: 79
Countries: Soviet Union vs. Lithuania
Years of Dispute: 1939–40
Disputed Territory: The Soviet Union sought the right to establish military bases and occupy bordering territories for purposes of defense against a possible German attack.
Outcome of Dispute: Under threat of invasion in October 1939 Lithuania acquiesced to Soviet demands as Soviet forces moved into the country to establish and occupy naval and air bases. Between May and June 1940 the Soviets demanded the right to occupy further bases and territory and by August all of Lithuania had been annexed.
Sources: Brecher and Wilkenfeld 1997; Rauch 1974.

Dispute Number: 80
Countries: Spain vs. Great Britain
Years of Dispute: 1919–95
Disputed Territory: Spain has claimed sovereignty over the eastern entrance to the Strait of Gibraltar and called on the British to withdraw from their naval base at Gibraltar.
Outcome of Dispute: Despite repeated rounds of negotiations over many decades there has been no resolution of Spanish claims to Gibraltar.
Sources: Allcock 1992; *Boundary and Security Bulletin 1993–95*; Dennis 1990; *Great Britain Foreign Office Archives 1923–25, 1951–60*; Hills 1974; Jackson 1987; O'Reilly 1992.

Dispute Number: 81
Countries: Sweden vs. Finland
Years of Dispute: 1920–1
Disputed Territory: Sweden claimed sovereignty over Aaland island.
Outcome of Dispute: In an October 1921 agreement Sweden recognizes Finnish sovereignty over the island but Finland provides specific guarantees to preserve the rights and culture of the Swedish population.
Sources: *League of Nations Official Journal, July–December 1920, January–April, September 1921*; *Survey of International Affairs 1920–23*.

Dispute Number: 82
Countries: Turkey vs. Great Britain
Years of Dispute: 1955–9
Disputed Territory: Turkey seeks the partition or annexation of Cyprus.
Outcome of Dispute: In February 1959 the London–Zurich Accords were signed which provided for the establishment of an independent Cypriot State with provisions for: (1) a Greek-Cypriot President and Turkish-Cypriot Vice-President; (2) a defense alliance between Greece, Turkey, and Cyprus; (3) the retention of two British military bases along the southern coast of Cyprus; and (4) a guarantee of Cypriot independence by Greece, Turkey, and Britain.
Sources: Alastos 1955; Alford 1984; Averoff-Tossizza 1986; Bahcheli 1990; Bitsios 1975; Ehrlich 1974; Ertekun 1984; *Keesing's 1951–59*; Purcell 1969; Sonyel 1985; Stephens 1966.

Dispute Number: 83
Countries: West Germany vs. Czechoslovakia
Years of Dispute: 1955–73
Disputed Territory: West Germany refused formally to accept its post-World War II borders with Czechoslovakia and therefore contested the Czech reincorporation of Sudetenland territory that had been ceded to Germany in 1938 (see dispute number 29).
Outcome of Dispute: In December 1973 West Germany signed a treaty in which it recognized the post-war borders of Czechoslovakia and therefore accepted the loss of the Sudetenland.
Sources: Busek and Spulber 1957; Griffith 1978; Hanrieder 1967, 1989; *Keesing's 1955–73*; McAdams 1993; Prittie 1974; Szulc 1971.

Dispute Number: 84
Countries: West Germany vs. East Germany
Years of Dispute: 1955–72
Disputed Territory: West Germany refused to recognize the independence of East Germany as a sovereign state.
Outcome of Dispute: In a treaty signed in December 1972 West Germany recognized the boundaries and territorial integrity of East Germany as a sovereign state (West Germany, however, did not renounce its policy of seeking a unified Germany).
Sources: Griffith 1978; Hanrieder 1967, 1989; *Keesing's 1955–72*; McAdams 1993; McGhee 1989; Prittie 1974; Whetten 1980.

Dispute Number: 85
Countries: West Germany vs. France
Years of Dispute: 1955–6
Disputed Territory: Germany sought the return of the Saar region which had been secured by France after World War II.
Outcome of Dispute: The results of a plebiscite held in 1955 strongly favored the return of the Saar to West Germany and in a treaty signed in October 1956 France ceded the Saar to West Germany.
Sources: Freymand 1960; *Keesing's 1955–56*.

Dispute Number: 86
Countries: West Germany vs. Poland

Years of Dispute: 1955–70

Disputed Territory: West Germany refused officially to recognize the post-war borders of Poland (the Oder–Neisse Line) in which Poland had gained territories from (East) Germany.

Outcome of Dispute: In the West German–Polish Treaty signed in December 1970 West Germany recognized the prevailing territorial status quo and post-war boundaries of Poland and renounced any territorial claims against Poland.

Sources: Griffith 1978; Hanrieder 1967, 1989; *Keesing's 1955–70*; Klafkowski 1972; Kulski 1976; McAdams 1993; McGhee 1989; Prittie 1974; Szaz 1960; Whetten 1980; Worster 1995.

Dispute Number: 89
Countries: Yugoslavia vs. Austria
Years of Dispute: 1919–20
Disputed Territory: Yugoslavia asserted claims to the Klagenfurt Basin.

Outcome of Dispute: In October 1920 a plebiscite was held in the disputed region and the results strongly favored Austria and Yugoslavia therefore withdrew its claims.

Sources: *A History of the Peace Conference of Paris* (vol. 4); Biger 1995; Sharp 1991; *Survey of International Affairs 1920–1923*; Wambaugh 1933.

Dispute Number: 90
Countries: Yugoslavia vs. Bulgaria
Year of Dispute: 1919
Disputed Territory: Yugoslavia claimed territory in Macedonia in the Strumica Valley.

Outcome of Dispute: Bulgaria cedes all of the disputed territory in the Treaty of Neuilly signed in November 1919.

Sources: *A History of the Peace Conference of Paris* (vol. 4); Biger 1995; *International Boundary Study* (#130).

Dispute Number: 91
Countries: Yugoslavia vs. Greece
Years of Dispute: 1925–9
Disputed Territory: Yugoslavia sought to establish effective sovereign control over the Port of Salonica.

Outcome of Dispute: In agreement reached in March 1929 Yugoslavia accepted a settlement of the dispute on terms generally favorable to Greece. Yugoslavia failed to obtain key concessions from Greece on issues such as enlargement of the free zone at the port and control over railway lines.

Sources: Biger 1995; *Survey of International Affairs 1926, 1928.*

Dispute Number: 92
Countries: Yugoslavia vs. Greece
Years of Dispute: 1945–6
Disputed Territory: After World War II Yugoslavia once again sought to gain territory in Greek Macedonia in order to secure the Port of Salonica.
Outcome of Dispute: At the Paris Peace Conference in 1946 Yugoslavia failed to secure support for its territorial claims and thus Greece retained control of the disputed territory (this outcome was formalized in the Paris Peace Treaty signed in February 1947).
Sources: Jelavich 1983; Jelavich and Jelavich 1965; Roucek 1948; *Survey of International Affairs 1946.*

Dispute Number: 93
Countries: Yugoslavia vs. Hungary
Years of Dispute: 1919–20
Disputed Territory: Yugoslavia claimed territory in Croatia-Slavonia and a section of the Banat region.
Outcome of Dispute: In the Peace Treaty signed in June 1920 Hungary conceded almost all of the disputed territory to Yugoslavia.
Sources: Biger 1995; Deak 1942; Sharp 1991.

Bibliography of sources listed in case summaries

A History of the Peace Conference of Paris (1920–4), vols. 1–2, 4, 6 (London: Henry Frowde and Hodder & Stoughton).
Alastos, Doros (1955) *Cyprus in History* (London: Zeno Publishers).
Albrecht-Carrie, René (1966) *Italy at the Paris Peace Conference* (Hamden: Archon Books).
Alford, Jonathan ed. (1984) *Greece and Turkey, Adversity in Alliance* (New York: St. Martin's Press).
Allcock, John ed. (1992) *Border and Territorial Disputes*, 3rd ed. (London: Longman).
Annual Register 1922–40 (1923–41) (New York: Longmans, Green and Co.).
Averoff-Tossizza, Evangelos (1986) *The Lost Opportunity* (New Rochelle, New York: Aristide D. Caratzas).
Bahcheli, Tozun (1990) *Greek–Turkish Relations Since 1955* (Boulder: Westview Press).

Beeley, Brian (1978) "The Greek-Turkish Boundary" *Transactions of the Institute of British Geographers*, 3, 3: 351–66.

Biger, Gideon (1995) *The Encyclopedia of International Boundaries* (New York: Facts on File).

Bitsios, Dimitri (1975) *Cyprus* (Thessaloniki: Institute for Balkan Studies).

Bogdan, Novak (1970) *Trieste 1941–1954* (Chicago: University of Chicago Press).

Boundary and Security Bulletin 1993–95 (1993–5) (Durham: International Boundary Research Unit).

Brecher, Michael and Jonathan Wilkenfeld (1997) *A Study of Crisis* (Ann Arbor: University of Michigan Press).

British Documents on Foreign Affairs, Part II, Series A (1984) vols. 3, 5 (Bethesda: University Publications of America).

British Documents on Foreign Affairs, Part II, Series B (1997) vol. 30 (Bethesda: University Publications of America).

Bullock, Alan (1962) *Hitler, A Study in Tyranny* (New York: Harper & Row).

Busek, Vratislav and Nicolas Spulber (1957) *East-Central Europe Under the Communists* (New York: Frederick A. Praeger Inc.).

Canning, Paul (1985) *British Policy Towards Ireland* (Oxford: Clarendon Press).

Carlgren, W. M. (1977) *Swedish Foreign Policy During the Second World War* (New York: St. Martin's Press).

Case Concerning Sovereignty over Certain Frontier Lands (Belgium/Netherlands) (1959) (Hague: International Court of Justice Reports).

Cassels, Alan (1970) *Mussolini's Early Diplomacy* (Princeton: Princeton University Press).

Charles, Max (1959) *Berlin Blockade* (London: Allan Wingate Publishers).

Chiper, Ioan (1995) "Bessarabia and Northern Bukovina" in Tuomas Forsberg ed. *Contested Territory* (Hants: Edward Elgar Publishing), 107–27.

Crampton, R. J. (1987) *A Short History of Modern Bulgaria* (Cambridge: Cambridge University Press).

Currey, Muriel (1932) *Italian Foreign Policy 1918–1932* (London: Ivor Nicholson & Watson).

Davies, Norman (1972) *White Eagle, Red Star* (New York: St. Martin's Press).

Davison, W. Phillips (1958) *The Berlin Blockade* (Princeton: Princeton University Press).

Day, Alan J. ed. (1982) *Border and Territorial Disputes* (London: Longman).

Dauksts, Bonifacijs and Arturs Puga (1995) "Abrene" in Tuomas Forsberg ed. *Contested Territory* (Hants: Edward Elgar Publishing), 178–87.

Deak, Francis (1942) *Hungary at the Paris Peace Conference* (New York: Columbia University Press).

Debicki, Roman (1962) *Foreign Policy of Poland 1919–39* (New York: Frederick A. Praeger).

Dennis, Philip (1990) *Gibraltar and Its People* (London: David & Charles).

Destani, Beytullah ed. (1999) *Albania & Kosovo* (Oxford: Archive Editions).

Drohobycky, Maria (1995) *Crimea, Dynamics, Challenges, and Prospects* (Lanham, MD: Rowman & Littlefield).

Ehrlich, Thomas (1974) *Cyprus 1958–1967* (New York: Oxford University Press).

Emmerson, James (1977) *The Rhineland Crisis* (London: M. Temple Smith).

Ertekun, N. M. (1984) *The Cyprus Dispute* (Oxford: K. Rustem & Brother).

Foreign Broadcast Information Service: Daily Reports – Central Eurasia 1991–95 (1991–5) (Washington DC: Foreign Broadcast Information Service).

Forsberg, Tuomas (1995) "Karelia" in Tuomas Forsberg ed. *Contested Territory* (Hants: Edward Elgar Publishing), 202–23.

Freymond, Jacques (1960) *The Saar Conflict* (London: Stevens).

Gehl, Jiurgen (1963) *Austria, Germany, and the Anschluss, 1931–1938* (London: Oxford University Press).

Great Britain Foreign Office Archives:
  Britain vs. France (case #6, 24) documents on relations between Britain and France regarding the Channel Islands dispute from 1945–50 beginning with FO 371/49232 and ending with FO 371/89204.

  Spain vs. Britain (case #80) documents on relations between Britain and Spain regarding Gibraltar 1923–5 beginning with FO 371/9489 and ending with FO 371/11079, and 1951–60 beginning with FO 371/96179 and ending with FO 371/153276.

Griffith, William (1978) *The Ostpolitik of the Federal Republic of Germany* (Cambridge: MIT Press).

Hanrieder, Wolfram (1967) *West German Foreign Policy, 1949–1963* (Stanford: Stanford University Press).

(1989) *Germany, America, Europe* (New Haven: Yale University Press).

Helmreich, Paul C. (1974) *From Paris to Sevres* (Columbus: Ohio State University Press).

Hills, George (1974) *Rock of Contention* (London: Robert Hale & Company).

Hitchens, Christopher (1984) *Cyprus* (London: Quartet Books).

Huth, Paul (1988) *Extended Deterrence and the Prevention of War* (New Haven: Yale University Press).

International Boundary Study (1961–72) (Washington DC: The Geographer, Bureau of Intelligence and Research, US Department of State).

International Boundary Study. No. 4 France–Italy Boundary, 19 May 1961.

International Boundary Study. No. 7 Belgium–Germany Boundary, 30 June 1961.

International Boundary Study. No. 31 Germany–Netherlands Boundary, 6 April 1964.

International Boundary Study. No. 41 Greece–Turkey Boundary, 23 November 1964.

International Boundary Study. No. 43 Romania–USSR Boundary, 30 December 1964.

International Boundary Study. No. 47 Hungary–Romania Boundary, 15 April 1965.

International Boundary Study. No. 53 Bulgaria–Romania Boundary, 30 June 1965.

International Boundary Study. No. 56 Bulgaria–Greece Boundary, 1 October 1965.

International Boundary Study. No. 58 Austria–Italy Boundary, 8 June 1966.

International Boundary Study. No. 66 Czechoslovakia–Hungary Boundary, 1 March 1966.

International Boundary Study. No. 74 Finland–USSR Boundary, 1 February 1967.

International Boundary Study. No. 81 Denmark–Germany Boundary, 14 June 1968.

International Boundary Study. No. 113 Albania–Greece Boundary, 18 August 1971.

International Boundary Study. No. 116 Albania–Yugoslavia Boundary, 8 October 1971.

International Boundary Study. No. 130 Bulgaria–Yugoslavia Boundary, 16 October 1972.

Jaats, Indrek (1995) "East of Narva and Petserimaa" in Tuomas Forsberg ed. *Contested Territory* (Hants: Edward Elgar Publishing), 188–201.

Jackson, William (1987) *The Rock of the Gibraltarians* (Cranbury, NJ: Associated University Press).

Jakobson, Max (1968) *Finnish Neutrality* (New York: Praeger).

Jelavich, Barbara (1983) *History of the Balkans*, vol. 2 (Cambridge: Cambridge University Press).

Jelavich, Charles and Barbara Jelavich (1965) *The Balkans* (Englewood Cliffs: Prentice-Hall).

Johnson, D. H. N. (1954) "The Minquiers and Ecrehos Case" *The International and Comparative Law Quarterly*, 3, 3: 189–216.

Keesing's Contemporary Archives 1940–86 (London: Keesing's Publications, 1940–86).

Keesing's Record of World Events 1987–95 (London: Keesing's Publications, 1987–95).

Kertesz, Stephen (1985) *The Last European Peace Conference* (Lanham, MD: University Press of America).

Kirby, D. G. (1979) *Finland in the Twentieth Century* (London: C. Hurst & Company).

Klafkowski, Alfons (1972) *The Polish–German Frontier After World War Two* (Poznon: Poznanskie).

Knox, MacGregor (1982) *Mussolini Unleashed, 1939–1941* (Cambridge: Cambridge University Press).

Kondis, Basil (n.d.) *The Greeks of Northern Epirus and Greek-Albanian Relations*, vols 1–4 (Athens: "Hestia" Publishers & Booksellers).

Kousoulas, Dimitrios (1953) *The Price of Freedom* (Syracuse: Syracuse University Press).

Kulski, W. W. (1976) *Germany and Poland* (Syracuse: Syracuse University Press).

League of Nations Official Journal, July–December 1920 (Geneva: League of Nations, 1920–1).

League of Nations Official Journal, January–April, September, December 1921 (Geneva: League of Nations, 1921–2).

League of Nations Official Journal, October 1924 (Geneva: League of Nations, 1924).

Lee, J. J. (1989) *Ireland 1921–1985* (Cambridge: Cambridge University Press).

Legal Status of Eastern Greenland (1933) (Hague: Permanent Court of International Justice).

Leiss, Amelia Catherine (1954) *European Peace Treaties After World War II* (Boston: World Peace Foundation).

Levie, Howard (1989) *The Cyprus Question and the Turkish Position in International Law* (New York: Oxford University Press).

Levine, Herbert (1973) *Hitler's Free City* (Chicago: University of Chicago Press).

Macartney, C. A. (1965) *Hungary and Her Successors* (London: Oxford University Press).

Macartney, C. A. (1956–7) *A History of Hungary 1929–1945*, Parts I & II (New York: Frederick A. Praeger).

Making the Peace Treaties, 1941–47 (Washington, DC: US Department of State, Government Printing Office, 1947).

McAdams, James (1993) *Germany Divided* (Princeton: Princeton University Press).

McGhee, George (1989) *At the Creation of a New Germany* (New Haven: Yale University Press).

Necatigil, Zaim (1985) *The Turkish Republic of Northern Cyprus in Perspective* (Nicosia: Tezel Offset and Printing).

(1989) *The Cyprus Question and the Turkish Position in the International Law* (New York: Oxford University Press).

Nevakivi, Jukka (1976) *The Appeal That Was Never Made* (London: C. Hurst).

O'Ballance, Edgar O. (1966) *The Greek Civil War* (New York: Praeger).

Olivova, Vera (1972) *The Doomed Democracy* (London: Sidgwick & Jackson).

Opie, Redvers (1951) *The Search for Peace Settlements* (Washington, DC: Brookings).

O'Reilly, J. G. (1992) *Gibraltar: Spanish and United Kingdom Claims* (Durham: International Boundary Research Unit).

Paris Peace Conference 1946 (Washington DC: US Department of State, Government Printing Office, 1946).

Polyviou, Polyvios G. (1980) *Cyprus – Conflict and Negotiation 1960–1980* (London: Gerald Duckworth & Co. Ltd.).

Preuss, Lawrence (1932) "The Dispute Between Denmark and Norway Over the Sovereignty of East Greenland" *American Journal of International Law*, 26, 3: 469–87.

Prittie, Terence (1974) *Willy Brandt* (New York: Schocken Books).

Pundeff, Marin V. (1994) *Bulgaria in American Perspective* (New York: Columbia University Press).

Puntila, L. A. (1974) *The Political History of Finland, 1809–1866* (Helsinki: Olava Publishing Co.).

Purcell, H. D. (1969) *Cyprus* (London: Ernest Benn Limited).

Rabel, Roberto (1988) *Between East and West: Triesto, the United States, and the Cold War, 1941–1954* (Durham, NC: Duke University Press).

Rauch, Georg Van (1974) *The Baltic States* (London: C. Hurst & Company).

Report of the Irish Boundary Commission 1925 (1969) (Shannon: Irish University Press).

Roucek, Joseph S. (1948) *Balkan Politics* (Stanford: Stanford University Press).

Sachar, Howard (1969) *The Emergence of the Middle East* (New York: Alfred A. Knopf).

Savchenko, N. (1997) *Anatomiia Neob'iavlennoi Voiny* (Kiev: Ukrainska Perspektiva).

Seton-Watson, Hugh (1962) *Eastern Europe Between the Wars 1918–1941*, 3rd ed. (Hamden: Archon Books).

Sharp, Alan (1991) *The Versailles Settlement* (New York: Macmillan).

Shorrock, William I. (1988) *From Ally to Enemy* (Kent: Kent State University Press).

Slusser, Robert (1973) *The Berlin Crisis of 1961* (Baltimore: Johns Hopkins University Press).

Sonyel, Salahi (1975) *Turkish Diplomacy 1918–1923* (London: Sage Publications).
 (1985) *The Turco-Greek Conflict* (Ankara: The Cyprus Turkish Cultural Association).

Stephens, Robert (1966) *Cyprus – A Place of Arms* (London: Pall Mall Press).

Stickney, Edith (1926) *Southern Albania or Northern Epirus in European International Affairs, 1912–1923* (Stanford: Stanford University Press).

Sula, Abdul (1967) *Albania's Struggle for Independence* (New York: Sula).

Survey of International Affairs 1920–48 (1925–52) (London: Oxford University Press).

Szaz, Z. Michael (1960) *Germany's Eastern Frontiers* (Chicago: H. Regnery).

Szulc, Tad (1971) *Czechoslovakia Since World War II* (New York: Viking Press).

Upton, Anthony (1974) *Finland, 1939–1940* (London: Davis-Poynter).

Van Creveld, Martin (1973) *Hitler's Strategy 1940–1941* (Cambridge: Cambridge University Press).

Vickers, Miranda (1995) *The Albanians* (London: I. B. Tauris).

Wambaugh, Sarah (1933) *Plebiscites Since the World War*, vol. 1 (Washington, DC: Carnegie Endowment for International Peace).

Weinberg, Gerhard (1970) *The Foreign Policy of Hitler's Germany* (Chicago: University of Chicago Press).
 (1980) *The Foreign Policy of Hitler's Germany, Starting World War II 1937–39* (Chicago: University of Chicago Press).

Whetten, Lawrence (1980) *Germany East and West* (New York: New York University Press).

Worster, Peter (1995) "The Northern Part of East Prussia" in Tuomas Forsberg ed. *Contested Territory* (Hants: Edward Elgar Publishing), 156–77.

Appendix C
Territorial disputes in the Near East, Middle East, and North Africa, 1919–1995

List of dispute cases

In this first section a summary list of the territorial disputes in the regions of the Near East, Middle East, and North Africa is presented. For each dispute the following information is provided: (a) the first state listed is the challenger while the second is the target, (b) the first and last year of the dispute, and (c) a brief description of the territorial claims of the challenger. For those disputes marked with an asterisk both states are challengers and therefore the dispute is listed a second time with the identity of the challenger and target reversed.

1. Armenia vs. Azerbaijan* 1919–20: Claims along border in districts of Zangezur, Nakhichevan, and Karabakh
2. Armenia vs. Georgia* 1919–20: Claims to Borchula district
3. Armenia/Soviet Russia vs. Turkey* 1919–21: Claims to Kars, Ardahan, and Turkish territory extending to Mediterranean Sea
4. Azerbaijan vs. Armenia* 1919–20: Claims along border in districts of Zangezur, Nakhichevan, and Karabakh
5. Azerbaijan vs. Georgia 1919–20: Claims to large section of territory from Daghestan to Batum
6. Chad vs. Libya 1973–94: Claim to regain Aozou Strip after Libya occupies it in 1972
7. Britain vs. France* 1919–20: Claims to areas along Syrian–Jordanian border
8. Britain vs. France* 1919–32: Claims to areas along Syrian–Iraqi border
9. Britain vs. France* 1919–20: Claims to areas along Syrian/Lebanese–Palestine border
10. Britain vs. Iraq 1919–20: Claim of mandate rights over Iraq
11. Britain/Iraq vs. Najd/Saudi Arabia* 1922–81: Claims to border areas of Saudi Arabia (UK is challenger 1922–31, Iraq is challenger 1932–81)

12. Britain/Jordan vs. Najd/Saudi Arabia* 1922–65: Claims to border areas extending to Aqaba (UK is challenger 1922–45, Jordan is challenger 1946–65)
13. Britain/Kuwait vs. Saudi Arabia (Najd)* 1920–95: Claims to land border areas as well as offshore islands (UK is challenger 1919–60 and Kuwait thereafter)
14. Britain/South Yemen/Yemen vs. Saudi Arabia* 1935–95: Claims to ill-defined border areas (UK is challenger 1935–66, South Yemen 1967–90 and Yemen thereafter)
15. Britain/UAE vs. Saudi Arabia* 1934–74: Claims to and around Buraimi Oasis as well as bordering territories along what becomes the Qatari coastline (UK is challenger 1934–70 and UAE thereafter)
16. Britain vs. Saudi Arabia* 1949–58: Claims to islands in close proximity to Bahrain
17. Britain vs. Turkey* 1922–6: Claims to Mosul region along Iraqi–Turkish border
18. Egypt vs. Britain 1922–56: Claims to Sudan as part of Egypt
19. Egypt vs. Sudan 1958–95: Claims to sections along border after Sudanese independence
20. Egypt vs. Britain 1922–54: Call for restrictions and then withdrawal of British military base rights and troops in Suez Canal Zone
21. Egypt vs. Israel* 1948–88: Initial disputes over sovereign rights to territory in demilitarized zones and desire to gain territory in Negev and then later claims to territory occupied by Israel after the Six Day War
22. Eritrea vs. Yemen 1995: Claim to Hanish islands in the Red Sea
23. France vs. Britain* 1919–20: Claims to areas along Syrian/Lebanese–Palestine border
24. France vs. Britain* 1919–20: Claims to areas along Syrian–Jordanian border
25. France vs. Britain* 1919–32: Claims to territory along Syrian–Iraqi border in the Jabel Sinjar area which forms border with Turkey
26. France vs. Spain* 1919–28: Claims to Tangier
27. France vs. Syria 1919–20: Claim to mandate rights over Syria
28. France vs. Turkey 1919–21: Claims to Cilicia and along what becomes Syrian border with Turkey
29. Georgia vs. Armenia* 1919–20: Claims to Borchula district
30. Hijaz vs. Najd* 1919–26: Claims to Khurma and Turba along border
31. Iran vs. Britain 1919–70: Claims to Bahrain Islands
32. Iran vs. Britain 1919–71: Claims to islands of Abu Musa and Greater and Lesser Tunb

33. Iran vs. Britain/Iraq 1920–75: Claims in Shatt-al-Arab Waterway and along several small sections of land border (UK is target 1921–31 and Iraq thereafter)
34. Iran vs. Saudi Arabia* 1949–68: Claims to offshore islands of Farsi and Al-Arabiyah
35. Iran vs. Soviet Union* 1919–57: Claims both east and west of the Caspian Sea as well as islands in the Caspian
36. Iran vs. Turkey* 1919–32: Claims to sections along border in the Khotur region
37. Iraq vs. Britain/Kuwait 1938–94: Claims to border areas, Bubiyan and Warba islands, and contesting status of Kuwait as an independent state (UK is target 1938–60 and Kuwait thereafter)
38. Iraq vs. Britain 1941: Call for greater restrictions and limits on British military base and troop rights
39. Iraq vs. Britain 1947–8: Call for greater restrictions and limits on British military base and troop rights
40. Iraq vs. Iran 1979–95: Claims in Shatt-al-Arab Waterway
41. Israel vs. Egypt* 1949–67: Disputes over sovereign rights to territory in demilitarized zones established after 1948 war
42. Israel vs. Jordan* 1949–67: Disputes over sovereign rights to territory in demilitarized zones established after 1948 war and Jerusalem
43. Israel vs. Syria* 1949–67: Disputes over sovereign rights to territory in demilitarized zones established after 1948 war
44. Italy vs. Britain/Egypt 1919–25: Claim to Jaghbub and Sallum areas along Libyan–Egyptian border (UK is defender 1919–21 and Egypt thereafter)
45. Italy vs. France 1919: Claims to territory along Libyan–Algerian border in areas of Ghadames, Ghat, and Tummo
46. Italy vs. France 1919–35: Claims to border rectifications following World War I along Chad–Libya border in areas of Borku and Tibesti
47. Italy vs. Turkey 1919–21: Claims to mandate rights in Adalia and Smyrna
48. Jordan vs. Israel* 1948–94: Initial claims to territory along demilitarized zones as well as limited claims to change border in return for recognition of Israel while later disputes center on Israeli occupation of West Bank and Jerusalem after the Six Day War
49. Libya vs. France/Chad 1954–72: Claim to the Aozou Strip (France is target 1954–59 and Chad thereafter)
50. Mauritania vs. Spain 1960–75: Claims to territory of Spanish Sahara

51. Morocco vs. France/Algeria 1956–72: Claims along border in south in the Tindouh area (France is target 1956–61 and Algeria thereafter)
52. Morocco vs. Spain 1956–95: Claims to Spanish enclaves and offshore islands
53. Morocco vs. Spain 1956–75: Claims to Spanish Sahara
54. Najd vs. Hijaz* 1919–26: Claims to Khurma and Turba along border
55. North Yemen vs. Asir 1919–26: Claims to border areas and contesting independence of Asir
56. North Yemen vs. Britain/South Yemen 1919–90: Initial claims to border areas of Aden and then all territory that becomes South Yemen (UK is target 1919–66 and South Yemen thereafter)
57. North Yemen vs. Najd-Hijaz (Saudi Arabia)* 1927–34: Claims to border areas in Asir and Najran
58. Oman vs. Saudi Arabia* 1971–90: Claims to territory in Buraimi Oasis
59. Oman vs. United Arab Emirates* 1971–93: Claims to Buraimi Oasis and then northern coast of Ras al-Khaimah
60. Oman vs. South Yemen/Yemen* 1981–92: Claims along border in Dhofar
61. Qatar vs. Bahrain 1971–95: Claims to Hawar islands and Dibal and Jarada shoals
62. Russia vs. Azerbaijan 1994–5: Call for military base rights
63. Russia vs. Georgia 1993–5: Call for military base rights
64. Saudi Arabia (Najd) vs. Britain/Iraq* 1922–81: Claims to border areas of Iraq (UK is target 1922–31 and Iraq thereafter)
65. Saudi Arabia (Najd) vs. Britain/Kuwait* 1920–95: Claims to land border areas of Kuwait as well as offshore islands (UK is target 1919–60 and Kuwait thereafter)
66. Saudi Arabia (Najd) vs. Britain/Jordan* 1922–65: Claims to border areas of Jordan extending to Aqaba region (UK is target 1922–45 and Jordan thereafter)
67. Saudi Arabia vs. Britain/South Yemen/Yemen* 1935–95: Claims to ill-defined border areas (UK is target 1935–66, South Yemen 1967–90 and Yemen thereafter)
68. Saudi Arabia vs. Britain/UAE* 1934–74: Claims to Buraimi Oasis, Sila and bordering territories along what becomes the Qatari coastline (UK is target 1934–70 and UAE thereafter)
69. Saudi Arabia vs. Britain/Oman* 1934–90: Claims to territory in Buraimi Oasis (UK is target 1934–70 and Oman thereafter)
70. Saudi Arabia vs. Britain* 1949–58: Claims to islands in close proximity to Bahrain

71. Saudi Arabia vs. Iran* 1949–68: Claims to offshore islands of Farsi and Al-Arabiyah
72. Saudi Arabia vs. Qatar 1992: Claims to small section of bordering territory along the Qatari coastline
73. Saudi Arabia (Najd-Hijaz) vs. North Yemen* 1927–34: Claims to border areas in Asir and Najran
74. Soviet Russia vs. Georgia 1920–1: Claims to small sections of border and then dispute over independence of Georgia
75. Soviet Union vs. Iran* 1919–57: Claims both east and west of the Caspian Sea as well as islands in the Caspian
76. Soviet Union vs. Turkey 1945–53: Call for military base rights and joint control of Straits as well as claims to Kars and Ardahan
77. Spain vs. France* 1919–28: Claims to Tangier
78. South Yemen/Yemen* vs. Oman 1981–92: Claims along border in Dhofar
79. Syria vs. Israel* 1948–95: Initial disputes over sovereign rights to territory in demilitarized zones and desire to gain territory beyond UN designated border and then subsequent claims to Golan Heights territory occupied by Israel after the Six Day War
80. Tunisia vs. France 1956–62: Call for France to withdraw from military bases
81. Tunisia vs. France/Algeria 1959–70: Claim to Sahara region along border (France is target 1959–61 and Algeria thereafter)
82. Turkey vs. Armenia/Soviet Russia* 1919–21: Claims to territory in Kars and Ardahan (Armenia is target 1919–20 and Soviet Russia in 1921)
83. Turkey vs. Britain* 1922–6: Claims to Mosul region along Iraqi–Turkish border
84. Turkey vs. France 1925–9: Claims along southern border with Syria
85. Turkey vs. France 1937–9: Claims to Alexandretta
86. Turkey vs. Georgia/Soviet Russia 1919–21: Claims to Artvin, Ardahan, and Batum (Georgia is target 1919–20 and Soviet Russia in 1921)
87. Turkey vs. Iran* 1919–32: Claims to small areas along border in the Khotur region as well as in the north in the Little Ararat region
88. United Arab Emirates vs. Iran 1971–95: Claims to islands of Abu Musa and Greater and Lesser Tunb
89. United Arab Emirates vs. Oman* 1971–93: Claims to Buraimi Oasis and several other sections of border including northern coast of Ras al-Khaimah

Case summaries of territorial disputes in the Near East,
Middle East, and North Africa 1919–1995

In this section a short summary is presented of each territorial dispute that
is listed above. In each summary a description of the territory in dispute is
provided along with information on the outcome of the dispute. For each
of the sources listed at the end of a case, a complete citation is provided
in the bibliography in the third section of this appendix.

Dispute Number: 1, 4
Countries: Armenia vs. Azerbaijan and vice versa
Years of Dispute: 1919–20
Disputed Territory: At the end of World War I fighting broke
   out between these two states along disputed sections of the
   border near the tripoint with Turkey, including Nakhichevan,
   Zangezur, Karabakh, and Sharur Daralaguez.
Outcome of Dispute: A British plan to evenly divide much of the
   disputed territory was presented to both sides by mid-1920 but
   no final settlement was reached prior to the collapse of each
   country and the re-establishment of Soviet rule in mid-to-late
   1920.
Sources: *Documents on British Foreign Affairs, Part II, Series A* (vols.
   1, 4); Kazemzadeh 1951; Pipes 1954; *Survey of International
   Affairs 1920–1923*.

Dispute Number: 2, 29
Countries: Armenia vs. Georgia and vice versa
Years of Dispute: 1919–20
Disputed Territory: With the end of World War I and the collapse of
   Turkish and Russian control in the Caucasus, a border dispute
   emerged between these two new states struggling to remain
   independent. The dispute centered over the Borchulu district.
Outcome of Dispute: The territory had been neutralized through
   an agreement reached in January 1919 but no resolution of
   rival claims had been achieved prior to the re-establishment of
   Soviet rule in each country.
Sources: *Documents on British Foreign Affairs, Part II, Series A* (vols.
   1, 4); Kazemzadeh 1951; Pipes 1954; *Survey of International
   Affairs 1920–1923*.

Dispute Number: 3, 82
Countries: Armenia/Soviet Russia vs. Turkey and vice versa
Years of Dispute: 1919–21

Disputed Territory: In the Brest-Litovsk Treaty of 1917 Soviet Russia ceded to Turkey the provinces of Kars and Ardahan in Russian Armenia. By 1919 the new Armenian government, however, laid claim to these and additional territories of Turkey, while the Turkish government claimed large sections of territory that were intended to be part of the new Armenian state.

Outcome of Dispute: In December 1920 Armenia renounced its claims to Kars and Ardahan in an agreement with Turkey, and in subsequent agreements between Turkey and Soviet Russia in March and October 1921 Turkey's control of Kars and Ardahan was confirmed while the Soviets secured Alexandropol.

Sources: Hemlreich 1974; *International Boundary Study* (#29); Pipes 1954; Sachar 1969; *Survey of International Affairs 1920–23*.

Dispute Number: 5
Countries: Azerbaijan vs. Georgia
Years of Dispute: 1919–20
Disputed Territory: Azerbaijan claimed a large section of territory from Daghestan to Batum.

Outcome of Dispute: Negotiations between the two states failed to produce a settlement before both countries were occupied by the Red Army and Soviet rule was re-established.

Sources: *Documents on British Foreign Affairs, Part II, Series A* (vols. 1, 4); Kazemzadeh 1951; Pipes 1954; *Survey of International Affairs 1920–1923*.

Dispute Number: 6
Countries: Chad vs. Libya
Years of Dispute: 1973–94
Disputed Territory: Following Libya's occupation and assumption of control over the Aozou Strip in 1972, Chad sought the withdrawal of Libyan forces and the restoration of sovereign control over the territory.

Outcome of Dispute: In 1990 the dispute was submitted to the ICJ. A ruling was issued in February 1994 in which sovereignty over the Aozou Strip was awarded to Chad. Libya withdrew from the territory in May of that year.

Sources: Allcock 1992; Biger 1995; *Boundary and Security Bulletin 1993–94*; *International Boundary Study* (#3); *Keesing's 1973–94*; Shaw 1986; Wright 1989.

Dispute Number: 7, 24
Countries: Great Britain vs. France and vice versa
Years of Dispute: 1919–20
Disputed Territory: After the conclusion of World War I, the Sykes–Picot Agreement divided territory in the Middle East once belonging to the Ottoman Empire between France and Britain. Britain secured a mandate over Transjordan while France gained control over Syria. Disputes quickly arose, however, as to the location of the border between the new mandates. Both the British and French wanted access to water in bordering areas as well the use of railway lines and pipelines.
Outcome of Dispute: An agreement was reached in December 1920 that established a border along lines generally favored by the French.
Sources: Biger 1995; Frichwasser-Ra'anan 1976; *International Boundary Study* (#94); Toye 1989 (vols. 2–3).

Dispute Number: 8, 25
Countries: Great Britain vs. France and vice versa
Years of Dispute: 1919–32
Disputed Territory: After the conclusion of World War I the Sykes–Picot Agreement divided territory in the Middle East once belonging to the Ottoman Empire between France and Britain. Britain secured a mandate over Iraq while France gained control over Syria. From the outset of talks in 1919 disputes arose along several sections of what was to become the new border between French Syria and British Iraq.
Outcome of Dispute: A League of Nations Border Commission took up the dispute in 1932 and issued a ruling that required both sides to make mutual concessions. Both sides accepted the ruling in November 1932.
Sources: Biger 1995; Frichwasser-Ra'anan 1976; *League of Nations Official Journal, November 1931, September 1932*; Schofield 1992 (vol. 8); *Survey of International Affairs 1925 1934* (vol. 1).

Dispute Number: 9, 23
Countries: Great Britain vs. France and vice versa
Years of Dispute: 1919–20
Disputed Territory: After World War I, the Sykes–Picot Agreement divided territory in the Middle East once belonging to the Ottoman Empire between France and Britain. Britain secured a mandate over Palestine while France gained mandate rights

over Lebanon and Syria. Disputes quickly arose, however, as
to the location of the new border between the mandates. The
British wanted access to the water of Litani, the Jordan river
and Lake Hula, and access to and use of railway lines and
pipelines. The French raised similar issues of control of water,
railways, and pipelines.

Outcome of Dispute: In an agreement reached in December 1920
the border between Palestine and Lebanon/Syria was delimited with both countries conceding territory, though the terms
generally favored the French.

Sources: Biger 1995, Frichwasser-Ra'anan 1976, Toye 1989
(vols. 2–3).

Dispute Number: 10
Countries: Great Britain vs. Iraq
Years of Dispute: 1919–20
Disputed Territory: After World War I Turkey relinquished
control over its Arab-populated territories in the Middle East.
The British, with the support of the League of Nations, sought
to establish mandate rights over Iraq. The leadership of Iraq,
however, resented the mandate system and instead sought
independence as a sovereign state.

Outcome of Dispute: An armed revolt by Iraq against attempts by
the British to secure their mandate rights erupted in mid-1920
but British forces crushed the revolt by October of that year.

Sources: *A History of the Peace Conference of Paris* (vol. 6),
Al-Marayati 1961; Kedourie 1987.

Dispute Number: 11, 64
Countries: Great Britain/Iraq vs. Najd/Saudi Arabia and vice versa
Years of Dispute: 1922–81
Disputed Territory: Both the UK/Iraq and Najd/Saudi Arabia laid
claims to areas along the length of the poorly defined border.

Outcome of Dispute: The conflicting claims to bordering territory
were resolved by a series of agreements. The first agreement
was signed in 1922 and established a provisional neutral zone
while a second agreement in 1975 further defined the neutral
zone and adjacent sections of the border. The third and final
agreement of December 1981 settled all remaining questions
of border alignment west of the neutral zone and established
a new border in detail in the divided neutral zone.

Sources: Abu-Dawood and Karan 1990; *British Documents on
Foreign Affairs, Part II, Series B* (vols. 11, 13); *International*

Boundary Study (#111); Kostiner 1993; Leatherdale 1983; Schofield 1992 (vol. 6), 1994a; *Survey of International Affairs 1925* (vol. 1), *1928, 1930*; Troeller 1976; Wilkinson 1991.

Dispute Number: 12, 66
Countries: Great Britain/Jordan vs. Najd/Saudi Arabia and vice versa
Years of Dispute: 1922–65
Disputed Territory: With the break-up of the Ottoman Empire, Transjordan became a British mandated territory. The border between Transjordan and Najd was poorly defined and disputed by both sides in areas such as Wadi-i-Sirhan, Maan, and the port of Aqaba.
Outcome of Dispute: In November 1925 the UK and the Nejd signed the Hadda Agreement, which delimited the central and northern sectors of the border. Disputes persisted between Jordan and Saudi Arabia over the southern sectors, including Aqaba. A final agreement was reached in August 1965 with both sides conceding territory, though Jordan retained control over Aqaba.
Sources: Abu-Dawood and Karan 1990; Biger 1995; *British Documents on Foreign Affairs, Part II, Series B* (vol. 13); Schofield 1992 (vol. 7); *Survey of International Affairs 1925* (vol. 1), *1928*; Troeller 1976.

Dispute Number: 13, 65
Countries: Great Britain/Kuwait vs. Najd/Saudi Arabia and vice versa
Years of Dispute: 1920–95
Disputed Territory: The British and Najd disputed the borders of Kuwait along its entire length as well as offshore islands based on differing interpretations and assessments of the terms and validity of the 1913 Anglo-Turkish Agreement. In 1922 a provisional neutral zone was established along a section of the border but the precise location and boundary of the neutral zone and adjacent territories remained in contention for decades.
Outcome of Dispute: The dispute over the neutral zone and other sections of the land border were settled in a July 1965 agreement through mutual concessions. The dispute over offshore islands, however, remains unresolved.
Sources: Abu-Dawood and Karan 1990; Albaharna 1975; *International Boundary Study* (#103); Kostiner 1993; Leatherdale

1983; Schofield 1992 (vol. 11); Schofield and Blake 1992 (vol. 13); Troeller 1976; Wilkinson 1991.

Dispute Number: 14, 67
Countries: Great Britain/South Yemen/Yemen vs. Saudi Arabia and vice versa
Years of Dispute: 1935–95
Disputed Territory: Both sides have claimed large sections of what is a very ill-defined border. The Saudis initially challenged various boundaries in the east proposed by the British in the 1930s and in recent decades southern sections of the border in the Rub al Khalil ("The Empty Quarter") desert have been disputed as well.
Outcome of Dispute: There has been no resolution of any of the disputes that affect the entire length of the border.
Sources: Abu-Dawood and Karan 1990; Biger 1995; *Boundary and Security Bulletin 1993–95*; Gause 1990; *Middle East Contemporary Survey 1980–95*; Schofield 1992 (vol. 20).

Dispute Number: 15, 68
Countries: Great Britain/United Arab Emirates vs. Saudi Arabia and vice versa
Years of Dispute: 1934–74
Disputed Territory: Both sides in this dispute claimed territory in and around the Buraimi Oasis as well as along what becomes the border with Qatar along the coastline.
Outcome of Dispute: At the time when the British withdrew from the Gulf in 1971 the dispute over Buraimi and the border near Qatar remained unsettled. In August 1974 an agreement was reached between UAE and Saudi Arabia that settled the dispute. Saudi Arabia conceded six of nine disputed villages in the Buraimi Oasis while the UAE ceded the Zararah oilfield, Khur al-Udaid, and a corridor to the sea to Saudi Arabia.
Sources: Abu-Dawood and Karan 1990; Al-Alkim 1989; Albaharna 1975; Biger 1995; Cordesman 1984; Kelly 1980; *Memorial of the Government of Saudi Arabia*; Schofield 1992 (vols. 18–19), 1994b (vol. 2); Schofield and Blake 1992 (vol. 13); Taryam 1987; Wilkinson 1991.

Dispute Number: 16, 70
Countries: Great Britain vs. Saudi Arabia and vice versa
Years of Dispute: 1949–58

Disputed Territory: Both sides claimed sovereignty over the islands of Lubayana al-Khabirah and Lubaynah al-Sagirah.

Outcome of Dispute: In an agreement signed in February 1958 the dispute was settled with the islands being split between the two. Lubayna al-Khabirah was awarded to Saudi Arabia while the British/Bahrain retained control over Lubaynah al-Saghirah.

Sources: Albaharna 1975; Wilkinson 1991.

Dispute Number: 17, 83
Countries: Great Britain vs. Turkey and vice-versa
Years of Dispute: 1922–26
Disputed Territory: The two countries disputed sovereignty over the Mosul region along the border between Turkey and Iraq.
Outcome of Dispute: In an agreement signed in June 1926 Turkey recognized Iraqi sovereignty over almost all of the Mosul but was granted future oil royalties.
Sources: *British Documents on Foreign Affairs Part II, Series B* (vol. 30); *International Boundary Study* (#27); *Survey of International Affairs 1925* (vol. 1).

Dispute Number: 18
Countries: Egypt vs. Great Britain
Years of Dispute: 1922–56
Disputed Territory: Egypt contested British control over the Sudan and sought to incorporate the Sudan as part of their country.
Outcome of Dispute: Negotiations in the inter-war period failed to resolve the dispute but after World War II an agreement was reached in February 1953. The agreement called for a transitional government to take over power in the Sudan and for Sudan to determine its future political status by 1956. By early 1956 the Sudan had announced that it intended to seek full independence as a sovereign state and the Egyptian government accepted this decision.
Sources: Marlowe 1965; Sabry 1982; *Survey of International Affairs 1925–1958*.

Dispute Number: 19
Countries: Egypt vs. Sudan
Years of Dispute: 1958–95
Disputed Territory: In February of 1958 the Egyptian government laid claim to Sudanese territory in two areas north of the 22nd Parallel (the Wadi Halfa salient and Hala'ib).

Outcome of Dispute: There has been no resolution of the dispute, with Egypt maintaining its claims. The dispute remained dormant for some time until the early 1990s when Sudan complained to the United Nations that Egyptian troops had moved into the disputed areas and were undertaking actions to establish a permanent presence.

Sources: *Boundary and Security Bulletin 1993–95*; *Keesing's 1958–1995*; *Middle East Contemporary Survey 1976–1995*.

Dispute Number: 20
Countries: Egypt vs. Great Britain
Years of Dispute: 1922–54
Disputed Territory: Beginning in 1922 Egypt sought the termination of British military base rights in the Suez Canal zone and the withdrawal of all British troops.

Outcome of Dispute: After extensive negotiations an agreement was reached in July 1954 in which the British agreed to a phased withdrawal of their troops and termination of their base rights. The agreement also established the condition under which British forces could return to the Canal Zone for defense support.

Sources: Brecher and Wilkenfeld 1997; Butterworth 1976; *Survey of International Affairs 1925–1954*.

Dispute Number: 21
Countries: Egypt vs. Israel
Years of Dispute: 1948–88
Disputed Territory: With the declaration of Israel's independence in 1948 and the war that followed, Egypt became embroiled in a dispute with Israel over its sovereignty and borders. Egypt refused to formally recognize Israel's status as a sovereign state and in the negotiations establishing demilitarized zones in 1949 claims were made to the Negev and disputes arose over the sovereignty of territory in the zones. Following their defeat in the 1967 war, Egypt sought the return of territory occupied by Israel in the Sinai.

Outcome of Dispute: The basis for settling the dispute was the 1979 peace treaty between the two states. Egypt formally recognized Israel's independence and borders and in turn Israel agreed to return the Sinai to Egypt. A limited disagreement developed as Israel withdrew from occupied territories over Taba. A UN commission arbitrated the rival claims from late 1986 to mid-1988 and issued an award that recognized Egyptian sovereignty (which Israel accepted).

Sources: Caplan 1997; *International Boundary Study* (#46); Kliot 1995; Lukacs 1997; *Middle East Contemporary Survey 1976–1988*; Morris 1993; Quandt 1986, 1993; Rabinovich 1991.

Dispute Number: 22
Countries: Eritrea vs. Yemen
Year of Dispute: 1995
Disputed Territory: Eritrea claimed the Hanish Islands which were under the control of Yemen. The dispute emerged in 1995 when Yemen allowed an Italian firm to set up a tourist resort on the island of Hanish al Kabir. Eritrea responded by sending forces to the island in November and ordered Yemeni forces to vacate the island. Soon afterward fighting between the armed forces of the two countries erupted on the islands.
Outcome of Dispute: Mediation attempts by the Ethiopians, the Egyptians, and the French failed to achieve a settlement as Eritrea maintained its claims to the islands.
Sources: *Boundary and Security Bulletin 1995–96*; *Keesing's 1995*; *Middle East Contemporary Survey 1995–96*.

Dispute Number: 26, 77
Countries: France vs. Spain and vice versa
Years of Dispute: 1919–28
Disputed Territory: France and Spain were both interested in establishing territorial control over Tangier in Morocco. In 1904 Tangier had been declared a neutral territory but both states sought to change that status quo by fully incorporating the city into their colonial spheres of influence.
Outcome of Dispute: By September 1928 a final agreement was reached in which the city of Tangier was internationalized and thus neither France nor Spain was able to establish dominant control over the city and surrounding territories.
Sources: Bennett 1994; Stuart 1955; *Survey of International Affairs 1925* (vol. 1), *1929*.

Dispute Number: 27
Countries: France vs. Syria
Years of Dispute: 1919–20
Disputed Territory: After World War I France sought to establish a mandate over Syria but King Faisal sought independence for Syria as a sovereign state.

Outcome of Dispute: By August of 1920 the French military took control of Syria by ousting King Faisal and occupying Damascus.

Sources: *A History of the Peace Conference of Paris* (vol. 6); Fromkin 1989; Kedourie 1987; Longrigg 1958; Yapp 1987.

Dispute Number: 28
Countries: France vs. Turkey
Years of Dispute: 1919–21
Disputed Territory: The French laid claim to Cilicia and sections of what later would become the Turkish–Syrian border. Kemal, the Nationalist leader in Turkey, strongly opposed the French occupation of what he saw as Turkish territory and claims to bordering territory.
Outcome of Dispute: In December 1919 France offered to concede much of the territory in Cilicia in return for economic concessions but Kemal rejected this offer. In May of 1920 France agreed to an armistice and a partial withdrawal of its forces in the region but the armistice broke down shortly thereafter. A final agreement was reached in October 1921 on terms favorable to Turkey.
Sources: *A History of the Peace Conference of Paris* (vol. 6); Busch 1976; Sachar 1969; Sonyel 1975.

Dispute Number: 30, 54
Countries: Hijaz vs. Najd and vice versa
Years of Dispute: 1919–26
Disputed Territory: As Turkish control in Arabia collapsed during World War I the new states of Hijaz and Najd contended for control over territory in the areas of Khurma and Turba.
Outcome of Dispute: Najd defeated Hijaz in a war from 1924–5 and in January 1926 Najd rule over the Hijaz and disputed territories was established.
Sources: *British Documents on Foreign Affairs, Part II, Series B* (vols. 1, 4); Burdett 1996 (vol. 8), Troeller 1976.

Dispute Number: 31
Countries: Iran vs. Great Britain
Challenger: Iran
Years of Dispute: 1919–70
Disputed Territory: Iranian claims to the island of Bahrain date back to the 1840s.
Outcome of Dispute: Several rounds of negotiations in the interwar period failed to resolve the dispute and Iranian claims

were pressed once again in the post-World War II period as the British prepared to withdraw from the Gulf region. A UN fact-finding mission was sent to the island in 1970 to determine the desire of the Bahraini people and when it was concluded that they strongly favored independence, the Iranian government in May renounced its claim to sovereignty over the island.

Sources: Adamiyat 1955; *British Documents on Foreign Affairs Part II, Series B* (vol. 15); Kelly 1980; Schofield and Blake 1992 (vol. 13); Taryam 1987.

Dispute Number: 32
Countries: Iran vs. Great Britain
Years of Dispute: 1919–71
Disputed Territory: The three islands of Abu Musa, the Greater Tunb and the Lesser Tunb, lie approximately mid-way between the United Arab Emirates and Iran in the Strait of Hormuz. Iranian claims to sovereignty over the islands date back to the nineteenth century.

Outcome of Dispute: Periodic negotiations over the islands had failed to resolve the dispute by the time the British intended to withdraw from the Persian Gulf. In November 1971 a small contingent of Iranian forces occupied the islands and effectively established control over them. The UAE, however, did not recognize Iranian sovereignty over the islands and since late 1971 has called for the withdrawal of Iranian forces and has maintained its claim to sovereignty over the islands (see dispute number 88).

Sources: Amirahamd 1996; Kelly 1980; Mclachlan 1994; Mehr 1997; Schofield and Blake 1992 (vol. 13); Toye 1993 (vols. 4–5).

Dispute Number: 33
Countries: Iran vs. Great Britain/Iraq
Years of Dispute: 1920–75
Disputed Territory: Iran sought to shift the boundary line in the Shatt al-Arab waterway to the Thalweg and also claimed several small sections of the land border, particularly in the Zohab district. After World War I Iran raised these claims and disputed the British and Iraqi claims that the 1913 treaty signed between Iran and Turkey had settled all questions regarding delimitation of the border.

Outcome of Dispute: An agreement signed in July 1937 provided the basis for a settlement but the border commission established prior to World War II to resolve points of disagreement along the border ended in failure. In the post-World War II period Iran continued to raise questions about the land border and sought to extend the use of the thalweg as the boundary line in the Shatt al-Arab. In a treaty signed in March 1975 all border questions were settled and the thalweg was adopted as the boundary line for further sections of the Shatt al-Arab as demanded by Iran.

Sources: Al-Izzi 1971; *British Documents on Foreign Affairs, Part II, Series B* (vols. 22–3, 26–8); *International Boundary Study* (#164); Mclachlan 1994; Schofield 1986, 1989 (vols. 6–9).

Dispute Number: 34, 71
Countries: Iran vs. Saudi Arabia and vice versa
Years of Dispute: 1949–68
Disputed Territory: Both states claimed sovereignty over the islands of Farsi and Al-Arabiyah in the Persian Gulf.
Outcome of Dispute: In an agreement signed in October 1968 ownership of the islands was split between the two countries with Iran gaining control over the island of Farsi and Saudi Arabia the island of Al-Arabiyah.
Sources: Albaharna 1975; Burdett 1997; Schofield and Blake 1992 (vol. 13).

Dispute Number: 35, 75
Countries: Iran vs. Soviet Union and vice versa
Years of Dispute: 1919–57
Disputed Territory: Both states had claims to various islands in the Caspian Sea and to small sections of the land border on either side of the Caspian.
Outcome of Dispute: A border agreement signed in late 1954 established the basis for a final settlement of the dispute through the creation of a border commission. The commission completed its work by late 1956 and a treaty signed in April 1957 settled all outstanding claims through mutual concessions.
Sources: *British Documents on Foreign Affairs Part II, Series B* (vols. 21–2); Dmytryshyn and Cox 1987; *International Boundary Study* (#25); Mclachlan 1994; Rezun 1981; Volodarsky 1994.

Dispute Number: 36, 87
Countries: Iran vs. Turkey and vice versa
Years of Dispute: 1919–32

Disputed Territory: Several small sections of the border were contested. In the north territory near Mt. Ararat was disputed while in the central region the Khotur sector was claimed by both sides. Finally, in the south the area near Rezaiyeh was disputed.

Outcome of Dispute: A final agreement was reached in May 1932 with the Tehran Convention, under which Turkey gained land in the northern section of the border while Iran gained land in the southern and central regions.

Sources: *British Documents on Foreign Affairs Part II, Series B* (vols. 31–2); *International Boundary Study* (#28); *League of Nations Official Journal, February 1935; Survey of International Affairs 1928, 1934.*

Dispute Number: 37
Countries: Iraq vs. Great Britain/Kuwait
Years of Dispute: 1938–94
Disputed Territory: Iraqi territorial claims included: (a) the islands of Warba and Bubiyan since the late 1930s, (b) small sections of the land border at Khwar al-Sabiya since the 1950s, and (c) all of Kuwait when calling for the incorporation of Kuwait as part of a larger Iraqi state at various times since the 1960s.

Outcome of Dispute: Despite repeated rounds of talks dating back to the 1930s no negotiated settlement of the dispute had been achieved prior to Iraq's invasion of Kuwait in 1990. After Iraq's defeat in the Gulf War, the UN carried out a comprehensive delimitation of the border which was accepted by Iraq in November 1994.

Sources: *Boundary and Security Bulletin 1993–94*; Finnie 1992; Schofield 1993a.

Dispute Number: 38
Countries: Iraq vs. Great Britain
Years of Dispute: 1941
Disputed Territory: In 1941 the Iraqi military led a revolt in which the premier was forced to resign and a government of National Defense under Rashid Ali was formed. The leaders of the new government in an attempt to reassert Iraqi control and sovereignty called for the British to restrict their military base rights and the movement and size of British troops at military bases in the country. The British refused to allow any restrictions on their base rights or forces and charged that the

treaty of 1930 defined those rights and could not be unilaterally modified.

Outcome of Dispute: A military conflict with British forces at the Habbniya military base during April–May resulted in heavy losses for Iraq. The Iraqi government fell as a result and the new government withdrew demands for restrictions on British military base rights in the country.

Sources: Brecher and Wilkenfeld 1997; Sachar 1969; *Survey of International Affairs 1939–1946: The Middle East in the War 1945–1950.*

Dispute Number: 39
Countries: Iraq vs. Great Britain
Years of Dispute: 1947–8
Disputed Territory: The Iraqi government sought reduction if not the elimination of British military bases on its national territory.

Outcome of Dispute: An agreement was reached between the two countries in January 1948 in which the British would be allowed to maintain bases only in time of war and not during peace time. However, after the terms of the agreement were announced there was widespread opposition in Iraq and the collapse of the Iraqi government. As a result, the treaty was never ratified and by the end of 1948 the British government decided to withdraw unilaterally all of its military bases on Iraq.

Sources: *Keesing's 1948*; Sachar 1969.

Dispute Number: 40
Countries: Iraq vs. Iran
Years of Dispute: 1979–95
Disputed Territory: The Shatt-al-Arab waterway and land border dispute between Iran and Iraq was settled by the Algiers Agreement of 1975. In that agreement Iraq conceded to the Iranian demand that the Thalweg form the boundary line in the waterway. In 1979 Iraq claimed that Iran was violating the treaty and subsequently denounced the treaty and declared that the Thalweg would no longer be accepted as the boundary line.

Outcome of Dispute: In 1990 just before the invasion of Kuwait by Iraqi troops, Saddam Hussein seems to have offered very favorable terms to Iran for settling the dispute by proposing that the 1975 agreement be accepted once again. No formal agreement was signed, however, before the Gulf War began and since the war Iraq has not been willing to offer the same favorable terms for a settlement.

Sources: Abdulghani 1984; *Boundary and Security Bulletin 1993–95*; Ismael 1982; Mclachlan 1994; Schofield 1986, 1993a, 1994a.

Dispute Number: 41
Countries: Israel vs. Egypt
Years of Dispute: 1949–67
Disputed Territory: Following the Armistice Agreement signed in February 1949 Israel disputed small sections of territory in demilitarized zones that separated the forces of the two countries.
Outcome of Dispute: With its victory in the Six Day War of 1967 Israel took control of all disputed areas.
Sources: Caplan 1997; *International Boundary Study* (#46); Morris 1993.

Dispute Number: 42
Countries: Israel vs. Jordan
Years of Dispute: 1949–67
Disputed Territory: Following the Armistice Agreement signed in April 1949 Israel disputed small sections of territory in demilitarized zones that separated the forces of the two countries as well as claims to all of Jerusalem.
Outcome of Dispute: The Israeli victory in the 1967 war enabled it to take control of all of Jerusalem as well as disputed areas in what had been demilitarized zones.
Sources: Caplan 1997; Morris 1993; Priestland 1996 (vol. 10); Rabinovich 1991; Schofield 1993b (vol. 1).

Dispute Number: 43
Countries: Israel vs. Syria
Years of Dispute: 1949–67
Disputed Territory: Following the Armistice Agreement signed in July 1949 Israel disputed small sections of territory in demilitarized zones that separated the forces of the two countries. In addition, Israel also pressed Syria to withdraw from territories it had occupied at the end of the 1948 war which were located beyond the borders of Israel as drawn up in 1947 by the UN.
Outcome of Dispute: With its victory in the 1967 war Israel took control of all disputed areas.
Sources: Caplan 1997; Morris 1993; Rabinovich 1991; Shalev 1993.

Dispute Number: 44
Countries: Italy vs. Great Britain/Egypt
Years of Dispute: 1919–25
Disputed Territory: Italy laid claims to the area along the Libyan–Egyptian border in the area of Jaghbub, an oasis, and the port of Sallum. In May of 1919 the United Kingdom presented Jaghbub to Italy but refused to concede the port of Sallum. Italy rejected this offer as it sought both areas along the border.
Outcome of Dispute: In December 1925 the Italians signed an agreement with Egypt (with British support). Under the terms of the agreement Italy secured control of Jaghbub but Egypt retained Sallum and gained access to the Ramallah wells near Sallum
Sources: Biger 1995; Brownlie 1979; *Survey of International Affairs 1924, 1925* (vol. 1).

Dispute Number: 45
Countries: Italy vs. France
Year of Dispute: 1919
Disputed Territory: Italy laid claims to the areas of Ghadames, Ghat and Tummo along what would become the Libyan–Algerian border.
Outcome of Dispute: In notes exchanged in September 1919 France ceded the territories to the Italians.
Sources: Biger 1995; Brownlie 1979; *Survey of International Affairs 1920–23.*

Dispute Number: 46
Countries: Italy vs. France
Years of Dispute: 1919–35
Disputed Territory: Italy sought to gain territory along the Chad–Libya border in the areas of Borku and Tibesti.
Outcome of Dispute: In a January 1935 agreement the Libyan border was moved south at the expense of Chad. This agreement, however, was never ratified by Italy.
Sources: Biger 1995; Brownlie 1979; Flandin 1947; Shorrock 1988.

Dispute Number: 47
Countries: Italy vs. Turkey
Years of Dispute: 1919–21
Disputed Territory: Italy sought to secure mandate rights to territory in Smyrna and Adalia.

Outcome of Dispute: In an agreement signed in March 1921 Italy withdrew its call for establishing control over mandated territory in Turkey.

Sources: *A History of the Peace Conference of Paris* (vol. 6); Busch 1976; Sonyel 1975; Yapp 1987.

Dispute Number: 48
Countries: Jordan vs. Israel
Years of Dispute: 1948–94
Disputed Territory: Following the Armistice Agreement signed in April 1949 Jordan disputed small sections of territory in demilitarized zones that separated the forces of the two countries and refused to recognize the independence of Israel as a sovereign state. After its defeat in the 1967 Six Day War, Jordan called for the withdrawal of Israeli forces from the West Bank, Jerusalem, and several other small sections of territory that Israel took control of.

Outcome of Dispute: By the mid-1990s Jordan had relinquished claims to the West Bank and to Jerusalem (except the holy places). In October 1994 the two countries signed a peace treaty which settled all outstanding border questions. In the treaty the entire border was delimited and required Israel to return several small sections of territory it had occupied for decades. In addition, some bordering territories, while recognized to be under Jordanian control, were to be leased to Israel for twenty-five years.

Sources: Caplan 1997; Luckas 1997; *Middle East Contemporary Record 1980–95*; Morris 1993; Priestland 1996 (vol. 10); Quandt 1986, 1993; Rabinovich 1991; Schofield 1993b (vol. 1); Shlaim 1990.

Dispute Number: 49
Countries: Libya vs. France/Chad
Years of Dispute: 1954–72
Disputed Territory: In January 1935 an agreement was signed between Italy and France in which France was to cede the Aozou Strip along the border of Libya and Chad (see dispute number 46). This agreement was never ratified by Italy and France never actually ceded the territory as a result. After gaining independence Libya called upon France and then Chad to cede the Aozou based on the terms of the 1935 agreement.

Outcome of Dispute: In 1972 Libya took advantage of domestic turmoil within Chad to move military forces into the Aozou Strip and took control of the disputed territory.

Sources: Allcock 1992; Neuberger 1982; Shaw 1986; Wright 1989.

Dispute Number: 50
Countries: Mauritania vs. Spain
Years of Dispute: 1960–75
Disputed Territory: Mauritania laid claim to the territory of the Spanish Sahara.
Outcome of Dispute: By the summer of 1975 Spain decided to withdraw from Spanish Sahara, leaving Morocco and Mauritania to work out an agreement on how to divide the territory of the Spanish colony. In November of that year Mauritania agreed to divide the Spanish Sahara with Morocco securing about two-thirds of the territory.
Sources: Allcock 1992; Damis 1983; Hodges 1983; *Keesing's 1960–75*; Thompson and Adloff 1980.

Dispute Number: 51
Countries: Morocco vs. France/Algeria
Years of Dispute: 1956–72
Disputed Territory: The Moroccan government laid claims to areas along the southern border of French Algeria in the district of Tindouh. Morocco proposed that a joint Franco-Moroccan commission be formed to delimit the border in this region but in subsequent negotiations a settlement could not be reached with France or Algeria.
Outcome of Dispute: A final settlement was achieved in a June 1972 agreement. Morocco withdrew its claim to the disputed territory and in turn Algeria agreed to permit Morocco the right to develop mineral resources in the border region. In addition, Algeria agreed not to oppose Moroccan claims to Spanish Sahara.
Sources: *Africa Contemporary Record 1969–72*; *Africa Research Bulletin 1963–72*; Damis 1983; *Documents Diplomatiques Français 1954–61*; Shaw 1986.

Dispute Number: 52
Countries: Morocco vs. Spain
Years of Dispute: 1956–95
Disputed Territory: Morocco has claimed the Chafarinas Islands off its northern coast as well as several Spanish enclaves, most notably Melilla and Ceuta.

Outcome of Dispute: There has been no settlement of the dispute with Morocco maintaining its claims and Spain has refused to withdraw from the islands or enclaves.

Sources: Allcock 1992; Biger 1995; *Keesing's 1956–95*; O'Reilly 1994.

Dispute Number: 53
Countries: Morocco vs. Spain
Years of Dispute: 1956–75
Disputed Territory: Morocco pressed claims to the Spanish Sahara on grounds of historical ties.

Outcome of Dispute: In 1956 and 1969 Spain ceded small sections of territory to Morocco and by 1970 Spain agreed in principle to hold a referendum in Spanish Sahara on self-determination but avoided discussion on dates for such a referendum until 1974. In December 1974 Mauritania and Morocco jointly filed an appeal in the International Court of Justice on the status of Spanish Sahara and the ICJ opinion issued in 1975 was that the region did not belong to any one country by the time of its colonization by Spain and that there were limited legal ties between the region and the countries of Mauritania or Morocco. Spain by this time, however, had decided to withdraw from the colony and in November 1975 Morocco and Mauritania reached an agreement to divide up the territory with Morocco gaining control over about two-thirds of the former Spanish colony.

Sources: *Africa Contemporary Record 1968–75*; Allcock 1992; Biger 1995; Dames 1983; Hodges 1983; *International Boundary Study* (#9); *Keesing's 1956–75*; Trout 1969.

Dispute Number: 55
Countries: North Yemen vs. Asir
Years of Dispute: 1919–26
Disputed Territory: Asir's independence had been recognized by the British in 1915 and British forces had been stationed in Asir during World War I. Yemen, however, claimed territories along the coastline, particularly the ports and towns of al-Hudayada and al-Luhayya and had larger aspirations of incorporating all of Asir into their country.

Outcome of Dispute: By the end of 1926 Yemeni forces had overrun much of southern Asir, including the disputed coastal regions. Northern sections of Asir were taken over by Najd and thus

Asir's bid for independence came to an end as its territories were annexed by its neighbors.
Sources: Schofield 1993b (vol. 4); Survey of International Affairs 1925 (vol. 1), 1928; Wenner 1967.

Dispute Number: 56
Countries: North Yemen vs. Great Britain/South Yemen
Years of Dispute: 1919–90
Disputed Territory: The initial attempt to delimit the border between the British Aden Protectorate and Yemen was in 1925 but disputes arose in a number of border regions and Yemen also claimed sovereignty over islands. After World War II Yemen governments extended their territorial claims to include all of the Aden Protectorate as their goal was to incorporate the British colony into a larger Yemeni state.
Outcome of Dispute: During the inter-war period negotiations on disputed border regions achieved very little and after World War II North Yemen supported rebel forces within Aden seeking to oust the British. Talks on reunification with South Yemen began in the 1970s and continued until a final agreement was reached in May 1990 for South Yemen to merge with North Yemen.
Sources: British Documents on Foreign Affairs Part II, Series B (vols. 8–10, 13); Gause 1990; Reilly 1960; Schofield 1993b (vol. 1); Survey Of International Affairs 1925 (vol. 1), 1928, 1939–1946; Wenner 1967; Wilkinson 1991.

Dispute Number: 57, 73
Countries: North Yemen vs. Saudi Arabia and vice versa
Years of Dispute: 1927–34
Disputed Territory: Following the collapse of Asir and its division between Najd and North Yemen in 1926 a dispute emerged in Asir and Najran over the new border between the two states.
Outcome of Dispute: In December 1931 limited concessions were made by Saudi Arabia to Yemen along sections of the Asiri border. By March 1934 the border conflict escalated to a full-scale war in which Saudi forces decisively defeated Yemen. In the peace treaty signed in May 1934 the disputed Najran region was gained by Saudi Arabia but the Saudis did not take any additional territory.
Sources: British Documents on Foreign Affairs Part II, Series B (vol. 10); Schofield 1993b (vol. 4); Survey of International Affairs 1925 (vol. 1), 1928, 1934; Wenner 1967; Wilkinson 1991.

Dispute Number: 58, 69
Countries: Oman vs. Saudi Arabia and vice versa
Years of Dispute: 1934–90
Disputed Territory: Saudi claims to the Buraimi Oasis and bordering territory of what becomes Oman dates back to the mid-1930s as did British claims (see dispute number 15). When Oman gained its independence in 1971 it claimed territory in the Buraimi Oasis and surrounding areas.
Outcome of Dispute: After repeated rounds of negotiations between the two countries starting in the early 1970s, a final agreement was reached in March 1990. Saudi Arabia withdrew its claims to the areas of the oasis claimed by Oman and mutual concessions were exchanged on remaining sections of the border.
Sources: Biger 1995; Cordesman 1984; Kechichian 1995; Riphenburg 1998; Schofield 1992 (vol. 19); Skeet 1992.

Dispute Number: 59, 89
Countries: Oman vs. United Arab Emirates and vice versa
Years of Dispute: 1971–93
Disputed Territory: Both states have laid claims to territory in the Buraimi Oasis as well as sections of the border along the northern coast of Ras al-Khaimah.
Outcome of Dispute: Limited agreements were reached in 1974 and 1978 and it was announced in April 1993 that a final settlement had been reached though the details remain unclear.
Sources: Biger 1995; Cordesman 1984, 1997a; Kechichian 1995; *Middle East Contemporary Survey 1977–93*; Schofield 1992 (vol. 19), 1994a.

Dispute Number 60, 78
Countries: Oman vs. South Yemen/Yemen and vice versa
Years of Dispute: 1981–92
Disputed Territory: The border between the states in the Dhofur region had been the source of dispute.
Outcome of Dispute: In October 1992 an agreement was signed that settled with mutual concessions on both sides.
Sources: Biger 1995; Cordesman 1984, 1997a; Kechichian 1995; *Middle East Contemporary Survey 1977–92*; Schofield 1992 (vol. 20).

Dispute Number: 61
Countries: Qatar vs. Bahrain

Years of Dispute: 1971–95

Disputed Territory: The Hawar Islands were awarded by the British to Bahrain in 1939 and this was opposed by the Qatari government on the grounds that the islands were closer to Qatar than they were to Bahrain. When Qatar gained its independence it maintained its claim to the islands.

Outcome of Dispute: Despite repeated rounds of talks there has been no settlement of the dispute. During 1993–5 the ICJ was studying the dispute.

Sources: *Boundary and Security Bulletin 1993–95*; Cordesman 1984, 1997a; *Middle East Contemporary Survey 1975–95*; Schofield 1992 (vol. 15); Zahlan 1979.

Dispute Number: 62

Countries: Russia vs. Azerbaijan

Years of Dispute: 1994–95

Disputed Territory: The Russians sought to secure military base rights in order to maintain troops and supporting operations for the Gabalin Radar Station.

Outcome of Dispute: By the end of 1995 the question of military base rights had not been settled despite several rounds of talks on the issue.

Sources: *Boundary and Security Bulletin 1994–95*; *Foreign Broadcast and Information Service: Daily Reports – Central Eurasia 1994–95*; *Keesing's 1994–95*.

Dispute Number: 63

Countries: Russia vs. Georgia

Years of Dispute: 1993–5

Disputed Territory: The Russians sought to secure military and naval base rights.

Outcome of Dispute: A tentative agreement was reached in March 1995 and then formalized in September in which the Russians received rights to four military bases for twenty-five years but this was contingent upon Russia forcing the political leadership of Abkhazi to end its self-determination efforts and to remain part of Georgia. At the end of 1995 Georgia was still seeking a political settlement with Abkhazi and therefore the military base agreement had not been ratified.

Sources: *Boundary and Security Bulletin 1993–5*; *Foreign Broadcast and Information Service: Daily Reports – Central Eurasia 1993–95*; *Keesing's 1993–95*.

Dispute Number: 72
Countries: Saudi Arabia vs. Qatar
Years of Dispute: 1992
Disputed Territory: In 1965 Qatar and Saudi Arabia signed a border agreement delimiting and defining the border area between the two countries. In 1992, however, Saudi Arabia laid claims to the Khafus region along the border and argued that the 1965 treaty included the territory within their country.
Outcome of Dispute: The dispute was settled in December 1992 with an agreement in which Qatari claims to the region of Khafus were upheld while the Saudis gained small territorial concessions in other areas. It was also decided to demarcate this region within a year to reflect the new boundaries that were drawn.
Sources: Biger 1995; Cordesman 1997a, 1997b; Schofield 1994a; Zahlan 1979.

Dispute Number: 74
Countries: Soviet Russia vs. Georgia
Years of Dispute: 1920–1
Disputed Territory: While the Soviet government recognized Georgia's independence in the spring of 1920 it nevertheless disputed the border in the Borchulu district (see dispute numbers 2, 29).
Outcome of Dispute: The dispute came to an end when Soviet armed forces invaded and occupied Georgia during February and March 1921 and declared Georgia to be a Soviet republic.
Sources: *British Documents on Foreign Affairs Part II, Series A* (vol. 4); Kazemzadeh 1951; Pipes 1954; *Survey of International Affairs 1920–1923*.

Dispute Number: 76
Countries: Soviet Union vs. Turkey
Years of Dispute: 1945–53
Disputed Territory: The Soviet Union laid claims to the areas of Kars and Ardahan. The Soviets also intended to establish a military base in the Turkish Straits and demanded rights to a base.
Outcome of Dispute: The Turkish government was unwilling to accept the claims of the Soviets and denied them access to any of the regions. In 1953 the Soviet government unilaterally withdrew its claims to the Kars and Aradahan regions as well as its claims to base rights in the straits.

Sources: Howard 1974; Kuniholm 1980; Lenczowski 1980; Vali 1972.

Dispute Number: 79
Countries: Syria vs. Israel
Years of Dispute: 1948–95
Disputed Territory: The dispute began with Syria refusing to recognize the independence of Israel and following the Armistice Agreement signed in July 1949 Syria disputed several sections of territory in demilitarized zones that separated the forces of the two countries. After its defeat in the 1967 Six Day War, Syria has demanded the withdrawal of Israeli forces from the Golan Heights.
Outcome of Dispute: There has been no settlement of Syrian claims throughout the dispute. With its defeat in 1967 Israel took control of disputed territory in demilitarized zones and Israel has continued to occupy the Golan Heights since 1967. Negotiations in the 1990s on the Golan Heights made some progress but no final agreement was reached.
Sources: Caplan 1997; Drysdale and Hinnebusch 1991; Ma'oz 1995; *Middle East Contemporary Survey 1977–95*; Morris 1993; Quandt 1986, 1993; Rabinovich 1998; Shalev 1993.

Dispute Number: 80
Countries: Tunisia vs. France
Years of Dispute: 1956–62
Disputed Territory: France granted Tunisia independence in 1956 but continued to maintain military bases in its former colony. Tunisia called for the withdrawal of French forces and the termination of all base rights, particularly the Bizerte base.
Outcome of Dispute: In 1958 France agrees to reduce its military presence in Tunisia and in a final agreement signed in January 1962 commits itself to withdraw completely from the remaining base at Bizerte within twenty-one months.
Sources: Brecher and Wilkenfeld 1997; Butterworth 1976; Gelpi 1994; *Keesing's 1956–62*.

Dispute Number: 81
Countries: Tunisia vs. France/Algeria
Years of Dispute: 1959–70
Disputed Territory: Tunisia laid claims to part of its border in the Sahara with Algeria, arguing that the border had not been established by prior agreements. France denied the Tunisian

claim and stated that the Tunisian government had approved the existing border.

Outcome of Dispute: In April 1968 an agreement was reached between the two sides which covered much of the disputed border and a final settlement was reached in January 1970. Tunisia withdrew its claims to the disputed areas and accepted the boundary line originally established in 1929.

Sources: *Africa Contemporary Record 1968–70*; *African Recorder 1967–70*; *Africa Research Bulletin 1967–70*; Biger 1995; Brownlie 1979; *Keesings's 1959–70*.

Dispute Number: 84
Countries: Turkey vs. France
Years of Dispute: 1925–9
Disputed Territory: Turkey laid claim to sections along its southern border with the French mandate of Syria.
Outcome of Dispute: A final settlement was reached in an agreement signed in June 1929 which required both sides to make mutual concessions.
Sources: *International Boundary Study* (#163); *Survey Of International Affairs 1925* (vol. 1), *1928*; *1930*.

Dispute Number: 85
Countries: Turkey vs. France
Years of Dispute: 1937–9
Disputed Territory: Beginning in 1937 Turkey called for limited changes along the border with Syria and by 1939 Turkey sought the annexation of Alexandretta.
Outcome of Dispute: During 1937 France agreed to minor border changes and then in July 1939 agreed to cede Alexandretta to Turkey.
Sources: *British Documents on Foreign Affairs Part II, Series B* (vol. 35); *International Boundary Study* (#163); *Survey of International Affairs 1936, 1938*.

Dispute Number: 86
Countries: Turkey vs. Georgia/Soviet Russia
Years of Dispute: 1919–21
Disputed Territory: Turkey laid claim to Artvin, Ardahan, and Batum.
Outcome of Dispute: In an agreement signed in March 1921 Turkey gains Artvin and Ardahan while Soviet Russia retains Batum.

Sources: *Documents on British Foreign Affairs Part II, Series A,* (vol. 4); Kazemzadeh 1951; Pipes 1954; *Survey of International Affairs 1920–1923.*

Dispute Number: 88
Countries: United Arab Emirates vs. Iran
Years of Dispute: 1971–95
Disputed Territory: In November 1971 Iran occupied the three islands of Abu Musa, the Greater Tunb and the Lesser Tunb which are located approximately mid-way between the United Arab Emirates and Iran in the Strait of Hormuz. The leadership of the UAE did not concede sovereignty over the islands to Iran and has called for the withdrawal of Iranian forces.
Outcome of Dispute: There has been no settlement of the dispute as both sides maintain claims of sovereignty and Iranian forces remain stationed on the islands.
Sources: Amirahamd 1996; *Boundary and Security Bulletin 1993–95*; Kelly 1980; Mclachlan 1994; Mehr 1997; Schofield and Blake 1992 (vol. 13); Toye 1993 (vols. 4–5).

Bibliography of sources listed in case summaries

Abdulghani, Jasim (1984) *Iran & Iraq* (Baltimore: Johns Hopkins University Press).

Abu-Dawood, Abdul-Razzak and P. Karan (1990) *International Boundaries of Saudi Arabia* (New Delhi: Galaxy Publications).

Adamiyat, Fereydoun (1955) *Bahrein Islands* (New York: Praeger).

Africa Contemporary Record 1968–75 (1969–76) (New York: African Publishing Co.).

African Recorder 1967–70 (New Delhi: M. H. Samuele, 1967–70).

Africa Research Bulletin 1963–72 (London: Africa Research Limited, 1963–72).

A History of the Peace Conference of Paris (1924) vol. 6 (London: Henry Frowde and Hodder & Stoughton).

Al-Alkim, Hassan (1989) *The Foreign Policy of the United Arab Emirates* (London: Saqi Books).

Albaharna, Husain (1975) *The Arabian Gulf States* (Beirut: Librairie Du Liban).

Al-Izzi, Khalid (1971) *The Shatt Al-Arab River Dispute* (Groningen: Groningen State University).

Allcock, John ed. (1992) *Border and Territorial Disputes*, 3rd ed. (London: Longman).

Al-Marayati, Abid (1961) *A Diplomatic History of Modern Iraq* (New York: Robert Sapeller & Sons).

Amirahamd, Hooshang ed. (1996) *Small Islands, Big Politics* (New York: St. Martin's Press).

Bennett, G. H. (1994) "Britain's Relations with France After Versailles" *European Historical Quarterly*, 24: 53–84.

Biger, Gideon (1995) *The Encyclopedia of International Boundaries* (New York: Facts on File).

Boundary and Security Bulletin 1993–96 (Durham: International Boundary Research Unit, 1993–96).

Brecher, Michael and Jonathan Wilkenfeld (1997) *A Study of Crisis* (Ann Arbor: University of Michigan Press).

British Documents on Foreign Affairs, Part II, Series A (1984) vols. 1, 4 (Bethesda: University Publications of America).

British Documents on Foreign Affairs, Part II, Series B (1985–97) vols. 1, 4, 8–11, 13, 15, 21–3, 26–8, 30–2, 35 (Bethesda: University Publications of America).

Brownlie, Ian (1979) *African Boundaries* (London: C. Hurst & Company).

Burdett, A. L. P. ed. (1996) *Records of the Hijaz 1798–1925*, vol. 8 (Oxford: Archive Editions).

(1997) *Records of Saudi Arabia 1761–1965* (Oxford: Archive Editions).

Busch, Briton (1976) *Mudros to Lausanne* (New York: State University of New York Press).

Butterworth, Robert (1976) *Managing Interstate Conflict* (Pittsburgh: University Center for International Studies).

Caplan, Neil (1997) *Futile Diplomacy*, vol. 3 (London: Frank Cass).

Cordesman, Anthony (1984) *The Gulf and the Search for Strategic Stability* (Boulder: Westview Press).

(1997a) *Bahrain, Oman, Qatar, and the UAE* (Boulder: Westview Press).

(1997b) *Saudi Arabia* (Boulder: Westview Press).

Damis, John (1983) *Conflict in Northwest Africa* (Stanford: Hoover Institution Press).

Dmytryshyn, Basil and Frederick Cox (1987) *The Soviet Union and the Middle East* (Princeton: Kingston Press).

Documents Diplomatiques Français 1954–61 (1987–98) (Paris: Ministère des Affaires Etrangères).

Drysdale, Alasdair and Raymond Hinnebusch (1991) *Syria and the Middle East Peace Process* (New York: Council on Foreign Relations Press).

Finnie, David (1992) *Shifting Lines in the Sand* (Cambridge: Harvard University Press).

Flandin, Pierre-Étienne (1947) *Politique Française, 1919–1940* (Paris: Les Editions Nouvelles).

Foreign Broadcast and Information Service: Daily Reports – Central Eurasia 1994–95 (Washington DC: Foreign Broadcast Information Service, 1994–5).

Frichwasser-Ra'anan, H. F. (1976) *The Frontiers of a Nation* (Westport: Hyperion Press).

Fromkin, David (1989) *A Peace to End All Peace* (New York: Avon Books).

Gause, F. Gregory (1990) *Saudi–Yemeni Relations* (New York: Columbia University Press).

Gelpi, Christopher (1994) "Power and Legitimacy" (PhD thesis, Department of Political Science, University of Michigan).

Hemlreich, Paul (1974) *From Paris to Sèvres* (Columbus: Ohio State University Press).

Hodges, Tony (1983) *Western Sahara* (Westport: Lawrence Hill & Co.).

Howard, Harry (1974) *Turkey, the Straits and US Policy* (Baltimore: Johns Hopkins University Press).

International Boundary Study (1961–78) (Washington DC: The Geographer, Bureau of Intelligence and Research, US Department of State).

International Boundary Study. No. 3 Chad–Libya Boundary, 5 May 1961.

International Boundary Study. No. 9 Morocco–Spanish Sahara Boundary, 14 September 1961.

International Boundary Study. No. 25 Iran–USSR Boundary, 30 December 1963.

International Boundary Study. No. 27 Iraq–Turkey Boundary, 30 January 1964.

International Boundary Study. No. 28 Iran–Turkey Boundary, 3 February 1964.

International Boundary Study. No. 29 Turkey–USSR Boundary, 24 February 1964.

International Boundary Study. No. 46 Israel–United Arab Republic Armistice Line, 1 April 1965.

International Boundary Study. No. 94 Jordan–Syria Boundary, 30 December 1969.

International Boundary Study. No. 103 Kuwait–Saudi Arabia Boundary, 15 September 1970.

International Boundary Study. No. 111 Iraq–Saudi Arabia Boundary, 1 June 1971

International Boundary Study. No. 163 Syria–Turkey Boundary, 7 March 1978.

Ismael, Tareq (1982) *Iraq and Iran* (New York: Syracuse University Press).

Kazemzadeh, Firuz (1951) *The Struggle for Transcaucasia* (Oxford: George Ronald).

Kechichian, Joseph (1995) *Oman and the World* (Santa Monica: Rand).

Kedourie, Elie (1987) *England and the Middle East* (Boulder: Westview Press).

Keesing's Contemporary Archives 1956–86 (London: Keesing's Publications, 1956–86).

Keesing's Record of World Events 1987–95 (London: Keesing's Publications, 1987–95).

Kelly, J. B. (1980) *Arabia, the Gulf and the West* (London: Weidenfeld and Nicolson).

Kliot, Nurit (1995) *The Evolution of Egyptian–Israeli Boundaries* (Durham: International Boundaries Research Unit).

Kostiner, Joseph (1993) *The Making of Saudi Arabia 1916–1936* (New York: Oxford University Press).

Kuniholm, Bruce (1980) *The Origins of the Cold War in the Near East* (Princeton: Princeton University Press).

League of Nations Official Journal, November 1931 (Geneva: League of Nations, 1931).

League of Nations Official Journal, September 1932 (Geneva: League of Nations, 1932).

League of Nations Official Journal, February 1935 (Geneva: League of Nations, 1935).

Leatherdale, Clive (1983) *Britain and Saudi Arabia 1925–1939* (London: Frank Cass).

Lenczowski, George (1980) *The Middle East in World Affairs*, 4th ed. (Ithaca: Cornell University Press).

Longrigg, Stephen (1958) *Syria and Lebanon Under French Mandate* (London: Oxford University Press).

Lukacs, Yehuda (1997) *Israel, Jordan, and the Peace Process* (New York: Syracuse University Press).

Ma'oz, Moshe (1995) *Syria and Israel* (Oxford: Clarendon Press).

Marlowe, John (1965) *Anglo-Egyptian Relations, 1800–1956* 2nd ed. (London: Frank Cass).

Mclachlan, Keith ed. (1994) *The Boundaries of Modern Iran* (London: UCL Press).

Mehr, Farhang (1997) *A Colonial Legacy* (Lanham: University Press of America).

Memorial of the Government of Saudi Arabia (1955) (Riyadh: Ministry of Foreign Affairs, Government of Saudi Arabia).

Middle East Contemporary Survey 1976–95 (New York: Holmes & Meir, 1978–85 and Boulder: Westview Press, 1986–97).

Morris, Benny (1993) *Israel's Border Wars 1949–1956* (Oxford: Clarendon Press).

Neuberger, Benyamin (1982) *Involvement, Invasion, and Withdrawal* (Tel Aviv: Shiloah Center for Middle Eastern and African Studies).

O'Reilly, Gerry (1994) *Ceuta and the Spanish Sovereign Territories* (Durham: International Boundary Research Unit).

Pipes, Richard (1954) *The Formation of the Soviet Union* (Cambridge: Harvard University Press).

Priestland, Jane ed. (1996) *Records of Jordan 1919–1965*, vol. 10 (Oxford: Archive Editions).

Quandt, William (1986) *Camp David* (Washington DC: Brookings).

(1993) *Peace Process* (Washington DC: Brookings).

Rabinovich, Itamar (1991) *The Road Not Taken* (Oxford: Oxford University Press).

(1998) *The Brink of Peace* (Princeton: Princeton University Press).

Reilly, Bernard (1960) *Aden and the Yemen* (London: HMSO).

Rezun, Miron (1981) *The Soviet Union and Iran* (Geneva: Sijthoff & Noordhoff).

Riphenburg, Carol (1998) *Oman* (Westport: Praeger).

Sabry, Hussein (1982) *Sovereignty for Sudan* (London: Ithaca Press).

Sachar, Howard (1969) *The Emergence of the Middle East* (New York: Alfred A. Knopf).

Schofield, Richard (1986) *Evolution of the Shatt al-'Arab Boundary Dispute* (Cambridgeshire: Middle East and North African Studies Press).

Schofield, Richard ed. (1989) *The Iran–Iraq Border 1840–1958*, vols. 6–9 (Trowbridge: Archive Editions).

(1992) *Arabian Boundary Disputes*, vols. 6–8, 11, 15, 18–20 (Oxford: Archive Editions).

(1993a) *Kuwait and Iraq*, 2nd ed. (London: Royal Institute of International Affairs).

(1993b) *Arabian Geopolitics 1*, vols. 1, 4 (Oxford: Archive Editions).

(1994a) *Territorial Foundations of the Gulf States* (New York: St. Martin's Press).

(1994b) *Arabian Boundaries, New Documents 1963*, vol. 2 (Oxford: Archive Editions).

(1997) *Arabian Boundaries, New Documents 1965*, vol. 2 (Oxford: Archive Editions).

Schofield, Richard and Gerald Blake eds. (1992) *Arabian Boundaries, Primary Documents 1853–1960*, vol. 13 (Oxford: Archive Editions).

Shalev, Aryeh (1993) *The Israel–Syria Armistice Regime, 1949–1955* (Tel Aviv: Jaffee Center for Strategic Studies, Tel Aviv University).

Shaw, Malcom (1986) *Title to Territory in Africa* (Oxford: Clarendon Press).

Shlaim, Avi (1990) *The Politics of Partition* (New York: Columbia University Press).

Shorrock, William (1988) *From Ally to Enemy* (Kent: Kent State University Press).

Skeet, Ian (1992) *Oman* (New York: St. Martin's Press).

Sonyel, Salahi (1975) *Turkish Diplomacy, 1918–1923* (Beverly Hills: Sage Publications).

Stuart, Graham (1955) *The International City of Tangier* (Stanford: Stanford University Press).

Survey of International Affairs 1920–58 (1925–62) (London: Oxford University Press).

Taryam, Abdullah (1987) *The Establishment of the United Arab Emirates 1950–85* (London: Croom Helm).

Thompson, Virginia and Richard Adloff (1980) *The Western Sahara* (London: Croom Helm).

Toye, Patricia ed. (1989) *Palestine Boundaries 1833–1947*, vols. 2–3 (Trowbridge: Archive Editions).

(1993) *The Lower Gulf Islands*, vols. 4–5 (Oxford: Archive Editions).

Troeller, Gary (1976) *The Birth of Saudi Arabia* (London: Frank Cass).

Trout, Frank (1969) *Morocco's Saharan Frontiers* (Geneva: Droz).

Vali, Ferenc (1972) *The Turkish Straits and NATO* (Stanford: Hoover Institution Press).

Volodarsky, Mikhail (1994) *The Soviet Union and its Southern Neighbors* (London: Frank Cass).

Wenner, Manfred (1967) *Modern Yemen* (Baltimore: Johns Hopkins University Press).

Wilkinson, John (1991) *Arabia's Frontiers* (London: I. B. Tauris).

Wright, John (1989) *Chad and the Central Sahara* (New York: Barnes and Nobles Imported).

Yapp, M. E (1987) *The Making of the Modern Middle East* (London: Longman).

Zahlan, Rosemarie (1979) *The Creation of Qatar* (London: Croom Helm).

Appendix D
Territorial disputes in Africa, 1919–1995

List of dispute cases

In this first section a list is provided of territorial disputes in Africa. For each dispute information is presented on the following: (a) the first state listed is the challenger and the second is the target, (b) the first and last years of the dispute, and (c) a brief description of the challenger's territorial claim. For those disputes marked with an asterisk both states are challengers and therefore the dispute is listed a second time with the identity of challenger and target reversed.

1. Belgium vs. Portugal* 1919–35: Claims to small sections of territory along Angola–Zaire border including islands and boundary line in Congo river
2. Belgium vs. Portugal 1926–7: Claims to territory of Matadi along Angolan–Congo border
3. Benin vs. Niger* 1960–5: Claim to Lete island
4. Botswana vs. Namibia 1992–5: Claim to islands in Chobe river
5. Britain vs. Ethiopia 1945–54: Claims to Ogaden and then western section of Eritrea
6. Britain vs. France* 1919: Claims to territory along Central African Republic–Sudan border
7. Britain/South Africa vs. Portugal* 1919–26: Claims to territory including Rua Cana Falls along South Africa–Angola border (UK is challenger 1919 and South Africa thereafter)
8. Britain vs. Portugal 1919–27: Britain contested small section of Mozambique border with Swaziland near tripoint with South Africa
9. Britain vs. Portugal* 1930–37: Claims to islands and location of boundary in Rovuma river along Mozambique–Tanzania border
10. Comoros vs. France 1975–95: Desire to annex Mayotte
11. Ethiopia/Italy vs. Britain/Kenya 1919–43, 1945–70: Claims to Gadaduma wells territory along border with Kenya (Ethiopia is challenger 1919–35 and Italy is challenger 1936–43, UK is target 1919–62 and Kenya thereafter)

12. Ethiopia/Italy vs. Britain/Sudan 1919–43, 1945–72: Claims to territory along border with Sudan (Ethiopia is challenger 1919–35 and Italy is challenger 1936–43, UK is target 1919–35, 1945–55 and Sudan thereafter)

13. Ethiopia vs. Italy* 1919–36: Claims to bordering territory of Italian Somaliland near tripoint with British Kenya

14. Ethiopia vs. Britain 1924–36, 1945–9: Claims to ports within British Somaliland

15. Ethiopia vs. France 1924–36: Claims to port of Djibouti

16. France vs. Britain* 1919: Claims to territory along Central African Republic–Sudan border

17. Gabon vs. Equatorial Guinea 1972: Claims to several small islands in Corisco Bay

18. Ghana vs. France/Ivory Coast 1959–66: Claim to Sanwi district along the south-eastern section of the border (France is target 1959 and Ivory Coast thereafter)

19. Ghana vs. France/Togo* 1958–66: Call for unification of Togo with Ghana (France is target 1958–9 and Togo thereafter)

20. Italy vs. Britain 1919–24: Claims to Jubaland region along border of Italian Somaliland and British Kenya

21. Italy vs. Britain 1924–30: Claims to territory along border of Italian and British Somaliland

22. Italy vs. Britain 1919–34: Claims to Sarra Triangle territory along Libya–Sudan border

23. Italy vs. Ethiopia* 1919–36: Claims to territory along Italian Somaliland–Ethiopia border near tripoint with British Kenya

24. Italy/Somalia vs. Ethiopia 1950–95: Claims to territory along (former) Italian Somaliland–Ethiopia border and then claims for union of Somalia populated areas of Ethiopia with Somalia (Italy is challenger 1950–9 and Somalia thereafter)

25. Italy vs. France 1919–43: Claims to territory of Djibouti including Djibouti–Addis Ababa railway line

26. Italy vs. France 1938–43: Claims to Corsica and bordering territory of Libya–Tunisia

27. Lesotho vs. South Africa 1966–95: Claims to large sections of territory within Orange Free State, Natal, and eastern Cape Province

28. Liberia vs. France 1919–60: Claim to bordering territory previously annexed by France along border with Ivory Coast

29. Liberia vs. France 1919–58: Claim to bordering territory of French Guinea previously annexed by France

30. Madagascar vs. France 1973–90: Claims to islands of Glorioso, Juan de Nova, Bassas da India, and Europa

31. Malawi vs. Zambia 1981–6: Claim to small section of territory along eastern province border
32. Mali vs. Mauritania 1960–3: Claims to Eastern Hodh and territory in western sector of border
33. Mali vs. Burkino Faso 1960–87: Claims to territory along Beli river in the Dori district
34. Mauritius vs. France 1976–95: Claim to island of Tromelin
35. Mauritius vs. Britain 1980–95: Claim to Diego Garcia islands
36. Morocco vs. France/Mauritania 1957–70: Desire for unification of Mauritania with Morocco (France is target 1957–9 and Mauritania thereafter)
37. Namibia vs. South Africa 1990–4: Claims to Walvis Bay and Penguin Islands
38. Niger vs. Benin* 1960–5: Claim to Lete island
39. Nigeria vs. Cameroon 1965–95: Claims to islands and territory in Bakassi peninsula
40. Portugal vs. Belgium* 1919–35: Claims to small sections of territory along Angola–Zaire border including islands and boundary line in Congo river
41. Portugal vs. Britain/South Africa* 1919–26: Claims to territory including Rua Cana Falls along South Africa–Angola border (UK is target 1919 and South Africa thereafter)
42. Portugal vs. Britain* 1930–7: Claims to islands and location of boundary in Ruvuma river along Mozambique–Tanzania border
43. Seychelles vs. France 1976–95: Claim to island of Tromelin
44. Somalia vs. Britain/Kenya 1960–81: Call for annexation of north-eastern province of Kenya populated by ethnic Somalis (UK is target 1960–2 and Kenya thereafter)
45. Somalia vs. France 1960–77: Desire for incorporation of Djibouti as part of Somalia
46. Togo vs. Ghana* 1960–95: Claim to southern bordering territory populated by Ewe tribe
47. Uganda vs. Tanzania 1974–9: Claim to Kagera Salient
48. Zaire vs. Zambia 1980–95: Claim to Kaputa district along northern border

Case summaries of territorial disputes in Africa, 1919–1995

In this section a short summary is provided of each dispute listed in section one. In each summary a description of the disputed territory is presented along with information on the outcome of the dispute. The complete citation for the sources listed at the end of each dispute summary is provided in the bibliography in section three.

Dispute Number: 1, 40
Countries: Belgium vs. Portugal and vice versa
Years of Dispute: 1919–35
Disputed Territory: The dispute arose over a small section of what is now on the border between Angola and Zaire, including conflicting claims to islands in the Congo river and the location of the boundary line in the river.
Outcome of Dispute: Talks began in 1922 and partial agreements settled limited areas in dispute by the end of the decade. A final agreement was concluded in August 1935 with both sides conceding territory with Portugal gaining more than the Belgians.
Sources: Braganca-Cunha 1937; Brownlie 1979; Bruce 1975; *International Boundary Study* (#144); Jentgen 1952.

Dispute Number: 2
Countries: Belgium vs. Portugal
Years of Dispute: 1926–7
Disputed Territory: Belgium sought minor border changes (to facilitate railway construction plans) close to the port of Matadi on the Congo river along the border between the Belgian Congo and Portuguese Angola.
Outcome of Dispute: An agreement was reached in July 1927 in which Belgium received one square mile of territory near the port while Portugal received in turn 480 square miles in the south-west corner of Congo.
Sources: *L'Afrique Française* 1927; *International Boundary Study* (#127); *Survey of International Affairs* 1929.

Dispute Number: 3, 38
Countries: Benin vs. Niger and vice versa
Years of Dispute: 1960–5
Disputed Territory: Both countries claimed sovereignty over Lete island in the Niger river.
Outcome of Dispute: The dispute was settled with an agreement in June 1965 to share sovereignty over the island.
Sources: *Africa Research Bulletin 1964–65*; Brownlie 1979; Shaw 1986; Touval 1972.

Dispute Number: 4
Countries: Botswana vs. Namibia

Years of Dispute: 1992–5

Disputed Territory: Botswana has claims to Kasikil and Sedudu Islands and bordering territory around these islands in the Chobe river.

Outcome of Dispute: There has been no settlement but in February 1995 the dispute was sent to the ICJ for arbitration.

Sources: *Africa Research Bulletin 1992–95*; *Boundary and Security Bulletin 1993–95*.

Dispute Number: 5

Countries: Great Britain vs. Ethiopia

Years of Dispute: 1945–54

Disputed Territory: Following the restoration of Ethiopian independence in late 1944, Great Britain sought to incorporate sections of the Ogaden and western Eritrea into British Somaliland.

Outcome of Dispute: Britain withdraws its claims to all of the territories in two agreements. The first was reached in August 1948 and the second in November 1954.

Sources: *Keesing's 1948–54*; Spencer 1984.

Dispute Number: 6, 16

Countries: Great Britain vs. France and vice versa

Year of Dispute: 1919

Disputed Territory: Both countries claimed sections of territory along the length of the border between French Equatorial Africa and the Sudan.

Outcome of Dispute: A convention was signed in September 1919 that defined the entire border. In the agreement France conceded most of the disputed territory to Britain.

Sources: Brownlie 1979; *L'Afrique Française (Supplement de Juin) 1924*; *L'Afrique Française 1920*; *Survey of International Affairs 1924*.

Dispute Number: 7, 41

Countries: Great Britain/South Africa vs. Portugal and vice versa

Years of Dispute: 1919–26

Disputed Territory: The dispute arose over the final delimitation of the border between Portuguese controlled Angola and South Africa. The main point of contention was the Kunene (Rua Cana) Falls, which provided water for irrigation and energy.

Outcome of Dispute: Negotiations began in 1918 and in an agreement reached in July 1926 Portugal secured sovereign rights over the falls but South Africa gained the right to use waters for irrigation and power.

Sources: Biger 1995; Braganca-Cunha 1937; Brownlie 1979; *British Command Papers, Nos. 2777, 2778*; Bruce 1975; *Great Britain Foreign Office Archives 1925–26*; *League of Nations Official Journal, November 1925*; *Survey of International Affairs 1929*.

Dispute Number: 8
Countries: Great Britain vs. Portugal
Years of Dispute: 1919–27
Disputed Territory: Beginning in 1905 Britain disputed the northern section of the border of Swaziland and Mozambique near the tripoint with South Africa.
Outcome of Dispute: In 1920 a commission was established to study the dispute and to make recommendations for a final settlement. The commission's work was completed during 1925 and in an agreement reached in October 1927 Great Britain accepted a definition of the border with minor changes on terms favored by Portugal.
Sources: Brownlie 1979, *Great Britain Foreign Office Archives 1920–25*.

Dispute Number: 9, 42
Countries: Great Britain vs. Portugal and vice versa
Years of Dispute: 1930–7
Disputed Territory: The dispute centered on rival claims to islands in the Rovuma river as well as the location of the boundary line in the river. The British proposed that islands lying above the confluence with the Domoni rivulet should belong to Tanganyika while islands below that belong to the Portuguese. In addition, the British asked for freedom of navigation for all citizens along the Rovuma as well as fishing rights.
Outcome of Dispute: In a series of notes exchanged during 1936–7 the two countries settled claims to islands and the location of the boundary line through mutual concessions on terms similar to those originally proposed by the British.
Sources: Brownlie 1979; *Great Britain Foreign Office Archives 1930, 1934–37*; *International Boundary Study (#39)*; McEwen 1971.

Dispute Number: 10
Countries: Comoros vs. France

Years of Dispute: 1975–95

Disputed Territory: In 1975 Comoros attained independence but a majority of the population of one of the Comoro islands, Mayotte (about 220 square miles), expressed a desire to remain a French dependency rather than be part of an independent Comoros. Comoros, however, maintains that Mayotte is part of its national territory, while the French government insists that the people of Mayotte have the right to self-determination.

Outcome of Dispute: Despite opposition from the United Nations Security Council and General Assembly, France has not altered its policy of support for Mayotte's continued status as a French dependency.

Sources: Allcock 1992; Berringer 1995; *Keesing's 1975–95*; Newitt 1984; *Yearbook of the United Nations 1976–95*.

Dispute Number: 11
Countries: Ethiopia/Italy vs. Great Britain/Kenya
Years of Dispute: 1919–43, 1945–70

Disputed Territory: Ethiopia claimed sovereignty over a small section of territory along the border where the Gadaduma and Gadama wells are located. In 1907 a border agreement had established the border between Ethiopian and British Kenya but a dispute subsequently arose over attempts to demarcate the border. As a result, Ethiopia disputed the location of the boundary line in the areas where the wells were located.

Outcome of Dispute: In several rounds of talks in the 1950s the British were firm in maintaining that the disputed territory remain a part of Kenya. Shortly before attaining independence in 1963, however, the Kenyan government reached a partial agreement to concede the Gadaduma wells to Ethiopia and, in turn, Ethiopia conceded the Gadaduma wells to Kenya. Further negotiations were held after independence and by June 1970 a comprehensive agreement was reached between Kenya and Ethiopia.

Sources: Brownlie 1979; *Great Britain Foreign Office Archives 1925–40, 1947–63*; *International Boundary Study* (#152); McEwen 1971; Taha 1983.

Dispute Number: 12
Countries: Ethiopia/Italy vs. Great Britain/Sudan
Years of Dispute: 1919–43, 1945–72

Disputed Territory: Ethiopia contested sections of its northern and southern border with Sudan. Earlier border agreements concluded between Ethiopia, Britain, and Italy at the turn of the century did not clearly establish the location of the border with Sudan, and as a result Ethiopia disputed the border as early as 1909 with a focus on the territory of the Umbrega Triangle.

Outcome of Dispute: All outstanding territorial issues were settled by an exchange of notes between the two governments in July 1972 in which Ethiopia accepted the existing borders of Sudan with minor exceptions.

Sources: *Africa Contemporary Record 1968–72*; *Africa Research Bulletin 1966–72*; Brownlie 1979; *Great Britain Foreign Office Archives 1923–39*; Shaw 1986; Taha 1983.

Dispute Number: 13, 23
Countries: Ethiopia vs. Italy and vice versa
Years of Dispute: 1919–36
Disputed Territory: Both Ethiopia and Italy claimed territory in the Ogaden, including the Walwal wells.

Outcome of Dispute: In December 1934 Ethiopian and Italian forces confronted each other in limited armed clashes in the area of the wells at Walwal. Negotiations followed with attempts at mediation by outside parties. In October 1935, however, Italy invaded Ethiopia and by the spring of 1936 had defeated Ethiopia bringing about an end to the dispute and Ethiopia's independence.

Sources: Baer 1967; Brecher and Wilkenfeld 1997; Brownlie 1979; Hardie 1974; *International Boundary Study* (#153); *Survey of International Affairs 1935* (vol. 2).

Dispute Number: 14
Countries: Ethiopia vs. Great Britain
Years of Dispute: 1924–36, 1945–9
Disputed Territory: Ethiopia sought the port of Zeila in order to gain access to the Red Sea.

Outcome of Dispute: In 1949 Ethiopia secured access to Eritrean ports through UN decisions and therefore decided to no longer seek a port at Zeila.

Sources: Sellassie 1976; Spencer 1984.

Dispute Number: 15
Countries: Ethiopia vs. France
Years of Dispute: 1924–36

Disputed Territory: Ethiopia sought access to the port of Djibuti and an economic free zone around the port and a road from the port to the interior of Ethiopia.

Outcome of Dispute: There was no settlement prior to Ethiopia's loss of independence in 1936 after its defeat in the war with Italy and after Ethiopia's sovereignty was restored the claim was no longer pursued.

Sources: Sellassie 1976.

Dispute Number: 17
Countries: Gabon vs. Equatorial Guinea
Year of Dispute: 1972
Disputed Territory: Gabon claimed sovereignty over islands in Corisco Bay.

Outcome of Dispute: A military confrontation over the disputed islands erupted during August and September but mediation efforts by November proved successful in resolving the dispute. Gabon conceded sovereignty over the islands based on the terms of a 1900 Franco-Spanish Treaty.

Sources: *Africa Diary 1972*; *African Recorder 1972*; Brownlie 1979.

Dispute Number: 18
Countries: Ghana vs. France/Ivory Coast
Years of Dispute: 1959–66
Disputed Territory: Under the regime of President Nkrumah, Ghana sought to annex the Sanwi district in the south-eastern section of the Ivory Coast.

Outcome of Dispute: Following the overthrow of President Nkrumah in 1966, the new leadership of Ghana withdrew its claim to the Sanwi district.

Sources: Thompson 1969; Touval 1972.

Dispute Number: 19
Countries: Ghana vs. France/Togo
Years of Dispute: 1958–66
Disputed Territory: Ghana sought to annex Togo and unify the two countries.

Outcome of Dispute: By mid-1966 the political leadership of Ghana had decided to drop its efforts to incorporate Togo into a larger unified country.

Sources: *Africa Research Bulletin 1964–66*; Allcock 1992; *International Boundary Study* (#126); Shaw 1986; Thompson 1969; Touval 1972.

Dispute Number: 20
Countries: Italy vs. Great Britain
Years of Dispute: 1919–24
Disputed Territory: Italy claimed the territory of Jubaland along the border of British Kenya and Italian Somaliland.
Outcome of Dispute: In an agreement reached in June 1924 the British cede large sections of Jubaland to Italy.
Sources: Brownlie 1979; Cassels 1970; *International Boundary Study* (#134); *L'Afrique Française 1920*; Macartney 1938; *Survey of International Affairs 1924*.

Dispute Number: 21
Countries: Italy vs. Great Britain
Years of Dispute: 1924–30
Disputed Territory: Italy sought to extend its colonial border in Somaliland into a small northern section of British Somaliland.
Outcome of Dispute: In an agreement signed in July 1930 Italy accepts the existing boundary line but Britain in turn grants grazing rights to tribes from Italian territory.
Sources: Bono 1979; *Great Britain Foreign Office Archives 1923–29*.

Dispute Number: 22
Countries: Italy vs. Great Britain
Years of Dispute: 1919–34
Disputed Territory: In 1919 at the Paris Peace Conference Italy presented a claim to the Sarra Triangle along the border of Libya and Sudan.
Outcome of Dispute: In an agreement reached in July 1934 Britain ceded the territory to Italy.
Sources: Albrecht-Carrie 1950; Brownlie 1979; Cassels 1970; *International Boundary Study* (#10).

Dispute Number: 24
Countries: Italy/Somalia vs. Ethiopia
Years of Dispute: 1950–95
Disputed Territory: Somalia has sought self-determination for, if not the annexation of, all Somali-inhabited areas of the Ogaden region in Ethiopia. Prior to Somalia's independence in 1960, Italian governments maintained that the Italian Somaliland border with Ethiopia was in dispute, but negotiations with Ethiopia failed to settle the conflict and by the late

1950s Somalian leaders were actively pressing their claims to the Ogaden.

Outcome of Dispute: There has been no resolution of the conflict over the Ogaden region. The OAU has consistently supported the Ethiopian position, but several attempts at mediation have proven unsuccessful. Intensified fighting in the Ogaden between rebels and Ethiopian forces occurred in 1982–3 and Italian mediation efforts in the mid and late 1980s failed to break the stalemate. Tensions were reduced with a joint agreement signed in 1988 in which both sides demilitarize the disputed region and stop supporting insurgency movements against one another. The dispute has not been a source of open conflict since civil war broke out in Somalia in 1990–1.

Sources: *Africa Contemporary Record 1968–90*; *Africa Research Bulletin 1964–70*; Allcock 1992; Farer 1979; *Boundary and Security Bulletin 1993–95*; Shaw 1986; *Yearbook of the United Nations 1950–60*.

Dispute Number: 25
Countries: Italy vs. France
Years of Dispute: 1919–43
Disputed Territory: Italy sought to annex the French colonial territory of what is now Djibouti for the primary reasons of gaining access to its port and the Djibouti–Addis Ababa railway line.
Outcome of Dispute: In January 1935 France ceded a very small piece of territory in Djibouti and sold some shares in the railway to Italy. Italy, however, did not view this agreement as a final settlement but France was not willing to make any further concessions.
Sources: Flandin 1947; Macartney 1938; Shorrock 1988.

Dispute Number: 26
Countries: Italy vs. France
Years of Dispute: 1938–43
Disputed Territory: Italy presented claims to Corsica and bordering territory along the Libya–Tunisia border.
Outcome of Dispute: France refused to concede any territory to Italy.
Sources: *Great Britain Foreign Office Archives 1938–39*; *Keesing's 1938–39*; Knox 1982; Shorrock 1988.

Dispute Number: 27
Countries: Lesotho vs. South Africa

Years of Dispute: 1966–1995

Disputed Territory: Lesotho claims sovereignty over large sections of territory within the Orange Free State and Natal and the eastern Cape Province of South Africa.

Outcome of Dispute: There has been no change in the positions of each state in the dispute despite an improvement in relations in the late 1980s.

Sources: Allcock 1992; Bardill and Cobbe 1985; *Boundary and Security Bulletin 1993–95*; Butterworth 1976; *International Boundary Study* (#143).

Dispute Number: 28

Countries: Liberia vs. France

Years of Dispute: 1919–60

Disputed Territory: Liberia had a long-standing dispute over its border with French West Africa, claiming that the French had unjustly annexed Liberian territory.

Outcome of Dispute: Shortly after the Ivory Coast's independence in August of 1960 the President of Liberia announced that all of his country's claims to the bordering territory of the Ivory Coast had been withdrawn.

Sources: Brownlie 1979; *International Boundary Study* (#132); *L'Afrique Française, Renseignements Coloniaux 1928–29*; Touval 1972.

Dispute Number: 29

Countries: Liberia vs. France

Years of Dispute: 1919–58

Disputed Territory: Liberia had a long-standing dispute over its border with French West Africa, claiming that the French had unjustly annexed Liberian territory.

Outcome of Dispute: Shortly after Guinea's independence in October 1958 the President of Liberia announced that all of his country's claims to the bordering territory of Guinea had been withdrawn.

Sources: Brownlie 1979; *International Boundary Study* (#131); *L'Afrique Française, Renseignements Coloniaux 1928–29*.

Dispute Number: 30

Countries: Madagascar vs. France

Years of Dispute: 1973–90

Disputed Territory: Madagascar has claimed sovereignty over the French islands of Glorioso, Juan de Nova, Bassas da India, and Europa.

Outcome of Dispute: In the 1970s Madagascar attempted to mobilize international support for its claims by pressing the issue at the United Nations. The General Assembly took up the question of the dispute at Madagascar's request, and in December 1979 a resolution was passed fully supporting Madagascar's claim. The French government, however, rejected the UN resolution in 1980 but after a decade of friendly relations indicated its willingness in June 1990 to accept United Nations resolutions, and, in return, Madagascar agreed to compensate French companies nationalized in 1972.

Sources: *Africa Contemporary Record 1973–90*; Allcock 1992; *Keesing's 1975–90*; Rabenoro 1986.

Dispute Number: 31
Countries: Malawi vs. Zambia
Years of Dispute: 1981–6
Disputed Territory: Malawi claimed the territory of Mwami along its eastern province border with Zambia.
Outcome of Dispute: Zambia withdrew its claim to the territory in August 1986.
Sources: *Africa Contemporary Record 1981–86*; *Africa Diary 1981–86*; Allcock 1992; *International Boundary Study* (#147).

Dispute Number: 32
Countries: Mali vs. Mauritania
Years of Dispute: 1960–3
Disputed Territory: Mali claimed sovereignty over the Eastern Hodh and territories along the western sector of the Mauritanian border (some 3,000 square miles), which had been ceded to Mauritania by France in 1944. The territory in dispute was largely desert and was sparsely populated.
Outcome of Dispute: A border agreement was reached in February 1963 in which Mauritania returned to Mali most of the territories ceded by France in 1944. In addition, it was agreed that nationals from each country would be guaranteed nomadic rights and the use of wells in the disputed areas.
Sources: Biger 1995; Butterworth 1976; *International Boundary Study* (#23); Touval 1972.

Dispute Number: 33
Countries: Mali vs. Burkino Faso
Years of Dispute: 1960–87
Disputed Territory: Since the independence of the two countries in 1960, Mali has claimed sovereignty over Burkino Faso territory

(approximately 500 square miles) along the Beli river in the Dori district.

Outcome of Dispute: Despite periodic negotiations throughout the 1960s and 1970s no resolution of the issue was achieved by the end of 1982. In 1983 the dispute was taken up by the ICJ, but a militarized confrontation occurred in December 1985 with casualties on both sides. The ICJ issued a ruling in December 1986 evenly dividing the disputed territory between the two countries, and the ruling was accepted by both countries in 1987.

Sources: *Africa Contemporary Record 1969–87*; *Africa Research Bulletin, 1985–86*; Allcock 1992.

Dispute Number: 34
Countries: Mauritius vs. France
Years of Dispute: 1976–95
Disputed Territory: Mauritius has claimed sovereignty over the French-controlled island of Tromelin which is less than one square mile and has little economic value.

Outcome of Dispute: The French rejected the Mauritius claim in December 1976, and there has been no change in the position of the opposing governments since then. Nevertheless, cooperative economic and political relations between the two countries have been maintained.

Sources: *Africa Research Bulletin 1976–95*; Allcock 1992.

Dispute Number: 35
Countries: Mauritius vs. Great Britain
Years of Dispute: 1980–95
Disputed Territory: Under an agreement reached in 1965 Mauritius recognized British sovereignty over Diego Garcia as part of the British Indian Ocean Territory. By 1980, however, Mauritius called for the return of Diego Garcia on the grounds that Britain had violated an agreement not to allow military bases on the island. Britain maintains that no such agreement on military bases (involving the United States) was ever reached and views the agreements of 1965 as valid and in force.

Outcome of Dispute: There has been no resolution of the disputing claims. The Mauritius claim of sovereignty over the entire Chagos Archipelago was formally endorsed by the OAU at a Summit in June 1980, and in the following month the OAU called for the demilitarization of Diego Garcia and its unconditional return to Mauritius. Periodic talks in the 1980s failed to resolve the dispute, and in 1992 and 1993 a newly elected Mauritius government renewed its claim to the islands and threatened to take the issue to the United Nations and the ICJ.

Sources: *Africa Research Bulletin 1980–95*; Allcock 1992.

Dispute Number: 36
Countries: Morocco vs. France/Mauritania
Years of Dispute: 1957–70
Disputed Territory: Morocco claimed sovereignty over all of Mauritania, arguing that in the pre-colonial period Mauritania had been a province of Morocco. As a result, Morocco withheld recognition of Mauritania's independence in 1960.
Outcome of Dispute: In 1969 Morocco formally recognized Mauritania, and in June 1970 a treaty was signed in which Morocco agreed to respect the territorial integrity of Mauritania.
Sources: Allcock 1992; Damis 1983, *Keesing's 1957–70*; Touval 1972.

Dispute Number: 37
Countries: Namibia vs. South Africa
Years of Dispute: 1990–4
Disputed Territory: Namibia claimed the territory know as Walvis Bay along with the Penguin Islands.
Outcome of Dispute: During negotiations in 1993 South Africa agreed to cede all of the territories over a short period of time and by March 1994 Walvis Bay and the islands were formally under the control of Namibia.
Sources: Allcock 1992; *Boundary and Security Bulletin 1993–94*; *International Boundary Study* (#125); Simon 1996.

Dispute Number: 39
Countries: Nigeria vs. Cameroon
Years of Dispute: 1965–95
Disputed Territory: The dispute began in the 1960s with Nigeria claiming islands and bordering territories in the Bakassi Peninsula and then in the 1990s conflicts emerged over the boundary line in Lake Chad. Nigeria maintains that a 1913 agreement between Britain and Germany in which the Bakassi Peninsula was ceded to Britain is not valid since the treaty was not ratified.
Outcome of Dispute: Despite repeated rounds of talks and attempts at negotiations, there has been no settlement of the dispute. In 1995 Cameroon sought to have the dispute submitted to the

ICJ but Nigeria was unwilling to do so at that time (later in 1996 Nigeria did agree to submit the case to the ICJ).

Sources: *Africa Research Bulletin 1965–95*; Allcock 1992; Biger 1995; *Boundary and Security Bulletin 1993–95*; Brownlie 1979; *Case Concerning the Land and Maritime Boundary Between Cameroon and Nigeria*; *International Boundary Study* (#92); Joseph 1995.

Dispute Number: 43
Countries: Seychelles vs. France
Years of Dispute: 1976–95
Disputed Territory: Since its independence Seychelles has claimed sovereignty over the French island of Tromelin.
Outcome of Dispute: France has refused to recognize Seychelles claims to sovereignty and has established military bases on Tromelin Island.
Sources: *Africa Research Bulletin 1976–95*; Allcock 1992; *Keesing's 1976–95*.

Dispute Number: 44
Countries: Somalia vs. Great Britain/Kenya
Years of Dispute: 1960–81
Disputed Territory: Somalia sought self-determination for, if not the annexation of, the Somali-inhabited areas of the north-eastern province of Kenya (approximately 50,000 square miles of territory).
Outcome of Dispute: In the Arusha Agreement of October 1967, mediated by the OAU, the two countries agreed to re-establish cooperative and normal diplomatic relations. As a result, Somalia did not actively press its claims against Kenya following the agreement. The OAU supported Kenya's position in the dispute and successive Kenyan governments called upon Somalia to renounce publicly its territorial claims. In September 1981 Somalia President Barre announced that his country had no territorial ambitions against Kenya and that ethnic Somalis in Kenya should be considered Kenyans. Since 1981 Somali governments have not issued irredentist claims against Kenya.
Sources: Adar 1994; *Africa Contemporary Record 1968–81*; *Africa Research Bulletin 1965–81*; Allcock 1992; McEwen 1971; Shaw 1986; Touval 1972.

Dispute Number: 45
Countries: Somalia vs. France
Years of Dispute: 1960–77

Disputed Territory: Somalia sought self-determination for, if not the annexation of, Djibouti.

Outcome of Dispute: In declarations in December 1976 and January 1977 the Somali government stated its intention to recognize the independence and sovereignty of Djibouti and to respect its territorial integrity after its attainment of independence. Djibouti became independent in June 1977 and Somalia carried through with its stated policy.

Sources: *Africa Contemporary Record 1968–77*; Butterworth 1976; Tholomier 1981; Touval 1972.

Dispute Number: 46
Countries: Togo vs. Ghana
Years of Dispute: 1960–95
Disputed Territory: Togo has laid claim to Ghanaian territory along their southern border populated by the Ewe tribe, which comprises one of the predominant ethnic groups within Togo.

Outcome of Dispute: Ghana has steadfastly refused to surrender any of the territory claimed by Togo, but Togo has not aggressively pressed its claims since the late 1970s. Relations during the 1980s, however, were strained as a result of a series of minor border incidents and political instability in both countries. Nevertheless, the territorial dispute did not re-emerge as a source of open conflict. Bilateral relations have improved since late 1991.

Sources: *Africa Research Bulletin 1965–95*; Allcock 1992; *International Boundary Study* (#126); Thompson 1969; Touval 1972.

Dispute Number: 47
Countries: Uganda vs. Tanzania
Years of Dispute: 1974–9
Disputed Territory: President Amin of Uganda laid claim to the Kagera Salient along the border of Tanzania. Anglo-German agreements signed in 1890 and 1914 had allocated the salient to German East Africa (Tanzania).

Outcome of Dispute: Following the removal of Amin from power following the war between Uganda and Tanzania in 1978–9, the Ugandan government renounced the territorial claim to the Kagera Salient.

Sources: *Africa Contemporary Record 1974–79*; *Africa Research Bulletin 1974–79*; Brecher and Wilkenfeld 1997; *International Boundary Study* (#55).

Dispute Number: 48
Countries: Zaire vs. Zambia
Years of Dispute: 1980–95
Disputed Territory: The dispute centers on a small area in and around Lake Mweru, which is located along Zambia's northern border with Zaire. The area in dispute is referred to as the Kaputa district.
Outcome of Dispute: It was announced in 1987, following several rounds of talks, that the two countries had reached an agreement on a general formula for eventually settling the dispute. Further progress was reported in 1989–90 but a final settlement has not been reached.
Sources: *Africa Contemporary Record 1980–90*; *Africa Research Bulletin 1980–95*; Allcock 1992; *Boundary and Security Bulletin 1993–95*.

Bibliography of sources listed in case summaries

Adar, Korena (1994) *Kenya's Foreign Policy Behavior Towards Somalia, 1963–1983* (Lanham: University Press of America).

Africa Contemporary Record 1968–1990 (New York: African Publishing Co., 1968–90).

Africa Diary 1972, 1981–86 (Delhi: Published by M. Chhabra for Africa Publications, 1972, 1981–6).

African Recorder 1972 (New Delhi: M. H. Samuel, 1972).

Africa Research Bulletin 1964–95 (London: Africa Research Limited, 1964–95).

Albrecht-Carrie, René (1950) *Italy from Napoleon to Mussolini* (New York: Columbia University Press).

Allcock, John, ed. (1992) *Border and Territorial Disputes*, rev. 3rd ed. (London: Longman).

Baer, George (1967) *The Coming of the Italian–Ethiopian War* (Cambridge: Harvard University Press).

Bardill, John and James Cobbe (1985) *Lesotho, Dilemmas of Dependence in Southern Africa* (Boulder: Westview Press).

Bekong, Njinkeng Julius (1997) "International Dispute Settlement" *African Journal of International and Comparative Law*, 9: 287–310.

Berringer, Huges (1995) "Mayotte, Une Collective Territoriale de L'Outre-Mer Français à Statut Particulier" *Revue Juridique et Politique*, 49, 3: 339–46.

Biger, Gideon (1995) *The Encyclopedia of International Boundaries* (New York: Facts on File).

Bono, Salvatore (1976) *Problemi di politica interna ed estera del l'Africa indipendente* (Roma: Istituto Italo-Africano).

Boundary and Security Bulletin 1993–1995 (Durham: International Boundaries Research Unit, 1993–5).

Braganca Cunha, Vicente de (1937) *Revolutionary Portugal: 1910–1936* (London: J. Clarke).

Brecher, Michael and Jonathan Wilkenfeld (1997) *A Study of Crisis* (Ann Arbor: University of Michigan Press).

British Command Paper, No. 2777 (xxx, 145): *Agreement between the Government of the Union of South Africa and the Government of the Republic of Portugal in Relation to the Boundary between the Mandated Territory of South-West Africa and Angola* (London: HMSO, 1926).

British Command Paper, No. 2778 (xxx, 149): *Agreement between the Government of the Union of South Africa and the Government of the Republic of Portugal Regulating the Use of the Water of the Kunene River for the Purpose of Generating Hydraulic Power and of Inundation and Irrigation in the Mandated Territory of South-West Africa* (London: HMSO, 1926).

Brownlie, Ian (1979) *African Boundaries: A Legal and Diplomatic Encyclopedia* (Berkeley: University of California University Press).

Bruce, Neil (1975) *Portugal: The Last Empire* (North Pomfret: David and Charles).

Butterworth, Robert (1976) *Managing Interstate Conflict, 1945–74* (Pittsburgh: University Center for International Studies, University of Pittsburgh).

Case Concerning the Land and Maritime Boundary Between Cameroon and Nigeria (Cameroon vs. Nigeria) (Geneva: International Court of Justice, 15 March 1996 reprinted in *African Journal of International and Comparative Law*, 8, 3 (1996): 671–708).

Cassels, Alan (1970) *Mussolini's Early Diplomacy* (Princeton: Princeton University Press).

Damis, John (1983) *Conflict in Northwest Africa* (Stanford: Hoover Institute Press).

David Simon (1996) "Strategic Territory and Territorial Strategy: The Geopolitics of Walvis Bay's Reintegration into Namibia" *Political Geography*, 15, 2: 193–219.

Farer, Tom (1979) *War Clouds on the Horn Of Africa* (New York: Carnegie Endowment for International Peace).

Flandin, Pierre-Étienne (1947) *Politique Française, 1919–1940* (Paris: Éditions nouvelles).

Great Britain Foreign Office Archives:

  Britain vs. Portugal (case #7, 41), documents on relations between Britain/South Africa and Portuguese Angola from 1925–6 beginning with FO 371/11090 and ending with FO 371/11933.

  Britain vs. Portugal (case #8), documents on relations between British Swaziland and Portuguese Mozambique from 1920–5 beginning with FO 371/4402 and ending with FO 371/11930.

  Britain vs. Portugal (case #9, 42), documents on relations between British Tanzania and Portuguese Mozambique from 1930–7 beginning with FO 371/15028 and ending with FO 371/21278.

  Ethiopia vs. Britain (case #11), documents on relations between Ethiopia and British Kenya from 1925–63 beginning with FO 371/10873 and ending with FO 371/172830.

Ethiopia vs. Britain (case #12), documents on relations between Ethiopia and British Sudan from 1936–54 beginning with FO 371/20176 and ending with FO 371/20425.

Italy vs. Britain (case #21), documents on relations between Italian and British Somalilands from 1923–9 beginning with FO 371/8412 and ending with FO 371/13884.

Italy vs. France (case #26), documents on relations between Italy/Libya and French Tunisia and Britain for 1938–9 beginning with FO 371/R713/7/22 and ending with FO 371/R4728/399/22 and FO 371/J393/33/63 to J1464/33/66.

Hardie, Frank (1974) *The Abyssinian Crisis* (Hamden: Archon Books).

International Boundary Study (1961–75) (Washington DC: The Geographer, Bureau of Intelligence and Research, US Department of State).

International Boundary Study. No. 10 Libya–Sudan Boundary, 16 October 1961.

International Boundary Study. No. 23 Mali–Mauritania Boundary, 16 December 1963.

International Boundary Study. No. 39 Mozambique–Tanzania Boundary, 30 October 1964.

International Boundary Study. No. 55 Tanzania–Uganda Boundary, 1 September 1965.

International Boundary Study. No. 92 Cameroon–Nigeria Boundary, 3 November 1969.

International Boundary Study. No. 125 South Africa–South-West Africa (Namibia) Boundary, 12 July 1972.

International Boundary Study. No. 126 Ghana–Togo Boundary, 6 September 1972.

International Boundary Study. No. 127 Congo–Zaire Boundary, 8 September 1972.

International Boundary Study. No. 131 Guinea–Liberia Boundary, 15 December 1972.

International Boundary Study. No. 132 Ivory Coast–Liberia Boundary, 2 January 1973.

International Boundary Study. No. 134 Kenya–Somalia Boundary, 14 May 1973.

International Boundary Study. No. 143 Lesotho–South Africa Boundary, 25 January 1974.

International Boundary Study. No. 144 Angola–Zaire Boundary, 4 April 1974.

International Boundary Study. No. 147 Malawi–Zambia Boundary, 27 November 1974.

International Boundary Study. No. 152 Ethiopia–Kenya Boundary, 15 October 1975.

International Boundary Study. No. 153 Ethiopia–Somalia Boundary, 5 November 1975.

Jentgen, Pierre (1952) *Les Frontières du Congo Belge* (Bruxelles: Académie Royale des Sciences d'Outre-Mer).

Joseph, Essombe Edimo (1995) "Considérations Juridiques sur le Différend Frontalier de la Peninsule de Bakasi" *African Journal of International and Comparative Law*, 7, 1: 98–128.

Keesing's Contemporary Archives 1938–86 (London: Keesing's Publications, 1938–86).

Keesing's Record of World Events 1987–95 (London: Keesing's Publications, 1987–95).

Knox, MacGregor (1982) *Mussolini Unleashed, 1939–1941* (Cambridge: Cambridge University Press).

L'Afrique Française. January 1920: 9–11, 133–4; November 1927: 471–3; May 1928: 293–320; November 1929: 585–94.

L'Afrique Française Renseignements Coloniaux. May 1928: 300–3; November 1929: 585–86.

League of Nations Official Journal November 1925 (Geneva: League of Nations, 1925).

Macartney, Maxwell (1938) *Italy's Foreign and Colonial Policy, 1914–1937* (London: Oxford University Press).

Maluwa, Tiyanjana (1993) "Disputed Sovereignty Over Sidudu Islands (Botswana vs. Namibia)" *African Journal of International and Comparative Law*, 5, 1: 113–38.

McEwen, A. C. (1971) *International Boundaries of East Africa* (Oxford: Clarendon Press).

Newitt, M. D. D. (1984) *The Comoro Islands* (Boulder: Westview Press).

Rabenoro, Césaire (1986) *Les Relations Extérieures de Madagascar, de 1960 à 1972* (Paris: L'Harm Han).

Sellassie, Haile (1976) *My Life and Ethiopia's Progress, 1892–1937* (Oxford: Oxford University Press).

Shaw, Malcolm (1986) *Title to Territory in Africa* (Oxford: Clarendon Press).

Shorrock, William (1988) *From Ally to Enemy* (Kent: Kent State University Press).

Simon, David (1996) "Strategic Territory and Territorial Strategy: The Geopolitics of Walvis Buy's Reintegration into Namibia" *Political Geography*, 15, 2: 193–219.

Spencer, John (1984) *Ethiopia at Bay* (Algonac: Reference Publications).

Survey of International Affairs 1924, 1929, 1935 (London: Oxford University Press, 1926–36).

Taha, Faisal Abdel Rahemm Ali (1983) *The Sudan–Ethiopia Boundary Dispute* (S. L.: Abu Dhabi Printers & Pub.).

Tholomier, Robert (1981) *Djibouti* (Meutchen: Scarecrow Press).

Thompson, Scott (1969) *Ghana's Foreign Policy 1957–1966* (Princeton: Princeton University Press).

Touval, Saadin (1972) *The Boundary Politics of Independent Africa* (Cambridge: Harvard University Press).

The Yearbook of the United Nations 1950–60, 1976–95 (New York: United Nations, 1951–61, 1977–96).

Appendix E
Territorial disputes in Central Asia, the Far East, and Pacific, 1919–1995

List of dispute cases

In this first section a summary list of territorial disputes in Central Asia, the Far East, and the Pacific is presented. For each dispute information is provided on: (a) the challenger and target with the former listed first, (b) the first and last years of the dispute, and (c) a brief description of the challenger's territorial claims. For those disputes marked with an asterisk both states are challengers and therefore the dispute is listed a second time with the identity of the challenger and target reversed.

1. Afghanistan vs. British India 1919–21: Claim to border area north of the Khyber Pass
2. Afghanistan vs. Iran* 1919–35: Claims along central border sector
3. Afghanistan vs. Pakistan 1947–95: Refusal to recognize Durand Line and desire for incorporation of Pathan-populated territory
4. Afghanistan vs. Soviet Union 1919–46: Claims to Pendjeh, islands in Amour and Pyandzh rivers, and disputes over river borders
5. Britain/India vs. France 1919–54: Initial dispute over territorial limits of French enclaves and then call by India for France to relinquish all control over enclaves of Pondichery, Karikal, Mahe, and Yanam
6. Cambodia vs. South Vietnam/Vietnam* 1954–85: Claim to sections of land border at several points as well as islands in the Gulf of Thailand
7. Cambodia vs. Thailand 1954–62: Claims to territory in and around Preah Vihear
8. China vs. Afghanistan 1919–63: Claims along border in Pamir region
9. China vs. Bhutan 1979–95: Claims to small sections of border
10. China vs. Britain 1919–30: Call for return of leased territory of Port Weihaiwei
11. China vs. Britain 1919–84: Call for termination of British control and resumption of Chinese sovereignty over Hong Kong

12. China vs. Britain/India 1919–62: Claims to bordering territory of India along eastern and western sectors (UK is target 1919–46 and India thereafter)

13. China vs. Britain/Burma 1919–60: Claims to small sections of border in Yunnan (UK is target 1919–47 and Burma thereafter)

14. China vs. France 1919–45: Call for return of leased territory of Port Kwangchou-wan

15. China vs. France/South Vietnam/Vietnam* 1932–95: Claims to Paracel and Spratly Islands as well as small sections of land border (France is target 1932–53 and South Vietnam 1954–75 and Vietnam thereafter)

16. China vs. Japan 1919–45: Claims to leased territories in Shantung (Kiaochaw Bay) and in Liaotung Peninsula (Port Arthur and Dairen)

17. China vs. Japan 1951–95: Claim to the Senkaku Islands

18. China vs. Nepal* 1949–61: Claims to bordering territory along the border with Tibet

19. China vs. Kazakhstan 1993–4: Claims along border

20. China vs. Kyrgystan 1993–5: Claims along border

21. China vs. Outer Mongolia 1946–62: Claims along border after China recognizes Outer Mongolia as independent state

22. China vs. Pakistan 1947–63: Claims along border between Kashmir and Xinjiang

23. China vs. Portugal 1919–75: Dispute over border location and then claims to sovereignty over Macau

24. China vs. Soviet Union/Russia 1919–95: Call for revision of unequal treaties defining the length of the border from Central Asia to Manchuria

25. China vs. Soviet Union 1948–55: Call for termination of Soviet base rights at Port Arthur and withdrawal of Soviet forces

26. China vs. Tajikistan 1993–95: Claims along sections of border

27. France vs. Japan 1939–45: Claim to Spratly Islands following Japanese occupation and annexation of the islands

28. France/South Vietnam/Vietnam vs. China* 1932–95: Claim to Paracel and Spratly Islands (South Vietnam until 1975 and Vietnam thereafter)

29. France vs. Thailand 1945–6: Claims to regain territories along border with Laos and Cambodia that had been conceded to Thailand in 1941

30. India vs. China 1963–95: Call for restoring status quo along border to pre-1962 war position

31. India vs. Pakistan/Bangladesh* 1947–95: Claims to sections of border including numerous small enclaves (Pakistan 1947–71 and Bangladesh thereafter)
32. India vs. Pakistan 1947–8: Claims to Jammu and Kashmir following independence
33. India vs. Pakistan 1947–8: Claims to Junagadh
34. India vs. Pakistan* 1947–68: Claims to Rann of Kutch
35. India vs. Portugal 1947–61: Call for Portugal to withdraw from Goa and other enclaves
36. Indonesia vs. Netherlands 1950–62: Claim to West Irian
37. Indonesia vs. Malaysia 1980–95: Claims to islands of Sipadan and Ligitan
38. Iran vs. Afghanistan* 1919–35: Claims along central border sector
39. Japan vs. China 1932–45: Claim to Manchukuo as an independent state and desire to extend occupation further into Manchuria
40. Japan vs. France 1938–9: Claim to Spratly Islands
41. Japan vs. France 1941: Demand for the right to establish military bases in southern Indo-China
42. Japan (Manchukuo) vs. Outer Mongolia 1935–40: Claims to bordering territory
43. Japan (Manchukuo) vs. Soviet Union 1935–45: Claims to bordering territory and sovereignty of islands in disputed rivers
44. Japan vs. Soviet Union 1951–95: Claims to Kurile Islands
45. Malaysia vs. China 1979–95: Claim to Spratly Islands
46. Malaysia vs. Singapore 1980–95: Claim to Pedra Branca Island
47. North Korea vs. South Korea 1948–95: Call for unification of South with North Korea
48. North Vietnam vs. South Vietnam 1954–75: Call for unification of South with North Vietnam
49. Pakistan vs. India* 1947–68: Claims to Rann of Kutch
50. Pakistan vs. India 1947–95: Claims to Jammu and Kashmir following independence
51. Pakistan/Bangladesh vs. India* 1947–95: Claims to enclaves along border and small sections of the border
52. Portugal vs. India 1962–74: Refusal to recognize Indian annexation of Goa and other enclaves and maintaining claim to sovereign rights
53. Nepal vs. China* 1949–61: Claims to territory along the border with Tibet
54. Papua New Guinea vs. Australia 1974–8: Claim to islands along coastline
55. Philippines vs. China 1971–95: Claim to Spratly Islands

56. Philippines vs. Malaysia 1962–95: Claim to Sabah
57. Portugal vs. Indonesia 1975–95: Refusal to recognize Indonesian annexation of East Timor and maintaining claims to sovereign rights
58. South Korea vs. Japan 1951–95: Claim to Takeshima Islands
59. South Vietnam/Vietnam vs. Cambodia* 1954–85: Claim to small sections of land border at several points as well as islands in the Gulf of Thailand (South Vietnam until 1975 and Vietnam thereafter)
60. Thailand vs. France 1919–41: Claims to boundary line and sovereignty of islands in Mekong and then larger claims to territory of Laos and Cambodia
61. Thailand vs. France/Cambodia 1949–53: Claims to territory in and around Preah Vihear (France is target 1949–52 and Cambodia thereafter)
62. Thailand vs. Laos 1984–95: Claims to territory in the north along Mekong and in Ban Rom Klao region
63. United States vs. Japan 1919–22: Dispute over Japan's mandate rights to Island of Yap
64. United States vs. Netherlands 1919–28: Claims to Palmas (Miangus) Islands
65. Vanuata vs. France 1982–95: Claim to Matthew and Hunter Islands

Case summaries of territorial disputes in Central Asia, the Far East, and Pacific

In this section a short case history is provided for each of the disputes listed in section one. In each summary information is presented on the territorial claims of the states and the outcome of the dispute. Complete citations for sources listed at the end of each case summary can be found in the bibliography in section three.

> *Dispute Number*: 1
> *Countries*: Afghanistan vs. British India
> *Years of Dispute*: 1919–21
> *Disputed Territory*: Afghanistan contested a small section of the British Indian border north of the Khyber Pass with the dispute emerging in the late nineteenth century.
> *Outcome of Dispute*: In a treaty signed in November 1921 the dispute was settled on terms favorable to Britain.
> *Sources*: Adamec 1974; *British Command Paper, Nos. 324, 1786*; Lamb 1968; Prescott 1977; Sareen 1981; *Survey of International Affairs 1925* (vol. 1).

Dispute Number: 2, 38
Countries: Afghanistan vs. Iran and vice versa
Years of Dispute: 1919–35
Disputed Territory: The boundary between Iran and Afghanistan was delimited in two different sections in the late nineteenth century. The southern border was delimited in 1872 while in 1891 the northern border was delimited by the British at the request of the two countries. The British, however, left a gap in the middle sector of the border (about 250 miles) that was left undefined and both countries disputed the boundary line in this area.
Outcome of Dispute: In 1934 both countries agreed that Turkey would act as an arbitrator and the Turkish award issued in May 1935 was accepted by both countries and required mutual concessions.
Sources: Adamac 1974; Biger 1995; Burrell 1997; *International Boundary Study* (#6); Mclachlan 1994; Prescott 1977; Rezun 1981; Volodarsky 1994;

Dispute Number: 3
Countries: Afghanistan vs. Pakistan
Years of Dispute: 1947–95
Disputed Territory: Afghan governments have refused to accept the boundary lines of its eastern border with Pakistan (the so-called Durand Line established in 1893 and further developed by agreements in 1905, 1921, and 1930) wherein Pathan tribes are populated. Afghanistan has called for the incorporation of all Pathan tribes within Afghanistan, including sections of Pakistani territory, or an autonomous or independent state of Pakhtoonistan. The Pakistani government has steadfastly maintained that the Durand Line is not open to question.
Outcome of Dispute: Afghan governments had actively pursued the dispute until the mid-to-late 1970s without any change in Pakistan's policy of refusing to discuss the issue. However, as a result of the Soviet invasion of Afghanistan in 1979 and the subsequent civil war in Afghanistan, the territorial dispute with Pakistan has not been a source of recent conflict.
Sources: Ahmed Dar 1986; Ali 1990; *Boundary and Security Bulletin 1993–95*; Kaur 1985; *Keesing's 1947–95*.

Dispute Number: 4
Countries: Afghanistan vs. Soviet Union
Years of Dispute: 1919–46

Disputed Territory: Afghanistan disputed the border area of Pendjeh along with islands and river borders in the region. Afghanistan and Russia were almost brought to war as Russia conquered the Panjdeh oasis and annexed Merv.

Outcome of Dispute: Afghan claims to islands in the Oxus river were settled on favorable terms in 1926 but a comprehensive settlement was not reached until 1946. In June of that year a border treaty was signed which resolved all outstanding issues on terms generally favorable to Afghanistan.

Sources: Adamac 1974; Dmytryshyn and Cox 1987; *Great Britain Foreign Office Archives 1934–36, 1945–46*; Carr 1953; *International Boundary Study* (#26); Lamb 1968; *Survey of International Affairs 1920–23*; Volodarsky, 1994.

Dispute Number: 5
Countries: Great Britain/India vs. France
Years of Dispute: 1919–54
Disputed Territory: British India disputed the territorial limits of the French enclaves of Pondicherry, Karikal, Mahe, and Yanam. The French argued that sovereign rights over bordering areas, including many small islands, had been exercised for many decades and that French sovereignty was recognized in a convention signed in 1903. Britain argued that by the treaties of 1814 and 1815 France was only entitled to the land it held in 1792 and that the boundary lines as fixed in 1839 did not include the territories and islands claimed by France. Furthermore, the British argued that the Anglo-French convention of 1903 contained no reference to the islands. Once India gained its independence it called for the complete withdrawal of France from all of the enclaves.

Outcome of Dispute: In 1954 France yielded all rights to the enclaves and recognized Indian sovereignty. The formal transfer of control over all the enclaves was completed by 1962.

Sources: Butterworth 1976; *Great Britain Foreign Office Archives 1928–54*; *Keesing's 1949–1954*.

Dispute Number: 6, 59
Countries: Cambodia vs. South Vietnam/Vietnam and vice versa
Years of Dispute: 1954–85
Disputed Territory: The length of the common border between Vietnam and Cambodia is approximately 760 miles long and is based on treaties negotiated between France and Cambodia

in the nineteenth century and from decrees issued by the Governor General of Indochina during the period of French colonial rule. South Vietnam and Cambodia, however, were unable to reach an agreement on the delimitation of their border following their independence. As a result, several sections of the border were in dispute, as was sovereignty over several islands in the Gulf of Thailand, with both sides claiming territory of the other. Disputes over the border existed in the following areas: (1) in the Prek Binh Gi area in junction with Bassac, (2) between Bassac and Mekong proper, (3) north-east of Loc Ninh between Dak Jerman and Dak Huyt, (4) between Srepok and the Se San, and (5) near the Laos tripoint. In most of these areas Cambodia claimed Vietnamese territory populated by sizeable Cambodian minorities. In the Gulf of Thailand, Vietnam and Cambodia disputed sovereignty over the offshore islands of Quan Phu Quoc and the smaller Wei Islands.

Outcome of Dispute: Following their invasion of Cambodia in December 1977, Vietnamese forces assumed control over disputed territory. An agreement was reached in February 1979 to begin negotiations on resolving the border dispute. In a series of agreements signed between 1982 and 1985 disputes over the land border and islands were settled with Vietnam generally accepting the definition of the border as provisionally established in 1954.

Sources: Amer 1997; *Asian Recorder 1963–85*; Pradhan 1987; St. John 1998; Van Minh 1978, 1979.

Dispute Number: 7
Countries: Cambodia vs. Thailand
Years of Dispute: 1954–62
Disputed Territory: Following Cambodia's independence a dispute emerged over the Temple of Preah Vihear and surrounding territory. Cambodia called on Thailand to withdraw its forces from their area and based its claims on the terms of the 1907 Franco-Siamese Treaty.

Outcome of Dispute: In 1959 Cambodia submitted the dispute to the International Court of Justice. In June 1962 the ICJ ruled that the territory belonged to Cambodia. Thailand objected to the ruling but then accepted and in 1963 Cambodia took possession of the Temple and surrounding territory.

Sources: Biger 1995; *International Boundary Study* (#40); *Keesing's 1954–62*; Leifer 1962; Prescott 1975; Smith 1965; St. John 1998.

Dispute Number: 8
Countries: China vs. Afghanistan
Years of Dispute: 1919–63
Disputed Territory: The eastern border of Afghanistan with China in the Wakhan valley – forty-seven miles in length – had never been carefully delimited by the British following the 1895 treaty with Russia that established the valley as the border. In the early twentieth century Chinese governments advanced claims to much of the mountainous Pamir region along this ill-defined border, and those claims were maintained by the new communist government after it came to power in 1949.
Outcome of Dispute: The Chinese did not pursue their claims for decades but finally sought a settlement following an improvement in relations in the early 1960s. A November 1963 agreement fully delimited the border between the two countries on terms favorable to Afghanistan and in accord with the provisions of the 1895 treaty that originally established the border.
Sources: *Asian Recorder 1963*; Biger 1995; Hyer 1990; *International Boundary Study* (#89); Prescott 1977.

Dispute Number: 9
Countries: China vs. Bhutan
Years of Dispute: 1979–95
Disputed Territory: The border between the two countries extends for about 300 miles and China lays claim to small sections of territory at several points.
Outcome of Dispute: Multiple rounds of talks have been held since 1984 with both parties expressing an interest in a friendly settlement. Nevertheless, no final resolution of the dispute has been achieved.
Sources: *Boundary and Security Bulletin 1993–95*; Day 1987; Hyer 1990. *Keesing's 1979–95*.

Dispute Number: 10
Countries: China vs. Great Britain
Years of Dispute: 1919–30
Disputed Territory: In 1919 China called for the return of all territories that had been leased to foreign powers, which included Port Weihaiwei controlled by the British.
Outcome of Dispute: Negotiations began in the early 1920s and an agreement was reached in October 1930 in which Britain terminated its lease and full Chinese sovereignty was restored.
Sources: *China Handbook 1924–31*; Lane 1990; Pollard 1933; *Survey of International Affairs 1920–23, 1925* (vol. 2), *1930*.

Dispute Number: 11
Countries: China vs. Great Britain
Years of Dispute: 1919–84
Disputed Territory: In 1919 at Versailles China called for the restoration of its full sovereignty over all territories lost as a result of leases and unequal treaties. While Britain was willing to negotiate with China over Port Weihaiwei (dispute number 10) it rejected talks on the status of Hong Kong and the New Territories throughout the inter-war period. After World War II China maintained its position that Hong Kong should be restored to China but did not press for immediate negotiations.
Outcome of Dispute: Negotiations began in 1982 and by the end of 1984 an agreement was reached that Hong Kong would be returned to China by July 1997.
Sources: Cottrell 1993; Lane 1990; Roberti 1984.

Dispute Number: 12
Countries: China vs. Britain/ India
Years of Dispute: 1919–62
Disputed Territory: In 1913 Britain attempted to delimit the border between India and China at the Simla Conference. An agreement was reached on what has become known as the "McMahon Line" but when the Chinese representative at the conference presented the terms of the agreement to the Chinese government in Beijing, the McMahon Line was rejected and the boundary was considered to be still undefined. The British, however, maintained that the border agreement signed at the conference was valid and that the McMahon Line established much of the new border. The Chinese government did not actively pursue its claims during the inter-war period while Britain attempted to conclude border agreements with Tibetan authorities. After World War II the dispute persisted as the new communist regime in China continued to reject the McMahon Line while Indian leaders insisted that the question of the boundary was settled by the agreements reached in 1913.
Outcome of Dispute: After the failure of negotiations over several years and many low level military confrontations along the border, China and India fought a short war in late 1962 in which the Indian army was defeated. As a result of its military victory China established a new *de facto* border that corresponded closely to the boundary line that its leaders had proposed in prior negotiations.

Sources: Bhim 1988; Heimsath 1971; Hoffman 1990; Hyer 1990; Jetly 1979; *Keesing's 1954–62*; Maxwell 1970; Rowland 1967; Sharma 1971; *Survey of International Affairs 1956–60*; Tzou 1990; Whiting 1975.

Dispute Number: 13
Countries: China vs. Great Britain/Burma
Years of Dispute: 1919–60
Disputed Territory: China disputed the British definition of the boundary line in two different sections of the far south-eastern border with Burma dating back to the late nineteenth century. In the inter-war period numerous rounds of negotiations were held and substantial progress towards a settlement was achieved by 1941. After World War II the dispute persisted with China directly negotiating with the Burmese government.
Outcome of Dispute: A final settlement was reached in a January 1960 agreement which required both sides to make mutual concessions. The terms of the agreement closely followed those negotiated back in 1941.
Sources: Biger 1995; *China Handbook 1950*; *Great Britain Foreign Office Archives 1919–41*; Hinton 1958; Hyer 1990; *International Boundary Study (#42)*; *Keesing's 1941–60*; Prescott 1975; Tzou 1990; Whittam 1961; Woodman 1962.

Dispute Number: 14
Countries: China vs. France
Years of Dispute: 1919–45
Disputed Territory: China desired that the Port of Kwangchou-wan to be returned from France. In 1919 at Versailles China first stated that it wanted all territory returned from foreign leases. In 1921 at the Washington Conference China again called for the return of the port and France countered that it would terminate the lease only if other powers with leases would do the same.
Outcome of Dispute: In an agreement reached in August 1945 France terminated its lease and Chinese sovereignty was restored over the port.
Sources: *China Handbook 1937–1945*; Pollard 1933; *Survey of International Affairs 1920–23*.

Dispute Number: 15, 28
Countries: China vs. France/South Vietnam/Vietnam and vice versa

Years of Dispute: 1932–95

Disputed Territory: The land and sea border between China and French territories in Asia were first delimited in 1887 and then again in 1895 but the agreements reached at that time became a source of dispute beginning in the 1930s. In 1932–3 France sought to establish sovereignty over the offshore islands of the Paracel and Spratlys but China rejected these claims. When France withdrew from Indochina, South Vietnam took up the claim to the disputed islands and with the collapse of South Vietnam in 1975 the islands dispute was carried on between China and Vietnam. A dispute has also existed over several small sections of the land border between China and Vietnam. It seems that China had expressed reservations about the land border to North Vietnam as far back as the 1950s but the dispute over conflicting claims was not actively pursued until the late 1970s.

Outcome of Dispute: There has been no settlement of either the land border dispute or of the conflicting claims to the offshore islands despite periodic negotiations since the late 1970s.

Sources: *Asian Recorder 1980–95*; *Boundary and Security Bulletin 1993–95*; Cheng 1986; Dzurek 1996; Englefield 1994; Gilks 1992; Hyer 1995; Lawson 1984; Lo 1989; Long 1991; Ross 1988; Samuels 1982; St. John 1998; *The Hoang Sa and Trong Sa Archipelagoes*; Thomas 1989; Tiet 1994; Valencia 1995.

Dispute Number: 16
Countries: China vs. Japan
Years of Dispute: 1919–45
Disputed Territory: Beginning at Versailles in 1919 China sought the return of the leased territories of Kiaochaw Bay in Shantung as well as Port Arthur and Dairen in the Liaotung Peninsula from Japan.

Outcome of Dispute: In February 1922 Japan agreed to return Kiaochaw Bay to Chinese control but refused to negotiate the return of either Port Arthur or Dairen. With Japan's defeat in World War II their control over Port Arthur and Dairen came to an end.

Sources: Pollard 1933; *Survey of International Affairs 1920–34*.

Dispute Number: 17
Countries: China vs. Japan
Years of Dispute: 1951–95

Disputed Territory: China disputes Japanese sovereignty over the Senkaku Islands. Japan claims that China accepted Japanese annexation of the islands in the 1895 peace treaty and in the peace treaties signed after World War II there is no commitment to restore Chinese sovereignty over the islands. China counters that the 1895 peace treaty did not transfer sovereignty over the islands to Japan and that with its defeat in World War II Japan renounced all claims to overseas territories.

Outcome of Dispute: There has been no formal settlement of the dispute. In the negotiations leading to the 1978 Peace treaty between the two countries the dispute over the islands was put on hold by the Chinese to avoid conflict but the Chinese have not renounced their claim of sovereign rights.

Sources: Deans 1997; Dzurek 1998; Eto 1980; Hiramatsu and Okonogi 1997; Jain 1981; Kenkyujo 1970; Kim 1990; Makino 1998; Ozaki 1972; Tretiak 1978.

Dispute Number: 18, 53
Countries: China vs. Nepal and vice versa
Years of Dispute: 1949–61
Disputed Territory: The dispute centered on the lack of a clearly defined border. As a result, both governments advanced opposing interpretations of where the 670-mile border between Tibet and Nepal was located. Several treaties were negotiated between Nepal and Tibet in the eighteenth and nineteenth centuries. However, the boundary lines established in the treaties were often unclear or contradictory. As a result, both countries advanced claims to the territory of the other along the border in twenty different sectors, including Rasua, Kimathauka, Nara Pass, Tingribode, Mt. Everest, and the Nelu River.

Outcome of Dispute: Border talks were initiated in late 1959, and by October 1961 a border pact was signed settling all outstanding issues. Most of the disputes were settled in favor of Nepal.

Sources: *Asian Recorder 1959–61*; Biger 1995; Hyer 1990; *International Boundary Study* (#50); Muni 1973; Prescott 1975.

Dispute Number: 19
Countries: China vs. Kazakhstan
Years of Dispute: 1993–94
Disputed Territory: China sought changes along the border of Kazakhstan that were based on its long-standing claims against the former Soviet Union (see dispute number 24).

Outcome of Dispute: In April 1994 a border agreement was signed which settled all points of dispute through mutual concessions.

Sources: *Asian Recorder 1993–94*; *Boundary and Security Bulletin 1993–94*.

Dispute Number: 20
Countries: China vs. Kyrgystan
Years of Dispute: 1993–5
Disputed Territory: China sought limited changes along the border of Kyrgystan that were based on its long-standing claims against the former Soviet Union (see dispute number 24).

Outcome of Dispute: Several rounds of negotiations were held from 1993–5 with progress reported but no settlement.

Sources: *Asian Recorder 1993–94*; *Boundary and Security Bulletin 1993–94*.

Dispute Number: 21
Countries: China vs. Outer Mongolia
Years of Dispute: 1946–62
Disputed Territory: In 1946 China recognized the Mongolian People's Republic but the boundary line between the two countries was not delimited with approximately 1,000 of the 2,900-mile border in dispute.

Outcome of Dispute: In December 1962 a border agreement was signed that settled all outstanding issues with China conceding most of its claims to bordering territory.

Sources: *Asian Recorder 1960–62*; Friters 1949; Hyer 1990; Prescott 1975; Tang 1959; Tzou 1990.

Dispute Number: 22
Countries: China vs. Pakistan
Years of Dispute: 1947–63
Disputed Territory: The territory centered on the 325-mile border between Pakistani-controlled Kashmir and the Chinese region of Xinjiang. Approximately 3,400 square miles were claimed by China.

Outcome of Dispute: In late 1959 Pakistan announced its willingness to consult on the boundary question and over the next four years talks were held. An agreement was signed between the two governments in March 1963 dividing up the disputed territory. A protocol to the agreement was added in March 1965.

Sources: *Asian Recorder 1959–63*; *International Boundary Study* (#85); Rais 1977; Syed 1974.

Dispute Number: 23
Countries: China vs. Portugal
Years of Dispute: 1919–75
Disputed Territory: In 1887 the Lisbon Agreement gave Portugal exclusive rights to govern Macau but problems of delimiting the border emerged by the early twentieth century. After World War II the Chinese government claimed sovereignty over Macau which Portugal rejected but China did not actively press for negotiations on the future of Macau.
Outcome of Dispute: The dispute came to an end during 1975 when the recently established Portuguese government renounced its claim to Macau as a colony. At this point, the only question that remained was when Macau would be restored to Chinese control.
Sources: Cohen and Chiu 1974; Cottrell 1993; Kao 1980; Lane 1990; Shipp 1997; Tung 1970.

Dispute Number: 24
Countries: China vs. Soviet Union/Russia
Years of Dispute: 1919–95
Disputed Territory: Chinese calls for revisions in its border with the Soviet Union date back to the early twentieth century. The Chinese position has been that the treaties defining the border (signed in the mid and late nineteenth century) are "unequal" and therefore subject to renegotiation. Chinese claims to Soviet territory amounted to over 500,000 square miles. Initially, the Soviets indicated a willingness to revise the border but preliminary negotiations broke down by the early 1920s and China did not press for border revisions for the remainder of the inter-war period. After World War II communist China did not press its territorial claims against the Soviet Union during the 1950s but by the early 1960s the dispute was a primary source of conflict between the two countries. China had disputes with the Soviets (now Russia) in the Far Eastern sector along the border between Manchuria and Eastern Siberia, and in the Central Asian sector between Xinjiang and the (former) Soviet Republics of Khazakhstan, Kirghizia, and Tajikistan.
Outcome of Dispute: Periodic rounds of talks were held from 1964–82 between the two governments without any substantial progress. In 1986 the Soviet leader Gorbachev indicated that his country was willing to make some concessions and further talks were held. In 1991 the Soviets made several concessions

to China in the Far Eastern sector, including the transfer of Damansky Island and the Amur, Argun, and Ussuri rivers and subsequent agreements have also been reached during 1992–4. Nevertheless, disputes persist over islands in the eastern sector as well as small sections of the more western sector of the border. With the collapse of the Soviet Union, Chinese territorial claims in the central sector are now the subject of negotiations with Kazakhstan, Kirghizia, and Tajikistan (see disputes numbers 19, 20, 26). Thus, a comprehensive settlement will require agreements with each of these states.

Sources: *Asian Recorder 1960–95*; Biger 1995; *Boundary and Security Bulletin 1993–95*; Cheng 1957, 1972; Ginsburgs and Pinkele 1978; Hyer 1990; Jones 1985; *Keesing's 1960–95*; Leong 1976; Tsui 1983; Wei 1956; Weigh 1928; Wun 1976.

Dispute Number: 25
Countries: China vs. Soviet Union
Years of Dispute: 1946–55
Disputed Territory: In 1945 the Sino-Soviet Treaty decreed that Port Arthur in Manchuria would be a naval base for "joint use" for the USSR and China and Port Dairen was decreed a free port to all countries for shipping trade. Half of the port installations were to be leased to the Soviet Union although administration of the port would be left to China. The Soviets, however, continued to occupy both ports preventing the Chinese from exercising any control. In 1948 China called for the withdrawal of Soviet forces from the two ports and argued that the 1945 treaty was no longer valid because of Soviet violations.

Outcome of Dispute: An agreement was reached in early 1950 for the Soviets to begin withdrawing from the ports but it was not until mid-1955 that the Soviets had fully withdrawn from the two ports, allowing the Chinese to resume full control.

Sources: *China Handbook 1950*; Wei 1956.

Dispute Number: 26
Countries: China vs. Tajikistan
Years of Dispute: 1993–5
Disputed Territory: China has sought changes along the border of Tajikistan that were based on its long-standing claims against the former Soviet Union (see dispute number 24).

Outcome of Dispute: Several rounds of negotiations have been held with progress reported but no settlement had been reached by the end of 1995.

Sources: *Asian Recorder 1993–95*; *Boundary and Security Bulletin 1993–95*.

Dispute Number: 27
Countries: France vs. Japan
Years of Dispute: 1939–45
Disputed Territory: During 1932–3 France had claimed control over the Spratly Islands but Japan had refused to recognize the French claim to sovereignty over the islands. In March 1939 Japan occupied and claimed sovereignty over the Spratly Islands. France refused to recognize the Japanese claim and called for Japan to withdraw.
Outcome of Dispute: Japan refused to withdraw from the islands but following its defeat in World War II French control over the islands was restored.
Sources: Iriye 1991; Kenkyujo 1970 (vols. 22, 26, 28); Nakamura 1990; Shinobu 1988.

Dispute Number: 29
Countries: France vs. Thailand
Years of Dispute: 1945–6
Disputed Territory: In 1941 Thailand, with the support of Japan, secured an agreement with France that required the French to concede large amounts of territory that it had previously gained in 1893, 1904, and 1907 (see dispute number 60). With World War II coming to an end in the Pacific, France called for Thailand to return all of the territories it had gained in 1941.
Outcome of Dispute: Thailand was forced to concede all of the territorial gains it had made in 1941 in the Washington Treaty signed in November 1946.
Sources: Hammer 1954; Santaputra 1985; St. John 1998; Wyatt 1984.

Dispute Number: 30
Countries: India vs. China
Years of Dispute: 1963–95
Disputed Territory: Following India's defeat in the border war in the fall of 1962 and the loss of territory to China (see

dispute number 12), Indian governments have maintained the position that the McMahon Line remains the legitimate border between the two countries and that China must withdraw from all territories that it has occupied since the war.

Outcome of Dispute: There has been no settlement despite periodic talks.

Sources: *Asian Recorder 1963–1995*; *Boundary and Security Bulletin 1993–95*; Hyer 1990; Jetly 1979; *Keesing's 1963–1995*; Sandhu 1988; Tzou 1990.

Dispute Number: 31, 51
Countries: India vs. Pakistan/Bangladesh and vice versa
Years of Dispute: 1947–95
Disputed Territory: At the time of their independence in 1947 many sections of the border between India and East Pakistan were not clearly defined. One of the most difficult issues in drawing a boundary line was how to treat hundreds of small enclaves on either side of the border. A border commission was established as early as 1948 to try and deal with the problems and negotiations have been held periodically for decades.

Outcome of Dispute: Several agreements have been reached on small sections of the border and enclaves since the late 1950s but disputes persist over a number of remaining enclaves and sections of the border.

Sources: Gupta 1969; Jha 1972; *Keesing's 1947–95*; Prakhar 1987; Prescott 1977; Razvi 1971; Saksena 1987; Shukla 1984.

Dispute Number: 32, 50
Countries: India vs. Pakistan and vice versa
Years of Dispute: 1947–95
Disputed Territory: At the time of independence the political and territorial status of Kashmir was uncertain because the Maharajah had not made a decision whether to join either state or seek independence for Kashmir as well. Both India and Pakistan desired the incorporation of Kashmir into their national territories. Fighting between the army of Kashmir and Muslim rebel forces was already underway at the time of independence and this armed confrontation escalated with the intervention of regular armed forces from both India and Pakistan.

Outcome of Dispute: By late 1948 a fragile ceasefire existed but India had taken control of nearly two-thirds of Kashmir and a *de facto* partition of Kashmir had been established. Pakistan was deeply opposed to the new established line of control in Kashmir and therefore has sought to overturn the new status quo whereas India was generally satisfied with the partition of Kashmir on such favorable terms. As a result, after 1948 Pakistan has been the challenger to the status quo in Kashmir, calling for the withdrawal of Indian military forces and the holding of a plebiscite. India in contrast has sought to preserve the territorial gains it achieved in the fighting of 1947–8 and has rejected calls for a plebiscite or withdrawing its forces from Kashmir. Since 1948 the dispute over Kashmir has escalated into military conflicts on many occasions and numerous rounds of negotiations have been held but no resolution has been achieved.

Sources: *Asian Recorder 1955–95*; Biger 1995; Bindra 1981; *Boundary and Security Bulletin 1993–95*; Gupta 1966; *Keesing's 1947–95*; Prakhar 1987; Wirsing 1994, 1998.

Dispute Number: 33
Countries: India vs. Pakistan
Years of Dispute: 1947–8
Disputed Territory: The territory of Junagadh had not signed the Instrument of Accession to India or Pakistan by the required date of 15 August 1947. The princely state was ruled by a Muslim leader but was 80 percent Hindu and did not have any contiguous land border with Pakistan. On 17 August 1947 Janagadh declared its accession to Pakistan which India strongly opposed.
Outcome of Dispute: India responded to the accession announcement by trying to pressure the Muslim leadership to reverse the decision. When that failed military pressure was applied and by November Indian forces had effectively occupied the state. Pakistan strongly denounced the actions of India but was not capable of a direct military response in the disputed territory. A plebiscite in February 1948 (the results were clearly in favor of union with India) effectively settled the dispute.
Sources: Brecher and Wilkenfeld 1997; *Keesing's 1947–48*.

Dispute Number: 34, 49
Countries: India vs. Pakistan and vice versa
Years of Dispute: 1947–68
Disputed Territory: Both Pakistan and India contested where the boundary line was to be drawn for a section of the border in the

Rann of Kutch. The areas in contention totaled some 3,500 square miles.

Outcome of Dispute: The dispute was settled in February 1968 by a ruling of the Indo-Pakistan Western Boundary Case Tribunal. In the award almost all of the disputed territory (about 90 percent) went to India and both states accepted the ruling.

Sources: *Asian Recorder 1968*; Gupta 1969; *International Boundary Study* (#86); Jha 1972; Razvi 1971; Saksena 1987.

Dispute Number: 35
Countries: India vs. Portugal
Years of Dispute: 1947–61
Disputed Territory: Following its independence, India advanced claims to several Portuguese port enclaves situated along the Adriatic Sea – Goa, Damao, and Diu.

Outcome of Dispute: In December 1961 Indian forces successfully invaded the Portuguese territories, and shortly thereafter the territories were incorporated into India.

Sources: Butterworth 1976; *Keesing's 1948–61*; Lawrence 1963; Rubinoff 1971.

Dispute Number: 36
Countries: Indonesia vs. Netherlands
Years of Dispute: 1950–62
Disputed Territory: Following its independence in 1949, Indonesia called for the complete incorporation of New Guinea (or West Irian as named by Indonesia) within its national territory. The Dutch maintained that the population had the right to self-determination and therefore would not permit Indonesia to incorporate West Irian.

Outcome of Dispute: By 1961 the dispute had escalated to armed conflict short of war. In August 1962 a settlement was reached between the two governments in which it was agreed that Indonesia would assume administrative control over the territory in 1963, and self-determination for the local population would be exercised by the end of 1969.

Sources: Agung 1973; *Asian Recorder 1955–1962*; *Keesing's 1950–1962*; Leifer, 1983; Palmier 1962; Pluvier 1965; Reinhardt 1971; Weistein 1976.

Dispute Number: 37
Countries: Indonesia vs. Malaysia
Years of Dispute: 1980–95

Disputed Territory: Indonesia and Malaysia have four sections to their maritime boundaries: (1) tri-junction with Thailand to the tri-junction with Singapore off the western entrance of the Johor Strait; (2) tri-junction with Singapore to the tri-junction with Vietnam; (3) this section extends northward into the South China Sea from Tandjung Datu; and (4) the eastern terminus of their land boundary on Borneo and reaches into the Celebes Sea. The first three sections have been delimited but Indonesia claims sovereignty over two islands in the Celebes Sea, Pulau Sipadan and Pulau Ligitan, that are controlled by Malaysia. Indonesia argues that the Anglo-Dutch Treaty of June 1891 established their claim to sovereignty over the islands.

Outcome of Dispute: Despite periodic talks there has been no settlement of the dispute.

Sources: *Asian Recorder 1980–95*; *Boundary and Security Bulletin 1993–95*; Haller-Trost 1995; *International Boundary Study* (#45).

Dispute Number: 39
Countries: Japan vs. China
Years of Dispute: 1932–45
Disputed Territory: In 1932 Japan began its occupation and expansion into Manchuria and shortly thereafter Japan established Manchukuo. From 1933 onwards Japan continued to seek further control over territory in areas along the borders of Manchukuo and Inner Mongolia.

Outcome of Dispute: With Japan's defeat in World War II Chinese sovereignty was restored over all territories in Manchuria and Inner Mongolia that had been controlled by Japan since 1932.

Sources: Brecher and Wilkenfeld 1997; *Cambridge History of Japan* (vol. 6); Morley 1983; Nish 1993; *Survey of International Affairs 1932–37*.

Dispute Number: 40
Countries: Japan vs. France
Years of Dispute: 1938–9
Disputed Territory: In 1917 a Japanese businessman established a private company on the Spratly Islands. During 1932–3 France established a claim to the islands but Japan requested that France withdraw its claim to sovereign rights over the islands.

Japan officially declared its own claims to sovereignty over the islands in 1938.

Outcome of Dispute: In the spring of 1939 Japan occupied the islands which France protests but does not counter with any military response.

Sources: Iriye 1991; Kenkyujo 1970 (vols. 15, 22); Nakamura 1990; Shinobu 1988.

Dispute Number: 41
Countries: Japan vs. France
Year of Dispute: 1941
Disputed Territory: In 1941 Japan sought to establish military bases and to station troops in French Indo-China in order to prevent military supplies from being shipped to China.

Outcome of Dispute: Under the threat of war France in September 1941 agreed to allow Japan to occupy territory for purposes of establishing military bases.

Sources: Hammer 1966; Morley 1983.

Dispute Number: 42
Countries: Japan (Manchukuo) vs. Outer Mongolia
Years of Dispute: 1935–40
Disputed Territory: By 1935 Japanese expansion into Manchukuo and Inner Mongolia created border problems with Outer Mongolia. Japan sought control over Dalai and Buyr lakes, the Halhin river, and surrounding territories. Attempts were made to settle the dispute through several rounds of talks and the formation of border commissions.

Outcome of Dispute: In a July 1940 agreement the Japanese concede on almost all of their territorial demands and recognize Outer Mongolian sovereignty over the disputed areas.

Sources: Coox 1985; Friters 1949; Kenkyujo 1970 (vol. 15); Kudo 1985; Prescott 1975.

Dispute Number: 43
Countries: Japan (Manchukuo) vs. Soviet Union
Years of Dispute: 1935–45
Disputed Territory: When Japan established Manchukou in 1932 it inherited China's disagreement with the USSR over the border between Manchuria and the USSR which centered on the Amur river as well as sections along the border in close proximity to Korea. Beginning in 1935 talks were held in an attempt to settle the border disputes.

Outcome of Dispute: There was no settlement of the dispute through negotiations and with Japan's defeat in World War II the dispute came to end.

Sources: Brecher and Wilkenfeld 1997; Coox 1977; Friters 1949; Kenkyujo 1970 (vol. 15); Kudo 1985; Morley 1983.

Dispute Number: 44
Countries: Japan vs. Soviet Union
Years of Dispute: 1951–95
Disputed Territory: Japan has contested Soviet (now Russian) occupation of a number of islands off the north-east coast of Japan. The islands are the Habomai group along with Shikotan, Kunashiri, and Etorofu, which were occupied by Soviet forces at the very end of World War II. In the 1951 peace treaty (which the Soviet Union did not sign), Japan accepted the loss of Sakhalin and the Kurile Islands, but with the provision that the latter did not include Kunashiri, Etorofu, Shikotan, or the Habomais. Japan claims sovereignty over all of these islands but the Soviet Union maintained that its sovereignty over the islands was established by agreements reached with allied powers just prior to the end of World War II. In total, approximately 3,000 square miles of territory are in dispute.

Outcome of Dispute: There has been no resolution of the competing claims, and Russia continues to control the disputed islands. Under Soviet leader Gorbachev, talks were resumed in 1986 and several rounds were subsequently held. Russian troops began to withdraw from the islands in 1991 and agreements were reached on fishing and travel rights in 1991–2. During 1992–3 the possibility of Russia exchanging the islands for large-scale economic aid from Japan was discussed between the two countries but no such agreement has been reached.

Sources: *Asian Recorder 1960–95*; *Boundary and Security Bulletin 1993–95*; Ishiwatari 1995; Jain 1981; *Keesing's 1960–95*; Kenkyujo 1970; Makino 1998; Tanaka 1993; Tomaru 1993; Wada 1990.

Dispute Number: 45
Countries: Malaysia vs. China
Years of Dispute: 1979–95
Disputed Territory: Malaysia has claimed sovereignty over several of the Spratly Islands that are located on its continental shelf.

Outcome of Dispute: There has been no resolution of the dispute. China proposed in 1990 the joint economic development of the Spratlys but Malaysia has not expressed a strong interest in the proposal.

Sources: *Asian Recorder 1979–95*; *Boundary and Security Bulletin 1993–95*; Dzurek 1996; Englefield 1994; Hyer 1995; *Keesing's 1979–95*; Thomas 1989; Tiet 1975; Valencia 1995.

Dispute Number: 46
Countries: Malaysia vs. Singapore
Years of Dispute: 1980–95
Disputed Territory: The dispute centers over Malaysian claims to the Pedra Branca Island.
Outcome of Dispute: Periodic negotiations have been made but no settlement has been reached.
Sources: *Asian Recorder 1980–95*; *Boundary and Security Bulletin 1993–95*; Haller-Trost 1993; Prescott 1985.

Dispute Number: 47
Countries: North Korea vs. South Korea
Years of Dispute: 1948–95
Disputed Territory: North Korea has sought to create a single unified Korea (by the use of force if necessary) and for decades has refused to recognize the independence of South Korea. In June 1950 North Korea invaded South Korea in an attempt at unification, which failed as a result of US and UN armed intervention in support of South Korea. The present border is a provisional line established by the 1953 armistice agreement, which brought an end to the Korean War.
Outcome of Dispute: The two countries have held numerous rounds of talks on reunification since the early 1970s without a general settlement. An important step towards a settlement, however, was taken when the two countries signed an "Agreement on Reconciliation, Non-Aggression, and Exchanges and Cooperation" in December 1991. In the accord North Korea formally recognized South Korea, pledged not to attack South Korea and to resolve all disputes peacefully, and agreed to promote economic, scientific, and cultural ties with South Korea. Since 1992 further progress in implementing the 1991 accord was blocked by the controversy over the potential development of nuclear weapons in North Korea and the failure of North Korea to permit full-scope inspections of nuclear facilities by the International Atomic Energy Agency.

Sources: Alexander 1986; *Asian Recorder 1960–95*; Blair 1987; *Boundary and Security Bulletin 1993–95*; Cummings 1990; Fehrenbach 1963; *Keesing's 1948–95*; Oliver 1978.

Dispute Number: 48
Countries: North Vietnam vs. South Vietnam
Years of Dispute: 1954–75
Disputed Territory: The Geneva agreements of 1954 provisionally split Vietnam into a northern and southern zone until reunification could be achieved through national elections to be held in 1956. The national elections, however, were not held and South Vietnam disassociated itself from the 1954 agreements for reunification. North Vietnam, however, continued to seek the reunification of Vietnam and therefore did not accept the independence of South Vietnam.
Outcome of Dispute: During the period from 1956 until late 1960 North Vietnam sought peaceful reunification with South Vietnam. By the fall of 1960, however, North Vietnam decided to support the Viet Cong armed struggle. By late 1964 regular armed forces of the North Vietnamese army were infiltrating into South Vietnam and were preparing to engage in direct combat with South Vietnamese and US forces. The Vietnam War ended with the capture of Saigon in 1975, and in 1976 a unified Vietnam under communist rule was proclaimed.
Sources: *Asian Recorder 1956–75*; *Keesing's 1954–75*; Thies 1980.

Dispute Number: 52
Countries: Portugal vs. India
Years of Dispute: 1962–74
Disputed Territory: Following its independence India advanced claims to several Portuguese port enclaves situated along the Adriatic Sea – Goa, Damao, and Diu. In December 1961 Indian forces successfully invaded the Portuguese territories and shortly thereafter the territories were incorporated into India. While Portugal did not resist with force the Indian invasion, it did not recognize Indian sovereignty over the enclaves.
Outcome of Dispute: It was not until 1974, with the change of regime in Portugal, that Indian sovereignty over the territories was recognized by the Portuguese government.
Sources: Butterworth 1976; *Keesing's 1961–74*; Lawrence 1963; Rubinoff 1971.

Dispute Number: 54
Countries: Papua New Guinea vs. Australia
Years of Dispute: 1974–8
Disputed Territory: Papua New Guinea claimed sovereignty over several small islands in the Torres Straits.
Outcome of Dispute: In a treaty signed in December 1978 Australia ceded the disputed islands to Papua New Guinea.
Sources: Prescott 1977, 1985; *The Torres Straits Treaty*.

Dispute Number: 55
Countries: Philippines vs. China
Years of Dispute: 1971–95
Disputed Territory: The Philippine government has claimed several of the Spratly Islands, all of which China has claimed sovereignty over since the 1930s. In 1956 the Philippine government indirectly laid claim to the islands, and in 1971 openly, and more formally, asserted its claim. In 1978 a presidential decree annexed several islands to the Philippine province of Palawan.
Outcome of Dispute: An agreement was reached between the two governments in March 1979 to resolve the dispute "in a spirit of conciliation and friendship," but no formal settlement has been concluded. Chinese proposals for the joint economic development of the Spratly Islands have not been well received by the Philippines. The Philippines has established a military presence on several of the disputed islands and has actively sought to develop oil deposits around the islands.
Sources: *Asian Recorder 1971–95*; *Boundary and Security Bulletin 1993–95*; Dzurek 1996; Englefield 1994; Hyer 1995; *Keesing's 1971–95*; Samuels 1982; Tiet 1975; Thomas 1989; Valencia 1995.

Dispute Number: 56
Countries: Philippines vs. Malaysia
Years of Dispute: 1962–95
Disputed Territory: In 1961 Great Britain and Malaya began discussing plans for the formation of a Malaysian federation which would include the territory of Sabah (North Borneo). The Philippine government, however, in 1962 claimed sovereignty over the territory itself on historical grounds.
Outcome of Dispute: In 1977 the Philippine government announced its intent to withdraw its claim to sovereignty over Sabah, and subsequent Philippine governments have not

renounced that policy. Several rounds of talks in the mid and late 1980s were held between the two countries, and in August 1988 the Philippine Foreign Secretary stated that his country was willing in principle to drop the claim. Nevertheless, no formal settlement has been reached in which the Philippine government has conclusively renounced its territorial claims.

Sources: Allcock 1992; *Asian Recorder 1962–95; Boundary and Security Bulletin 1993–95*; Mackie 1974.

Dispute Number: 57
Countries: Portugal vs. Indonesia
Years of Dispute: 1975–95
Disputed Territory: Following the outbreak of civil war in East Timor in August 1975, Indonesian armed forces intervened in December, and by August 1976 East Timor was proclaimed Indonesia's twenty-seventh province. Portugal condemned the Indonesian action, refused to accept Indonesian annexation of East Timor, and has maintained its claims to East Timor.
Outcome of Dispute: The United Nations condemned the Indonesian invasion and called for East Timor to be given the right of self-determination. Indonesian leaders, however, continued to insist that East Timor is a province of their country and denied charges of widespread human rights abuses against the local population and Fretilin resistance movement. Portugal, in turn, has refused in several rounds of talks in the 1980s and 1990s to recognize Indonesian sovereignty and supports UN resolutions for self-determination in East Timor.
Sources: Allcock 1992; *Asian Recorder 1975–95; Boundary and Security Bulletin 1993–95*; Cranna 1994; Krieger 1997; Taylor 1990.

Dispute Number: 58
Countries: South Korea vs. Japan
Years of Dispute: 1951–95
Disputed Territory: South Korea has contested Japanese sovereignty over the small group of islands known as Takeshima (or Tak-do as named by the South Koreans). The islands are located in the southern portion of the Sea of Japan, approximately equidistant between the two countries. Japan had formally annexed the islands in 1905, but following World War II South Korea challenged the legitimacy of the Japanese annexation, claiming that it was an act of imperialism and therefore

illegal and that Japan relinquished all rights to the islands after its defeat in World War II.

Outcome of Dispute: Negotiations were held over the islands in the 1950s and 1960s with South Korea pressing for full sovereignty over the islands while declining Japanese proposals for international arbitration. An agreement, however, was reached in the mid-1960s to neutralize the islands, and since the late 1970s South Korea has exercised *de facto* sovereignty over the islands. Nevertheless, Japan has not formally conceded sovereignty of the islands to South Korea, and therefore the dispute has not been officially settled.

Sources: Allcock 1992; Hiramatsu and Okonogi 1997; Kenkyujo 1970 (vols. 26, 28); Makino 1998; Tsukamato 1994.

Dispute Number: 60
Countries: Thailand vs. France
Years of Dispute: 1919–41
Disputed Territory: Following the signing of a border treaty in 1893 Thailand raised claims to islands in the Mekong and where the boundary line was to be drawn along the river. In addition, during the inter-war period Thailand called for the return of several enclaves that had been ceded to France in 1904 and 1907.

Outcome of Dispute: By 1939 France sought to secure its position in Indo-China by signing a non-aggression pact with Thailand. Thailand would only sign the pact in return for territorial concessions over the areas in dispute. The government in Paris was willing to make the concessions but the colonial governors were not and therefore no final settlement could be reached during 1939 and early 1940. By November of 1940 war broke out between Thailand and France as Thailand pressed for concessions. Confronted with the threat of Japanese intervention in support of Thailand, France signed a border treaty in March 1941 that satisfied all of the territorial demands of Thailand and restored all of the territories lost to France by the agreements of 1893, 1904, and 1907.

Sources: Crosby 1945; Decoux 1949; Flood 1969; Levy and Roth 1941; Morlat 1995; Prescott 1975; Santaputra 1985; Sivaram 1941; Thompson 1941; Vadakarn 1941; Wyatt 1984.

Dispute Number: 61
Countries: Thailand vs. France/Cambodia
Years of Dispute: 1949–53

Disputed Territory: Following the return in 1946 of the provinces of Siem Reap and Battambang to France, Thailand raised a claim to the ancient Khmer Temple of Preah Vihear and its surrounding territory, arguing that the Franco-Siamese Treaty of 1907 established that the Temple was within Thai national territory.

Outcome of Dispute: Shortly before Cambodia's independence in 1953 Thai military forces moved into the disputed territory and established control.

Sources: Biger 1995; *International Boundary Study* (#40); Leifer 1962; Prescott 1975; Smith 1965; St. John 1998.

Dispute Number: 62
Countries: Thailand vs. Laos
Years of Dispute: 1984–95
Disputed Territory: Thailand disputes two areas along its border with Laos. The first centers on approximately twenty square kilometers of territory along the northern border west of the Mekong. The second area covers eighty square kilometers of bordering territory between the Laos province of Sayaboury and the Thai province of Phitsanuloke, referred to as Ban Rom Klao.

Outcome of Dispute: Multiple rounds of talks were held between 1984 and 1988 with some limited progress reported. A border commission was established during 1988 and surveys and inspections of the border areas were carried out during 1989–90 but no settlement has been reported.

Sources: Allcock 1992; *Asian Recorder 1984–95*; Biger 1995; *Boundary and Security Bulletin 1993–95*; Ngaosyvathn and Ngaosyvathn 1994; St. John 1998.

Dispute Number: 63
Countries: United States vs. Japan
Years of Dispute: 1919–22
Disputed Territory: In May 1919 the Council of Four awarded mandate rights to Japan for the Yap Islands. The US protested and maintained its own claim to mandate rights over the islands.

Outcome of Dispute: In February 1922 the US signed an agreement recognizing Japan's mandate rights and in return Japan agreed to permit the US to use communication lines located on the island.

Sources: Buckingham 1983; Buell 1922; Ichiashi 1928.

Dispute Number: 64
Countries: United States vs. Netherlands
Years of Dispute: 1919–28
Disputed Territory: In 1906 a US official visited Palmas Islands and found a Dutch flag flying. In response the US protested the Dutch presence and claimed that the island was under US sovereignty.
Outcome of Dispute: In 1925 both states agreed to submit the dispute to The Hague for arbitration. The Hague ruling in April 1928 upheld the Dutch claim to sovereignty which the US accepted.
Sources: *Survey of International Affairs 1929*; *The Island of Palmas Arbitration*.

Dispute Number: 65
Countries: Vanuatu vs. France
Years of Dispute: 1982–95
Disputed Territory: The dispute over the Matthew and Hunter Islands arose in 1982 when Vanuatu contested French sovereignty. In 1976 the French had declared that the islands were part of New Caledonia but Vanuatu has rejected the validity of this 1976 action.
Outcome of Dispute: In the early and mid-1980s relations between the two countries suffered as a result of the islands dispute. Relations have improved since 1988 but there has been no resolution of the conflicting claims.
Sources: Allcock 1992; *Asian Recorder 1982–95*; *Keesing's 1982–95*.

Bibliography of sources listed in case summaries

Adamac, Ludwig (1974) *Afghanistan's Foreign Affairs to the Mid-Twentieth Century* (Tuscon: University of Arizona Press).

Agung, Ide Anak Agung Gde (1973) *Twenty Years Indonesian Foreign Policy, 1945–1965* (Mouton: The Hague).

Ahmed Dar, Saeedudin (1986) *Selected Documents on Pakistan's Relations with Afghanistan, 1947–1985* (Islamabad: National Institute of Political Studies).

Alexander, Bevin (1986) *Korea, the First War We Lost* (New York: Hipporcrene Books).

Ali, Mehrunnisa, ed. (1990) *Pak–Afghan Discord* (Karachi: Pakistan Study Centre, University of Karachi).

Allcock, John, ed. (1992) *Border and Territorial Disputes*, 3rd ed. (Essex: Longman).

Amer, Ramses (1997) "Border Conflicts between Cambodia and Vietnam" *Boundary and Security Bulletin*, 5, 2: 80–91.

Asian Recorder 1959–1995 (New Delhi: K. K. Thomas, 1959–95).

Bhim, Sandhu (1988) *Unresolved Conflict: China and India* (New Delhi: Radian Publishers).

Biger, Gideon (1995) *The Encyclopedia of International Boundaries* (New York: Facts on File).

Bindra, Sukhawant Singh (1981) *Indo-Pak Relations* (New Delhi: Deep & Deep Publications).

Blair, Clay (1987) *The Forgotten War: America in Korea 1950–1953* (New York: Times Books Inc.).

Boundary and Security Bulletin 1993–1995 (Durham: International Boundaries Research Unit, 1993–5).

Brecher, Michael and Jonathan Wilkenfeld (1997) *A Study of Crisis* (Ann Arbor: University of Michigan Press).

British Command Paper, No. 324 (xxxvii, 1183) *Papers Regarding the Hostilities with Afghanistan, 1919* (London: HMSO, 1919).

British Command Paper, No. 1786 (xxv, 7) *Treaty Between the British and Afghan Governments* (London: HMSO, 1923).

Buckingham, Peter (1983) *International Normalcy* (Wilmington: Scholarly Resources Inc.).

Buell, Raymond (1922) *The Washington Conference* (US: Russell and Russell).

Burrell, Robert (1997) *Iran Political Diaries 1881–1965*, vols. 9–10 (Oxford: Archive Editions).

Butterworth, Robert (1976) *Managing Interstate Conflict, 1945–74* (Pittsburgh: University Center for International Studies, University of Pittsburgh).

The Cambridge History of Japan (1988) vol. 6 (Cambridge: Cambridge University Press).

Carr, Edward Hallet (1953) *A History of Soviet Russia*, vol. 3 (New York: Macmillan).

Cheng, Peter (1972) *A Chronology of the People's Republic of China from October 1 1949* (Totowa: Rowan and Littlefield).

——— (1986) *A Chronology of the People's Republic of China, 1970–79* (Metuchen: Scarecrow Press).

Cheng, Tien-Fong (1957) *A History of Sino-Russian Relations* (Washington DC: Public Affairs Press).

China Handbook 1924–31, 1937–45, 1950 (New York: Rockport Press, 1924–31, 1937–45, 1950).

Cohen, Jerome and Hungdah Chiu (1974) *People's China and International Law* (Princeton: Princeton University Press).

Coox, Alvin (1977) *The Anatomy of a Small War* (Westport: Greenwood Press).

——— (1985) *Nomonhan* (Stanford: Stanford University Press).

Cottrell, Robert (1993) *The End of Hong Kong* (London: John Murray).

Cranna, Michael, ed. (1994) *The True Cost of Conflict* (New York: New Press).

Crosby, Sir Josiah (1945) *Siam* (London: Hollia and Carter Ltd.).

Cummings, Bruce (1990) *The Origins of the Korean War* (Princeton: Princeton University Press).

Day, Alan (1987) *Border and Territorial Disputes*, 2nd ed. (Harlow: Longman).

Deans, Phil (1997) "The Diaoyutai/Senkaku Dispute" (unpublished manuscript) http://sipe.ukc.ac.uk/international/papers.dir/deans.htm

Decoux, Amiral (1949) *À la Barre de L'Indochine* (Paris: Libraia Plon).

Dmytryshyn, Basil and Frederick Cox (1987) *The Soviet Union and the Middle East: A Documentary Record of Afghanistan, Iran, and Turkey, 1917–1985* (Princeton: Kingston Press).

Dzurek, Daniel (1996) *The Spratly Islands Dispute* (Durham: International Boundaries Research Unit).

Englefield, Greg (1994) "Managing Boundaries in the South China Sea" *Boundary and Security Bulletin*, 2, 2: 36–8.

Eto, Shinkichi (1980) "Recent Developments in Sino-Japanese Relations" *Asian Survey*, 20, 7: 726–43.

Fehrenbach, T. R. (1963) *This Kind of War* (New York: Macmillan Company).

Flood, Thadeus (1969) "The 1940 Franco-Thai Border Dispute and Phibuun Sonkhraam's Commitment to Japan" *Journal of Southeast Asian History*, 7: 304–25.

Friters, Gerard (1949) *Outer Mongolia and Its International Position* (Baltimore: Johns Hopkins University Press).

Gilks, Anne (1992) *The Breakdown of the Sino-Vietnamese Alliance, 1970–1979* (Berkeley: Instiute of East Asian Studies, University of California, Center for Chinese Studies).

Ginsburgs, George and Carl Pinkele (1978) *The Sino-Soviet Territorial Dispute, 1949–64* (New York: Praeger).

Great Britain Foreign Office Archives:

    Afghanistan vs. Soviet Union (case #4), documents on relations between Afghanistan and the Soviet Union from 1934–6 beginning with FO 371/18258 and ending with FO 371/20320 and from 1945–6 beginning with FO 371/45217 and ending with FO 371/52287.

    Britain/India vs. France (case #5), documents on relations between France and British India/India from 1928–54 beginning with FO 371/13348 and ending with FO 371/112209.

    China vs. Britain (case #13), documents on relations between China and British Burma from 1920–41 beginning with FO 371/5318 and ending with FO 371/31669.

Gupta, Hari Ram (1969) *The Krutch Affair* (New Delhi: U. C. Kapur & Sons).

Gupta, Sisir (1966) *Kashmir: A Study in India–Pakistan Relations* (Bombay: Asia Pub. House).

Haller-Trost, R. (1993) *Historical Legal Claims: A Study of Disputed Sovereignty over Pulau Batu Puteh (Pedra Branca)* (Durham: International Boundaries Research Unit).

    (1995) *The Territorial Dispute Between Indonesia and Malaysia over Pulau Sipadan and Pulau Ligitan in the Celebes Sea* (Durham: International Boundaries Research Unit).

Hammer, Ellen (1954) *The Struggle for Indochina* (Stanford: Stanford University Press).

    (1966) *Vietnam Yesterday and Today* (New York: Rinehart and Winston).

Heimsath, Charles (1971) *Diplomatic History of Modern India* (Bombay: Allied Publishers).

Hinton, Harold (1958) *China's Relations with Burma and Vietnam* (New York: Institute of Pacific Relations).

Hiramatsu, Shigeo, and Masao Okonogi (1997) "Takeshima wo meguru Kokusaikankei" in Tomoyuki Kojima ed., *Higashi Ajia no Kiki no Kozu* (Tokyo: Tokyo Keizai Shinpo-sha).

Hoang Sa and Truong Sa Archipelagoes (Paracels and Spratly) (1981) (Hanoi: Vietnam Courier).

Hoffman, Steven (1990) *India and the China Crisis* (Berkeley: University of California Press).

Hyer, Eric (1990) "The Politics of China's Boundary Disputes and Settlements" (Ph.D. Thesis, Department of Political Science, Columbia University).

—— (1995) "The South China Sea Disputes: Implications of China's Earlier Territorial Settlements" *Pacific Affairs*, 68, 1: 34–54.

Ichiashi, Yamato (1928) *The Washington Conference and After* (Stanford: Stanford University Press).

International Boundary Study (1961–9)(Washington DC: The Geographer, Bureau of Intelligence and Research, US Department of State).

International Boundary Study. No. 6 Afghanistan–Iran Boundary, 20 June 1961.

International Boundary Study. No. 26 Afghanistan–USSR Boundary, 30 December 1963.

International Boundary Study. No. 40 Cambodia–Thailand Boundary, 1 November 1966.

International Boundary Study. No. 42 Burma–China Boundary, 30 November, 1964.

International Boundary Study. No. 45 Indonesia–Malaysia Boundary, 15 March 1965.

International Boundary Study. No. 50 China–Nepal Boundary, 30 May 1965.

International Boundary Study. No. 85 China–Pakistan Boundary, 15 November 1968.

International Boundary Study. No. 86 India–Pakistan Boundary, 15 November 1968.

International Boundary Study. No. 89 Afghanistan–China Boundary, 1 May 1969.

Iriye, Akira (1991) *Taiheiyo Senso no Kigen* (Tokyo: Tokyo University Press).

Ishiwatari, Toshiyasu (1995) "The Northern Territories" in Thomas Forsberg ed., *Contested Territory: Border Disputes at the Edge of the Former Soviet Empire* (Brookfield: Elgar).

Island of Palmas Arbitration, Memorandum of the United States of America (1925) (Washington DC: US Government Printing Office).

Jain, Rajendra (1981) *The USSR and Japan, 1945–1980* (Atlantic Highlands: Humanities Press).

Jetly, Nancy (1979) *India–China Relations 1947–1977* (New Delhi: Radiant Publishers).

Jha, Dinesh Chandra (1972) *Indo-Pakistani Relations* (Patna, India: Bharati Bhawan).

Jones, Peter and Sian Kevill, eds. (1985) *China and the Soviet Union 1949–84* (New York: Facts on File Publications).

Kao, Ting Tsz (1980) *The Chinese Frontiers* (Palatine: Chinese Scholarly Pub. Co.).

Kaur, Kulwant (1985) *Pak–Afghanistan Relations 1947–1977* (New Delhi: Deep & Deep Publications).

Keesing's Contemporary Archives 1947–86 (London: Keesing's Publications, 1947–86).

Keesing's Record of World Events 1987–95 (London: Keesing's Publications, 1987–95).

Kenkyujo, Kashima Heiwa, ed. (1970) *Nihon Gaikoushi*, vols. 15, 22, 26, 28 (Tokyo: Kajima Kenkyujo Shuppan Kai).

Kim, Youngtae (1990) "Sino-Japanese Relations: The Making of the Peace and Friendship Treaty" (Ph.D. Thesis, The Graduate School of Arts and Sciences, George Washington University).

Krieger, Heike ed. (1997) *East Timor and the International Community* (Cambridge: Cambridge University Press).

Kudo, Michihiro (1985) *Nisso Churitsu Joyaku no Kenkyu* (Tokyo: Nansosha).

Lamb, Alastair (1968) *Asian Frontiers: Studies in a Continuing Problem* (London: Pall Mall Press).

Lane, Kevin (1990) *Sovereignty and the Status Quo* (London: Westview Press).

Lawrence, Leo (1963) *Nehru Seizes Goa* (New York: Pagent Press).

Lawson, Eugene (1984) *The Sino-Vietnamese Conflict* (New York: Praeger).

Leifer, Michael (1962) "Cambodia and Her Neighbors" *Pacific Affairs*, 36, 4: 361–74.

——— (1983) *Indonesia's Foreign Policy* (London: Allen & Unwin).

Leong, Sow-Theng (1976) *Sino-Soviet Diplomatic Relations, 1917–1926* (Canberra: Australian National University Press).

Levy, Roger and Andrew Roth (1941) *French Interests and Policies in the Far East* (New York: Institute of Pacific Relations Inquiry Series).

Lo, Chin-kin (1989) *China's Policy Towards Territorial Disputes: The Case of the South China Sea Islands* (London: Routledge).

Long, Simon (1991) *Taiwan, China's Last Frontier* (New York: St. Martin's Press).

Mackie, J. A. C. (1974) *Konfrontasi: The Indonesia-Malaysia Dispute* (Kuala Lumpur: Oxford University Press).

Makino, Yoshihiro (1998) *Senkaku, Takeshima, Hoppoyonto* (Tokyo: Asahi Shinbun-sha).

Maxwell, Neville (1970) *India's China War* (New York: Pantheon Books).

Mclachlan, Keith (1994) *The Boundaries of Modern Iran* (London: UCL Press).

Morlat, Patrice (1995) *Les Affaires Politiques de L'Indochine, 1895–1923, Les Grand Commis, du Savoir au Pouvoir* (Paris: Harmattan).

Morley, James, ed. (1980) *The Fateful Choice: Japan's Advance into Southeast Asia, 1939–1941* (New York: Columbia University Press).

——— (1983) *The China Quagmire* (New York: Columbia University Press).

Muni, S. D. (1973) *Foreign Policy of Nepal* (Delhi: National Publishing House).

Nakamura, Akira (1990) *Daitoa Senso he no Michi* (Tokyo: Tenten-sha).

Ngaosyvathn, Mayoury and Pheuiphanh Ngaosyvathn (1994) *Kith and Kin Politics: The Relationship Between Laos and Thailand* (Manila: Journal of Contemporary Asia Publishers).

Nguyen-vo, Thu-Huong (1992) *Khmer–Viet Relations and the Third Indochina Conflict* (London: McFarland).

Nish, Ian (1993) *Japan's Struggle with Internationalism* (London: K. Paul International).

Oliver, Robert (1978) *Syngman Rhee and American Involvement in Korea 1942–1960* (Seoul: Panmun Book Company).

Ozaki, Shigenori (1972) "Senkaku Shoto no Kizoku ni Tsuite" *The Reference*, 263: 30–48.

Palmier, Leslie (1962) *Indonesia and the Dutch* (London: Oxford University Press).

Patrice, Morlatm (1995) *Les Affaires Politiques de L'Indochine, 1895–1923* (Paris: Harmattan).

Pluvier, Jan (1965) *Confrontations: A Study in Indonesian Politics* (Kuala Lumpur: Oxford University Press).

Pollard, Robert (1933) *China's Foreign Relations: 1917–1931* (New York: Macmillan).

Pradhan, P. C. (1987) *Foreign Policy of Kampuchea* (London: Sagam Books).

Prakhar, Gulab Mishra (1987) *Indo-Pakistan Relations* (New Delhi: Ashish).

Prescott, John (1975) *Map of Mainland Asia by Treaty* (Melbourne: Melbourne University Press).

(1977) *Frontiers of Asia and Southeast Asia* (Melbourne: Melbourne University Press).

(1985) *The Maritime Political Boundaries of the World* (New York: Methuen).

Rais, Rasul Bux (1977) *China and Pakistan: A Political Analysis of Mutual Relations* (Lahore: Progressive).

Razvi, Mujtaba (1971) *The Frontiers of Pakistan* (Karachi: National Publishing House).

Reinhardt, Jon (1971) *Foreign Policy and National Integration* (New Haven: Yale University Southeast Asia Studies).

Rezun, Miron (1981) *The Soviet Union and Iran* (Geneva: Sythaff and Noordhaff Publishers).

Roberti, Mark (1984) *The Fall of Hong Kong* (New York: John Wiley & Sons).

Ross, Robert (1988) *The Indochina Tangle: China's Vietnam Policy, 1975–1979* (New York: Columbia University Press).

Rowland, John (1967) *A History of Sino-Indian Relations* (Princeton: Van Nostrand).

Rubinoff, Arthur (1971) *India's Use of Force in Goa* (Bombay: Popular Prakashan).

Saksena, Ajay (1987) *India and Pakistan: Their Foreign Policies* (Delhi: Anmol).

Samuels, Marwyn (1982) *Contest for the South China Sea* (New York: Methuen).

Sandhu, Bhim (1988) *Unresolved Conflict, China and India* (New Delhi: Radiant Publishers).

Santaputra, Charivat (1985) *Thai Foreign Policy 1932–1946* (Bangkok: Thai Khadi Research Institute).

Sareen, Anurandha (1981) *India and Afghanistan* (Dehli: Seema Publications).

Sharma, Surya (1971) *India's Boundary and Territorial Disputes* (New Delhi: Vikas Publications.

Shinobu, Seitaro (1988) *Mouhitotsu no Taiheiyo Senso* (Tokyo: Keiso Shobo).

Shipp, Steve (1997) *Macau, China* (London: McFarland & Company).

Shukla, S. P. (1984) *India and Pakistan* (New Delhi: Deep & Deep).

Sivaram, M. (1941) *The Mekong Clash and Far East Crisis* (Bangkok: Thai Commercial Press).

Smith, Roger (1965) *Cambodia's Foreign Policy* (Ithaca: Cornell University Press).

St. John, Ronald (1998) *The Land Boundaries of Indochina, Cambodia, Laos and Vietnam* (Durham: International Boundaries Research Unit, University of Durham).

Survey of International Affairs 1920–23, 1925, 1929–30, 1932–37, 1956–60 (Oxford: Oxford University Press, 1925–64).

Syed, Anwar Hussain (1974) *China & Pakistan: Diplomacy of an Entente Cordiale* (Amherst: University of Massachusetts Press).

Tanaka, Takahiko (1993) *Nisso Kokko Kaihuku no Shiteki Kenkyu: Sengo Nisso Kannkei no Kiten* (Tokyo: Yuhikaku).

Tang, Peter (1959) *Russia and Soviet Policy in Manchuria and Outer Mongolia 1911–1931* (Durham: Duke University Press).

Taylor, John (1990) *The Indonesian Occupation of East Timor, 1974–1989* (London: Catholic Institute for International Relations).

Thies, Wallace (1980) *When Governments Collide: Coercion and Diplomacy in the Vietnam Conflict, 1964–1968* (Berkeley: University of California Press).

Thomas, Bradford (1989) *The Spratly Islands Imbroglio* (Durham: International Boundaries Research Unit).

Thompson, Virginia (1941) *Thailand: The New Siam* (New York: Paragon).

Tiet, Tran-minh (1975) *L'Agression Sino-Communiste des Îles Paracel Vietnami-ennes* (Paris: Nouvelles Editions Latines).

Tomaru, Hiroyasu ed. (1993) *Shinbun Shuusei: Hoppuo Ryuodo* (Tokyo: Ozorasha).

Torres Straits Treaty (1979) (Canberra: Australian Government Publishing Service).

Tretiak, Daniel (1978) "The Sino-Japanese Treaty of 1978: The Senkaku Incident Prelude" *Asian Survey*, 18, 12: 1235–49.

Tsukamoto, Takashi (1994) "Heiwa Joyaku to Takeshima: Sairon" *The Reference*, 518: 31–56.

Tsui, Tsien-Hua (1983) *The Sino-Soviet Border Dispute in the 1970s* (Oakville: Mosaic Press).

Tung, William (1970) *China and the Foreign Powers* (New York: Oceana Publications).

Tzou, Byron (1990) *China and International Law: The Boundary Disputes* (New York: Praeger).

Vadakarn, Luang Vichitr (1941) *Thailand's Case* (Bangkok: Thai Commercial Press).

Valencia, Mark (1995) *China and the South China Sea Dispute* (Oxford: Oxford University Press).

Van Minh, Tran (1978) "Terrestrial Borders between Cambodia and Vietnam" *Juridical and Political Journal: Independence and Cooperation*, 32, 2: 647–73.

—— (1979) "The Nautical Borders between Cambodia and Vietnam" *Juridical and Political Journal: Independence and Cooperation*, 33, 1: 37–66.

Volodarsky, Mikhail (1994) *The Soviet Union and its Southern Neighbors* (Essex: Frank Cass).

Wada, Haruki (1990) *Hopporyodo Mondai wo Kangaeru* (Tokyo: Iwananmi shoten).

Wei, Henry (1956) *China and Soviet Russia* (Princeton: D. Van Nostrand Company).

Weigh, Ken Shen (1928) *Russo-Chinese Diplomacy* (Shanghai: Commecial Press).

Weinstein, Franklin (1976) *Indonesian Foreign Policy and the Dilemma of Dependence: From Sukarno to Soeharto* (Ithaca: Cornell University Press).

Wirsing, Robert (1994) *India, Pakistan, and the Kashmir Dispute: On Regional Conflict and its Resolution* (New York: St. Martin's Press).

(1998) *War or Peace on the Line of Control? The India–Pakistan Dispute over Kashmir Turns Fifty* (Durham: International Boundaries Research Unit).

Whiting, Allen (1975) *The Chinese Calculus of Deterrence: India and Indochina* (Ann Arbor: University of Michigan Press).

Whittam, Daphne (1961) "The Sino-Burmese Border Treaty" *Pacific Affairs*, 34, 1: 174–83.

Woodman, Dorothy (1962) *The Making of Burma* (London: Cresset).

Wun, Kin Wah (1976) *A Documentary Analysis of Sino-Soviet Relations: The Border Negotiations* (Singapore: Institute of Humanities and Social Sciences, Nanyang University).

Wyatt, David (1984) *Thailand: A Short History* (New Haven: Yale University Press).

Appendix F
Territorial disputes in North and South America, 1919–1995

List of dispute cases

In this section a summary list is provided of territorial disputes in the Americas. For each dispute information is presented as follows: (a) the first state listed is the challenger while the second is the target, (b) the first and last years of the dispute, and (c) a brief description of the challenger's territorial claims. For those disputes marked with an asterisk both states are challengers and therefore the dispute is listed a second time with the identity of challenger and target reversed.

1. Argentina vs. Britain 1919–95: Claim to Falkland Islands
2. Argentina vs. Chile 1919–95: Claims along Andean border in Palena and Laguno del Desierto as well as islands in the Beagle Channel
3. Argentina vs. Paraguay* 1919–45: Claims to border along Pilcomayo river
4. Argentina vs. Uruguay* 1919–73: Claims to islands in the Rio de la Plata river and boundary line in the river
5. Bolivia vs. Argentina 1919–25: Claims along length of border
6. Bolivia vs. Chile 1919–95: Claims to provinces of Tacna and Arica
7. Bolivia vs. Paraguay 1919–38: Claims to border in Chaco Boreal region
8. Brazil vs. Argentina 1919–27: Claims to boundary line along bordering rivers and islands
9. Brazil vs. Bolivia 1919–28: Claim to boundary line along bordering rivers and islands
10. Brazil vs. Britain 1919–26: Claims along border of British Guyana
11. Brazil vs. Colombia* 1919–1928: Claims along border
12. Brazil vs. Paraguay* 1919–27: Claims to boundary line along bordering Paraguay river and islands
13. Canada vs. Britain 1919–27: Claims to border with Newfoundland in the Labrador Peninsula
14. Colombia vs. Brazil* 1919–28: Claim to small section along southern section of border

15. Colombia vs. Nicaragua* 1919–28: Claims to section of Mosquito coastline and Corn Islands
16. Colombia vs. Peru* 1919–34: Claims to territory in Leticia and Loreto regions
17. Colombia vs. United States 1919–28: Claim to Serrana Bank Islands
18. Colombia vs. Venezuela* 1919–24: Claims along southern section of border including the La Goajira Peninsula
19. Cuba vs. United States 1959–95: Call for US withdrawal from military base at Guantanamo
20. Dominican Republic vs. Haiti* 1919–35: Claims along length of border
21. Ecuador vs. Peru* 1919–42: Claims to border in the Maranon region
22. Ecuador vs. Peru 1950–95: Claims to border in the Maranon region
23. El Salvador vs. Honduras* 1919–92: Claims along border and to islands in the Gulf of Fonseca
24. Guatemala vs. Britain 1936–95: Call for incorporating Belize as part of Guatemala as well as claims to territory in order to gain outlet to sea (UK is target until 1980 and Belize thereafter)
25. Guatemala vs. Honduras* 1919–33: Claims along length of border
26. Haiti vs. Dominican Republic* 1919–35: Claims along length of border
27. Haiti vs. United States 1919–95: Claim to Navassa Island
28. Honduras vs. El Salvador* 1919–92: Claims to border and islands in the Gulf of Fonseca
29. Honduras vs. Guatemala* 1919–33: Claim along length of border
30. Honduras vs. United States 1921–71: Claim to Swan Islands
31. Mexico vs. United States: 1919–63: Claims to El Chamizal along Texas border
32. Mexico vs. France 1919–32: Claim to Clipperton Island
33. Nicaragua vs. Colombia* 1919–28: Claim to archipelago of San Andreas and Providencia
34. Nicaragua vs. Colombia 1980–95: Claim to archipelago of San Andreas and Providencia
35. Nicaragua vs. Honduras 1919–60: Claim to territory along eastern section of the border
36. Nicaragua vs. United States 1969–70: Claim to Corn Island
37. Netherlands/Suriname vs. Britain/Guyana 1928–95: Claim to bordering territory near the New River (Netherlands is challenger 1928–74 and Suriname thereafter, UK is target 1928–65 and Guyana thereafter)

38. Netherlands/Suriname vs. France 1919–95: Claim to bordering territory of French Guiana near the Maroni river (Netherlands is challenger 1919–74 and Suriname thereafter)
39. Panama vs. Costa Rica 1919–41: Claim to border between coridilleras and Caribbean Sea
40. Panama vs. United States 1923–77: Claims to restore full sovereignty over the Canal Zone
41. Paraguay vs. Argentina* 1919–45: Claims to border along Pilcomayo river
42. Paraguay vs. Brazil* 1919–27: Claims to boundary line along bordering Paraguay river and islands
43. Peru vs. Chile 1919–29: Claims to Tacna and Arica
44. Peru vs. Colombia* 1919–34: Claims to territory in Leticia and Loreto regions
45. Peru vs. Ecuador* 1919–42: Claims to border in Maranon region
46. United States vs. Canada 1973–95: Claims to Seal Island and North Rock in the Gulf of Maine and Bay of Fundy
47. Uruguay vs. Argentina* 1919–73: Claims to islands in the Rio de la Plata river and boundary line in the river
48. Uruguay vs. Brazil 1919–95: Claim to Brasilera Island and boundary line in the Arroyo de la Invernda area
49. Venezuela vs. Britain 1919–42: Claim to the island of Patos
50. Venezuela vs. Britain/Guyana 1951–95: Claims to the Essequibo region (UK is target 1951–65 and Guyana thereafter)
51. Venezuela vs. Colombia* 1919–24: Claims along southern section of border including the La Guajira Peninsula

Case summaries of territorial disputes in the Americas

In this section a case history is presented for each of the disputes listed in section one. For each dispute information is provided on the territorial claims of the states and the outcome of the dispute. At the end of each case history is a list of sources and the complete citation for those sources can be found in the bibliography in section three of this Appendix.

> *Dispute Number*: 1
> *Countries*: Argentina vs. Great Britain
> *Years of Dispute*: 1919–95
> *Disputed Territory*: Argentina has disputed the British claim to sovereignty over the Falkland Islands (or Malvinas) and their dependencies which are located in the South Atlantic some 300 miles off the Argentine coastline since 1833. In the

post-World War II period Argentina began actively pressing its claim in 1965. The Argentine claim is based on geographic proximity and occupation of the islands prior to 1833. Britain, in turn, claims sovereignty as a result of its occupation of the islands since 1833 and because the expressed preference of the local population is to remain under British rule.

Outcome of Dispute: The conflicting claims to sovereignty over the islands persist. Multiple rounds of negotiations were held between the mid-1960s and the early 1980s but no settlement was reached. In 1982 Argentina and Britain went to war when Argentina attempted to seize the islands, but Argentine military forces were compelled to withdraw after a successful British counter-attack. Since 1982 there has been no change in the position of either side on the basic issue of sovereignty despite several rounds of talks. Trade relations, however, were resumed between the two countries in the course of the mid-1980s and since 1990 full diplomatic relations have been restored and the two countries have cooperated on joint fishing rights around the disputed islands.

Sources: *Boundary and Security Bulletin 1993–95*; Calvert 1982; Child 1985; Davis 1977; Ireland 1938; Kinney 1989; Waldock 1948.

Dispute Number: 2
Countries: Argentina vs. Chile
Years of Dispute: 1919–95
Disputed Territory: Three areas have been in dispute between the two countries. The claims of Argentina have a long history that can be traced back to each country's independence from Spain in the early nineteenth century. At the time of independence the borders between the two former Spanish provinces in certain regions were only vaguely, or even inaccurately, defined by treaties and agreements. As a result, the two newly independent countries presented differing interpretations of where their common border was located. Agreements signed in 1881 and 1902 failed to resolve disputes in three regions. The first area of contention centered on a small strip of territory approximately forty-five miles in length along the north–south Andean border referred to as the Palena region. The second area centered on the Laguno del Desierto region along the southern portion of the Andean frontier. The third and most contentious area of dispute involved a group of small

islands – primarily Picton, Nueva, and Lennox – at the southern tip of the continent in the Beagle Channel.

Outcome of Dispute: The disputes over the Palena and the Laguna
del Desierto regions were not a source of open and acute conflict after the mid-1960s, when British arbitration helped resolve many of the disputes; a comprehensive settlement, however, was not reached over all of the disputed territory in each
region. It was not until August 1991 that an agreement was
signed between the two countries settling almost all points
of contention through mutual concessions, except for small
sections of the Laguna del Desierto. It was agreed, however,
that the remaining dispute in this region would be submitted
to a panel of judges from the OAS for a final decision. Both
countries submitted their claims to the panel in August 1993
and a ruling issued in the fall of 1995 on terms favorable to
Argentina settled the dispute. The dispute over islands in the
Beagle Channel, however, was resolved in November 1984 in
a Treaty of Peace and Friendship signed by the two countries.
A panel of former ICJ judges had issued a ruling in 1977 favoring Chile, but Argentina refused to accept the panel's decision.
Papal mediation eventually helped bring about an agreement.
In the 1984 treaty Argentina recognized Chilean sovereignty
over the disputed islands, but Chile did accept tight restrictions on its maritime rights to the Atlantic in close proximity
to the islands.

Sources: Barros 1970; *Boundary and Security Bulletin 1993–95*;
Burr 1965; Butterworth 1976; Encina 1959; Espinosa Moraga
1969; Fitte 1978; Garrett 1985; *International Boundary Study*
(#101); Lagos Carmona 1966; Lanus 1984; Levene 1984;
Moreno 1961; *Relaciones Chileno-Argentinas, La Controversia
del Canal Beagle*; Sepulveda, 1960.

Dispute Number: 3, 41
Countries: Argentina vs. Paraguay and vice versa
Years of Dispute: 1919–45
Disputed Territory: Argentina and Paraguay disputed sections
of their border which had originally been established by the
Spanish under colonial rule. Several treaties, dating back to
1811, had been signed in attempts to settle the border dispute.
In 1856 Argentina recognized Paraguayan independence and
sovereignty but no agreement was reached on a final adjustment of the disputed sections of the border. Paraguay challenged Argentina, Brazil, and Uruguay in the War of Triple

Alliance (1866–70). This war was concluded with a border treaty that was signed by the disputants in 1875 but was rejected by Paraguay. In an 1876 border treaty, Paraguay relinquished its claim to Misiones and Chaco between the Pilcomayo and Tenco-Bermego rivers in exchange for sovereignty over northern Chaco Boreal between the Bahia Negra and Verde river. The question of disputed sovereignty over the Chaco Boreal between the Verde and Pilcomayo rivers was submitted to US arbitration. In 1878 President Hayes awarded the entire area south of the main branch of the Pilcomayo river to Paraguay but problems arose in interpreting the award. In 1905 Argentina and Paraguay signed an agreement, which was modified in 1907, for a committee to study the border at the Pilcomayo river. The committee report was the focus of talks in the 1920s but no further efforts towards settling the dispute were taken until 1939.

Outcome of Dispute: On 1 June 1945 the Supplementary Treaty of Definitive Boundaries was signed by the two countries. The treaty delimited the border in Pilcomayo between Punto Horqueta and Salto Palmer, where no fixed water course existed. The treaty was ratified by both countries shortly thereafter in 1945 (Argentina in July and by Paraguay in August).

Sources: Biger 1995; Davis 1977; *International Boundary Study* (#166); Ireland 1938; *Keesing's 1945*; Marchant 1944.

Dispute Number: 4, 47
Countries: Argentina vs. Uruguay and vice versa
Years of Dispute: 1919–73
Disputed Territory: The Uruguay river and the Rio de la Plata were considered to form in principle the boundary between Argentina and Uruguay since the preliminary Peace Convention of August 1828 that was signed by the two countries. A treaty to delimit the boundary was signed in September 1916 but neither country ratified the agreement. The dispute centered on exactly where the boundary between the two countries should be located along the Rio de la Plata river, including sovereignty over several islands and rights to oil deposits under the river. Uruguay's position was that the boundary should be located at the geographic center of the river, while Argentina insisted that the boundary should follow the deep channel.

Outcome of Dispute: A partial agreement was reached in April 1961 when a treaty was signed allocating islands between the two countries in the Uruguay river. Following agreements on joint development of oil resources, a general settlement was concluded in November of 1973. The treaty contained the following provisions: (a) the center of the Rio de la Plata river was accepted as the boundary, (b) international use of the river channels was established, and (c) possession of various small islands was determined.

Sources: Biger 1995; Bruno 1981; Del Castillo Laborde 1996; Espiell 1963; *International Boundary Study* (#68); Ireland 1938; Lanus 1984; Lichtschein 1969; Marchant 1944; Taboada 1969.

Dispute Number: 5
Countries: Bolivia vs. Argentina
Years of Dispute: 1919–25
Disputed Territory: The border dispute between Bolivia and Argentina can be traced back to the early nineteenth century. A treaty of friendship, commerce, and navigation was signed by the leaders of both countries in 1868, but was later rejected by Bolivia. In 1889, a boundary treaty was signed at Buenos Aries; it was ratified by Bolivia in 1889 and by Argentina in 1891 with modifications. A final treaty was ratified in 1893 by Bolivia. In 1899 demarcation efforts began but eventually broke down as Bolivia disputed sections of the border in the Chaco district along the Pilocomayo river.
Outcome of Dispute: A border treaty was signed on 9 July 1925 between the two countries which delimited the entire border and settled all disputed sections on terms largely in favor of Argentina.
Sources: Biger 1995; Fifer 1972; *International Boundary Study* (#162); Ireland 1938; Marchant 1944; *Survey of International Affairs 1925* (vol. 2).

Dispute Number: 6
Countries: Bolivia vs. Chile
Years of Dispute: 1919–95
Disputed Territory: Bolivia has sought a territorial outlet to the Pacific Ocean ever since the loss of coastal territory to Chile in the Pacific War of 1879–84. Bolivia has called for a port in the region along the border between Chile and Peru in the Tacna and Arica provinces. While Chile has refused to cede the territory requested by Bolivia, it has granted Bolivia duty-free use of the ports of Africa and Antofagasta and of the railroads connecting them.

Outcome of Dispute: The two countries, along with Peru, have exchanged proposals for a resolution of the issue, particularly since the mid-1970s. At one point Chile proposed to grant to Bolivia a corridor to the sea but only in exchange for Bolivian territorial and financial compensation. In 1987 Bolivia proposed that Chile cede 1,000 square miles of territory, which Chile rejected. By the end of 1992 Bolivia was moving in the direction of seeking a rapprochement with Chile, and there was discussion within Bolivia about possibly dropping its demand for a sea outlet. However, by the summer of 1993 Bolivia was reaffirming its demand for a sea outlet and criticizing Chile for refusing to adopt a more flexible policy. As a result, there had been no settlement of the dispute by the end of 1995.

Sources: Biger 1995; *Boundary and Security Bulletin 1993–95*; Carrasco 1920; Cusicanqui 1975; Girot, 1994; *International Boundary Study* (#67); Ireland 1938; Marchant 1944.

Dispute Number: 7
Countries: Bolivia vs. Paraguay
Years of Dispute: 1919–38
Disputed Territory: Following President Hayes' award of the territory between the Pilcomayo and the Verde rivers to Paraguay in 1878, Bolivia demanded a settlement for an old claim to the Chaco Boreal. Bolivia argued that this region had been given to them by the king of Spain in colonial times. In 1907, both states agreed to submit the dispute to Argentinian arbitration and to refrain from advancing beyond existing positions, but the protocol was never ratified by either party. Bolivia continued to advance into Chaco Boreal while negotiations continued. In 1913, the parties signed a protocol to negotiate the final treaty within two years and to accept the status quo position of 1907 until an agreement was reached. The protocol was later extended to June 1918. At that time, the treaty was once again postponed until a commission could decide on how to delimit the border. Armed hostilities ensued as both countries extended their reach into the Chaco Boreal. In 1933 Paraguay declared a state of war with Bolivia that lasted until 1936.

Outcome of Dispute: On 21 July 1938, the Treaty of Peace, Friendship, and Limits between the Republics of Bolivia and Paraguay was signed to settle the disputing claims to the Chaco Boreal. The area between the Pilcomayo and the Verde rivers was kept by Paraguay and the region north of Bahia Negra, which provided Bolivia access to the Paraguay river, was ceded to Bolivia. Paraguay gained extensive territorial concessions but Bolivia did secure free transit on the Paraguay river to the Atlantic.

Sources: Biger 1995; Farcau 1996; *Foreign Relations of the United States 1924, 1926–28* (vol. 1); *International Boundary Study* (#165); Ireland 1938; Marchant 1944; Rout 1970; *Survey of International Affairs 1930, 1936*; *The Chaco Peace Conference 1935*.

Dispute Number: 8
Countries: Brazil vs. Argentina
Years of Dispute: 1919–27
Disputed Territory: The governments of Brazil and Argentina signed an initial boundary treaty in 1857. Argentina, however, never ratified the treaty. In 1885, Brazil and Argentina created a commission to study the controversial rivers and territory between the Rio Pepri Gauzu and the Rio San Antonio. In 1895, President Cleveland was brought in to arbitrate the dispute. Progress towards a settlement was achieved with the signing of a treaty in 1898. In October 1910 another boundary convention was signed but never ratified by Argentina which amended the 1898 treaty but this treaty left unresolved the southern terminus of the border along the Uruguay river near Brazilera Island.
Outcome of Dispute: On 27 December 1927 a border agreement was signed which settled all outstanding questions through mutual concessions. Most importantly, the east bank of the Uruguay river was assigned to Brazil while the west bank went to Argentina.
Sources: Biger 1995; *International Boundary Study* (#168); Ireland 1938; Marchant 1944; *Survey of International Affairs 1930*.

Dispute Number: 9
Countries: Brazil vs. Bolivia
Years of Dispute: 1919–26
Disputed Territory: In July 1899 Brazilian rubber gatherers with the backing of the Brazilian government contested Bolivian control of territory in Puerto Acre. They seized the territory, although Bolivian authority was re-established in 1901. In the same year, Bolivia established the Bolivia Trading Company which introduced laborers into this area. Brazil retaliated

by closing all of the Amazon river to Bolivian commerce. In 1903 Brazilian colonists revolted against Bolivian authority again. Brazilian troops soon occupied the area. The Treaty of Petropolis signed in November 1903 concluded hostilities. In the treaty Brazil gained the territory of Acre while Bolivia received £2 million sterling and the use of territory for a railway to provide Bolivian access to the sea. Nevertheless, disputes persisted as Brazil maintained claims to islands in the Madeira river and along the Paraguay river.

Outcome of Dispute: On 25 December 1928, a final treaty was signed that settled all disputed claims. In the treaty the islands in the Madeira river along the frontier were divided according to which shore the islands were closest to and small sections of border were clarified to correct for errors in the 1903 treaty. Brazil received the entire area of Acre while Bolivia received railway access to a sea port. Brazil acknowledged Bolivia's claim to the entire western bank of the Paraguay river from Bahia Negra southward (which was occupied by Paraguay) whereas Bolivia confirmed Brazil's sovereignty over the east bank of the Paraguay river between the outlet of Bahia Negra and the mouth of the Apa.

Sources: Davis 1977; Ireland 1938; Marchant 1944; *Survey of International Affairs 1925* (vol. 2).

Dispute Number: 10
Countries: Brazil vs. Great Britain
Years of Dispute: 1919–26
Disputed Territory: By 1840 a dispute had emerged as Brazil contested the British policy of asserting control over the former Dutch area of Pirara. Brazil claimed a right to all territory that was originally Portuguese, while Britain claimed the right to all territories that once belonged to the Dutch. The dispute was submitted to Italian arbitration and the award of 1904 proposed delimitation of the border on terms favorable to the British. The 1904 award, however, failed to settle the dispute as Brazil asserted that errors and inaccuracies in the award rendered it unworkable.

Outcome of Dispute: On 22 April 1926 a general border treaty and boundary convention was signed to delimit the border by correcting the inaccuracies of the 1904 award. By the time delimitation had been completed in 1930, 5,400 miles of territory were assigned to Brazil and 7,600 miles to Britain.

Sources: Biger 1995; *British Command Papers, Nos. 3341, 3538; Great Britain Foreign Office Archives 1925*; Ireland 1938; Marchant 1944; *Survey of International Affairs 1925* (vol. 2), *1930.*

Dispute Number: 11, 14
Countries: Brazil vs. Colombia and vice versa
Years of Dispute: 1919–28
Disputed Territory: The dispute centered on the southern section of the border along the Amazon river where the borders of Brazil and Colombia converge with those of Peru. Conflicting claims were presented as far back as the 1820s. On 24 April 1907 Brazil and Colombia signed a treaty of boundaries and navigation, which defined the border from Cuchy Rock to the mouth of the Apaporis but left open the question of the very southern section border until Colombia resolved its border conflicts with Peru and Ecuador. In 1922 Brazil protested against the terms of the recently negotiated border treaty between Colombia and Peru. Brazil argued that the territory that was being allocated in this treaty included sections of the disputed border between Brazil and Colombia.
Outcome of Dispute: In 1925 Brazil withdrew its objections to the 1922 treaty following US arbitration. Shortly after the exchange of treaty ratifications by Colombia and Peru in 1928 a final border treaty was signed in November of that year in which both sides made territorial concessions.

Sources: Biger 1995; *Foreign Relations of the United States 1924–25* (vol. 1); Ireland 1938; Marchant 1944.

Dispute Number: 12, 42
Countries: Brazil vs. Paraguay and vice versa
Years of Dispute: 1919–27
Disputed Territory: After both Paraguay and Brazil gained independence, much of the border between the two states was disputed. By the second half of the nineteenth century the dispute centered on the location of the frontier in the Apa region along the Paraguay river as well as conflicting claims to islands in the river. Despite border treaties signed in the 1870s both countries retained claims against the other.
Outcome of Dispute: On 21 May 1927 a complementary boundary treaty was signed between the two countries. In the treaty the Paraguay river was delimited as the border up to the entrance of the Bahia Negra and all islands were allocated according to their proximity to respective shores.

Sources: Biger 1995; Ireland 1938; Marchant 1944; *Survey of International Affairs 1930*.

Dispute Number: 13
Countries: Canada vs. Great Britain
Years of Dispute: 1919–27
Disputed Territory: In 1907 Canada disputed the border between Labrador and Newfoundland (at that time a British colony). The Canadian government referred the matter to Judicial Committee of the Imperial Privy Council for resolution.
Outcome of Dispute: In March 1927 the Lords of the Judicial Committee of the Imperial Privy Council upheld almost all of the claims of Newfoundland and awarded limited territory to Canada.
Sources: *Documents on Canadian External Relations 1919–30* (vols. 3–4).

Dispute Number: 15, 33
Countries: Colombia vs. Nicaragua and vice versa
Years of Dispute: 1919–28
Disputed Territory: Nicaragua had claims to islands off the Mosquito Coast, including San Andreas, Providence, and Santa Catalina while Colombia had claims to the Corn islands and sections of the Mosquito coast. In 1925 Colombia proposed a settlement in which it would withdraw its claims and recognize Nicaraguan authority over the Mosquito coast and Great and Little Corn islands if Nicaragua recognized Colombian sovereignty over San Andreas and Providence islands. Nicaragua rejected this proposal and offered a counter-proposal that the Mosquito coast and Great and Little Corn islands would become Nicaraguan while San Andreas and Providence islands were to be open to arbitration. In 1927 Colombia proposed to grant San Andreas Archipelago to Colombia and the Corn islands and Mosquito coast to Nicaragua.
Outcome of Dispute: In March 1928 Colombia's 1927 proposal was accepted by Nicaragua and this agreement settled the dispute.
Sources: *Foreign Relations of the United States 1925, 1928* (vol. 1); Ireland 1938; *Survey of International Affairs 1930*.

Dispute Number: 16, 44
Countries: Colombia vs. Peru and vice versa
Years of Dispute: 1919–34

Disputed Territory: This dispute, whose history can be traced back to the early nineteenth century, centered on the Leticia and Loreto regions of the border between the two countries. In May of 1904 Colombia and Peru signed an arbitration treaty but Colombia withdrew from the arbitration because of heavy domestic pressure. In July 1906 the two countries agreed to a treaty in which both sides were to withdraw from the disputed areas. Colombia withdrew but many Peruvian rubber companies stayed and pushed into Colombian territory. In March 1922 a treaty on boundaries and free rivers drawn up by Peru and Colombia provided the basis for a settlement of the border dispute in which Leticia would be ceded to Colombia while Loreto would be given to Peru. Opposition to the treaties in both countries, however, prevented their full and complete implementation. By the fall of 1932 the dispute over Leticia had escalated to a military confrontation threatening war which prompted direct intervention by the League of Nations.

Outcome of Dispute: An agreement was reached in May 1934 between the two states in accordance with the terms of the treaty of 1922. As a result, Peru agreed that most of Leticia would become Colombian territory.

Sources: Biger 1995; Brecher and Wilkenfeld 1997; *Foreign Relations of the United States 1919* (vol. 1); Ireland 1938; Marchant 1944; *Survey of International Affairs 1930, 1933*.

Dispute Number: 17
Countries: Colombia vs. United States
Years of Dispute: 1919–28
Disputed Territory: Colombia disputed US control over the Serrana Banks Islands.
Outcome of Dispute: In April 1928 an agreement was reached in which Colombia recognized US sovereignty over the islands but was granted fishing rights in the waters around the islands.
Sources: *Foreign Relations of the United States 1919* (vol. 1), *1928* (vol. 2); Ireland 1941.

Dispute Number: 18, 51
Countries: Colombia vs. Venezuela and vice versa
Years of Dispute: 1919–24
Disputed Territory: Colombia and Venezuela had disputed territory in the Goajira Peninsula since they both gained independence. Repeated efforts at a negotiated settlement were

attempted but no agreement was reached. In 1883 the dispute was submitted to the Spanish and in 1891 the Spanish awarded the whole peninsula to Colombia. While both governments accepted the award in 1894 subsequent efforts to demarcate the border resulted in new disputes emerging over many small sections of the border. Colombia was willing to cede some of the peninsula to Venezuela, but the Colombian Congress would not approve. In 1894 the Spanish line was accepted and a demarcation committee was established but no further agreements were reached.

Outcome of Dispute: In 1917 a Swiss Federal Council was named to arbitrate the conflict and the commission issued a series of rulings between 1922 and 1924 that resolved all of the remaining disputes. In accepting the Swiss rulings both Colombia and Venezuela settled the dispute on the basis of mutual territorial concessions.

Sources: Biger 1995; Ireland 1938; Marchant 1944.

Dispute Number: 19
Countries: Cuba vs. United States
Years of Dispute: 1959–95
Disputed Territory: Following Fidel Castro's assumption of power in Cuba, the Cuban leader has condemned the US military base at Guantanamo as an illegal occupation of Cuban territory and has demanded that the United States withdraw from the base. The United States has countered that it has full jurisdiction and control over the base and its surrounding territory (117 square miles), based on treaties signed with Cuba in 1903 and 1934, and that it has no intention of withdrawing. The Cuban claim to Guantanamo was reaffirmed in 1976 when, by referendum, a provision was included in the Cuban constitution declaring that all international treaties signed under conditions of inequality and pressure were null and void.

Outcome of Dispute: The dispute remains deadlocked in stalemate. The United States continues to use the base at Guantanamo and has given no indication that it intends to change its policy despite continuing Cuban calls for complete withdrawal.

Sources: *Foreign Relations of the United States 1958–60* (vol. 6), *1961–63* (vol. 10); *Keesing's 1959–95*; *New York Times 1959–95*.

Dispute Number: 20, 26
Countries: Dominican Republic vs. Haiti and vice versa
Years of Dispute: 1919–35

Disputed Territory: By the 1870s the two countries began efforts to define a common boundary and in 1874 signed a treaty which defined the border in general terms. Nevertheless, disputes quickly developed and persisted for decades over the meaning and interpretation of the 1874 treaty. By the early 1900s the dispute had become centered on questions relating to jurisdiction over the River Massacre and rival claims to Lake El Fundo and surrounding territories. Plans to submit the dispute to The Hague were never implemented. In 1929 the governments established border commissions to try and resolve the remaining areas of dispute.

Outcome of Dispute: In February 1935 the presidents of the two countries signed an agreement that finally settled all rival claims. In the agreement both parties were required to make concessions.

Sources: Biger 1995; *Foreign Relations of the United States 1920–31* (vol. 1); Ireland 1941; Marchant 1944.

Dispute Number: 21, 45
Countries: Ecuador vs. Peru and vice versa
Years of Dispute: 1919–42
Disputed Territory: Since their independence in the early nineteenth century Ecuador and Peru had claimed large sections of the Amazon Basin of northern Peru known as the Orient. For Ecuador, control of the disputed territory would have provided direct access to the Amazon river and therefore the Atlantic Ocean. The territories in dispute covered some 125,000 square miles and included the Amazon and Maranon rivers and Peru's primary oil-producing region.

Outcome of Dispute: On 29 January 1942 the Protocol of Peace Friendship and Boundaries terminated military hostilities between the two states and settled the disputed border. The protocol assigned to Peru almost all of the territory that it claimed and had seized during the military conflict of 1941. As a result, Ecuador failed to gain direct access to the Amazon and lost much of the territory it had claimed in the Orient, including territory near its oil-producing areas.

Sources: Biger 1995; Brecher and Wilkenfeld 1997; Child 1985; Ireland 1938; Krieg 1986; Maier 1969; Marchant 1944; *The Question of Boundaries Between Peru and Ecuador*; *Survey of International Affairs 1925* (vol. 2), *1930*.

Dispute Number: 22
Countries: Ecuador vs. Peru
Years of Dispute: 1950–95
Disputed Territory: Since its independence in the nineteenth century Ecuador has laid claim to a large section of the Amazon Basin of northern Peru, known as the Orient, in an attempt to gain direct access to the Amazon river and therefore the Atlantic Ocean. The territory it claimed totaled 125,000 square miles and included the Amazon and Maranon rivers as well as Peru's primary oil-producing region. Following its defeat in armed conflict with Peru in 1941, Ecuador signed the Rio Protocol in 1942, which awarded most of the disputed territory to Peru and denied Ecuador direct access to the Amazon river. By 1950 Ecuador was openly calling for the revision of the Rio Protocol based upon (a) the discovery of the Rio Cenepa river which was not a part of the Protocol and, if controlled by Ecuador, would provide it with access to the Amazon river, and (b) the charge that the Protocol was invalid because it had been signed under duress. In 1960 Ecuador unilaterally declared the Rio Protocol null and void and called on Peru to reopen border negotiations. Peru, however, has maintained that the Rio Protocol remains in force and that therefore there is no dispute over the delimitation of the border between the two countries.

Outcome of Dispute: The dispute persists because Peru has not been willing to negotiate with Ecuador on a revision of the Rio Protocol. Militarized confrontations along the border occurred in 1991, but some movement towards a possible settlement did take place during late 1991 until early 1993. Peru offered joint economic development projects and navigation rights to Ecuador on the Amazon, and the two countries were working on an agreement for mediation by the Vatican and the possibility of permitting an outside expert to help resolve the dispute. The apparent movement towards a more accommodative position by Peru, however, ended when the Peruvian president announced in September 1993 and again in March 1994 that the Rio Protocol remained fully in force and should not be revised. There has been no settlement or change in the border by 1995.

Sources: Allcock 1992; Biger 1995; *Boundary and Security Bulletin 1993–95*; *Keesing's 1980–95*; Krieg 1986.

Dispute Number: 23, 28
Countries: El Salvador vs. Honduras and vice versa
Years of Dispute: 1919–92
Disputed Territory: The two countries disputed numerous small
    sections of their land border as well as sovereignty over islands
    in the Gulf of Fonseca. The dispute had a long history going
    back to the nineteenth century. In particular, the provisions of
    an 1884 border convention were the center of conflict.
Outcome of Dispute: The dispute was settled with an Interna-
    tional Court of Justice judgement in September 1992. Hon-
    duras was awarded about two-thirds of the land border in dis-
    pute while El Salvador was awarded two of the three islands in
    dispute.
Sources: Biger 1995; Blanco 1991; *Case Concerning the Land and
    Maritime Frontier Issue: El Salvador/Honduras 1992*; Ireland
    1938; *Keesing's 1969–92*; Marchant 1944.

Dispute Number: 24
Countries: Guatemala vs. Great Britain
Years of Dispute: 1936–95
Disputed Territory: Guatemala had claimed sovereignty over the
    neighboring territory of Belize (formerly British Honduras)
    since its independence from Spain in the mid-nineteenth cen-
    tury. Guatemala claimed Belize on the grounds that it had in-
    herited the territory (8,866 square miles) from Spain. In 1859
    Guatemala signed a treaty with Britain recognizing British
    sovereignty over Belize and delimiting the border. Adherence
    to the treaty was contingent upon the building of a road across
    the jungle from Guatemala to the Caribbean coast (article 7).
    By 1936 Guatemala officially claimed that Britain had nullified
    the Boundary Treaty of 1859 by failing to meet the require-
    ments of article 7. In turn, Britain has denied that it bears sole
    responsibility for the failure to implement article 7. Further-
    more, Britain has maintained that the colony had the right to
    self-determination and that the population favored indepen-
    dence as opposed to annexation by Guatemala.
Outcome of Dispute: Despite periodic rounds of talks between
    the two countries in the 1960s and 1970s, a negotiated settle-
    ment could not be reached providing for the independence of
    Belize on terms acceptable to Guatemala. Accordingly, Britain
    went ahead with plans for independence, which was achieved
    by Belize in 1981. By 1983 Guatemala had greatly reduced the

size of its territorial claims against Belize, and by 1989 relations between the two countries had improved. In mid-1990 it was agreed that a joint commission would be formed to draft a treaty in which Guatemala would recognize Belize independence and in late 1992 the president of Guatemala decided to recognize Belize officially. Guatemala, however, still maintained limited claims to territory along the border through 1995.

Sources: Bianchi 1959; Biger 1995; Bloomfield 1953; *Boundary and Security Bulletin 1993–95*; *Controversy Between Guatemala and Great Britain Relative to the Convention of 1859 on Territorial Matters*; *Foreign Relations of the United States 1937* (vol. 5), *1939* (vol. 5), *1940* (vol. 5); Ireland 1938; *Keesing's 1946–95*; Mendoza 1959; "The Belize Controversy between Great Britain and Guatemala"; Zammit 1978.

Dispute Number: 25, 29
Countries: Guatemala vs. Honduras and vice versa
Years of Dispute: 1919–33
Disputed Territory: Both states claimed territory along the length of the border with the conflicting claims dating back to the 1840s. A convention of 1904 called for a boundary commission to settle the remaining areas of dispute but repeated efforts failed by 1920.
Outcome of Dispute: Both countries signed a border treaty in July 1930 which established provisions for arbitration. In January 1933 an arbitration award was accepted by both sides in which mutual concessions were required. The border was fully demarcated between 1933 and 1936.
Sources: *Foreign Relations of the United States 1919–21* (vol. 1), *1923* (vol. 1), *1928–30* (vol. 1), *1932* (vol. 5), Ireland 1941; Marchant 1944;

Dispute Number: 27
Countries: Haiti vs. the United States
Years of Dispute: 1919–95
Disputed Territory: Haiti maintains claims to sovereignty over Navassa Island which the US rejects.
Outcome of Dispute: There has been no resolution of the dispute with both sides maintaining their claims.
Sources: Allcock 1992; *Foreign Relations of the United States 1932* (vol. 5); Ireland 1941.

Dispute Number: 30
Countries: Honduras vs. United States
Years of Dispute: 1921–71
Disputed Territory: Honduras claimed sovereignty over the Swan Islands which the United States had secured control over after signing a lease agreement in 1863.
Outcome of Dispute: In a November 1971 agreement the United States terminated its lease and returned the island, restoring full sovereignty to Honduras.
Sources: *Foreign Relations of the United States 1935* (vol. 5), *1938–40* (vol. 5), *1948* (vol. 9); Ireland 1941; *US Department of State Bulletin* (15 December 1969); *United States Treaties and Other International Agreements 1972, Part 3.*

Dispute Number: 31
Countries: Mexico vs. United States
Years of Dispute: 1919–63
Disputed Territory: The controversy over the El Chamizal territory began in 1895 due to the shifting course of the Rio Grande and the problems this created for defining the border area near El Paso. In 1910 Mexico and the US agreed to arbitration but the tribunal's award, which favored Mexico, was rejected by the US in 1911. Several rounds of negotiations before and after World War II failed to resolve the dispute.
Outcome of Dispute: In August 1963 the dispute was settled by a treaty in which both sides made territorial concessions with the US conceding more than Mexico.
Sources: *Foreign Relations of the United States 1925* (vol. 2), *1929–30* (vol. 3), *1933* (vol. 5); Gregory 1963; Ireland 1941; Jessup 1973; Lamborn and Mumme 1988; Liss 1965; Wilson 1980.

Dispute Number: 32
Countries: Mexico vs. France
Years of Dispute: 1919–32
Disputed Territory: In 1898 a dispute arose over sovereign rights to Clipperton Island with Mexico calling on France to give up its control of the island. In 1909 the two countries agreed that the King of Italy would arbitrate the dispute.
Outcome of Dispute: In January 1931 the arbitration award by Victor Emmanuel affirmed French claims to sovereign rights and by December 1932 Mexico had accepted the unfavorable decision.

Sources: Ireland 1941; "Judicial Decisions Involving Questions of International Law, France-Mexico"; Skaggs 1989.

Dispute Number: 34
Countries: Nicaragua vs. Colombia
Years of Dispute: 1980–95
Disputed Territory: In 1980 Nicaragua declared null and void a 1928 treaty establishing Colombian sovereignty over the Caribbean archipelago of San Andras and Providencia. Nicaragua argued that the 1928 treaty was invalid because it had been imposed under pressure by the US. Colombia argued that the issue of the archipelago was settled in the 1928 treaty and was not open to change.
Outcome of Dispute: There has been no resolution of the dispute.
Sources: Allcock 1992; Biger 1995; *Boundary and Security Bulletin 1993–95*; *Keesing's 1980–95*.

Dispute Number: 35
Countries: Nicaragua vs. Honduras
Years of Dispute: 1919–60
Disputed Territory: In 1906 an arbitration award by the king of Spain awarded much of the disputed territory along the north-eastern border of Nicaragua to Honduras. Nicaragua, however, expressed reservations and refused to comply with the terms of the award. Repeated efforts at settling the dispute through negotiations were attempted in the inter-war period with the US acting as a mediator. Honduras insisted that Nicaragua must accept the validity of the 1906 award as the basis for a settlement but Nicaragua was unwilling to do this.
Outcome of Dispute: The discovery of oil in the disputed area threatened military hostilities between the two countries in the late 1950s. When Honduras strengthened administrative control over the disputed territory, Nicaragua opposed the move and both countries sent troops into the territory. In 1958 the dispute was taken up by the ICJ which upheld the 1906 decision in a judgement that was issued in November 1960. Nicaragua finally accepted the 1906 award and the dispute was settled.
Sources: Biger 1995; *Foreign Relations of the United States 1919–23* (vols. 1–2), *1929–31* (vol. 1), *1937–41* (vol. 5); Ireland 1941; Marchant 1944; Somarriba-Salazar 1957.

Dispute Number: 36
Countries: Nicaragua vs. United States
Years of Dispute: 1969–70
Disputed Territory: In 1914 the Bryan-Chamorro Treaty granted the US the right to lease the Corn Islands for 99 years and gave Nicaragua the right to develop an inter-oceanic canal in Nicaragua along with a naval base. In 1965 Nicaraguan President Schick declared that Nicaragua would seek the termination of the Bryan-Chamorro Treaty if the Nicaraguan canal site was rejected. In 1969 the US rejected the Nicaraguan site to build a canal and Nicaragua therefore pressed for the return of the Corn Islands.
Outcome of Dispute: In a July 1970 agreement the US returned the islands to Nicaragua.
Sources: *Convention with Nicaragua Terminating the Bryan-Chamorro Treaty of 1914*; Ireland 1941.

Dispute Number: 37
Countries: Netherlands/Suriname vs. Great Britain/Guyana
Years of Dispute: 1928–95
Disputed Territory: The Dutch prior to 1975 and Suriname since then have claimed a triangular area of land (approximately 6,000 square miles) with little economic value near the New river along the southern border of Guyana.
Outcome of Dispute: Movement towards a settlement in the 1930s was halted with the outbreak of World War II and intermittent negotiations in the post-war period have failed to resolve the dispute.
Sources: Allcock 1992; Biger 1995; *Great Britain Foreign Office Archives 1925–61*; *Keesing's 1970–95*.

Dispute Number: 38
Countries: Netherlands/Suriname vs. France
Years of Dispute: 1919–95
Disputed Territory: The Dutch prior to 1975 and Suriname since have claimed a triangular area of land (approximately 3,000 square miles) near the Maroni river along the southern border of French Guiana.
Outcome of Dispute: A proposed 1977 treaty called for Suriname to recognize French sovereignty over the disputed territory in return for French economic aid to develop resources in the disputed territory. The proposed treaty, however, has not been

pursued by Suriname since the late 1970s and the dispute therefore persists.

Sources: Allcock 1992; Henry 1981; *Keesing's 1980–95.*

Dispute Number: 39
Countries: Panama vs. Costa Rica
Years of Dispute: 1919–41
Disputed Territory: The boundary dispute between the two parties carried over from colonial days and centered in the sector of the border between the coridilleras and the Caribbean Sea. In 1900 President Loubet of France arbitrated the border dispute between Colombia and Costa Rica but neither party was willing to ratify his judgement. Panama inherited the dispute when it gained its independence in 1910. In 1913 the two parties submitted their cases to Chief Justice Edward White of the US to arbitrate the dispute. Costa Rica accepted his decision but Panama rejected it and repeated attempts at a negotiated settlement in the inter-war period failed.
Outcome of Dispute: On 1 May 1941 the border dispute was finally settled with a treaty that delimited the border and provided for a mixed border commission. The border line followed the terms agreed to in the proposed 1938 treaty and required mutual concessions. By 1944 the new border line had been demarcated.
Sources: Biger 1995; *Foreign Relations of the United States 1921, 1925, 1926, 1929, 1940* (vols. 1, 5); *International Boundary Study* (#156); Ireland, 1941; Marchant 1944; *Survey of International Affairs 1925* (vol. 2), *1930.*

Dispute Number: 40
Countries: Panama vs. United States
Years of Dispute: 1923–77
Disputed Territory: The Panamanian government desired complete sovereignty over the Panama Canal Zone. The United States exercised sovereignty over the Canal Zone based on a treaty signed in 1903, which granted the United States sovereign rights for 99 years.
Outcome of Dispute: After multiple rounds of negotiations and tentative agreements being signed since the 1950s, a general settlement was reached in 1977. In the treaty the two governments agreed that Panama would assume full sovereignty and operational control of the Canal Zone by the year 2000.

Sources: Farnsworth and McKenney 1983; *Foreign Relations of the United States 1924–26* (vol. 2); LaFeber 1978; Leonard 1993; *New York Times 1964–77*; Storrs 1977.

Dispute Number: 43
Countries: Peru vs. Chile
Years of Dispute: 1919–29
Disputed Territory: The dispute emerged in the 1880s as Peru laid claims to the territories of Tacna and Arica following Chilean efforts to assert more effective administrative control over the territories. Peru protested against these efforts and argued they violated the Treaty of Ancon. In 1895 the two nations tried to reach an agreement based on a plebiscite but they could not agree on the terms of the plebiscite and for the next three decades repeated attempts to agree on the terms of a plebiscite failed despite US mediation on many occasions.
Outcome of Dispute: A treaty signed in July 1929 settled the dispute with the two countries dividing the land between them with Peru gaining Tacna and Chile retaining Arica.
Sources: Biger 1995; *Foreign Relations of the United States 1919–22* (vol. 2); *International Boundary Study* (#65); Ireland 1938; Marchant 1944.

Dispute Number: 46
Countries: United States vs. Canada
Years of Dispute: 1973–95
Disputed Territory: The disputed territory between the US and Canada is Machias Seal Island and North Rock in the Bay of Fundy in the Gulf of Maine. The dispute centers on conflicting interpretations of treaties (1783 and 1814) and the Canadian claim is also based on the long-time exercise of unchallenged sovereignty over Machias Seal Island by British and Canadian authorities since the early nineteenth century.
Outcome of Dispute: There has been no settlement of the dispute.
Sources: *Cumulative Digest of the United States Practice in International Law 1981–1988* (vol. 2); *Digest of the United States Practice in International Law 1970–1980*; Smith and Thomas 1998.

Dispute Number: 48
Countries: Uruguay vs. Brazil
Years of Dispute: 1919–95
Disputed Territory: Two short sections of the border are contested by Uruguay. The first is the Arroyo de la Invernda area of

the Rio Quarai, and the second centers on islands situated at the confluence of the Rio Quarai and the Uruguay. A treaty signed in October 1851 delimited the border between the two countries, but the boundary disputes are based on opposing interpretations of the treaty by each country. According to the treaty the boundary follows the Cuchilla Negra to the headwaters of the Arroyo to the Rio Quarai. Brazil and Uruguay, however, identify different streams as the Arroyo de la Invernada, and thus the dispute centers on the area between the different streams as well as the sovereignty of Brasilera Island at the confluence of the Uruguay and the Rio Quarai. Uruguay claims that the boundary follows the more easterly rivers, while Brazil claims the more westerly rivers. Established boundary pillars favor the Brazilian position. The 1851 treaty states that islands in the Rio Quarai at its embouchure into the Uruguay belong to Brazil, but Uruguay claims that Brasilera Island is in the Uruguay river and does not belong to Brazil.

Outcome of Dispute: The dispute has not been a source of acute conflict between the two countries, and periodic talks have been held but no settlement has been reached.

Sources: *International Boundary Study* (#170); Ireland 1938; Marchant 1944; *Survey of International Affairs 1930*.

Dispute Number: 49
Countries: Venezuela vs. Great Britain
Years of Dispute: 1919–42
Disputed Territory: The dispute between the two nations was over Patos Island. The dispute dates back to the mid-nineteenth century with Venezuela claiming sovereignty over the island.

Outcome of Dispute: In February 1942 Britain and Venezuela signed a treaty in which the UK conceded sovereignty to Venezuela and in return Venezuela agreed to cooperate with the British on anti-submarine warfare in the Gulf of Paria.

Sources: *Great Britain Foreign Office Archives 1941–42*; Ireland 1938.

Dispute Number: 50
Countries: Venezuela vs. Great Britain/Guyana
Years of Dispute: 1951–95
Disputed Territory: Venezuela claims a large section of Guyanese territory (50,000 square miles) west of the Essequibo river, which includes areas rich in oil deposits. In 1899 the territory

in dispute was awarded by a court of arbitration to the British. In 1951 Venezuela publicly questioned the validity of the award and reopened the border issue, and in 1962 Venezuela officially announced that it no longer would accept the 1899 ruling.

Outcome of Dispute: The June 1970 Protocol of Port of Spain signed by Britain, Guyana, and Venezuela placed a twelve-year moratorium on the territorial dispute. Venezuela announced in December 1981, however, that it would not extend the moratorium and that it still claimed the Essequibo territory. United Nations mediated talks were held in the mid-1980s without a breakthrough, but by the end of the 1980s relations between the two countries had improved as economic ties were developed. Nevertheless, Venezuela maintains its claim to the Essequibo territory.

Sources: Allcock 1992; Biger 1995; Braveboy-Wagner 1984; *Great Britain Foreign Office Archives 1957–60*; *Keesing's 1962–95*.

Bibliography of sources listed in case summaries

Allcock, John, ed. (1992) *Border and Territorial Disputes*, 3rd ed. (Essex: Longman).

Barros, Mario (1970) *Historia Diplomatica de Chile 1541–1938* (Barcelona: Ediciones Ariel).

"The Belize Controversy between Great Britain and Guatemala" (1947) *British Yearbook of International Law*, 26: 406–9.

Bianchi, William (1959) *Belize: The Controversy between Guatemala and Great Britain over the Territory of British Honduras in Central America* (New York: Las Americas Publishing Co.).

Biger, Gideon (1995) *The Encyclopedia of International Boundaries* (New York: Facts on File).

Blanco, Geraldo Martinez (1991) *Enfoque Historio y Juridico de la Controversia Limitrofe entre Honduras y El Salvador* (Tegucigalpa: Universidad Nacional Autonoma De Honduras).

Bloomfield, Louis (1953) *The British Honduras–Guatemala Dispute* (Toronto: Carswell).

Boundary and Security Bulletin 1993–1995 (Durham: International Boundaries Research Unit, 1993–5).

Braveboy-Wagner, Jacqueline Anne (1984) *The Venezuela–Guyana Border Dispute* (Boulder: Westview Press).

Brecher, Michael and Jonathan Wilkenfeld (1997) *A Study of Crisis* (Ann Arbor: University of Michigan Press).

British Command Paper, No. 3341 (xxxi, 21) *Treaty and Convention Between Britain and Brazil for the Settlement of Boundary Between British Guiana and Brazil* (London: HMSO, 1929).

British Command Paper, No. 3538 (xxxi, 29) *Agreement Between Britain and Brazil for the Demarcation of the Boundary Between British Guiana and Brazil* (London: HMSO, 1930).

Bruno, José Luis (1981) *Actos Internacionales Uruguay–Argentina 1830–1980* (Montvideo: Ediciones del Institutio Artigas del Servicio Exterior).

Burr, Robert (1965) *By Reason or By Force* (Berkeley: University of California Press).

Butterworth, Robert (1976) *Managing Interstate Conflict* (Pittsburgh: University Center for International Studies).

Calvert, Peter (1982) *The Falkland Crisis: The Rights and the Wrongs* (New York: St. Martin's Press).

Carrasco, José (1920) *Bolivia's Case for the League of Nations* (London: Selwyn & Blount).

Case Concerning the Land Island and Maritime Frontier Issue: El Salvador/Honduras (1992) (Geneva: Reports of Judgments Advisory Opinions and Orders, International Court of Justice).

Chaco Peace Conference (1935) (Washington DC: Department of State, US Government Printing Office).

Child, Jack (1985) *Geopolitics and Conflict in South America* (New York: Praeger).

Controversy Between Guatemala and Great Britain Relative to the Convention of 1859 on Territorial Matters (1938) (Guatemala: Ministry of Foreign Affairs, Government of Guatemala).

Convention with Nicaragua Terminating the Bryan-Chamorro Treaty of 1914 (1971) (Washington DC: US Government Printing Office).

Cumulative Digest of the United States Practice in International Law 1981–1988 (1994) vol. 2 (Washington DC: Department of State, Office of the Legal Adviser, US Government Printing Office).

Cusicanqui, Jorge Escobari (1975) *The Diplomatic History of Bolivia* (Bolivia: La Paz Print).

Davis, Harold Eugene (1977) *Latin American Diplomatic History* (Baton Rouge: Louisiana State University Press).

Del Castillo LaBorde, Lilian (1996) "Legal Regime of the Rio de la Plata" *Natural Resources Journal*, 36, 2: 251–95.

Digest of the United States Practice in International Law 1977–1980 (1970–80) (Washington DC: Department of State, Office of the Legal Adviser, US Government Printing Office).

Documents on Canadian External Relations 1919–1930 (1970–1) vols. 3–4 (Ottawa: Department of External Affairs, Canada).

Encina, Francisco (1959) *La Cuestion de Limites entre Chile y Argentina disde la Independencia hasta el Tratado de 1881* (Santiago: Editorial Nascimento).

Espiell, Hector Gros (1963) "El Protocolo del Rio de la Plata" *Anuario Uruguayo de Derecho Internacional*, 2: 414–27.

Espinosa Moraga, Oscar (1969) *El Precio de la Paz Chileno-Argentina*, vol. 3 (Santiago: Editorial Nascimiento).

Farcau, Bruce (1996) *The Chaco War* (New York: Praeger).

Farnsworth, David and James Mckenney (1983) *US–Panama Relations, 1903–1978* (Boulder: Westview Press).

Fifer, Valerie (1972) *Bolivia, Land, Location, and Politics Since 1825* (Cambridge: Cambridge University Press).

Fitte, Ernesto (1978) *Los Limites con Chile*, 2nd ed. (Argentina: Editorial Plus Ultra).

Foreign Relations of the United States 1919–33, 1935, 1937–41, 1948, 1958–63 (1934–97) (Washington DC: Department of State, US Government Printing Office).

Garrett, James (1985) "The Begal Channel Dispute: Confrontation and Negotiation in the Southern Cone" *Journal of InterAmerican Studies and World Affairs*, 27: 81–109.

Girot, Pascal, ed. (1994) *The Americas* (London: Routledge).

Great Britain Foreign Office Archives:

Brazil vs. Britain (case #10), documents on relations between Brazil and British Guyana for 1925 in FO 371/10609.

Netherlands vs. Britain (case #37), documents on relations between Netherlands and British Guyana from 1925–61 beginning with FO 371/11085 and ending with FO 371/160713.

Venezuela vs. Britain (case #49), documents on relations between Venezuela and Britain from 1941–2 beginning with FO 371/26308 and ending with FO 371/30745.

Venezuela vs. Britain (case #50), documents on relations between Venezuela and British Guyana from 1957–60 beginning with FO 371/126740 and ending with FO 371/148666.

Gregory, Gladys (1963) "The Chamizal Settlement" *Southwestern Studies*, 1, 2: 1–52.

Henry, Arthur (1981) *La Guyane Française* (Cayenne: Le Mayouri, 1981).

International Boundary Study (1966–79) (Washington DC: The Geographer, Bureau of Intelligence and Research, US Department of State).

International Boundary Study. No. 65 Chile–Peru Boundary, 28 February 1966.

International Boundary Study. No. 67 Bolivia–Chile Boundary, 15 March 1966.

International Boundary Study. No. 68 Argentina–Uruguay Boundary, 30 May 1966.

International Boundary Study. No. 101 Argentina–Chile Boundary, 25 May 1970.

International Boundary Study. No. 156 Costa-Rica–Panama Boundary, 2 July 1976.

International Boundary Study. No. 162 Argentina–Bolivia Boundary, 8 November 1977.

International Boundary Study. No. 165 Bolivia–Paraguay Boundary, 1 September 1978.

International Boundary Study. No. 166 Argentina–Paraguay Boundary, 30 January 1979.

International Boundary Study. No. 168 Argentina–Brazil Boundary, 10 May 1979.

International Boundary Study. No. 170 Brazil–Uruguay Boundary, 23 November 1979.

Ireland, Gordon (1938) *Boundaries, Possessions, and Conflict in South America* (Cambridge: Harvard University Press, 1938).

(1941) *Boundaries, Possessions, and Conflicts in Central and North America and the Caribbean* (Cambridge: Harvard University Press).

Jessup, Philip (1973) "El Chamizal" *American Journal of International Law*, 67: 423–45.

"Judicial Decisions Involving Questions of International Law France-Mexico" (1932) *American Journal of International Law*, 26: 390–4.

Keesing's Contemporary Archives 1936–86 (London: Keesing's Publications, 1936–86).

Keesing's Record of World Events 1987–95 (London: Keesing's Publications, 1987–95).

Kinney, Douglas (1989) *National Interests/National Honor* (New York: Praeger).

Krieg, William (1986) *Ecuador–Peruvian Rivalry in the Upper Amazon*, 2nd ed. (Washington DC: Department of State, US Government Printing Office).

LaFeber, Walter (1978) *The Panama Canal* (New York: Oxford University Press).

Lagos Carmona (1966) *Guillermo: Las Fronteras con Chile* (Santiago: Empresa Editora Zig Zag).

Lamborn, Alan and Stephan Mumme (1988) *Statecraft, Domestic Politics, and Foreign Policy Making* (Boulder: Westview Press).

Lanus, Juan Archibaldo (1984) *De Chapultepec a Beagle, Politica Exterior Argentina 1945–1980* (Buenos Aires: Emece Editores).

Latin American Weekly Report 1979–95 (London: Latin American Newsletters, 1979–95).

Leonard, Thomas (1993) *Panama, the Canal, and the United States* (Claremont: Regina Books).

Levene, Gustavo Gabriel (1984) *Nueva Historia Argentina* (Buenos Aires: O. R. Sanchez Tenuelo).

Lichtschein, Domingo Sabate (1969) "El Acuerdo Saenz-Pena-Ramirez y los Problemas Juridicos del Rio de la Plata" *Estrategia*, 1: 89–95.

Liss, Sheldon (1965) *A Century of Disagreement* (Washington, DC: University Press of Washington, DC).

Maier, George (1969) "Ecuadorian–Peruvian Boundary Dispute" *American Journal of International Law*, 63, 1: 28–46.

Marchant, Alexander (1944) *Boundaries of the Latin American Republics* (Washington DC: Department of State, US Government Printing Office).

Mendoza, José Luis (1959) *Britain and Her Treaties on Belize* (Guatemala: Ministry for Foreign Affairs, Government of Guatemala).

Moreno, Ruiz (1961) *Historia de las Relaciones Exteriores Argentinas, 1810–1955* (Buenos Aires: Editorial Perrot).

New York Times, 1959–1995.

Question of Boundaries Between Peru and Ecuador (1936) (Baltimore: Reese Press).

Relaciones Chileno–Argentinas: La Controversia del Canal Beagle: Algunos Documentos Informativos (1978) (Geneva: Government of Chile).

Rout, Leslie B. Jr. (1970) *Politics of the Chaco Peace Conference, 1935–39* (Austin: University of Texas Press).

Sepulveda, Rodriguez and Juan Agustin (1960) *Chile en el Canal Beagle Mares Australes, Compendio Historico, Geografico y Juridico*, 2nd ed. (Valparaiso: Imprenta de la Armada).

Skaggs, Jimmy (1989) *Clipperton* (New York: Walker & Co.).

Smith, Robert and Bradford Thomas (1998) *Island Disputes and the Law of the Sea* (Durham: International Boundaries Research Unit).

Somarriba-Salazar, Jaime (1957) *Les Limites Entre Le Nicaragua et Honduras* (Leyde: A. W. Sijthoff's).

Spinner, Thomas (1984) *A Political and Social History of Guyana 1945–1983* (Boulder: Westview Press).

Storrs, Keith (1977) *A Chronology of Events Relating to Panama Canal* (Washington, DC: US Government Printing Office).

Survey of International Affairs 1920–36 (London: Oxford University Press, 1925–37).

Taboada, Diogenes (1969) "Las Relaciones Argentino–Uruguayas y su 'Status' Juridico" *Estrategia*, 1: 96–8.

US Department of State Bulletin December 15, 1969, vol. 61, no. 1590 (Washington DC: Department of State, US Government Printing Office, 1969).

United States Treaties and Other International Agreements 1972, Part 3 (Washington DC: Department of State, US Government Printing Office, 1973).

Waldock, C. H. M. (1948) "Disputed Sovereignty in the Falkland Islands Dependencies" *British Yearbook of International Law*, 25: 311–53.

Wilson, Larman (1980) "The Settlement of Boundary Disputes" *International and Comparative Law Quarterly*, 29, 1: 38–53.

Zammit, Ann (1978) *The Belize Issue* (London: Latin American Bureau, 1978).

Bibliography

The items listed in this bibliography refer to three general types of scholarly literatures: (a) existing theoretical and empirical work on the democratic peace, (b) theoretical works from political science and social psychology that we drew upon in developing the theoretical models of political institutions in Chapters 4–6, and (c) the literatures and sources that were consulted in designing, measuring, and empirically testing models of political institutions in Chapters 7–9. Bibliographies for the sources consulted in identifying and constructing the diplomatic and military histories of the 348 territorial disputes are located in Appendices B–F.

Achen, Christopher (1986) *The Statistical Analysis of Quasi-Experiments* (Berkeley: University of California Press).

Adler, Emanuel and Michael Barnett (1998) *Security Communities* (Cambridge: Cambridge University Press).

Ajzen, Icek (1989) "Attitudes, Structure and Behavior" in Anthony Pratkanis, Steven Breckler, and Anthony Greenwald eds., *Attitude Structure and Function* (Hillsdale, NJ: Lawrence Erlbaum Associates), 241–74.

Aldrich, John, John Sullivan, and Eugene Borgida (1989) "Foreign Affairs and Issue Voting: Do Presidential Candidates 'Waltz' Before a Blind Audience?" *American Political Science Review*, 83, 1: 123–41.

Alesina, Alberto and Howard Rosenthal (1995) *Partisan Politics, Divided Government, and the Economy* (Cambridge: Cambridge University Press).

Alt, James and Gary King (1994) "Transfers of Governmental Power: The Meaning of Time Dependence" *Comparative Political Studies*, 27, 2: 190–210.

Alvarez, R. Michael and Jonathan Nagler (1998) "When Politics and Models Collide: Estimating Models of Multiparty Elections" *American Journal of Political Science*, 21, 1: 55–96.

Alvarez, Mike, Jose Antonio Cheibub, Fernando Limongi, and Adam Przeworski (1996) "Classifying Political Regimes" *Studies in Comparative International Development*, 31, 2: 3–36.

Amemiya, Takeshi (1985) *Advanced Econometrics* (Cambridge: Harvard University Press).

Anderson, Lisa, ed. (1999) *Transitions to Democracy* (New York: Columbia University Press).

Annual Register 1920–95 (1959–96) (New York: Longmans, Green & Co., 1921–58, Longman).

Auerswald, David (1999) "Inward Bound" *International Organization*, 53, 3: 469–504.

(2000) *Disarmed Democracies: Domestic Institutions and the Use of Force* (Ann Arbor: University of Michigan Press).

Auvinen, Juha (1997) "Political Conflict in Less Developed Countries 1981–89" *Journal of Peace Research*, 34, 2: 177–95.

Axelrod, Robert (1984) *The Evolution of Cooperation* (New York: Basic Books).

(1986) "An Evolutionary Approach to Norms" *American Political Science Review*, 80, 4: 1095–1112.

Backman, Carl (1985) "Identity, Self-Presentation, and the Resolution of Moral Dilemmas: Towards a Social Psychological Theory of Moral Behavior" in Barry Schlenker ed., *The Self and Social Life* (New York: McGraw-Hill), 261–89.

Baldwin, David (1979) "Power Analysis and *World Politics*: New Trends Versus Old Tendencies" *World Politics*, 31, 2: 161–94.

(1985) *Economic Statecraft* (Princeton: Princeton University Press).

(1999) "Force, Fungibility and Influence" *Security Studies*, 8, 4: 173–82.

Banks, Arthur (1996) *Cross-Polity Time Series Data Archive* (Binghamton, NY: Department of Political Science).

Barnett, Michael (1992) *Confronting the Costs of War: Military Power, State, and Society in Egypt and Israel* (Princeton: Princeton University Press).

(1998) *Dialogues in Arab Politics Negotiations in Regional Order* (New York: Columbia University Press).

Barnett, Michael and Jack Levy (1991) "Domestic Sources of Alliances and Alignments: The Case of Egypt, 1962–73" *International Organization*, 45, 3: 369–95.

Bass, Gary Jonathan (2000) *Stay the Hand of Vengeance: The Politics of War Crime Tribunals* (Princeton: Princeton University Press).

Bates, Robert (1997) *Open-Economy Politics* (Princeton: Princeton University Press).

Beck, Nathaniel (1998) "Modeling Space and Time: The Event History Approach" in Elinor Scarbrough and Eric Ranenbaum, eds., *Research Strategies in the Social Sciences* (Oxford: Oxford University Press), 192–212.

Beck, Nathaniel, Jonathan Katz and Richard Tucker (1998) "Taking Time Seriously: Time-Series-Cross-Section Analysis with a Binary Dependent Variable" *American Journal of Political Science*, 42, 4: 1260–88.

Bennett, Andrew, Joseph Lepgold and Danny Unger (1994) "Burden-Sharing in the Persian Gulf War" *International Organization*, 48, 1: 39–76.

Bennett, Scott (1996) "Security, Bargaining, and the End of Interstate Rivalry" *International Studies Quarterly*, 40, 2: 157–84.

(1997) "Measuring Rivalry Termination, 1816–1992" *Journal of Conflict Resolution*, 41, 2: 227–54.

(1998) "Integrating and Testing Models of Rivalry Duration" *American Journal of Political Science*, 42, 4: 1200–32.

Bennett, D. Scott and Timothy Nordstrom (2000) "Foreign Policy Substitutability and Internal Economic Problems in Enduring Rivalries" *Journal of Conflict Resolution*, 44, 1: 33–61.

Bennett, Scott and Allan Stam (1996) "The Duration of Interstate Wars, 1816–1985" *American Political Science Review*, 90, 2: 239–57.

(1998) "The Declining Advantages of Democracy: A Combined Model of War Outcomes and Duration" *Journal of Conflict Resolution*, 42, 3: 344–66.

(2000) "Research Design and Estimator Choices in the Analysis of Interstate Dyads" *Journal of Conflict Resolution*, 44, 5: 653–85.

Benoit, Kenneth (1996) "Democracies Really Are More Pacific (in General)" *Journal of Conflict Resolution*, 40, 4: 636–57.

Benson, Michelle and Jacek Kugler (1998) "Power Parity, Democracy, and the Severity of Internal Violence" *Journal of Conflict Resolution*, 42, 2: 196–209.

Bercovitch, Jacob and Richard Jackson (1997) *International Conflict: A Chronological Encyclopedia of Conflicts and Their Management, 1945–1995* (Washington, DC: Congressional Quarterly).

Berinsky, Adam (1999) "The Two Faces of Public Opinion" *American Journal of Political Science*, 43, 4: 1209–30.

Bidwell, Robin (1973) *Bidwell's Guide to Government Ministries: The Major Powers and Western Europe 1900–1971* (London: Frank Cass & Company Limited).

Bienen, Henry and Nicolas Van de Walle (1991) *Of Time and Power* (Stanford: Stanford University Press).

Binder, Sarah (1999) "The Dynamics of Legislative Gridlock, 1947–96" *American Political Science Review*, 93, 3: 519–33.

Bond, Jon and Richard Fleisher (1990) *The President in the Legislative Arena* (Chicago: University of Chicago Press).

Brace, Paul and Barbara Hinckley (1992) *Following the Leader: Opinion Polls and the Modern Presidents* (New York: Basic Books).

Bratton, Michael and Nicolas Van de Walle (1997) *Democratic Experiments in Africa* (Cambridge: Cambridge University Press).

Braumoeller, Bear (1997) "Deadly Doves" *International Studies Quarterly*, 41, 3: 375–402.

Brecher, Michael (1993) *Crises in World Politics* (New York: Pergamon Press).

Brecher, Michael and Jonathan Wilkenfeld (1997) *A Study of Crisis* (Ann Arbor: University of Michigan Press).

Bremer, Stuart (1992) "Dangerous Dyads" *Journal of Conflict Resolution*, 36, 2: 309–41.

(1993) "Democracy and Militarized Interstate Conflict, 1816–1965" *International Interactions*, 18, 3: 231–49.

Breslauer, Geroge (1982) *Khrushchev and Brezhnev as Leaders: Building Authority in Soviet Politics* (Boston: Allen & Unwin).

Brewer, Marlynn and Norman Miller (1996) *Intergroup Relations* (New York: Brook's/Cole).

Brody, Richard (1991) *Assessing the President: The Media, Elite Opinion, and Public Support* (Stanford: Stanford University Press).

Bueno de Mesquita, Bruce (1981) *The War Trap* (New Haven: Yale University Press).

Bueno de Mesquita, Bruce and David Lalman (1992) *War and Reason* (New Haven: Yale University Press).

Bueno de Mesquita, Bruce, James Morrow, Randolph Siverson, and Alastair Smith (1999) "An Institutional Explanation of the Democratic Peace" *American Political Science Review*, 93, 4: 791–808.

Bueno de Mesquita, Bruce, James Morrow, and Ethan Zorick (1997) "Capabilities, Perceptions, and Escalation" *American Political Science Review*, 91, 1: 15–27.

Bueno de Mesquita, Bruce and Randolph Siverson (1995) "War and the Survival of Political Leaders" *American Political Science Review*, 89, 4: 841–55.

(1997) "Nasty or Nice? Political Systems, Endogenous Norms, and the Treatment of Adversaries" *Journal of Conflict Resolution*, 41, 1: 175–99.

Bueno de Mesquita, Bruce, Randolph Siverson, and Gary Woller (1992) "War and the Fate of Regimes" *American Political Science Review*, 86, 3: 638–46.

Byman, Daniel and Stephen Van Evera (1998) "Why They Fight" *Security Studies* 7, 3: 1–50.

Calvert, Peter (1970) *A Study of Revolution* (Oxford: Clarendon Press).

Carment, David and Patrick James (1997) "Secession and Irredenta in World Politics: The Neglected Interstate Dimension" in David Carment and Patrick James eds., *Wars in the Midst of Peace: The International Politics of Ethnic Conflict* (Pittsburgh: University of Pittsburgh Press), 194–231.

Carment, David, Patrick James, and Dane Rowlands (1997) "Ethnic Conflict and Third Party Intervention: Riskiness, Rationality, and Commitment" in Gerald Schneider and Patrica Weitsman eds., *Enforcing Cooperation: Risky States Intergovernmental Management of Conflict* (New York: St. Martin's Press), 104–31.

Cederman, Lars-Erik (2001) "Back to Kant: Reinterpreting the Democratic Peace as a Macrohistorical Learning Process" *American Political Science Review*, 95, 1: 15–32.

Cha, Victor (2000) "Abandonment, Entrapment, and Neoclassical Realism in Asia: The United States, Japan, and Korea" *International Studies Quarterly*, 44, 2: 261–91.

Chan, Steve (1984) "Mirror, Mirror on the Wall...Are Freer Countries More Pacific?" *Journal of Conflict Resolution*, 28, 4: 617–48.

(1997) "In Search of the Democratic Peace: Problems and Promise" *Mershon International Studies Review*, 41, 1: 59–91.

Chanley, Virginia (1999) "US Public Views of International Involvement from 1964 to 1993: Time-Series Analyses of General and Military Internationalism" *Journal of Conflict Resolution*, 43, 1: 23–44.

Checkel, Jeffrey (1999) "Norms, Institutions, and National Identity in Contemporary Europe: The Degree to Which International Norms Are Affecting Debates over Citizenship and National Minorities in Contemporary Germany" *International Studies Quarterly*, 43, 1: 83–114.

Christensen, Thomas and Jack Snyder (1990) "Chain Gangs and Passes Bucks: Predicting Alliance Patterns in Multipolarity" *International Organization*, 44, 2: 137–67.

Cialdini, Robert and Melanie Trost (1998) "Social Influence: Social Norms, Conformity and Compliance" in Daniel Gilbert, Susan Fiske, and Gartner Lindzey eds., *The Handbook of Social Psychology*, vol. 2, 4th ed. (New York: McGraw-Hill), 151–85.

Clarke, Harold, Allan Kornberg, Chris McIntyre, Petra Bauer-Kaase, and Max Kaase (1999) "The Effect of Economic Priorities on the Measurement of Value Change: New Experimental Evidence" *American Political Science Review*, 93, 3: 637–47.

Clodfelter, Micheal (1992) *Warfare and Armed Conflicts: A Statistical Reference to Casualty and Other Figures, 1618–1991* (Jefferson, NC: McFarland).

Cohen, Raymond (1994) "Pacific Unions" *Review of International Studies*, 20, 3: 207–24.

(1995) "Needed, A Disaggregate Approach to the Democratic-Peace Theory" *Review of International Studies*, 22, 3: 323–5.

Conge, Patrick (1996) *From Revolution to War: State Relations in a World of Change* (Ann Arbor: University of Michigan Press).

Coser, Lewis (1956) *The Functions of Social Conflict* (Glencoe, IL: Free Press).

Cox, Gary and Samuel Kernell eds. (1991) *The Politics of Divided Government* (Boulder: Westview Press).

Crescenzi, Mark and Andrew Enterline (1999) "Ripples from the Waves? A Systemic, Time-Series Analysis of Democracy, Democratization, and Interstate War" *Journal of Peace Research*, 36, 1: 75–94.

Cronin, Bruce (1999) *Community Under Anarchy: Transnational Identity and the Evolution of Cooperation* (New York: Columbia University Press).

Dahl, Robert (1998) *On Democracy* (New Haven: Yale University Press).

David, Steven (1991) *Choosing Sides: Alignment and Realignment in the Third World* (Baltimore: Johns Hopkins University Press).

Davis, David and Will Moore (1997) "Ethnicity Matters: Transnational Ethnic Alliances and Foreign Policy Behavior" *International Studies Quarterly*, 41, 1: 171–84.

DeNardo, James (1985) *Power in Numbers: The Political Strategy of Protest and Rebellion* (Princeton: Princeton University Press).

Denver, David (1994) *Elections and Voting Behavior in Britain*, 2nd ed. (New York: Harvester Wheatsheaf).

Diehl, Paul, ed. (1998) *The Dynamics of Enduring Rivalries* (Urbana-Champaign: University of Illinois Press).

Diehl, Paul and Gary Goertz (2000) *War and Peace in International Rivalry* (Ann Arbor: University of Michigan Press).

DiPalma, Giuseppe (1991) "Legitimation from the Top to Civil Society: Politico-Cultural Change in Eastern Europe" *World Politics*, 44, 1: 49–80.

Dittmer, Lowell (1990) "Patterns of Elite Strife and Succession in Chinese Politics" *The China Quarterly*, 123: 405–30.

Dixon, William (1993) "Democracy and the Management of International Conflict" *Journal of Conflict Resolution*, 37, 1: 42–68.

(1994) "Democracy and the Peaceful Settlement of International Conflict" *American Political Science Review*, 88, 1: 1–17.

(1998) "Dyads, Disputes and the Democratic Peace" in Murray Wolfson ed., *The Political Economy of War and Peace* (Boston: Kluwer), 103–26.

Domínguez, Jorge and James McCann (1996) *Democratizing Mexico: Public Opinion and Electoral Choice* (Baltimore: Johns Hopkins University Press).

Downs, George and David Rocke (1990) *Tacit Bargaining, Arms Races, and Arms Control* (Ann Arbor: University of Michigan Press).

(1995) *Optimal Imperfection* (Princeton: Princeton University Press).

Downs, George, David Rocke, and Peter Barsoom (1996) "Is the Good News about Compliance Good News about Cooperation?" *International Organization*, 50, 3: 379–406.

Doyle, Michael (1986) "Liberalism and World Politics" *American Political Science Review*, 80, 4: 1151–70.

Druckman, Daniel (1986) "Stages, Turning Points, and Crises: Negotiating Military Base Rights, Spain and the United States" *Journal of Conflict Resolution*, 30, 2: 327–60.

Druckman, Daniel and Richard Harris (1990) "Alternative Models of Responsiveness in International Negotiation" *Journal of Conflict Resolution*, 34, 2: 234–51.

Dudley, Ryan and Ross Miller (1998) "Group Rebellion in the 1980s" *Journal of Conflict Resolution*, 42, 1: 77–96.

Duffield, John (1992) "International Regimes and Alliance Behavior-Explaining NATO Conventional Force Levels" *International Organization*, 46, 4: 819–55.

   (1995) *Power Rules: The Evolution of NATO's Conventional Force Posture* (Stanford: Stanford University Press).

Dupuy, Ernest and Trevor Dupuy (1993) *The Collins Encyclopedia of Military History: From 3500 B.C. to the Present*, 4th ed. (New York: HarperCollins).

Edwards, George (1989) *At the Margins: Presidential Leadership of Congress* (New Haven: Yale University Press).

Edwards, George, Andrew Barrett, and Jeffrey Peake (1997) "The Legislative Impact of Divided Government" *American Journal of Political Science*, 41, 2: 545–63.

Edwards, George and George Gallup (1990) *Presidential Approval* (Baltimore: Johns Hopkins University Press).

Edwards, George, and B. Dan Wood (1999) "Who Influences Whom? The President, Congress, and the Media" *American Political Science Review*, 93, 2: 327–44.

Ellingsen, Tanja (2000) "Colorful Community or Ethnic Witches Brew?" *Journal of Conflict Resolution*, 44, 2: 228–49.

Elman, Miriam Fendius (2000) "Unpacking Democracy: Presidentialism, Parliamentarism, and Theories of Democratic Peace" *Security Studies*, 9, 4: 91–126.

Elman, Miriam Fendius ed. (1997) *Paths to Peace* (Cambridge: MIT Press).

Emmons, Juliann and Randolph Siverson (1991) "Birds of a Feather: Democratic Political Systems and Alliance Choices in the Twentieth Century" *Journal of Conflict Resolution*, 35, 2: 285–306.

Enterline, Andrew (1996) "Driving While Democratizing" *International Security*, 20, 4: 183–96.

   (1998) "Regime Changes and Interstate Conflicts" *Political Research Quarterly*, 51, 2: 385–409.

Etzioni-Halèvy, Eva (1993) *The Elite Connection: Problems and Potential of Western Democracy* (Cambridge: Polity Press).

Europa World Year Book 1960–95 (London: Europa Publications, 1960–95).

Eyerman, John and Robert Hart (1996) "An Empirical Test of the Audience Cost Proposition" *Journal of Conflict Resolution*, 40, 4: 597–616.

Facts on File 1940–95 (New York: Facts on File Inc., 1940–95).

Farber, Henry and Joanne Gowa (1995) "Polities and Peace" *International Security*, 20, 2: 123–46.

(1997a) "Building Bridges Abroad" *Journal of Conflict Resolution*, 41, 3: 455–56

(1997b) "Common Interests or Common Polities?" *Journal of Politics*, 59, 2: 393–417.

Fearon, James (1994a) "Signaling versus the Balance of Power and Interests" *Journal of Conflict Resolution*, 38, 2: 236–69.

(1994b) "Domestic Political Audiences and the Escalation of International Disputes" *American Political Science Review*, 88, 3: 577–92.

(1995) "Rationalist Explanations for War" *International Organization*, 49, 3: 379–414.

(1997) "Signaling Foreign Policy Interests" *Journal of Conflict Resolution*, 41, 1: 68–90.

(1998a) "Domestic Politics, Foreign Policy, and Theories of International Relations" in Nelson Polsby ed., *Annual Review of Political Science*, vol. 1 (Palo Alto: Annual Reviews), 289–314.

(1998b) "Bargaining, Enforcement, and International Cooperation" *International Organization*, 52, 2: 269–305.

Feng, Yi and Paul Zak (1999) "The Determinants of Democratic Transactions" *Journal of Conflict Resolution*, 43, 2: 162–77.

Finnemore, Martha (1996) *National Interests in International Society* (Ithaca: Cornell University Press).

Finnemore, Martha and Kathryn Sikkink (1998) "International Norm Dynamics and Political Change" *International Organization*, 52, 4: 887–917.

Fiorina, Morris (1981) *Retrospective Voting in American National Elections* (New Haven: Yale University Press).

(1992) *Divided Government* (New York: Macmillan Publishing Co.).

Fishbein, Martin and Icek Ajzen (1975) *Beliefs, Attitudes, Intention, and Behavior: An Introduction to Theory and Research* (Reading, MA: Addison-Wesley Publications).

Florini, Ann (1996) "The Evolution of International Norms" *International Studies Quarterly*, 40, 3: 363–89.

Forsythe, David (1992) "Democracy, War, and Covert Action" *Journal of Peace Research*, 29, 4: 385–95.

Freeman, John (1989) "Systemic Sampling, Temporal Aggregation, and the Study of Political Relationships" *Political Analysis*, 1: 61–98.

Friedberg, Aaron (2000) *In the Shadow of the Garrison State: American's Anti-Statism and Its Cold War Grand Strategy* (Princeton: Princeton University Press).

Frieden, Jeffrey and Ronald Rogowski (1996) "The Impact of the International Economy on National Politics: An Analytical Overview" in Robert Keohane and Helen Milner eds., *Internationalization and Domestic Politics* (Cambridge: Cambridge University Press), 25–47.

Gallup, George (1972) *The Gallup Poll: Public Opinion 1935–71*, vol. 1 (New York: Random House).

(1976a) *The Gallup International Public Opinion Polls: Great Britain 1937–1975*, vols. 1–2 (New York: Random House).

(1976b) *The Gallup International Public Opinion Polls: France 1939, 1944–1975* (New York: Random House).

(1985) *The Gallup Poll: Public Opinion 1984* (Wilmington, DE: Scholarly Resources).

Ganguly, Sumit (1997) *The Crisis in Kashmir* (New York: Cambridge University Press).

Garrett, Geoffrey (1998) "Global Markets and National Politics: Collision Course or Virtuous Circle?" *International Organization*, 52, 4: 787–824.

Gartner, Scott and Randolph Siverson (1996) "War Expansion and War Outcome" *Journal of Conflict Resolution*, 40, 1: 4–15.

Gartzke, Erik (1998) "Kant We All Just Get Along?" *American Journal of Political Science*, 42, 1: 1–27.

(2000) "Preferences and the Democratic Peace" *International Studies Quarterly*, 44, 2: 191–212.

Gartzke, Erik and Michael Simon (1999) " 'Hot Hand': A Critical Analysis of Enduring Rivalries" *Journal of Politics*, 61, 3: 777–98.

Gasiorowski, Mark (1995) "Economic Crisis and Political Regime Change: An Event History Analysis" *American Political Science Review*, 89, 4: 882–97.

(1996) "An Overview of the Political Regime Change Dataset" *Comparative Political Studies*, 29, 4: 469–83.

Gates, Scott, Torbjorn Knutsen, and Jonathan Moses (1996) "Democracy and Peace" *Journal of Peace Research*, 33, 1: 1–10.

Gaubatz, Kurt (1991) "Election Cycles and War" *Journal of Conflict Resolution*, 35, 2: 212–44.

(1995) "Intervention and Intransitivity: Public Opinion, Social Choice, and the Use of Military Force Abroad" *World Politics*, 47, 4: 534–54.

(1999) *Elections and War: The Electoral Incentive in the Democratic Politics of War and Peace* (Stanford: Stanford University Press).

Gellner, Ernest (1983) *Nations and Nationalism* (Ithaca: Cornell University Press).

Gelpi, Christopher (1997) "Crime and Punishment" *American Political Science Review*, 91, 2: 339–60.

(1999) "Alliances as Instruments of Intra-Allied Control" in Helga Haftendorn, Robert Keohane, and Celeste Wallander eds., *Imperfect Unions: Security Institutions over Time and Space* (Oxford: Oxford University Press), 107–39.

Gelpi, Christopher and Joseph Grieco (2001) "Democracy, Leadership Tenure, and the Targeting of Militarized Challenges" *Journal of Conflict Resolution*, 45, 6: 794–817.

Gelpi, Christopher and Michael Griesdorf (2001) "Winners or Losers? Democracies in International Crisis, 1918–94" *American Political Science Review*, 95, 3: 633–48.

Gibson, James (1996) "A Mile Wide but an Inch Deep (?): The Structure of Democratic Commitments in the Former USSR" *American Journal of Political Science*, 40, 2: 396–420.

(1998) "A Sober Second Thought: An Experiment in Teaching Russians to Tolerate" *American Journal of Political Science*, 42, 3: 819–50.

Glaser, Charles (1994/5) "Realists as Optimists" *International Security*, 19, 3: 50–90.

(1997) "Security Dilemma Revisited" *World Politics*, 50, 1: 171–201.

Gleditsch, Nils Petter and Havard Hegre (1997) "Peace and Democracy: Three Levels of Analysis" *Journal of Conflict Resolution*, 41, 2 (April): 283–310.

Gleditsch, Kristian and Michael Ward (2000) "War and Peace in Space and Time: The Role of Democratization" *International Studies Quarterly*, 44, 1: 1–29.

Goemans, Hein (2000) *War and Punishment: The Causes of War Termination and the First World War* (Princeton: Princeton University Press).

Goertz, Gary and Paul Diehl (1992) "Towards a Theory of International Norms" *Journal of Conflict Resolution*, 36, 4: 634–64.

(1993) "Enduring Rivalries: Theoretical Constructs and Empirical Patterns" *International Studies Quarterly*, 37, 2: 147–71.

Goldgeiger, James (1994) *Leadership Style and Soviet Foreign Policy: Stalin, Khrushchev, Brezhnev, Gorbachev* (Baltimore: Johns Hopkins University Press).

Goldstein, Judith (1993) *Ideas, Interests, and American Trade Policy* (Ithaca: Cornell University Press).

Goldstein, Judith and Robert Keohane (1993) *Ideas and Foreign Policy: Beliefs, Institutions, and Political Change* (Ithaca: Cornell University Press).

Gorvin, Ian (1989) *Elections Since 1945: A Worldwide Reference Compendium* (Chicago: St. James Press).

Gowa, Joanne (1994) *Allies, Adversaries, and International Trade* (Princeton: Princeton University Press).

(1999) *Ballots and Bullets* (Princeton: Princeton University Press).

Gowa, Joanne and Edward Mansfield (1993) "Power Politics and International Trade" *American Political Science Review*, 87, 2: 408–20.

Greene, William (1997) *Econometric Analysis*. 3rd ed. (Upper Saddle River, NJ: Prentice Hall).

Grieco, Joseph (1988) "Anarchy, and the Limits of Cooperation: A Realist Critique of the Newest Liberal Institutionalism" *International Organization*, 42, 3: 485–508.

Gruber, Lloyd (2000) *Ruling the World: Power Politics and the Rise of Supranational Institutions* (Princeton: Princeton University Press).

Gurr, Ted Robert (1993) *Minorities at Risk: A Global View of Ethnopolitical Conflict* (Washington DC: United States Institute of Peace Press).

Gurr, Ted Robert and Mark Lichbach (1986) "Forecasting Internal Conflict" *Comparative Political Studies*, 19: 3–38.

Gutmann, Amy (1980) *Liberal Equality* (Cambridge: Cambridge University Press).

Gutmann, Amy and Dennis Thompson (1996) *Democracy and Disagreement* (Cambridge: Belknap Press).

Hanneman, Robert and Robin Steinback (1990) "Military Involvement and Political Instability: An Event History Analysis 1940–1980" *Journal of Political and Military Sociology*, 18: 1–23.

Hardin, Russell (1995) *One For All* (Princeton: Princeton University Press, 1995).

Harff, Barbara and Ted Robert Gurr (1988) "Toward an Empirical Theory of Genocides and Politicides: Identification and Measurement of Cases Since 1945" *International Studies Quarterly*, 32, 3: 357–71.

Hart, Robert and William Reed (1999) "Selection Effects and Dispute Escalation" *International Interactions*, 25, 3: 243–64.

Hausman, Jerry (1978) "Specification Tests in Econometrics" *Econometrica*, 46, 6: 1251–71.

Hausman, Jerry and Donald McFadden (1984) "Specification Tests for the Multinomial Logit Model" *Econometrica*, 52, 5: 1219–40.

Heckman, James (1979) "Sample Selection Bias as a Specification Error" *Econometrica*, 47, 1: 153–61.

Hegre, Havard, Tanja Ellingsen, Scott Gates, and Nils Petter Gleditsch (2001) "Toward a Democratic Civil Peace? Democracy, Political Change, and Civil War, 1816–1992" *American Political Science Review*, 95, 1: 33–48.

Henderson, Errol (1997) "Culture or Contiguity: Ethnic Conflict, the Similarity of States, and the Onset of War, 1820–1989" *Journal of Conflict Resolution*, 41, 5 (1997): 649–68.

(1998) "The Democratic Peace Through the Lens of Culture" *International Studies Quarterly*, 42, 3: 461–84.

(1999) "Neoidealism and the Democratic Peace" *Journal of Peace Research*, 36, 2: 203–31.

(2002) *Democracy and War: The End of an Illusion?* (Boulder: Lynne Rienner).

Henderson, Errol and J. David Singer (2000) "Civil War in the Post-Colonial World, 1946–92" *Journal of Peace Research*, 37, 3: 275–99.

Hensel, Paul (1996a) "Charting a Course to Conflict" *Conflict Management and Peace Science*, 15, 1: 43–74.

(1966b) "The Evolution of Interstate Rivalry" (Urbana-Champaign: Ph.D. Dissertation, Department of Political Science, University of Illinois).

Hermann, Margaret and Charles Kegley (1995) "Rethinking Democracy and International Peace" *International Studies Quarterly*, 39, 4: 511–34.

(2001) "Democracies and Intervention: Is there a Danger Zone?" *Journal of Peace Research*, 38, 2: 237–46.

Hermann, Richard, Philip Tetlock, and Penny Visser (1999) "Mass Public Decisions on Going to War" *American Political Science Review*, 93, 3: 553–74.

Hewitt, Joseph and Jonathan Wilkenfeld (1996) "Democracies in International Crises" *International Interactions*, 22, 2: 123–42.

Hewstone, Miles (1990) "The Ultimate Attribution Error? A Review of the Literature on Intergroup Causal Attribution" *European Journal of Social Psychology*, 20, 4: 311–35.

Higley, John and Michael Burton (1989) "The Elite Variable in Democratic Transitions and Breakdowns" *American Sociological Review*, 54, 1: 17–32.

Higley, John and Richard Gunther eds. (1992) *Elites and Democratic Consolidation in Latin America and Southern Europe* (Cambridge: Cambridge University Press).

Higley, John, Judith Kullberg, and Jan Pakulski (1996) "The Persistence of Postcommunist Elites" *Journal of Democracy*, 7, 2: 133–47.

Hobsbawm, Eric (1990) *Nations and Nationalism Since 1780: Programme, Myth, Reality* (Cambridge: Cambridge University Press).

Hogg, Michael (1992) *The Social Psychology of Group Cohesiveness: From Attraction to Social Identity* (New York: Harvester).

Hogg, Michael and Dominic Abrams (1988) *Social Identifications: A Social Psychology of Intergroup Relations and Group Processes* (New York: Routledge).

Holsti, Kalevi (1991) *Peace and War* (Cambridge: Cambridge University Press).
  (1996) *The State, War, and the State of War* (Cambridge: Cambridge University Press).
Horowitz, Donald (1985) *Ethnic Groups in Conflict* (Berkeley: University of California Press).
Hough, Jerry (1980) *Soviet Leadership in Transition* (Washington DC: Brookings Institution).
Huber, John (1996) "The Vote of Confidence in Parliamentary Democracies" *American Political Science Review*, 90, 2: 269–82.
Huntington, Samuel (1968) *Political Order in Changing Societies* (New Haven: Yale University Press).
  (1991) *The Third Wave: Democratization in the Late Twentieth Century* (Norman: University of Oklahoma Press).
  (1996) *The Clash of Civilizations and the Remaking of World Order* (New York: Simon & Schuster).
Hurrell, Andrew (1998) "An Emerging Security Community in South America" in Emanuel Adler and Michael Barnett eds., *Security Communities* (Cambridge: Cambridge University Press), 228–64.
Huth, Paul (1988) *Extended Deterrence and the Prevention of War* (New Haven: Yale University Press).
  (1996) *Standing Your Ground* (Ann Arbor: University of Michigan Press).
  (1997) "Reputation and Rational Deterrence Theory" *Security Studies*, 7, 1: 72–99.
  (1998) "Major Power Intervention in International Crises, 1918–1988" *Journal of Conflict Resolution*, 42, 6: 744–70.
  (2000) "Territory: Why are Territorial Disputes Between States a Central Cause of International Conflict?" in John Vasquez ed., *What Do We Know About War?* (Boulder: Rowman & Littlefield), 85–110.
Huth, Paul and Ellen Lust-Okar (1998) "Foreign Policy Choices and Domestic Politics: A Re-examination of the Link between Domestic and International Conflict" in Frank Harvey and Ben Mor eds., *Conflict in World Politics: Advances in the Study of Crisis, War and Peace* (New York: St. Martin's Press), 62–95.
Huth, Paul and Bruce Russett (1984) "What Makes Deterrence Work: Cases from 1900 to 1980" *World Politics*, 36, 4: 496–526.
  (1988) "Deterrence Failure and Crisis Escalation" *International Studies Quarterly*, 32, 1: 29–46.
Jackman, Robert (1993) *Power Without Force* (Ann Arbor: University of Michigan Press).
Jaggers, Keith and Ted Robert Gurr (1995) "Transitions to Democracy: Tracking Democracy's Third Wave with the Polity III Data" *Journal of Peace Research*, 32, 4: 469–82.
James, Patrick and Glenn Mitchell (1995) "Targets of Covert Pressure" *International Interactions*, 21, 1: 85–107.
Jelavich, Barbara (1983) *History of the Balkans* (Cambridge: Cambridge University Press).
Jensen, Lloyd (1988a) *Negotiating Nuclear Arms Control* (Columbia: University of South Carolina Press).

(1988b) *Bargaining for National Security* (Columbia: University of South Carolina Press).

Jentleson, Bruce and Rebecca Britton (1998) "Still Pretty Prudent: Post-Cold War American Public Opinion on the Use of Military Force" *Journal of Conflict Resolution*, 42, 4: 395–417.

Jervis, Robert (1970) *The Logic of Images in International Relations* (Princeton: Princeton University Press).

Kacowicz, Arie (1995) "Explaining Zones of Peace" *Journal of Peace Research*, 32, 3: 265–76.

(1998) *Zones of Peace in the Third World: South America and West Africa in Comparative Perspective* (Albany: State University of New York Press).

Kahler, Miles, ed. (1997) *Liberalization and Foreign Policy* (New York: Columbia University Press).

Kahnemann, Daniel (1992) "Reference Points, Anchors, Norms, and Mixed Feelings" *Organizational Behavior and Human Decision Processes*, 51, 2: 296–312.

Katzenstein, Peter, ed. (1996) *The Culture of National Security: Norms and Identity in World Politics* (New York: Columbia University Press).

Kaw, Marita (1990) "Choosing Sides: Testing a Political Proximity Model" *American Journal of Political Science*, 34, 2: 441–70.

Keesing's Contemporary Archives 1935–86 (London: Keesing's Publications, 1935–86).

Keesing's Record of World Events 1987–95 (London: Keesing's Publications, 1987–95).

Kegley, Charles and Margaret Hermann (1995) "Military Intervention and the Democratic Peace" *International Interactions*, 21, 1: 1–21.

(1997) "Putting Military Intervention into the Democratic Peace" *Comparative Political Studies*, 30: 78–107.

Keohane, Robert (1984) *After Hegemony* (Princeton: Princeton University Press).

Keohane, Robert (1986) "Reciprocity in International Relations" *International Organization*, 40, 1: 1–27.

Keohane, Robert and Joseph Nye (1977) *Power and Interdependence: World Politics in Transition* (Boston: Little Brown).

Kivimaki, Timo (2001) "The Long Peace of ASEAN" *Journal of Peace Research*, 38, 1: 5–26.

Klotz, Audie (1995) *Norms in International Relations: The Struggle Against Apartheid* (Ithaca, NY: Cornell University Press).

Knopf, Jeffrey (1998) "How Rational is 'The Rational Public'?" *Journal of Conflict Resolution*, 42, 5: 544–71.

Kocs, Stephen (1995) "Territorial Disputes and International War, 1945–1987" *Journal of Politics*, 57, 1: 159–75.

Krain, Matthew (1997) "State-Sponsored Mass Murder: The Onset and Severity of Genocides and Politicides" *Journal of Conflict Resolution*, 41, 3: 331–60.

Krain, Matthew and Marissa Myers (1997) "Democracy and Civil War: A Note on the Democratic Peace Proposition" *International Interactions*, 23, 1: 109–18.

Kratochwil, Friedrich (1989) *Rules, Norms, and Decisions: On the Conditions of Practical and Legal Reasoning in International Relations and Domestic Affairs* (Cambridge: Cambridge University Press).

Krebs, Ronald (1999) "Perverse Institutionalism" *International Organization*, 53, 2: 343–78.

Kruglanski, Arie, Mark Baldwin, and Shelagh Towson (1983) "The Lay-Epistemic Process in Attribution-Making" in Miles Hewstone ed., *Attribution Theory: Social and Functional Extensions* (Oxford: Basil Blackwell), 81–97.

Kugler, Jacek and Douglas Lemke (1996) *Parity and War: Evaluations and Extensions of the War Ledger* (Ann Arbor: University of Michigan Press).

Kullberg, Judith and William Zimmerman (1999) "Liberal Elites, Socialist Masses, and Problems of Russian Democracy" *World Politics*, 51, 3: 323–58.

Lai, Brian and Dan Reiter (2000) "Democracy, Political Similarity and International Alliances, 1816–1992" *Journal of Conflict Resolution*, 44, 2: 203–27.

Lake, David (1992) "Powerful Pacifists: Democratic States and War" *American Political Science Review*, 86, 1: 24–37.

(1999) *Entangling Relations: American Foreign Policy in its Century* (Princeton: Princeton University Press).

Lamborn, Alan (1991) *The Price of Power* (Boston: Unwin Hyman).

(1997) "Theory and the Politics in World Politics" *International Studies Quarterly*, 41, 2: 187–214.

Larson, Eric (1996) *Casualties and Consensus: The Historical Role of Casualties in Domestic Support for U.S. Military Operations* (Santa Monica: Rand).

Laver, Michael and Norman Schofield (1998) *Multiparty Government* (Ann Arbor: University of Michigan Press).

Layne, Christopher (1994) "Kant or Cant" *International Security*, 19, 2: 5–49.

(1995) "On the Democratic Peace" *International Security*, 19, 4: 175–7.

Lee, Hong Yung (1991) *From Revolutionary Cadres to Party Technocrats in Socialist China* (Berkeley: University of California Press).

Leeds, Brett Ashley (1999) "Domestic Political Institutions, Credible Commitments, and International Cooperation" *American Journal of Political Science*, 43, 4: 979–1002.

Leeds, Brett Ashley and David Davis (1999) "Beneath the Surface: Regime Type and International Interaction, 1953–78" *Journal of Peace Research*, 36, 1: 5–21.

Leeds, Brett Ashley, Andrew Long, and Sara McLaughlin Mitchell (2000) "Alliance Reliability: Specific Threats, Specific Promises" *Journal of Conflict Resolution*, 44, 5: 686–99.

Legro, Jeffrey (1995) *Cooperation Under Fire: Anglo-German Restraint During World War II* (Ithaca, NY: Cornell University Press).

Lemke, Douglas and William Reed (1996) "Regime Type and Status Quo Evaluations" *International Interactions*, 22, 2: 143–64.

Leng, Russell (1993) *Interstate Crisis Behavior, 1816–1980* (Cambridge: Cambridge University Press).

Levy, Jack and Michael Barnett (1992) "Alliance Formation, Domestic Political Economy, and Third World Security" *Jerusalem Journal of International Relations*, 14, 4: 19–40.

Lewis-Beck, Michael (1988) *Economics and Elections: The Major Western Democracies* (Ann Arbor: University of Michigan Press).

Lian, Bradley and John Oneal (1993) "Presidents, the Use of Military Force, and Public Opinion" *Journal of Conflict Resolution*, 37, 2: 277–300.

Liao, Tim Futing (1994) *Interpreting Probability Models: Logit, Probit, and Other Generalized Linear Models*, Sage University Paper series on Quantitative Applications in the Social Sciences, 07–101 (Thousand Oaks, CA: Sage).

Lichbach, Mark (1995) *The Rebel's Dilemma* (Ann Arbor: University of Michigan Press).

Lichbach, Mark and Ted Robert Gurr (1981) "The Conflict Process" *Journal of Conflict Resolution*, 25, 1: 3–29.

Lieberman, Elli (1994) "The Rational Deterrence Theory Debate: Is the Dependent Variable Elusive?" *Security Studies*, 3, 3: 384–427.

—— (1995) "What Makes Deterrence Work? Lessons from the Egyptian–Israeli Enduring Rivalry" *Security Studies*, 4, 4: 833–92.

Lijphart, Arend (1984) *Democracies* (New Haven: Yale University Press).

Lindsay, James (1994) *Congress and the Politics of U.S. Foreign Policy* (Baltimore: Johns Hopkins University Press).

Linz, Juan and Alfred Stepan (1996) *Problems of Democratic Transition and Consolidation* (Baltimore: Johns Hopkins University Press).

Lohmann, Susanne (1997) "Linkage Politics" *Journal of Conflict Resolution*, 41, 1: 38–67.

Lohmann, Susanne and Sharyn O'Halloran (1994) "Divided Government and U.S. Trade Policy" *International Organization*, 48, 4: 595–632.

London Times, 1919–95.

Londregan, John and Keith Poole (1990) "Poverty, the Coup Trap, and the Seizure of Executive Power" *World Politics*, 42, 2: 151–83.

Long, J. Scott (1997) *Regression Models for Categorical and Limited Dependent Variables* (Thousand Oaks, CA: Sage).

Luard, Evan (1986) *War in International Society* (London: I. B. Tauris and Company).

Lupia, Arthur and Kaare Strom (1995) "Coalition Termination and the Strategic Timing of Parliamentary Elections" *American Political Science Review*, 89, 3: 648–65.

Lutz, James (1989) "The Diffusion of Political Phenomena in Sub-Saharan Africa" *Journal of Political and Military Sociology*, 17, 2: 93–114.

McFadden, Daniel (1978) "Modelling the Choice of Residential Location" in A. Karlquise et al. eds. *Spatial Interaction Theory and Residential Location* (Amsterdam: North-Holland).

—— (1981) "Econometric Models of Probabilistic Choice" in C. F. Manski and Daniel McFadden, eds. *Structural Analysis of Discrete Data* (Cambridge, MA: MIT Press).

Macartney, Maxwell (1938) *Italy's Foreign and Colonial Policy* (New York: Oxford University Press).

Mackie, Thomas and Richard Rose (1991) *The International Almanac of Electoral History*, 3rd ed. (Washington DC: Congressional Quarterly Inc.).

Maddala, G. S. (1983) *Limited Dependent and Qualitative Variables in Econometrics* (New York: Cambridge University Press).

Mainwaring, Scott and Matthew Shugart (1997) *Presidentialism and Democracy in Latin America* (Cambridge: Cambridge University Press).

Mansfield, Edward and Jack Snyder (1995) "Democratization and the Danger of War" *International Security*, 20, 1: 5–38.

Maoz, Zeev (1997) "The Controversy over the Democratic Peace" *International Security*, 22, 1: 162–98.

(1998) "Realist and Cultural Critiques of the Democratic Peace" *International Interactions*, 24, 1: 3–89.

Maoz, Zeev and Nasrin Abdolali (1989) "Regimes Types and International Conflict, 1816–1976" *Journal of Conflict Resolution*, 33, 1: 3–35.

Maoz, Zeev and Bruce Russett (1992) "Alliance, Contiguity, Wealth, and Political Equality" *International Interactions*, 17, 3: 245–67.

(1993) "Normative and Structural Causes of the Democratic Peace" *American Political Science Review*, 87, 3: 624–38.

Martin, Lisa (1993) "Credibility, Costs, and Institutions: Cooperation on Economic Sanctions" *World Politics*, 45, 3: 406–32.

(2000) *Democratic Commitments* (Princeton: Princeton University Press).

Mayhew, David (1991) *Divided We Govern: Party Control, Lawmaking, and Investigations, 1946–1990* (New Haven: Yale University Press).

Mearsheimer, John (1990) "Back to the Future" *International Security*, 15, 1: 5–56.

Mercer, Jonathan (1995) "Anarchy and Identity" *International Organization*, 49, 2: 229–52.

The Military Balance 1970–95 (1971–96) (New York: Oxford University Press).

Miller, Warren and Merrill Shanks (1996) *The New American Voter* (Cambridge: Harvard University Press).

Millett, Allan and Williamson Murray eds. (1987–8) *Military Effectiveness*, 3 vols. (Boston: Allen & Unwin).

Milner, Helen (1997) *Interests, Institutions, and Information* (Princeton: Princeton University Press).

Milner, Helen and Peter Rosendorff (1997) "Democratic Politics and International Trade Negotiations: Elections and Divided Government as Constraints on Trade Liberalization; Testing the Schelling Conjecture" *Journal of Conflict Resolution*, 41, 1: 117–46.

Mintz, Alex and Nehemia Geva (1993) "Why Don't Democracies Fight Each Other?" *Journal of Conflict Resolution*, 37, 3: 484–503.

Mitchell, Sara McLaughlin, Scott Gates, and Havard Hegre (1999) "Evolution in Democracy-War Dynamics" *Journal of Peace Research*, 43, 6: 771–92.

Morgan, Clifton and Kenneth Bickers (1992) "Domestic Discontent and the External Use of Force" *Journal of Conflict Resolution*, 36, 1: 25–52.

Morgan, Clifton and Sally Howard Campbell (1991) "Domestic Structure, Decisional Constraints, and War: So Why Kant Democracies Fight" *Journal of Conflict Resolution*, 35, 2: 187–211.

Morgan, Clifton and Valerie Schwebach (1992) "Take Two Democracies and Call Me in the Morning" *International Interactions*, 17, 4: 305–20.

Morrow, James (1989) "Capabilities, Uncertainty, and Resolve: A Limited Information Model of Crisis Bargaining" *American Journal of Political Science*, 33, 4: 941–72.

(1991) "Alliances and Asymmetry: An Alternative to the Capability Aggregation Model of Alliances" *American Journal of Political Science*, 35, 4: 905–33.

(1993) "Arms vs. Allies" *International Organization*, 47, 2: 207–34.

(1994a) "Alliances, Credibility, and Peacetime Costs" *Journal of Conflict Resolution*, 38, 2: 270–97.

(1994b) "Modeling the Forms of International Cooperation" *International Organization*, 48, 3: 387–424.

(1999) "The Strategic Setting of Choices" in David Lake and Robert Powell eds., *Strategic Choice and International Relations* (Princeton: Princeton University Press), 77–114.

Morrow, James, Randolph Siverson, and Tressa Taberes (1998) "The Political Determinants of International Trade" *American Political Science Review*, 92, 3: 649–61.

(1999) "Correction to 'The Political Determinants of International Trade'" *American Political Science Review*, 93, 4: 931–34.

Mousseau, Michael (1998) "Democracy and Compromise in Militarized Interstate Conflicts, 1816–1992" *Journal of Conflict Resolution*, 42, 2: 210–30.

(2000) "Market Prosperity, Democratic Consolidation, and Democratic Peace" *Journal of Conflict Resolution*, 44, 4: 472–507.

Mousseau, Michael and Yuchang Shi (1997) "Democracy and Militarized Interstate Collaboration" *Journal of Peace Research*, 34, 1: 73–87.

(1999) "A Test for Reverse Causality in the Democratic Peace Relationship" *Journal of Peace Research*, 36, 6: 639–64.

Mueller, John (1994) *Policy and Opinion in the Gulf War* (Chicago: University of Chicago Press).

Muller, Edward and Erich Weede (1994) "Cross-National Variation in Political Violence: A Rational Action Approach" *Journal of Conflict Resolution*, 34, 4: 624–51.

(1999) "Theories of Rebellion" *Rationality and Society*, 6, 1: 40–57.

Murray, Shoon (1996) *Anchors Against Change* (Ann Arbor: University of Michigan Press).

Murray, Shoon and Jonathan Cowden (1999) "The Role of 'Enemy Images' and Ideology in Elite Belief Systems" *International Studies Quarterly*, 43, 3: 455–81.

Murray, Shoon, Jonathan Cowden, and Bruce Russett (1999) "The Conversion of American Elites' Domestic Beliefs with their Foreign Policy Beliefs" *International Interaction*, 25, 2: 153–80.

Nalebuff, Barry (1991) "Rationalist Deterrence in an Imperfect World" *World Politics*, 43, 3: 313–35.

Neustadt, Richard (1990) *Presidential Power and the Modern Presidents: The Politics of Leadership from Roosevelt to Reagan* (New York: Free Press).

New York Times, 1919–95.

Nincic, Miroslav (1992) *Democracy and Foreign Policy: The Fallacy of Political Realism* (New York: Colombia University Press).

Nincic, Miroslav and Barbara Hinckley (1991) "Foreign Policy and the Evaluation of Presidential Candidates" *Journal of Conflict Resolution*, 35, 2: 333–55.

O'Donnel, Guillermo and Phillipe Schmitter (1986) *Transitions from Authoritarian Rule* (Baltimore: Johns Hopkins University Press).

O'Halloran, Sharyn (1994) *Politics, Process, and American Trade Policy* (Ann Arbor: University of Michigan Press).

O'Kane, Rosemary (1987) *The Likelihood of Coups* (Aldershot: Avebury).

Oneal, John, Frances Oneal, Zeev Maoz, and Bruce Russett (1996) "The Liberal Peace" *Journal of Peace Research*, 33, 1: 11–28.

Oneal, John and James Lee Ray (1997) "New Tests of the Democratic Peace Controlling for Economic Interdependence, 1950–1985" *Political Research Quarterly*, 50, 3: 751–775.

Oneal, John and Bruce Russett (1997a) "Escaping the War Trap" (Manuscript).

(1997b) "The Classical Liberals Were Right" *International Studies Quarterly*, 41, 2: 267–94.

(1999a) "Is the Liberal Peace Just an Artifact of the Cold War" *International Interactions*, 25, 3: 213–41.

(1999b) "Assessing the Liberal Peace with Alternative Specifications" *Journal of Peace Research*, 36, 4: 423–42.

(1999c) "The Kantian Peace" *World Politics*, 52, 1: 1–37.

Oren, Ido (1995) "The Subjectivity of the Democratic Peace" *International Security*, 20, 2: 147–84.

Owen, John (1994) "How Liberalism Produces Democratic Peace" *International Security*, 19, 2: 87–125.

Owen, John (1997) *Liberal Peace, Liberal War* (Ithaca: Cornell University Press).

Page, Benjamin and Robert Shapiro (1992) *The Rational Public: Fifty Years of Trends in Americans' Policy Preferences* (Chicago: University of Chicago Press).

Partell, Peter (1997) "Executive Constraints and Success in International Crises" *Political Research*, 50, 3: 503–28.

Partell, Peter and Glenn Palmer (1999) "Audience Costs and Interstate Crises" *International Studies Quarterly*, 43, 2: 389–406.

Peceny, Mark, Caroline Beer, and Shannon Sanchez-Terry (2002) "Dictatorial Peace?" *American Political Science Review*, 96, 1: 15–26.

Peterson, Paul (1994) "The President's Dominance in Foreign Policy Making" *Political Science Quarterly*, 109: 215–34.

Pierce, Roy (1995) *Choosing the Chief: Presidential Elections in France and the United States* (Ann Arbor: University of Michigan Press).

Poe, Steven and C. Neal Tate (1994) "Repression of Human Rights to Personal Integrity in the 1980s: A Global Analysis" *American Political Science Review*, 88, 4: 853–72.

Political Handbook of the World 1926–39 (New York: Harper and Row, 1927–39).

Powell, Bingham (1982) *Contemporary Democracies* (Cambridge: Harvard University Press).

(2000) *Elections as Instruments of Democracy* (New Haven: Yale University Press).

Powell, Robert (1991) "Absolute and Relative Gains in International Relations Theory" *American Political Science Review*, 85, 4: 1303–20.

(1993) "Guns, Butter, and Anarchy" *American Political Science Review*, 87, 1: 115–32.

(1994) "Anarchy in International Relations Theory: The Neorealist – Neoliberal Debate" *International Organization*, 48, 2: 313–44.

(1999) *In the Shadow of Power: States and Strategy in International Politics* (Princeton: Princeton University Press).

Power, Timothy and Mark Gasiorowski (1997) "Institutional Design and Democratic Consolidation in the Third World" *Comparative Political Studies*, 30, 2: 123–55.

Powers, Denise and James Cox (1997) "Echoes from the Past: The Relationship between Satisfaction with Economic Reforms and Voting Behavior in Poland" *American Political Science Review*, 91, 3: 617–33.

Przeworski, Adam (1991) *Democracy and the Market: Political and Economic Reforms in Eastern Europe and Latin America* (New York: Cambridge University Press).

Przeworski, Adam, Michael Alvarez, Jose Antonio Cheibub, and Fernando Limongi (1996) "What Makes Democracies Endure?" *Journal of Democracy*, 7, 1: 39–55.

(2000) *Democracy and Development: Political Institutions and Well-Being in the World, 1950–1990* (New York: Cambridge University Press).

Putnam, Robert (1976) *The Comparative Study of Political Elites* (Englewood Cliffs, NJ: Prentice-Hall).

(1988) "Diplomacy and Domestic Politics" *International Organization*, 42, 3: 427–60.

Raknerud, Arvid and Hvard Hegre (1997) "The Hazard of War: Reassessing the Evidence for the Democratic Peace" *Journal of Peace Research*, 34, 4: 385–404.

Ray, James Lee (1995) *Democracy and International Conflict* (Columbia: University of South Carolina Press).

Ray, James Lee (1998) "Does Democracy Cause Peace?" in Nelson Polsby ed., *Annual Review of Political Science*, vol. 1 (Palo Alto: Annual Reviews), 27–46.

Raymond, Gregory (1994) "Democracies, Disputes, and Third-Party Intermediaries" *Journal of Conflict Resolution*, 38, 1: 24–42.

Reed, William (2000) "A Unified Statistical Model of Conflict Onset and Escalation" *American Journal of Political Science*, 44, 1: 84–93.

Reed, William and David Clark (2000) "War Initiators and War Winners: The Consequences of Linking Theories of Democratic War Success" *Journal of Conflict Resolution*, 44, 3: 378–95.

Reiter, Dan (1995) "Exploding the Powder Keg Myth: Preemptive Wars Almost Never Happen" *International Security*, 20, 2: 5–34.

(1996) *Crucible of Beliefs: Learning, Alliances, and World Wars* (Ithaca, NY: Cornell University Press).

Reiter, Dan and Allan Stam (1998a) "Democracy, War Initiation, and Victory" *American Political Science Review*, 92, 2: 377–89.

(1998b) "Democracy and Battlefield Military Effectiveness" *Journal of Conflict Resolution*, 42, 3: 259–77.

(2002) *Search for Victory* (Princeton: Princeton University Press).

Remmer, Karen (1995) "New Theoretical Perspectives on Democratization" *Comparative Politics*, 28, 1: 103–22.

Reus-Smit, Christian (1999) *The Moral Purpose of the State: Culture, Social Identity, and Institutional Rationality in International Relations* (Princeton: Princeton University Press).

Riker, William (1986) *The Art of Political Manipulation* (New Haven: Yale University Press).

Risse-Kappen, Thomas (1995) *Cooperation Among Democracies: The European Influence on U.S. Foreign Policy* (Princeton: Princeton University Press).

Rosen, Stephen (1996) *Societies and Military Power: India and its Armies* (Ithaca: Cornell University Press).

Rosenau, James (1990) *Turbulence in World Politics* (Princeton: Princeton University Press).

(1997) *Along the Domestic–Foreign Frontier: Exploring Governance in a Turbulent World* (Cambridge: Cambridge University Press).

Ross, Marc (1986) "The Limits to Social Structure: Social Structural and Psychocultural Explanations for Political Conflict and Violence" *Anthropological Quarterly*, 59, 4: 171–6.

Rousseau, David (1996) "Domestic Political Institutions and the Evolution of International Conflict" (Ann Arbor: Ph.D. Dissertation, Department of Political Science, University of Michigan).

Rousseau, David, Christopher Gelpi, Dan Reiter, and Paul Huth (1996) "Assessing the Dyadic Nature of the Democratic Peace" *American Political Science Review*, 90, 3: 512–33.

Ruggie, John Gerard (1998a) *Constructing the World Polity: Essays on International Institutionalization* (London: Routledge).

(1998b) "What Makes the World Hang Together? Neo-Utilitarianism and the Social Constructivist Challenge" *International Organization*, 52, 4: 855–85.

Rummel, R. J. (1983) "Libertarianism and International Violence" *Journal of Conflict Resolution*, 27, 1: 27–71.

(1985) "Libertarian Propositions on Violence Within and Between Nations" *Journal of Conflict Resolution*, 29, 3: 419–55.

(1994) *Death by Government* (New Brunswick: Transaction Publishers).

(1995a) "Democracies ARE Less Warlike Than Other Regimes" *European Journal of International Relations*, 1, 4: 459–79.

(1995b) "Democracy, Power, Genocide, and Mass Murder" *Journal of Conflict Resolution*, 39, 1: 3–26.

(1997) *Power Kills: Democracy as a Method of Nonviolence* (New Brunswick: Transaction Publishers).

Russett, Bruce (1990) *Controlling the Sword: The Democratic Governance of National Security* (Cambridge, Mass: Harvard University Press).

(1993) *Grasping the Democratic Peace* (Princeton: Princeton University Press).

(1995) "And Yet it Moves" *International Security*, 19, 4: 164–75.

Russett, Bruce and James Lee Ray (1995) "Raymond Cohen on Pacific Unions" *Review of International Studies*, 21, 3: 319–25.

Russett, Bruce and John Oneal (2001) *Triangulating Peace: Democracy, Interdependence, and International Organizations* (New York: W. W. Norton).

Sabrosky, Alan (1980) "Interstate Alliances: Their Reliability and the Expansion of War" in David Singer ed., *The Correlates of War II: Testing Some Realpolitik Models* (New York: Free Press), 161–98.

Saideman, Stephen (2001) *The Ties that Divide: Ethnic Politics, Foreign Policy, and International Conflict* (New York: Columbia University Press).

Schelling, Thomas (1960) *The Strategy of Conflict* (Cambridge: Harvard University Press).

(1966) *Arms and Influence* (New Haven: Yale University Press).

Schultz, Kenneth (1995) "The Politics of the Political Business Cycle" *British Journal of Political Science*, 25, 1: 79–99.

(1998) "Domestic Opposition and Signaling in International Crises" *American Political Science Review*, 92, 4: 829–44.

(1999) "Do Democratic Institutions Constrain or Inform?" *International Organization*, 53, 2: 233–66.

(2001a) "Looking For Audience Costs" *Journal of Conflict Resolution*, 45, 1: 32–60.

(2001b) *Democracy and Coercive Diplomacy* (Cambridge: Cambridge University Press).

Schweller, Randall (1992) "Domestic Structure and Preventive War" *World Politics*, 44, 2: 235–69.

(1998) *Deadly Imbalance: Tripolarity and Hitler's Strategy of World Conquest* (New York: Columbia University Press).

Sellers, Patrick (1998) "Strategy and Background in Congressional Campaigns" *American Political Science Review*, 92, 1: 159–71.

Senese, Paul (1996) "Geographical Proximity and Issue Salience" *Conflict Management and Peace Science*, 15, 2: 133–61.

(1997a) "Between Dispute and War" *Journal of Politics*, 59, 1: 1–27.

(1997b) "Dispute to War" (Manuscript).

(1999) "Democracy and Maturity" *International Studies Quarterly*, 43, 3: 483–502.

Seton-Watson, Hugh (1962) *Eastern Europe Between the Wars, 1918–1941*, 3rd ed. (Hamden: Archon Books).

Shannon, Vaughn (2000) "Norms are What States Make of Them" *International Studies Quarterly*, 44, 2: 293–316.

Sherif, Muzafer (1966) *In Common Predicament: Social Psychology of Intergroup Conflict and Cooperation* (Boston: Houghton Mifflin).

Shimshoni, Jonathan (1988) *Israel and Conventional Deterrence: Border Warfare from 1953 to 1970* (Ithaca, NY: Cornell University Press).

Shugart, Matthew and John Carey (1992) *Presidents and Assemblies: Constitutional Design and Electoral Dynamics* (Cambridge: Cambridge University Press).

Signorino, Curtis (1999) "Strategic Interaction and the Statistical Analysis of International Conflict" *American Political Science Review*, 93, 2: 279–98.

Simmel, Georg (1955) *Conflict* (Glencoe: Free Press).

Simmons, Beth (1994) *Who Adjusts?: Domestic Sources of Foreign Economic Policy During the Interwar Years* (Princeton: Princeton University Press).

(1999) "See You in 'Court'? The Appeal to Quasi-Judicial Legal Processes in the Settlement of Territorial Disputes" in Paul Diehl ed., *A Road Map to War* (Nashville: Vanderbilt University Press).

Simon, Michael and Erik Gartzke (1996) "Political System Similarity and the Choice of Allies: Do Democracies Flock Together or Do Opposites Attract?" *Journal of Conflict Resolution*, 40, 4: 617–35.

SIPRI Yearbook: World Armaments and Disarmament 1970–95 (New York: Humanities Press 1970–3; Cambridge: MIT Press, 1974–7; London: Taylor & Francis, 1978–85; New York: Oxford University Press, 1986–95).

Siverson, Randolph ed. (1998) *Strategic Politicians, Institutions, and Foreign Policy* (Ann Arbor: University of Michigan Press).

Siverson, Randolph and Bruce Bueno de Mesquita (1996) "Inside-Out: A Theory of Domestic Political Institutions and the Issues of International Conflict" (paper presented at the 1996 annual meeting of the American Political Science Association).

Slaughter, Anne-Marie (1995) "International Law in a World of Liberal States" *European Journal of International Law*, 6, 2: 503–38.

Small, Kenneth and Cheng Hsiao (1985) "Multinomial Logit Specification Tests" *International Economic Review*, 26, 3: 619–27.

Small, Melvin and David Singer (1976) "The War Proneness of Democratic Regimes" *Jerusalem Journal of International Relations*, 1, 1: 46–61.

 (1982) *Resort to Arms: International and Civil Wars, 1816–1980* (Beverly Hills: Sage Publications).

Smith, Alastair (1995) "Alliance Formation and War" *International Studies Quarterly*, 39, 4: 405–26.

 (1996) "Diversionary Foreign Policy in Democratic Systems" *International Studies Quarterly*, 40, 1: 133–53.

 (1998) "International Crises and Domestic Politics" *American Political Science Review*, 92, 3: 623–38.

 (1999) "Testing Theories of Strategic Choice: The Example of Crisis Escalation" *American Journal of Political Science*, 43, 4: 1254–83.

Snyder, Glenn (1997) *Alliance Politics* (Ithaca, NY: Cornell University Press).

Snyder, Jack (1984) *The Ideology of the Offensive: Military Decision Making and the Disasters of 1914* (Ithaca, NY: Cornell University Press).

 (2000) *From Voting to Violence: Democratization and Nationalist Conflict* (New York: W. W. Norton).

Snyder, Jack and Karen Ballentine (1996) "Nationalism and the Marketplace of Ideas" *International Security*, 21, 2: 5–40.

Sorokin, Gerald (1994) "Arms, Alliances, and Security Tradeoffs in Enduring Rivalries" *International Studies Quarterly*, 38, 3: 421–46.

Spiro, David (1994) "The Insignificance of the Liberal Peace" *International Security*, 19, 2: 50–86.

 (1995) "The Liberal Peace – And Yet it Squirms" *International Security*, 19, 4: 177–80.

Stam, Allan (1996) *Win, Lose, or Draw: Domestic Politics and the Crucible of War* (Ann Arbor: University of Michigan Press).

Starr, Harvery (1991) "Democratic Dominoes: Diffusion Approaches to the Spread of Democracy in the International System" *Journal of Conflict Resolution*, 35, 2: 356–81.

Stein, Arthur (1990) *Why Nations Cooperate* (Ithaca, NY: Cornell University Press).

Stepan, Alfred and Cindy Skach (1993) "Constitutional Frameworks and Democratic Consolidation: Parliamentarism versus Presidentialism" *World Politics*, 46, 1: 1–22.

Stoll, Richard and Andrew McAndrew (1986) "Negotiating Strategic Arms Control, 1969–1979" *Journal of Conflict Resolution*, 30, 2: 315–26.

Sutter, Daniel (1995) "Settling Old Scores" *Journal of Conflict Resolution*, 39, 1: 110–28.

Swaminathan, Siddharth (1999) "Time, Power, and Democratic Transitions" *Journal of Conflict Resolution*, 43, 2: 178–91.

Tajfel, Henri (1978) *Differentiation Between Social Groups* (London: Academic Press.

(1982) *Social Identity and Intergroup Relations* (Cambridge: Cambridge University Press.

Tajfel, Henri, M. G. Billig, R. P. Bundy, and Claude Flament (1971) "Social Categorization and Intergroup Behavior" *European Journal of Social Psychology*, 1 (1971): 149–78.

Tajfel, Henri and John Turner (1979) "An Integrative Theory of Intergroup Conflict" in William Austin and Stephen Worchel eds., *The Social Psychology of Intergroup Relations* (Monterey: Brooks), 33–47.

Tarar, Ahmer (2001) "International Bargaining with Two-Sided Domestic Constraints" *Journal of Conflict Resolution*, 45, 3: 320–40.

Tarrow, Sidney (1994) *Power in Movement* (Cambridge: Cambridge University Press).

Tetlock, Philip (1992) "The Impact of Accountability on Judgment and Choice: Towards a Social Contingency Model" *Advances in Experimental Social Psychology*, 25: 331–76.

Thompson, William (1973) *The Grievances of Military Coup-Makers* (Beverly Hills: Sage Publications).

(1995) "Principal Rivalries" *Journal of Conflict Resolution*, 39, 2: 195–223.

(1996) "Democracy and Peace" *International Organization*, 50, 1: 141–74.

Thompson, William and Richard Tucker (1997) "A Tale of Two Democratic Peace Critiques" *Journal of Conflict Resolution*, 41, 3: 428–54.

Tillema, Herbert (1991) *International Armed Conflict Since 1945: A Bibliographic Handbook of Wars and Military Interventions* (Boulder: Westview Press).

Tures, John (2001) "Democracies as Intervening States: A Critique of Kegley and Hermann" *Journal of Peace Research*, 38, 2: 227–36.

Turner, John, R. J. Brown, and Henri Tajfel (1979) "Social Comparison and Group Interest in In-group Favoritism" *European Journal of Social Psychology*, 9, 2: 187–204.

Van Belle, Douglas (1997) "Press Freedom and the Democratic Peace" *Journal of Peace Research*, 34, 4: 405–14.

Vanhanen, Tatu (1979) *Power and the Means of Power: A Study of 119 Asian, European, American, and African States, 1850–1975* (Ann Arbor: University Microfilm International).

Vasquez, John (1993) *The War Puzzle* (New York: Cambridge University Press).

(1995) "Why Do Neighbors Fight – Proximity, Contiguity, or Territoriality?" *Journal of Peace Research*, 32: 277–93.

(1996) "Distinguishing Rivals that Go to War from Those that Do Not" *International Studies Quarterly*, 40, 4: 531–58.

Vaszquez, John and Marie Henehan (2001) "Territorial Disputes and the Probability of War, 1816–1992" *Journal of Peace Research*, 38, 2: 123–39.

Verba, Sidney (1987) *Elites and the Idea of Equality: A Comparison of Japan, Sweden, and the United States* (Cambridge: Harvard University Press).

Wagner, Harrison (2000) "Bargaining and War" *American Journal of Political Science*, 44, 3: 469–84.

Wallensteen, Peter and Margareta Sollenberg (1996) "The End of International War? Armed Conflict 1989–1995" *Journal of Peace Research*, 33, 3: 353–70.

Walt, Stephen (1987) *The Origins of Alliances* (Ithaca: Cornell University Press).

(1996) *Revolution and War* (Ithaca: Cornell University Press).

Wang, Kevin and James Lee Ray (1994) "Beginners and Winners: The Fate of Initiators of Interstate Wars Involving Great Powers Since 1495" *International Studies Quarterly*, 38, 1: 139–54.

Ward, Michael and Kristian Gleditsch (1998) "Democratizing for Peace" *American Political Science Review*, 92, 1: 51–61.

Warwick, Paul (1992) "Economic Trends and Government Survival in West European Parliamentary Democracies" *American Political Science Review*, 86, 4: 875–87.

(1994) *Government Survival in Parliamentary Democracies* (Cambridge: Cambridge University Press).

Weart, Spencer (1998) *Never at War: Why Democracies Will Not Fight One Another* (New Haven: Yale University Press).

Weaver, Kent and Bert Rockman (1993) *Do Institutions Matter?: Government Capabilities in the United States and Abroad* (Washington, DC: Brookings Institution).

Weede, Erich (1984) "Democracy and War Involvement" *Journal of Conflict Resolution*, 28, 4: 649–64.

(1992) "Some Simple Calculations on Democracy and War Involvement" *Journal of Peace Research*, 29, 4: 377–83.

Weingast, Berry (1997) "The Political Foundations of Democracy and the Rule of Law" *American Political Science Review*, 91, 2: 245–63.

Wendt, Alexander (1999) *Social Theory of International Politics* (Cambridge: Cambridge University Press).

Werner, Suzanne (1996) "Absolute and Limited War: The Possibility of Foreign-Imposed Regime Change" *International Interactions*, 22, 1: 67–88.

(1999) "Choosing Demands Strategically: The Distribution of Power, the Distribution of Benefits, and the Risk of Conflict" *Journal of Conflict Resolution*, 46, 6: 705–26.

Werner, Suzanne and Douglas Lemke (1997) "Opposites Do Not Attract: The Impact of Domestic Institutions, Power, and Prior Commitments on Alignment Choices" *International Studies Quarterly*, 41, 3: 529–46.

Whitten, Guy and Harvey Palmer (1996) "Heightening Comparativists Concern for Model Choice: Voting Behavior in Great Britain and the Netherlands" *American Journal of Political Science*, 40: 231–60.

Wintrobe, Ronald (1998) *The Political Economy of Dictatorship* (Cambridge: Cambridge University Press).

Wood, B. Dan and Jeffrey Peake (1998) "The Dynamics of Foreign Policy Agenda Setting" *American Political Science Review*, 92, 2: 173–84.

World Military Expenditures and Arms Transfers 1970–95 (1979–96) (Washington DC: United States Arms Control and Disarmament Agency).

Yoon, Mi Yung (1997) "Explaining U.S. Intervention in Third World Internal Wars, 1945–1989" *Journal of Conflict Resolution*, 41, 4: 580–602.

Zakaria, Fareed (1997) "The Rise of Illiberal Democracy" *Foreign Affairs*, 76, 6: 22–43.

Zaller, John (1992) *The Nature and Origins of Mass Opinion* (Cambridge: Cambridge University Press).

Zimmerman, William (2002) *The Russian People and Foreign Policy* (Princeton: Princeton University Press).

Zimmermann, Ekkart (1983) *Political Violence, Crises, and Revolutions: Theories and Research* (Boston: Schenkman).

Zorn, Christopher (2002) "U.S. Government Litigation Strategies in the Federal Appellate Courts" *Political Research Quarterly*, 55,1: 145–66.

Index

CAMBRIDGE STUDIES IN INTERNATIONAL RELATIONS